15.00
100k

Adrian Snodgrass

The Symbolism of the Stupa

Studies on Southeast Asia

SEAP

Southeast Asia Program
120 Uris Hall
Cornell University, Ithaca, New York
1985

ISBN 0-87727-700-1

PREFACE

The stupa is a symbolic form that pullulates throughout South, Southeast, and East Asia. In its Indian manifestations it is an extreme case in terms of architectural function: it has no usable interior space and its construction has a basic simplicity. In this "state of the art" study Adrian Snodgrass reads the stupa as a cultural artifact. The monument concretizes metaphysical principles and generates multivalent meanings in ways that can be articulated with literary texts and other architectural forms.

Mr. Snodgrass came to his scholarly studies by a route increasingly untravelled in the second half of the twentieth century. Trained as an architect, he is self-taught in the complexities of the Asian cultures that interest him. At the age of twenty-five he went to India and Sri Lanka where he lived and worked for more than six years and acquired knowledge of Tamil and Sanskrit. He then spent seven years in Japan where he taught English and learned Chinese, followed by two years each in Indonesia and Hong Kong. He returned to Australia in 1976 and now holds a joint appointment in religious studies and architecture at the University of Sydney. He is currently finishing a doctoral dissertation, using Chinese, Indic, pre-Columbian, African, Christian and Islamic materials to analyze how temporal concepts and cycles of time are incorporated in buildings. Another as yet unpublished work, based on Chinese and Japanese sources, is a massive study of two mandalas in Shingon Buddhism.

Craig J. Reynolds
Sydney April 1984

3927331

TABLE OF CONTENTS

PART II - THE PILE

INTRODUCTION

1. THE NATURE OF ARCHITECTURAL SYMBOLISM

In the traditional Indian view[1] a building, if it is properly conceived, satisfies both a physical and a metaphysical[2] indigence. It has a twofold function : it provides "commodity, firmness and delight" so as to serve man's psycho-somatic, emotional and aesthetic needs, and also serves him intellectually,[3] acting as a support for the contemplation of supra-empirical principles.

In this view an adequately designed building will embody meaning. It will express the manner in which the phenomenal world relates to the Real and how the One "fragments" into multiplicity; it will carry intimations of the non-duality (advaita) of the sensible and the supra-sensible domains. The fully functioning building will aid the attainment of the state of intellectual consciousness that the Indian traditions consider to constitute the goal and perfection of human life, that non-differentiated awareness or state of being "in which there is no longer any distinction of knower from known, or being from knowing".[4]

To the extent that the building embodies meanings conducive to an intellectual vision of the non-duality of principial Unity and manifested multiplicity, it functions as a symbol, that is to say, as a "representation of reality on a certain level of reference by a corresponding reality on another".[5] The belief that the building is capable of performing this symbolic function is founded on the Indian doctrine that there exists an analogous, or anagogical correspondence between the physical and the metaphysical orders of reality, that the sensible world is a similitude of the intellectual, in such a way that, "This world is the image of that, and vice versa".[6] Everything that exists derives its reality from a

---

1. The following considerations on symbolism derive in the main from the writings of René Guénon, A.K. Coomaraswamy and Mircea Eliade. See esp. Guénon, 1945a, pp. 130 ff.; 1962, *passim*; 1953, pp. 115 ff. For an excellent summary of Coomaraswamy's writings on symbolism, with references, see Livingstone, 1962, pp. 55 ff.; and valuable indications on Eliade's thought on symbolism are given in Saliba, 1976, pp. 54 ff., and Allen, 1978, pp. 140 ff.

2. The term "metaphysics" is used in this study as it is by Guénon and Coomaraswamy, to indicate that which lies beyond the physical. It does not refer to the "metaphysics" of modern philosophy. See Guénon, 1945a, pp. 108 ff.

3. "Intellect" here refers to the supra-individual "organ" whereby metaphysical realities are perceived and is a synonym for buddhi of Vedantic and Buddhist formulations. For buddhi see Guénon, 1945, pp 65 ff.

4. Coomaraswamy, 1946, p. 41.

5. Ibid., p. 115.

6. AB VIII. 2.

transcendent, supra-empirical principle and translates or expresses that principle in accordance with the limitations and modalities that characterize its own level of existence. The orders of reality, that is, the multiple states of being and the multiple states of existence, are so many reflections one of the other, since each in turn is a reflection of the Unity whence it derives.[7] This being so the objects of our sensory experience are seen as so many images or reflections, in varying degrees of obscuration, of paradigmatic forms existing at higher levels, and the laws operating at a lower domain can be taken to symbolize realities belonging to a superior order, "wherein resides their own profoundest cause, which is at once their principle and their end".[8]

In one sense all things that exist - images, words, language, physical and mental phenomena - are symbols of the supra-empirical levels of reality. Every existent thing is the "reflection" of an archetypal Form. In contrast to its accidental or actual form, which is its material cause, every thing also has an exemplary and essential Form, "the purely intellectual and immaterial cause of the thing being what it is as well as the means whereby it is known".[9] The essential Form and the material substance of the entity respectively constitute its intelligible and sensible aspects, that by which it is recognized from other things, and that which gives it its perceptible existence. By the fact that it partakes of an essence or is the reflection of an essential archetype, every phenomenal entity is "not only what it is visibly but also what it represents - so that man may find in any object whatever an intimation of the supra-sensible reality that informs it".[10] That is to say, every object of the senses or of thought is a symbol.

In a more specific and restricted sense, however, there is also a deliberate and calculated symbolism, one that crystallizes the doctrinal teachings of a tradition in the form of a prescribed figurative or spatial representation. From this arises the convention of confining the term "symbol" to objects or images which pertain directly to doctrinal formulations, and in which the symbolic content is clearly and explicitly manifest. Symbols, in this more specific sense, are clearer and more perfect reflections of principial relationships and processes, more cogent,

---

7. Guénon, 1962, Ch. L ("Les symboles de l'analogie"), pp. 319 ff.

8. Guénon, 1958a, p. xii; cf. 1962, p. 36. The doctrine that considers nature as a symbol of the supra-physical is not confined to the East. It was also current in Europe of the Middle Ages, and more particularly in the doctrines of the Franciscans, where it is enunciated with unambiguous clarity by St. Bonaventura. It is also implicit in the Thomist doctrine of *analogia entis*. See Guénon, 1962, p. 37, n. 1.

9. Coomaraswamy, 1946, pp. 72 f.

10. Coomaraswamy, 1977, 1,p. 295. The entity is a "reflection" of essential Form (*forma*) in matter (*materia*), which correspond at the level of phenomenal existences to Essence and Substance at the universal level, a concept that is explained in the following (see pp. 210 ff). In the Indian formulations *forma* and *materia* correspond to *nāma* and *rūpa*, lit. "name" and "form", that is, the denominational and apparitional, the name and likeness, the noumenal and phenomenal aspects of things. See below, p. 29, n.4, for clarifications on the word *materia*, "matter".

direct and succinct expressions of transcendent truths, than are the generality of things. They possess dimensions of meaning and a resonance of significance lacking in ordinary objects.

These latter symbols, possessed of greater transparency than the usual run of sensible entities, are characterized by "adequacy",[11] by an efficacy in producing in a qualified and receptive person an adaequatio rei et intellectus, which is to say a condition of true, intellectual knowledge. They are capable of provoking a recollection of a supra-mundane paradigm and, by that fact, are imbued with the sacred.

The adequate, or sacred symbol is deemed to have been "given"; it is revealed to the tradition from a non-human source. It is adequate precisely because it is not a mere contrivance of the human mind and thus a matter of imagined or supposed resemblances, but is a true imitation of a supernal exemplar, "not a matter of illusory resemblances, but of proportion, true analogy and adequacy, by which we are reminded of the intended referent".[12] An adequate symbol is "true, analogical, accurate, canonical, hieratic, anagogic and archetypal".[13]

It is seen that the term "symbol" as it is used in the Indian context and as it is understood in this study, has a significance quite other than that given it in everyday language, by psycho-analysis, linguistics, "symbolist" art or in the current semiological theories of architecture. In these, what are termed "symbols" indicate something within the empirical world, knowable by the senses or conceivable by the mind, so that the symbol and its referent stand at the same level of reality, whereas here it is taken to indicate a referent that stands at a supra-empirical level, where it cannot be known by sense perception or by thought or by any means other than by analogy. In its Indian meaning the symbol points beyond itself,[14] to a domain that transcends the sensible and the rational.[15] The symbol (from Gk. sym + ballō, "to throw together", suggesting the way the symbol carries the mind to its referent), in the Indian sense is anagogic (from Gk. anagō, "to lead up to"),[16] leading the understanding upward to a metaphysical meaning. Whereas symbols, as understood in contemporary thought, have but one level of reference, in Indian thought they have two : in Indian iconography, for example, the lotus refers on one level to the flower of our sensible experience, while on the other it means the Waters of All-Possibility, a concept that that is totally unsusceptible to any direct representation.[17]

* * * * *

Architectural forms are eminently appropriate to act as symbols. Every symbolic construct is of necessity grounded in the phenomenal; the ascent to exemplary levels must begin from the base of our sensible experience, must be expressed in the mode of the knower. In our world space occupies a fundamental position in our awareness; it is a primary datum of our consciousness of the corporeal world, and yet is itself

---

11. "Ad-equate", a "making equal to". On adequate symbolism see Coomaraswamy, 1946, pp. 135 ff.; Livingstone, 1962, pp. 59 ff.

12. Coomaraswamy, 1946, p.135.

13. Livingstone, 1962, p. 60.

14. See Allen, 1978, pp. 143 f.

15. Ibid., pp. 158 f.

16. Livingstone, 1962, p. 57.

17. Ibid., p. 58.

etherial[18] and of a most rarefied corporeality. As such it is a suitable medium for conveying metaphysical notions and, as this study will show, spatial analogies and metaphors abound in the Brahmanic and Buddhist literatures : the properties of space provide a cogent means for symbolic expression. Space is also the medium and first concern of architecture, and buildings, perhaps more fully and more directly than any other art form, are capable of rendering spatial concepts in sensible forms. By way of its manipulation of space the built form incorporates an adequate symbolism.

In traditional India, therefore, architecture is viewed as symbolic in both content and import. It acts as an intellectual bridge between the visible and the invisible, the corporeal and the formless, the expressible and the ineffable; it affirms the analogical correspondence of the orders of reality; it is intended to function both physically and metaphysically; and its forms are largely determined by the exigencies of intellectual speculation[19] and contemplation. The architectural work embodies in a tangible form, that is to say corporealizes, what is intangible and incorporeal. As a symbol it is a formal expression in and through which a supra-formal reality is perceived. It belongs to that "real art", which "is one of symbolic and significant representation, a representation of things that cannot be seen except by the intellect".[20]

* * * * *

The aim of this study is to exemplify, by way of the stupa, the manner in which the spatial forms of Indian and Indian-influenced architecture are symbols and function to express metaphysical notions. The stupa is particularly suited for this purpose since it clearly shows the spatial conformations that carry the main symbolic content of Indian buildings : a defined centre, an axis, orientation, a precise and succinct geometry, and the use of basic symbolic forms, such as the square and the circle and the cube and the sphere. The stupa also has advantages as a subject for the study of Indian architectural symbolism in that it is, in terms of its architectural function, an extreme case : it has no usable interior space and its construction is of basic simplicity, obviating explanations of its forms as resulting from functional or structural necessity. On the contrary, it exists solely to satisfy the needs of symbolism and it has a clear and unambiguous metaphysical reference. In the stupa, therefore, the operation of symbolism as a determinant of architectural form can be viewed in sharp focus; in the stupa we can see, in their uncomplicated simplicity, symbolic patterns that are equally applicable, _mutatis mutandis_, to the layout of other Indian building forms, from cities and towns, to palaces, houses and temples.

---

18. Skt. _ākāśa_ is both "space" and "Ether", the quintessential Element. See below, p. 37.

19. "Speculation" in its etymological sense, deriving from Lat. _specula_, "mirror", referring to the reflection of Forms in the Intellect (_buddhi_).

20. Livingstone, 1962, p. 57, quoting Coomaraswamy.

2. THE ANALYSIS OF THE SYMBOLISM OF THE STUPA

This study attempts to analyse a pattern of interrelated meanings generated by the form of the stupa. It does so by reference to myth, to ritual and to doctrine, viewing the architectural form from within the conceptual framework of the tradition to which it belongs. This approach involves questions of aim and methodology.

The referent of the symbol, lying in the transcendent realms of archetypal paradigms,[21] is ineffable : in the last analysis the meaning of the stupa cannot be expressed. The symbol, however, refers not only to realities of the principial order, but also to realities belonging to a superimposed hierarchy of levels and to realities belonging to any one from among those levels. The symbol contains a plurality of meanings; it is multivalent both vertically and horizontally. A causal relationship operates between the levels : the higher ones act as secondary causes to those that lie below, and since an effect expresses something that inheres within the nature of the cause, the things of the lower level participate in those of the higher, and can therefore be taken to represent them. This is the vertical multivalence of the symbol.[22]

The symbol also has a plurality of meanings on the horizontal level.[23] Every symbol forms part of a schema of interlocking referents; it forms part of a *pattern* of concordant interrelationships. It does not stand in isolation but interconnects with other symbols, which fit together to form a mutually reinforcing web of meaning. A deeper understanding of a symbol is gained by studying the grid or net formed by its symbolic homologues. The pattern of meaning that emerges from the juxtaposition of cognate symbols does not exhaust the significance of the symbol, which, as we have seen, is ultimately beyond words, but it reinforces its intimations, indicating a logical cohesion and integrity which in itself is an intimation of the all-pervasiveness of Principle. It is precisely this pattern of inter-reflecting symbols that this study attempts to delineate. By bringing together cognate symbols in apposition, that is, symbols that have a commonality of reference on the horizontal plane, it attempts to mark out the "field" of symbolic interactions which the stupa generates.

---

21. That is, the domain of the universal and the unmanifested. These terms are clarified by Guénon, 1945, pp. 32 ff., where he also gives the following table showing the distinction of the universal and individual domains :

Universal	The Unmanifested	
	Formless Manifestation	
Individual	Formal Manifestation	Subtle State
		Gross State

The "Gross State" is corporeal existence; the "Subtle State" includes all the extra-corporeal modalities of the individual states of existence, whether human or other.

22. Guénon, 1958a, pp. xii-xiv.

23. Symbols "have a capacity to express simultaneously a number of meanings whose continuity is not evident on the plane of immediate experience" (Eliade, 1959b, pp. 98 f.). Eliade repeatedly stresses the multivalence or polyvalence of symbols. See e.g., 1958b, p. 450; 1959b, p. 99; and Allen, 1978, pp. 161 ff.

The metaphor of the Net of Indra given in the Hua Yen (Jap. Kegon) school of Buddhism indicates the nature of this process of discerning pattern in symbolic constructs. The Net, which hangs in Indra's Palace, has a jewel at each of the crossings of its threads. Each of these jewels reflects each and every other jewel and is in turn reflected in each of them.[24] Symbolic correlates form a similar net : an exegetical analysis of a symbol's homologues throws light on the symbol; and as its meanings are thus clarified it in turn illuminates the other symbols. Further, the discernment of interlocking and inter-reflecting patterns is integrative;[25] in the same way that the many jewels of the Net are reflected or "focused" within a single jewel, so all symbolic constructs can be found within the single symbol studied and can be unified within it. Thus Eliade can say that "the search for symbolic structures is not a work of reduction but of integration. We compare or contrast two expressions of a symbol not in order to reduce them to a single, pre-existing expression, but in order to discover the process whereby a structure is likely to assume enriched meanings".[26]

The net of symbolic cognates is formed not only by visual and spatial symbols, but also by symbolic constructs expressed in other modes : *myth*, which is symbol expressed in a verbal or narrative form; *ritual*, which expresses the symbolic concepts by gestures and words; and *doctrine*, which expresses them conceptually.

What the architectural symbol is spatially the myth is verbally. The one expresses the supra-physical referent in a geometric or figurative mode, the other in a verbal and narrative mode.[27] As used here the word "myth" is not, as in popular speech, synonymous with "fable", meaning an untrue story. It is, on the contrary, used in its strict etymological sense : whereas "fable", from Lat. <u>fabula</u>, derives from <u>fari</u>, "to speak", "myth" is from the Gk. <u>muthos</u>, which derives from the root <u>mu</u>, "to speak with the lips closed", which is to say, silently.[28] This suggests the true nature of myth : it is a spoken narrative that refers to silence and the inexpressible. As do graphic symbols, the myth affirms the silence that lies beyond words : the narrator of the myth remains silent while speaking.[29]

Understood in this sense, myth is "the proper language of metaphysics"[30] and "represents the deepest knowledge man has".[31] Myth unveils a mystery and reveals a primordial cosmogenetic act;[32] it "reveals more profoundly than any rational experience ever could the actual presence of the divinity which transcends all attributes and reconciles all contraries".[33] Therefore to speak of the Buddha's life as a "myth" is not pejorative but is rather

---

24. See below, pp. 125 f. for references and further developments of this metaphor.

25. Eliade, 1958b, pp. 451 ff.; 1961, p. 163; 1959b, p. 96. See also Allen, 1978, pp. 144 f.

26. Eliade, 1959b, p. 97. 27. Guénon, 1953, pp. 120 f.

28. From the same root, <u>mu</u>, comes Lat. <u>mutus</u>, "mute"; as also do the Gk. <u>muein</u>, "to close the mouth, to be silent", and by extension, "to close the eyes"; and <u>mueo</u>, "to initiate", that is, to instruct wordlessly, and to consecrate. See Guénon, 1953, p. 125.

29. Guénon, 1962, Ch. II ("Le verbe et le symbole"), pp. 33 ff.

30. Coomaraswamy, 1944a, p. 19. 31. Coomaraswamy, 1946, p. 122.

an affirmation of its timeless significance,[34] since "a myth is true now, or it was never true at all"[35] and "myth spins out into a tale that is simultaneous and eternal".[36]

Ritual is similarly symbolic. Myth, symbol and the rite are strictly linked.[37] Every rite incorporates a symbolic meaning; it is a repetition of the sacred actions described in the myths, expressed by way of a series of gestures and words. The actions performed in the ritual - bodily and auditory - are symbols "put into action"; every ritual gesture is a symbol "acted". In reverse, the graphic representation of a symbol is a fixation of a ritual gesture and also, as in the delineation of the stupa plan described in the following,[38] the drawing of a symbol is itself a rite. Rites, myths and symbols are various, closely interlocking expressions of a single reality.

Likewise, in the Buddhist view, the canonical texts, the sutras and commentaries which are a main source for this study, are also symbols. This concept is conveyed by the Mahāyāna doctrine that the teachings are not the Truth in any absolute sense but are expedients (upāya) to aid men to an understanding of the Real.

The network of homologous symbols, myths, rituals and doctrines that can be delineated by a process of comparative juxtaposition is capable of indefinite extension. Since all symbols within a tradition are so many variant reflections of one and the same Principle, they are all inter-connected by way of this common reference, so that the analysis of the pattern of homologies generated from a given symbol as datum, if taken far enough, will eventually extend out to include all the symbolic forms of the whole tradition and even further to include the symbolic forms of all traditions. Guénon, Coomaraswamy, Eliade and others have traced the manifold correspondences and parallels that exist for various symbolic expressions among geographically and chronologically divergent peoples, demonstrating the universality of the web of symbolic affinities. Given the unlimited extent of this field of interconnected meanings, it is necessary to establish bounds to the analysis, and here it has been limited to materials from Brahmanic and Buddhist sources. Space permitting, however, these materials could be matched by cognates and homologues from a wide range of cultures. Many of the symbolic configurations demonstrated by reference to the stupa apply to architecture universally and, in the analogy of a philosophia perennis, it is possible to speak of a body of

---

32. See Saliba, 1976, p. 49.

33. Eliade, 1958b, p. 428.

34. Coomaraswamy, 1946, p. 164. Cf. Eliade, 1963, p.5 : "Myth narrates a sacred history; it relates an event that took place in primordial time, the fabled time of the 'beginnings'". Cf. Eliade, 1970, p. xii; 1973 p. 100; etc. This is a recurrent theme in Eliade's writings. For a constructive criticism, see Gaster, 1954, where the punctually present relevance of the myth is emphasised.

35. Coomaraswamy, 1946, p. 232.

36. Coomaraswamy, 1944b, p. 8, quoting an article by Murray Fowler.

37. See Guénon, 1953, Ch. XVI ("Le rite et le symbole"), pp. 115 ff. Saliba, 1977, pp. 53 ff., gives a summary of Eliade's extensive writings on the meaning of the rite.

38. See below, pp. 14 ff.

architectural principles that are of universal application. In this view the regional styles of architecture are dialects of a single architectural language.

The stupa is a Buddhist building, but the field of analytical enquiry has been extended beyond the borders of Buddhism to include the symbolic formulations of Brahmanism. The Brahmanic texts are a particularly rich source of explanatory material and an appeal to them for indications of the meanings of the Buddhist formulae follows a precendent set by scholars of the calibre of Coomaraswamy, Mus, and many others, who not only demonstrated the interrelatedness and continuity of Brahmanic and Buddhist formulations but showed that they derive from a common cultural source. Insofar as architectural symbols and rituals are concerned we are justified in speaking of an Indian rather than a specifically Brahmanic or Buddhist tradition.

This approach admittedly runs the risk of "denaturing" the *specific* content of the symbol - in the present case the specifically Buddhist significance of the stupa - but it can be argued that "it is only through the use of universal conceptions making possible significant critical comparisons between singulars of the same kind that we are able to discover and express clearly what is distinctive of the singular phenomenon",[39] and "An emphasis of universal religious structures need not reduce or compromize that which is singular".[40]

* * * * *

In the Indian view the symbol has a horizontal reference that is indefinitely extended and a vertical reference that is truly infinite. An exegesis that does justice to the fullness of the symbol in both its horizontal and vertical dimensions will leave its meaning "open" and not confine it within the limiting configuration of a closed hypothesis. The nature of the symbol precludes a reductionist methodology.

When, for example, texts are cited to show that the stupa axis is homologous with the World Tree, this is not to be taken (as it was by Bosch)[41] to show that the stupa is "nothing but" a development of tree imagery or that the stupa can be fully explained by this single reference. In the same way, the many references to the sun in connection with the stupa are not to be taken (as they were by Senart)[42] as indicating that the stupa form arose exclusively as a three dimensional diagram of solar movements. By contrast, to retain the "openness" of the stupa symbolism, the Tree and the Sun are to be seen as parts of a schema or pattern of interlocking and mutually reflecting symbols, no one of which predominates in significance over the others. Far from being self-sufficient as an explanation, the Tree is merely one among a number of equivalent and interchangeable axial symbols - Mountain, Pillar, Cosmic Person, the Vajra, etc., - whose referent is beyond themselves and is only to be known by a direct, intellectual insight. So likewise, when the spatial configuration of the stupa is referred to the movements of the sun or the other heavenly bodies, it is to be understood that the astronomical movements are not the

---

39. Smith, 1965, pp. 65 f., citing a point made by Cassirer. See also Allen, 1978, p. 164, n. 52.   40. *Idem*.

41. Bosch, 1960, *passim*.   42. Senart, 1882, *passim*.

43. Guénon, 1958a, pp. xiii & 14; 1962, p.36.

"meaning" of the symbol but another interlocking schema of symbolic expression, in which the celestial phenomena are in turn taken to represent, by way of analogy, principles of a supra-physical order.[43]

* * * * *

Approaching the study of the stupa from within the Buddhist tradition and with the intention of deciphering the pattern of symbolic constructs that it generates presupposes a synchronic method of analysis.

According to the traditional Indian concepts of the symbol, meanings are not "read into" symbols or added to them as a conceptual garnish. On the contrary, they are deemed to inhere within the form of the symbol in a manner analogous to that in which natural laws inhere within physical phenomena, or as mathematical principles reside in the very nature of numerical or geometrical phenomena. The significance of the stupa form, for example, is integral with the form itself, and lies there prior to its perception. This is one sense in which every religion and tradition ascribes a "non-human" origin to sacred symbols. Their principle traces back further and higher than do the constructs of the human mind. Because of this "the 'validity' of the symbol does not depend on its being understood; archetypal symbolisms preserve their structures and 'reappear spontaneously', even unconsciously, in non-religious phenomena... they 'are present' even if not consciously understood".[44] The symbol addresses not only the waking consciousness but the whole man; "symbols speak to the whole human being and not only to the intelligence".[45] Symbols communicate their "messages" even if the conscious mind remains unaware of the fact.[46]

This being so, the hermeneutic of a symbolic form such as the stupa is freed from the necessity of asking "how many individuals in a certain society and at a given historical moment understood all the meanings and implications of that symbol".[47] If the stupa can be shown to have clearly expressed a meaning at a certain moment of its history one is justified in supposing that the meaning inhered within its form at an earlier epoch, even if not consciously perceived or explicitly affirmed in the writings of those who built it. In the same way, meanings continue to inhere within the stupa even when they have been forgotten by later generations. "The 'cipher' of a symbolism carries in its composition all the values that man has progressively discovered in the course of centuries..." and "history does not basically modify the structure of an archetypal symbol".[48]

These considerations are deemed sufficient to justify a non-historical and a-temporal exegesis of the symbolism of the stupa. The stupa itself provides the model for this methodological approach. The stupa plan, as

---

44. Allen, 1978, pp. 209 f., citing Eliade, 1957a, p. 129; 1958a, p. 450; 1961, pp. 24 f. On the "non-human" origin of symbols see Guénon, 1962, p. 35.

45. Eliade, 1957a, p. 129. Cf. 1958b, p. 56; 1960, p. 16.

46. Eliade, 1965, p. 210.

47. Eliade, 1963, p. 102; Allen, 1978, p. 44. There are dangers in this approach if applied indiscriminately. Allen, 1978, is a book devoted to clarifying the methological implications of Eliade's position. Cf. Eliade, 1959b.

48. Allen, 1978, p. 176; cf. p. 183, etc.

will be shown, is a diagram of synchronicity; in the plan time is 'fixed', crystallized, rendered static; it is transmuted from a sequential and successive mode to an instantaneous pattern of relationships. The four seasons, for example, are "frozen" into the geometric configuration of the oriented cross; and in this cross they are seen in their momentaneity. So similarly, the aim of this study is to show the "successive" meanings of the stupa in their immediate, "spatial" pattern, as a structural lattice or web which, as does the symbol itself, lies beyond the limitations of historical contingency.

THE PLAN

1 THE SPATIAL CONFIGURATION OF THE STUPA.

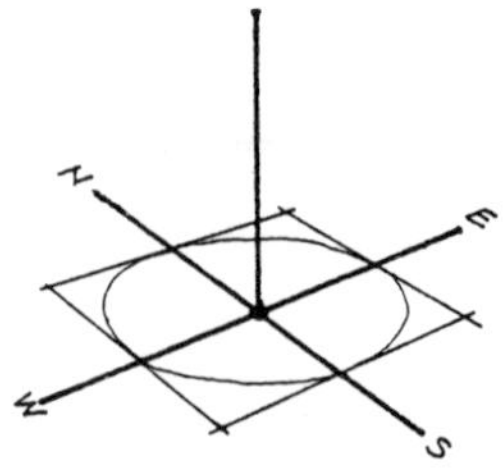

Fig. 1. Characteristics of the stupa: a centre, a vertical axis, and orientation.

The stupa has many and various forms. The differences between domed, towered and pyramidal stupas is sufficiently marked to suggest that they are the unrelated products of isolated architectural traditions. Despite their dissimilarities, however, all forms of the stupa have characteristics in common :

1. Every stupa plan develops symmetrically about a central point;
2. Every stupa volume develops symmetrically about an axis that rises vertically from that central point;
3. Every stupa mass is oriented in accordance with the directions of space.

These characteristics - centrality, axiality and orientation - are constants underlying the disparate aspects of the stupa form. It is precisely in these shared features that the essential significance of the stupa is to be found.

* * * * *

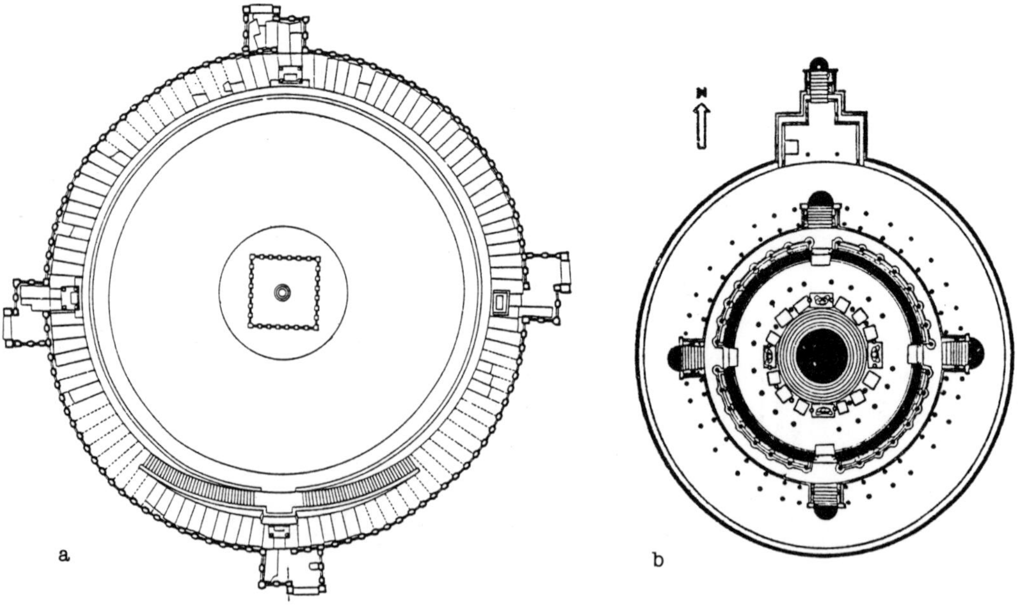

Fig. 2 : Typical stupa plans. Each is oriented in accord- with the cardinal directions. a. Stupa 1, Sāñcī. b. The Wat-da-ge, Sri Lanka. c. A Burmese terrace stupa. d. A Chinese tower stupa. e. Borobudur, Java. g. A Japanese tower stupa. h,i. Small Java- nese stupas. j. The Great Stupa of Rawak, Sinkiang.

Each and every form of the stupa is centred by a vertical axis. The axis is its fundamental and indispensable element. In the context of symbolic significance the axis *is* the stupa; the stupa exists to emphasise the presence of a perpendicular; it is the celebration of a vertical. The stupa's other components are so many developments, embellishments and adornments of the meanings contained within the axis.

The body of the stupa grows out into space from the axis, evolving equally in all directions from this fulcrum. The plan shape is invariably regular - a circle, or one of the regular polygons that can be inscribed within a circle. The centre governs the geometry : the plan shape and the volumes of the stupa expand symmetrically and centrifugally.

The geometry of the stupa form develops outwards from the centre in the cardinal directions : every stupa plan is oriented. The presence of directional axes is marked by gateways, niches, pillar groups (*āyaka-stambha*), podia (*vāhalkada*) and, in polygonal stupas, by the faces of the supporting base.

* * * * *

The first volume of this study is devoted to an examination of the proliferation of meanings generated by the centre, the vertical axis and the orientation (which is to say the emanation of the four cardinal directions from the centre) of the stupa plan. These meanings derive in large part from the ritual whereby the plan is delineated, described in the following section.

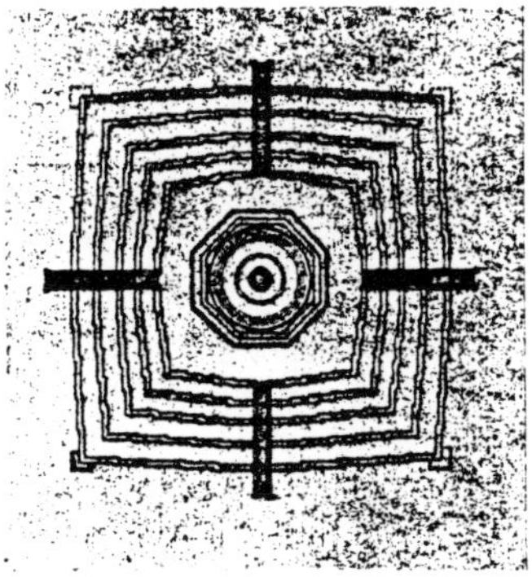
c

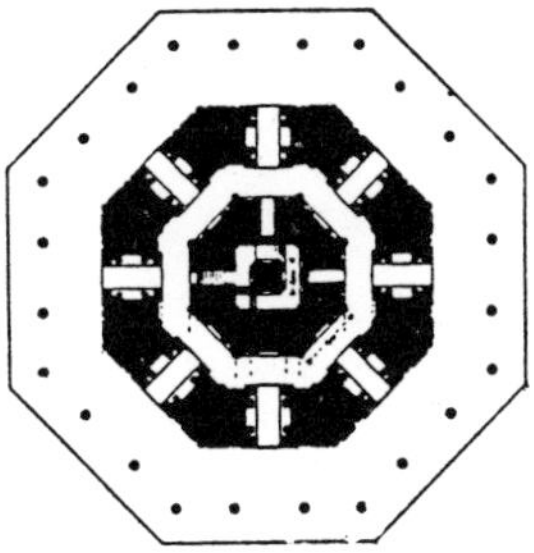
d

e

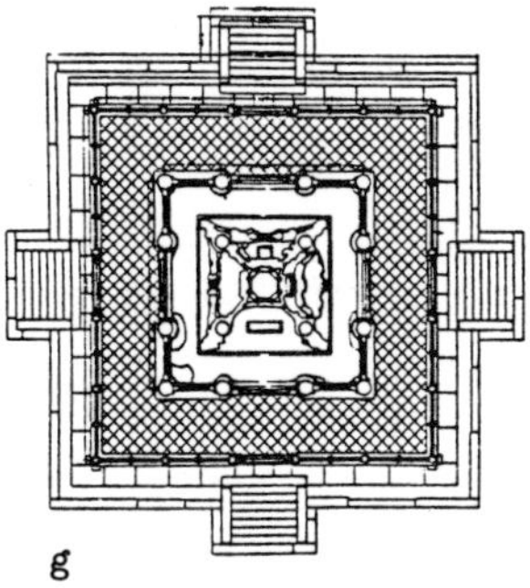
g

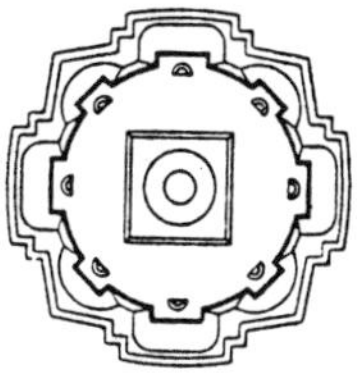
h

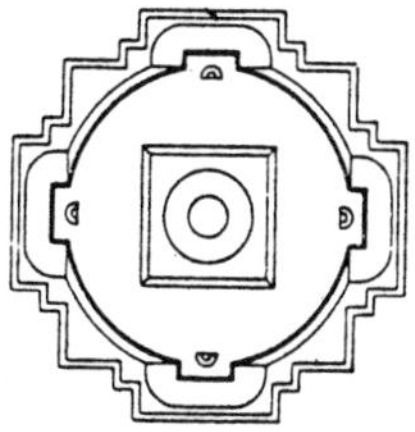
i

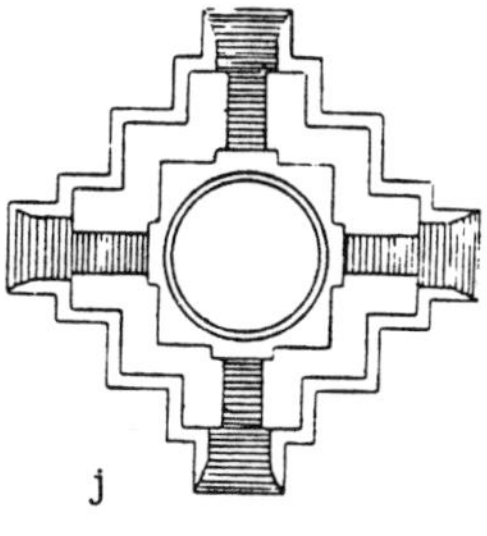
j

2 THE RITUAL DEMARCATION OF THE STUPA PLAN.

The stupa plan is determined by ritual means. The ritual procedures, detailed in the Indian building manuals, the *Śilpaśāstras*,[1] and summarized in the description of fig. 3, are used by Hindus, Buddhists and Jains to orient and define the boundaries of architectural projects - cities, temples, palaces and houses. The same method is employed to lay out mandalas.[2] The ritual forms part of a cultural heritage shared by all Indian traditions[3] and is one that dates from very early times.[4]

The ritual uses the shadows cast by a gnomon-pillar set up at the centre of a circle to determine an East-West axis. From this the North-South axis is derived geometrically, and then, by describing a series of arcs, a square is delineated whose sides are aligned with the four directions.

The ritual orients and delimits space and in so doing renders it meaningful. It creates spatial order from disorder, cosmos out of chaos. It sacralizes space, establishing a sacred area in the midst of profane environs.[5] The periphery of the square separates a formal area, a space with form, from an amorphous surrounding; it marks out a defined, and therefore knowable, space, from an indefinite and inconceivable extension; it specifies a relevant area, a field of ritual operation, from an irrelevant expanse.

---

1. See *Mayamata*, VI.1-10; *Mānasāra*, VI; Mallaya, 1949, pp. 124-125, where further references are given; Mus, 1935, pp. 131-133; Burckhardt, 1967, pp. 23-24; Dumarçay, 1978, p. 19; Combaz, 1935, pp. 33-34; Kramrisch, 1946, p. 227, and cf. pp. 23 & 39-40. Cf. Acharya, 1934; Bhattacharya, 1963; Johes, 1973; Pisharati, 1937.

2. On the method of laying out a mandala, see below, pp. 104 ff. For the setting out of Buddhist temple compounds, see Giteau, 1969; and for similar material relating to the orientation of buildings in Kampuchea, see Porée-Maspero, 1961.

3. Mus, 1935, pp. 131 ff., and Combaz, 1935, p. 32 both assume that the stupa was set out and oriented according to the same ritual procedures that are described in the Hindu *Śāstras*. The *Śāstras* make occasional reference to Buddhist buildings and indicate that Hindus and Buddhists employed similar building rituals. See e.g., *Mayamata*, IX. 70, XIII. 60 et seq. The ritual is of widespread occurrence in traditions other than the Indian, to the extent that it is possible to say that it belongs to the ritual repertoire of mankind as a whole. See Burckhardt, 1967, p.24. For Chinese parallels see Wheatley, 1971, pp. 425-6; and for its use in ancient Rome, ibid., pp. 423-4. I have seen variations of the ritual performed in Japan (cf. Nitschke, 1974, 764f., on the *tokoro shizume matsuri*, the "Earth Quietening Ritual"), in Thailand and by the Dayak of Kalimantan.

4. Its use is implied in ancient texts such as Asvalayana's *Grihya-sūtra*, II. 7-8 and Gobila's *Grihya-sūtra*, IV.7, both in Oldenberg and Muller, 1892. Cf. Toganoo, 1932, p. 22

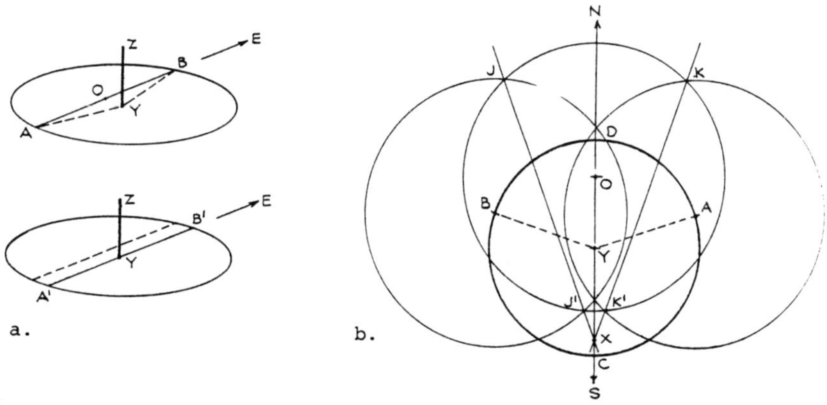

Fig. 3 : The determination of the orients.

The ritual described in the *Mānasāra Śilpaśāstra*, VI, is typical of those found in the other building manuals. It instructs the performer of the rite to erect a gnomon (YZ) at the point selected to be the centre of the building. From this centre, Y, a circle with a radius twice the length of YZ is described on the ground. The points where the ends of the shadow thrown by the gnomon touches the circumference of the circle in the morning and the evening are marked (A and B). The vector AB lies in the East-West direction.

The line AB cannot act as the spine (pṛṣṭhyā) of the building since it does not pass through the centre, Y. The midpoint of AB (marked O in the figure) only coincides with the centre Y at the time of the equinoxes, when the shadow cast by the gnomon points to the West during the morning and to the East after midday. At all other times of the year O and Y are not coincident. From the equinoxes the distance between them progressively increases until it reaches its maximum at the time of the solstices when the declension of the sun is at its minimum. Thus if the ritual is performed on any day other than the two equinoxes it is necessary to draw a second line (A'B') running parallel to AB and passing through the centre Y.

The *Mānasāra Śilpaśāstra* gives no indication of how this is ritually accomplished, but another text, the *Tantrasamuccaya* (in Mallaya, 1949, pp. 124-5), which is the building manual most used in the Tamil South, describes an alternative method of determining the directions that avoids the necessity of relocating the first-found axis. By marking the end of the shadow cast by the gnomon at three equally spaced times during the day - in the morning, the afternoon, and a time half way between them - three points are obtained, two on the circumference of the circle and one within its area (A, B and O in fig. b). With these points as centres three circles are drawn, cutting each other at the points J, J', K and K'. The line XY that joins the gnomon to X, the point of intersection of the lines JJ' and KK', marks the North-South direction. Its extension gives the points C and D on the circumference of the principal circle.

Having thus determined one of the two cardinal axes, the next step is to determine its complement. From A and B (fig. a) or C and

5. The concept of the demarked space as cosmos as opposed to a surrounding chaos is developed by Eliade in several places. See e.g., Eliade, 1957, pp. 60 ff.; 1956b, pp. 367 ff.; 1959, pp. 9 & 18. Cf. Wheatley, 1971, pp. 418-9; Altizer, 1963, pp. 125 ff.

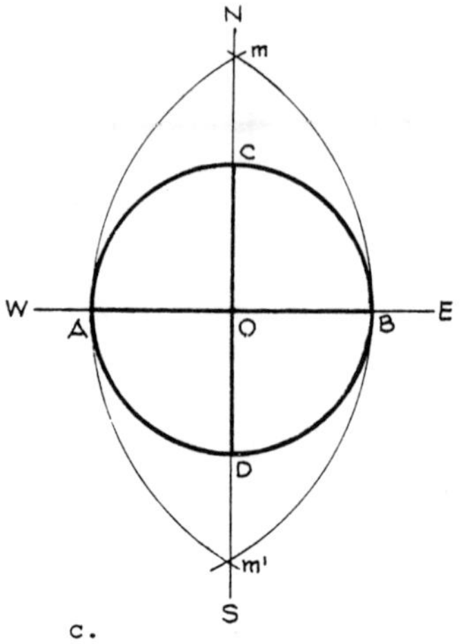

c.

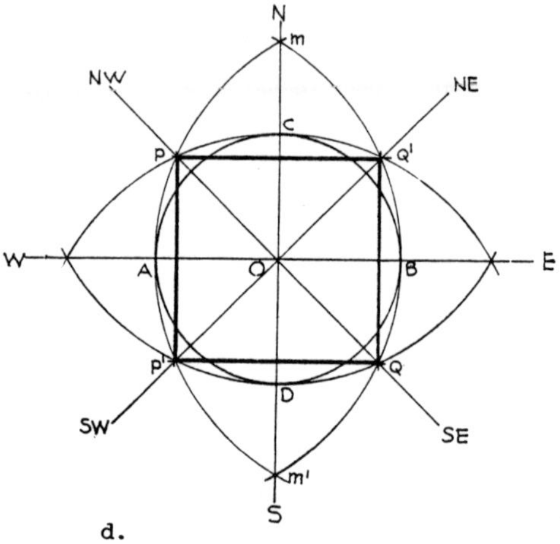

d.

What we now have is a circle with two diagonals cutting at right angles and oriented in accordance with the cardinal directions, the basic layout of the stupa with a circular plan. In order to determine the plan form for stupas with a square base, a second schema of geometrical construction is followed. From A, B, C and D as centres and with the diameter of the circle as radius four segments of circles are described so as to intersect at the points p, p', q and q' (fig. d). By joining these four points the square pp'qq' is obtained. The diagonals of this square, pq and p'q', mark the axes of the intermediate directions NE-SW and SE-NW respectively. Thus we get a second schema of orientation derived from the first : a square whose sides face the four cardinal directions and whose corners lie on the axes of the ordinal directions.

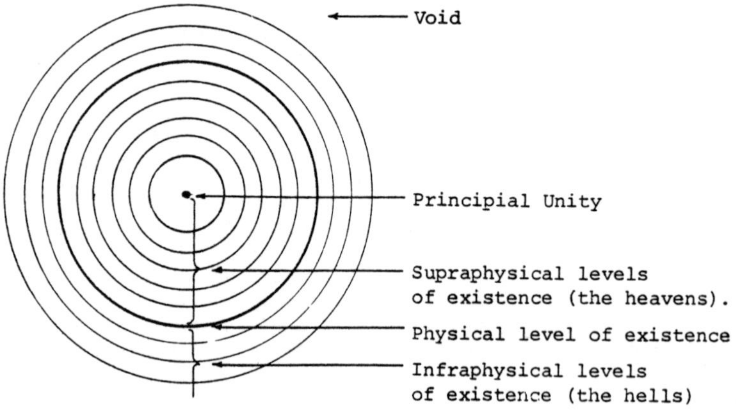

Fig. 4 : The states of existence
represented by concentric
spheres.

The ritual is equivalent to a creation of cosmos from chaos because it re-enacts or reproduces the manner in which the total universe is instantly and perpetually brought into existence. The measuring out and orienting of the enclosure is a reflected likeness, a mimesis, of the momentary and punctual process of the world's manifestation. The ritual is seen as a creation of cosmos because it retraces the original _modus operandi_ whereby the total cosmos is ordered from primordial chaos.[6]

The significance of this ritual transformation of chaotic and profane space to cosmic and sacred space can be clarified by reference to a diagrammatic model of the universe or, more correctly, a model of the manner of the generation of the universe.[7] It consists of a series of hollow spheres of diminishing radius arranged one within the other about a common centre. Figure 4 shows a median section through this disposition of concentric spherical shells. This configuration represents the totality of all the possibilities of manifestation, whether belonging to the informal, subtle or gross levels.[8] Each of the spheres (or the circles in the sectional representation) is a "world", that is to say, a given ensemble of possibilities making up a level of existence. One of the spheres will represent our own particular plane of existence; the spheres above it, that is, closer to the centre, represent the heavens or the supra-human levels; and the spheres below, those that are further from the centre, represent the hells or the infra-human levels of existence. The configuration as a whole thus shows a hierarchy of states of existence; and it should be noted in passing that in this schema heavens and hells are relative to a given plane of existence : our world is a hell for its superior states but is in turn a heaven for the underlying hells.

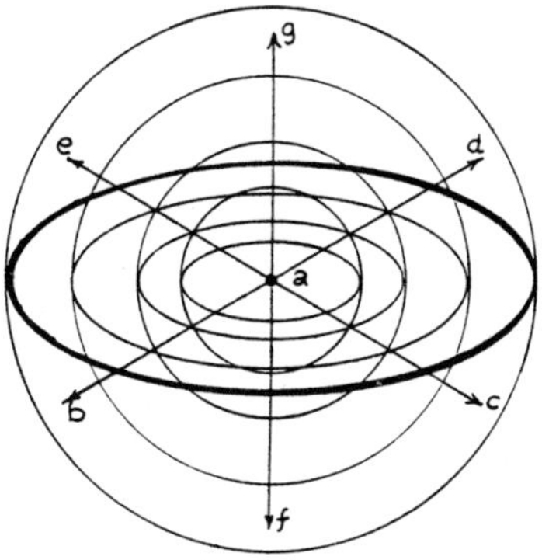

Fig. 5 : Deployment of space in the six directions from the Centre.

6. For ritual as mimesis, see Eliade, 1959, pp. 18 & 20 ff.; 1958c, p. 6; and below, pp. 19 f.

7. This model is a three-dimensional development of the wheel symbolism demonstrated by Coomaraswamy, 1977, 1, pp. 178-180 & 221-222. Cf. Guénon, 1957a, Ch. 23 ("La Roue Cosmique"). Other aspects of the symbolism of the wheel are developed below, pp. 78 ff.

8. For clarifications concerning the use of the terms "subtle", "gross", "manifestation" and "non-manifestation", see Guénon, 1945, pp. 33-35, and above, p. 5, n. 21.

For any point on the surface of one of the spheres there is a radius that passes through it and connects it to the centre; and just as there are innumerable points on the surface, so also are there innumerable radii passing through them to the centre. Taking one of these radii as typical it is seen that it not only connects the points on the surface of the sphere to the centre but also passes through each of the spheres lying between that particular surface and the centre. That is to say, the radius connects the state of existence which is being considered with all the superior states. Again if the radius is extended outwards it similarly connects this state of existence with all the underlying hells. In this way each and every one of the indefinite number of radii tending from the centre pierces each of the multitude of states of existence, connecting it to each of the others as well as to the point that centres them all.

This model relates to the ritual demarcation and orientation of the stupa site : the point selected to be the centre of the stupa plan is where the radius from the centre (a) strikes the plane of the earth. It is taken as the typical exemplar of the indefinitude of points where radii meet the ground. The ritually selected point is now _the_ point. The line that connects it back to the centre of the spheres is similarly _the_ radius, and the gnomon-pillar is that radius made visible and marks the line that connects this world to all the superior planes of existence and ultimately back to the centre whence all derive. When the performer of the ritual measures out in the four directions of space upon the ground he is mimetically repeating what happens at the centre : the innumerable radii emanating in all directions from the centre can be reductively typified by the six radii that emanate in the six primary directions, those which are the coordinates of the concentric spheres, namely, the four forming the arms of a right angle cross on the horizontal plane (ab, ac, ad and ae in fig. 5), plus the two directions on the vertical axis, one directed towards the Nadir (af) and the other towards the Zenith (ag).

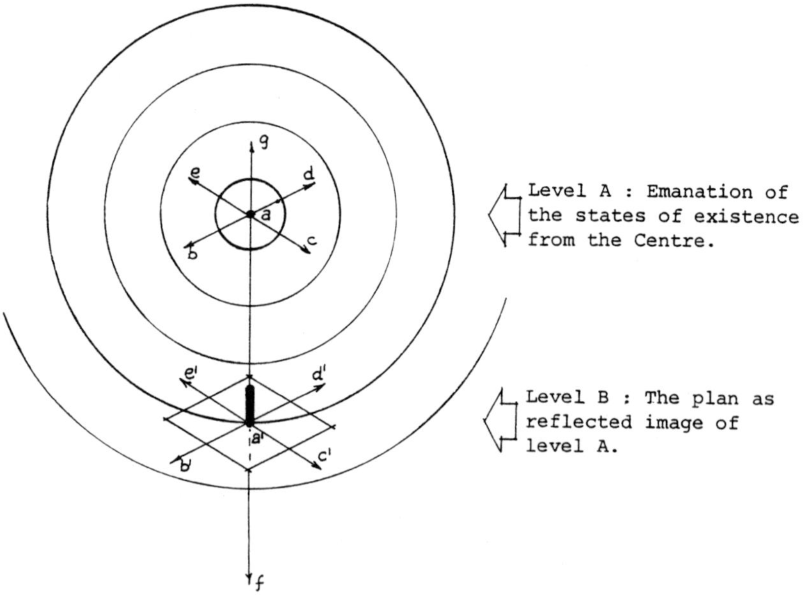

Fig. 6 : The orientation of the plan as a mimesis of the cosmogenesis.

The model is a conventionalized representation of the manner in which the states of existence are generated. The process of their manifestation from Principle is analogous to a "radiation" of spheres from the centre along the coordinates in the six directions, in the manner of ripples spreading from a stone dropped into a still pond of water, but conceived in a three-dimensional rather than a two-dimensional way : a series of spherical "waves" or "pulsations" emanating from a point source of origin. The genesis of the multiple states of existence that together make up the totality of the manifested universe can thus, in a sense, be thought of as "measuring out" from the Void; and it is precisely this process of measuring out the total cosmos that is imitated in the ritual demarcation of the site. The ritual repeats what happens as the worlds come into existence. The space defined in the ritual is symbolically a cosmos because the manner of its measuring out is a mimesis of the measuring out of the total cosmos; its ordering and delimitation is an image of the process whereby that cosmos is defined. The centre of the cosmos-in-a-likeness laid out upon the ground of the building site is charged with meaning because it is a reflection of the supreme Centre, the progenitive source of all manifestation.

The cosmological model thus derived is shown in fig. 6. The lines ab, ac, ad, etc., at level A are the coordinates of the universe radiating in the six directions from the Centre (a). The square plane shown at level B is to be thought of as delineated on the inner surface of the sphere that represents the terrestrial level of existence. It can be considered as a horizontal plane if the sphere is thought of as indefinitely remote from its centre. This horizontal plane is the area measured out along the four cardinal directions in the ritual : the line aa' is the radius, vertical with respect to the plane, that connects the centre of the ritual space with the principial Centre.

* * * * *

The point upon the ground selected to be the centre of the stupa plan is symbolically the trace or reflection at the terrestrial level of the supernal and primordial Centre whence existence derives by emanation. By reflection and by symbolic equivalence the visible centre is identified with the transcendent Centre. It is seen as the <u>omphalos</u>, the navel and fulcrum of the world, the progenitive source point of manifestation.

Trace of the axis that joins the worlds to each other and to their transcendent Source, the centre of the plan marks a place of communication and of passage, a gateway to the celestial and infernal realms, a point of initiatic entry to the pathway ascending to the supernal Sun. It is the <u>locus</u> of a rupture in the divisions between the planes of existence. It is the place of the manifestation of the divine, a point of hierophany, of an irruption of the real into the realm of the illusory. It is the source whence all celestial influences and graces flow into the world.[9]

The centre (a') is the point where the vertical axis from the Centre (a) strikes the plane of earth. In their symbolic significance point and axis are correlative; they are the alternate expressions of cosmic centrality : the vertical radius seen in plan is a point; seen in elevation it is a perpendicular axis. The place of the world's centre is simultaneously and always the place of its axis : <u>umbilicus mundi</u> and <u>axis mundi</u> are coincident.

---

9. The concept of the centre as the locus of an hierophany is a recurrent theme in the works of Eliade. See e.g., Eliade, 1957, *passim*; 1958b, pp. 367 ff.; 1961, pp. 27 ff.; etc.

The gnomon erected at the centre of the plan is the axis mundi, the axial pivot that centres the states of existence, linking them to each other as beads upon a string, and each to the centre whence it derives. It is the way whereby communication with the other states of existence is effected and whereby the influences from above flow down into their various levels. It is the axis of the World Wheel, whose spokes are the emanating radii and whose felly is our plane of existence. The vertical ray is the trunk of the Cosmic Tree or Tree of Life, whose branches are the multiple states; it is the Mountain that stands at the centre of the Universe; the Ladder whose rungs are the states of existence leading up to Heaven; it is the mast of the Ship and also the smoke that rises from the Hearth at the centre of the House of the Universe.

The ritual of site demarcation and orientation is to be understood in this context of significance. By means of the ritual the builder identifies the centre of his structure with the axis of the universe; by measuring out from the centre he repeats by analogy the process of cosmogony. The space he delineates is a reflected likeness of the total cosmos, its area made meaningful by way of its connection with the supra-physical realms located along the axis that centres it.

* * * * *

Several qualifications are necessary in connection with the cosmogonic model described in the preceding. Firstly, a description of the genesis of the universe in terms of an emanation from a point outwards in the six directions is, if taken literally, an error, since space is a condition of existence peculiar to our own level in the hierarchy of the states of manifestation. Spatial concepts are not applicable at other levels : the model is to be taken as a spatial representation of processes that are spatial by analogy only.

This points up what was said above on the nature of symbolism : whatever transcends our level of existence is no longer subject to its characteristic limiting conditions such as space and time. It cannot be described in modes of expression that partake of those limitations, but only by way of analogy, which is to say by way of symbols. The symbol is not to be taken literally : the builder who measures out the cosmos in the ritual of demarcation is not repeating the process of cosmogenesis in any literal sense but solely in a likeness. He is repeating, in the modes proper to our state of existence, processes that are essentially indescribable since they lie beyond those modes.

Secondly, it is to be emphasised that the above is only one of a number of possible ways of explaining the symbolism of axiality. Every true and adequate symbol is, as was stated in the Introduction, multivalent in its meaning. To the extent that it reflects universal realities the symbol possesses a universal content of significance, which can be viewed from many points of view. To allow but a single interpretation of a symbol is to limit its referent, which is unlimited.

3 THE SYMBOLISM OF THE CENTRE.

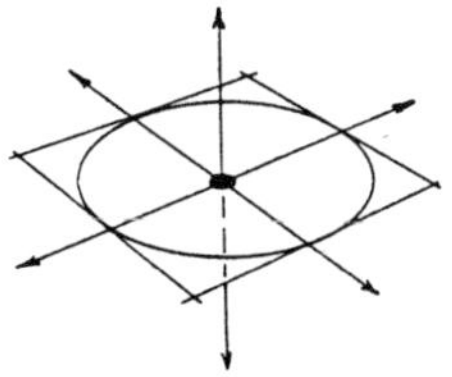

1. THE GEOMETRIC CENTRE.[1]

The cosmogony is symbolically expressed as an expansion or radiation into the six directions from a central point. The three-dimensional cross, with its six arms radiating from a common centre, is the universally recurrent symbol of this process of cosmogenetic evolution. The arms are the coordinates of our sensible world; they indicate how space deploys into existence from a point centre and, by analogy, how time evolves from punctuality. The centre of the cross, where its six arms come together, symbolizes the Principle that generates the universe; it is the point of origin of all things. Itself dimensionless and timeless, it is the Principle of extension and duration. Lying beyond all spatial and temporal limitations it nevertheless engenders the entirety of spatio-temporal manifestation. The arms of the cross depend upon and radiate from their centre; without the centre they could not exist. So likewise the totality of universal manifestation depends upon and radiates from - and is irradiated by - its Principle, lacking which it would be nothing.

The concept of the genesis of space as an expansion or radiation from a point is reflected in language. The Sanskrit word nābhi, "the hub or nave of a wheel" and also "centre" and "navel", derives from the root nabh, "to expand". With reference to the human body, the navel corresponds to space,[2] and in the *Ṛg Veda* the cosmos is frequently spoken of as "expanded" from a chthonic navel.[3] Also, in the *Vedas* space is often designated by the word diś, which is literally "cardinal point" or "direction".[4]

The six directions of spatial extension - before, behind, left and right, above and below - and the three divisions of time - past, present and future - are contained in dimensionless momentaneity at the centre. All phenomena, all entities, all events in space and time are held there in an atemporal nowhere that is now and here.

Because the geometric point-centre is formless, dimensionless and without duration it is an adequate symbol of primordial Unity,[5] the

---

1. The works of Guénon provide insights that are indispensable for an understanding of the symbolism of the centre and the following relies heavily on his analysis. See esp. Guénon, 1958a, Ch.7 and *passim*; 1962, Ch. 8 and *passim*. The concepts introduced by Guénon are developed in the writings of Coomaraswamy and Eliade : see Coomaraswamy, 1977, 1, pp. 454 ff. and 2, pp. 221 ff.; Eliade, 1957, *passim*; 1958a, pp. 143 ff.; 1959, pp 12 ff.; 1960, pp. 49 ff.; 1961, pp. 27 ff. & 73 ff. See also Chevalier and Gheerbrant, 1973, 1, pp. 299 ff., s.v., Centre ; Cirlot, 1962, pp. 39 ff.; Wheatley, 1971, pp. 428 ff.; Perry, 1971, pp. 771 ff.

2. MU VI.6. 3. Coomaraswamy, 1977,2, p.222. 4. Mus, 1935, p.139.

5. That is, metaphysical rather than arithmetical unity, which latter represents Unity by analogical correspondence at the level of quantity. See Guénon, 1946, p. 28; 1957, Ch. 5; 1962, p. 84.

Principle of manifestation. The radiation of the worlds from the centre is a realization, a bringing into existence, of virtualities lying dormant within Unity[6] : it is a procession from Unity to multiplicity, from the imperishable One to perishable plurality.[7] It is a disintegration and division of the One into the many : activating itself, the One spreads out and scatters its light into the opacity, and there "rests in a wavering refraction which appears other than itself".[8]

In the same way that Unity produces all numbers without being modified or affected in its essence by their production, so similarly the central point produces all things and yet remains unaltered. So it is that the Brahmanic texts can say that "It (Brahman) became the all"[9] and yet add that "Only one Fire is kindled manifold, only one Sun is present to one and all, only one Dawn illumines this All"[10] and "He maketh his single form to be manifold".[11] Similarly, the Buddha, who is the personification of the point of Unity, says, "I, being one become many, and being many become one".[12]

This is conveyed by the geometry of the figure laid out in the ritual demarcation of the stupa site. The ground on which it is drawn is the Ground of the Void or Non-Being, mathematically Zero. The centre is Unity, the first and principial number, One; and, since the circle can have but a single centre, inconnumerable. The circumference, made up of an indefinitude of points, represents the numbers of multiplicity; and the square expresses the procession from Unity to quadrature,[13] which reductively typifies the fragmentation of the One.

* * * * *

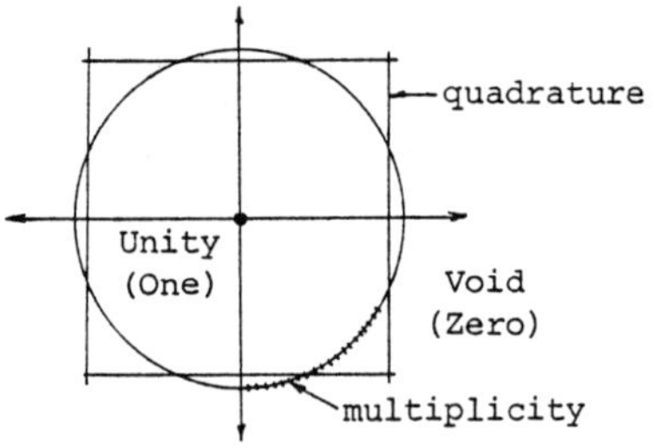

The centre has another significance. It is not only the point of origin whence all things issue forth but is also the point of their ultimate return. There are two possible directions of movement along the radii that join the points on the circumference of the circle to their centre, firstly, from the centre to the circumference, and secondly, from the circumference back to the centre. These complementary phases of movement, centrifugal and centripetal, comparable to those of respiration or the action of the heart, give the image of the successive manifestation and reabsorption of existences. From the centre as nucleus proceed the cosmic tendencies of emergence and divergence, of expansion and emanation : the One gives forth the multiple, the most inward proceeds outward, the unmanifest becomes manifest and the eternal unfolds to reveal the cycles of time. In the complementary phase the cosmic forces of reintegration and convergence, of concentration and conjunction, tend back towards the centre : multiplicity returns to Unity, the outward turns wholly inward, manifestation is occulted and time is absorbed into the still point of the timeless.

---

6. Guénon, 1958a, pp. 20 ff.; Eliade, 1957a, p. 44.

7. Edgerton, 1924, p. 20; cf. Wu, 1963, p. 10.

8. Tucci, 1961, p. 57. 9. BU I.4.10. 10. RV VIII.58.2

11. MU VI.26. 12. S II.212.

13. Guénon, 1962, Ch. 14 ("Le *Tetraktys* et le carré de quatre"), treats of the quaternary as the number of universal manifestation. See also Kramrisch, 1946, p. 123, n. 84.

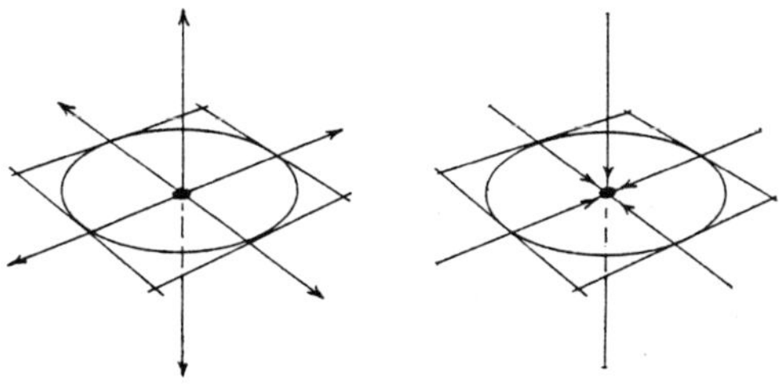

This concept of emanation frcm and return to the centre forms one of the most fundamental bases of architectural symbolism. If beings are entirely dependent on Principle in everything they are, then they must all, consciously or unconsciously, aspire to return to it, and this centripetal tendency is rendered into built forms by means of ritual orientation, which directs the construction towards a centre, a terrestrial and sensible image of the true Centre of the World. The orientation of the stupa is thus seen to be an embodiment of man's striving to retrace the steps of his becoming, back along the radii of the Wheel of Existence to its central hub. The stupa, as every other form of traditional architecture, materializes man's most fundamental intent, that of a return to his own true centre.

* * * * *

Lying equidistant from all the points on the circumference, the centre divides each diameter into two equal parts. It is the point where extremes, or opposing tendencies, represented by points opposite each other on the circumference, are reconciled and joined in perfect equilibrium. The centre is the place where all contraries are unified and all oppositions are resolved.[14] The coming into existence of the worlds is the genesis of oppositions, the creation of a cosmic dialectic of contrasts and irreconcilables. The cross with arms expanding from a common point of origin in the contrary directions - north versus south, east versus west, and the nadir opposed to the zenith - is the archetypal formulation of this deployment of contraries. It subsumes the cosmic interplay of antithetical, antipodean counteractions and interactions, the polarity of contradictory energies. The central point is the place of the nativity of oppositions; it is also the place of their reconciliation, of their union in a coincidentia oppositorum. At the centre all oppositions are fused in a coincident and concurrent merging. From one viewpoint the marriage of contraries is an equilibrium of complementaries, subsisting in a harmonious balance of mutual compensation. In this view the centre is an abode of tranquility, the paradisical locus where antinomies are transcended and the dualities inherent within existence are subsumed within a non-dual concordance, the place where all evil and suffering, the anguish and anxiety deriving from the clashing conflict of contraries, disappear within the perfect peace and repose of their central merging. Viewed from another position, however, it is a focus of dynamic intensity, the place where all energies and forces are concentrated, where all oppositions inherent within the cosmos coexist in a state of prepotent virtuality.

---

14. Guénon, 1958a, p. 38; 1962, p. 88; Chevalier and Gheerbrant, 1973, 1, p. 299.

2. THE SUN AS CENTRE.

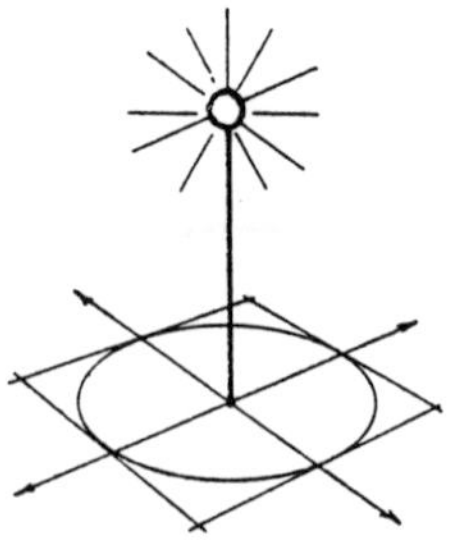

The orientation of the stupa plan is determined by reference to the movements of the sun; the plan is a geometric diagram of the solar cycle; its axes locate the successive positions of the sun's course. This has a more than merely astronomical significance and expresses the symbolism of the metaphysical Sun, the source and centre of the worlds.

In both the Brahmanic and Buddhist traditions the sun is the symbol of the supreme Principle,[15] the transcendent Centre of the universe. In the Brahmanic texts the Sun is Cosmic Intelligence and the light it radiates is intellectual Knowledge;[16] it is the abode of Brahman and Purusa and the seat of the cyclic legislator, Manu. The Sun's rays measure out the worlds, bring all things into existence, quicken all beings : "Thou alone, O Sun, art born about the whole world".[17] The Sun is the sacrificial Person who is "poured out upon the earth from East to West".[18] It divides itself to fill the worlds[19] but yet remains undivided and whole among divided things,[20] "for inasmuch as he is that (Sun) in yonder world he is one, and inasmuch as he is numerously divided here on earth among living beings, he is manifold".[21] By this manifold division of itself the Sun's light is progenitive, "for progeny indeed is all the light".[22] The Sun's rays are his sons and every animate being is filiated from the Sun; and the Enlightened know that "the rays of him (the Sun) who burns there, are the righteous"[23]: they <u>are</u> the solar rays, and true sons of the Sun.[24]

The symbolism is Buddhist as well as Brahmanic. The Buddhist literature contains a group of stories in which the future Buddha has the form of a golden animal or bird that daily leaps or flies to the top of a tree.[25] These legends have reference to the ascension of the golden Sun to the apex of the world axis. The Buddha's birth is compared to the triumphal rising of the Sun, which lights the whole world.[26] In the Pali texts the Buddha is "the kinsman of the Sun" (P. <u>adhicca-bandhu</u>); he is also the "Eye of the World" (P. <u>cakkhumā-loke</u>),[27] evoking the recurrent Brahmanic identification of the Sun and the Cosmic Eye, which "surveys the whole" and "sees all things"[28]: from its solar centre the whole circumference of the cosmic wheel is visible; the Buddha, like the Sun, sees all things simultaneously.

---

15. Perry, 1971, pp. 317 ff.

16. Chevalier and Gheerbrant, 1973, 4, p. 216, s.v. <u>Soleil</u>.

17. AV XIII.2.3. 18. RV X.90.5. 19. MU VI.26.

20. BG XIII.16 and XVIII.20. 21. ŚB X.5.2.16

22. ŚB VIII.7.1.16; cf. TS VII.1.1.1.

23. ŚB I.9.3.10; cf. RV I.109.7. 24. JUB II.9.10.

25. See Przyluski, 1930, pp. 457 ff.; 1929, pp. 311 ff.; Bosch, 1961, p. 144.

26. *Buddhacarita*, I.28. On solar symbolism in the Buddha legend, see Rowland, 1938, and Soper, 1949.

27. SN I.599 & III.9.6; D II.158.

28. RV I.164.44 and *passim*; AV III.22.5; BU I.3.8.14; KU V.11; S I.38; *Atthasālinī* 38; etc.

In the Vajrayāna the identity of the Buddha and the Sun is explicit. The supreme Tathāgata is termed the "Great Sun" (Mahāvairocana, Jap. Dainichi), the supreme Eye of all the Buddhas and Bodhisattvas, who is "without centre or circumference and never increases or diminishes".[29] He is the Solar Source from which all Buddhas and Bodhisattvas issue forth as beams of light; and he is the Solar Body of Fruition to which they all return. The Great Sun, Mahāvairocana, stands upon the summit of the World Mountain, Meru, where he eternally reveals the Dharma by radiating forth the Diamond World Mandala from his effulgent Body.

The Great Sun, which is the metaphysical Sun, is not to be confused with the physical sun of our everyday experience. "Whereas the light of the physical sun is partite, shining in the daytime but not at night, the light of the Sun of Wisdom shines brilliantly in all places and at all times....and everywhere throughout the Dharma World. The Great Sun cannot truly be likened to the physical sun except by analogy; the physical sun is subject to the limitations of causality, whereas the Great Sun is wholly transcendent. Therefore it is called the Great Sun, Mahāvairocana".[30] The supernal Sun "after elevation to the zenith shall no more rise nor set, but stand single in the Centre. Hence this text : 'There it has not set, nor did it ever rise...' It neither rises nor sets; once for all it stands in heaven for him who knows the doctrine of the Brahman".[31] The perceptible sun is merely the likeness of the supernal Sun; it moves, and by its motion measures out the rhythms of time; but the imperceptible Sun is stationary, fixed in an eternal Present, in the punctual and Principial Instant whence time evolves. The metaphysical Sun stands beyond time and remains forever motionless; within the Sun the nunc fluens is forever the nunc stans and time is congealed in punctuality.

* * * * *

The central point of the stupa plan is identified with the Sun, the Centre of the cosmos, located at the navel of the universe at the summit of the World Mountain. From the terrestrial viewpoint the Sun is at the top of the universe, at the "eye" of the celestial vault; but in truth the Sun is positioned at the Centre of the total universe. Viewed from the felly of the World Wheel the Sun at the hub is at the zenith of the circle's radius, which is at once a solar ray and the axis of the universe; but viewed with the Solar Eye and from the position of the Sun itself, it is centrally located.[32]

The Sun is homologous to other symbols of the Centre : it is "the one lotus of the zenith";[33] it is the circular roof plate (kaṇṇikā-maṇḍalam)[34] and eye of the dome in which the rafters converge as the rays of the sun or radii of a wheel;[35] it is the hub of the chariot wheel, Heaven's only opening, enveloped by rays of light, which must be withdrawn before the orb can be clearly seen.[36] It is also the axis mundi, since centre and radius, in the view of the Sun's Eye, are coincident. Thus the Sun is itself the Pillar that holds apart the worlds,[37] and the Tree

---

29. MKDJT, p. 1522, s.v., *Dainichi Nyorai*, quoting the *Kongōchō-kigetsu*.

30. *Idem*, quoting Śubhākarasiṃha, 1.

31. CU III.11.1-3; cf. Eliade, 1961, p.75.

32. Cf. Coomaraswamy, 1977, I, p. 420, n.11.

33. BU VI.36. 34. RV I.146.4. 35. Coomaraswamy, 1977,1, p.440.

36. Īśā Up. 15, 16; JUB I.3.5; I.111.33; CU VIII.6.1; etc.

37. RV VI.86.1; VIII.41.10; X.17.11; X.121.1; JUB I.10.9.

of Light.[38] In many traditions the sun is a symbol of the ruling Principle or Law of the cosmos, and analogically represents the king as the embodiment of Law within the empire.[39] So also in the Buddhist tradition the Sun is the symbol for the sovereign Buddha, personification of the Cosmic Dharma, and analogically the emblem of the cakravartin-king.

The stationary Sun stands at the apex of the world axis. It rests in the topmost branches of the Cosmic Tree and is the same Sun that stands unmoving above the tree when the child Siddhartha, the Buddha-to-be, entered the first meditation (dhyāna).[40] It shines from the summit of the World Mountain : it is the "one Sun that never leaves Mt. Meru",[41] and Meru is "the support of the Sun".[42] The head of the Sun Pillar, extending from the centre of the vault of heaven to the navel of the earth,[43] is the omniform and omniscient Sun-Spirit whose kiss endows all things with life and being.[44] The symbolism is expressed in Buddhist iconography by the frequently recurrent motif of the Wheel (cakra) supported by a pillar : the Wheel is identified with the Sun[45] and located at the top of the column is at once the Wheel of the Dharma and the Buddha-Sun set motionless at the apex of the world.[46]

The Buddhist story book, the *Vikramacharita*,[47] tells us that on the summit of a high mountain there lies a lake from whose centre rises a pillar of gold to support a golden throne. "From sunrise to noon-time the column rises gradually till it reaches the disc of the sun and after that it sinks little by little till at sundown it touches the water again. This happens day by day". The story continues by describing how the cakravartin Vikramāditya ("Sun of Heroism"), sitting upon this throne, rises with it towards

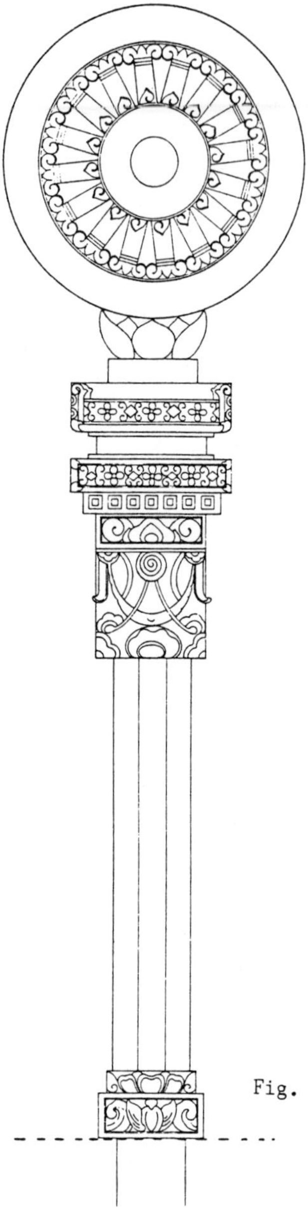

Fig. 7 : The Sun Disc, homologue of the Wheel of the Dharma, standing stationary at the top of the World Axis.

---

38. Coomaraswamy, 1977, 1, p 387.

39. Chevalier and Gheerbrant, 1973, 4, p. 217, s.v., Soleil.

40 See below, p. 182.   41. AB XIV.6.44, Comm.

42. Kramrisch, 1946, p. 355, quoting the Hansot Plate, 757 A.D., (Broach), Ep. Ind., XII, 203.

43. AB V.28.1; II.1.   44. ŚB VII.3.2.12-13.

45. R.V I.174.5; I.175.4; IV.16.12; IV.7.14; VI.56.3; etc.

46. Cf. Bosch, 1961, p. 159.

the Sun, and then redescends with it to enter the subterranean world, where a glittering golden sacrificial post (yūpa) is set up upon a golden altar. Beside the post stands Prabha ("Splendour"), the Mother of the World and the beloved of the Sun. Seated on his throne, once more the king rises to the surface of the lake at the moment of the sun's rising. In this manner the cakravartin and the throne follow the ascent of the sun to the zenith and then its nightly descent into the subterranean worlds.[48] In this connection it is to be noted that the Great Goddess is assimilated to the cosmic axis that holds apart the worlds and upholds the Sun God, Sūrya.[49]

The cakravartin's throne supported at the summit of the Pillar is a variation on the theme of the cakravartin's palace which "rests on a single column" (ekastambha-prāsāda)[50]: "If I raised a palace on a single column, I would be first among all kings", says a monarch in the *Jātakas*,[51] and the *Culavaṃsa* relates how the Sinhalese king Parakkamabāhu had just such a palace constructed : "Rising from a makara, it rose aloft as if it had split open the earth. It was adorned with a golden chamber placed upon a golden column and possessing the beauty of a cave of gold for this lion among kings..."[52] This in turn relates to the symbolism of a town supported by a pillar, typified by Dvāravāti, the city of the cakravartin, which, at the approach of enemies and at a cry from the demon who guarded it, would rise up into space as if supported by an island in the middle of the sea. When all danger had passed the town sank down to its usual level.[53]

These legends, associating the pillar-supported Sun, the cakravartin, his throne, his palace and his city, ultimately refer to the Buddha, who is the supreme Cakravartin, the Solar King who dwells at the summit of the universe.[54]

As shall be shown in greater detail in the following[55] the macrocosmic symbolism of the Sun located at the zenith of the cosmic Mountain, Tree or Pillar has a microcosmic counterpart. In the individual being the Sun "of a thousand rays" is synonymous with the sahasrāra, the thousand petalled lotus stationed at the foramen (brahmarandhra) at the crown of the head and the summit of the merudaṇḍa, which is homologous with the solar ray and the microcosmic axis.[56]

The full implications of this symbolism of the Sun fixed stationary at the summit of the axis mundi - Pillar, Mountain or Tree - will become apparent when the imagery of the Sun Door is examined at a later place.[57]

---

47. Also called the *Siṃhāsanadvātriṃsika*, "The Thirty Two Stories of the Throne". Cited in Bosch, 1961, p. 96; Auboyer, 1949, pp. 78 ff.; 1954, p. 183; Wales, 1977, p. 132; Féer, 1883, pp. 127 ff.; and mentioned below, p. 70, in connection with the symbolism of the Pillar.

48. A similar symbolism appears in the *Cakkavati-sīhanāda-suttanta* (SBB 4, 26) but there the motion of the pillar follows the life of the cakravartin in its ascendency and subsequent decline. Elsewhere the pillar rises and falls in accordance with the length of the kalpa (cf. Auboyer, 1949, p. 79).

49. See below, p. 166. Cf. Combaz, 1935, p. 114.

50. *Jātaka* 121 & 454; Auboyer, 1949, p. 80, n.3, p.117, n.6 & p. 128.

51. *Jātaka* 465. 52. *Culavaṃsa* II.11-12. 53. *Jātaka* 454.

54. This theme is developed in the following. See pp. 88 ff.

55. See below, pp. 317 ff. 56. Eliade, 1957, pp. 77-78.

57. See below, pp. 268 ff.

4 THE SYMBOLISM OF MEASURING.

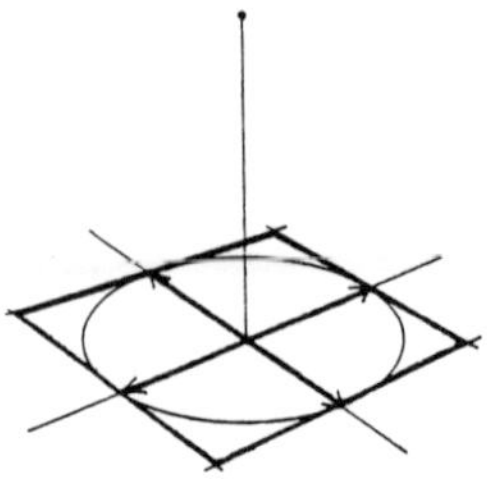

1. MEASURING OUT FROM THE CENTRE.

The ritual of laying out the confines of the stupa to accord with the directions of space is the demarcation of an ordered, or cosmic space from out of the chaos of unlimited extension. It is the determination of the indeterminate; a limitation of the unlimited; a making finite or definite of what is undefined and indefinite. It is a process of measuring out so as to give bounds to the unbounded : in its unbounded state space is amorphous; by its bounding it is given form. By its measuring out space is brought from virtuality to actuality; it is rendered real, made to exist.

The manner in which undefined space is measured out in the ritual is analogous to that in which the possibilities contained within Principle are determined in the process of cosmogenesis. The generation of existences is precisely their definition from All-Possibility. From the central point, which is itself the first determination of the Ocean of Possibility, there is an irradiation that illuminates the tenebrous Waters of potentiality, and they are made manifest. The Waters are measured. The possibilities of manifestation are defined and bounded. Just as the radii that emanate in the cardinal directions from the centre in the rite can be said to realize space by causing it to pass from virtuality to actuality, the extension of the radii being the measure of the actualized, or realized space, so analogously the radii issuing from the cosmic Centre realize the potentialities inherent within the Waters and thereby bring forth order - cosmos - from dark chaos. The radii are like the rays of the sun; they illuminate the obscurity of substantial chaos, making apparent that which they illumine so that the possibilities of phenomenal existence are made visible. The rays make things manifest and, symbolically speaking, manifest them. The possibilities of manifestation are actualized, brought from potentiality to act.

In this process "the 'non-measured' is that which has not yet been defined; the 'measured' is the defined or finite content of the universe, that is, of the 'ordered' universe; the 'non-measurable' is the Infinite, which is the source both of the indefinite and the finite, and remains unaffected by the definition of whatever is definable, that is to say by the realization of the possibilities of manifestation that it carries in itself".[1]

The significance of the ritual of demarcation thus lies in the fact that it is a mimesis of the measuring out of cosmos from the dark and limitless Ocean of Universal Possibility. The ritual is a reenactment of this cosmic generation : it is mimetically an illumination, a making manifest and a making real. Prior to its determination by the radii emanating from the centre, space has no real existence, remaining outside manifestation as disembodied, indistinguishable extension, nothing more than a virtuality. The projection of the radii and the bounding of the space is the realization of space. The perimeter of the bounded space marks the effective extension of the radii from the centre, which extension is the measure of the space realized. Just as the primordial measuring

---

1. Guénon, 1953a, pp. 37 f., paraphrasing Coomaraswamy, 1938c, p. 91, n. 2.

is a comprehension or an encompassing of potentialities, so too the builder's simulated demarcation is a division of the graspable, that is, comprehensible, from the incomprehensible, of the knowable from the indefinitude of the unknown.

The rite, as are all others, is a reflected reproduction at its own level of the original and momentarily persisting process of the production (that is, literally, "a leading forth") of order, a concept that is conveyed by the word "rite", which is connected with the Sanskrit word ṛta, "order", and also by its root with the Latin ordo.[2] To ritually measure the unmeasured is to regulate it (from the Latin regula, "a rule"), to order it, to create cosmos or an ordered world.

To measure (mā) is to give existence to a thing, to actualize it, to give it reality. In the beginning the principial Unity divides itself to give existence to divided things, and this fragmentation of the One is a measuring out of the universe. The cosmogonic procession is a measuring out, and in this sense is per artem. It is māyā, an illusory or "magical" process. Saṃsāra, the world of becoming, is māyā-maya, "natured", of the stuff of māyā. Māyā is "art", that by which an artefact, an appearance (rūpa), is produced; it is an artifice, that which brings the world into existence.[3] The word māyā comes from the same root mā, "to measure", as does mātra, "measure", which in turn is etymologically linked to the Latin materia, from which our word "matter" derives.[4] Materia not only relates to mater, "mother", and to matrix, but also to metiri, "to measure, to lay out (a place)", that is, to define it by boundaries, and "to erect, to set up", thus involving the twofold concept of generative principle and of measure : the measuring out of the world is the very process of its genesis.

The material world, even etymologically, is intimately connected with measure. This relationship is clearly expressed in Buddhist myth, where Māyā is the Buddha's mother and where the Buddha appears in the world in his "body of measurement" or "measured body" (nirmāṇakāya) : the body of the Buddha is coterminous with the measured body of the universe and his nativity is a paradigm of its production into existence.[5]

The concept of the cosmogenesis as a process of measuring out of the directions from a centre is inherent within many aspects of Indian thought. The measuring out of the directions is a reiterated theme in the Brahmanic and Buddhist mythologies. Prajāpati, who is the Year, measures out the world with his Eye, the Solar Orb.[6] So similarly the Sun measures the dimensions of space and time to produce the cosmos.[7]

---

2. Ibid., p. 338, n.10.

3. Zimmer, 1946, pp. 24-25. For other valuable insights into the nature of māyā see Eliade, 1979, pp. 201-202.

4. It must be stressed that the term materia as used here and as conceived by the Scholastics has nothing whatever to do with the "matter" of contemporary science. However vague and ambiguous this term might be when used in the modern world it nevertheless always refers to the sensible order of reality, whereas in the traditional context materia belongs to the principial order and thus lies in a realm that cannot be penetrated or cognized by the sensible or mental faculties. It is totally beyond the level of apperception belonging to the senses or the discursive mind. See Guénon, 1953a, pp. 25 ff.; Coomaraswamy, 1977, 1, p. 376, n. 1.

5. See Coomaraswamy, 1938a, *passim*, and esp. p. 83.

6. See below, pp. 31 f.

7. See below, pp. 30 ff.

Puruṣa (= Prajāpati), the non-supreme (apara) and first form of the supreme Brahman (para-brahman),[8] identified with Viśvakarman, the Architect of Universe,[9] "bears the measuring rod (māna, from mā), knows divisions and thinks himself composed of parts".[10] Thus divided and measured out, Puruṣa thinks of himself as the Goddess Umā, whose name, like māyā, is from the root mā, "to measure" : she is "the measured out", the manifested world come into existence by the thinking of Puruṣa.[11] By thinking himself as divided and composed of parts he measures out the cosmos.

2. MEASURING OUT BY THE SUN.

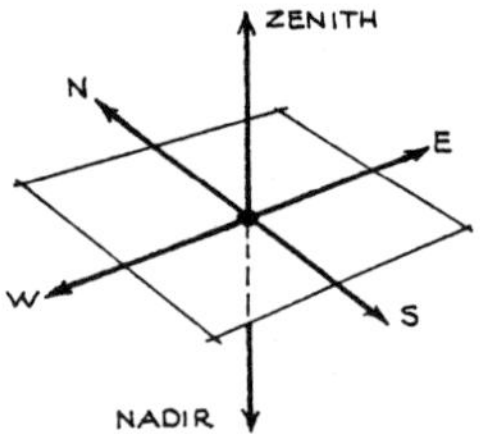

Fig. 8 : The seven rays, viz., the rays in the six directions (the four cardinals, the Zenith and the Nadir) plus the Centre, the "seventh ray".

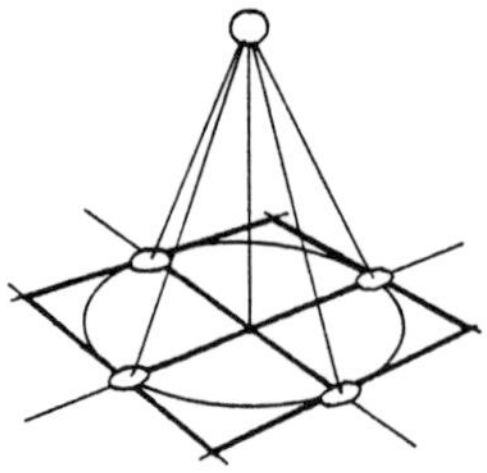

The method of orienting the stupa plan in the ritual of its demarcation is a mimesis of the manner in which the sun measures out the directions in its diurnal and annual cycle. This, in turn, is a physical likeness of the metaphysical Sun's deployment into space, its passage from Unity to quadrature, from the One to multiplicity.

The Sun is the Centre, in which there is no distinction of directions, the "locus" of Brahman who "is endless in all directions, though for him assuredly directions such as 'East' etc., cannot be predicated"[12] and in whom "the directions are submerged".[13] Manifestation expands or extends outwards in the six directions from the Sun as its Principle, which is therefore "seven rayed", with reference to the six arms of a three dimensional cross and the point of their junction, which is the trace of a seventh "ray" that is coincident with the centre. The Sun, "set aloft", at first "was unstable, it seemed, it did not flame, it seemed, it did not burn aloft", and only when made firm by the gods did it "burn upwards, hitherwards and crosswise",[14] that is, shine from the Centre (the "seventh and best ray") in the six directions.

The seven rays of the Sun typify the 4,5,8,9, 1000 or innumerable rays that shine from it in all the indefinitude of directions that part from it as centre. Of the six radiating rays those of the zenith and the nadir coincide with the Cosmic Axis, while those of the four directions on the horizontal plane determine the extension of the "world", or a particular ensemble of possibilities of manifestation. The seventh ray, coincident with the Sun-Centre itself, as it were passes "through" the Solar Orb to the supra-solar Brahma-worlds, where "no sun shines". By his passage through the Sun the Wayfarer begins his "ascent" of the seventh ray, which is the brahma-pātha, the continuing Path of Brahman. This Path, being dimensionless, is incapable of description by geometric representation except by analogy; it is ineffable, non-human, uncommunicable, knowable only by the Intellect and not by any physical or mental means.[15]

* * * * *

8. Śvet. Up.III.19; *Viṣṇupurāṇa* I.1.2. 9. *Mānasāra* II.2-5.

10. *Vāyu-purāṇa* IV.30-31, cited by Kramrisch, 1946, p. 131.

11. Kramrisch,1946, p.131. 12.MU VI.17. 13.JUB III.1.9. 14.JUB I.55.

The universe is measured out from the Sun as Centre. Viṣṇu, using the Sun as his measuring instrument, measures the earth;[16] and by the same means Indra measures out the six regions and so brings the wide earth and the high heavens into existence.[17] Varuṇa also, "employing the Sun as his rule, measures out the earth"[18] and "stretches out the earth as a butcher stretches out a hide, so that it should be the carpet of the Sun".[19] Elsewhere it is the Sun himself who "measures out the chthonic regions";[20] and Savitṛ, the Sun, measures the universe.[21] The Sun is the point of attachment to which the worlds are tied by means of the six directions; the warp of the world stuff is fastened by six pegs or rays of light.[22] "The Sun is the fastening (or pivot) to whom these worlds are linked by means of the quarters",[23] and hence the Sun is "four-cornered, for the quarters are his corners".[24] In other numerous texts Heaven and Earth are wheels, whose radii, determining the extension of their circumferences, are the rays of the supernal Sun : spatial extension deploys from the Sun as Centre; the Sun is the architect of space. "He (the Sun) has measured out with his rays the boundaries of Heaven and Earth";[25] and "it is through the Sun that the Earth becomes the support of all things".[26]

Analogously, the Sun measures out the cycles of time. Prajāpati is the Year and "The eye of Prajāpati's crudest from, his cosmic body, is the Sun. For Puruṣa's great dimensioned world (<u>mātra</u>) depends upon the eye, since it is with the (solar) eye that he moves about among dimensioned things".[27] "What precedes the Sun[28] is timeless (<u>akāla</u>) and undivided (<u>akala</u>); but what begins with the Sun is Time that has divisions (<u>sakala</u>) and its form is the Year".[29]

The procedure from Unity to quadrature by means of the Sun is mythically expressed in the Vedic account of the three Ṛhbus making four cups from Tvaṣṭṛ's one. The etymology of the term Ṛhbu is indicative of the import of this story : it derives from the root <u>rabh</u>, "to undertake, to fashion", and hence the Ṛhbus are "fashioners" or "creators". They are also "props" or "supports" (<u>rambhu</u>, also from the root <u>rabh</u>).[30] They are "the men of Midspace", associated with the cosmogonic action of diremption whereby Midspace separates Heaven and Earth and the four directions deploy from the centre. They divide Tvaṣṭṛ's cup "as it were measuring out a field (<u>kṣetra</u>)".[31] Tvaṣṭṛ's cup is the disc or plate of the Sun.[32] "Savitṛ (the Sun).. is this only feeding vessel of the Titan (Father)";[33] it is "the bowl wherein is set the glory omniform".[34]

* * * * *

---

15. Coomaraswamy, 1977,1, p. 420, n. 11. 16. RV VI.49.13.

17. Keith, 1925, 1, p. 80. 18. RV V.85.5; cf. VIII.42.1.

19. RV V.85.1. 20. RV V.81.3. 21. Idem. 22. AV X.7.42.

23. ŚB VI.1.1.17; VIII.7.3.10. 24. ŚB XIV.3.1.17.

25. RV VIII.25.18. 26. *Mānasāra* III.7. 27. MU VI.6.

28. Cosmologically, "what precedes the Sun" is the timeless epoch before time began; soteriologically, it indicates that he who attains the Sun is liberated from the toils of time : he is a <u>jivan-mukta</u>, "liberated in this life". Cf. Eliade, 1961, p. 74.

29. MU VII.11.8. 30. Cf. Coomaraswamy, 1977, 1, p. 416.

31. RV I.130.1-5. 32. RV I.110.3 & 5. 33. RV I.110.5.

34. AV X.8.9.

The directional axes of the stupa plan are the projections of the cross marked out upon the celestial sphere by the sun in its diurnal and annual movements. In its daily procession from dawn to sunset the sun measures out the extent of the earth along the East-West axis. Its inclination to the South (or North) from the zenith at midday, and its corresponding inclination to the North (or South) from the nadir at midnight, when projected upon the plane of earth subtends a short North-South axis. In this manner the sun marks out the four directions in its diurnal course.

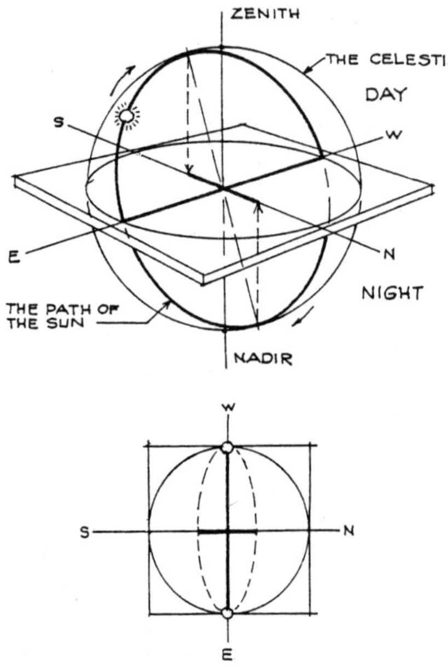

Fig. 9 : The cross projected by the diurnal movement of the sun.

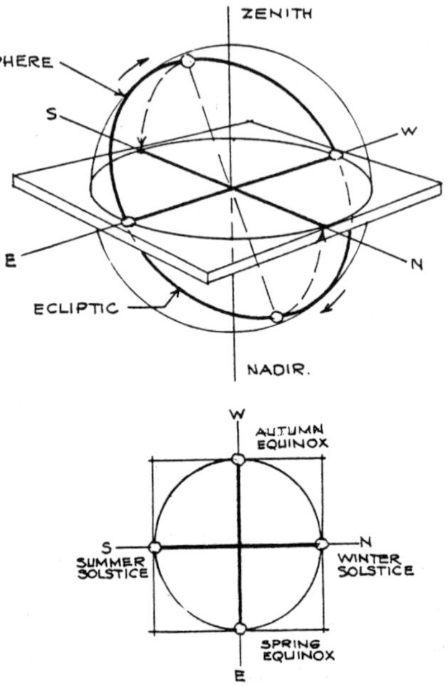

Fig. 10 : The cross projected by the annual movement of the sun on the ecliptic.

In relation to the plane of earth the sun rises daily in the East; in relation to the sphere of the heavens it rises successively in the East, the South, the West and the North. In its annual course the position of its daily rising is progressively displaced along the pathway of the ecliptic, moving one degree each day to trace a great circle upon the spherical surface of the celestial globe. The progress is coincident with the succession of the seasons : the sun reaches its Northernmost position at the time of the winter solstice; at the summer solstice it is in the South; and the spring and autumn equinoxes mark the times of its risings in the East and West.[35]

Thus by its diurnal and annual movements the sun simultaneously measures out the directions of space and determines the seasons. The four extremities of spatial extension and the four nodes of the temporal cycle of the year are married in the motions of the solar orb.

---

35. Guénon, 1962, p. 121; Mus, 1935, p. 227. For a description of spherical astronomy see Smart, 1931. A useful summary is given in Needham, 1959, pp. 178 ff. The correspondence of the seasons and directions is, of course, reversed in the Southern hemisphere, where North is the direction of summer and South is that of winter.

The stupa's plan is the projection of a celestial geometry : its directional axes are a projection onto the ground of the axes that join the sun's positions on the sphere of the heavens at the solstices and the equinoxes; its square is the terrestrial reflection of the supernal square determined by the nodal points of the year; its quarters are the four seasons of the year.

Each quarter of the cycle of the ecliptic comprizes three months and their three corresponding zodiacal signs, namely, one of the solstitial or equinoctial signs and its two adjacent signs. The twelvefold division of the circle of the ecliptic symbolically defines twelve aspects of the Sun, which are personified in the Brahmanic texts as the twelve Ādityas.[36] The circle of the ecliptic, divided into months, is translated to the earth as a square, with its twelve signs located in groups of three at each of the four sides.[37] This zodiacal square is the frequent basis for architectural forms : buildings and towns of the ancient and Asian world were laid out as squares with twelve doors or gates arranged three to a side so as to correspond with the twelve positions of the sun in its movement through the twelve months.[38]

The twelve months, which correlate with twelve positions of the sun on the ecliptic, are twelve aspects of the stationary Sun that stands at the apex of the world. The axes of the zodiacal square, joining the extreme positions of the sun's annual course on the great circle of the ecliptic, cross at right angles. The point of their crossing lies upon the world's vertical axis, which issues from the Sun fixed motionless at the zenith of the celestial vault. The cardinal axes which quarter the celestial sphere are centred on a pillar surmounted by the Sun. Moving through its twelve positions the sun revolves around this Solar Pivot : the ecliptic is a sun wheel turning about a Sun-Axle.

The essential ritual associated with the stupa, the circumambulation (pradakṣina) in a clockwise direction, keeping the centre to the right, repeats the solar symbolism. The ritual is a mimesis of the movements of the sun, passing through the four directions and the four seasons of the year. The performer of the ritual follows the ascending progress of the sun from the South to the North, where Liberation is attained,[39] and then its descending course back into the world, repeating the redescent of the Bodhisattvas who return to aid all suffering beings.

* * * * *

Both the diurnal and the annual cycles of the sun are reflected in the oriented square of the stupa's plan. The cross formed by the directional axes is a geometric representation of both the lesser and the greater cycles. They can both be represented by the same diagram because one is the image of the other : the daily projectory of the sun partially reflects its annual progress. So also something of the movement of the annual cycle is apparent in the successive positions of the sun's risings on the horizon, which are daily displaced by some degrees to the North or South of true East. There is a similar correspondence between the ascending and descending movements of the sun in the annual cycle and the two halves of

---

36. See below, p. 108. 37. Kramrisch, 1946, pp. 29 ff.

38. Typical of the many examples that could be cited are the Celestial Jerusalem and the Chinese Ming T'ang.

39. The North is the direction of the Sun Gate leading out of the cosmos. See below, pp. 269 ff.

the day. The ascending half of the day is from midnight to midday and the descending half is from midday to midnight. Midnight corresponds to the winter solstice and the North, and midday corresponds to the summer solstice and the South; morning corresponds to spring and the East (the direction of the sun's rising) and evening to autumn and the West (the direction of the sun's setting). The phases of the day, like those of the month, analogically reproduce at a reduced scale the phases of the year. The same can be said of a cycle of any length : it always follows the same quarternary law.[40]

The day, therefore, is a condensed image of the year. The year, in turn, is an image of the Great Day; and Great Days combine to form a Great Year. By these correspondences the significance of the stupa plan is expanded to encompass all the cycles of time, from the parts of the day to the total duration of the universe. By way of a series of reducing reflections time in both its totality and its subdivisions is focussed in the stupa plan. All time is geometrically reproduced within its confines.

The Pali texts speak of the periodic contraction (P. saṃvaṭṭati) and evolution (P. vivaṭṭati) of the world.[41] The time which thus evolves is divided into aeons (P mahākappa), each consisting of four periods called "uncountables" (P. asaṃkheyya) : the uncountable period of contraction, the uncountable period in a contracted state, the uncountable period of evolution, and the uncountable period in an evolved state.[42] Like space, time evolves and contracts and, like space, is reabsorbed into the timless centre. Time in its expanded state constitutes the Great Year. But the revolution of the wheel of the year through the four seasons has no beginning and no end. Every point of the sun's progress is simultaneously the end of a complete cycle and the commencement of a new one. The point of the beginning of the wheel of time is not on its rim, but can only be at its centre. The directions evolve from a centre and so similarly the four seasons evolve from a "fifth season", which is for time what the centre is for space. The fifth season is symbolically identified with the timeless days of the intercalary period and in the schema of temporal and spatial correspondences is located at the summit of the celestial pole, locus of the supernal Sun, the timeless source of all duration.

* * * * *

The stupa plan geometrizes time. It is a "crystallization" of temporal cycles, a fixation of time's movements. In the stupa plan time is transmuted into space, its motions frozen into geometric correspondences. In this way the two coordinates of the sensible world, the warp and weft of the tissue of the empirical universe - space and time - are woven together into the buiding fabric of the stupa.[43]

So, likewise, the stupa plan is a geometric graph of the cycles of renewal. The course of the sun is the paradigm of recurrent regeneration and decline : the sun's daily rising in the East is the image of rebirth and new beginnings, just as its setting in the West is the image of decay and death; and the sun's yearly journey through the seasons delineates a similar pattern, passing from the spring of new awakenings to the winter of dormancy. The axial cross of the stupa plan captures these transformations in momentary stasis.

* * * * *

---

40. Guénon, 1968, p. 240, n.2.

41. E.g., in the *Brahmajāla-sūtra* and *Aggañña-sutta*.

42. Gombrich, 1975, p. 137.

43. This theme is developed below, pp. 109 ff.

There is a microcosmic as well as macrocosmic application of the solar symbolism. The cosmological significance of the sun's progress through the four quarters has a psychological counterpart, as is evidenced by the *Chāndogya Upaniṣad*,[44] where the sun rises in the East, the South, the West or the North depending on one's level of spiritual advancement. For the Sādhyas it rises in the Zenith and sets in the Nadir; and for the Comprehensor, "the supernal Sun, risen in the Zenith, stands there in the middle, neither setting nor rising but evermore high noon". All these risings and settings take place "within you", "in the space of the heart".[45]

This internal schema of solar movement is explained by reference to the accompanying figure, in which "A" represents an individual positioned on the circle of the World Wheel. For reasons that will be developed in a later place the centre of the Wheel lies in the North;[46] South lies opposite, at the circumference; and East and West are as shown, to accord with the turning of the Wheel in a clockwise direction. The spiritual condition of the individual is a function firstly of his distance from the centre, and secondly of the direction he faces. At the beginning of his spiritual progress he turns from the centre and proceeds against the turning of the Wheel, facing the East, where he sees the sun to rise. Moving thus in an outward, extensive and centrifugal spiral he reaches a maximum distance from the centre, and now faces South. This is the winter solstice of his spiritual life and the "dark night" of his soul : the sun rises in the South. Now he "turns about in the deepest seat of consciousness" and, facing the West, moves in the direction of the Wheel's turning, retracing the spiral in an inward, intensive and centripetal direction. The sun is

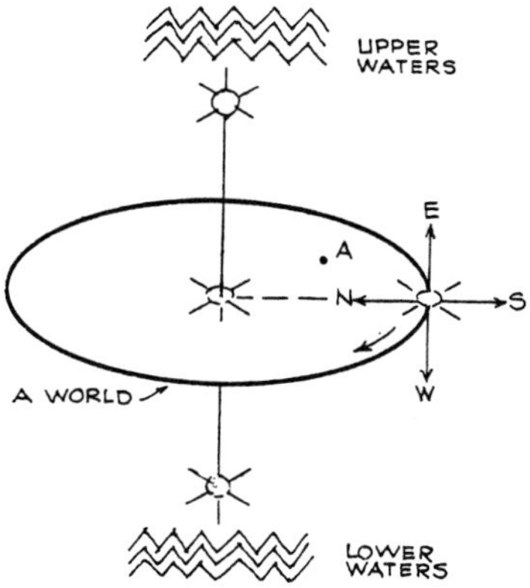

Fig. 11 : The solar movement in the microcosm (based on the illustration given in Coomaraswamy, 1976, p. 108).

44. CU III.10-11. 45. Coomaraswamy, 1976, pp. 90-91, n. 65.

46. See below, pp. 269 ff.

seen to rise in the West. In the fourth stage he comes to stand near the centre of the wheel, which is coincident with the centre of his own being. He faces North, and now the sun is seen to rise in that direction.[47]

Finally, when the journey of spiritual pilgrimage is completed, the aspirant is reunified within the centre. He becomes one with the nave of the world. For such a one the sun rises in the Zenith and sets in the Nadir. Henceforth his journey is along the "seventh ray", until, "laying aside both manifestation and non-manifestation, he is Brahman"[48] or, in Buddhist terms, he has attained _anuttara-saṃyak-saṃbodhi_, the Highest Perfect Awakening : the _axis mundi_ has contracted to a point and the sun "is forever risen; there is no more rising or setting. He is verily One, in the middle place".[49]

---

47. Coomaraswamy, 1976, pp. 109-111. The sun lies to the South at the winter solstice of the spiritual year, and to the North in summer. Hence East is the direction of autumn and the West is that of spring. The discrepancy with the evidence of our sensible experience of the movements of the physical sun exemplifies the axiomatic law of symbolic expression that the images of the empirical plane reflect those of the spiritual world as in a mirror, which is to say reversed.

48. BU III.5.

49. Coomaraswamy, 1976, p. 114.

5 THE SYMBOLISM OF THE DIRECTIONS OF SPACE

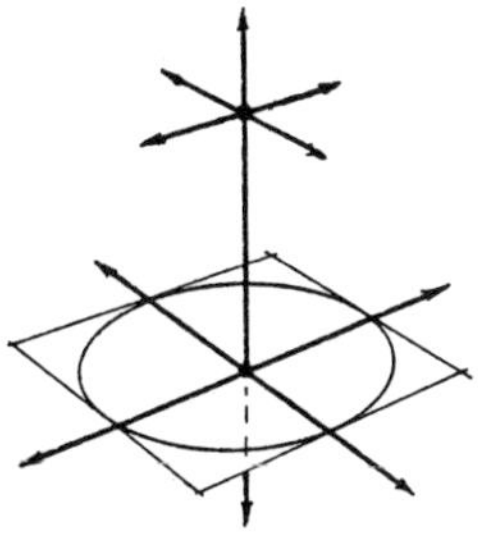

1. THE DEPLOYMENT OF THE DIRECTIONS.

The Buddhist tradition of laying out the stupa in accordance with the directions goes back to the earliest texts. The Sinhalese chronicles show that the ancient stupas of Sri Lanka were laid out in this manner. The *Mahāvaṃsa*, for example, tells how the spear of the Sinhalese king Duṭṭagamāṇi, having been planted in the earth could not be moved and was therefore taken to form the central axis of a stupa that was built around it.[1] The chronicle then goes on to describe how the king paid homage to the eight directions and to four monks in the cardinal directions and then placed eight sacred bricks in the eight directions, starting from the East.[2]

The *Mahā-parinibbāna-sutta* records that the Buddha, instructing Ānanda on the appropriate way to honour his remains after his parinirvāṇa, says that they are to be treated as those of a cakravartin and are to be installed within a stupa built "at the crossing of four great roads".[3] Scholars have been unanimous in seeing this as a reference to the four directions of space.[4]

A famous passage in the *Saddharma-puṇḍarīka-sūtra* adds depth of meaning to the symbolism of the crossroads. The sutra tells the story of a wealthy merchant whose house burst into flames while his children were playing within. To bring them to safety he calls to them that there are three carts outside, drawn by a ram, a deer and an ox, and urges them to come out and ride upon them. By this expedient (upāya) the children were enticed to leave the blazing building and were saved. "The children came out safely", the sutra says, "and seated themselves in the open space (ākāśe) at the crossroads".[5] The parable is rich in meanings : the burning house represents the world of saṃsāra; the flames are those of suffering and illusion. The children represent ignorant men, who must be enticed to safety by way of the expedient means - the provisional truths - of the Buddha's teachings; the carts drawn by the three animals are the Three Vehicles of the Buddhist Doctrine; and the "open space at the crossroads" is the locus of Liberation. The word used for "open space" is ākāśe, from ākāśa, literally "space", but more specifically and technically referring to the "spaceless space" at the axle point of a wheel[6] and synonymous with the principial Void-point whence the spatio-temporal world deploys. The children of the parable are safe from the flames of saṃsāra when they reach the ākāśa at the unmoving hub of the World Wheel, the crossing point of the

---

1. *Mahāvaṃsa* XXV.1. Cf. Mus, 1935, p. 118.

2. *Mahāvaṃsa* XXIX.64; cf. XXIX.59 and *Thūpavaṃsa* 104-105.

3. MV 10; cf. D XVI.5.

4. See Bénisti, 1960, p. 53; Viennot, 1954, p. 236; Bareau, 1960, p. 234; Combaz, 1935, pp. 32 & 51; 1932, p. 208; Volwahsen, 1969, p. 89; Govinda, 1976, p. 3.

5. SPS Ch. III (Kern, 1884, pp. 72 ff.).

6. Coomaraswamy, 1977, 2, pp. 20 ff.

axes marking the directions of space - which is precisely where the Buddha instructs Ānanda to build the stupa that will contain his ashes. Commentaries on the *Saddharma-puṇḍarīka-sūtra* explain that the crossroads also refer to the Four Noble Truths of the Buddhist Doctrine, so that when the children seat themselves in the "open space at the crossroads" they are at the very heart of truth.[7]

2. THE DEPLOYMENT OF SPACE IN THE BRAHMANIC MYTHS.

The Indian literature, both Brahmanic and Buddhist, contains many accounts, expressed in myth, of the cosmogonic deployment of space into the directions. One typical example tells how the opposing armies of the Gods (deva) and Titans (asura) fought for possession of the cardinal directions. The earth was unsteady, trembling like a lotus leaf agitated by the wind. The Gods seized it and made it firm, in the way that a hide is stretched and pegged by its corners. Using this as a stable support they set fires upon it and thus prevented their rivals from approaching. The earth having been secured, the struggle continued in the Midspace. The battle was fought in the East, then in the South, the West and the North, and in each of these directions the Titans were victorious. It was only when the fight reached the North-East, "the invincible region", that the Gods were able to repulse the enemy, but having lost the four directions the Gods were disoriented and confused and in great danger of losing the Midspace to the forces of disorder and disruption. The five regions were confused together, and were only recognized again when five divinities appeared, each in his appropriate place : by Pathyā Svasti the Gods recognized the region of the North...by Agni, the East...by Soma, the South...by Savitar, the West...by Aditi, the upper region. With the regions once more recognizable the Gods were able to overcome the Titans, and triumphantly ascended to the zenith of the sky.[8]

The import of the myth is clear : it tells of the simultaneous measuring out of the four directions and the vertical axis. The five points - the four at the horizon and the fifth at the zenith - are fixed in their positions and the stable cosmos of spatial extension is established.

The best known expression of the concept of the cosmogonic deployment of the spatial directions is Brahmā, the god of Creation, whose four heads, facing the quarters, symbolize the directional emanation of space. Brahmā is the source, the seed, of all that is. He is the embodiment of space-creating and time-creating power. Whereas Brahman, the unoriented and boundless Immensity, the Void, offers no room for existence, Brahmā, the Immense Being, Brahman's masculine or personified form and first affirmation, is the Principle of space and time : he punctuates the Void so that space and time may originate within its non-determination. He is qualified Brahman (saguṇa-brahma); he is identified with the Golden Egg (hiraṇya-garbha) from which the universe develops; he is similarly identified with Prajāpati, the god from whom the world is formed.

---

7. Parenthetically it should be noted that the term used to translate "open space" (ākāśe) in Kumarajiva's translation of the SPS is roji in Sino-Japanese, which is the term that the great Japanese tea master Sen-no-Rikyū uses in his *Nambōroku* to designate the small garden passed through when entering the tea house. Sen-no-Rikyū summarizes his reasons for adopting this nomenclature by saying, "The term roji sums up the whole realm of boundless tranquility that is the tea room". Rikyū used the term to signify the purity of the mind that has taken leave of all wordly toil and defilement. See Furuta, 1964, pp. 79 f.

8. Lévi, 1898, pp. 48 ff.; Mus, 1935, p. 168.

The lightning-thunderbolt (vajra) with which Indra slays Vṛtra[10] is "four-cornered", which is to say square,[11] as is its symbolic equivalent, the Cosmic Mountain, Meru, each of whose sides is assigned to one of the four castes : the Brahmins to the white side, the East; the Kṣatryas to the red side, the North; the Vaiṣyas to the yellow side, the South; and the Śudras to the black side, which is to the West.[12] Town and village plans in ancient India were disposed accordingly, with each caste occupying its appropriate direction on the square plan.[13]

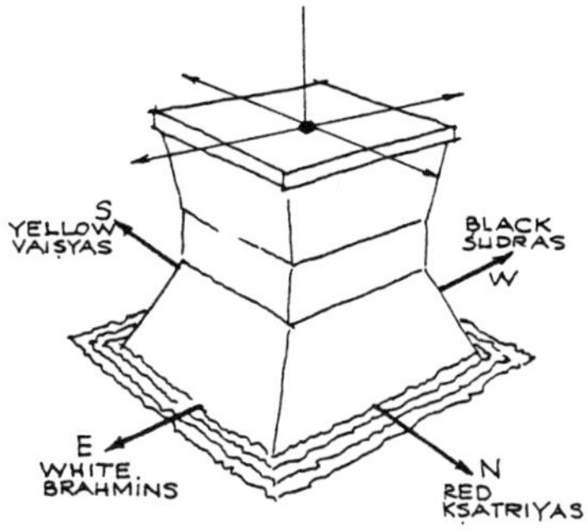

Fig. 12 a : The five prong vajra. The four outer prongs are arranged in the four directions around the fifth, axial prong.

b : Brahmā. His four heads, facing the four directions, refer to the deployment of space from the Centre.

c : Mount Meru. Its four sides, each correlated with a colour and a caste, face the four directions of space.

3. THE DEPLOYMENT OF SPACE IN THE BUDDHA LEGEND.

The legend of the Buddha's life contains many references, both implicit and explicit, to the concept of the directions of space deploying from a centre.

Before his descent into the world the future Buddha chose the place of his birth. The place he selected was the "Middle Country", defined in the *Vinayas* as lying centrally among towns, hills and rivers in the eight directions.[14] His mother, Māyā, conceived the future Buddha in a dream, in which the Guardian Gods of the Four Directions lifted her to a mountain top and placed her beneath a Sal Tree, where her son entered her womb in the form of a white elephant.[15] At his birth the Guardian Gods of the

---

9. Daniélou, 1964, pp. 232-234. 10. See below, pp. 64 f.

11. RV IV.22.2.

12. Guénon, 1938, p. 21; 1962, p. 120; Kramrisch, 1946, p. 42, n. 57.

13. *Bṛhat-saṃhitā* LII.67-68, cited by Kramrisch, 1946, p. 42.

14. Warren, 1922, p. 41. 15. Ibid, p. 42.

16. The significance of the net is discussed below, pp. 111 ff.

Directions appeared again, this time to receive the infant in a golden net[16] when he issued from Māyā's right side as she held fast to a Sal Tree.[17]

Each of these events has a spatial import, indicated by the presence of the regents of the cardinal directions and the Sal Tree, which symbolizes the central axis of the world.

Placed upon the ground the future Buddha stood upright and contemplated the regions in the ten directions (the four cardinals, the four intermediates, the Nadir and the Zenith) and could see no one in them to equal him. Then he took seven steps and declared, "I am the summit of the world, I am the best in the world, I am the eldest in the world".[18] As will be explained in detail in later chapters[19] the seven steps refer to the six directions of space plus the centre whence they deploy (that is, the "seventh ray"). On his seventh step the Buddha reaches the Centre of the universe and is thereby entitled to proclaim his primacy in the cosmos.

A story in the *Jātakas*, told of the Bodhisattva Jotipāla ("Keeper of the Light") but also understood to describe acts performed by Siddhartha to win his bride Yasodhara,[20] gives an account of how in an archery competition he set up four banana trunks in the four corners of the courtyard and, "fastening a thread to the feathered end of the arrow, aimed at and struck one of the trees; the arrow penetrated it, and then the second, third and fourth in succession and finally the first again, which had already been pierced, and so returned to his hand, while the trees stood encircled by the thread".[21] In the manner of the Sun the Buddha has measured out the four sectors of the world, tying them to himself by a thread of light : the directions are thus attached to the Sun, and "The Sun is the pivot, for to the Sun these worlds are linked by means of the quarters".[22]

The accounts of the Enlightenment tell us that the Buddha-to-be, having bathed and eaten, came to the Tree of Awakening, ascended the throne of Wisdom and stood on its Southern side, facing North. Immediately the South side of the world sank, tilting down as far as the hells, while the Northern side rose up to the highest heavens. Walking round the Tree with his right side towards it he came to the West and faced East, whereupon the Western half of the world sank, "as though it had been a huge cartwheel lying on its hub, and someone were treading on its rim".[23] Proceeding to the North the same thing happened and it was only when he arrived at the Eastern side and faced West that the world remained stable. "Now it is on the Eastern side of their Bo Trees that all Buddhas have sat

17. Warren, 1922, p. 46.

18. Fausböll, *Jātaka* I.53; Rhys Davids, 1880, p. 67; Mus, 1935, p. 483.

19. See below, pp. 242 ff & 275 ff.

20. Cf. *Jātaka* I.58; Warren, 1922, p. 56; *Lalita Vistara* XII.

21. *Jātaka* III.372; Coomaraswamy, 1943b, p. 111 and n. 16; 1944a, pp. 120-121. When the assembled people wonder at these marvels the gods explain that "former Buddhas have likewise, with the arrows of emptiness (śūnya) and impersonality (nairatma) smitten the enemy, depravity, and pierced the net of heretical views, with intent to attain the supreme Enlightenment". See *Jātaka* I.58; Coomaraswamy, 1943b, p. 117, n. 45.

22. ŚB VI.7.1.19; cf. VIII.7.3.10; BU III.6.2; BG VII.7.

23. Warren, 1922, p.75.

crosslegged, and that side neither trembles nor quakes".[24] The Great Being, saying, "This is the immovable spot on which all the Buddhas have planted themselves:, turned his back to the Tree to face the East and seated himself crpsslegged in an unconquerable position. Now Māra appeared and laid claim to the throne occupied by the Bodhisattva but is put to rout when Śākyamuni calls upon the Earth to witness his virtues. The victory over Māra was achieved before the setting of the sun, and as darkness pervaded the world the Bodhisattva concentrated his mind and began a meditational ascent of the world's axis, rising to ever higher planes of insight and understanding until, at daybreak, he attained perfect Enlightenment, bursting in total Freedom from the apex of the world.[25]

Directional and axial symbolism inheres in every detail of this story. In the context of the legend of the Enlightenment East is the location of the hub of the World Wheel. The East locates one aspect of the World Axis, namely, the Pillar of the Dawn, the column of light that sunders the darkness and props the sky from the earth.[26] The Wheel of the World tilts when the Bodhisattva steps upon its rim in the South, the West and the North - each of these positions is off centre - but remains steady when he reaches the East, the point of beginnings, here identified with the centre.[27]

Māra's claiming of the throne relates to the same themes. The World Wheel of the unenlightened is caused to turn by ignorance, craving and passion; the wheel of birth and death revolves about an axis of these three poisons. It is as the humanized embodiment of the poisons, the incarnation of delusion, that Māra claims the centre of the world as rightfully his. By contrast, the World Wheel of the enlightened Buddhas is seen by them to be the Wheel of the Dharma, the wheel of the cosmos ordered by the Norm and turning on the Buddha as its unmoving axle-tree.[28]

The Buddha's attainment of Enlightenment is the realization of his centrality. From the centre of our world he rises through the upper worlds, ascending the perpendicular that leads up to the Centre of centres, where he breaks free from the confines of the cosmos.

The symbolism of centrality is equally evident in the events immediately following the Buddha's attainment of Enlightenment, in the period called "the seven week's retreat".[29] In these forty nine days the Wakened One remains within the circle of the Tree of Awakening. For the first week he remains seated and motionless, realizing the bliss of nirvāṇa. Then, rising, he stands for seven days more, steadfastly gazing with unblinking eyes at the Bodhi Tree. In the following three weeks he makes, in seven day

---

24. Ibid., p. 76. 25. Ibid., p. 83. This event in the Buddha's life is discussed in greater detail below, p. 279.

26. See below, pp. 163 ff.

27. The East is identified with the centre at the foot of the world axis : the Supernal Sun "rises" in the Nadir and "sets" in the Zenith, which directions are identified with the East and the West, the directions in which the sidereal sun rises and sets. Cf. Coomaraswamy, 1976, p. 86, n. 48.

28. For a fuller analysis of this theme, see below, pp. 84 ff.

29. *Nidānakathā*, pp. 102 ff.; MVU III.281,1 ff.; *Lalita Vistara* XXIV; Coomaraswamy, 1956a, pp. 29-30; Warren, 1922, pp. 83 ff; etc. There are considerable variations in the accounts of the Buddha legend (see Lamotte, 1947, pp. 37-71; Foucher, 1951) and the times and the details of the events of the forty nine days show divergences. Nevertheless the accounts are in general agreement on the events referred to here.

periods, a journey within the bodhimaṇḍa, which can be interpreted as taking possession of the universe, comparable to that effected by the seven steps taken at his nativity.[30] He rises into the air to convince the spirits of his attainment; he paces to and fro along a cloistered path running from East to West and extending from the throne beneath the Tree to the place of the steadfast gazing, tracing the diurnal path of the sun that "measures out" the worlds, extending them out from the centre and then retracing that path, retracting them into the central Tree.[31] This perambulation is described in the *Lalita Vistara* as taking place in the "three thousand thousands of worlds".[32] Having once more resisted the temptations of Māra the Buddha takes up his position at the foot of the Mucalinda Tree and again

Fig. 13 a : The meditating Buddha protected by the Serpent Mucalinda. The spatial reference of the event is indicated by the association of the image with a liṅga-like caitya, the other three sides of which show the Bodhisattvas Vajrapāṇi, Prajñāpāramitā and Avalokiteśvara. Angkor, late 10th Century.

b : A relief from Amarāvatī showing a stupa fronted by the Buddha protected by Mucalinda.

enters meditation. For seven days a furious storm rages, and the serpent king Mucalinda, emerging from his underground lair at the foot of the Mucalinda Tree, wraps him about with his coils and extends his hoods to shelter his head.

The story of the forty nine days following the Enlightenment is an account of the cosmic peregrinations of the Buddha. Starting from the centre of the universe, the Tree, he ascends to the supernal worlds; then he encompasses the four directions of space; and finally he descends into the

---

30. See below, pp. 275 ff.

31. For the measuring out of the worlds by the sun, see above, pp. 30 ff.

32. *Lalita Vistara*, XXIV, cited by Viennot, 1954, p. 180.

underworlds by being fully enwrapped by the coils of the chthonic serpent. He has traversed the six directions of the universe : the zenith, the four directions on the horizontal plane, and the nadir, recomposing them within the centre, which is himself.

On the last day of the seven week's retreat the Buddha desired to eat. He was offered food by two merchants who were passing but had no bowl to receive their offering. Seeing this the Guardians of the Four Directions appeared before him, each with a bowl. Taking the four bowls the Buddha placed them one above the other and made them to be one, showing four lines around the rim. In this single bowl he received the food and ate.

Fig. 14 : The offering of the four bowls by the Regents of the Four Directions.

This unification of the bowls of the four directions is the mythic converse of the process symbolized in the Brahmanic story of the Ṛhbu's fourfold division of the Sun Bowl cited above : by this miraculous act the Buddha reverses the process of manifestation. The centrifugal expansion of the directional rays is reversed; they are withdrawn to the centre, quadrature returns to Unity and space is reconcentrated within the centre whence it derived. This is an outward indication of the inward process whereby the Buddha attained Enlightenment : by a one-pointed concentration of his mind he has withdrawn his senses back to the dimensionless centre of his being, thereby freeing himself from the bonds of the spatial and temporal world. The full significance of this symbolism of the bowl as it relates to the stupa becomes apparent when it is remembered that the archetypal shape of the stupa, revealed by the Buddha himself, is that of the alms bowl. The tradition is recorded by the Chinese pilgrim Hsuan-tsang : "The Buddha took his three cloths, folded each one into a square, and piled them on the earth, beginning with the largest and finishing with the smallest. Then, turning over his alms bowl, he placed it on top of them and set up his begging staff upon the whole. 'Thus', he said, 'is a stupa made', and this was its first model".[33] The term "upturned bowl" (Jap. fukubachi)

---

33. Quoted by Foucher, 1905, pp. 63-64 and in Mus, 1935, pp. 62-63 & 288-289; cf. Combaz, 1932, pp. 176-177; Bénisti, 1960, p. 43; Saunders, 1960, p. 168.

designates the dome of the stupa to this day in Japan.[34]

* * * * *

The symbolism of the cosmogonic expansion of the point-centre into the directions is developed more fully in the Mahāyāna, where the geometric procession from Unity to quadrature and fragmented multiplicity is mythically humanized so that it is the Buddha himself who divides to fill the universe with his proliferated Person. This theme will be returned to in the following.[35]

Fig. 15 : A relief panel showing the birth of the Buddha, whose presence is aniconically implied by the insignia of royalty, the parasol and fly whisks. He is received in a golden net by the Regents of the Four Directions. The net is marked with seven small footprints, representing the seven steps taken by the infant Buddha to encompass the seven directions of space and thereby proclaim his lordship over the spatial and temporal universe (see below, pp. 275 ff.).

34. 伏鉢 , Jap. fukubachi, Ch. fu-po, "upturned bowl". See also below, p. 65, n. 90.

35. See below, pp. 52 ff.

6 THE DEPLOYMENT OF SPACE AND THE SACRIFICE

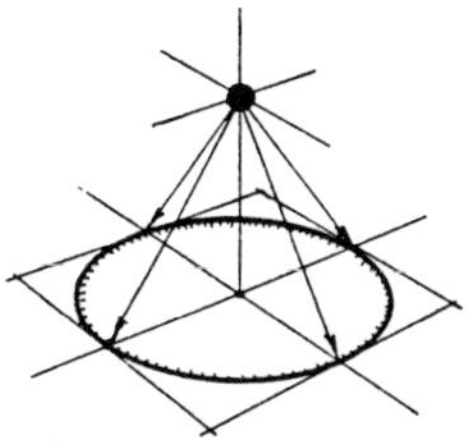

The deployment of the directions of space from the centre of the stupa plan refers to the cosmogonic procession from Unity to multiplicity and the reintegrative return of multiplicity to Unity : the plan is a diagram of the manner in which Unity is fragmented into phenomena; and simultaneously it is a diagram of the way in which the divided cosmos is momentarily reunified within its Principle. The symbolism relates to concepts of sacrifice, formulated in the Brahmanic literature and physically expressed in the construction of the Vedic fire altar. It is to these sources that we must look for clarifications concerning the meaning of the oriented stupa plan.

1. THE VEDIC FIRE ALTAR

The stupa is not the only construction whose plan is laid out according to the directions of space determined by the movements of the sun. This method of laying out plans is characteristic of Indian architecture as a whole, so that Mus has said that, "In the history of Indian ideas this spatio-temporal pentagram and the world structure to which it corresponds constitute a common factor or an autonomous system which is taken for granted by the most diverse religions, which merely fill it out with sectarian specifics".[1] The prototype of the oriented plan is to be found in the Vedic fire altar.

The agnicayana, the rite of constructing the High Altar,[2] lasts a year, since Prajāpati is the Year. Constantly repeated, it represents the periodic reconstruction of Prajāpati, enabling him to continue his creative work. When the construction of the High Altar begins, a horse, which is the manifestation of Prajāpati and a symbol of the Sun, is made to approach the site and snuffle upon the first layer of bricks.[3] A lotus leaf, which represents the Earth as foundation, the primordial Waters, place of the birth of Fire,[4] is laid where the horse places his hoof. On this leaf is laid a golden plate, the symbol of the Sun[5] and immortality[6] and above this lies a statuette of a Golden Man, upon its back and turned to the East. The Golden Man is Prajāpati, the immortal Person of the sacrifice.[7] Homage having been paid to this figure, bricks are built above it and a live turtle, representing the vital sap of the world,[8] a human head[9] and the

---

1. Mus, 1935, p. *234; cf. Bénisti, 1971, p. 150 and also above, p.14.

2. The rite is described in ŚB. See Eggeling, 1882, 41, p. 143; Keith, 1925, p. 354; Gonda, 1962, 1, pp. 231 ff.; Kramrisch, 1946, pp. 68 ff.

3. On the symbolism of the horse's snuffling upon the self-perforated bricks of the altar, see Coomaraswamy, 1940, pp. 47 ff. The horse is the Sun and the bricks all beings and the worlds; and "just as he, the Priest, makes it snuffle at these bricks, so yonder Sun strings to himself these worlds upon a thread" (ŚB VII.3.2.12) and "so bestows the Breath indeed upon them" (TS V.2.8.1; V.3.7.4). This is the sūtrātman doctrine discussed below, pp. 111 ff. See also Coomaraswamy, 1977, 1, p. 387. n. 28.

4. TS V.2.6.5. 5. ŚB VII.4.1.17. 6. TS V.2.7.2. 7. ŚB VII.4.1.15.

8. ŚB VII.5.1.1. 9. "The human head can be that of one from the

heads of four animals - horse, ox, ram and goat - are built into the five layers of the altar. These five layers are the five seasons and the five directions.[10]

The construction of the High Altar is a mimesis of the construction of the cosmos[11]: the water used for mixing the clay of the bricks is primeval Water; the clay is the Earth; the side walls of the altar are Midspace, and so on.[12] The altar is also the cosmos in its temporal aspect and the building up of its layers is a reconstruction of time. To use Mus' phrase, the altar is "time materialized".[13] "The altar of fire is the Year...the nights are the stones surrounding it and there are 360 of them because there are 360 nights in the year; the days are the yajuṣmati bricks, for there are 360 of them; and there are 360 days in the year".[14] The altar is built up with 10,800 bricks, one for each hour of the year (the day and the night each having fifteen hours).[15] At the building of the enclosing wall 15 x 80 syllables are recited at the laying of each stone, and since there are 360 stones there are 15 x 80 x 360 = 432,000 syllables built into the altar,[16] which is not only the total number of syllables in the *Ṛg Veda*, but also the number of years in a manvantara or total world cycle. This number in turn relates to 25,920, the number of years in the precession of the equinoxes.[17] Further, the 10,800 bricks of the altar correspond to the 10,800 paṅkti of the *Ṛg Veda*, that is, the number of metres formed by five elements or octosyllabic verses.[18]

The altar is piled up in five layers, which are the seasons : "...of five layers consists the fire altar, and five seasons make a year, and the year is Agni (that is, the altar)";[19] "...and that Prajāpati who became relaxed is the year; and those five bodily parts (tanū)[20] of his which became relaxed are the seasons; for there are five seasons, and five are those layers : when he builds up the five layers he thereby builds him up with the seasons".[21] The piling up of the altar thus replicates the course of the year, which is a reduced image of the Great Year, identified with Prajāpati. The five layers are also identified with the five directions : "... and those five bodily parts of his, the seasons, which became relaxed, are the regions (the four directions and the Zenith); for five in number are the regions and five those layers : when he builds up the five layers he builds up Prajāpati with the regions".[22]

The altar is an image of the universe in both its spatial and temporal aspects, for not only does it embody the days and nights and seasons of the year but is also oriented according to the four directions, each governed by a season.[23] The five layers of the altar are simultaneously identified with the five seasons and the five directions; and the seasons and the directions compose the spatio-temporal cosmos, which is the body of Prajāpati.

---

third or fourth class, killed in battle or by a thunderbolt" (*Āpastambīya-śrautasūtra* XVI.6.2, quoted by Gonda, 1962, 1, p. 231).

10. See below. 11. ŚB VI.5.1.1 ff. 12. ŚB X.9.2.29.

13. Mus , 1935, p. 384; Eliade, 1957, p. 68; 1958a p. 372; 1961, p. 25.

14. ŚB X.5.4.10 . 15. ŚB. X.4.2.18 .

16. ŚB X.4.2.30; and see Eggeling, 1882, 43, p. 354, n. 2, on the method for determining the number 360. Cf. Mus, 1935, p. 281.

17. Guénon, 1970, p. 22; 1938, *passim*.

18. Mus , 1935. p. 280. 19. ŚB VI.1.8.15 .

20. On the five tanū of Prajāpati, see below, p. 47. 21. ŚB VI.1.2.18 .

22. ŚB VI.1.2.19. 23. See above, pp. 32 f., and Mus, 1935, p. *97 and pp. 733-789; Eliade, 1957, p. 68.

"The altar is imbued with the substance of the world";[24] it is the hypostasis of the cosmos; its construction brings together all directions, all the Breaths, all times - the seasons, the months, the days and nights - into a single, reintegrated whole. It is the coalescence of all space and all time within a compounded unity.

The five layers of the altar are identified with two groups of five qualities or "powers" (tanū), which constitute the "inherent body" or bodily Self of Prajāpati.[25] There are five that are mortal (hair, skin, flesh, bones and marrow) and five that are immortal (mind, speech, breath, sight and hearing).[26] The five layers also represent the Three Worlds (Heaven, Midspace and Earth) and the two intermediate spaces.

2. THE DIVISION AND REUNIFICATION OF THE BODY OF PRAJĀPATI - THE SACRIFICE.

According to the Brahmanic outlook the cosmogenesis is a sacrifice (yajña),[27] and the sacrifice is Prajāpati, who divides himself into the cosmos.

In the beginning, teach the *Brāhmaṇas*, Prajāpati, who is Ātman[28] and the unmanifested Unity-Totality, desired to multiply, to become multiple.[29] He emanated (visṛj, in which sṛj is "to flow, to speed", and vi- indicates dispersal in all directions) from himself the Word (vāc), and thence the Waters. Desiring to reproduce himself he penetrated the Waters and an Egg developed, whose shell became the Earth. The gods, demons, men, plants, etc., appeared.[30]

By this emanation of the worlds, Prajāpati is completely emptied out, exhausted, without power.[31] Before the cosmogenetic act he is the One, concentrated and integral; after, he is decomposed, dispersed, differentiated into the world of multiplicity : "After Prajāpati had emitted the living beings, his joints were disjointed. Now Prajāpati is certainly the Year, and his joints are the two joinings of day (that is, dawn and twilight), the full moon and the new moon, and the beginnings of the seasons. He was unable to rise with his joints loosened; and the gods healed him by (the ritual of) the agnihotra, strengthening his joints".[32]

Man's performance of the ritual of sacrifice repeats the archetypal and primordial Sacrifice. The dismemberment of Prajāpati, which is the production of the universe, is reflected in the ritual as in a mirror, inversely. The sacrifice is a reversal of the cosmo-generative process whereby the manifold proceeds from the One. The sacrificer disjoins the mere-seeming cohesion of the partitite sacrifice so as to reveal its impartible essence, which is one and whole. Whereas Prajāpati divides himself, makes himself many to enter into his offspring in whom he is swallowed up and hidden, so in their turn his progeny empty themselves out, dismembering

---

24. Mus, 1935, p. *112. 25. ŚB VI.1.2.17 ff. 26. ŚB X.1.3.4.

27. On the sacrifice see Levi, 1898; "*Ātmayajña* : Self Sacrifice", in Coomaraswamy, 1977, 2, pp. 107 ff; Coomaraswamy, 1943a, pp. 19 ff.; Eliade, 1979, pp. 227 ff.; 1958a, pp. 109 ff.; Gonda, 1962, pp. 227 ff.; Mus, 1935, pp. *144 ff.

28. JB I.68. 29. ŚB VI.1.1.8.

30. ŚB VI.1.1.8; cf. Eliade, 1979, p. 228; Gonda, 1962, p. 227.

31. ŚB III.9.1.1. 32. ŚB I.6.3.35-36.

here for a remembering there. The body and self of the sacrificer, or of his ritual surrogate, the victim or holocaust, are taken apart at the terrestrial level to be reassembled supernally. Multiplicity is immolated, Unity restored. The oblation, disintegrated here, is reintegrated above.

The ritual of sacrifice has a twofold function, on the one hand macrocosmic and on the other microcosmic. Functioning macrocosmically as a repetition of the original act of creation, it is a ritual of renewal of the world. The universe is recreated anew in the analogy of the year that exhausts itself in completing its cycle and annually begins again. Microcosmically, the sacrificial offering is the externalization of an inner act. The proper sacrificial victim is the soul, the appetitive and greedy mind, the sense of separate selfhood. The psycho-physical self is the truly appropriate holocaust.

* * * * *

The building of the altar is a sacrificial act. The body of Prajāpati, which had been fragmented and dispersed by the cosmogenesis, is reconstituted and rearticulated - healed - by the sacrificial ritual of constructing the altar : "This Prajāpati who became disjointed is now the same fire altar built formerly".[33]

The being, who is a portion of Prajāpati's body, is likewise scattered, dispersed, discontinuous and deprived of cohesion. The creature and the creation are both subject to time - and time is the destroyer; the Year is Death.[34] Days and nights are the arms of Death that squeeze man. They are the waves that swallow everything.[35] Partite and divided, the being partakes of desolation, disorder and death.[36]

The construction rite restores Prajāpati's lost unity and by the rite the sacrificer is likewise made whole again. Prajāpati, who was dismembered in the beginning, is reassembled (samskṛi) in the altar. By its construction the sacrificer identifies himself with Prajāpati. The sacrificer, the altar and Prajāpati are identified in the building ritual : the extent of the base is that of the outstretched arms of the sacrificer, the bricks are the length of his foot, the navel (nabhi) is a square with the dimension of his span. The Golden Man, built into the courses of the altar, represents the immolated sacrificer. In analogous ways the sacrificer is identified with the sacrificial animal and with the consuming fire : the officiant is the altar, the holocaust, the sacrificial fire and the God to whom the sacrifice is offered.[37]

When the sacrificer builds the altar he is renewing himself in unity. By the performance of the sacrifice he is reintegrated. Retracing the course of Prajāpati's descent into the world he returns from multiplicity to unity. He passes beyond space and time, is reborn, and attains immortality.[38]

The altar is the world and includes both its spatial and temporal parameters. The spatial extension of the cosmos is embodied in the altar both by its orientation in accordance with the directions and also by the sacrificial animals built into its five layers.[39] The myth, given in the

33. ŚB II.6.1.3. 34. ŚB X.4.3.3. 35. Gonda, 1962, p.236.

36. Ibid., p. 228. 37. Burckhardt, 1967, pp. 20-21.

38. Ibid., p. 233; Eliade, 1979, p. 230.

39. The considerations that follow are elaborated in Mus, 1935, pp. 495 ff., Ch. XV :"La reconstruction de Prajāpati et l'unité de l'universe."

Śatapatha Brāhmaṇa, establishes the connection : - The altar, in both name and ritual identification, is Agni, the Fire. Agni is the son of Prajāpati, engendered in the Dawn (Uṣas). When first born the infant boy began to weep because he had no name. Prajāpati called him Rudra, "Howler", "for Rudra is Agni". But the boy-god said, "Give me yet a name", and Prajāpati successively bestowed seven more names upon him : Sarva, Paśupati, Ugra, Aśani, Bhava, Mahān Deva and Iśana. The child entered into these forms in turn.[40]

The eight forms of Agni, plus Agni himself at the centre, are the regent-gods of the directions of space.[41] By entering into them Agni has realized a unification - the directions have been reintegrated within their centre - and Prajāpati, desiring this wholeness for himself, pursued Agni, who escaped by hiding within the five sacrificial animals. But Prajāpati recognized him in them and prepared to sacrifice the five animals to five gods : the man to Viśvakarman, the horse to Varuṇa, the ox to Indra, the ram to Tvaṣṭṛ, and the goat to Agni. These five gods are also regents of the directions : Agni is the god who governs the East, Varuṇa governs the West, Tvaṣṭṛ the North, Indra the South, while the centre is given over to Viśvakarman, the Architect and Creator, the Maker of all things, whose four faces turn towards the four winds of the world and who is identified with Prajāpati himself and with his cosmo-progenitive activity. The five gods constitute a schema of the five directions; they form a pentagram of the manifested world; they are the divided portions of Prajāpati, "emptied out" into the world. The five gods are emanations of Prajāpati, and a dispersal into multiplicity of his original unity.

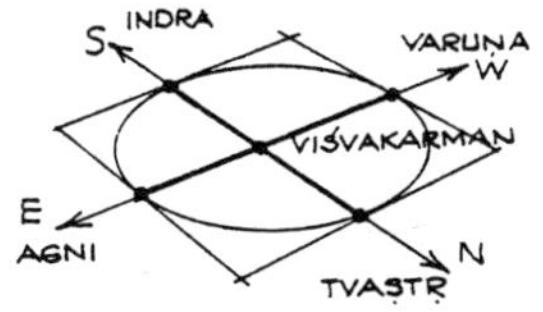

For Prajāpati to sacrifice to these five gods would be a fatal error. By so doing he would be obscured within his own dismembered parts. By sacrificing to the gods of the directions he would endorse their dispersal and reinforce his own exhaustion. Thus, as time passed, he began to reflect. "He thought, 'For different deities, indeed, I mean to sacrifice now; but I myself desire Agni's forms; well then, I will sacrifice them as (the objects of my) desire'",[42] that is to say, the disjointed god decided to sacrifice the animals to Agni so as to rediscover himself. Thinking thus, he seized the five animals and sacrificed them, but at the same time constructed the five-layered altar, identifying each layer with an animal[43] and thus with a direction. But these five animals are the five parts of Agni, and by incorporating them within a single altar Prajāpati builds a single, whole Agni - with whom he is identified. Thus Agni becomes Prajāpati's own self : "(the victims) are five; for there are those five Agnis, to wit, the five layers. For them he thus lays down five homes; and seeing that, Agni turns unto him".[44]

---

40. ŚB VI.1.3.8-19.

41. With the exception of Aśani, who is replaced by Bhima, the list of names is that of the eight regent gods of the cardinal and intermediate directions given in the later Hindu texts, where they are described as eight forms of Śiva.

42. ŚB VI.2.1.6. 43. ŚB VI.2.1.11; VI.2.1.16.

44. ŚB VI.2.1.16 This concept of interactive or reciprocal sacrifice is parallelled in Shingon Buddhism and is represented by the Bodhisattvas of Reciprocal Offering in the Diamond World Mandala. See below, pp. 150 f.

The building of the altar is thus a reintegration of the spatial extension of the cosmos back within the unity whence it came. The complementary coordinate of the physical world, time, is similarly reintegrated within the altar. The five Agnis also preside over the five seasons. "Assuredly, these (five) layers are the seasons";[45] and the full year is thus Agni in his unity : "The fire altar has five layers, (each layer is a season), the five seasons make a year, and Agni is the year".[46] Prajāpati is the Year and in the altar Prajāpati, the Year, is reconstituted.

* * * * *

Prajāpati is Unity or Being fragmented into the diversity and flux of manifestation. In his essence he is Puruṣa, the Person, the unchanging, eternal and indivisible Essence of man and the cosmos. In an alternative version of the cosmogonic myth it is Puruṣa who is scattered into manifestation. Puruṣa is sacrificed by the gods (deva) at the beginning of the world. From his dismembered body proceed the animals, the liturgical elements, the castes, the sky and the earth, the gods.[47] This is the mythological theme that identifies the manifested universe with the body of the god, a theme that is recurrent in the Vedic literature : the bodily parts of Skambha,[48] Brahmā,[49] Brahman-Puruṣa,[50] and Viṣṇu[51] are identified with the constituent components of the world. An analogous concept is found among the Jains.[52] Prajāpati creates all creatures by drawing them from himself, the demons from his abdomen, the gods from his mouth, the waters from his ears and animals from his "breaths".[53] This leads back to the considerations just now examined : Prajāpati "creates" the five sacrificial animals of the Vedic altar with his "breaths". The sacrificial victims, identified with the directions and the seasons, are disjunct portions of Prajāpati's body : the man is Prajāpati's Self (ātman), the horse is his eye, the ox his breath, the ram his ear, the goat his voice. Built into the altar they are reunited, as are the divinities with whom they are identified. By building the altar the sacrificer retracts spatial extension and temporal duration to the centre of his being; and microcosmically he withdraws the outflowing "breaths" of his senses back to the source of their dispersal.[54]

* * * * *

---

45. ŚB VI.2.1.36.

46. ŚB VI.8.1.15. There is a play of words in the Sanskrit text, for which see Mus, 1935, p. 462, n.1.

47. RV X.90.1 Cf. Eliade, 1979, p. 224; Burckhardt, 1967, pp. 17 ff. Kramrisch, 1946, p. 68; Auboyer, 1949, p. 144; Muir, 1868, 5, pp. 367 ff.; Muṇḍ. Up. II.1.4. Burckhardt is at pains to emphasise that "this must not be understood as 'pantheism', for Puruṣa is not divided in himself, nor is he 'localized' in ephemeral beings; it is only his manifested and apparent form that is sacrificed, while his eternal nature remains as it ever was... Multiplicity is not in the nature of God but in the nature of the world" (Burckhardt, 1967, p. 20). For the nature of the gods who sacrifice Puruṣa, see below, pp. 63 f.

48. AV X.7.10; Muir, 1868, 5, p. 381.

49. ŚB XI.2.3.1ff.; Muir, 1868, 5, pp. 388-390. 50. AV X.10.

51. BG XI.7 & 15; Rawson, 1973, pls. 23 & 48.

52. Auboyer, 1949, p. 145; Guérinot, 1926, p. 172 and pl. V.

53. ŚB VII.5.2ff.; Muir, 1868, 1, pp. 24 & 28.

54. See below, pp. 65 f.

The symbolism of the immolation of the forms of Agni in the altar also has a microcosmic significance, one that pertains directly to the attainment of immortality by the celebrant of the sacrifice.[55] The *Śatapatha Brāhmaṇa* enumerates five "forms" of Agni, which are identified with "powers" of the performer of the ritual : Agni is the voice, he is the eye, the mind, the ear, and finally he is the breath, which is his supreme form, since the other forms are sustained by and dependent upon it.[56] The text then goes on to indicate cosmic equivalents : the voice is fire, the ear is the four directions of space, the eye is the sun, the mind is the moon, and the breath is the wind.[57] The passage concludes by stating that at death he who understands the doctrine" passes into fire by his speech, into the sun by his eye, into the moon by his mind, into the quarters by his ear, and into the wind by his breath; and being composed thereof, he is identified with that one among their divinities who corresponds and is at peace".[58]

By ritual means the sacrificer is identified with the altar, which as we have seen, is in turn identified part by part with the total body of the universe. His five "breaths" - voice, eye, mind, ear and breath - are identified one by one with the layers of the altar, which in their turn are identified with the directions and the seasons and with fire, the sun, the moon, the quarters and the wind. Those who practise the sacrificial ritual come to realize this identification of the "breaths" or faculties with those of the universe and likewise realize their reconstitution within the Unity which the altar represents : at his death he does not perish, but returns to the One.[59]

To construct the altar is to reunite the scattered parts of Prajāpati; it is to bring multiplicity back to unity; it is to transform finitude to totality and mortality to immortality. To perform the rite is to return to the centre : spatial extension is brought back to the geometric centre, the navel (nābhi) of the altar; temporal duration is reconcentrated at the viśuvat, the central day of the ceremonies; and the bodily elements and mental faculties of the person performing the ritual are withdrawn to the centre of his being, the "immortal centre", which is coincident with the centre of Prajāpati. These three centres coalesce in the rite, and whatever operates for one operates for all : the construction rites performed in space are simultaneously performed in time, and exercise their influence on the celestial powers, on the universe, and on the person of the sacrificer.[60]

* * * * *

Prajāpati is seen to have several aspects : "in the beginning" he is primordial Unity, the principle of manifestation prior to its deployment; then he is the spatial and temporal universe, issued forth by his dismembering; and finally he is the One that has been recomposed from his differentiated parts. That is to say, he is first the unmanifested Spirit, in its concentrated Unicity; then he is the cosmogenetic power of the Spirit, raying out to form the worlds; and finally, he is that power once more concentrated and returned within itself.

---

55. Mus, 1935, pp. *144 ff.

56. Cf. this doctrine with that given in CU V.1.7-15 and BU VI.7-14, where it is taught that when these functions cease man becomes dumb, blind, mad or deaf, but when breath is withdrawn, he dies. See also below, p. 61.

57. ŚB X.3.3.1-6. 58. ŚB X.3.3.8.

59. Cf. Mus, 1935, p. *146. 60. Gonda, 1962, p. 234.

3. BUDDHIST PARALLELS - THE PROLIFERATION OF THE BODY OF THE BUDDHA.

There is a close analogy, evidenced in both literature and iconography, between Prajāpati and the Buddha of the Mahāyāna. "The Buddha as Supreme Person (puruṣottama) ... is, from the standpoints of ontology and psychology, as well as verbal correspondences, virtually identified with Brahmā-Prajāpati".[61] Prajāpati is "Father of the World" (lokapitā), and similarly "He, the Tathāgata, endowed with Buddha-Knowledge, powers, absence of hesitation and the other qualities proper to a Buddha, mighty with supernatural power, is the Father of the World (lokapitā)".[62] Prajāpati is literally "Lord of Progeny" and with analogous import the Buddha is the "Lord of begotten existences" (sarvaprajāna-nātha)[63] : in the same way that Prajāpati's dispersal into the world is "an emanation of children", a sending forth of rays as from a central sun[64] so that we are all divided and fragmented portions of his body, so likewise the Mahāyāna teaches that all entities (dharma) and all beings possess the Buddha Nature, even though obscured by our ignorance and attachment. Prajāpati-Viśvakarman has faces turned to every direction and has innumerable hands and feet that reach into the farthest points of the extended universe, signifying that he is omnipresent, "goes" everywhere to organize these points by his presence : he is present in each and every point of the cosmos. The Buddhist pantheon provides many matching examples of divinities whose multiple arms and multiple heads signify the omnipresence of the Essence of Buddhahood. Like Prajāpati, the Buddha divides himself to be present in every tiniest grain of dust in the universe.

Fig. 16 :
A Chinese "Thousand Buddha stele" depicting the proliferation of the Body of the Buddha.

---

61. Coomaraswamy, 1935a, p. 47. 62. SPS III (Kern, 1884, p. 77).

63. SPS XV.21 (Kern, 1884, p. 309). 64. For the solar rays as children of the sun, see JUB II.9.10; ŚB III.9.2.6; VII.3.2.12; VIII.7.1.16-17; X.2.6.5

Brahmanism identifies the cosmos with the body of the God; Buddhism identifies it with the body of the Buddha. The *Lalita Vistara* says : "The Buddha is called the caitya of the world...; three thousand worlds come together to form the caitya of his body".[65] There are several places in Nāgārjuna's *Mahā-prajñā-pāramitā-śāstra* where the Buddha's body is equated with the universe. His essential body is said to "fill space in the ten directions; it is immense, endless (ananta)... like space", and "Showing his great Body (mahākāya) of pure light and varied colours, he filled space (ākāśa)". "'My body', said the Buddha, 'is inconceivable (acintya). Brahmā, the king of the gods..., the gods and the elders... desired to measure my body and discover my voice; they were unable to fathom them'". In another passage the Bodhisattvas, seeing the body of the Buddha, cried, "to attempt to measure his body would be a never-ending task. It goes beyond the world of space..."[66]

Fig. 17 :
Kongōzōō Bosatsu (the Bodhisattva "Diamond Storehouse King"), who typifies those Bodhisattvas whose multiple heads and arms represent a deployment of Buddha qualities throughout the cosmos.

Expressing a similar concept, the *Avataṃsaka-sūtra* contains several passages assimilating elements of the cosmos with transformations of the body of the Buddha,[67] and the same sutra speaks of the body of Samantabhadra as having "incalculable Buddha Lands, innumerable as particles of dust, in each of the pores of his skin".[68] The *Karanda-vyūha-sūtra* similarly says that each of the pores of the skin of Avalokiteśvara contains the whole universe.[69]

---

65. Quoted by Auboyer, 1949, p. 148.

66. Lamotte, 1944, pp. 5-6, 18 &19; quoted in Auboyer, 1949, p. 148.

67. Snellgrove, 1978, p. 201; cf. Auboyer, 1949, p. 148, where she describes 7th Cent. bronzes from China and Turkestan which show the Buddha wearing a cloak representing elements of cosmological symbolism.

68. *Avataṃsaka-sūtra*, quoted MKDJT, p. 1915b, s.v., Fugen Bostatsu.

69. Snellgrove, 1978, p. 326.

Fig. 18.
a. The Body of the Buddha as a cosmos. The robe shows Mt. Meru as its axis, with the Tuṣita Heaven above and the hells below.

b. An eight-armed Avalokiteśvara. The body shows a multitude of small Buddhas, with reference to the passages in the *Karaṇḍa-vyūha-Sūtra* which teach that each of the pores of Avalokiteśvara's skin contains a universe.

The sutras contain many accounts of a proliferation of the Buddha's body, which can be interpreted as referring to the deployment of his body into the directions of space so as to fill the universe. One such is the legend of the Great Miracle at Śrāvastī, which tells how the Buddha, having been repeatedly requested by King Prasenajit to display his powers, rose into the sky and walked in the air, while emitting flames from the upper part of his body and waves of water from the lower part, like a multi-coloured aura. Then he multiplied his form, radiating images of himself up to heaven and in all directions so that the sky was filled with Buddhas preaching the Dharma. The twin miracle was completed by the raging of a violent storm. The heterodox were overthrown and an immense multitude were converted.[70]

70. *Dhammapada-Aṭṭhakathā* XVI; also mentioned in the *Nidāna-kathā*; *Jātaka* 483; Mil; introduction to the *Aṭṭhasālinī*, etc. See Foucher, 1917, p. 152, and 1909, *passim*. The *Mahāvaṃsa* 137, 241 & 254 and the *Jātaka* Commentary (Fausböll, 1881, 1, pp. 77,88 etc.) call it "the miracle at the foot of the mango tree" with reference to their versions of the myth, according to which the miraculous occurrences began with the Buddha causing an enormous mango tree to grow immediately from a mango seed.

In the *Divyāvadāna* account of the same story the Buddha seated himself on the corolla of a marvellous lotus that was created for him by the Nāga Kings Nanda and Upananda. The Buddha sat upon this lotus with the gods Śakra (Indra) and Brahmā to his right and left. Then he caused another lotus with a Buddha seated upon it to appear above the first, and then others in front, behind, to either side, and then proliferating until a crowd of Buddhas in the four consecrated attitudes (standing, walking, sitting and recumbent) filled the heavens up to the Akaniṣṭha, that it, the heaven at the final limit of the World of Form.[71]

The *Saddharma-puṇḍarīka-sūtra* records another miracle of analogous import. It tells how, from the circle of hair on his brow (ūrṇā), the Buddha darted a ray of light in which were made visible Buddhas preaching in thousands of myriads of koṭis of Buddha fields throughout the ten directions.[72] These uncountable myriads of Buddhas assembled in all the directions around Śākyamuni. All these Buddhas are emanated from the body of Śākyamuni, who says, "I have miraculously created from my own body many Tathāgata forms, which in the ten directions of space in separate Buddha fields, in thousands of worlds, preach the Law to creatures".[73] The Chinese version of the text is even more explicit : "The moment has come to bring together here all the Buddhas that I have produced by dividing my body and who preach the Law in the ten directions of space".[74] A little later the Buddha says, "...from the moment when I began to preach the Law to creatures in the Saha world and in hundreds of thousands of myriads of koṭis of worlds, the venerable Tathāgatas... such as the Tathāgata Dipaṃkara and others... have all been miraculously produced by me".[75]

The same sutra also describes how the two Buddhas, Śākyamuni and Prabhutaratna, seated side by side in the stupa that had miraculously appeared in the sky at the time when Śākyamuni was preaching the Law, "smiled at each other, and from their open mouths gave tongue, so that their tongues extended to the Brahmaloka, and from these two tongues there issued forth countless myriads of rays, and from each ray countless myriads of Bodhisattvas, of golden body... who, stationed in every quarter, preached the Law... so that every existence in every Buddha field heard that voice from the sky".[76]

Another example of this theme of the multiplication of Buddhas to fill the ten directions of space, taken from the *Bommōkyō*, is given at a later place,[77] and many other texts could be cited to demonstrate the theme. It is a commonplace in the sutras of the Mahāyāna.

* * * * *

The Buddhas proliferate not only in space but also in time. The concept is expressed in the doctrine of the three thousand Buddhas of the three kalpas. A kalpa is a vast aeon, of incalculable length.[78] The three kalpas are those of the past, the present and the future. In each of these periods a thousand Buddhas appear. Shingon Buddhism teaches that

---

71. *Divyāvadāna* 162; Foucher, 1917, p. 159.

72. SPS XI (Kern, 1884, pp. 227 ff : "Apparition of the Stupa").

73. SPS XI (Kern, 1884, p. 231). 74. Taishō, Vol.9, No. 262, p. 32.

75. SPS XI. Cf. Mus, 1935, p. 603. 76. SPS XX (Kern, 1884, p. 364 f.)

77. See below, pp. 207 f.

78. For the meaning of the term kalpa see Ishizuka and Coates, 1949 p. 367, n. 19.

the three thousand Buddhas are various and innumerable[79] transformation bodies of the five Jina Buddhas who abide eternally, which is to say timelessly and instantaneously, in the Pure Land of the Great Sun Buddha (Mahāvairocana, Jap. Dainichi) on the summit of Mr. Meru, where they occupy the terrace of the Jewel Stupa.[80]

* * * * *

A persisting preoccupation of the Mahāyāna generally and the Vajrayāna in particular is the concept of the five Buddhas who dwell in and rule over the five directions of space : Vairocana at the Centre, Akṣobhya in the East, Ratnasambhava in the South, Amitābha in the West, and Amoghasiddhi in the North.[81] The spatial arrangement of these five Buddhas - Vairocana at the centre surrounded by the four others in the cardinal directions - is that of the Diamond World Mandala (vajra-dhātu-maṇḍala), which occupies an extremely important position within the Vajrayāna schools of Buddhism.[82] The mandala of the five Buddhas is a diagrammatic representation of the emanation of Buddhas from the unique and unitary Buddha who occupies the axial hub of the Wheel of the Universe. The mandala is a conventional abstraction and the five Buddhas do not constitute a limiting schema : these are not the five Buddhas of the world, but five Buddhas who represent innumerable Buddhas ruling over Buddha Lands of limitless extent. The entire cosmos is filled with "Tathāgatas crowded into the whole extension of space, with Vairocana, Akṣobhya, Ratnasambhava, Amitābha and Amoghasiddhi at their head".[83]

The sutras of Pure Land Buddhism, far from claiming exclusiveness for Amitābha's Pure Land, continually emphasise that it is one among a limitless number. Prior to his attainment of Enlightenment and as the monk Dharmākara, Amitābha Buddha was shown "the perfection of all the excellences and good qualities of Buddha countries belonging to eighty one hundred thousand niyutas of koṭis of Buddhas..."[84] This is a repetitive refrain in the sutras, which speak of "the Buddhas in immeasurable, incomparable, immense Buddha countries in the ten quarters", of "the blessed Buddhas excelling in number the grains of the sands of the Ganges", and so on. In the *Sukhāvatī-vyūha* Amitābha's Pure Land is located "over a hundred thousand koṭis of Buddha countries from here".[85] The Smaller *Sukhāvatī-vyūha* describes the Buddhas in the East, led by Akṣobhya, Merudhvaja, Mahāmeru... and Tathāgatas equal in number to the sand of the river Gaṅga...", and gives similar lists for each of the six directions.[86] The *Saddharma-puṇḍarīka-sūtra* contains the same sort of teaching : Akṣobhya is the regent of the East, but close to him dwells the Tathāgata Merukūṭa; Amitāyus rules in the West, but close to him is the Tathāgata Sarvalokadhātupadravodvegapratyuttīrṇa; and so on for the principal Buddhas of the Directions. They are countless, for in the East alone there are five

---

79. Innumerable since the number one thousand is to be taken analogically.

80. See MKDJT, p. 468, s.v. *Gengōsenbutsu*; p. 813, s.v., *Sanzenbutsu*; p. 468, s.v., *Gengō*; BKDJT, p. 940, s.v., *Gengōsenbutsu*; Ishizuka and Coates, 1949, p. 308. The thousand Buddhas of the present kalpa are shown in the Diamond World Mandala. 81. See below, pp. 135 ff.

82. See below, p. 136. 83. Bhattacharyya, 1931, Intro. p. 2.

84. MSV 5 (Cowell, Muller and Takakusu, 1894, p. 91); cf. MSV 8.5; 8.9; etc.

85. SV 2 (Cowell, Muller and Takakusu, 1894, p. 91).

86. SV 11-16.

hundred thousand myriads of millions of Buddhas, preaching the Dharma in their own Buddha Lands.[87] In the *Amitāyur-dhyāna-sūtra* the Buddha grants Queen Vaidehi a vision of all the Buddha Lands that fill the universe in every direction, each centred by a Buddha seated beneath a Bodhi Tree and preaching the Dharma. It says, "At that moment the World Honoured One flashed forth a golden ray from between his eyebrows. It extended to all the innumerable worlds of the ten quarters. On its return the ray rested on top of the Buddha's head and transformed itself into a golden pillar just like the Mt. Sumeru, wherein the pure and admirable countries of the Buddhas in the ten quarters appeared all at once illuminated".[88]

87. SVS VII.59; XI (Burnouf, 1852, pp. 113 ff., and pp. 147 ff.; Kern, 1884, pp. 177 ff., and pp. 231 ff.); cf. Mus, 1935, p. 601.

88. ADS I.5 (Cowell, Muller and Takakusu, 1894, p. 166).

7 THE DEPLOYMENT OF SPACE AND THE SOLAR BREATH

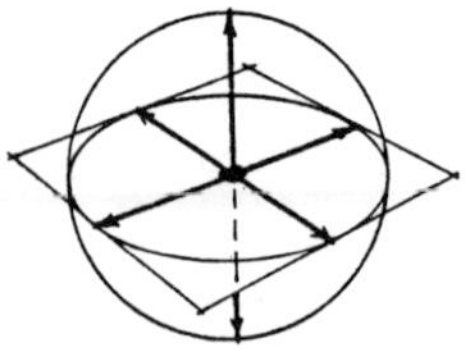

1. THE PNEUMATIC DEPLOYMENT OF THE MACROCOSM.

The cosmogenesis can be expressed as the deployment of space from a central Point, as an irradiation from the central Sun, or as an outblowing of Breath from the central Gale. The spatial, solar and pneumatic symbolisms are complementary, interlocking and interchangeable. The Void (śūnyatā), the Ground, Non-Being, Para-Brahman, is alternately likened to Infinite Space, to Darkness or to an unbounded field of Breath; the first affirmation of the Void is alternately the Point, the Sun or the Gale; and the measuring out of the cosmos from the Void is alternately a deployment of the directions of space, a radiation of Light or an exhalation of Breath. The seven directions - the centre plus the six arms of the three-dimensional cross that emanates from it - are assimilated to seven rays of the Sun and to seven Breaths. They at once form a nimbus of light and a flatus of Breath, "halo" and "halation". They are the "glories" that radiate from the Sun, the exhalations of his fiery Breath. The outbreathing of this solar respiration is kalpa, the Day of manifestation; the inbreathing is pralaya, the Night wherein the world is reabsorbed.

The Sun is identified with the Breath-Spirit : "The Sun is the Spirit (ātman) of all that is in motion or at rest";[1] and "The Spirit of both gods and men, the Spirit arisen from the sea, is yonder Sun".[2] The Sun is the Spirit or Breath of everything that exists in the Three Worlds of Heaven, Midspace and Earth.[3] Its rays are spirations and every being is filiated from the Sun, connected to it by a thread of Breath (sūtrātman) that is also a ray of light, an indwelling Gale-thread that is the support of life.[4] "It is by the rays of that Sun that all these creatures are endowed with vital breaths, and therefore the rays extend downwards to these breaths".[5] Living beings are the children of the Sun; their life depends upon their Solar Father;[6] they are quickened by his rays, the Breaths. All beings, all entities, the worlds, are connected with the Sun in what Coomaraswamy terms "literally one vast conspiracy".[7] They are joined back to the Solar Source by rays of light or threads of Breath, so that it is said that "Yonder Sun connects the worlds by a thread and what that thread is is the Gale";[8] "All this is strung on Me like a row of gems on a thread";[9] "The Sun is the fastening to whom these worlds are linked by means of the quarters... He strings these worlds to Himself by a thread; the thread is the Gale of the Spirit";[10] "All these elemental beings are on the Spirit, as on a jewel thread";[11] "Even as a thread might be threaded through a gem, even so is all this strung (upon the Sun's ray), namely, Gandharvas, Apsarasas, beasts and men";[12] and "I know the extended thread wherein these progeny are inwoven : the thread of the thread I know; what else (should it be) but the Great (the Sun), of the nature of Brahman?".[13]

---

1. RV I.115.1. 2. JUB III.2-3. 3. RV I.115.1.

4. The sūtrātman doctrine is a recurrent theme in the writings of Coomaraswamy. See, e.g. Coomaraswamy, 1977, *passim*; 1940; 1944; 1945; etc.

5. ŚB II.3.3.7 6. JUB II.9.10; III.10.4; ŚB VII.3.2.12.

7. Coomaraswamy, 1977, 1, p. 387, n. 28. 8. ŚB VIII.7.3.10.

9. AV IX.8.38; BG VII.7. 10. ŚB VI.1.1.17; VIII.7.3.10.

11. *Dhyāna Up.* VIII. 12. JUB III.4.13; III.5.1. 13. AV X.8.38.

By their radiating extension from the Sun-Centre, the thread-rays weave the worlds and quicken all beings. Conversely, their withdrawal is world's end or, microcosmically, death. When the world ends "the wind cords are severed"[14] and "they say of a man who has departed (from this life) that his limbs are unstrung; for it is by the Gale, indeed as thread, that they are tied together".[15] Hence the life-giving Sun is also Death : "That Man in Yonder (Sun's) orb is no other than Death",[16] who "slays and quickens".[17] "Now that Man in yonder orb (the Sun) and that Man in the right eye truly are no other than Death; - his feet (which are the rays of the Sun) have stuck fast in the heart, and having pulled them out he comes forth; and when he comes forth then that man dies : whence they say of him who has passed away, 'He has been cut off'".[18] The withdrawal of the Sun's light is also the retraction of the animating Breath and is the death of the person.

* * * * *

The deployment of the directions is a radiation of light from the Sun. It is also an emanation of radiant Breath, a "measuring out" by Spirit. In the cosmogenetic process Midspace is filled with Air; the world, in the manner of a vast aeolian bellows or balloon, is inflated by the Gale (*vāyu*). The creation is an insufflation. The cosmic extension or dilation is a spiration. The world is filled, animated and measured out by Breath. The Dawn Breeze blows open the directions of space. As the engenderer of spatial extension, Prajāpati is the Gale; his seven Breaths flow out to inflate the worlds and enliven forms. His cosmic Egg, floating upon the Waters, is a bubble of Air.[19] The etymology of the word *nirvāṇa* leads back to the same conceptions : it is the Breath that "passes out" or "blows out" from the envelope of *samṣāra*.

The directions of space emanate from the Sun; they likewise emanate from the Gale. When the Sun sets it returns into the Gale, the directions return into the Mansion of the Wind, and all things, the moon, the constellations, fire, day and night, the rain, the waters, plants and trees, return into the Air.[20]

The Breaths blow out in the directions to measure out Midspace. The inflation of space is its quartering, so that Indra proclaims, "I am the Breath; thou art that (Breath); all elemental beings art that (Breath); he (the Sun) that shines yonder is that (Breath). It is in this form (*rūpa*) that I pervade all the quarters, thereof is my food".[21] Similarly, "... that Prajāpati, the Year, who became relaxed is that very Gale who blows yonder. And those five bodily parts of his, the seasons, which became relaxed, are the quarters".[22] The *Śatapatha Brāhmaṇa* gives numerically different lists of the Breaths or vital airs and connects them with equal numbers of directions of space and seasons : six vital airs, six directions, six seasons; ten vital airs, ten directions, ten seasons; and so on.[23]

---

14. MU I.4. 15. BU III.7.2. 16. ŚB X.5.2.3.

17. RV XIII.3.3; cf. IV.53.3. 18. ŚB X.5.2.13.

19. Which, it will be shown, is the very image the Sinhalese chronicles give as a model for the stupa. See below, p. 194 f.

20. JUB III.1.1-2.

21. AĀ II.2.3. 22. ŚB VI.1.2.19.

23. ŚB VI.7.1.16, 18 & 20; VI.2.2.34.

2. PNEUMATIC DEPLOYMENT IN THE MICROCOSM.

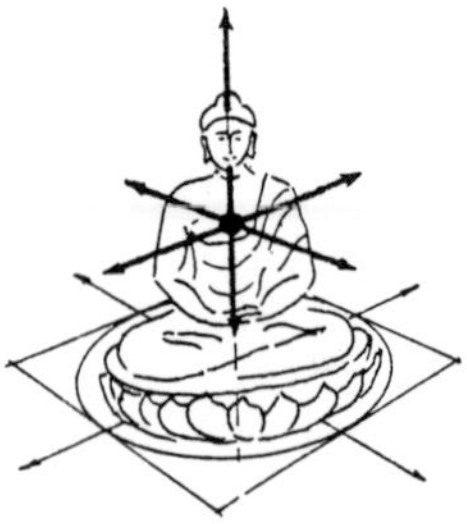

The genesis of the world by pneumatic dilation and inflation has its microcosmic counterpart. As for the world so also for man. In the same way that the universe is breathed into existence, so also life and space are breathed into the human embryo. The *Harivaṃsa*, transmitting ancient traditions, describes how the foetal flesh is penetrated by the Wind of the Spirit and, thus suffused, puts forth its members, dividing the Breath five-fold into the five Winds or vital functions; five modalities of the Breath as it relates to respiration : aspiration (prāṇa), respiration in its ascending phase; inspiration (apāna), its descending phase; and intermediate phase (vyāna); expiration (udāna), the projection of the breath beyond the confines of the individuality; and assimilation (samāna).[24] The *Aitareya Āranyaka* speaks of the breath of the nostrils entering the mouth and the brow : here the human head is homologous with the sphere of the world, the mouth being Earth and the brow Heaven, sundered by Midspace, the Breath of the nostrils.[25] Elsewhere in the same text Brahman as Breath enters the feet of the embryo and thence rises through the body, inflating its organs and members : from the feet it rises to the thighs, to the stomach, to the chest, and finally to the head.[26] The genesis and animation of man, like that of the integument of the world, is the inflation of a corporeal bag of skin.

Here again, in a microcosmic context, the Breaths emanate from a centre to the quarters. The *Upaniṣads* specifically correlate the five subtle vectors (nādi) of the heart[27] with the five vital airs, the five functional organs, the five regents of the directions and with the Sun, the Moon, Fire, Water and Space:[28]

Vector	Breath	Organ	Regent	
East	prāṇa	sight	Āditya	Sun
South	vyāna	hearing	Candramas	Moon
West	upāna	speech	Agni	Fire
North	samāna	thought	Parjanya	Water
Zenith	udāna	-	Vāyu	Air (Space)

"These, verily, are the five Brahma-Persons, the door keepers of the world of Heaven".[29]

The *Śatapatha Brāhmaṇa*[30] describes the rite that bestows the five breaths upon the new born child. Five Brahmans, who represent the winds of the four quarters and the Zenith and the corresponding Breaths that bring the victim in the horse sacrifice to life again, are requested to breathe over the baby. Alternately, the father breathes over the child, circumambulating around him in a clockwise direction and passing through the quarters.

* * * * *

24. Filliozat, 1933, pp. 415-416; Mus. 1935, pp. 455-456. For the doctrine of the five vāyus, see Guénon, 1945, pp. 77 ff.; *Brahma-Sūtra* II.4.8-13; CU V.19-23; MU II.6.

25. AĀ II.1.4; Keith, 1909, 2, pp. 102 f.& 201 f.; cf. Belvalkar and Ranade, 1927, 2, p. 154.

26. AĀ II.1.2; Keith, 1909, p. 103 f.; Mus, 1935, p. 456.

27. See below, pp. 317 ff. 28. CU III.13.1-6. Cf. Mus, 1935, p. 450.

The senses and the faculties are identified as breaths. In several places in the *Upaniṣads* it is recorded how the faculties dispute among themselves as to which is supreme among them. Prajāpati gives the answer : "Whichever one, quitting the body, leaves it in the worst condition, is the best among you". Speech, sight, hearing and mind left the body in turn, leaving it dumb, blind, deaf and mindless, but still breathing and alive. The turn of breath now came and "when breath was about to depart, tearing up the other senses, even as a spirited horse might tear up the pegs to which he is tethered, they gathered around him and said, 'Reverend Sir, remain, you are the best of us, do not depart'", and each in turn acknowledged the superiority of the breath. The passage concludes : "Verily, they do not call them speeches or eyes or ears or minds. They call them breaths, for all these are Breath".[31]

Thus Prajāpati, who is identified with the Breath, "divides himself to quicken his children"[32] while remaining "undivided among the divisions".[33] He divides himself among the five senses,[34] and so awakens his offspring and supports the body.[35] He goes out from the centre into the directions to animate the voice, the eye, the mind and the ear. "Breaking through these openings (the five apertures of the senses) he enjoys the objects by means of the five reins (or rays, raśmibhi). These reins are the faculties of perception (buddhindriyāṇi). His horses are the faculties of action (karmendriya). His chariot is the body. The Mind is the charioteer. His nature (prakṛti) is the whip. Thus driven by him, this body spins like a potter's wheel. So this body is set up as possessing consciousness; he alone is its mover".[36]

Thus divided the fivefold Breath-body of Prajāpati is synonymous with the five forms of Agni, which are personified as Viśvakarman, the Breath, at the Centre or Zenith; Agni, the Fire that animates the voice, in the East; Indra, the Sun that animates the eye, in the South; Varuṇa, the Moon that animates the mind, in the West; and Tvaṣṭṛ, the quarters that animate the ear, in the North.[37] These are the measures (mātra) of Fire, or the measures of Breath.[38] Thus Agni, identified with the Wind or Breath, blows out through the senses; and therefore it is said that he who knows Agni becomes speech, becomes seeing, becomes thought, becomes audition, which four functions return to Agni, to the Breath, during sleep and issue forth again at waking.[39]

Prajāpati's dismemberment, the genesis of the world, is an emanation of radiant Breath, a measuring out of space by Spirit. In the same way that the Ideas or Images of things are projected out from the source of light to reflect from the Waters of Substance, just so do the Seven Breaths flow out from Prajāpati to enliven forms; and to the extent that the individual so-and-so has shattered the illusions of selfhood and is thereby unified with his own true Self, has remembered the body of Prajāpati, so

---

29. CU III.13.6. 30. ŚB XI.8.3.6; cf. Coomaraswamy, 1940, pp. 55 f.

31. CU V.1.7.15; Senart, 1930, p. 62; cf. BU VI.7-14.

32. MU II.6. 33. BG XVIII.20.

34. For alternative meanings of the text see Coomaraswamy, 1977, 2, p. 399, n. 27. 35. Praśna Up. II.3; MU II.6; VI.26.

36. MU II.6; cf. RV VI.75.6; KU III.3 ff.; *Jātaka* VI 252.

37. See above, p. 49.

38. See "Measures of Fire" in Coomaraswamy, 1077, 2, pp 159-165.

39. ŚB X.3.31-36; cf. Belvalkar and Ranade, 1927, pp. 146 ff.; Mus, 1935, p. 449.

too, are his seven breaths, the senses flowing out through the eye, the ear and the other sense organs, so many outbreathings of fiery Air, scintilla of effulgent Breath, scattering out to measure cosmos from chaos. The expiration of the Self is the inspiration of forms, transforming them from an inert virtuality to an animate actuality.

* * * * *

The same concept is otherwise expressed in the Indian and traditional doctrine of sense perception. According to this it is the Inner Spirit or, in Buddhist terms, the immanent Buddha who sees, and not the eye; the Spirit or Buddha that hears, and not the ear; and so on for the other senses and powers of consciousness. The sense powers move outwards, as "breaths" (prāṇa), to objects, which are cognizable because foreknown.[40] "It is by the outbreath that one smells a scent".[41] "Inhalation is the swallower; exhalation the taster".[42] Inhalation is merely a preparation for smelling; it is by exhalation that the odour is perceived. In vision the object is seen by a "ray" projected by way of the retina, and not by a reflected light that strikes the eye; and so similarly for the other powers of perception. Sensation involves reactions by the sense organs to physical stimuli (the "inhalation"), but these are only known as scents, sounds, etc., when the light, or Breath, of the Intellect is projected upon them. Sensible reactions are in themselves unintelligent; sensibility is a passion, but perception is an act of the will, a function of the Inner Spirit.[43]

The five senses are termed "the five powers of Indra" (pañcendriya). The powers or "forces" of consciousness, the senses, are conceived in the image of the powers or forces which Indra, the archetypal King located at the Centre and Zenith of the spatial world, projects throughout his cosmic kingdom. According to the traditional Buddhist exegesis the term indriya means "supreme" (parama), the "Lord" (iśvara) and "Ruler" (adhipati). "What then is the meaning of the word indriya? It derives from the root idi, indicating 'absolute supremacy'..."[44] The term indriya is expressive of power, dominance or suzerainty (P. adhipacca, issarya).[45]

---

40. JUB I.60.5. The correlation of the breaths and the senses is not always direct in the early texts. In ŚB the series is breath, speech, sight, hearing and mind; in Kauṣ. Up. II.15 the father transmits his indriyas to his son, contact being made "sense to sense", and here they are enumerated as speech, breath, sight, hearing and taste. In CU they are sight, hearing, speech, thought and what is undoubtedly breath. These series connect with the senses by way of the openings in the head : sight and hearing relate to the eyes and ears, speech to the mouth and thus to taste, the breath with the nostrils and thus to smell. The sense of touch has no apparent correlation in the primitive series. Cf. Mus, 1935, pp. 457-458. - The following analysis of the indriyāṇi as Breaths relies heavily on Coomaraswamy's article "On the Indian and Traditional Psychology, or Rather Pneumatology", in Coomaraswamy, 1977, 2, pp. 333 ff. See esp. pp. 344 ff.

41. BU III.2.2. 42. AĀ II.2.1.

43. Coomaraswamy, 1940, pp. 60-63 and n. 32; 1977, p. 497, n. 15.

44. Yaśomitra's *Abhidharmakośa-śāstra-vyākya* II, quoted by Sōgen, 1912, p. 146.

45. *Visuddhimagga*, in Rhys Davids, 1920a, pp. 491 ff., quoted by Karunadasa, 1967, p. 49; cf. Rhys Davids and Stede, PTS Dictionary, s.v., indriya; Rhys Davids, 1924, pp. 121 & 168; Mus, 1935, p. 456 and n. 6.

The Brahmanic Indra, the divine personification of the Regnum, is identified with the central Sun and the sovereign Breath. He symbolizes the Breath as the Inner Person (antaḥpuruṣa) and Inner Spirit (antarātman), who is the "Lord of the Breaths" and "Leader of the Breaths and of the body",[46] the "Lord of all",[47] the "Lord of the Gods and Lord of beings".[48] He is the regnant Breath whom all hail as King and to whom the Breaths gather at death,[49] in whom the gods who are the Breaths, inhere.[50]

Whoever speaks, hears, thinks, etc., does so by Indra's ray;[51] he is the Inner Controller, "other than whom there is no seer, hearer, thinker or knower".[52] The powers (indriyāṇi) are his subject Spirations or Breaths (prāṇa),[53] Gods or Angels (deva) who participate in and depend upon him.[54] They are the Maruts[55] and the "fires".[56] Indra is the indwelling and regnant Spirit and "even as sparks proceed in all directions from a blazing fire, even so from this prescient Spirit the Breaths and other substances disperse to their respective stations".[57] The indriyāṇi "are of the Spirit; it is the Spirit that proceeds in them and controls them".[58] The faculties of vision, audition, etc., are not ours but "only the names given to forces that He projects and reabsorbs".[59]

The outflow of the senses into space from Indra as the regnant Spirit corresponds to the outflow of Indra's power in his function as archetypal King. As King in divinis he sits enthroned at the centre of the Trāyastriṃśa Heaven surrounded by his 32 attendant Gods, positioned round him in the 32 directions of space. The Gods are his delegated powers and regulate the kingdom according to his commands. Indra rules his domain by "projecting" the Law by way of his delegated mandatories into the 32 directions of space and to the outermost confines of his kingdom. He thus puts bounds to disorder in mimetic repetition of the ordering of chaos in the cosmogenesis. The functioning of society and the actions of his subjects are thereby regulated (are "measured") to accord with metaphysical paradigms. The terrestrial kingdom of the cakravartin-king on earth is structured in accordance with this same supernal model.

In an analogous manner the senses, the "powers", are projected out through the portals of the body - the sense organs - from the centre of consciousness, the throne of the Inner Controller, Indra within Everyman, called the Breath and Solar Gale in the Brahmanic texts and the Mind King, the indwelling Tathāgata as Dharma-Cakravartin, in the Buddhist.

The indriyāṇi are elemental beings (bhūta), divisions of the Great Being (mahābhūta), who is Brahman, Breath or Indra who, "indwelling the secret cave (of the heart), looks round about through these elemental beings".[60] They are Gods or Intelligences, "distributive essences"

---

46. Muṇḍ. Up. II.2.8. 47. AV XI.4.1.10.

48. AV VIII.1; TS VI.1.11.4; MU V.2. 49. MU IV.3.37-38.

50. Kauṣ. Up. III.3; AĀ II; BU I.4.7. 51. JUB I.28-29.

52. BU III.7.23; III.8.11. 53. JUB IV.7.4; II.4.5.

54. BU I.5.21; CU.5.1.15; cf. Coomaraswamy, 1977, 2, p. 162, n. 15; 1939, p. 68, n. 4. 55. AB III.16. 56. RV III.26.4.

57. Kauṣ. Up. III.3; IV.20; Muṇḍ. Up. II.1.1; MU VI.26.31.

58. MU VI.31. 59. BU I.4.7; I.5.2; I.6.3; etc. 60. KU IV.4.6.

(vibhūtaya),[61] whose operation is our consciousness.[62] They are the powers of the soul, the delegations and extensions of the Power of the Spirit, sent forth by him to do his bidding. And just as the Spirit indwells the man, so also do the powers of the Spirit : "Having made him their mortal house, the Gods[63] inhabited man";[64] "All these Gods are in me";[65] "They are neither in the sky nor on earth : whatever breathes, therein they are".[66] Obeying the command of the Spirit the God of Fire enters into man's mouth to become the voice; so similarly the Sun, the Moon, and the Quarters enter the eyes, the mind, the ears.[67] They serve the Spirit-Breath as subjects serve a king.[68] To Him they bring tribute,[69] to Him they resort[70] and by Him they are protected.[71] They are solar rays, by which the Spirit, who is the Only Seer and Only Thinker, sees, hears, thinks and eats within us.[72] "Assuredly, the Self of one's self is called the leader, immortal, perceiver, thinker, the goer, the evacuator, the delighter, the doer, the speaker, the taster, the smeller, the seer, the hearer and the toucher".[73] "Whoever sees it is by His ray that he sees",[74] that is, "he sees by the ray of the Only Seer, Himself unseen".[75]

The outflowing of the Breaths from the Inner Controller is directly assimilated to the expansion of the directions of space from their centre, that is, to the seven directions. The Solar Indra is "seven rayed", and it is "by the power of these seven rays that everything that thinks, thinks, everything that sees, sees..." and so on for the other faculties. The outflowing of Breaths to their objects is likened to the pouring out of streams or rivers. "The Self-existent pierced the opening (khāni) outwards",[76] and thence looks forth. The khāni are sluices or floodgates : "Ye, Indravaruṇau, have pierced the sluices (khāni) of the waters".[77] These outpourings are sevenfold. The *Atharva Veda* asks the question, "Who pierced the seven apertures (khāni) in the head, these ears, the nostrils, eyes and mouth.... who divided up the Waters for the flowing of the rivers in this man?"[78] The answer is given in the *Ṛg Veda's* account of Indra's smiting of Vṛtra[79]:

---

61. AĀ II.1.7; BG X.10.

62. Coomaraswamy, 1977, 2, p. 337. The indriyas have a twofold aspect, one psychic, pertaining to the subtle realm, and one corporeal, belonging to the realm of gross manifestation. They are at one and the same time faculties and organs : on the one hand the indriyas are the faculties or powers belonging to the five senses of touch, taste, smell, sight and hearing; and on the other hand, and by extension, they are the five associated bodily organs - the skin, the tongue, the nose, the eye and the ear. The sense faculty and its bodily organ, described by the same word, together constitute a single instrument, either of knowledge (buddhi, jñāna) or of action (karma) (Guénon, 1945, pp. 62 & 72-73) : "The various faculties of sensation and action are eleven in number, five of sensation (buddhindriya, or jñānendriya), five of action (karmendriya), and Mind (manas)". (*Brahma-Sūtra* II.4.1 ff.; cf. Guénon, 1945, p. 72).

63. The equivalent of Intelligences or Angels in the Christian terminology. 64. AV XI.8.18.b. 65. JUB I.14.2 ff. 66. ŚB IX.2.1.15.

67. AĀ II.4.2. ff. 68. BU I.4.7; Kauṣ.Up. III.2; IV.20.

69. AV X.7.37; X.8.15; XI.4.19; JUB IV.24.9; Kauṣ. Up. II.1; etc.

70. ŚB VI.1.1.4. 71. AV X.2.27; BU IV.3.12.

72. MU II.6; VI.31; BU III.7.23; JUB I.29-30; etc. For the doctrine of the median Spirit who "eats" the subject senses, see Coomaraswamy, 1977, 2, p. 122 and the references for "swallow" there given.

73. MU VI.7. 74. JUB I.28.8 75. BU III.7.23. 76. KU II.1.1.

77. RV VII.82-83. 78. AV X.2.6.1. 79. Cf. below, pp. 184 & 313.

Indra "with his bolt pierced the sluices of the streams",[80] thus releasing the "Seven Rivers" by which we see, hear, etc.[81] When he smote the Serpent, Indra "sent forth the Seven Rivers, opened the doors that had been closed".[82] The Seven Rivers are simultaneously the faculties of sense, the seven rays of the Sun, the seven Breaths, and the seven directions of space.[83] The slaying of Vṛtra is at once a freeing of both the macroscosmic and the microcosmic waters of existence, which flow out to fill the worlds.

The same correlations are expressed in the symbolism of the Seven Ṛṣis (named from the root ṛṣ, "to flow, to shine"), the Seven Seers, identified with the Seven Breaths : "From the Not-being arose the Seven Breaths (prāṇa) in the shape of the Seven Seers : they were kindled up by the Breath in the middle as Indra, whereupon they produced the Seven Puruṣas".[84] "Who were the Ṛṣis? The Ṛṣis doubtless were the Breaths... (and) this same median Breath doubtless is Indra. He by his power (indriya) kindled those Breaths from the midst; and inasmuch as he kindled (indh) he is the kindler (indha).. the Breaths, being kindled, created seven separate Persons (puruṣa)".[85] The seven separate Persons are the Seven Breaths who surround the central Breath; they are the six indriyāṇi (the powers of vision, audition, breathing, speech, etc.), plus Mind (manas); their openings are in the head. They serve Indra, "the One beyond the Ṛṣis", "the mover of the Ṛṣis",[86] offering him sacrifice and homage in the hope of finding the Sun Door or of entering into Indra himself. This attendance upon the axial divinity is likened in astronomical symbolism to the revolution of the seven stars of the Great Bear or Great Dipper (Ursa Major) around the Pole Star, which stands at the centre of the turning heavens.[87]

The concept returns us to the form of the stupa, for the *Bṛhadāranyaka Upaniṣad* speaks of the Seven Ṛṣis, which it identifies with the Breaths, as seated on the rim of the "upturned bowl", the head, which, together with Speech (vāc), is "the eighth".[88] The "upturned bowl", the head, is homologous with the sphere of the World Egg, the mouth being Earth, the brow Heaven, held apart by the axial Breath of the nostrils;[89] and, as we have seen, the term "upturned bowl" is also the name given the Egg (garbha) or dome of the stupa.[90]

* * * * *

For the unregenerate and unannihilate self the stimulations of sense seem centripetal, passing from the outer object through the gateways of the sense organs to consciousness; but for the realized Self it is not the inward flow of breath, but by its outflowing, that the sense of smell "measures" or grasps olfactions; it is by a radiation of light outward

---

80. RV II.15.3. 81. RV *passim*. 82. RV IV.2.8.1. 83. JUB I.29.8-9.

84. Keith, 1925, 2, p. 454, citing ŚB VI.1.1.1.

85. ŚB VI.1.1.1-2; cf. VIII.4.1.5; VIII.4.3.6; IX.1.1.21; IX.2.1.13. For further references, see Coomaraswamy, 1977, 2, p. 356, n. 72, and for the doctrine see ibid., p. 156. 86. RV VIII.51.3; cf. I.23.24.

87. Coomaraswamy, 1977, 2, p. 356, n. 73, gives the following references : RV I.164.15; X.73.1; X.82.2; TS V.7.4.3; AV X.8.5.9; XI.12.19; XIX.41.1; ŚB II.1.2.4; VI.6.1.1ff.; JUB I.45; I.46.1-2; I.48.3; IV.14.5-6; IV.26.2; BU II.2.4.

88. BU II.2.3. Cf. AV X.2.6 and AĀ I.5.2, which also speak of seven Breaths in the head, with speech as the eighth, "not mingled with the others". 89. AĀ II.1.2; cf. above, p. 60.

90. The terminology traces to Sino-Japanese usage, where the dome of the stupa is called the fukubachi, 伏鉢 , literally, "the upturned bowl".

through the eye that forms are illumined and comprehended; and so similarly for each of the senses. Sensing is a centrifugal flowing. Inversely, for the follower of the meditational path, it is by withdrawing the senses towards the centre of consciousness that the abode of the Self within the heart is entered, whence the Inner Controller, the Mind King, looks outward to survey the world.

* * * * *

The deployment of the directions in the stupa plan embodies these concepts. The centre of the plan is the centre of Consciousness, the location of the Mind King. The six arms of the three-dimensional cross that radiate from that centre are rays of Breath or Consciousness projected outwards through the sense portals to the objects of the sensible world. The stupa plan is the graphic schema of the manner in which the world is momentarily "created" by Consciousness emanating outwards to "in-form" phenomena.

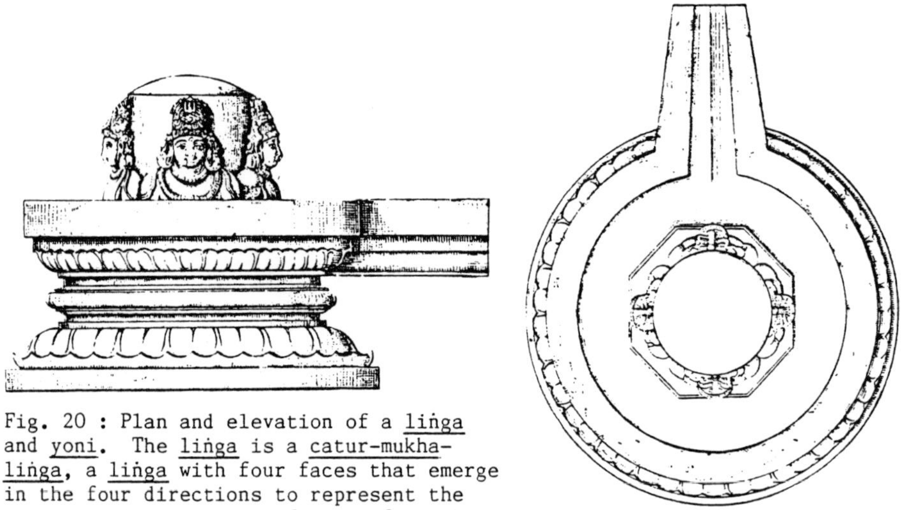

Fig. 20 : Plan and elevation of a liṅga and yoni. The liṅga is a catur-mukha-liṅga, a liṅga with four faces that emerge in the four directions to represent the cosmogenetic emanation of space from the Pillar of the Universe. See the following chapter.

8 THE DEPLOYMENT OF SPACE IN ICONOGRAPHY, ARCHITECTURE AND THE BUDDHIST KINGDOM.

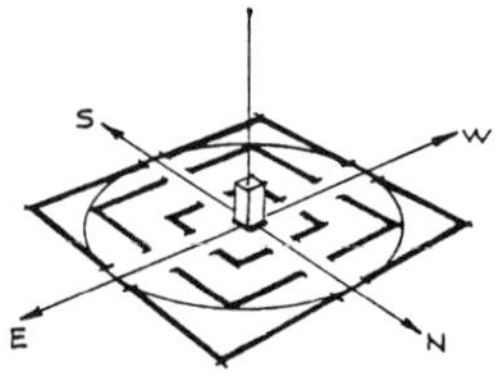

The multi-headed God or Bodhisattva, a commonplace in both Hindu and Buddhist iconography, expresses the emanation of the directions from their point source of origin. The four heads of Brahmā face the cardinal directions to represent the expansion of existence into space from its cosmogenetic centre. A similar concept is conveyed by the eleven-headed Avalokiteśvara (Jap. Jūichimen Kannon) and the numerous other examples of multicephalous divinities that appear in the Brahmanic and Buddhist pantheons.

Fig. 21 : Eleven headed Avalokiteśvara (Jap. Jūichimen Kannon). The heads are aspects of Compassion (karuṇa) and also the eleven directions of space : the cardinals, the ordinals, the zenith, nadir, and centre.

Fig. 22 : Vajrasattva, who represents Enlightenment innate within the person. He has four heads facing the cardinal directions, he carries a five prong vajra and his stupa-like crown shows Buddhas emerging in the four directions: his revelation within the heart of the person is symbolically expressed as a spatial deployment from a centre. Nālandā, India, 13 - 14th century.

The theme is translated directly into architecture in the famous Khmer monument, the Bayon in Kampuchea, where Jayavarman II had his own face carved in the likeness of Vajradhara on the four sides of each of the 54 towers.[1] The eyes painted upon the four sides of the harmikā of the Nepalese stupa embody an analogous symbolism.

---

1. Coedes, 1963, Ch. VI. See also Wheatley, 1971, for analogous concepts in the Chinese tradition.

a

b

c

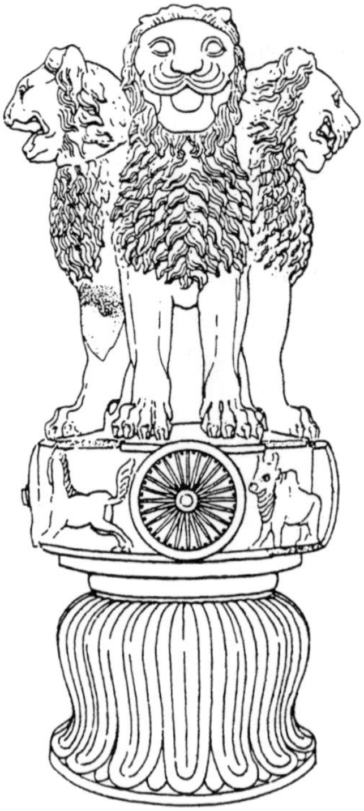

d

e

Fig. 23 : a. The 54 towers of the Bayon, Angkor, have the head of Jayavarman II, as Vajradhara, carved on each of the four sides.

b. A Nepalese stupa, with eyes painted on each side of the square harmikā.

c. Liṅga with protuberances in the four directions.

d. Aśoka's lion capital from Sārnāth.

e. A relief from Sāñcī showing the Sun-Wheel of the Dharma supported by four lions facing the four directions.

The concept of a deployment, a flowing outwards from a centre towards the cardinal points of the compass, was expressed in the Asian tradition of urban planning by the construction of massive gates, of a size far exceeding the requirements of access or defense. Whereas the *Mānasāra-śilpa-śāstra* prescribes a maximum of 12 storeys for temples and dwellings, it authorizes gateways having as many as 17 storeys for towns and cities.[2] The architectural canons of South and South-East Asia specify the reason for the construction of these enormous entrances : spiritual power, generated at the axis, flowed out from the confines of the ceremonial complex formed by the city, diffusing outwards towards the cardinal points of the compass in a perpetually recurrent mimesis of the primordial cosmogenetic process.[3] From the central point of the town the four horizons were projected outwards to the "bounds of space" in the four directions, so delimiting and orienting the surrounding countryside, assimilating it as sacred territory within the continuum of profane space, subjecting it to cosmic order, sacralizing it, rendering it fit for human habitation and cultivation.[4]

The same order of ideas is expressed on a smaller scale by the numerous examples of pillar forms with four-way projections. Bosch describes four-headed liṅga or liṅga with four spherical protuberances.[5] The four lateral prongs of a five-prong vajra have a similar significance.

A clear example of this iconography is provided by the so-called lion pillar at Sārnāth, erected there by Aśoka. This column has been closely analyzed and shown to be an iconographic representation of the deployment of space in the four directions from a central axis.[6] The capital of the column is decorated by four wheels alternating with four animals, an ox, a lion, a horse and an elephant, proceeding in a sun-wise direction. Przyluski was the first to demonstrate that each of the four wheels corresponds to a direction, to a planet, a colour, a precious stone, etc. The clue to this correspondence is given by the four animals. The Buddhist literature speaks of Lake Anavatapta, fed by hot springs and possessing healing powers. Buddhas, Bodhisattvas and arhats fly there to bathe in its sacred waters. Four streams flow from the lake in the four directions through fountain-heads in the shape of the four animals and thence flow down into the world as four great rivers : the river Gaṅgā flows to the East from the mouth of a silver ox; Sindhu flows to the South from the mouth of a golden elephant; Śītā to the North from the mouth of a crystal lion; and the river Oxus flows to the West from the mouth of a lapis lazuli horse.[7] An account is given in the *Vikramacharita* of a golden pillar that daily rises from the centre of this same Lake Anavatapta to touch the sun at noon.[8] The Sārnāth pillar is a representation of this golden column : the lions standing upon its capital originally supported a fifth wheel, which is at one and the same time the disc of the stationary Sun at midday and the Wheel of the Dharma. As Mus has so ably demonstrated, the wheel at the summit of the column is the apical direction while the four wheels on its sides are the four directions in the horizontal plane.[9]

---

2. *Mānasāra* XX, XXX & XXXIII. 3. Wheatley, 1971, p. 435.

4. Ibid., pp. 417 f. 5. Bosch, 1961, pp. 212 f.

6. Przyluski, 1932a; Mus, 1935, pp. 145 ff,; cf. Bénisti, 1960, p. 52; Auboyer, 1949, p. 88.

7. *Bommōkyō (Brahmajāla-sūtra)*, cited by Elisséeff, 1936, p. 95. See also Zimmer, 1955, p. 225; Coedes, 1963, pp. 50 f.; Smith, 1911, pp. 59 f. & 95; Vogel, 1936, p. 11; Rowland, 1953, pp. 45 f. & 216; 1953a, p. 15; Paranavitana, 1954, p. 155; Wales, 1977, p. 135.

8. See above, pp. 26 f. 9. Mus, 1935, pp. 148 ff.

a

b

d

c

Fig. 24 : Examples of iconographic forms expressing the deployment of space in the four directions.
a. A *liṅga* with four heads (*catur-mukha-liṅga*). The heads face the four directions of space and emerge from the *liṅga*, the principial pole of the universe.
b. A five-prong *vajra*. The upper and lower groups of prongs represent the emanation of space into the directions in the Diamond and Matrix Worlds respectively.
c. A *karma-vajra*, consisting of a pair of three-prong *vajras* crossed at right angles. The twelve prongs represent the twelve divisions of the ecliptic and the spatial division of the heavens.
d. A Wheel of the Dharma (*dharma-cakra*), whose eight spokes represent both the Noble Eightfold Path and the eight directions of space (the cardinal and ordinal directions) emanating from their principial centre.

The Sārnāth pillar is rich in symbolic associations. The column is a hieroglyph of the dissemination of the Buddha's Dharma throughout the worlds; at the same time it represents the sovereignty of Aśoka who, as a Buddhist king and earthly reflection of the Buddha as universal cakravartin, rules the world according to that Law. The power of the Buddha's Law and the power of his kingly representative spread out, regulate, and thereby "cosmicize", the four quarters.[10]

Fig. 25 : The Sun-Wheel of the Dharma supported by dig-gajas, the elephants of the four directions (see below, pp. 314 ff.).

Fig. 26 : The hair of Śiva, which represents the deployment of space. The River Gaṅgā flows down into the hair and is divided into the directions of space so as to irrigate the earth. In this image the Goddess Gaṅgā is shown seated within Śiva's hair.

The Buddhist formulation of the outflowing of the four rivers into the world has its counterpart in the Hindu myth of the descent of the Gaṅgā. The waters of the river flow down with such force that they threaten to destroy the world, but Śiva receives them in his hair, whence they flow with life-giving efficacy onto the plain of India. [11] The hair of Śiva is explicitly identified with the directions of space.[12]

The quartering of space figured by the column capital relates closely to the significance of the inverted lotus that supports it. Opening from above downwards, it is rooted in the Upper Waters, the Ground of all existences. Its downward flowering is the deployment of the world.[13]

---

10. These concepts are developed in the section dealing with kingship. See below, pp. 88 ff.

11. Zimmer, 1946, pp. 112-116; 1959, pp. 98 f.

12. Guénon, 1958a, p. 17, n. 4.

13. For the symbolism of the lotus, see below, pp. 97 ff. & 203 ff.

Paranavitana gives the symbolism a Theravāda flavour by identifying the four animals with the "perils" of birth, decay, disease and death, which, following each other in a never-ending cycle, are taken to represent the round of samṣāra. The animals of the four quarters of the Sārnāth column are shown running. Their movement is the turning of the Wheel of Existence.[14] With similar import the directions of Thai temples are associated with birth (East), life (South), dying (West) and death (North), and the monks' quarters are accordingly located to the South of the temple. Stupas show representations of the Buddha's nativity, his meditation, or his death, in the appropriate directions.[15]

The symbolism of the Sārnāth pillar is directly translated into architectural forms. The animals of the four directions appear on the "moonstones" at the foot of the stairs leading to Sinhalese shrines.[16] Bronze figurines of the four animals, together with representations of the guardian deities of the quarters (dikpāla), were buried under the floors of each of the porches in the cardinal directions of early Sinhalese monasteries;[17] similar figures were placed in nine depressions arranged according to the directions in the foundation stones at the base of Malayan temples.[18] The stelae (vāhalkada) at Anuradhāpura in Sri Lanka were surmounted by the animal figures, elephants to the East, lions to the North, and so on. Friezes of the four animals decorated other Sinhalese stelae and guardstones,[19] and it is common in many parts of Asia to find four animals shown in friezes decorating the step at the entrance of the stupa.

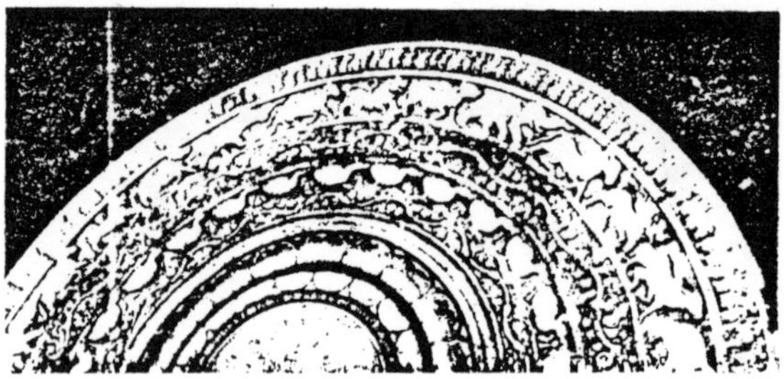

Fig. 27 : A "moonstone" at Anuradhāpura, Sri Lanka. The band second in from the outer edge shows a procession of the animals of the four directions : the lion, the ox, the elephant and the horse.

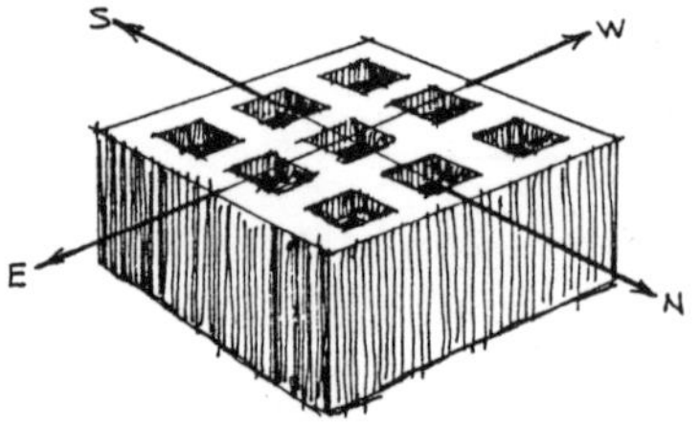

Fig. 28 : Images of the animals of the four directions were placed at the appropriate positions in the depressions of the foundation stones of Malayan temples.

The Neak Pean temple of the Angkor complex in Kampuchea has a small central sanctuary that stands as an island in the midst of a square pool. From this central pool the water poured into four smaller tangential pools through four fountain-heads having the form of a lion, an elephant, a horse and a man. Despite this substitution of a man for an ox there is little doubt that the structure was intended to represent the sacred Lake Anavatapta with its four outflowing rivers.[20] A later expression of the same

---

14. Paranavitana, 1946, pp. 54 f. 15. Idem.

16. Paranavitana, 1954, *passim*; Zimmer, 1959, p. 255.

17. Paranavitana, 1954, p. 198; 1946, pp. 54 f.; Smith, 1911, pp. 59f.

18. O'Connor, 1966, pp. 53 f. 19. Paranavitana, 1946, pp. 54 f.

20. Coedes, 1963, pp. 50 f.; Wales, 1977, pp. 128 ff.

symbolism is found at the Wat Samplum in Bangkok, where four springs flow from the heads of the four animals located on the four sides of the main temple.[21]

* * * * *

The geometric schema of expansion into the directions is reflected in the spatial configuration of Buddhist kingdoms. An extensive literature exists on the profusion of five and nine unit systems, that is, units having a centre plus four or eight surrounding political units, in the social structures and symbolic constructs of government in the South East Asian world.[22] The Burmese king had four principal and four secondary wives, whose titles, "Northern Queen of the Palace", "Queen of the West", etc., associated them with the directions. Their chambers formed a circle around the hall of the king. He sat upon a throne embellished with symbols of the Guardian Kings of the Four Directions (lokapāla), who provided the model for the four chief ministers, each governing one quarter of the capital and one quarter of the empire, and having flags of the colours associated with the four sides of Mt. Meru.[23] This cosmological structuring of the bureaucracy carried on down through every level of the official hierarchy.[24] The structure of the old Sinhalese kingdom was similar. The four chief ministers in Kandy were called "Lords of the Quarters",[25] and their functional relationship to the king was modelled on that of the four Lokapāla to the Buddha, who entrusted the four segments of the world to their care when he entered nirvāṇa.[26] Exactly analogous configurations of power operated at Anuradhāpura and in Java.[27]

Royal capitals of Buddhist kingdoms were modelled on the cities of the gods. The monarch's palace was built according to the descriptions of Indra's Palace, Vejayanta, given in the sacred writings. The *Jātakas* and the Sri Lankan chronicles both speak of this practice.[28]

In more complex developments of this schema the kingdom was conceived as a multi-layered mandala. However irregular its boundaries might be in topographical fact, the kingdom was nevertheless symbolically considered as a square mandala, divided four-fold by the directional axes crossing at its centre. This spatial conformation is repeated on a reduced scale through a series of cosmic images, one within the other. The cosmic square of the kingdom is repeated in the capital that stands at its centre, then in the palace that centres the capital, in the throne room, and then in the throne, located at the common midpoint of this expanding series of concentric squares.

A clear instance is provided by Pegu in Burma. The kingdom, the city and the palace were diminishing mandalas, each a reflection of the others, symmetrically oriented upon East-West and North-South axes. At the centre of the palace was the pyatthat (= prāsadā), a storied tower of pyramidal

---

21. Wales, 1977, p. 135.

22. See e.g., Tambiah, 1976, pp. 102 ff.; MacDonald, 1957, pp. 204 ff.; de Jong, 1952; Schrieke, 1957; Shorto, 1963, pp. 581 ff.; Moertono, 1968; Wheatley, 1971.

23. Sarkisyanz, 1965, p. 85 and n. 6; Wales, 1977, p. 139; Heine-Geldern, 1956, p. 5.

24. Heine-Geldern, 1956, p. 5.

25. Hayley, 1923, pp. 39-49; Hocart, 1927a, p. 107; Mus, 1935,p,296.

26. *Mahāvaṃsa* XXI.29 ff; XXX.89; Przyluski, 1923, pp. 168 & 399 ff.

27. Hocart, 1927a, p. 109; Mus, 1935, p. 296.

28. Mus, 1935, p. 298.

form rising from the throne room and symbolically identified with Mt. Meru. The throne, placed on the vertical axis of the pyatthat, was a smaller representation of the cosmic mountain, adorned with figures of Indra, the 32 attendant gods of his heaven, the four regents of the cardinal points, and a peacock and hare to indicate the sun and the moon. The centre of the reducing series was occupied by the king, who was identified with the Golden Germ (hiraṇyagarbha), the cosmogenetic centre of the universe. He was seen as the personification of Mt. Meru; he was the most interior and central of the multiple representations of the Cosmic Mountain.[29] By a process of concentration each of the cosmic images is fully contained within the next, until they are all enveloped in the person of the sovereign.

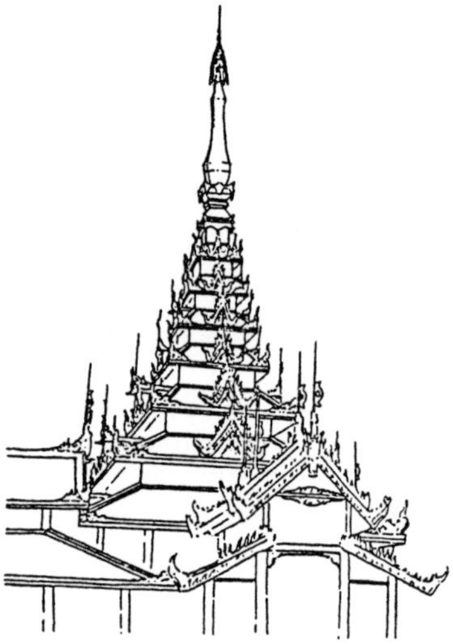

Fig. 29 : The Burmese pyatthat at Mandalay. It represents Mt. Meru, the central axis of the world, and stands above the king's throne.

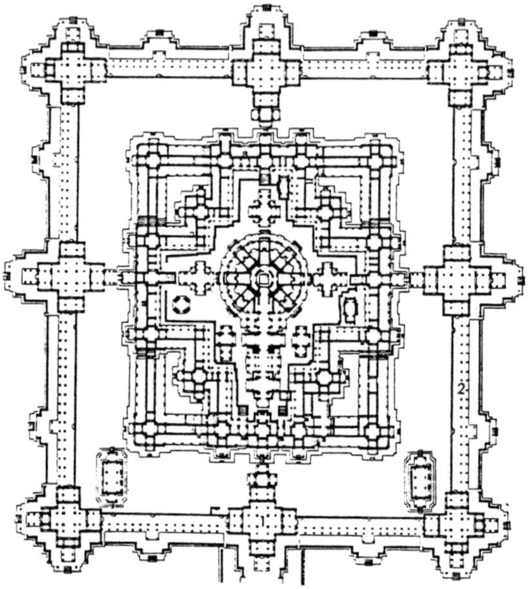

Fig. 30 : The plan of the Bayon, Angkor, an example of a cruciform plan aligned to the cross of the four directions.

Mandalay, built as recently as 1857, was planned according to these principles. A square with sides facing the cardinal directions, it had three gates on each of its sides to give a total of twelve, each marked with a sign of the zodiac. The city was conceived in the likeness of the heavenly constellations revolving about Mt. Meru, which was represented by the royal palace.[30] The Meru-palace was not located at the geometric centre of the city but was slightly displaced to the East, the direction of the rising sun, and recalling the symbolism of the dawn and the imagery of the

29. Heine-Geldern, 1930, pp. 57-59; Mus, 1935, pp. 301 f.; Auboyer, 1949, p. 92; Tambiah, 1976, p. 109; Shorto, 1963, p. 590.

30. The square city plan with twelve gates connected by straight roadways dividing the enclosure into sixteen blocks is that prescribed in the Indian *Śāstras*, e.g., *Arthaśāstra* II.4, and is a common pattern for the layout of towns throughout Asia. Exact parallels exist in many traditions.

sun at daybreak as the cosmic pillar or "the palace supported on a single pillar" (P. ekattambha pāsāda).[31] Above the audience hall rose a seven-tiered Meru tower, beneath which stood the Lion Throne, adorned with representations of the 33 gods of Indra's Heaven.[32]

In other cases the kingdom is laid out in the likeness of Indra's Heaven on the summit of Mt. Meru, where Indra, the prototypic King, sits within his centrally located palace surrounded by a retinue of 32 gods, each assigned a point on a circle divided into 32 segments.[33] The guiding concept is a 32-fold division of space around a centre : the four cardinal directions, the four ordinals and their intermediate divisions and subdiv-

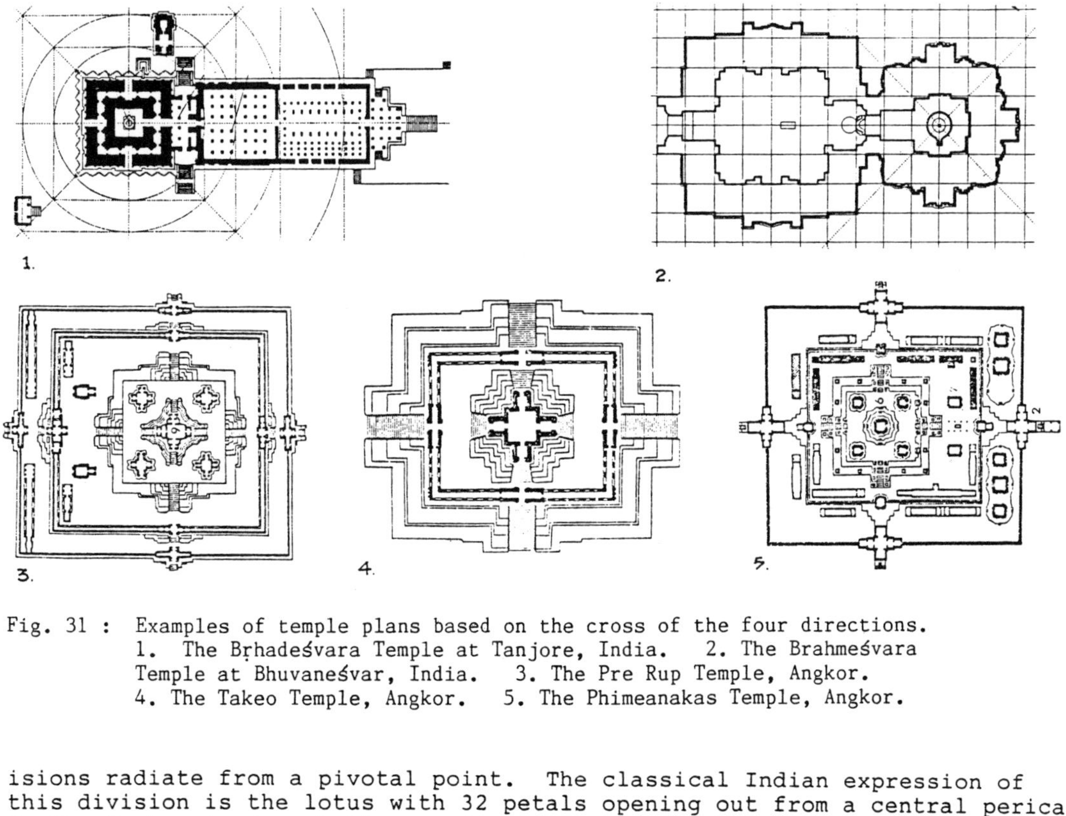

Fig. 31 : Examples of temple plans based on the cross of the four directions. 1. The Bṛhadeśvara Temple at Tanjore, India. 2. The Brahmeśvara Temple at Bhuvaneśvar, India. 3. The Pre Rup Temple, Angkor. 4. The Takeo Temple, Angkor. 5. The Phimeanakas Temple, Angkor.

isions radiate from a pivotal point. The classical Indian expression of this division is the lotus with 32 petals opening out from a central pericarp. In the Brahmanic formulations Indra is surrounded by the Regents of the Four Directions (lokapāla) and 28 zodiacal "houses", representing the phases of the moon, so that the celestial mandala combined spatial and temporal elements. The Buddhist texts differ from this, relocating the Regents of the Four Directions to the slopes of Meru and encompassing Indra with 32 gods.[34] The geometric structuring of Indra's Heaven is reflected in the

31. See above pp. 27 f.; Auboyer, 1949, p. 80.

32. Heine-Geldern, 1930, p. 59; 1956, p. 4; Auboyer, 1949, p. 142; Wales, 1977, pp. 138f.; Sarkisyanz, 1965, pp. 84f.; Shorto, 1963, pp. 588 f.

33. See M I.253. A detailed description of Indra's Heaven is given in Coedes and Archaimbault, 1973, summarized in Wales, 1977, pp. 54 f.

34. Mus, 1935, p. 299, n.1.

layout of Buddhist kingdoms, which are divided into 32 directionally oriented provinces, centred by the sovereign's palace. Right up until the late 19th Century there still existed Buddhist kingdoms structured in accordance with this paradigm. The ancient Burmese kingdom of Pyu had 32 provinces, each with a regional head and centred by the capital, Śrikṣetra (Old Prome), which was built in the likeness of Sudarśana, Indra's city and capital of the Trāyastriṃśa Heaven, with a golden palace at its midpoint and 32 gates, each carrying the name of a corresponding province.[35] The old Burmese chronicles say that Śrikṣetra was designed by Indra on the model of Sudarśana. At the foundation of the city Indra laid out the circuit with a rope attached to an indhakhīla pillar, which became the symbolic Meru at the centre of the capital.[36] Similarly, the kingdom of Pegu in Burma in the 14th Century had 32 provinces grouped around the capital on the pattern of the Trāyastriṃśa.[37] The kingdom of Java in the 9th Century had 32 high dignitaries, including four ministers corresponding to the lokapālas, and 28 regents to govern the 28 vassal states.[38] The ruler of Mataram in the 17th Century was called "Lord of the 33 Islands";[39] and the Shan state of Keng tung was known as the "32 towns of the Khun", in which "Khun" was the name of the ruler.[40] With similar reference the *Mahāvaṃsa* relates that the Sinhalese king defeated the invading Tamils in 28 battles, taking 32 kings prisoner. When the final assault was mounted on Anuradhāpura his forces were drawn up in 32 battalions.[41]

* * * * *

The same themes are evident in the rites of consecration (rājasuya) performed at the installation of a king. In the Brahmanic ritual, which forms the basis for the Buddhist ceremonies, water, drawn from rivers, lakes and ponds throughout the kingdom, was sprinkled on the king's head, and by this aspersion he was symbolically impregnated with the essence of the whole territory. At another moment in the ceremony he was ritually identified with Prajāpati, prototypic Father and King, who contains all the gods within himself. By his equation with Prajāpati the king brings together within himself the god-regents of the directions of space. The total spatial extension of the world and, by reflection, the total extension of its microcosmic counterpart, the kingdom, passes into his bodily person. The state is embodied in the monarch.[42]

---

35. Heine-Geldern, 1930, pp. 48-50; 1956, p. 4; Wales, 1977, p. 137; Sarkisyanz, 1965, p. 84; Mus, 1935, pp. 296-298; Harvey, 1925, p. 12; Shorto, 1963, p. 580.

36. Luce and Pe Maung Ting,1923, pp. 14 f.; Shorto, 1963, p. 577, n. 1; Mus, 1935, p. 297.

37. Heine-Geldern, 1956, p. 5; Wales, 1977, pp. 137 f.; Mus, 1935, p. 299; Sarkisyanz, 1965, p. 84; Shorto, 1963, pp. 572 & 577, n. 2. A 15th Cent. inscription of King Dhammaceti records that when the Buddha visited Burma he prophesied that in the future one of his teeth would return to that country and be in 33 places in the Mon empire. After the parinirvāṇa his tooth was brought to Burma and miraculously multiplied into 33 teeth, which were enshrined in 33 stupas marking the centres of the capital and the 32 provinces of Pegu (Shorto, 1963, pp. 573 f.).

38. Heine-Geldern, 1956, pp. 5f.; Shorto, 1963, p. 581; Mus, 1935, p. 299.

39. Shrieke, 1955, 2, p. 222; Shorto, 1963, p. 581.

40. Wales, 1977, p. 138; Heine-Geldern, 1956, p. 5; Mus, 1935, p. 299.

41. *Mahāvaṃsa* XXV.7 ff.; XXV.55; XXV.75.

42. ŚB V.3.4.1 ff.; Mus, 1935, pp. 238 & 245.

In the analogous Kampuchean ritual the king thinks of his body as Meru, his right and left eyes as the sun and the moon, his arms and legs as the four directions. The six-tiered parasol held above him represents the six abodes of paradise; his crown is the spire of Indra's paradisial palace; his sword is the Sword of Wisdom; his slippers are the Earth, supporting the Mountain, and his red cloak is Mt. Yugandhara, the covering of Meru, expressing a symbolism that traces to the *Purāṇas*, in which Mt. Meru is equated with the Golden Embryo (hiraṇya-garbha) and the encircling mountain ranges that mark the boundaries of the universe are the caul that contains the Embryo.[43]

The coronation ceremonies of Burma, Thailand and Kampuchea include a ritual circumambulation of the capital by which the king takes possession of the city and, by way of the symbolic analogies that tie them together, of the kingdom and the cosmos.[44] The procession starts from the Eastern gate and proceeds clockwise, halting at the cardinal directions to pour out libations to the Earth Goddess. At each of the stops the king changes his vehicle (palenquin, chariot, horse and elephant) and his headdress so as to correspond with symbolic analogies with the Regents of the Directions.[45] In the Thai ceremonies of royal inauguration the Four Regents of the Directions are invoked,[46] as they also were in ancient Sri Lanka.[47] In the Burmese ritual the king, who was identified with the Sun, with Indra and with Viśvakarman, the divine Architect,[48] sat upon a throne representing Mt. Meru placed within a structure called "Indra's Palace" (thagyanan), surrounded by eight Brahmin priests who were the eight Lokapāla, the guardian gods of the eight directions. At one point in the ceremony four maids of honour, one for each direction, render him homage.[49]

* * * * *

These examples of the deployment of space in iconography, architecture and polity could be multiplied, and it is possible to add many analogous instances from other fields of thought and activity. The spatial symbolism of the radiation or expansion of the six arms of the three-dimensional cross from the central point of their meeting is a dominant theme in the Buddhist arts and sciences. In each case the symbolic reference is the same : the divided segments of the whole are organized to accord with a supernal paradigm; they are related to the principial point-centre whence they derive and whereon they depend. These are precisely the values conveyed by the six-armed cross delineated in the stupa plan.

---

43. Thiounn, 1906, *passim*; Mus, 1935, p. 302, n.2; Senart, 1882, pp. 56 & 62; Auboyer, 1949, p. 92; Wales, 1976, p. 142; Heine-Geldern, 1956, p.6. Cf. Winstedt, 1947, for Malayan parallels.

44. Heine-Geldern, 1956, p. 3; Wales, 1977, p. 137.

45. Sarkisyanz, 1965, p. 138; Shorto, 1963, p. 588.

46. Wales, 1931, p. 31. 47. *Mahāvaṃsa* XXX.89; XXI.29 ff.; *Culavaṃsa* LXXII.59.

48. Heine-Geldern, 1956, pp. 6 & 8. 49. Ibid, p. 6.

9 THE STUPA PLAN AS WHEEL.

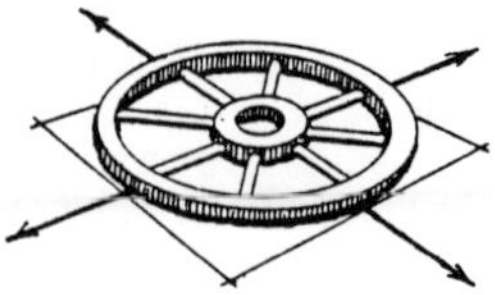

The symbolism of the wheel[1] is implied within the plan of the stupa. The circle drawn about the gnomonic post in the ritual of laying out the stupa plan is the Cosmic Wheel; the axes of orientation identify it as the Wheel of the Year, whose turning is the movement of the sun on the circle of the ecliptic.

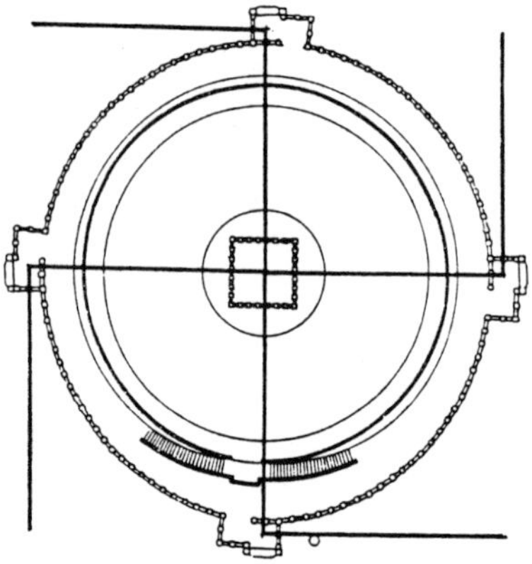

Fig. 32 : The entrances to Sāñcī are turned at right angles to the axes to form a svastika.

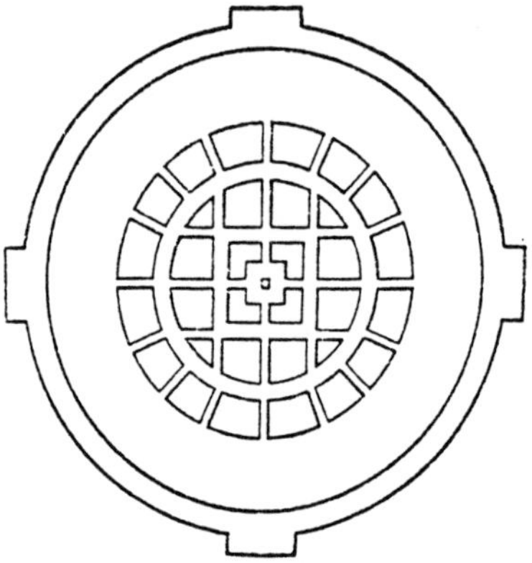

Fig. 33 : The ground plan of the stupa at Ghantaśāla, South India.

In many cases the presence of the wheel is explicitly represented in the stupa. At Sāñcī and Bhārhut the gateways of the stupa are turned at right angles to the axes to indicate movement, in the manner of the arms of the svastika.[2] The domes of the large Indian stupas were rarely constructed of solid masonry but were more often filled with rubble and earth. To support the outer shell of the cupola the builders used a system of internal walls, and these were laid out in the form of wheels, with spokes radiating from a central hub. This is the arrangement found in the oldest surviving stupa at Piprahwā and again in another of the earliest of the stupas, that at Bhaṭṭprolu, which has a wheel shaped central portion.[3] Four of the numerous stupas at Nāgārjunakoṇḍa enclose walls built to delineate a svastika; all the others are constructed on the plan of a wheel, usually with 4 or 8 spokes, but some having 6 or 10. The larger stupas show concentric walls joined by radials in a staggered formation having 8 walls in the inner, 12 in the middle, and 16 in the outer circle. One stupa, the

1. See Guénon, 1962, Ch. XL ("Le dome et la roue"); 1957a, Ch. XXIII ("La roue cosmique"); 1958a, Ch. XXIX ("Centre et circumference"); Chevalier and Gheerbrant, 1973, 4, pp. 119ff., s.v., Roue; Saunders, 1960, pp. 95 ff.

2. Govinda, 1976, p. 8; Volwahsen, 1969, p. 93; Pant, 1976, pp. 119 f.

3. Sarcar, 1966, p. 88; Pant, 1976, pp. 99 & 129.

largest, has eight spokes in the inner space and 16 in each of the two others.[4] The stupa at Ghantaśāla consists of two concentric walls joined by 16 radial walls; the space within the inner circle is divided by a series of walls at right angles to one another, arranged around the square mass at its centre to form a mandala.[5] The interior of the stupa at Kankālī-Tīlā near Mathura is similarly constructed, with two concentric walls joined by 8 walls radiating from the centre. The same method of construction occurs regularly in the stupas of Gandhāra.[6]

* * * * *

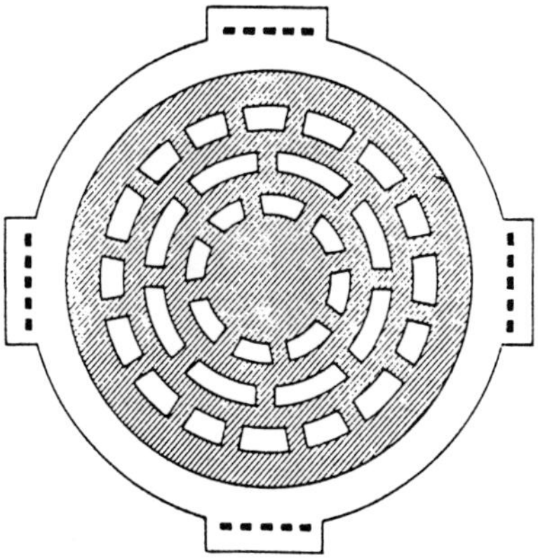
Fig. 34 : The ground plan of the Great Stupa at Nāgārjunakoṇḍa.

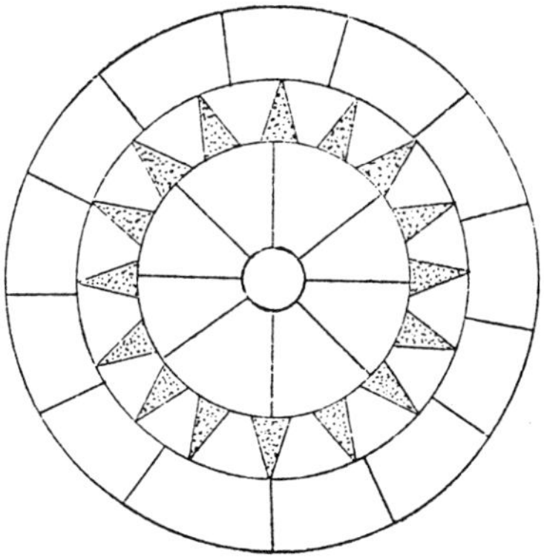
Fig. 35 : Plan of the centre of the stupa at Bhaṭṭprolu.

The wheel represents the cosmos in cross section. The felly is Earth, the level of multiplicity, the human world (loka); the nave (nābhi) is a heaven, representative of all the angelic, or intellectual states that lie above the human plane. The spokes are the axial radii that join beings to their principial centre. Each spoke is the integration of a whole individuality (nāma-rūpa), the totality of an individual consciousness in all its multiple states : the junction of the spoke with the felly marks the locus of the operation of this consciousness at the human and phenomenal (rūpa) level and its junction with the nave its operation at the archetypal and ideal (nāma) level. "As all the spokes are held together in the hub and felly of a wheel, just so, all beings, all gods, all worlds, all breathing

4. Sarcar, 1966, p. 86; Volwahsen, 1969, p. 95; Longhurst, 1938, pp. 12-14; Combaz, 1932, pp. 206 & 303 f.; Pant, 1976, p. 131.

5. Combaz, 1932, p. 206. The literal meaning of the word maṇḍala is "circle", whence it is used to refer to any centred space. It is usual in Indian Hindu buildings to use the square maṇḍala form, derived from the circle, for the plan, but despite the transformation of the plan shape, the symbolic significance remains unchanged, in the same way that the Indian zodiac is laid out on a square but has a cyclical and wheel-form referent. The relation of the circle to the square is discussed in greater detail in the following (below, pp. 101 ff.). Cf. Guénon, 1962, p. 87.

6. Combaz, 1932, p. 206.

creatures, all these selves are held together in this Self".[7] The axle point (āṇi) is the First Principle, Supernal Sun, Being and, theologically, God : "The notions of all created things inhere in him, who is, as it were, the hub within the wheel".[8] It is the receptacle and source of all formative ideas, of order (ṛta = dharma) and all felicities.[9] Finally, the ambient of the wheel is Non-Being, theologically Godhead, and in Buddhist parlance, the Void (śūnyatā), which is simultaneously immanent and transcendent.[10]

A world (loka) or level of existence is a defined modality, or set, of possibilities, and in these terms the wheel as a whole represents the entirety of the possibilities of manifestation : the felly represents the possibilities of the human order, inclusive of both their physical and mental forms; the nave represents the totality of informal possibilities; the axle point is the Principle of the possibilities of manifestation; and the ambient is All-Possibility, including the possibilities of both manifestation and non-manifestation.

When referred to the cosmic diagram shown on the right the wheel is seen to relate to several levels of significance: the wheel turning upon the hub at A is the wheel of the whole cosmos, including the totality of the multiple states of existence; and the felly, X, is one from among those states. The wheel that revolves about the centre C is the wheel of one world, the Wheel of Becoming, rotating about a centre that is a reflection of the Cosmic Centre, A. The two levels are symbiotic, since the fellies of both wheels refer to the same level of existence.[11]

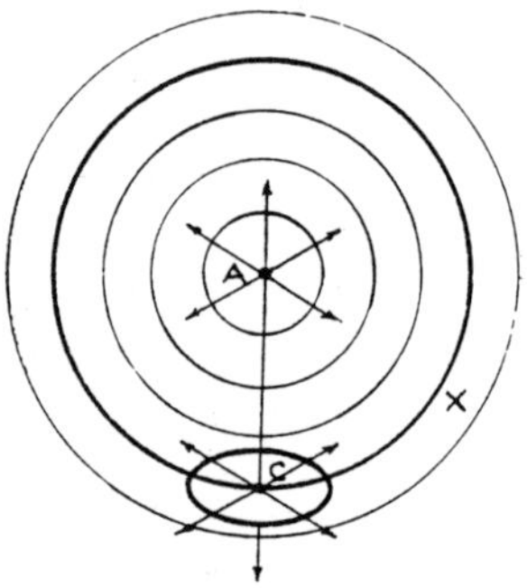

These considerations refer to the wheel in its static, spatial significance; but it is in the nature of the wheel to revolve, and this turning is the unfolding of cyclic time. The significance of the wheel includes both a spatial and a temporal reference : it refers to both space and time, the two coordinates that structure the empirical world. The genesis of the world can be expressed in spatial terms as a spreading out in a systole and diastole of pulsations from a centre, as a series of concentric waves, each reproducing the two phases of concentration and expansion of the original vibration. Alternately, it can be described in terms of a succession of

---

7. BU II.5.15. Cf. the following passage from a Buddhist Tantric text : "...then imagine that all the spokes assume the aspect of the Goddess: as eternally the rays shine forth from the sun, thus also the Goddesses arise from the body of the Great Goddess" (*Gandharvatantra*, quoted in the *Sāktānandataraṅginī* and cited by Tucci, 1961, p. 26).

8. RV VIII.41.6. To avoid confusion it is to be noted that the nave (nābhi) is usually the space within the hub (āṇi) and occasionally the hub itself. The term nābhi is from the root nabh, "to expand", and in the *Ṛg Veda* the cosmos is recurrently referred to as "expanded", from the nave. Nābhi is also "navel", which connects the symbolism of the wheel with that of the navel and that of the World Egg, discussed below. See Coomaraswamy, 1977, 2, p. 222; Bosch, 1960, p. 158; and above, pp. 21 f.

9. RV II.28.5; VIII.41.6; IV.28; etc. 10. See Coomaraswamy, 1977, 2, pp. 221-225 & 178f. 11. Cf. Ezekiel I.16 for a Biblical expression of this concept.

cycles evolving from an Eternal Present, a timeless Now which is time's source and Principle.[12] As fundamental experiences of the world we live in space and time provide the source materials for the symbolic expressions of the Real. Just as chaos is ordered by an "expansion" of space from the centre, so also chaos is ordered into a cohesive and comprehensible pattern by the cycles of time, by the ordered succession of temporal events : the seasons, the year, the waxing and waning of the moon, the equinoctial precessions, the repetitious schema of the revolution of the planets and the movements of the constellations.

Spatial and temporal symbolisms coalesce in the wheel. Its spokes mark not only the directions of space developing from the dimensionless point of their origin, but also the divisions of the cycles of time. The felloe simultaneously circumscribes the limits of cosmic space and traces the turning of time about an atemporal Present. It is portion of a continuous spiral evolving from a motionless hub. The wheel is thus a symbol of the world in its two aspects : the hub is the Principle of both space and time; the felly is manifestation in its twofold modality.

In its temporal connotations the wheel is the everlasting sequence of the Year, the eternal Prajāpati dismembered into time. It is the ceaseless flux of phenomena.[13] Its revolution is the ever-repeating rotation of the cycles, turning and returning in an endless motion of renewal. The wheel of time is the wheel of becoming : all existent things are parts of a revolving universe governed by laws of periodicity and rhythms of recurrence, spinning in ceaseless cycles of birth, growth, decline and death.

In Brahmanic symbolism the wheel of time is the Sun Wheel, since time is dependent on the sun.[14] The sidereal sun is the source of the year, and so analogically the supernal Sun is the origin of Time. In Vedic formulations Sūrya, the Sun, is figured by a chariot wheel of 5, 12 or 360 spokes, which are the seasons, the months and the days of the solar year.[15] In the sense that a circle is its centre[16] Time is the Sun, and Time, the Sun and the Wheel are identified. The Sun, or Solar Wheel, is constantly spoken of as "revolving" or as being revolved.[17] In an alternate symbolism the Sun is a Chariot that runs on twin wheels connected by an axle-tree, one being the Wheel of Heaven and the other the Wheel of Earth,[18] while the axle is the axis mundi that holds Heaven and Earth apart.[19] There is also a three-wheeled Chariot, whose wheels are Heaven, Earth and "the Secret Name" (nāma-guhyam), corresponding to the Buddha's three Bodies (trikāya).[20]

---

12. The word "eternal" is not used here in the sense of an indefinitely prolonged duration of time, which is more properly the "aeviternal". It refers to what is unconditioned by time, lying outside of time in the timeless Instant. See Coomaraswamy, 1947, *passim*.

13. AB II.17; RV I.155.6 & I.164.2, 11, 13, 14, 48; AV X.8.4-7; KB XX.1; JUB I.35; BU I.5.15; Śvet. Up. I.4; Praśna Up. VI.5.6. Cf. Coomaraswamy,1977, 2, p. 222.

14. MU VI.14 - 16.

15. RV I.164.2, 11, 13, 14, 48; I.174.5; I . 175.4; IV.7.14; IV.16.12; VI.56.3; etc. See Bosch, 1960, p. 159; Coomaraswamy, 1935a, p. 25.

16. See below, pp. 189 ff.

17. Coomaraswamy, 1935a, p. 25.

18. RV I.30.19 and X.85.18.

19. RV V.29.4 and X.89.4; cf. Coomaraswamy, 1935a, p. 28.

20 Coomaraswamy, 1935a, p. 28.

The significance of the wheel correlates with the number of its spokes. The four-spoked wheel is a model of the solar-structured world, its divisions denoting the four directions and the four seasons; but it also refers to the four parts of the day, the four ages of man, the quaternary rhythms of the moon, the four stages (aśrama) in the life of the Hindu,[21] the four yugas.[22] The six-spoked wheel is the Sun, the wheel of fire descending from the summer solstice,[23] its spokes the horizontal projection of a six-branched cross. It is the six days of the week, the seventh being the Sun-Wheel itself : "The seven yoke the chariot to the single wheel; a single steed with sevenfold name moves the triple-naved wheel, the immortal wheel which nothing stops, on which all things abide".[24] The six-spoked wheel is the Buddhist Wheel of Existence (saṃsāra-cakra, bhava-cakra), a diagram of the disposition, at once spatial and temporal, of the six realms (loka) through which beings migrate in an unending round of rebirths. The eight-spoked wheel is the wheel of the eight directions of space. It is also the wheel of renewal and regeneration. It is the Wheel of the Dharma, its spokes the Noble Eightfold Path, the Wheel set in motion by the preaching of the Buddha, who is the Cakravartin, the "Turner of the Wheel". The wheel of twelve spokes is the wheel of the months and the zodiac; wheels with thirty spokes refer to the division of the lunar cycle; and finally, the wheel with 360 spokes is the wheel of the year divided into days.

* * * * *

The wheel is cognate with the Sun, the lotus, the svastika, and all other symbols of the centre. The eight-spoked wheel is assimable to the eight-petalled lotus,[26] and in early Buddhist iconography, as represented for example in the Amarāvatī and Gupta sculptures, the wheel is shown with a lotus, or the pericarp of a lotus, in place of the hub.[27] The theme is repeated to this day in Japanese depictions of the wheel.[28]

Fig. 35 : Japanese Wheel of the Dharma (rimbō) with lotus pericarp.

The svastika, commonly used as an aniconic representation of the Buddha, is also homologous with the wheel.[29] If the svastika is compared with the figure of the cross inscribed within a circle, the basic equivalence of the two symbols is apparent, the rotation of the wheel being indicated in the first case by the circumference of the circle and in the svastika by the lines at right angles to the four arms of the cross, which are to be thought of in the manner of ribbons streaming in the wind. Like the wheel, the svastika represents movement about a fixed and unmoving axis and, like the wheel, it is a symbol of the generation of universal cycles

21. For the doctrine of the four yugas, the four ages that subdivide the total world cycle, see Guénon, 1938; Zimmer, 1946, pp. 13 ff.

22. Guénon, 1962, pp. 85 f. 23. Eliade, 1958b, pp. 147 f.

24. RV III.45.6 and I.50; cf. Chevalier and Gheerbrant, 1973, 4, p. 120. 25. This is of direct relevance to methods of orientation.

26. See Guénon, 1962, Ch. X ("Les fleurs symboliques"), Ch. L ("Les symboles des analogies"), and p. 87.

27. Auboyer, 1949, p. 93; Mus, 1935, pp. 204 ff.; Coomaraswamy, 1935a, p. 27 and n. 60. 28. See e.g., Saunders, 1960, p. 188, fig. 104.

29. Guénon, 1958a, Ch. X ("The Swastika"); 1962, pp. 89-92; Chevalier and Gheerbrant, 1973, 4, pp. 247 ff., s.v, "Svastika".

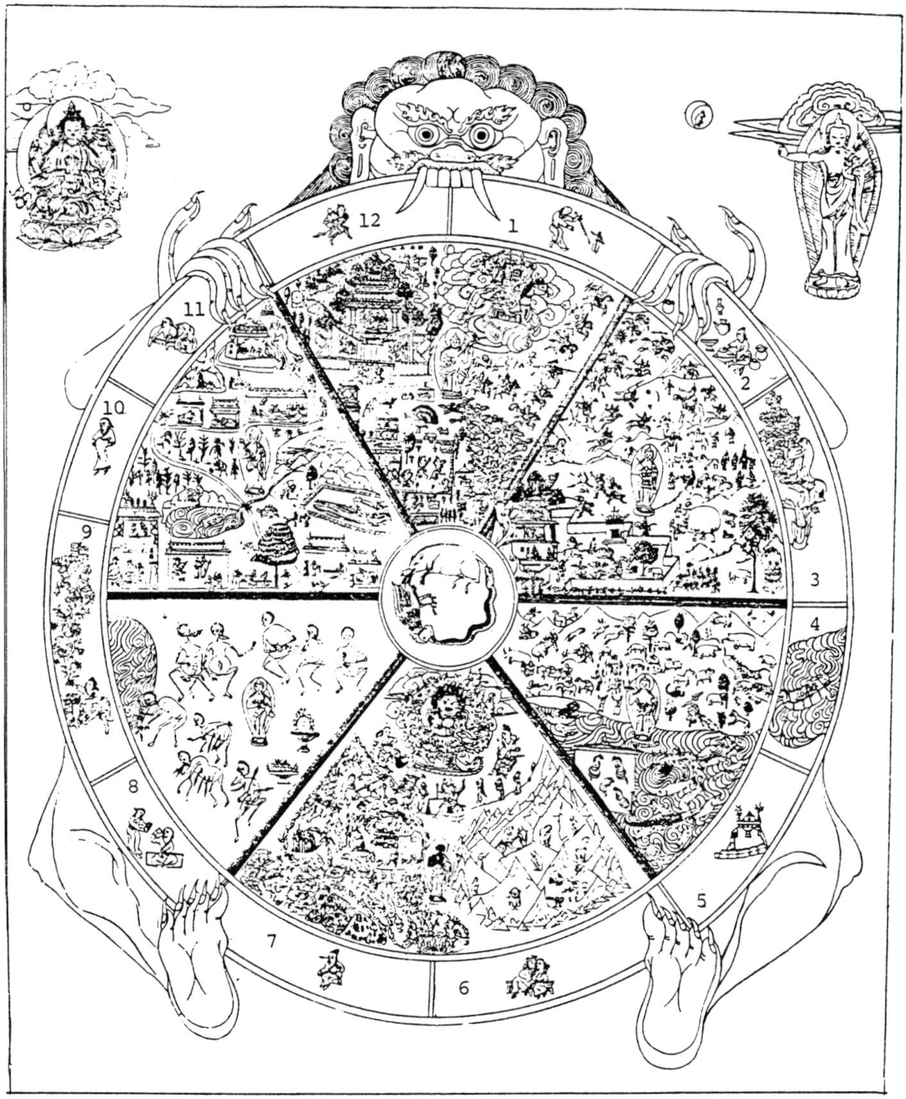

Fig. 36 :
The Wheel of Becoming. At the pivot of the Wheel are a black pig that stands for ego-delusion (moha), a green snake to represent hatred, enmity, revulsion (dveṣa), and a red cock that is desire, attachment, clinging (rāga). Encircling these are the six realms, shown as six divisions of the Wheel. At the top is the realm of the gods (deva), beings who live in states of bliss lasting through long aeons but who are nevertheless still subject to the turning of the Wheel and must inevitably sink back to the lower levels. The reverse of these felicitous abodes are the hells (nirāya), the realm of various degrees of intense suffering, shown in the lowest section of the Wheel. The tortures suffered there, like the delights enjoyed in the heavens, are not eternal and, in accordance with the ineluctable work-

from a forever-Present Centre. It represents the generation of currents of energy, and is a symbol of the action of immutable Principle, the "unmoved mover", within manifestation.[30]

* * * * *

The wheel takes two forms in Buddhism : the Wheel of Becoming (*saṃsāra-cakra* or *bhava-cakra*) and the Wheel of the Dharma (*dharma-cakra*). The Wheel of Becoming is the recurrent cycle of birth and death.[31] Beings are turned about on the wheel of rebirths, passing from one level of existence to the next in an unending sequence. The root causes (*hetu*) of the wheel's incessant turning are the "three poisons" : delusion (*moha*), the illusory notion of a separate self-hood; desire-attachment (*dveṣa*), the craving for and clinging to all that serves to maintain the sense of ego; and aversion (*rāga*), the hatred of whatever opposes or threatens this sense.

---

ings of the Wheel, the damned will rise again into less painful realms. Above the hells, moving in an anti-clockwise direction, is the realm of animals, whose lives are controlled by blind necessity and instinct. This realm is symmetrical with the realm of hungry spirits (*preta*), the abode of those who incarnate unsatisfied passions and unfulfilled desires and lead a life of ghost-like craving. Between the realms of the *pretas* and the heavens is the abode of men, symmetrical with the realm of the titans (*asura*), the "anti-gods" who embody disruptive and destructive power. Outside the six realms is shown the Twelve Linked Chain of Dependent Origination (*pratītya-samutpāda*). The twelve links of the chain of becoming are figured in twelve divisions of the circle : the first panel shows an old, blind woman, who represents ignorance (*avidyā*) (1), from which arises form-creating activity (*saṃskāra*), indicated by a potter (2). Just as a potter creates the shapes of pots, our volitional acts of body, speech and mind give rise to consciousness (*vijñāna*), shown as a monkey grasping a branch (3). Consciousness is like a monkey, jumping from object to object. Consciousness, however, not only restlessly grasps objects of sense and imagination, but polarizes itself into mental functions and physical form (*nāma-rūpa*), the basis of the psycho-physical combination which is the precondition of the individual existence. The next panel (4) shows *nāma* and *rūpa* as two people in a boat propelled by a ferryman. The psycho-physical organism is further differentiated through the formation and action of the six senses (*saḍāyatana*), represented by a house with six windows (5). This leads to contact (*sparśa*) of the senses with their objects, shown in the sixth frame as the contact of lovers (6). The sensation (*vedanā*) that results from the contact of the senses with their objects is represented in the next drawing by a man whose eye has been pierced by an arrow (7). The eighth picture shows a drinker, served by a woman, figuring thirst for life (*tṛṣna*), the craving that arises from sensation (8). From craving arises grasping and attachment (*upādāna*) to objects of desire, shown in the ninth panel by a man picking fruit (9). The result of attachment is a new process of becoming (*bhava*), represented by the sexual union of a man and a woman (10), whence there is rebirth (*jāti*) shown by a woman giving birth to a baby (11). The twelfth picture shows a man carrying a corpse on his back to the cremation ground (12). The Wheel has turned through birth, life and old age, and now comes death (*jaramarana*), giving rise to ignorance and setting the cycle in motion once again, to be repeated countless times until man can interrupt the causal chain and break free from its bonds.

---

30. Guénon, 1958, p. 56; Chevalier and Gheerbrant, 1973, 4, p. 248, Cf. below, p. 88.

31. On the Wheel of Becoming, see Govinda, 1959, pp. 236 ff.; Pallis, 1939, pp. 145 ff.; MacGovern, 1968, Ch. VI.

The three poisons are the pivot on which the Wheel of Becoming revolves and, represented by a pig, a snake and a cock, are accordingly shown in paintings of the Wheel as occupying the central hub. Encircling this hub of the passions, and impelled to turn by their presence, is the circle of the six realms, representing all the multiple states of existence through which the unenlightened being passes from aeon to aeon, driven from state to state in an unending cycle. The outer rim of the Wheel shows another aspect of the cycle of births and deaths, the Twelve-Linked Chain of Dependent Origination (pratītya-samutpāda),[32] the connected series of twelve causal nexuses (nidāna) whereby conditioned existence is produced, comparable to a series of transformations through various states, each containing the potentiality of the next. The fearsome monster who clutches the Wheel in his teeth and talons is Yama (Tib. Shindjé), the Lord and Judge of the Dead, who is also the Dharma-rāja, Lord of the Dharma, ruler of cosmic order. Death governs the world and his domination of the Wheel indicates the inexorable nature of the Law of Causation that ensures that all beings shall die. The Wheel of Becoming is the wheel of death; the round is cognate with mortality.[33]

By contrast, the Wheel of the Dharma (dharma-cakra), set in motion by the Buddha when he preaches the Doctrine (dharma), is the wheel of Principle, the wheel that rotates around the central axle-point of Truth. It is the Wheel of Reality, of the realm of Thusness (tathatā), the eternal and immutable world that the Buddha perceives with his Eye of Omniscience. It signifies the first preaching of the Dharma, the Dharma itself or, alternately, the Buddha,[34] as in reliefs at Bhārhut,[35] where the Buddha is represented by a wheel within a vihāra.[36] Similarly, the rolling of the Wheel is equivalent to the Buddha's walking through the worlds, leaving his vestigia pedis as evidence of his omnipresence. It is perfectly consequent that the prints of his feet carry the mark of the Wheel.[37]

* * * * *

The Wheel of Becoming pertains to the relative, phenomenal, individual and conditioned, while the Wheel of the Dharma pertains to the absolute, real, supra-individual and unconditioned : the former is the wheel of existences in their ceaseless flux and impermanence and the latter is the wheel of the Buddha's immutable Word, the wheel of the permanent Principle that eternally governs all things. Seen with the fleshly eye (māṃsa-cakṣus), the eye of the unenlightened wayfarer who is still turned about on the Wheel of Existence, the two Wheels appear separate and irreconcilable; but to the Eye of Wisdom (prajñā-cakṣus), the Eye of the Awakened (buddha-cakṣus), of the Comprehensor who has taken up his station at the unmoving hub, they are the inseparable, non-dual (advaita) faces of a single Reality. They are two aspects of Suchness (tathatā) : the wheel of the transient and ever-changing world is not other than the wheel of the never-changing Law. As perceived by the Enlightened the entities (dharma) of the world, spinning through the cycles of change, are seen in their unchanging instantaneity. The Wheel of Becoming is seen to be coincident with the Buddha's own intrinsic form.

---

32. Evola, 1951, pp. 73 f.

33. Kramrisch, 1946, p. 42; Pallis, 1939, p. 175 (Yama = Tib. Shindjé); Daniélou, 1964, p. 132.

34. Coomaraswamy, 1956a, pp. 20 f.; quoted in Bénisti, 1971, p. 144.

35. See Pl. VIII, fig. 25 and pl. X, fig. 28 in Coomaraswamy, 1956a, pp. 47 & 48.

36. Cf. Bénisti, 1971, p. 144.

37. Coomaraswamy, 1956a, p. 21, n.4.

a

b

c

d

e

f

g

Fig. 37 : The Wheel of the Dharma.
a. On a gateway lintel at Sāñcī, where it represents the preaching of the Buddha's first sermon. b. At the summit of the World Pillar. The Pillar stands within a sacred space marked out by an enclosing fence. c. On the feet of the Buddha.
d. In an example from Thailand.
e. Supported on the backs of lions facing the four directions in the manner of the Aśokan Pillar at Sārnāth. f. As an object of adoration. g. At the top of the Tree that grows from the stupa <u>harmikā</u>. The stupa stands on the Wheel of Becoming, the two Wheels are identical.

The non-duality of the Wheel of Becoming and the Wheel of the Dharma is implicit in the Pali texts of the Theravāda, which teach that, "He who sees Dependent Origination sees the Dharma and who sees the Dharma sees Dependent Origination";[38] and it is explicit in the Sanskrit and Chinese texts of the Mahāyāna, such as the *Saddharma-puṇḍarīka-sūtra* in which the Buddha is addressed with the words, "The Wheel of the Dharma was put in motion by thee, O thou that art unrivalled in the world, at Varanasi, O great hero, that wheel which is the rotation of the rise and decay of all aggregates (skandha) of existence".[39]

The identity of the Wheel of Becoming and the Wheel of the Dharma is an expression of the fundamental Mahāyāna doctrine of the sameness (sama) of saṃsāra and nirvāṇa : "Error (kleśa) is Awakening (bodhi), world flux (saṃsāra) and Extinction (nirvāṇa) are the same: "Ignorance (avidyā) and Awakening are the same";[40] and "Form is Emptiness (śūnya) and the very Emptiness is form; Emptiness does not differ from form, nor does form differ from Emptiness; whatever is Emptiness, that is form".[41]

One aspect of the Buddha's Total Knowledge consists of a realization of this sameness (sama). The Knowledge of Sameness (samatajñāna), personified by the Buddha Ratnasambhava, is the Knowledge that perceives the essential identity of all entities (dharma) and their Principle, and views the non-duality of their ephemeral transitoriness and absolute immutability.[42]

The identity of the two Wheels explains the dismay of the gods when, following his attainment of Enlightenment, the Buddha hesitates to set the Wheel of the Dharma in motion. Brahmā cries, "Alas, the world is altogether lost", and prays that the Doctrine may be preached,[43] for unless the principial Wheel is set turning the existential Wheel on which the gods depend is a non-existence, a mere nothing. A god brings the Wheel to the Buddha to be turned; by consenting to do so he does what all the previous Awakened Ones have done, recreating the Law of the World for another aeon (kalpa).[44]

Thus, for those who see it solely in its existential aspect, the Wheel is the round of suffering; they are bound to it by cords of selfhood and forever sustain the torment of its turning. For them Liberation lies in stopping the Wheel's motion. To arrest the Wheel is to attain the tranquil stillness of nirvāṇa. But one who achieves this Liberation perceives that the cycle of the Wheel of phenomena is not distinct from the turning of the Wheel of the Dharma; he sees that the Wheel of Becoming is cognate with the Wheel of his own Word, that the Wheel of the universe is of twofold nature but single essence, and that its motion is at once a metaphysical and an existential turning.

* * * * *

---

38. M XXVIII   39. SPS III.33.

40. *Maitreya-Asaṅga*, *Sūtrālaṃkāra*, XIII, 12 (Commentary).

41. *Prajñā-pāramitā-hṛdaya-sūtra* ("The Sutra of the Heart of Perfect Wisdom"), Short Form, II.1-3, in Conze, 1973, p. 142. Cf. Conze, 1967, pp. 148-167.

42. Jap. byōdō shō chi, "Knowledge of the Identity of Essences", one of the five aspects of the Buddha's Knowledge (pañca-jñāna), personified by the five Jina Buddhas of the Diamond World Mandala. It corresponds to Ratnasambhava Tathāgata (Jap. Hōshō Nyorai), who is located in the South of the mandala. See MKDJT, pp. 620 ff., s.v., Gochi; BKDJT, pp. 1246 ff, s.v. Gochi.

43. *Jātaka* I.81.   44. *Lalita Vistara*, Foucaux, 1884, 1,p. 345, cited in Combaz, 1935, pp. 110 f.

The wheel incorporated in the plan of the stupa is seen to have a multivalent significance : it is the cycle of the Sun that measures out the Year; it is the Wheel of the Universe, whose spokes are the deployment of cosmic space; it is the cycle of Dependent Origination and the revolving round of rebirths; and it is the Wheel of the Dharma.

To build a stupa is to repeat mimetically the Buddha's primordial action of setting the Wheel of the Dharma in motion; it is to recreate the Buddha's cosmogonic and ordering action, that whereby chaos is structured and the Way revealed.

* * * * *

In India the spiritual path has always been seen as a return to the Centre. "The seeker, having gone forth, returns; home is the desire of all things that proceed; abandoning his never-completed task he comes back again",[45] and having returned, "in him are all beings, and the eye that oversees; intellect (manas), breath (prāṇa) and noumenon (nāma) coincident; in him when he comes forth all his children enjoy; sent by him and born of him, it is in him that all this universe is established".[46] Having returned, he is the One "on whom the parts stand fast, as spokes in the nave of the wheel".[47]

So likewise the Buddhist Way, which is called the Way of the Centre, is one of return to the axial hub of the Wheel, and the stupa, cognate with the Wheel, marks the location of the sacred centre to which the Wayfarer directs his life's pilgrimage. The stupa locates a focus of spiritual force, drawing the pilgrim with centripetal magnetism. The stupa signals the centre of the pilgrim's cosmos; it stands at the unmoving hub of the World Wheel and is the axle of its turning.

In Buddhism to attain the centre is to be Awakened. The Buddha, the Wake, is one who has moved inward from the receding, whirling felly to the immobile nave. By a process of concentration he has contracted the circle's radius and brought the enclosing circumference ever closer to the centre until it is itself enclosed within that principial point, the point of unitary being where the multiple is compacted in the One. Established at the pivot he is the Eye (cakṣus) that surveys the whole and "sees all things at once in their diversity and coincidence".[48]

* * * * *

Returned to the centre of the Wheel and stationed within the Void-pleroma of its axle-tree, the Buddha is the unmoved mover of its turning; its revolving depends upon the "actionless activity" of his pivotal presence. He is the dharma-cakra-pravartana, the setter in motion of the Wheel of the Dharma, and the cakravartin, the "Turner of the Wheel".[49] The latter term is used to designate a king and, since the motion of the cosmic Wheel is wholly governed by his action of actionless presence, he is the universal Ruler and cosmic Sovereign, spiritual analogue of the the terrestrial king and emperor whose rule encompasses the empire.[50]

---

45. RV II.38.6   46. AV XIX.53.6-9.   47. Praśna Up. VI.6.

48. RV X.187.4; cf. VS XXXII.8; BG VI.29-30.   49. P. cakkavatti.

50. For the Buddhas as Cakravartins see Sarkisyanz, 1965, pp. 86 f.; Saunders, 1960, p. 167; Auboyer, 1959, p. 187; Viennot, 1954, p. 103; Tambiah, 1976, p. 96; Rahula, 1956, p. 66.

At his nativity the soothsayers of his father's court predict that if Siddhartha remains in lay life he will become a universal monarch (cakravartin) and if he renounces the world he will be a Buddha.[51] His choice is seemingly between success in the temporal or in the spiritual domain,[52] but in choosing the path of renunciation and winning dominion over the realm of the spirit the Buddha also attains sovereignty over the earth : the spiritual wheel encompasses the terrestrial wheel and by returning to its centre the Buddha becomes the Cakravartin-King in both the natural and supernatural orders.

This idea is conveyed in the *Mahāpadana Sutanta*,[53] which gives the life story of a previous Buddha, Vipassi, who, in the manner of all Buddhas including his successor, Śākyamuni, is born into a royal family, shows the 32 distinguishing marks of a great man (mahā-puruṣa), and has two destinies open to him - that of a cakravartin, who rolls the wheel of conquest to the four quarters, or that of a Buddha, who rolls back the veil of ignorance from the world. By choosing the way of renunciation over that of dominion the Buddha attains both ends. He becomes the turner of both wheels.[54]

The Buddha and the World Monarch are two aspects of one universal principle. The Buddha is the transcendent Law and Norm (dharma), and he is also that Law as it is manifested in the governance of the world. The Buddha is cakram vartayati, "he who sets the sacred wheel (of the world pacifying monarchy) in motion". He is a world conqueror who marches in victorious triumph to the four quarters of the world, starting from Mt. Meru at the centre of the universe,[55] preceded by the Sun-Wheel, which he causes to roll before him as he advances, opening the way of his conquest.[56] The *Digha-Nikaya* describes the process of the Cakravartin's subjugation of the world : he solemnly invokes the wheel to roll on; it rolls on successively toward the East, the South, the North and the West; and when the Cakravartin, following the wheel, appears in each of the quarters, the king of that region bows down in submission and is allowed to continue to rule but in accordance with the Law.[57] When the Cakravartin returns to the summit of the central Mountain his Law radiates out through the cardinal directions and governs the kingdoms of the entire world.

In the Brahmanic theory of government the spiritual authority of the Dharma, the Law which governs all things, resides in the brahmans, the priestly caste, while the kṣatriyas, the royal caste, are the mandatories of its temporal governance. The conservation, continuity and correct understanding of the Dharma belong with the sacerdotium; implementing its ordinances and acting upon its edicts is the function of the regnum. The former function is essentially contemplative and intellectual, the latter active and instrumental. These values were adopted by Buddhism. At the first Buddhist Council at Rajagṛha (in the 5th Cent. B.C.) Ajatasattu is reported to have said to the assembled monks, "Yours is the authority of the spirit, as mine is of power".[58] The Buddha combines both functions : he possesses

51. *Jātaka* I.56. Cf. Warren, 1922, pp. 51 f.; Coomaraswamy, 1943a, p. 52; Coomaraswamy and Nivedita, 1916, p. 9; Bénisti, 1960, p. 51.

52. *Mahāvastu* II.158 f. 53. Rhys Davids, 1910, 3, 2.

54. Cf. Tambiah, 1976, p. 43.

55. Reynolds, 1972, p. 20, quoted in Tambiah, 1976, p. 46.

56. Zimmer, 1951, pp. 128-130; 1955, pp. 245 f.

57. D II & III, quoted by Tambiah, 1976, p. 44.

58. Gokhale, 1966, p. 22.

both spiritual authority and temporal power. As the embodiment of the Dharma he includes both its spiritual and temporal aspects within his single Person. He is a cakravartin in a twofold sense : he is the Turner of both the Wheel of spiritual Law and the Wheel of temporal authority. As the turner of the Law Wheel he is the ideal of the Bodhisattva, preeminent in the spiritual domain; and as turner of the Wheel of Dominion (P. anucakka) he is the ideal of the leader in the temporal realm.[59]

* * * * *

The Buddha as Cakravartin is a common theme in Buddhist literature and art. In the *Mahā-sudassana-sutta*, for example, Gautama is described as having been a Universal King in a previous birth.[60] Throughout the Buddhist texts he is addressed with the epithets of sovereignty[61]: the *Mahāvaṃsa* calls him "the Conqueror", "the Vanquisher";[62] and his cognate, the Dharma, is "the Ruler of rulers" and "the highest in the world".[63] Stupas, the symbolic equivalents of the Buddha and the Dharma, are referred to as repositories of the Buddha's "power of conquest".[64] Entry into nirvāṇa is likened to entry into a royal city and from this derives the Burmese literary convention of calling nirvāṇa "the Golden City".[65] Before his parinirvāṇa the Buddha gave instructions that his remains were to be accorded the funeral honours due to a Cakravartin-King, saying, "They will not fail to honour the remains of the Tathāgata in the same way one honours the remains of a Cakravartin".[66] In the Mahāyāna the Pure Lands of the Buddhas are called Buddha Kingdoms (buddha-kṣetra).

The Buddha is born with the 32 great distinguishing marks (mahā-vyañjana) and the numerous secondary marks (anuvyañjana) of the Cakravartin King;[67] and at the moment of his birth the seven great symbols of the Cakravartin also appear in the world : the sacred wheel; the divine white elephant (hastiratna), the vehicle of the monarch; the milk-white horse (aśvaratna), the sun-steed, mount and chariot animal of the king; the magic jewel (cintāmaṇi), the "thought jewel" or wishing stone that illumines the darkness and fulfils every desire; the perfect Queen Consort (strīratna) the ideal woman, faultless in beauty and virtue; the perfect Minister (gṛhapāti), whose able and trustworthy administration provides lavish funds for charity and good works; and the perfect General (pariṇāyaka).[68] In the Far East these seven "Jewels" are placed around the image of the Buddha upon the altar.

---

59. The concept of the Cakravartin and the Ruler by Law (P. dhammiko dhammaraja) is discussed in Ghoshal, 1959; Gokhale, 1966; Reynolds, 1972; Ling, 1973; Tambiah, 1976.

60. *Mahā-sudassana-sutta* II.37 & 42, in Rhys Davids, 1881, pp. 285 & 289. Many passages in the Pali literature compare the Buddha and the cakravartin, e.g., the *Mahā-sudassana-sutta* D III. 26 and the *Cakkavatti-sihanāda-sutta*. The attributes of the Cakravartin are described in D III. 1-5. Cf. Zimmer, 1951, pp. 127 ff.

61. Reynolds, 1972, p. 17; Tambiah, 1976, p. 44.

62. Tambiah, 1976, p. 44. 63. *Idem*. 64. *Ibid*., p.43.

65. Sarkisyanz, 1965, p. 86.

66. D XVI.5.10-12; cf. Zimmer, 1951, p. 133; Kern, 1896, pp. 43f.; Sarkisyanz, 1965, p. 87.

67. See Tucci, 1961, p. 44; Snellgrove, 1959, p. 213.

68. Zimmer, 1951, pp. 129 f.; BKDJT, 1922, s.v., Shichihō ("Seven Jewels"); p. 3826 f., s.v., Tenrinjōō.

The identification of the sacerdotium and the regnum in the Person of the Enlightened One is expressed iconographically by representations that show the Buddha wearing the turban or topknot of royalty (the so-called "crowned Buddhas"),[69] making the hand sign of turning the Wheel (dharma-cakra-mudrā), or sitting in the posture of "kingly ease" (pralambapādāsana).[70]

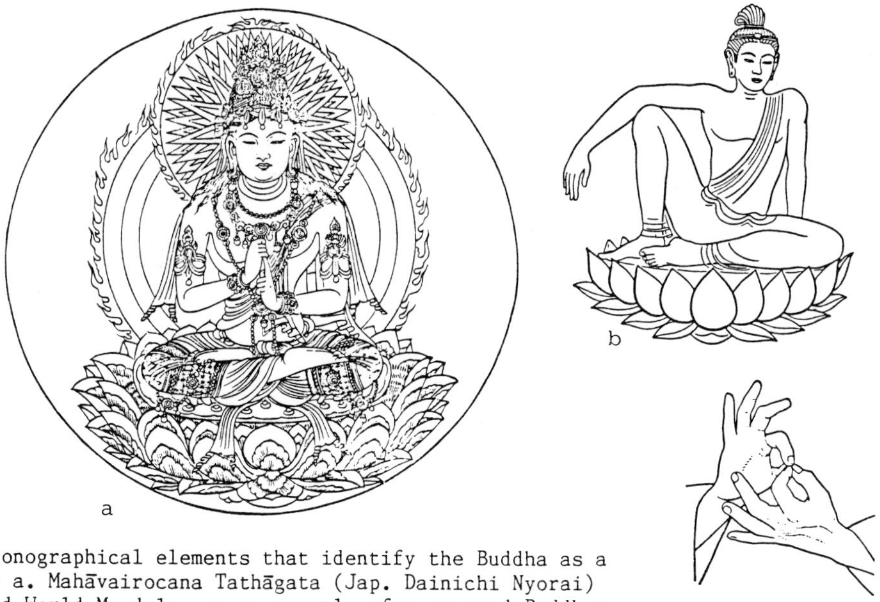

a

b

c

Fig. 38 : Iconographical elements that identify the Buddha as a cakravartin : a. Mahāvairocana Tathāgata (Jap. Dainichi Nyorai) in the Diamond World Mandala, as an example of a crowned Buddha; b. the posture of Royal Ease (rājalīlāsana); c. the hand gesture of Turning the Wheel of the Law (dharma-cakra-mudrā).

The assimilation is particularly apparent in the Vajrayāna. The description of the Buddha Ratnaketu ("Jewel Standard") given in the *Mañju-śrīmūlakalpa* explicitly identifies him as a Cakravartin : "(Ratnaketu), the great Cakravartin-chief, is to be placed at the centre (of the mandala). He has the colour of saffron and is like the rising sun.[71] He holds a great wheel which is turning... He is like a great king with his palace and his decorations, a great being who is crowned and adorned with all adornments... In his left hand he holds the wheel, which is wreathed in blazing light. He is turning it as he sits in semi-paryaṅka posture".[72]

Many Buddhist mandalas represent the Buddha enthroned at the centre of Indra's palace on the summit of Meru,[73] wearing the "crown" and adornments of a sovereign.[74] The preeminent example is the Diamond World

---

69. Mus, 1928, pp. 1f. 70. Auboyer, 1959,p. 187; Saunders,1966,p. 167.

71. Cf. the symbolic association of Ratnaketu and the dawn, described below, pp. 168 f. 72. Snellgrove, 1959, pp. 206 f.

73. Tucci, 1961, p. 44; Eliade, 1958a, pp. 220 f.

74. Mus, 1928, has given an admirable analysis of the meaning of the Buddha dressed with the headdress and adornments of a king. Cf. Auboyer, 1959, p. 213.

Fig. 39 : Mandala of the Great Buddha-Uṣṇīṣa (Jap. Daibutchō-mandara). The Great Buddha-Uṣṇīṣa (Mahā-buddha-uṣṇīṣa, Jap. Daibutchō) sits on the pericarp-hub of a lotus-wheel, surrounded by the Seven Jewels of a Cakravartin, eight Bodhisattvas and, on the petals of the lotus, the eight Great Mantra Kings (Jap. Dai Myō-ō). The remaining layers of the mandala show Bodhisattvas and Gods from the Diamond World Mandala.

Fig. 40 : A variant version of the Mandala of the Great Buddha-Uṣṇīṣa. Mahā-buddha-uṣṇīṣa sits upon the pinnacle of Mt. Meru. Above his head sits "Golden Wheel Śākyamuni" (Jap. Shaka Kinrin), Śākyamuni's aspect as a Cakravartin. Around these figures are gathered the Cakravartin's Seven Jewels, a water pot and a vajra, which represent the Matrix and the Diamond Worlds. In the foreground are two nāga kings.

Mandala, in which Mahāvairocana Tathāgata (Jap. Dainichi Nyorai) sits enthroned within the Vejayanta Palace at the centre of the Trāyastriṃśa Heaven, occupying the position of Indra, the prototypic King and regnum in divinis. He wears the headdress and adornments of a monarch : as his name "Great Sun" implies, he is the Solar Sovereign who centres the kingdom of the total manifest universe; as also, microcosmically, within each and every being, he is the Mind King (cittarāja), the innermost and central Ruler of the realm of the mind, Lord of the total person.[75]

The concept of the Royal Buddha is personified in the Buddha-Cakravartins[76] of Japanese Shingon Buddhism. They are called "Uṣṇīṣa-Wheel-Kings" (uṣṇīṣa-cakra-rāja, Jap. chōrinnō) or "Buddha-Uṣṇīṣas" (Jap. butchō). Their significance is an evocative construct of interconnected symbols : the uṣṇīṣa, the protuberance at the top of the Buddha's head, is one of the thirty two distinguishing marks of a Great Person (mahā-puruṣa) or Cakravartin and, as is explained in greater detail in the following,[77] these Buddhas embody the universal powers of the Cakravartin that radiate from the central point of the cosmos at the summit of Meru, microcosmically coincident with the summit of the Buddha's head. The symbolism of the

---

75. See above p. 63. MKDJT, p. 1522 ff., s.v. Dainichi Nyorai.

76. Jap. butsu rinnō, lit. "Buddha Wheel King". See MKDJT, p. 1939, s.v. Butchō. 77. See below, pp. 260 ff.

Fig. 41 : The Golden Wheel Mandala (Jap. Kinrin mandara). The Buddha-Uṣṇīṣa "Golden Wheel" (Jap. Kinrin Butchō) sits upon the pericarp of an eight-petalled lotus. On the petals are shown the Seven Jewels of the Cakravartin and the "Buddha Eye" (Jap. Butsugenson), personified as a Buddha, seated on the lowermost petal.

Fig. 42 : A variant version of the Golden Wheel Mandala. The Buddha-Uṣṇīṣa "Golden Wheel" is seated on a seven-lion throne within a Sun Disc surrounded by the Seven Jewels and "Buddha Eye" to the viewer's lower right.

Buddha-Uṣṇīṣa Wheel-Turning King is developed in a series of mandalas showing one or other of their number sitting at the hub of a wheel, on the pinnacle of Mt. Meru, on the pericarp of an eight-petalled lotus, or on a lion throne, and surrounded by various divinities and the seven Jewels of the Cakravartin.

The Buddha-Uṣṇīṣa brings together two symbolisms within his person : the Wheel that turns about the world's central point, located at the summit of the Cosmic Mountain and also at the summit of the Buddha's head; and the uṣṇīṣa as the repository of the Buddha's powers of Knowledge and Conquest, located within the thousand-petalled lotus (uṣṇīṣa-kamala) whose flowering in the uṣṇīṣa is at one and the same time the attainment of Enlightenment, the deployment of the worlds and the revelation of the all-vanquishing power of the Dharma.

The identity of terrestrial king and supra-terrestrial Buddha is specifically expressed in the initiatic rites (abhiṣeka) of Shingon Buddhism.[78] These rites are performed within a mandala that is identified with a king's palace and duplicate the previously mentioned rituals of aspersion (rājasuya) whereby Indian kings were consecrated.[79] In the

---

78. See BKDJT, p. 811, s.v. Kwanjō; MKDJT, p. 409, s.v. Kanjō; Ishizuka and Coates, 1949, pp. 172 ff.

79. On the consecration of Indian kings, see above, pp. 76 f.; Eliade, 1965, pp.153-155; Heesterman, 1957; Hocart, 1927, pp. 189 ff.; Raglan, 1964, pp. 163 ff.

ancient Indian ceremonies waters from the four seas were sprinkled on the head of the new monarch to symbolize his power over the four directions of the world. Similarly, in the Buddhist rituals the initiate is anointed with water from five vases (kalaśa), which are placed within the mandala in the four directions and at the centre. The waters from the vases represent five aspects of the Buddha's Knowledge, which correspond to the five Jina-Buddhas who abide in the five directions. The aspersion confers upon the recipient, at least in virtual mode, the five types of Knowledge possessed by the Enlightened. This ceremony of esoteric initiation corresponds to that described in the exoteric literature, in which it is told how the Buddha sprinkles water on the head of the Bodhisattva entering the last of the Ten Stations of the Way to Highest Perfect Awakening (anuttara-saṃyak-saṃbodhi), thus conferring on him the Wisdom of Buddhahood.[80] Eliade indicates that in the ritual of abhiṣeka the disciple is assimilated to the sovereign because his initiation raises him above the play of cosmic forces. He attains autonomy and freedom, which are the prerogatives of the king.[81] By his anointment with the waters from the five vases the initiate ritually "conquers" the world in the manner of the cakravartin.

* * * * *

Fig. 43 : The Cakravartin with the Seven Jewels, shown on a relief on the stupa at Jaggayyapeṭa.

Fig. 44 : The stupa adorned with garlands, lion columns, parasols and other insignia of royalty. Relief from Amarāvatī.

Fig. 45 : A stupa supported on the back of an elephant. Relief from the Yun-kang caves, China.

---

80. MKDJT, p. 410, s.v. Kanjō; Ishizuka and Coates, 1949, p. 172; cf. Tucci, 1961, p. 44; Snellgrove, 1959, pp. 207 f. & 213 ff. Cf. below, pp. 345 ff.

81. Eliade, 1958a, p. 221; cf. Tucci, 1961, p. 51.

The stupa embodies the Wheel in its two aspects. It signifies the deployment of both the spiritual and the temporal Law. It is the centre from which the twofold Dharma radiates through the cosmos. In accordance with this significance, some stupas, and notably Borobudur, marked the metaphysical, religious and political centre of the empire. Frequently a large stupa is found within the confines of the palace in the royal or imperial cities of Buddhist Asia. A famous example is the white marble stupa built in 1651 by the Chinese Emperor Shun Ch'ih at the summit of the Jade Fountain Hill in Peking, which stupa dominates the entire imperial city.[82]

* * * * *

The Buddha is a Cakravartin-King and so the stupa, the symbol of the Buddha, is accorded the honours owing to a monarch. The *Mahāvaṃsa* relates that the Sri Lankan king ritually relinquished his sovereign powers to the relics contained within the stupa, which is equivalent to their bestowal on the stupa itself : "He worshipped the relics with the offering of a parasol and investing them with the kingship over Lanka... with joyful heart he thrice conferred on the relics the kingship of Lanka";[83] "With believing heart did the king worship the relics by (offering) a white parasol, and conferred on them the entire over-lordship of Lanka, for seven days";[84] and "Five times, each time for seven days, I have bestowed (glad at heart) the rank of ruler of this island upon the doctrine".[85]

The iconography of the stupa reflects that assimilation. The formula of the stupa embellished with the insignia of royalty is common in the reliefs of Amarāvatī and other early Buddhist monuments : the stupa is adorned with parasols, standards, scarves, lion thrones and jewel garlands.[86]

Associated with the same symbolism is the depiction of the seven Jewels of the Cakravartin on the early stupas. At Jaggayyapeṭa, one of the most ancient of Indian stupas, a stone slab shows the cakravartin surrounded by the seven Jewels,[87] and analogous versions of the same theme are to be found in reliefs at Amarāvatī and Nāgārjunakoṇḍa.

Fig. 46 : Stupa supported on elephants. Anuradhāpura, Sri Lanka.

Fig. 47 : Stupa with parasols.

---

82. Combaz, 1935, p. 72.

83. *Mahāvaṃsa* XXXI.90 f.

84. *Ibid*, XXXI.111.

85. *Ibid*, XXXII.36

86. Auboyer, 1949, p. 110.

87. Zimmer, 1955, p. 349 and pl. 37; Combaz, 1935, pp. 89, fig. 35 & 89; Coomaraswamy, 1935a, figs. 19 & 20.

The assimilation of the Buddha and the World Monarch is also expressed in a striking manner in the stupas at Taxila and in Sri Lanka and Thailand which have their lowest terrace supported on the backs of elephants who stand in rows with heads and shoulders protruding from the wall.[88] The significance is primarily cosmological - the elephants represent the Waters whereon the stupa as cosmos floats - but it also indicates the royal nature of the stupa since in ancient India to be carried on an elephant was the exclusive privilege of the king.[89]

The parasol that rises from the summit of the stupa is also an indication of its regnal character. Throughout Asia from earliest times the parasol has been the emblem of kingship.[90] The form of the parasol recalls the wheel - the ribs coming together at the pole resemble the junction of the spokes of the wheel at its hub - and it is therefore preeminent among the insignia of the cakravartin, the universal monarch who is located at the centre of the wheel. Placed above the stupa the parasol indicates the royal nature of the building it shelters. It shows that the stupa is a symbol of the Buddha as Universal Monarch, the Wheel-Turning King, whose Dharma rules the cosmos.

---

88. Combaz, 1935, pp. 71 f.; 1932, p. 238, fig. 35.

89. Combaz, 1935, pp. 71-72.

90. Ludowyck, 1958, p. 95; Bosch, 1961, p. 75. On the symbolism of the parasol, see below, pp. 324 ff.

10 THE STUPA PLAN AND THE LOTUS.

The stupa plan is delineated by measuring out the directions from a centre. This measuring out is a mimesis of the process of cosmogenesis, replicating the manner in which manifestation deploys from Principle. This expansion of the worlds from their Centre is likened to the opening of a lotus.[1] The petals of the lotus are the points of the compass, indicating directions of indefinite extension; their opening is the deployment of space from the Centre, the emanation of the One into the multiple.[2] "What is the lotus and of what is it made?", asks the *Maitri Upaniṣad*, and then answers, "That lotus, assuredly, is the same as space, and the four intermediate quarters are its petals".[3]

"Through the dawn, shining in the lights of Heaven, the lotus is brought to birth",[4] and "the world-lotus naturally blooms in response to the rising of the Sun 'in the beginning', in answer to and as a reflection of the light of Heaven mirrored on the surface of the Waters".[5] The pillaring apart of Heaven and Earth by the Column of the Rising Sun is the opening of the cosmic Lotus, a symbolism that is reflected in etymology : the word puṣkara, "blue lotus", derives from the root puṣ, "to grow, increase", as well as "to support" : "Dawn brings forth the growth of growth (puṣṭasya puṣṭam)",[6] which, says Coomaraswamy, "is tantamount to puṣkara, the World Lotus rising from the Waters at the dawn of the creation, just as the day-lotus opens at sunrise in actual experience".[7]

The moment of the pillaring apart of Heaven and Earth is also that of the diremption of the Upper and Lower Waters. The Waters represent the possibilities of manifestation contained within Substance (prakṛti), the potential aspect of Being; the Lower Waters are those containing the formal possibilities of manifestation and the Upper Waters are those containing its formless possibilities. The connection of this with the Sun and the opening Lotus is expressed in the iconography of the Sun-God, Sūrya, who holds a lotus in either hand, representing the two Waters, para- and apara-prakṛti.[8] So too the nimbus of the Buddha image generally shows lotuses - the Upper Waters - to complement the lotus on which he sits or stands - the Lower Waters.[9]

* * * * *

---

1. On lotus symbolism see Coomaraswamy, 1935a, pp. 17ff. & 39 ff.; Bosch, 1960, *passim*; Saunders, 1960, pp. 159 ff.; Zimmer, 1955, pp. 158 ff.; 1946, pp. 90 ff; BKDJT, pp. 5036 ff., s.v. Renge; MKDJT, pp. 2294 ff., s.v. Renge; Chevalier and Gheerbrant, 1973, 3, pp. 141 ff., s.v. Lotus; Cirlot, 1962, pp. 184 f., s.v. Lotus; Guénon, 1962, Ch. IX ("Les fleurs symboliques") Getty, 1962, pp. 192 f., s.v. Padma; Ward, 1952, *passim*.

2. Tucci, 1961, p. 27; cf. Mus, 1935, pp. 297 f.

3. MU VI.2; cf. CU VIII.1-3; Coomaraswamy, 1935a, p. 18; 1977, 1,p. 172.

4. *Pañcaviṃśa Brāhmaṇa* XVIII.8.6; see Coomaraswamy, 1935a, p. 21 & n. 39; Ward, 1952, p. 137; Saunders, 1960, p. 250, n.1.

5. Coomaraswamy, 1935a, p. 20. 6. RV X.55.4. 7. Coomaraswamy, 1935a, p. 71, n. 40.

8. Rao, 1914, 1, p. 306; Sastri, 1916, p. 236 and fig. 143.

9. Coomaraswamy, 1935a, p. 20.

Lotus symbolism indicates a further significance of the stupa plan delineated in the ritual. The lotus or, variantly, the lotus leaf, is the support of the world. It is identified with the Waters that uphold the total cosmos, including all its multiple states of existence; or it is identified with the ground (pṛthivī) of existence, the Earth, extended on the back of the Waters [10] and representing one from among those multiple states, "whereon and wherein existence is established firmly amidst the sea of possibility". [11] It is identified with the Earth Mother, Lakṣmi, Padma ("Lotus"), who gives birth to, nourishes and supports all life.[12] "The lotus means the Waters, and this earth is a leaf thereof : even as a lotus leaf here lies spread on the water, so that earth lies spread on the Waters. Now this same earth is Agni's womb".[13] This symbolic concept is built into the Vedic Fire Altar, during the construction of which a lotus leaf is laid at its centre as a chthonic support and to represent the birthplace of Agni. On the lotus leaf is placed a golden disc to symbolize the Sun, and upon this lies a figure of the Golden Man (puruṣa), which is the image of Agni-Prajāpati, the Person in the Sun.[14]

Fig. 48 : Sūrya, the Sun God. The lotuses he holds represent the Upper and the Lower Waters.

Fig. 49 : The Buddha Amitābha (Jap. Amida) attended by the Bodhisattvas Avalokiteśvara (Jap. Kannon) and Mahāsthamaprapta (Jap. Daiseishi). He sits upon a supporting lotus (the Lower Waters) and has a lotus nimbus (the Upper Waters).

---

10. *Nirukta* V.14; MU VI.2.

11. Coomaraswamy, 1935a, p. 20; cf. Paranavitana, 1954, pp. 207 f.; Combaz, 1935, p. 95.

12. Zimmer, 1946, pp. 90 ff.; 1955, pp. 158 ff. See also this latter work for a lengthy discussion of the lotus in Indian art.

13. ŚB VII.4.1.7-8. Cf. Sayana, Commenting on RV VI.16.13, quoted in Coomaraswamy, 1935a, p. 19.

14. ŚB VII.4.1.7-8; VIII.3.1.11; X.5.2.8; and X.5.2.12; Coomaraswamy, 1935a, p. 20; Kramrisch, 1946, p. 111.

The identification of the Lotus with the supporting foundation of the universe - Water or Earth - is sufficient to explain its use as the support of Buddhist images and buildings, each of which is an imago mundi. Buddhas, Bodhisattvas and celestials sit upon lotus thrones or stand upon lotus bases.[15] Innumerable passages in tantric and other texts direct the meditator to visualize the divinity seated upon a lotus. Buddhist buildings rest on bases with lotus-petal mouldings and have supporting columns with lotus capitals. Architecture and image alike are firmly based upon the Lotus of the Earth-Waters and the Dharma.[16]

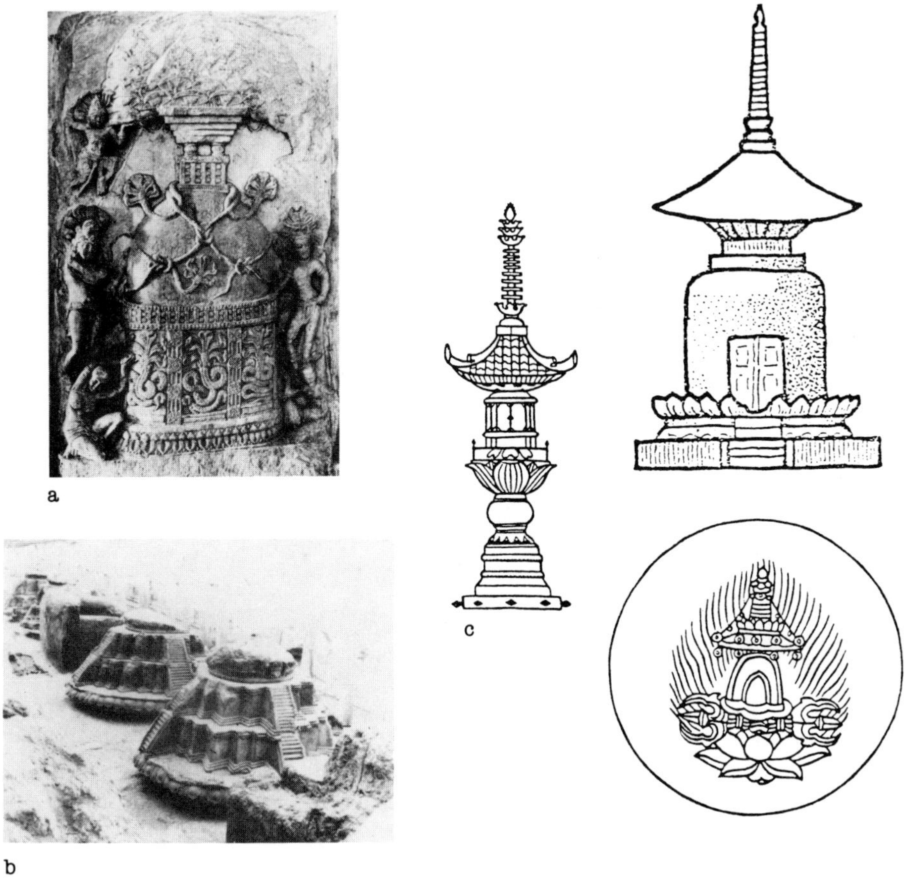

Fig. 50 : Stupas supported by lotuses. a. A relief panel from Amarāvatī showing a stupa adorned with nāgas and resting on a lotus base. b. Lotus-based stupas from Tapar Sadār, Ghazni, Afghanistan. The lotuses are raised above the ground. The sides of one stupa are decorated with a profusion of small Buddha images, suggesting the irradiation of Buddhas to all the points of the universe. c. Three drawings of Japanese stupas supported by lotuses.

15. ADS gives a lengthy description of the lotus throne of Amitābha in the Land of Supreme Bliss (sukhāvatī); the theme is reiterated in SPS XXIV.32 and MSV 16.40 & 41.

16. Further aspects of Lotus symbolism are developed below, pp. 203 ff.

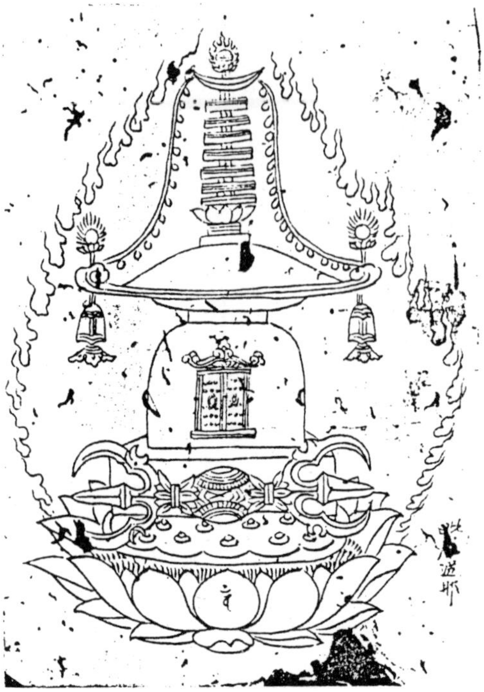

Fig. 51 : Japanese drawing of a stupa supported on a lotus. The stupa is a Tahōtō ("Prabhutaratna stupa"), that which appears in the sky at the time of Śākyamuni's preaching of the *Saddharma-puṇḍarīka-sūtra*. In Esoteric Buddhism it represents the Cosmic Body of Mahāvairocana, combining in its single form the two aspects of Buddhahood, Principle and Knowledge, represented by the two Buddhas Śākyamuni and Prabhutaratna (Jap. Shakamuni and Tahō), who sit together within its dome. The emergence of the stupa from the lotus represents the manifestation of the cosmos as seen by the Eye of Knowledge in its adamantine perfection, indicated by the vajra that lies on the lotus pericarp. (From *Taishō Shinshū Daizōkyō, Zuzō* 1, p. 1029).

Fig. 52 : The central eight petal section of the Matrix World Mandala. Mahāvairocana sits on the pericarp, four Buddhas sit on the petals in the cardinal directions (Ratnaketu to the East, Saṃkusumitarāja to the South, Amitābha to the West, and Divya-dundubhi-megha-nirghoṣa to the North), and four Bodhisattvas sit on the petals in the diagonal directions (Samantabhadra to the South East, Mañjuśrī to the South West, Avalokiteśvara to the North West and Maitreya to the North East). In its microcosmic significance this eight petal lotus mandala represents the stages in the attainment of perfect Buddhahood, which is compared to the opening of the lotus of the heart-mind. The four Bodhisattvas are "causal stages" which result in the attainment of Enlightenment, the aspects of which are embodied in the four Buddhas. Macrocosmically, the eight petal lotus mandala conveys the concept of the unfolding of the world of phenomena from the Womb-Lotus, which is identified with the Dharma-Body of Principle of Mahāvairocana Tathāgata.

11 THE CIRCLE AND THE SQUARE.

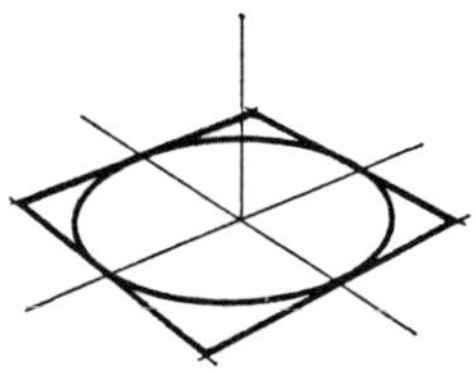

The stupa plan is a diagram of the diurnal and annual movements of the sun. The cycles of the sun are pinned to the four directions and in this way the circle of the sun's rotation is squared. In the world of appearances the plane of earth is round, circumscribed by the circle of the horizon. When structured by the cardinal points, determined by the movements of the sun, it is converted to a square and in this respect is called "four cornered" (caturbhṛṣṭi).[1] The plan of the stupa is the circle of earth and space squared by the fourfold-divided cycles of time.

The earth is a circle since the visible horizon that circumscribes the expanse of the terrestrial plane is circular. The nature of the celestial world, by contrast, is expressed in the quaternary rhythm of the heavenly cycle, a rhythm that translates geometrically into the figure of the square. The circle drawn about the gnomon is the earth in its apparent aspect, the square that is laid out upon it is the square of the ecliptic projected down from the heavens onto the plane of earth. By this projection earth is fixed and regulated by time.

* * * * *

The prototypic example of this symbolic construct is found in the arrangement of the fire altars built for the Vedic sacrifice. They are described in the *Śatapatha Brāhmaṇa* and the *Śulva-Sūtras*. Within a sacrificial shed there are three altars laid out along the "easterly spine" (prācīvaṃsa), the East-West axis determined by the points of the sun's rising and setting. The gārhapatya, a circular hearth to the West, represents the World of Earth; the āhavanīya, a square hearth to the East, represents the World of Heaven; and the dakṣināgni, a semi-circular altar lying to the South of the East-West spine, represents the intermediate region, the World of Mid-space, or the Atmosphere.[2] These three hearths symbolize the manifested universe : the Earth, or corporeal state of manifestation; Midspace, which is the subtle state of mental phenomena; and Heaven, which is the informal state.

The arrangement is repeated in the great altar ground (mahāvedi), which is laid out to the East of the sacrificial pavilion housing the three hearths. The altar ground is the symbol of Earth : "As large as is the altar ground (vedi) so large is the Earth".[3] At its eastern end is the High Altar (uttara-vedi)[4] which, like the āhavanīya hearth, is square and denotes the Heaven World. It is the main altar of the group. At its centre is a small square, termed its navel (nābhi).[5] As do the three hearths, the altar ground (vedi) and the High Altar (uttara-vedi) together symbolize the cosmos: "The vedi is the Earth and the uttara-vedi is the Heaven World".[6]

---

1. RV X.58.3; cf. VII.99.1 and ŚB VI.1.2.29, where it is similarly "four-cornered" (catuṣsvakti).

2. ŚB XII.4.1.3. Detailed descriptions of the altars of Heaven and Earth are given in ŚB VII.1.1.37 and VII.2.2.2 ff.

3. Kramrisch, 1946, p. 17, citing RV I.164.35; *Mādhyandina Saṃhitā* XIII.62; ŚB III.7.2.1 (vedi = pṛthivī); RV X.110.4; AB I.5.28; TB.II.1.1; ŚB IX.4.2.3; XII.8.2.36.

4. The proportions of the mahāvedi, involving the numbers 24, 30 and 36, are susceptible of an extended exegesis.

5. Kramrisch, 1946, p. 23. 6. ŚB VII.3.1.27; Kramrisch, 1946, p. 24.

The same symbolism is apparent in the Vāstu-puruṣa-maṇḍala of the Hindu temple, which is a square diagram of the cycles of the sun, the moon and the planets. It is a diagram of the cycles of time plotted as a square upon the circle of earth (pṛthivī-maṇḍala).

* * * * *

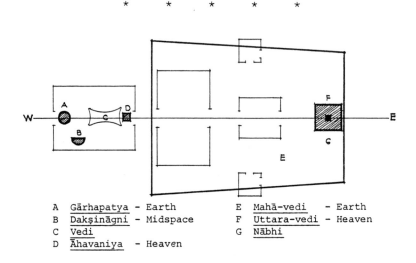

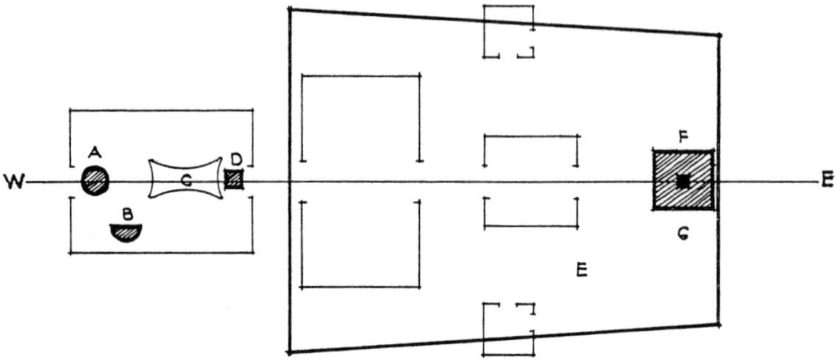

A Gārhapatya - Earth
B Dakṣināgni - Midspace
C Vedi
D Āhavaniya - Heaven
E Mahā-vedi - Earth
F Uttara-vedi - Heaven
G Nābhi

Fig. 53 : Plan of the Vedic sacrificial ground.

The *Śatapatha Brāhmaṇa* says that the square hearth is the Heaven World and the round hearth is the World of Earth.[7] The circle, as the most dynamic of geometric, two-dimensional forms, in this context is associated with the flow and flux, the mutability, of the terrestrial realm, while the square, as the most static of forms, is associated with the immutability of Heaven.[8] The symbolism of the conjunction of the circle of Earth and the square of Heaven within the stupa plan can be interpreted at several levels. At one level of significance the squaring of the circle is a marriage of space and time, the two parameters of our state of existence. At another level, and as will be shown in the following, Heaven and Earth, and hence the square and the circle, are respectively the formless and formal states of existence, the Upper and Lower Waters that represent the diremption of All-Possibility into the possibilities of form and those without form.[9] The union of the square and the circle in the stupa plan represents the cosmogenetic marriage of the Waters. At a yet higher level the conjunction of the two geometric forms is the marriage of the Essential and Substantial poles of manifestation, a doctrine that will be fully analyzed in the later chapter dealing with the symbolism of the sphere and the cube.[10]

* * * * *

7. E.g., ŚB XII.4.1.3; VII.1.1.37; etc.

8. In other contexts these values can be reversed, as will be shown in the analysis of the cube and the sphere given in the following.

9. See below, pp. 295 ff.

10. Below, pp. 209 ff.

All these symbolic references are incorporated within the stupa plan, which unifies the circle and the square and the principles they signify. The same relationships are found elsewhere in the stupa. In the domical type of stupa, for example, the square *harmika* that stands on the summit of the dome is a High Altar (*uttara-vedī*) and equates the square of Heaven,[11] thus duplicating at a higher level the square of Heaven incorporated within the plan.

---

11. See below, pp. 250 ff.

12 THE STUPA PLAN AS MANDALA.

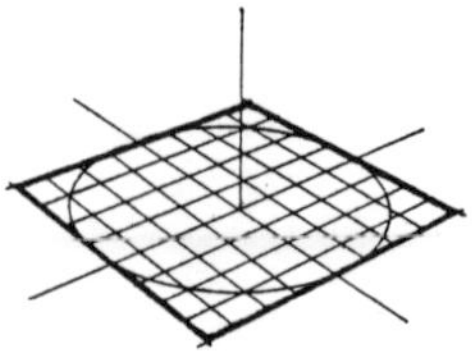

The mandala is basically a circle inscribed within a square, drawn on the ground with coloured powders or outlined with threads or, for convenience, drawn as a painting on cloth or paper. The characteristics of the mandala are those of the stupa plan : like the plan, the mandala is laid out by a ritual "squaring of the circle", is centred, is square, and is strictly oriented in accordance with the directions of space. The square of the mandala is subdivided into smaller squares by a gridwork of lines, and within these squares Buddhas, Bodhisattvas and Gods are installed, arranged according to the structuring principles of a paradigmatic model that expresses the cosmic pattern of the universe in the image of a network of theophanies. This grid pattern of theophanic nodal points is rich in associations and symbolic correlations, all directly relevant to the significance of the stupa plan.

* * * * *

The plan of the stupa laid out in the ritual is a mandala. The rituals for setting out the stupa plan are closely parallelled by those described in the Tantric texts for the delineation of mandalas.[1]

1. THE MEANING OF THE MANDALA

The Sanskrit word maṇḍala[2] means "circle", and by extension comes to indicate a centred space used for ritual action. In Tibetan texts it is translated as "centre" or "what surrounds".[3] In Chinese, when not simply transliterated as man t'u lo (Jap. mandara), it is translated as t'an (Jap. dan), "terrace, platform, world, arena", or as tao tch'ang (Jap. dōjō), "place of the Way" and synonymous with bodhimaṇḍa.[4] The mandala is a centred world, an area whose centre has been determined and whose boundaries have been clearly defined. It is a sacred enclosure, a world or field from which demonic, which is to say disordered and distracting, influences have been expelled and within which rituals can be performed without hindrance or danger. It is a cosmicized space, ordered from out of the unlimited extension of unstructured chaos.

---

1. The rituals for laying out the Matrix Mandala (garbha-kośa-maṇḍala, Jap. taizōkai mandara) on the ground, the so-called "Seven Day Ritual" (shichi nichi sa dan hō), are described in the *Dainichikyō*, pp. 4 et seq., and summarized in MKDJT, pp. 974 f., s.v., Shichi nichi sa dan hō. Cf. also the summary of the description in the *Daranishukyō* found in BKDJT, pp. 1912 ff., and the instructions for setting up a mandala in the *Hevajra Tantra*, Snellgrove, 1961, 1, pp. 82f., & 113. For additional material, see Tucci, 1961, pp. 85 ff., and de Visser, 1935, 1, pp. 160 ff.

2. For the theory and meaning of the mandala see BKDJT, p. 4757, s.v., Mandara; p. 2509, s.v. Shuhōdan; MKDJT, p. 2095, s.v. Mandara; Toganoo, 1932; Tucci, 1961, 1932, 1934, 1938; Eliade, 1958a, pp. 219 ff. & 408; 1958b, pp. 373 ff.; Tajima, 1959; B.L.Suzuki, 1936; Sawa, 1972, pp. 137 ff.; Foucher, 1900, 2, pp. 8ff.; de Visser, 1935, pp. 159 ff.; Finot, 1934, pp. 13 ff.; Steinilber-Oberlin, 1938, pp. 109 ff.; Mus, 1935, pp. 320 ff.; Lin Li-kouang, 1935; Chou Yi-liang, 1945; Chevalier and Gheerbrant, 1973, 3, p. 177, s.v., "Mandala"; Eliot, 1935, pp. 344 ff.; Snellgrove, 1957, pp. 64-90; 1971, p. 38; 1961, 1, pp. 19-33.

3. Eliade, 1958a, p. 219; 1958b, p. 373. 4. See below, pp. 157 ff.

The term maṇḍala means "circle" in other senses : it is a totality, a whole formed by an association of parts. The circle, always and everywhere, has been the sign of completeness and perfection. In Buddhism it symbolizes the perfection of Buddhahood. With these associations in mind the Chinese translators sometimes rendered maṇḍala as louen yuan kiu tsou (Jap. rinengunku), "a circle-like completeness", defined as "the totality formed by the various qualities and virtues of the Buddhas and Tathāgatas, just as a wheel is a whole formed by the assemblage of its various parts, its hub, its felly, spokes, etc".[5]

The mandala is also a circle in the sense in which we speak of "a circle of friends" : it is an assembly or gathering together of Buddhas and Bodhisattvas. "Maṇḍala means an assembly. The differentiations of Wisdom throughout the worlds, innumerable as particles of dust, come together like the spokes of a wheel to support the Mind King, Vairocana (Jap. Dainichi)".[6]

The texts of Japanese Shingon Buddhism give further specifications. The *Dainichikyō* says that the mandaḷa is a circle; it gives birth to Buddhas; and it has "incomparable flavour".[7] In his commentary on the sutra Śubhākarasiṃha explains these enigmatic references. The mandala "gives birth to Buddhas" because it represents the growth of the seed of Buddhahood which, when planted in "the earth of the mind", moistened by the water of Great Compassion, heated by the sun (or fire) of Great Wisdom, animated by the air of Great Method, grows into the space of the Great Void, and thus develops into the sprout of the Dharma-Nature, which grows outward into the Dharma-World and finally becomes the full-grown Buddha Tree.[8]

This is the functional and pragmatic definition of the mandala. According to this definition the mandala is the means whereby Buddhahood is attained. The mandala produces Enlightenment and, in this sense, gives birth to Buddhas, the Enlightened Ones. The mandala is a schema of the progressive stages in the ascent of the Way to Buddhahood, the Way that leads from the Awakening of the seed of bodhicitta up to the full perception of Method (upāya), the activity of the Buddha whereby all beings are aided to gain a perception of the Real.

In speaking of the "incomparable flavour" of the mandala the Sutra employs a metaphor that is recurrent in the Buddhist literature, that of churning milk to make butter and curds. The word maṇḍala comprizes maṇḍa, "ghee", and la, "composed of"; just as ghee is the concentrated essence of milk, so the mandala is the pure and quintessential distillation of the universe, cognate with amṛta, the ambrosial fluid of immortality obtained by the churning of the Milky Ocean. The Hindu myth, given in detail in the following,[9] tells how the Milky Ocean, which represents the Waters of potentiality, that is, the unformed, unstructured and chaotic Substance of the universe, is churned by the World Mountain revolving in the manner of a churning rod, so causing the Milk to solidify and produce forms. In this present Buddhist context the myth is given a new dimension : the Milky Ocean is also the Dharma-Nature (dharmatā), lying as an unrealized potentiality within the mind of the person, where it remains "uncoagulated" and "unformed" because of illusion. When "churned", that is to say awakened

---

5. BKJT, p. 1116, s.v., Rinengunku.
6. Śubhākarasiṃha, p. 626.a.9.
7. *Dainichikyō*, p. 5.b.26.
8. Śubhākarasiṃha, p. 625.a.
9. See below, pp. 177 f.

and actualized by the practice of meditational rituals, it passes through the stages of the "five flavours",[10] which are five levels of understanding, and is transformed into the essence of Supreme and Perfect Enlightenment.

"Maṇḍala", says Śubhākarasiṃha, "means the most purified and refined part of butter... the part which is unchanging, firm, of excellent flavour, homogeneous, without residue (of impurity). This is why the Buddha says that the mandala has incomparable flavour. The milk of the Buddha-Nature is churned by the three types of esoteric method[11] and, passing through the stages of the five flavours, forms the ghee of wondrous Awakening, which is of such purity that it cannot be further refined. (The mandala)... is the supremely sweet flavour of the true, the pure and the immutable".[12]

2. THE MANDALA AND COSMOS.

Man seeks to discern order in the universe. Through art, science and religion he searches for meaningful patterns, for a cohesive order underlying the ever-changing current of forms. The order man seeks and but dimly discerns is seen with absolute clarity by the Awakened Ones, the Buddhas. They perceive the forms of the world in their instantaneous and perfect harmony.

Shingon Buddhism, maintaining a doctrine that derives from Indian formulations, teaches that the maelstrom of forms perceived by ignorant beings and the underlying harmony and order perceived by the Buddhas are the inseparable aspects of a non-dual Reality : the chaotic confusion of forms is inseparable from their perfect ordering; their ceaseless flux is another aspect of their adamantine immutability. The forms of the phenomenal world, in all their impermanence, imperfection and disorder, are an aspect of Universal Form, which is synonymous with the Dharma Body of Vairocana. His Dharma Body is co-extensive with the forms of the conditioned cosmos; it completely pervades the innumerable modalities of formal phenomena; the manifold forms of the universe are manifestations of the qualities of the Buddha.

The mandala is the configuration of forms, cognate with Buddha qualities, as they abide in perfect equilibrium and symmetry within the Dharma Body of Vairocana. The mandala is a circle encompassing the Buddha's Dharma Body. Since that Body is totally and inseparably merged with the world of forms, it is at the same time an "all encompassing totality" (Ch. louen yuan kiu tsou) that includes within its area all the forms of the universe

---

10. The metaphor of the "five flavours" (Jap. gomi) is one that is commonly used in Buddhist writings to illustrate progressively refined levels of understanding. In the Tendai school, for example, it is used to describe five stages in the Buddha's preaching of the Dharma to audiences of increasing receptivity : firstly, the preaching of the *Avataṃsaka-sūtra* for śravakas and pratyekabuddhas is the flavour of fresh milk; secondly, the preaching of the *Agama-sūtras* for the followers of the Hīnayāna is the flavour of cream; thirdly, the preaching of the *Vaipulya-sūtras* is the flavour of curd; fourthly, the preaching of the *Prajñā-sūtras* is the flavour of butter; and finally, the preaching of the *Saddharma-puṇḍarīka-sūtra* and the *Mahā-parinirvāṇa-sūtra* is the flavour of ghee.

11. I.e., the practice of the Three Mysteries of Body, Speech and Mind.

12. Śubhākarasiṃha, p. 625.a.

as seen in their perfection and regulated order through the eyes of the Enlightened. The mandala simultaneously shows the Dharma Body of Vairocana Tathāgata and the ideal configuration of the cosmos of forms.

The mandala is a compressed schema of the cosmos of forms in its essential cohesion and integrality. It is the "focussed" or concentrated image of the total universe as it abides in non-dual coalescence within the immutability of Suchness. Within the confines of the mandala the world is contained in its original and undefiled purity, inseparably permeated by the virtues and qualities of the Buddhas.

* * * * *

In its microcosmic import the mandala is a model or image of the transcendent world existing within the mind of every being. "That is called a mandala which abides in the Mind of the Great Being (Mahāsattva).[13] It is located in the minds of all (followers of) the Shingon. Knowing this, the complete fruition (of Buddhahood) is attained".[14] The mandala drawn on the ground or as a painting is not the true mandala, but a meditational support for the realization of the mandala in the mind. It is a paradigm of the spiritual structure of the universe infused with the Buddha-Nature; and likewise of the spiritual world that lies within the being, the inner world through which he must pass in his pilgrimage back to his own centre, the locus of his indwelling Enlightenment.

The formal mandala delineated on the ground can simultaneously depict both worlds, the inner and the outer, because of the strict analogy that exists between them. Each part of the universe is analogous to every other part and to the whole, so that the total cosmos is reflected within the mind of every being and the centre of the total cosmos is located at the centre of each mind. When the initiate enters the mandala he is ritualistically traversing his inner states; in his innermost mind he is crossing the flood of saṃsāra, tracing his way to the centre of the cosmos, which is the bodhimaṇḍa, the place where the Buddhas attain Enlightenment.

3. THE MANDALA AS PLAN : THE *VĀSTU-PURUṢA-MAṆḌALA*

The square of the mandala is characteristically divided into a number of smaller squares so as to form a chessboard-like figure. The manner in which this grid configuration relates to the symbolism of an architectural plan is indicated by the example of the Vāstu-puruṣa-maṇḍala, which is laid out as a metaphysical prefiguration of the plan form of the Hindu temple.[15]

The square that was delineated in the ritual of orientation is divided into smaller squares, their number depending on symbolic correspondences with the location and intended use of the temple, the identity of the

---

13. That is, Vajrasattva, who embodies the Enlightenment that lies innate within the mind of the unawakened being.

14. *Dainichikyō*, p. 41.b.18

15. Kramrisch, 1946, pp. 21 ff., gives the definitive description and analysis of the Vāstu-puruṣa-maṇḍala. Burckhardt, 1967, pp. 28 ff., gives a summary. Cf. also Volwahsen, 1969, pp. 43 ff.

divinity enshrined, the caste of the donor and a number of other connected factors.[16] There are 32 types of mandala that are used, forming by gnomonic increase an arithmetical series, starting with a mandala of one square and increasing to mandalas with as many as 32 x 32 = 1,024 squares. The most commonly used from among these are the ones having 8 x 8 = 64 and 9 x 9 = 81 squares.[17]

The squares of the mandala are assigned to various divinities, who are invited in rituals to descend into the mandala and there take up their positions. The central squares are those of the Brahmāsthāna, the station of Brahmā, the Creator, personification of Principle and the Centre whence manifestation deploys. Surrounding Brahmā are 44 devatas, whose number and relative positions remain constant in mandalas of whatever number of subdivisions : in the squares at the periphery are stationed 32 gods, called "Enclosing Gods" (prakara-devata) or "Occupying Gods" (pada-devata), comprizing 28 gods who personify the lunar mansions (nakṣatra) plus the four regions of the directions. Between them and the Brahmāsthāna are the eight Ādityas, who represent the eight positions of the sun upon the ecliptic,[18] corresponding to the eight directions and the eight planets. As well, there are four other gods who also relate to the directions.

* * * * *

The symbolism brings together several of the themes examined in the preceding. The Brahmāsthāna, where Brahmā takes his stand at the centre of the mandala, is the place of the hiraṇyagarbha, the Golden Womb, the progenitive point and "primordial germ of cosmic light", from which effulgent source "proceeds the light of all times and in every direction",[19] shining through the Suns (the Ādityas) and thence the planets and the moons. The mandala is a radiation of light into the directions of space.

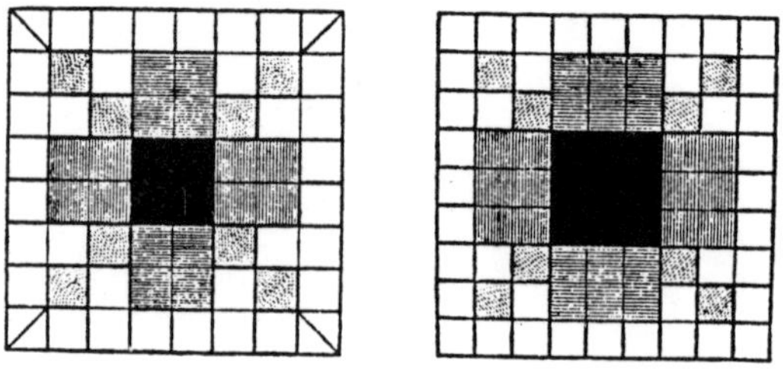

Fig. 54 : Two examples of the *Vāstu-puruṣa-maṇḍala*. The one on the left has 8 x 8 = 64 divisions, and that on the right has 9 x 9 = 81 divisions.

---

16. See Kramrisch, 1946, pp. 58 ff.

17. The Numbers 64 and 81 are fractions of 25,920, the number of years in a precession of the equinoxes and a fundamental cyclical number. See Guénon, 1970, pp. 22 ff. For the symbolic correspondences of the mandalas of 64 and 81 squares, see Kramrisch, 1946, pp. 46-50.

18. Cf. above, p. 33. The twelve Ādityas are here reduced to eight, thus forming four hierogamic pairs.

19. Kramrisch, 1946, p. 89.

It is also a geometrizing, a "crystallization", of the cycles of time, fixed in the mandala of space and the earth.[20] Time is fixed within the mandala in two ways : firstly, the diurnal movements of the sun are graphed upon the mandala by way of the process of gnomonic quadrature; and secondly, the divisions of the cycles of time are established within the mandala by way of an apotheosis. Personified and divinized, the divisions of the cycles of the moon, the planets and the sun are brought down from their celestial realms to take up their places upon the gridwork of the mandala, where they occupy positions that correspond to their celestial locations.

The mandala thus combines spatial and temporal references. The gridwork of its squares images the emanating production of spatial extension and temporal duration from the principial point of Unity. The laying out of the mandala delineates the genesis of space from the primordial Centre, and also, shown in an instantaneous and static mode, the unfolding of the great cycles of time. The two coordinates of the sensible world, space and time, the warp and weft of the empirical universe, are woven together in the tissue of the mandala.

By fixing the divine personifications of the temporal cycles upon the squares of the mandala time is transmuted into space, its movements frozen and rendered motionless. Time is thereby linked by geometry to the central point, the Source of the universe.

Every symbol is multivalent in meaning and the mandala, as a geometric diagram of the solar, lunar and planetary cycles, can be interpreted at several levels. At its least significant level it is a graph of the movements of the physical and perceptible heavenly bodies, an astrological chart for the preparation of horoscopes. At a more profound level of interpretation the movements of the stars are visible analogies of invisible principles and the mandala is a diagram of the modes of principial functioning; it is a symbolic representation of the manner in which the great rhythms of the perceptible cosmos, representing the processes of becoming, derive from primordial Being. It shows how space disperses from a dimensionless centre, how the revolutions of time evolve from a timeless instant, how multiplicity, in its spatial and temporal aspects, relates to Unity; how the One becomes many. By spatializing time in the mandala the partite segments of its cycles are geometrically referred to the One, the central hub about which the wheel of time revolves.

* * * * *

The mandala on which the Hindu temple is built is called the _Vāstu-puruṣa-maṇḍala_. _Vāstu_, literally "a dwelling place, a building", from the root _vās_, "to dwell, to exist", refers specifically and in its narrow sense to the building site defined by the periphery of the mandala. In its wider and metaphysical sense it refers to the total extent of manifested existence which the mandala symbolically defines. _Vāstu_ is the field of existence marked out by the borders of the building plan, which, as a mandala, is coextensive with the structured cosmos.

Puruṣa, the second term in the name of the mandala, is literally "Person", and refers to Universal Man, the personification of the informing Spirit, the primeval Male from whom Existence evolves. Identical with the

20. Cf. above, p. 34.

Word, with Knowledge, he is the anthropomorphic expression of the Essential Principle of manifestation, the Essence of Existence. Considered in relation to the individual man, Puruṣa is the principial and unconditioned Self, the universal Ātman residing at the vital centre of the individuality as in a city (puri-ṣaya).[21] The term Vāstu-puruṣa-maṇḍala can thus be translated as "the mandala of spiritual Essence immanent within Existence" and, in one of its meanings, the mandala is a figuration of Essence (puruṣa) immanent within forms, referring to the progenitive marriage of the principial poles of manifestation, Essence and Substance (puruṣa and prakṛti).[22]

Puruṣa, the Essential Principle of manifestation, is also Universal Man, man insofar as he is identified with his informing Essence. In the symbolic imagery of the ritual it is therefore appropriate to represent Puruṣa anthropomorphically, and he is so delineated on the Vāstu-puruṣa-maṇḍala, in the position of the sacrificial victim, face downwards, head to the East and feet to the West. Drawn in this way upon the mandala Puruṣa is identified with the cosmic victim, Puruṣa-Prajāpati. As we have seen, the generation of spatial extension and temporal duration from their dimensionless and timeless Principle is symbolically expressed as a fragmentation of primordial Unity. The cohering integrity of Being is shattered to become multiple; the impartite becomes partite. Mythologically, this is the sacrifice of the divine Person, Puruṣa, who divides himself in order to enter into existence. The discrete parts of manifestation are his disjointed members; the manifold portions of the universe are the fractions of his dismembered body, taken apart in a perpetually proceeding and ever-renewed act of sacrifice. Thus emptied out and dispersed into manifestation, Puruṣa is Prajāpati, Lord of Progeny (prajā), the personification of total Existence, who, his oneness fragmented into time, is identified with the cycle of the Year.[23] The sacrificial ritual is a reversal of this progression of the One into the many. By taking apart the body of multiplicity Unity is restored.[24] The body of Puruṣa delineated in the Vāstu-puruṣa-maṇḍala is the body of the God "incarnated" into the ground of existence - the divine Presence immanent within and divided among the multiplicity of forms - and simultaneously that partite body sacrificed for the renewal of Unity.

The figure of the immolated body drawn upon the mandala has an alternative connotation. The figure is also that of brute and titanic existence, conquered and transformed by the gods. The *Bṛhat Saṃhitā* tells how "Once there was some existing thing not defined by name. Unknown in its proper form it blocked Heaven and Earth; seeing that, the devas seized it of a sudden and laid it on the earth face downwards. In the same position as they were when they seized it, the devas stayed on it where it lay. Brahmā made it full of gods and called it Vāstu-puruṣa".[25]

At first sight this account seems to contradict what has gone before, but in fact it is a variant symbolic expression of the same concept, emphasising another of its aspects. The "pinning" by the gods of the undefined, nameless "thing" lacking intelligible form, is the ordering of chaos, directly assimable to the informing "actionless activity" of Essence

---

21. According to a derivation by nirukta. See Guénon, 1945, p. 45, n. 1.

22. This concept is explained in the following.

23. See above, p. 54. 24. See above, pp. 54 ff.

25. *Bṛhat Saṃhitā* LII.2-3, quoted in Kramrisch, 1946, p. 73. See also Volwahsen, 1969, p. 43; Burckhardt, 1967, p. 26.

upon Substance. The "thing" is the unformed void, the tenebrous root of existence; the gods (*deva*) are the divine qualities, so many luminous aspects of the effulgence of Being; their firm establishment on the body of the shapeless "thing" is the *fiat lux* whereby the unformed, the void, is filled with divine reflections and transformed from the amorphous disorder of chaos into the cosmos of ordered formality. Insofar as it appears as the opposite of light and of Essence, the formlessness of Substance is identified with the *asuras*, the titan-demons, the hosts of darkness and disorder, forever engaged in battle with the *devas*, the gods or angels, the forces of light and order, a warfare that mythically expresses the ever-continuing interaction of the dark and light Principles, the polar bifurcation whereby Being descends into Existence. The victory of the *devas* over the tenebrous and amorphous "thing" is the establishment of cosmos within chaos and therefore synonymous with the measuring out of the defined space of the mandala from out of undefined extension. The chaos of Substance becomes the ground of distinctive and clearly defined qualities, the support of manifestation.[26]

4. THE SYMBOLISM OF THE MANDALA GRIDWORK.

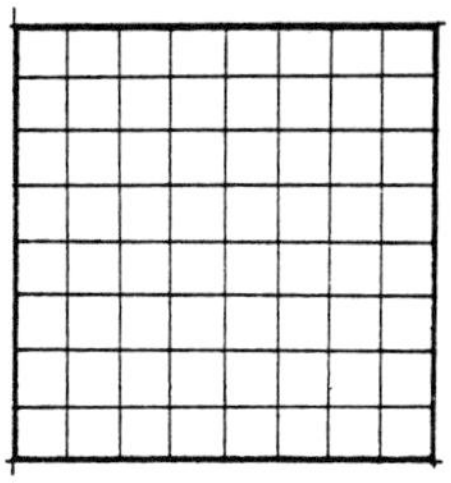

a. The Lines as Pneumatic Measures.

The lines that subdivide the mandala plan have more than a merely geometric significance. They are lines of Breath (*prāṇa*), having symbolic reference to the pneumatic structuring of the world and man. The body of man and the body of the cosmos are suffused with Breath; they are held together by a pneumatic net. The "ground" or "field" of the world is criss-crossed with lines of Breath; and the psycho-physical "field" of man is a network of subtle, pneumatic arteries (*nāḍi*).[27] The macrocosmic and microcosmic worlds are "measured out" by these lines of Breath. Hence *prāṇa* is a prototypic measure, the width of the line (*sūtra*) used to lay out the mandala. It is also a measure of time : in early systems the *prāṇa* is the shortest measure of concrete time, being the time needed for inspiration and expiration.[28] In Indian architectural manuals[29] *prāṇa*, "Breath", and the related concept *vāyu*, "Wind", are listed as units of measure.[30] The lines that delineate and divide the mandala are pneumatic measuring cords.

---

26. The fixing of tenebrous chaos is analogously expressed in rituals of stabilizing the earth, discussed below, pp. 184 ff. The chthonic serpent represents the Waters of Chaos, and the stake that pins the ophidian head, transfixing and stabilizing the amorphous, is the vertical ray that strikes the horizontal plane of Substance.

27. See also pp. 317 ff. 28. Kramrisch, 1946, p. 51 and n. 88.

29. E.g., the *Kamikāgama*, cited by Kramrisch, 1946, p. 51.

30. The Breaths (*prāṇa*) and Winds (*vāyu*) are identified in RV XI.4.15.

b. Breath-threads, Breath-knots and Breath-nets.

The lines of the mandala are lines of Breath. The concept pertains to the multivalent and complex symbolism of threads of Spirit (sūtrātman),[31] according to which the life and essential nature of each person depends on a pneumatic thread, cognate with a ray of light, that connects him to the Sun.

The thread or ray of attachment is the vertical axis, equivalent to the Cosmic Tree, Pillar, Ladder or Mountain. It strings the worlds together like beads upon a necklace, connecting them to each other and all to their common source. So also the worlds contained within the microcosm of man are strung through their centres upon the pneumatic cord.[32] As we have seen, the directions that emanate from this axis of Air are exhalations of Breath : the microcosm and the macrocosm both come into existence by an expiration, a projection of Breath-lines into the directions.[33] In a complementary symbolism, the person is a pneumatic coagulation; he is a spiritual aggregate, a cohesion of Breath, a knot in the Breath-cord (sūtrātman).[34] The Breath-knot is the focus of the forces that determine the plexus of individual existence, and hence knots and names are homologous : "The thread is his (the Breath's) Word (vāc) and the knots are names; and so with his Word as the cord and names as knots all this universe is tied up".[35] The knot in the cord of Breath is the "vital node" that holds together the component elements of individuality.[36]

---

31. It was one of Coomaraswamy's main concerns to expound the doctrine of the Breath-thread (sūtrātman) and it is a recurrent theme in his writings. See e.g., 1977, 1, pp. 465 ff, "*Svayamātṛṇṇa:* Janua Coeli"; ibid, 2, pp. 333 ff., "On the Indian and Traditional Psychology, or Rather Pneumatology"; 1945a, *passim*.

32. See Guénon, 1962, Ch. LXI, "La chaine des mondes", pp. 365-373. The thread that leads back to the origin and centre is the line of transmission of the doctrine, the line that runs from one generation to the next and traces back to a divine and revelatory source. The unbroken continuity of this line of transmission is seen as the surety that the doctrine derives from an in-Spiration and is not mere threads of thought unwinding from the fallible mind of man. The sermons of the Buddha, which are so many sonorous reverberations of his Breath, the "Thunderous Sound of the Celestial Drum" (divya-dundubhi-megha-nirghoṣa), are transmitted in the sacred writings, the sūtras and the tantras, which two words both literally mean "thread". Sūtra is translated in Sino-Japanese by the character 經 (Ch. king, Jap. kyō), literally "warp", in which 糸 is the "thread" radical and 巠 is "a subterranean watercourse", that is, a secret and hidden stream. The sutras are the warp of the doctrine; the commentaries form its weft, 緯 (Ch. wei, Jap. i) which is how they are designated in China and Japan. See Guénon, 1945, pp. 19-20; 1958a, p. 65; 1947, p. 101; Chevalier and Gheerbrant, 1973, 2, pp. 318 f., s.v., Fil (tissage).

33. See above, pp. 72 ff.

34. For the symbolism of knots, see Guénon, 1962, Ch. LXVIII ("Liens et noeuds"), pp. 400 ff.; Coomaraswamy, 1944a; Eliade, 1961, pp. 110 ff.; Chevalier and Gheerbrant, 1973, 3, pp. 267 ff., s.v., Noeud.

35. AĀ III.1.6. For the doctrine of names (nāma), see Coomaraswamy, 1977, 2, pp. 257 ff., etc. Among the Egyptian hieroglyphics the knotted cord designates the man's name or his distinctive individual existence, that is, the person so-and-so.

36. Guénon, 1962, p. 342. Elsewhere (1977, 1, pp. 9f.) Guénon refers to the "*point sensible*", which exists in every cathedral "built according to the rules of the art". This point corresponds to the "vital node" within the body of man. When this nodal point is "pierced" (in a symbolic sense) there is an immediate and complete disintegration of the body.

The symbolism of knots overlaps that of the net. The knot of individual existence corresponds to the point of intersection of the threads of the net. The lines of the net are the Breath-threads that animate and structure the cosmos. Macrocosmically, and taking the net to represent the "field" formed by a plane of existence, each of the crossing points represents an individuality, a nodal aggregation or knot of being; microcosmically, and taking the net to represent the "field" formed by an individual existence, the crossings are the vital nodes within the body, the places where the Breaths or Winds channelled by the nāḍis converge to vital centres.

The body of man and the body of the world are held together by a pneumatic net. Cosmic Wind-cords hold the universe together. A net of Spirit-cords defines the field of the cosmos, so that the *Upaniṣads* speak of "that God who, having spread out one net after another, in various ways wanders (transmigrates) in the field",[37] that is, he is "the one who spreads the net, who rules with his ruling powers".[38] Analogously, Breath-cords hold together and articulate the body of man. The organs are held together by the Breath of Ātman, by the Spirit of Brahman : "I know the stretched thread on which these living beings are woven; I know the thread of the thread, and also the great Brahman";[39] "Do you know, O Kāpya, the thread by which this world and all beings are held together?...He who knows that thread, O Kāpya, and that Inner Controller, indeed knows Brahman, he knows the worlds, he knows the Gods, he knows the *Vedas*, Being, Self and everything".[40] The wind-ropes bind the cosmos, and when cut the cosmos will fall apart.[41] The same is true of the person : the Breaths are the immortal parts of the body[42] and "by Wind, as by a thread, this world, the other world and all beings are held together. Therefore, verily, they say of a person who dies that his limbs have been loosened...for it is the Wind that binds them like a thread".[43] The ultimate reference is to the sacrifice of Prajāpati, whose body is "unstrung" when divided into multiplicity : "With his joints unstrung he was incapable of standing up, and the gods put them together again by means of sacrifices",[44] a restoration that is ritually repeated in the putting together of the Fire Altar, equated with Prajāpati's body. In this way the sacrificer "reunites Prajāpati, totally and entirely".[45]

* * * * *

The symbolism is ambivalent[46] : for those who are still attached (tied, bound) to saṃsāra, the knot of individual existence is a good; its untying is death,[47] and hence in Chinese Buddhism the endless knot, sign of longevity, is one of the eight auspicious signs.[48]

From the essential viewpoint, however, the knot is a constraint, a complication, a complex, an entanglement; it is the knot of individuality that ties the Spirit in bonds, binds the person to a determined state, and holds him within the limits of contingent being. To untie the knot is to be liberated, so that a prayer is addressed to Soma to "untie as it were a knot the entangled straight and tortuous paths".[49] "When all the knots that

---

37. Śvet. Up. V.3.7. 38. Śvet. Up. III.1. 39. AV X.8.38. 40. BU III.7.1.

41. MU I.4. 42. ŚB X.1.4.1. 43. BU III.7.2. 44. I.6.3.35-36.

45. ŚB VI.2.2.11; cf. above, pp. 47 ff. 46. Eliade, 1961, p. 112; Guénon, 1962, p. 401; Coomaraswamy, 1944, p. 117.

47. In French, *dénouement*, the "untying", is both the dramatic solution of the problem, and the final crisis, death.

48. Williams, 1960, p. 155, s.v. "Eight Treasures", and p. 289, s.v., "Mystic Knot". 49. RV IX.97.18.

fetter the heart are cut asunder, then a mortal becomes immortal".[50] The image is employed in a famous section in the *Śuraṅgama Sūtra* : to untie the knots of the being, teaches the Buddha, is to attain the perfect freedom of Buddhahood; but "having been tied in a certain order, they can only be untied in the reverse order", and the Buddha prescribes a rigorous sequence of meditations to unbind the constraints of individual existence.[51] The untying - or "penetration" - of the knots (*granthi*) is an aim of tantric practice; and to pierce the *ajñācakra*, the *plexus*[52] between the eyebrows, is to untie the knot of Rudra (*rudragranthi*) and thereby open the third eye.

To untie the knots is to transform the cord that binds into the cord that connects all things together and to their Principle. It is to see the true nature of the binding cord, to see it as the single and continuous clew that leads back to the Centre.[53]

Similarly the net, which has a beneficent aspect when viewed as the pattern of order, the trace of the Dharma that regulates the world and "rules out" chaos and confusion and the net that binds together the world and the being, is also a net of Death, a constraint and a constriction, that must be cut away if the transcendent realms of unrestricted Freedom are to be attained.

* * * * *

Fig. 55 : Stupas adorned with serpents and serpent-knots.

---

50. KU II.15. For "knots (*granthi*) of the heart", see also CU VII.26.

51. *Śuraṅgama-sūtra*, in Luk, 1966, pp. 118 ff.

52. The words "plexus", "complex", "perplex", etc., are from Lat. *plectere*, "to plait", that is, "to knot".

53. The symbolism of the clew relates closely to that of the labyrinth for which see Guénon, 1962, Ch. LXVI, "Encadrements et labyrinthes", pp. 391 ff.; Coomaraswamy, 1944a, pp. 110 ff.; Chevalier and Gheerbrant, 1973, 3, pp. 99 ff., s.v., *Labyrinthe*.

The lines of the gridwork drawn upon the surface of the mandala are Breath-lines (prāṇa-sūtra) which define the Breath-form (prāṇa-rūpa) of the Cosmic Person, Puruṣa. The body of Puruṣa is composed of Wind : "The city (pur) doubtless is these worlds and Puruṣa is he that blows here (the Wind, vāyu); he dwells (ṣī) in this city; hence he is Puruṣa".[54] The intersections of the gridlines define vulnerable points or tender spots (marma) within the body of Puruṣa, corresponding to the Breath-knots and centres within both the macrocosmic and microcosmic pneumatic bodies.[55] In the laying out of the plan of the Hindu temple and also that of the stupa the location of these marmas affect the positions of the building's elements : the crossing points of the lines must not be encroached upon, or else the body of the donor and the field of the surrounding environment could be harmed.[56]

c. The Symbolism of Weaving.

The symbolism of the gridwork of lines corresponds to that of weaving.[57] To weave is to produce cosmos. The world of space and time is woven from the thread of Breath. In the *Vedas* the two sisters, Night and Dawn, weave the web of time, as "two weavers in happy agreement weave the taut thread together".[58]

The Sun that joins the universe to itself by a Gale-thread is the cosmic weaver : "The weaver of the cloth is certainly he who shines down there, for he moves across the worlds as if across a cloth",[59] and "the yonder Sun is indeed well-meshed, for he weaves together the days and nights".[60] In the *Upaniṣads* the world is woven by Brahman. In answer to the question, "... if the Waters are the web on which all is woven, on what web are the Waters woven?", the reply is given that it is the Inner Controller, which is the Breath-thread (sūtrātman).[61] Similarly, "... that which is above the Sky, that which is beneath the Earth, that which people call the past, the present and the future, across space is that woven like warp and woof. Across what is space woven...?" The reply is given : "That ... which the knowers of Brahman call the Imperishable",[62] which is Brahman or the Self, "He in whom the Sky, the Earth and Midspace are woven as also the mind along with all the vital breaths, know him alone as the one Self".[63] Theistically expressed, Kṛṣṇa is the Supreme Person "by whom this universe is woven";[64] and he declares, "All this is woven on me".[65]

The to-and fro movement of the shuttle upon the cosmic loom is the alternation of life and death, of the coming into and going out of existence, whether of a person or a world; it is the alternation of both the macrocosmic and microcosmic in-breathing and out-breathing; it is the rhythmic pulse of movement and of change in both the universe and the individual.

---

54. ŚB XIII.6.2.1.

55. See Kramrisch, 1946, pp. 51-53, 55-57 & 51, n. 87.

56. *Ibid.*, p. 55, lists the marmas that are not to be encroached upon.

57. For the symbolism of weaving, see esp. Guénon, 1958a, pp. 65 ff.; Eliade, 1965, pp. 170 ff.

58. RV II.3.6. On the weaving of time see RV V.5.6; IV.13.4; V.10.7. 42 ff.; X.8.37-39. 59. ŚB XIV.2.2.22. 60. ŚB IX.4.1.8.

61. BU III.6.1; cf. Eliade, 1965, pp. 172 f.

62. BU III.8.7-8. 63. Muṇḍ. Up. II.2.5. 64. BG VIII.22.

65. BG IX.4; cf. XI.38.

The warp threads are the immutable and principial radii originating from the Centre and passing through the states of existence; the weft threads are those states themselves, the variable and contingent applications of the Principle to particular conditions. The image is that of the rays of the Sun (the warp threads) irradiating the worlds (the weft threads), with the Sun removed an infinite distance so that its rays are parallel,[66] and the concentric circles they traverse, being circumferences of infinite extent, having become straight lines.[67]

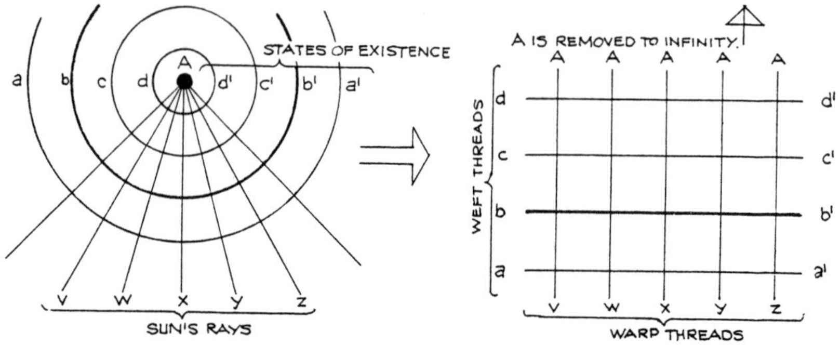

Fig. 56 : The assimilation of Sun and loom symbolisms

The loom is the cosmos. The warp (top) beam is the Essential pole of the universe; the bottom beam is its Substantial pole; or, transposing the symbolism, the upper beam is Heaven and the lower beam is Earth. The weft threads are the planes of existence or the levels of being; the warp threads are the rays of informing Light or Breath, linking the upper and lower Principles. Joined together by its supporting side beams the loom forms a rectangle framing an interlaced gridwork of threads, which is precisely the form of the mandala.[68]

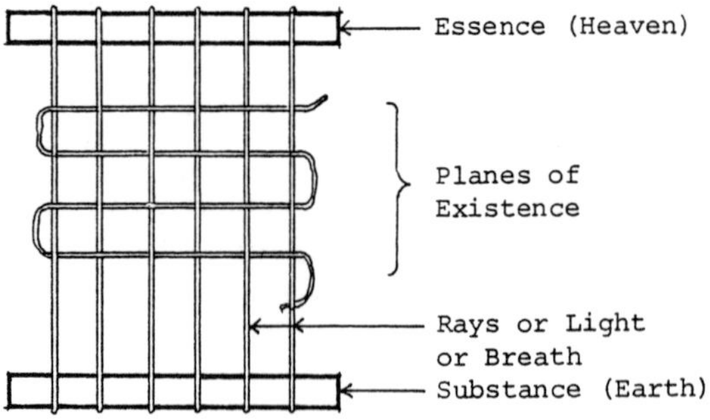

Fig. 57 : The loom as an image of the cosmos.

In this symbolism the plane of the mandala is seen as vertical, with Heaven above and Earth below, so as to represent a cross section through the multiple states of existence. Whether the loom stands vertically or

66. As they are considered to be in the physics of light.

67. There are cases where the warp threads are strung from a centre or from a ring rather than from a warping beam.

68. See above, p. 104.

horizontally, the same symbolic considerations apply, since it is possible to transpose a vertical symbolism of this type to a horizontal plane by taking one of the directions as "up". When oriented in this way the grid-lines of the mandala can be taken to represent the Breath-threads of Essence, running vertically, and the Breath-threads of Substance, running at right angles to them and horizontally. The nodal points of their crossings are then so many "concentrations" of Breath, each representing an "object" or a phenomenon of the plane of existence or plane of being under consideration and each in this way representing a pneumatic hierophany.

Alternately, in a complementary symbolism, the plane of the grid-lines can be taken as horizontal rather than vertical and in this case it represents the plan of a level of existence : the warp and weft Breath-threads are so many reproductions of the directions emanating from the centre of the plane. Each crossing is implicitly a three-dimensional cross; a vertical passes through each and every point upon the plane of existence (or of being) that the cloth represents, linking that point back to the Centre. In this symbolism, as in the former, the points of intersection are so many "specifications" of Breath; at each point Breath reveals itself as some aspect of form.

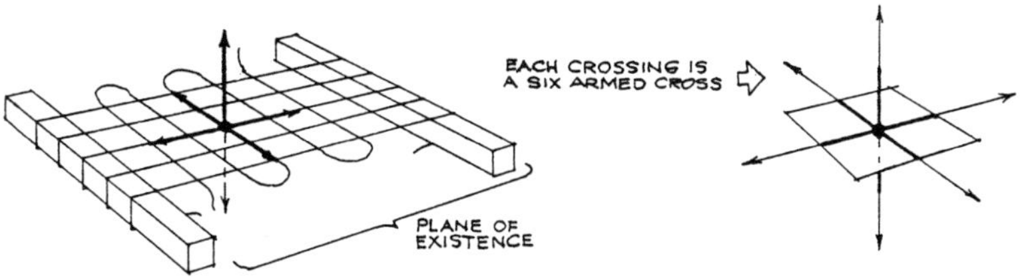

Fig. 58 : The loom as a horizontal plane or level of existence.

d. The Symbolism of the Spider's Web.

The same formula is expressed in the image of the spider and its web.[69] In the myths of many cultures the spider is associated with the Moon, which weaves the destinies of men,[70] but in the *Brāhmaṇas* it is specifically equated with the Sun that centres the cosmos.[71] "Like a spider, the one God surrounds himself with threads drawn from primordial Substance (pradhāna)";[72] "As a spider spins its threads... even so from the Self comes forth all breaths, all worlds, all divinities, all beings";[73] "Just as a spider emanates and draws in (its thread)... so from the Imperishable the universe comes into being";[74] and "Just as a spider produces its own threads itself... even so Brahman creates the world unaided by any extraneous means".[75]

---

69. The symbolism of the spider's web is developed by Coomaraswamy, 1935b, pp. 396 ff.; 1977, 2, p. 76, n. 40; Eliade, 1965, p. 172; Chevalier and Gheerbrant, 1973, 1, p. 92, s.v., Araignée.

70. Eliade, 1958b, p. 181; Cirlot, 1962, p. 290. 71. KB XIX.3.

72. Śvet. Up. VI.10. 73. BU II.1.20. 74. Muṇḍ. Up. I.1.7.

75. BSSB II.1.25.

The weaving of the web is the world's manifestation (kalpa); its withdrawal is the return to non-manifestation (pralaya). The radii and concentric rings of the spider's web are the warp and weft of the world. The web models the multiple levels of existence irradiated by lines of Breath.

The spider's web is a spiral net converging to its centre, where sits the spider who spun it out from his own substance. The spider is the point-source and Principle of the world and is thus associated with the vulva (yoni)[76] and the cosmic navel (nābhi) : "Whence those seven rays spin forth there is my (Agni's) navel".[77] The Sun shines with seven rays "to form the web".[78]

* * * * *

Ophidian and arachnoid symbolisms coalesce in the myth of Indra's smiting of the Serpent Vṛtra to release the "seven rivers" of universal manifestation. Invoking Indra, the *Ṛg Veda* says, "Thou clavest the spidery (aurṇavabham) Vṛtra, son of Dānu".[79] The term auṇavabha derives from ūrṇā-vabha, "thread spinner", which is to say, "spider". Vṛtra, who is Principle in privative mode, prior to the deployment of the worlds, is both the Serpent who contains the Waters hidden within his coils, and the Spider who has not yet spun the world web. He is the "stark and far-famed Aurṇavabha" who, when conquered by Indra, together with the Serpent Ahīṣuva, becomes the co-creator of the cosmos.[80]

e. The Symbolism of the Buddha's Ūrṇā

These associations of spinning out of threads from a centre are implicit in the usual designation of the spider in the *Brāhmaṇas* and *Upaniṣads*, namely ūrṇā-nābhi, in which nābhi is "hub" or "navel" and ūrṇā is "spider's thread"; but ūrṇā also designates one of the thirty-two characteristic marks (lakṣana) of a Buddha, the hair tuft on his brow, which emits rays of brilliant light that illumine the worlds.[81] The theme is recurrent in the Mahāyāna literature, where this emission of light from the ūrṇā is the usual means whereby the Buddha affords a vision of the multitude of Buddha Lands that fill all the directions of the sphere of the universe. The *Amitāyur-dhyāna-sūtra* provides an example : "At that moment, the World Honoured One flashed forth a golden ray from between his eyebrows. It extended to all the innumerable worlds of the ten quarters. On its return the ray rested on the top of the Buddha's head and transformed itself into a golden pillar just like the Mount Sumeru, wherein the pure and admirable countries of the Buddhas in the ten quarters appeared all at once illuminated".[82] Similarly, in the *Laṅkāvatāra Sūtra* : "Then the Blessed One... emitted rays of light from the tuft of hair between the eyebrows... emitting rays of light which shone flaming like the fire at the end of a kalpa, like a luminous rainbow, like the rising sun, blazing brilliantly, gloriously..."[83] And in the *Saddharma-puṇḍarīka-sūtra* it says : "At that moment

---

76. Coomaraswamy, 1935b, p. 396 & n. 32. 77. RV I.105.9.

78. RV I.164.5. 79. RV. II.11.8

80. Coomaraswamy. 1935b, pp. 393 & 396.

81. E.g., in SPS; *Lalita Vistara* 397.17; *Laṅkāvatāra-sūtra* XIII.4. (Suzuki, 1932, p. 13); etc.

82. DS I.5 (Cowell, Muller and Takakusu, 1894, p. 166).

83. *Laṅkāvatāra-sūtra* XIII.4 (Suzuki, 1932, p. 13).

there issued a ray from within the circle of hair between the eyebrows of the Lord. It extended over eighteen hundred thousand Buddha-fields in the Eastern quarter, so that all these Buddha-fields appeared wholly illuminated by its radiance..."; [84] and in like manner at the time of the apparition of the stupa [85] described in the same sutra the Buddha darts a ray of light from his ūrṇā in which become visible the "many hundreds of thousands of koṭis of Buddha fields, similar to the sands of the Ganges", in each of the ten directions. [86] Many paintings of the Buddhas and the Bodhisattvas show them with the ūrṇā emitting rays of light. [87]

The meaning of the imagery is clear : the Buddha, the Sun-Hub (nābhi) and central Eye of the World (cakkhum loke), fills the worlds with lucent thread-rays, spun out from the point of concentrated Buddha-Consciousness located in the cavernous plexus (ājñā-cakra, "the cakra of command, or ordering") between the brows, and identified with the Buddha Eye (buddha-cakṣus), the "third eye" of popular Buddhism. [88]

Fig. 59 : The head of the Buddha showing the ūrṇā or hairtuft in the forehead.

Fig. 60 : a. The Bodhisattva Bhṛkuti (Jap. Bikutei, "the Frown"), here shown in her benign aspect.
b. The Bodhisattva Tathāgata-orṇā (Jap. Nyorai Gōsō), who embodies the qualities of the Buddha's forehead hairtuft. He carries a shining hairtuft on a lotus.
c. The Bodhisattva Krodha-candra-tilaka (Jap. Gatten, "the Wrathful Moon Spot").

a b c

84. SPS I (Kern, 1884, pp. 20f.). 85. See above, pp. 55f.

86. SPS XI (Kern, 1884, pp. 231f.)

87. See e.g., (Okazaki, 1977, p. 107, & pls. 81-83 & 89.

88. Supposedly by analogy with the third eye of Śiva.

The qualities of the ūrṇā are personified in the Bodhisattva Tathāgataorṇā (Jap. Nyorai Gōsō Bosatsu) who is shown as a reflex of Śākyamuni Buddha in the Matrix Mandala of Shingon Buddhism,[89] where he appears carrying a lotus which supports an ūrṇā radiating flames of light.[90] Another hypostasis of the ūrṇā is the Bodhisattva Krodha-candra-tilaka (Jap. Funnugatten Bosatsu), who also appears in the Matrix Mandala as a reflex of Vajrasattva. The term "moon-spot" (candra-tilaka, Jap. gatten) in his name, which is literally "Wrathful Moon Spot", is the ūrṇā, the light from which burns away the hindrances of the passions. In this connection Śubhākarasiṃha says that "this Diamond-dweller is born from the hairtuft on the Buddha's brow, and this is the reason for his name; the radiance of the hairtuft is like that of a full moon and it is therefore called a 'moon spot'".[91] Analogous associations are implicit in the person of another Bodhisattva in the mandala, Bhṛkuti ("the Frown", Jap. Bikutei), who sprang forth in a form of extreme ferocity from the ūrṇā of Avalokiteśvara when that Bodhisattva frowned because the Bodhisattvas who embody Wisdom seemed about to destroy the whole world by the uncontrolled power of their analytical, and therefore disintegrative, Knowledge. In the myth the necessary equilibrium of Wisdom and Compassion - and an ordered world - is restored when the Bodhisattvas of Wisdom are overawed by the fearsome appearance of Bhṛkuti, who represents the power of the integrative aspect of Avalokiteśvara's Compassion.[92]

f. Noose and Net Symbolism in the Myth of Varuṇa.

The creation of the cosmos is the spreading out of a pneumatic net; the universe is ordered by the criss-cross of Spirit cords. The concept is hypostatized in the person of Varuṇa,[93] who is the master of māyā, of the artifice that produces cosmos[94]: "He bound together the hours of the day by artifice (māyā)";[95] and, as we have seen, māyā is measure.[96] Varuṇa's artifice is the measuring out of the worlds by his cord; he casts his net upon the surface of the Waters. His measuring is by the Sun, his Eye, wherewith he surveys the whole universe;[97] he is the god who, "keeping himself in Midspace, has measured out the Earth with the Sun as measure";[98] who "has made for the Sun a wide route which he is to follow",[99] and who "has separated the earth as a butcher separates a skin in order to spread it under the sun".[100] Hence, like the cosmocrators Brahmā and Viśvakarman, he has four faces, one of which "is like unto the face of Agni".[101] He measures out the seven dirèctions : "Thou art a great god, O Varuṇa; from thy mouth flow the seven rivers, as through a deep channel".[102] The seven rivers likewise flow from the mouth of the Serpent Vṛtra when made to gape by Indra's bolt,[103] and in this regard the symbolic meanings of Varuṇa and

---

89. See MKDJT, P. 1751, s.v., Nyorai Gōsō Bosatsu.

90. MKDJT, p. 519, s.v., Gōsō.

91. Śubhākarasiṃha, quoted in MKDJT, p. 1966, s.v., Funnu Gatten Bosatsu.

92. Śubhākarasiṃha, quoted in MKDJT, p. 1845, s.v., Bikutei Bosatsu.

93. See Eliade, 1952, pp. 95 ff.; 1958b, pp. 67 ff.; Dumézil 1934, *passim*; 1940, *passim*; Levi, 1898, pp. 153 ff.; Hopkins, 1920, pp. 116 ff.; Bergaigne, 1978, 3, pp. 114 ff.; Daniélou, 1964, pp. 118 ff.

94. RV VI.48.14; X.99.10. 95. RV VIII.41.3. 96. See above, p. 29.

97. RV I.164.44; cf. VII.61.1. 98. RV V.85.5; cf. above, p. 31.

99. RV I.24.8; cf. RV VII.87.1. 100. RV V.85.1; cf. Bergaigne, 1978, p. 123. 101. RV VII.88.2. 102. RV VII.58.12.

103. See above pp 64 f., below, pp. 184 & 313, etc.

Vr̥tra coalesce. Both names relate to the root vr̥, "to surround, to cover", or "to restrain, to check" : "He covers, or binds, all things and hence he is (called) Varuṇa (vr̥ + unan)".[104] The two names have reference to the Waters, and especially to the "contained Waters" : "The Great Varuṇa has hidden the sea..."[105] Indra smites the Serpent to release the Waters; so likewise he rescues the victims "bound" by Varuṇa and "unlooses" them.[106] Further, it is noteworthy, since the serpent (nāga) is closely associated with the Waters, that Varuṇa's noose is a snake.[107]

Fig. 61 : In Japanese Buddhist iconography Varuṇa, (Jap. Suiten) is shown seated on a turtle in the midst of the waters. He wears a nāga crown and holds a serpent-noose in the left hand.

He is the "thousand eyed" (sahasrāksa),[108] and oversees the actions of men, punishing with "bondage" those who infringe the universal Law laid down and defined by the pattern of his net.[109] He is "the binder" who envelops or imprisons the wicked in his toils; he is "the Lord who punishes; he is the king whose duty it is to punish".[110] His name reflects this function, deriving from the Indo-European root uer, "to bind", whence also derive words such as Sanskrit varatrā, "strap, cord".[111] The *Vedas* contain many petitions for release from Varuṇa's cord or net : "O deliver from their bonds those who are bound".[112] Similarly, the paired gods Mitrā-Varuṇau "have many bonds";[113] and the attribute is also that of the whole group of

---

104. *Uṇadī Sūtra* 3.53, in Daniélou, 1964, p. 120. On the etymological relationship of the two names see also Bergaigne, 1978, 3, pp. 115 ff.; Coomaraswamy, 1942, pp. 29 ff.; but cf. the alternative and now more widely accepted etymology given below. Even if, however, the name Varuṇa does not directly derive from the root vr̥, it relates to it.

105. RV IX.73.3. It is by way of this association that in later times Varuṇa becomes the God of the Waters, the giver of rain and the ruler of the Nāgas (e.g., in Mbh II.9), which role he plays in both Hinduism and Buddhism. See Daniélou, 1964, p. 119.

106. Dumézil, 1934, pp. 79 ff. 107. *Hayaśārṣa Pāñaratna*, quoted by Daniélou, 1964, p. 120. 108. AV IV.16.2-7,etc.; RV I.35.7ff.; VII.34.10.

109. Bergaigne, 1978, pp. 215 ff., discusses aspects of the Vedic concept of law; and see also Eliade, 1952, p. 97.

110. *Manu Smr̥ti* IX.245, quoted in Daniélou, 1964, p. 119.

111. See Eliade, 1952, p. 95; 1958a, p. 70; etc. Cf. n. 12 above.

112. AV VI.121.4; cf. RV I.24.15; VI.74.4; VII.65.3; X.85.24; etc.

113. RV VII.65.3.

Ādityas, who "have bonds prepared for the perfidious, for the deceiver".[114] This is the significance of the rope Varuṇa carries. It is the noose (pāśa), the snare, used to catch animals in the hunt and the "animals" Varuṇa hunts are unregenerate "living beings" (paśu) : the animal is caught in the snare and the living being is tied by the limiting conditions that bind him in his particular state of existence. To escape the snare is to escape those limitations, to be freed from the web of space, the toils of time, the bonds of selfhood, so that it is no longer true of him to say that "thinking 'I am he', 'This is mine', he binds himself with his self like a bird in a snare".[115]

The word pāśa is essentially "loop", but it is also "the eye of the needle", which is the Sun Door and "strait gate" through which the Worthies (arhat) escape from the cosmos.[116] To slip through the noose without being caught is to have passed unscathed through the jaws of Death.[117]

Varuṇa is not the only god who employs the noose to bind those who break the universal Law. In the same way that Varuṇa casts his net of measure upon the worlds so it is said of Indra also that Mid-space is his snare in which he traps his enemies;[118] and likewise it is said that he brought a "bond" for Vṛtra[119] and bound him without cords.[120] The bonds of Yama ("the Binder"), who is the "King of the Law" (dharma-rāja) and its very embodiment, are the bonds of Death.[121] "He who controls all beings without distinction is Yama, the binder", "who binds, who assesses the actions of living beings as fruitful or not fruitful",[122] who "as the restrainer of men is called Yama",[123] and who is the judge and punisher of the dead, called Death (mṛtyu), the End (antaka), Time (kāla), the Noose-Bearer (pāśin).

So also Nirrti binds those intended for destruction[124] and hymns are addressed to the gods, asking to be kept from "the bonds of Nirrti".[125] The noose held by the elephant headed god Ganeśa, the creator and remover of obstacles, is the means of restraining the recalcitrant and of leading the worthy.

g. Noose and Net Symbolism in Buddhism.

Buddhism provides parallels for these formulations. Laying a network of Breaths upon a "field" (kṣetra) or world is a common metaphor in the sutras. The *Amitāyur-dhyāna-sūtra* describes sixteen meditations on the Buddha Amitābha, which include meditations in which Amitābha's Pure Land, in the form of a mandala, is laid out on the ground of the mind. The first meditation is on the sun (the establishment of the centre); the next meditation is on water, which is visualized as changing to ice and then to lapis lazuli, transparent and shining, and supported by a golden banner extending to the eight points of the compass and completely filling the field. "Over the surface of the ground of lapis lazuli there are stretched golden ropes intertwined crosswise, and divided by strings of seven jewels ..."[126] The golden ropes that reticulate the Buddha Land are cords of breath, laid down upon the inward mind-field of the meditator by techniques

114. RV II.27.16. 115. MU III.2. 116. For the Sun Door, see below, pp. 268 ff.

117. Coomaraswamy, 1977, 2, pp. 308f., s.v. pāśa; Guénon, 1962, p.340.

118. RV VIII.8.5-8. 119. RV II.30.2. 120. RV II.13.9.

121. AV VI.96.2; VIII.7.28; VIII.2.2; etc. 122. Mbh XII.3446.

123. Mbh III.16813. 124. AV VI.63.1-2; TS V.2.4.3; ŚB VII.2.1.15.

125. AV I.31.2. 126. ADS 9-10 (Cowell, Muller and Takakusu, 1894, pp. 169-171).

of controlled respiration (prāṇayāma). The interior mandala is measured out, articulated spatially and temporally, by measured breathing. A common Far Eastern Buddhist painting, the Pure Land Mandala (Jap. Jōdo Mandara), which serves as a meditational support for the sixteen visualizations prescribed in the sutra, shows a ground divided by the golden gridlines. The same reticulated ground is a convention in mandalas of all Buddhist schools.[127]

* * * * *

Fig. 62 : The visualization of the reticulated ground of the Buddha Amitābha's Pure Land, one of the sixteen meditations described in the *Amitāyur-dhyāna-sūtra*.

Vairocana Tathāgata in the Matrix Mandala of Japanese Shingon Buddhism embodies Principle (理 , Ch. li, Jap. ri), the innate pattern of order that pervades and sustains the phenomenal world. The character stands for the markings on jade, the grain of a piece of bamboo, the fibres of a muscle or the threads of a fabric, that is, the network formed by the "inner Law" of things.[128] The Buddha Vairocana (Jap. Dainichi, "Great Sun"), in his aspect as the Body of Principle (Jap. rishin) embodies this concept of the net of order that pervades the world, and thus shares characteristics

Fig. 63 : A detail of the central section of the Matrix World Mandala showing the reticulated ground on which the 8-petal lotus is painted.

Fig. 64 : Mahāvairocana Tathāgata (Jap. Dainichi Nyorai) in the Matrix World Mandala, where he represents the Principle that sustains the universe.

126. ADS 9-10 (Cowell, Muller and Takakusu, 1894, pp. 169-171).

127. See e.g., the illustrations of the sixteen visualizations shown in BKDJT, pp. 2406-8, s.v. Jūrokukan.

128. Sze, 1957, pp. 30-31 & 101; cf. Cook, 1977, p. 128, n. 15.

with the Vedic Varuṇa, who similarly personifies the structuring Law inherent within the cosmos. Vairocana abides at the hub of the World Wheel, which is the receptacle and source of all order, locus of the Principle that governs phenomenal existences, the point that is coincident with cosmic and supra-cosmic Law.[129] This is also the abode of Varuṇa, so that the hymnists chant, "May we, O Varuṇa, win they nave of Law".[130] When the Vedic texts describe the procession of the (Brahman-) Yakṣa Varuṇa[131] as "a Great Yakṣa at the centre of the world, proceeding in a glowing (that is, as the Sun) on the back (that is, on the surface) of the ocean, wherein are set the deities, as it were branches round about the Tree's trunk",[132] they could be describing Mahā-vairocana at the centre of the Matrix Mandala.

* * * * *

The net is personified in the Bodhisattva Jālinīprabha, "Net of Splendour" (Jap. Kōmō Bosatsu), who represents the myriad qualities of the Wisdom of Mañjuśrī, which qualities form a net-like splendour of mutually reflecting lights, drawing beings towards Enlightenment. Her attribute is the noose of Wisdom or the net.[133] The symbolism is ambivalent and has a negative aspect, since the word jālinī also means the "ensnaring net of illusion" and "enchantress" and is used synonymously with tṛṣṇa, "thirst", the ultimate obstruction to Liberation.[134]

Fig. 65 : Some noose- and net- bearing divinities from the Buddhist pantheon : a. Jālinīprabha Bodhisattva ("Net of Splendour"), who carries a net in the right hand. b. Another form of Jālinīprabha, who carries a noose. c. Vajrapāśa Bodhisattva, ("Diamond Noose"), who also carries a noose. d. Acalanatha Vidyarāja (Jap. Fudō Myō-ō), "Immovable", who holds the Sword of Wisdom in the right hand and a noose in the left.

The noose (pāśa) is the attribute of other Buddhist divinities, most notably the wrathful figure of Acalanatha (Jap. Fudō Myō-ō, "the Dhāraṇī-King, Immovable"), who embodies the Wisdom that cuts away the passions and the erroneous forms of knowledge that impede the attainment of Enlightenment. He holds the sword of Wisdom in the right hand, with which he severs these hindrances, and in his left he holds the "binding rope" (Jap. baka no nawa) with which he hobbles the demons of obstruction and draws in beings towards Liberation.[135]

* * * * *

---

129. MKDJT, p. 1937, s.v., Busshin. 130. RV II.28.5.

131. Yakṣa is equated with Varuṇa in RV VII.88.6 and X.88.3.

132. AV X.7.38; cf. RV X.82.6. 133. MKDJT, p. 545, s.v., Kōmō Bosatsu.

134. See Edgerton, 1970, s.v., Jālinī.

135. See MKDJT, 1955, s.v. Fudō Myō-ō; BKDJT, p. 4486, s.v., Fudō Myō-ō; Getty, 1962, p. 35; Saunders, 1960, pp. 172 f., s.v., Kensaku ("Noose"), and p. 182.

The Hua-Yen (Jap. Kegon) sect of Buddhism uses this metaphor of Indra's Net to elucidate the concept of the identity and mutual intercausality of all phenomena. In Indra's Heaven there hangs a wondrous net with a jewel set at each of its "eyes" or crossings in such a way that each of these innumerable gems reflects all the others and is in turn reflected in each of them. The whole is mirrored in the part and the part is mirrored in every portion of the whole, so as to form an immeasurable radiance of mutual reflection.[136] The phenomena of the world interrelate in an analogous manner. Their static relationship is one of mutual identity,[137] and their dynamic relationship is one of mutual intercausality (pratītya-samutpāda).[138]

In terms of the cosmogonic model described earlier, the Centre (A) is reflected in each and every point on each and every one of the surfaces of the spheres that surround it; and any one of these points could be taken as the point that centres all the others. This gives the image of a space indefinitely extended in all directions and "packed" with contiguous points, each the centre of a series of contiguous and concentric spheres. If the point A in the model is taken as the Centre and B is its reflection on the plane of the earth, it is apparent that the latter can equally well be taken as the centre of a series of spheres in the same manner as A, and so similarly for all the points (C,D,E, etc.,) on the surface of the sphere on which it lies, and for the points ($B^1,B^2,B^3...; C^1,C^2,C^3...$ etc.,) which correspond to them on the surfaces of the other spheres. The points are mutually reflecting and the spheres they centre are interpenetrating and interfused.

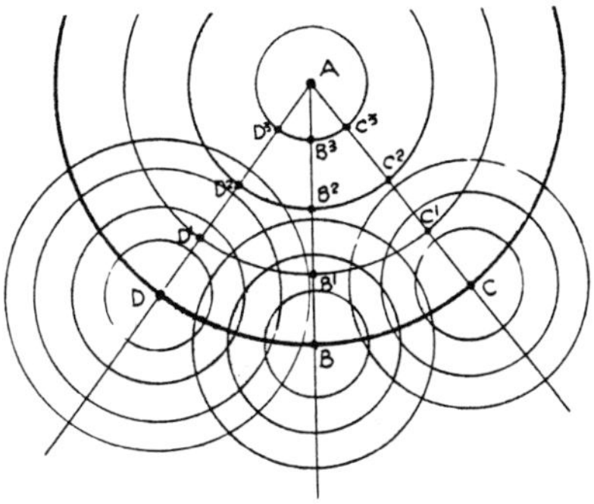

Fig. 66 : The mutual reflection of centres and interpenetration of spheres in the cosmos.

A circumference cannot exist without a centre; remove the centre and the circumference ceases to exist. To remove any one of the points in the exemplary model is to render non-existent all the spheres that surround it; all the points are dependent on each one among them.

This total interdependence of the whole and the parts gives a model of the Hua-Yen doctrine concerning the operation of causation. The parts of the cosmic whole, and the whole and its parts, are bound together by causal interdependence (pratītya-samutpāda). Each phenomenal entity (dharma) is the cause (hetu) for the totality of other phenomenal entities; the totality of phenomena depends upon and is supported by each single phenomenon; and the whole is the cause of the single entity. Each entity is the cause of the whole and is caused by the whole: this is the Hua-Yen concept of the dharma-dhātu, a universe of mutually interpenetrating parts,

136. Cook, 1977, p. 2. 137. 相卽, Ch. hsiang chi, Jap. sōsoku.

138. 相由, Ch. hsiang yu, Jap. sōyu.

connected together in an indissoluble non-duality (advaita) by causal interdependence. The dharma-dhātu, the universe, "arises" by interdependent causation; phenomenal entities have no self-essence (svabhāva) other than in this interdependence; they have no independent existence and derive wholly from interdependent causation; and in this is their Emptiness (śūnyatā). All entities of the cosmos interpenetrate unobstructedly[139] in their mutual dependence, and thus constitute the dharma-dhātu-kāya, the Body of the Buddha, synonymous with the tathāgata-garbha.

The tathāgata-garbha doctrine posits "a conjunctively whole universe, correctly seen as the mutual identity and interdependence of all the disjunctively separate objects that constitute it, this totality being none other than the One Mind and the One Body of the Buddha. This is the identity of phenomena with phenomena. The dharma-dhātu Buddha is totally present not only in human beings but in ants, grass and dirt. This is Mind Only, or the One Mind, the mutual identity and interdependence of all phenomena. It is the reality that is dharma-kāya, and it is tathāgata-garbha to the extent that all phenomena without exception participates in this fundamental reality".[140]

5. THE MANDALA EXPRESSED IN THE STUPA.

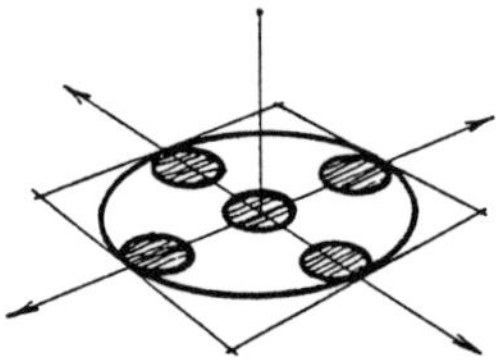

a. The Stupa Plan as Mandala.

The oriented plan of the stupa is a mandala. The orientation and crossed axes of the stupa plan proclaim the presence of the mandala. The ritual of laying out a stupa plan is the same as that for setting up a mandala. The mandala-plan is a prefiguration of the symbolic content that

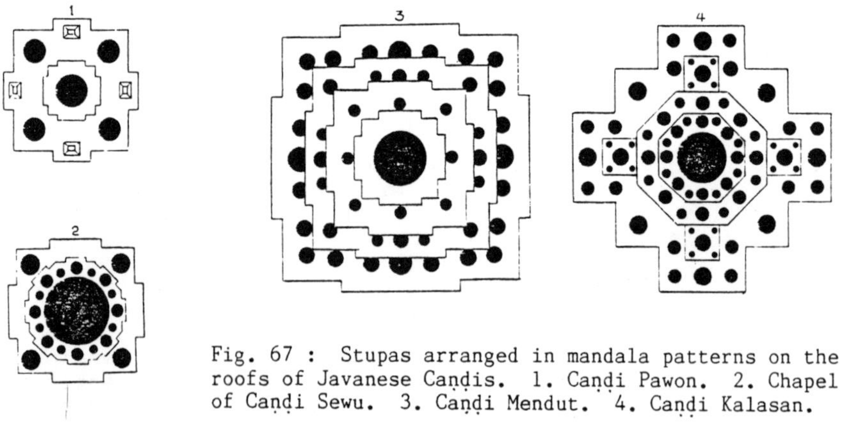

Fig. 67 : Stupas arranged in mandala patterns on the roofs of Javanese Caṇḍis. 1. Caṇḍi Pawon. 2. Chapel of Caṇḍi Sewu. 3. Caṇḍi Mendut. 4. Caṇḍi Kalasan.

---

139. 事事無礙 , Ch. shih shih wu ngai, Jap. jijimuge. See Cook, 1977, p. 36; cf. BKDJT, p. 1617, s.v. Jijimuge hokkai.

140. Cook, 1977, p. 52.

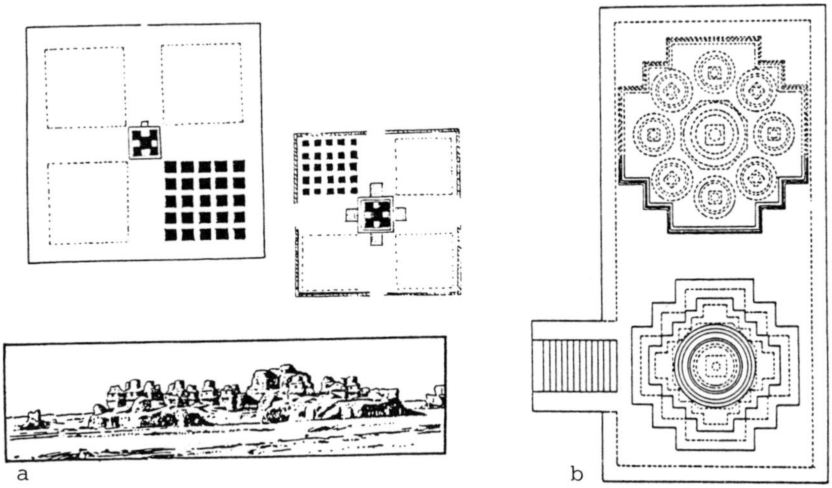

Fig. 68 : Stupas arranged to form mandalas. a. Stupas in groups of 25 arranged in the diagonal directions around a central group of 5 stupas at Chotscho, Sin-kiang, Turfan. b. Plan of stupas on Caṇḍi Bungsu, Muara Takus, Sumatra.

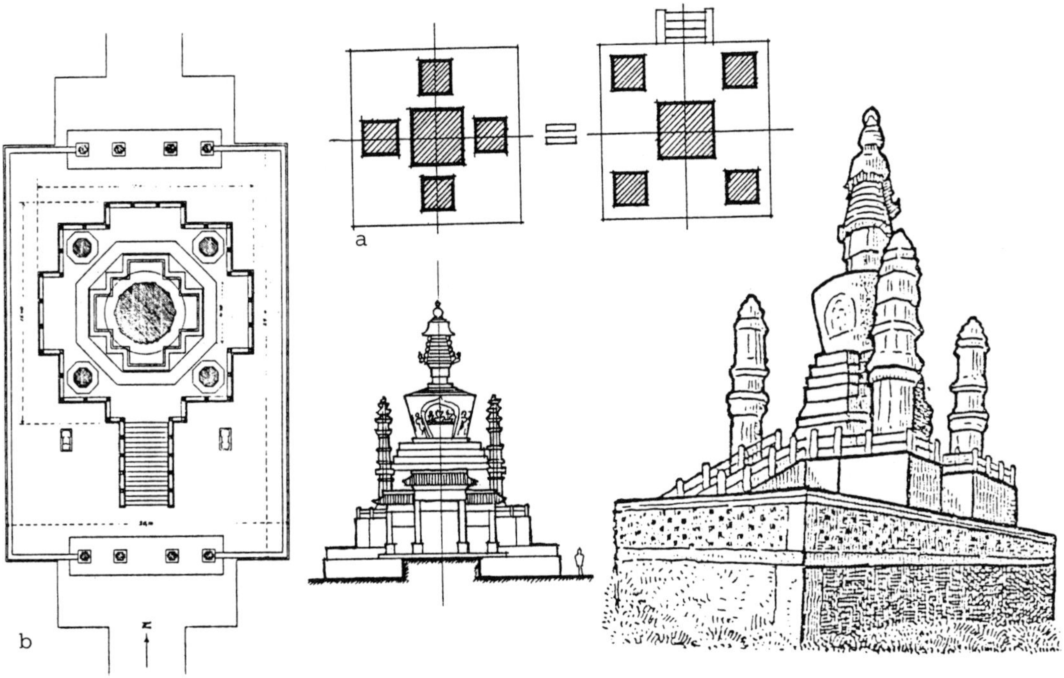

Fig. 69 : Stupas with ancillary towers arranged to form mandalas. In each case the five towers represent Mt. Meru and the four lesser mountains that surround it in the four directions of space. To allow for access stairs and entry along axes in the cardinal directions the ancillary towers are moved to the intermediate directions, but this does not affect the symbolism of the mandala. a. Plans with towers in the cardinal and the intermediate directions. The two mandala forms are symbolically equivalent. b. A lamaist stupa in Peking, China.

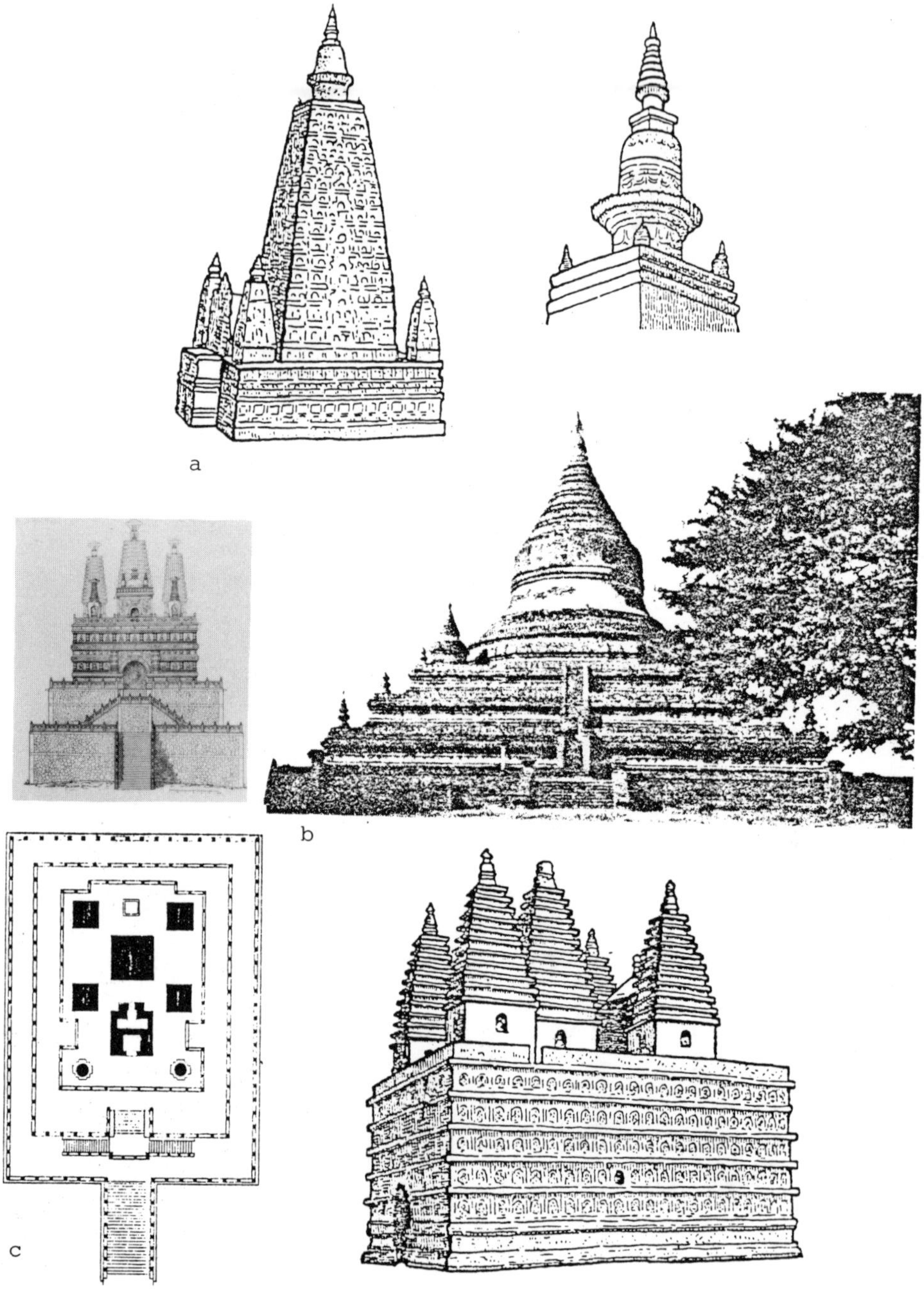

Fig. 70 : Stupas with towers arranged to form mandalas. a. The Mahābodhi stupa at Bodhgayā, India. This is the prototypic tower-stupa having ancillary towers in the four directions to form a mandala. The formula is repeated at the summit of the tower. b. The Mingalazedi stupa, Pagan, Burma. There is a large and a small stupa in each of the four corners of the uppermost terrace and a small stupa in the corners of each of the lower terraces. c. The Wu t'a sze stupa, China. d. Plan and elevation of a Chinese lamaist stupa.

is to be embodied in the structure. Just as its square masonry base is its physical foundation so the mandala marked upon the ground is the stupa's metaphysical foundation, a prognostic program or forecast of what the building as a whole will signify; it is a preliminary abstract of the stupa's essential meanings. The stupa pile is a three-dimensional development of the metaphysical meanings contained as potentialities within the mandala.

Single stupas are laid out as mandalas and groups also are arranged in mandala patterns. In Central Asia, Tibet, Burma and China are to be found groups of five stupas, one central and the others disposed in the four directions, and Central Asia shows an arrangement in which this five-fold stupa is accompanied by four groups of 25 tower-like stupas.

b. The Mandala Within the Stupa.

The mandala does not belong exclusively to the Tantric sects of Buddhism but is also explicitly present in the stupas of the Hīnayāna and in those of the non-Tantric schools of the Mahāyāna. Giving an example of a mandala set up within a Hīnayāna stupa, the *Mahāvaṃsa* relates how King Duṭṭagāmani placed within the relic chamber of the Great Stupa of Sri Lanka an image of the Buddha seated beneath a Bodhi Tree of gold and silver and set with precious stones.[141] To this were added seven other Buddha images, "facing the other seven regions of the heavens", and images of Brahmā, Indra and the other gods.[142] The group, surrounded by a balustrade enriched with gems, is laid out in a classic mandala form, with the Tree at the centre surrounded by Buddhas in the eight directions.

The deposit boxes that are placed at the level of the foundation stone in many stupas often have the form and function of a mandala. The type is represented by the yantragala of Sri Lankan stupas, a square stone slab containing 9, 17 or 25 square holes arranged in 3, 4 or 5 rows. These "can be seen at almost any ancient site in Ceylon".[143] The holes contained images of the dikpālas, the guardians of the ten regions of space (the cardinals, the ordinals, the zenith and the nadir), the animals of the four directions (the bull, the lion, the horse and the elephant),[144] and images of the Hindu divinities connected with the directions of space and with the cycles of time. The mandala formed in this way was often centred by a representation of Mt. Meru.[145]

The concept of the mandala is alternately conveyed in some Sri Lankan and many Nepalese stupas by a small room of stone built at the centre of

141. The Tree is the axis mundi (see below, pp. 180 ff) and the cognate of the Cosmic Mountain (see n. 144 below). 142. *Mahāvaṃsa* XXX.72.

143. Paranavitana, 1946, p. 23; see also O'Connor, 1966, p. 57; cf. Gail, 1980. p. 263.

144. For these animals of the four directions see above, pp. 70 ff. Arranged in the manner described, the four animals have been found within stupas in other places. See O'Connor, 1966, p. 54.

145. Paranavitana, 1946, pp. 20-23; O'Connor, 1966, p. 57; cf. Gail, 1980, p. 263; Marshall, 1918a, pp. 40f. & 45f. In some cases a Bodhi Tree replaces the Meru. The *Mayamata* XII.60, speaking of the foundation deposit of Buddhist buildings, says, "The foundation of a Sugata (=Buddhist) sanctuary includes an aśvattha (= Bodhi Tree), a vase, a lion, and a golden umbrella. The aśvattha must be in front, the umbrella behind it, the vase to the left and the lion to the right". (Dagens, 1970, p. 6). The arrangement is that of a mandala.

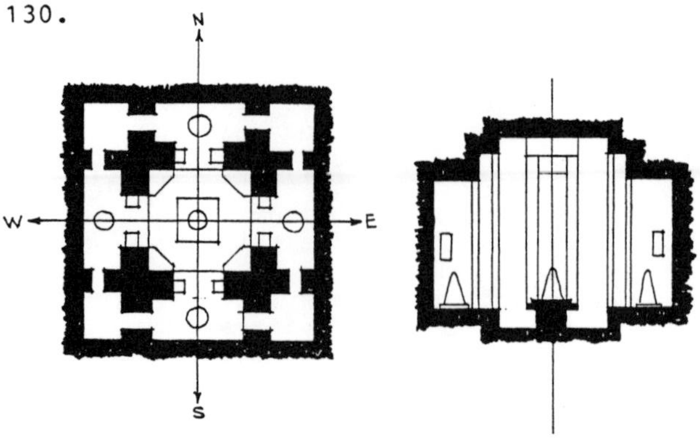

Fig. 71 : Plan and section of the relic chamber of the Kiri-Vehera stupa, Polonnāruwa, Sri Lanka, laid out as a mandala with a Mt. Meru in each of the four cardinal directions and at the centre.

Fig. 72 : Foundation stone of the Asuka Dera, Nāra, Japan. It has a square cavity at the centre to receive the foundation deposit; from this cavity grooves run in the N-S and E-W directions; and a third groove runs from a position slightly West of South to one slightly East of North to indicate the Gates of the Forefathers and the Gods respectively.

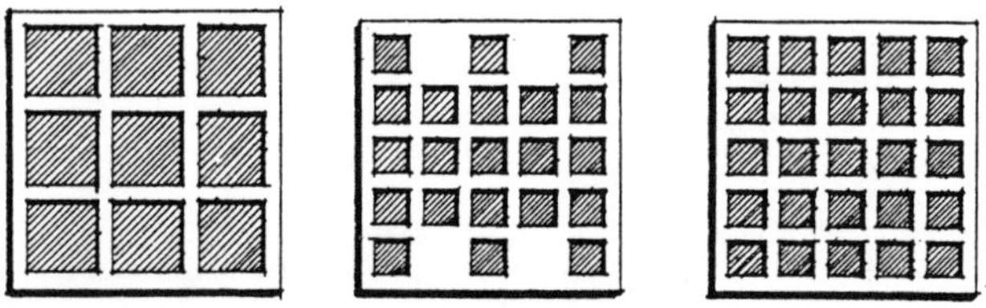

Fig. 73 : The mandalas formed by the yantragalas of Sri Lankan stupas. They characteristically show 9, 17 or 25 squares.

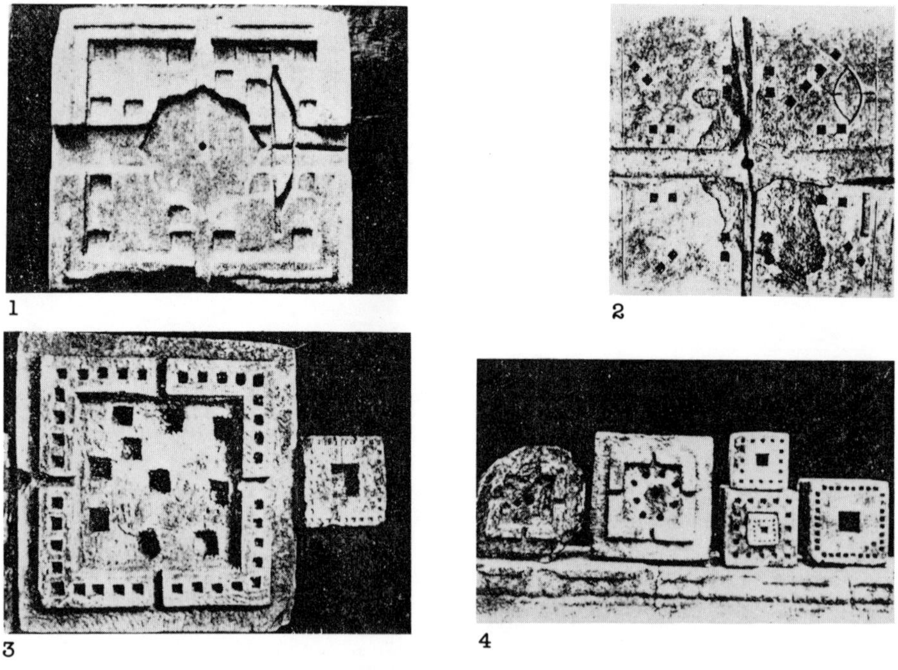

Fig. 74 : Deposit stones from Angkor. 1 and 2 are deposit stones from the summit of the tower, and 3 and 4 show the upper and lower deposit stones to left and right respectively.

the garbha, divided into a central space surrounded by eight compartments in the directions. In the Nepalese stupas each of these spaces contained a so-called dharmakāya ("Dharma Body") verse, symbolizing some aspect of the Ādi Buddha.[146]

The yantragala of the Sri Lankan stupa is a particular case of the foundation stone (ādhāraśilā) that is laid down at the centre of the plan of Hindu and Buddhist buildings.[147] It takes the form of a stone slab or box divided into compartments or recesses, one located at the centre and 8, 16, 24 or 32 others surrounding it in the directions. In these are placed precious stones, metal discs, seed syllables or other objects identified with the divinities of the directions.[148] In some cases the stone takes the form of a lotus, with seed syllables carved on its petals.[149]

Another type of foundation stone is divided into four equal sections by two grooves running in the cardinal directions and forming a right angle cross. This type of stone often shows supplementary cavities or a secondary groove indicating the North-East.[150] The symbolic significance of this is explained by the considerations developed in the following in connection with the Sun Gate leading out of the cosmos, which is located in the North-East. This form of foundation stone is found in locations as far apart as Kampuchea[151] and Japan, where it is found in many ancient stupas such as those at Asuka-dera.[152]

c. The Stupa as a Mandala of the *Manuṣi* Buddhas.

Every stupa embodies a mandala. In some its presence is outwardly expressed by those elements, such as gates or stairways, which indicate a cross-form arrangement of the axes; in others it is made apparent by images of Buddhas or other divinities located in the four directions. Of this type are the early Hīnayāna stupas showing the four Manuṣi Buddhas in niches attached to the surface of the dome or to the base.[153]

The Manuṣi Buddhas are the Buddhas of the present aeon. According to both the Hīnayāna and Mahāyāna teachings Śākyamuni was not the only Buddha to appear in the present kalpa, but was preceded by the Buddhas Krakucchanda, Kanakamuni and Kāśyapa, thus forming part of a group of four Buddhas of this world era. This group is frequently enlarged to a quinary by the addition of Maitreya, the Buddha who is yet to come, and there are also frequent textual references and representations of seven, and occas-

---

146. Descriptions of the Nepalese examples are given in Toganoo, 1971, p. 466; Oldfield, 1880, pp. 210 ff.; Hodgson, 1874, p. 30. The Sri Lankan examples are mentioned in Paranavitana, 1946, p. 23.

147. On the ādhāraśilā in the Hindu temple, see Kramrisch, 1946, p. 127 and esp. n. 91. For the ādhāraśilā in the temples at Angkor, see Coedes, 1935, pp. 43-47; in Malaya, see O'Connor, 1966; Lamb, 1960, p. 74. On deposit boxes and stones in S.E.Asia and Angkor, see Coedes, 1935; Boisselier, 1963, p. 133; Parmentier, 1906, pp. 291-295; 1918, 2, p. 414; 1909, p. 350; Finot, 1903, pp. 63-70; 1935, pp. 283f.; Lunet de Lajonquière, 1902, p. 313.

148. Wales, 1977, p. 116; O'Connor, 1966, pp. 54 & 57; Lamb, 1960, pp. 71-81.

149. Coedes, 1952, *passim;* O'Connor, 1966, p. 59; Wales, 1977, pp.115f.

150. See below, p. 272. Cf. Coedes, 1940, p. 332.

151. See Coedes, 1940, p. 332.

152. Kidder, 1972, p. 89; *Sekai Bijutsu Zenshu*, 1962, pp. 147 f.

153. Wales, 1977, p. 60.

ionally eight, Buddhas of the past. Each of these Buddhas, whether he belongs to a group of four, five, seven or eight, commemorates the beginning of a world age.[154]

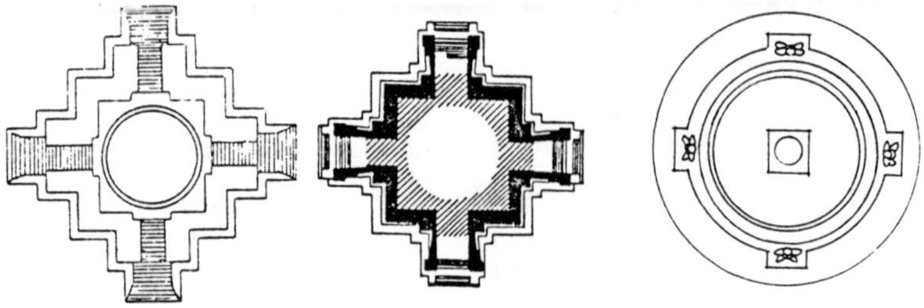

Fig. 75 : Plans of stupas having stairways or Buddha images in the four directions.

Each of the Manuṣi Buddhas is associated with a direction of space. The correspondence is usually given as Krakucchanda at the centre, Kanakamuni to the East, Kāśyapa to the South, Śākyamuni to the West, and the future Buddha, Maitreya, to the North.[155] But on the stupa another schema of correspondences operates : Maitreya, who is distinguishable by his Bodhisattva garb, is concealed at the centre, and the first of the terrestrial Buddhas, Krakucchanda, is moved to the North.

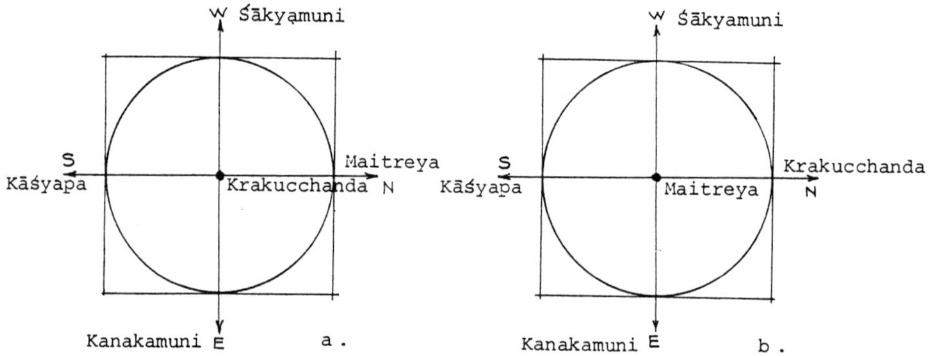

Fig. 76 : The five Manuṣi Buddhas and the directions of space. a. The usual correspondence of the five Manuṣi Buddhas and the directions. b. The location of the five Manuṣi Buddhas in the stupa.

Arranged in this manner, the Manuṣi Buddhas appear on stupas in many parts of Asia. They are present among the sculptures at Sāñcī.[156] The celebrated Nanda temple in Burma enshrines statues of the four Manuṣi Buddhas in the four directions, and the later three-tiered stupa-temples of Burma often have a central Buddha image at the second storey and the four Manuṣi Buddhas in chapels at the cardinal points of the storey below.

154. Bénisti, 1971, pp. 149 f.

155. Mus, 1935, p. 75, and cf. p. 435; Waddell, 1895, pp. 305 f.; Soekmono, 1976, pp. 8 f.; Getty, 1962, p. 28.

156. Marshall, 1918, pp. 35 & 77.

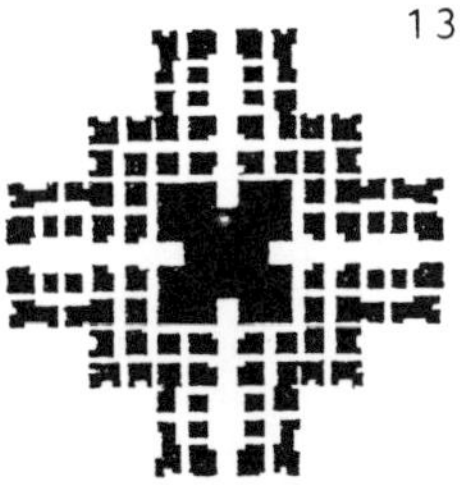

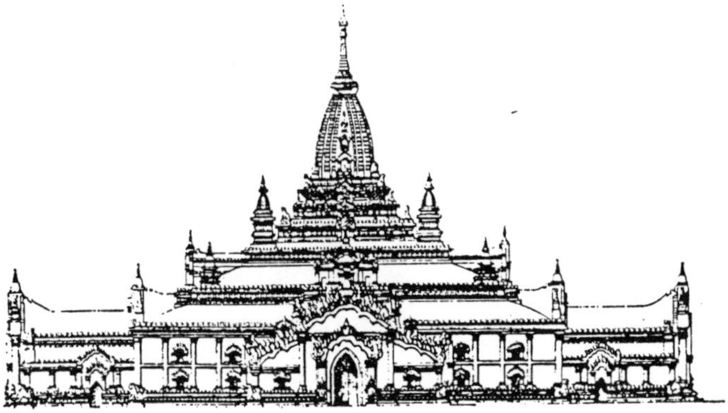

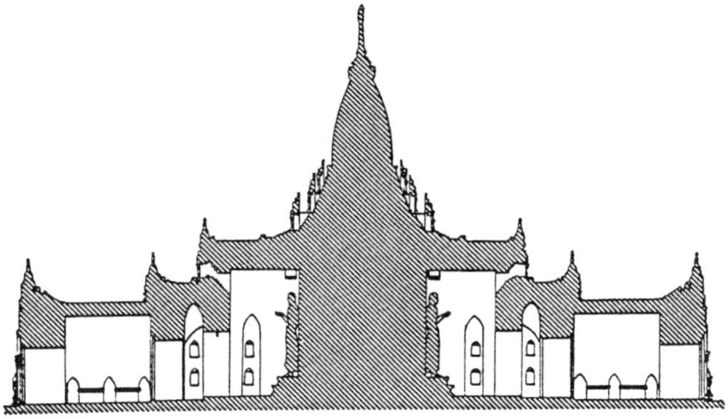

a

b

c

d

c

Fig. 77 : Examples of stupas with Manuṣi Buddhas in the four directions. a. The Ānanda Temple, Burma, which enshrines the Manuṣi Buddhas in niches on four sides of a central mass. b. A Manuṣi Buddha stupa from Nepal. c. A Manuṣi Buddha stupa from Nālandā, India. d. The Shwe Dagon, Burma, which contains relics of the Manuṣi Buddhas. e. A Manuṣi Buddha reliquary.

The Shwe Dagon in Rangoon is said to contain relics of the Manuṣi Buddhas, buried within the building in the four directions.[157] The arrangement is found in Sri Lanka (notably in the Wat-da-ge) and in Nepal, where legend says that Aśoka established the prototype for the form by building four stupas in the four directions to commemorate the four ages of the world.[158] The formula recurs in Thailand, Laos and Kampuchea.[159]

With the Manuṣi Buddhas arranged in the four directions of the stupa we once again encounter a familiar theme. By way of their presence the stupa marries the directions of space with the divisions of time. The Buddhas of the present kalpa, each presiding over an age of the world, also rules an orient. The two coordinates of our physical cosmos, space and time, are captured in the conformation of the structure : time is crystallized in a spatial figuration.

d. The Stupa as a Mandala of the Regents of the Quarters.

The mandala form is also overtly expressed in the stupa by the presence of images of the four Regents of the Quarters (lokapāla).[160] The regent-gods of the four directions, called the "Four Kings" - Dhṛtarāṣṭra in the East, Virūḍhaka in the South, Virūpākṣa in the West and Vaiśravaṇa (or Kuvera) in the North - are guardian deities, whose function it is to protect

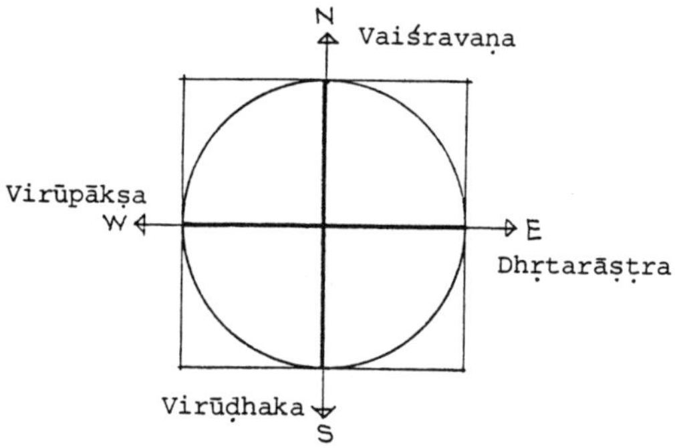

Fig. 78 : The Regents of the Directions: Virūḍhaka (top left), Vaiśravana (top right), Dhṛtarāṣṭra (bottom left) and Virūpākṣa (bottom right). Above is the mandala of the Regents of the Directions

157. Shorto, 1971, p. 79. 158. Combaz, 1935, p. 90.

159. Bénisti, 1971, pp. 149 f.

160. For the Lokapālas, see Sawa, 1971, pp. 130 ff.; BKDJT, 1958, s.v., Shitennō; Getty, 1962, pp. 166 ff.; Combaz, 1933, pp. 142 f.

the Dharma and, more specifically, to protect the borders of the mandala, preventing the entry of disruptive or demonic forces into its sacred area. Shown as warriors dressed in armour they are frequent in bas-reliefs at the base of stupas in Central Asia, China, Japan and Tibet. Sometimes they are shown alone, and sometimes paired with the Buddhas of the cardinal directions. Occasionally they decorate the base of the stupa while the Buddhas are shown at a higher level.[161]

e. The Stupa as a Mandala of the *Jina* Buddhas.

The stupas built by the Vajrayāna schools of Buddhism are explicitly identified with the mandala. Such is the case with the Ādi-Buddha stupas of Nepal and Tibet, the "mountain stupas" of Burma and Thailand, some of the stupas of the Esoteric Buddhist (mikkyō) sects of Japan and China, and first and foremost among them all, the great Javanese stupa of Borobudur. These are all stupas built by the Tantric sects, for whom the mandala occupies a position of prime importance in both their doctrine and their practice.

These stupas are solid mandalas. They embody the mandala of the five Buddhas of Victory (jina-buddha), each of whom rules over a direction : Vairocana, "the Sun" or "the Brilliant", is at the centre, (which is called "the undecaying condition", askaram padam);[162] Akṣobhya, "the Unshakable", is in the East; Ratnasambhava, "Jewel Birth", is in the South; Amitābha, "Infinite Light", is in the West; and Amoghasiddhi, "Attainment that is not Void", is in the North.[163]

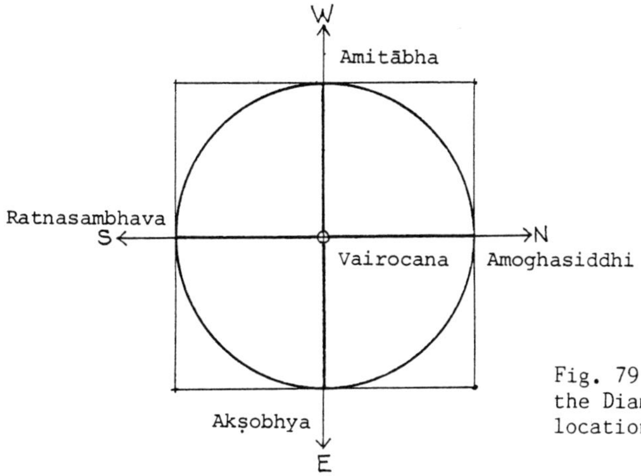

Fig. 79 : The five Jina Buddhas of the Diamond World Mandala and their locations in the directions of space.

Stupas with the five Jina Buddhas are expressions of the Diamond World Mandala (vajra-dhātu-maṇḍala), a mandala depicting the world of multiplicity and division as it abides eternally in non-dual syzygy with indivisible and adamantine Suchness (tathatā). It is a mandala of the cosmos as perceived through the Buddha's Wisdom Eye; it is the world seen in the light of the Total Knowledge that accrues with perfect Enlightenment.

---

161. Combaz, 1933, pp. 142 f.; 1935, p. 90.

162. *Guhyasamāja* 90, translated by Tucci, 1961, p. 49.

163. The five Buddhas are erroneously called Dhyāni Buddhas by early scholars. Despite criticism of the usage by orientalists of the stature of Conze (see e.g., 1975, pp. 174 f.) it still sometimes recurs.

Fig. 80 : The Diamond World Mandala, which is a mandala of the five Jina Buddhas and their attendant Bodhisattvas in the five directions of space. See also fig. 85 on p. 144.

According to Advayavajra, at one level of correspondences the five Jina Buddhas are transcendent personifications of the five constituent "aggregates" (skandha) that make up the individual being.[164] Vairocana is the personification of form (rūpa), Amoghasiddhi is that of volition (saṃskāra), Amitābha is discernment (saṃjñā), Ratnasambhava is sensation (vedanā), and Akṣobhya corresponds to consciousness (vijñāna). This identification is an expression of the doctrine of the non-duality of

164. See Mus, 1935, p. 439; Tucci, 1961, p. 52; Toganoo, 1932, pp. 453 & 454; Snellgrove, 1971, pp. 38 f. & 70-75; Bhattacharyya, 1958, pp. 2 & 47; Bénisti, 1971, p. 153; Dasgupta, 1958, pp. 84 f.

nirvāṇa and *saṃsāra*. In the non-Tantric schools of Buddhism the individual is analyzed into the five constituent *skandhas* in order to show its lack of permanency : the being is nothing other than the aggregates, or "heaps", that come together in patterns that are momentarily changing,[165] and therefore, it is taught, Reality lies solely in the transcendent Buddha realms, in the domain of *nirvāṇa*. In the esoteric doctrine of the Vajrayāna, however, the world of ever-changing phenomena and the Buddha's world of adamantine immutability are non-dual : the world-body formed by the ephemeral *skandhas*, coming together in fleeting conjunctions, constitutes the Diamond-Body of the Tathāgata. Each of the *skandhas*, just as it is, in all its evanescent transience, is an aspect of perfect and transcendent Enlightenment. Taken solely as they pertain to *saṃsāra*, the *skandhas* are lacking in self-nature; but as they pertain to Knowledge they are the immutable essences of all beings, the very Self-Nature of the Buddha.

In the light of the Vajrayāna doctrine of non-duality there is no contradiction in identifying the five Buddhas with the five *skandhas*. The Buddhas comprize the two-fold aspect of the *skandhas*, on the one hand their mundane and temporary aspect, which pertains to change, and on the other their supra-mundane and eternal aspect, which pertains to transcendent Buddha Knowledge.

A complementary interpretation, postulated in the Shingon school of Japanese Buddhism, identifies the Buddhas with five forms of consciousness that constitute the total consciousness of the individual being. According to this doctrine the five types of consciousness are so many forms of the Buddha's Knowledge.[166] What is seen as a faculty of consciousness by the unenlightened is, in the eyes of the Awakened, nothing other than a form of Total and Perfect Knowledge.

The five *Jina* Buddhas are thus simultaneously identified with forms of consciousness and with aspects of Total Knowledge. With the attainment of Enlightenment the five types of consciousness (or nine types, if the single consciousness of sense is counted as five, dividing it to give one for each of the five senses) are transformed, not in that their nature is

---

165. All Buddhist schools subscribe to the teaching that the personality is an aggregate of five constituent parts (*skandha*, lit. "heap"), which are continually changing. There is no permanent entity that underlies this flux. The person is only a body, which is the physical support, or "form" (*rūpa*) compounded of the five Elements, Earth, Water, Fire, Air and Space; and a psyche, comprizing the sensations (*vedanā*) whereby he perceives the world, the power of discernment (*saṃjñā*), whereby things are differentiated or discriminated, volition (*saṃskāra*), which is the force or coefficient of *karma*, and, finally, consciousness (*vijñāna*). For the five aggregates, see Soothill and Hodous, 1934, p. 126a, s.v., 五蘊 JEBD, p. 91a, s.v., *Goun*; BKDJT, p. 1094, s.v., *Goun*; Tucci, 1961, p. 52; Sangharakshita, 1957, pp. 177 ff.

166. See MKDJT, p. 663, s.v., *Gobutsu*; p. 620, s.v., *Gochi*; p. 1171, s.v., *Jōjinne*; BKDJT, p. 1283, s.v., *Gobutsu*; p. 1246, s.v., *Gochi*; and under the heads of each of the five Buddhas in both works. See also Toganoo, 1932, pp. 210 ff.; Tajima, 1959; *passim*. B.L. Suzuki, 1936, incorrectly correlates the five types of Knowledge with the five Buddhas of the Matrix World, rather than with those of the Diamond World.

in any way changed but in that they are now seen as inseparable from the Buddha's Wisdom.[167]

Fig. 86 : the five Jina Buddhas (Tibetan). From the left : Ratnasambhava, Amitābha, Vairocana, Akṣobhya and Amoghasiddhi. Each is recognizable by his distinctive hand gesture (mudrā).

The correlations of the five Buddhas, the directions, the types of consciousness[168] and the aspects of Knowledge are shown in the following diagram : -

	Direction	Consciousness	Knowledge
Vairocana	Centre or Zenith	Undefiled Consciousness	Knowledge of the Essential Nature of the Dharma World
Akṣobhya	East	Storehouse Consciousness	Mirror Knowledge
Ratnasambhava	South	Mind Consciousness	Knowledge of the Identity of Essences
Amitābha	West	Thought Consciousness	Knowledge of Wondrous Perception
Amoghasiddhi	North	Sense Consciousness: Sight Hearing Smell Taste Touch	Knowledge of the Perfection of Action

167. The term "Mind King" (Jap. shinnō) is used of both the faculties of consciousness and the Buddhas with whom they are identified. The doctrine relates to that of the buddhindriyas outlined above. The Mind Kings rule over the faculties of consciousness - and indeed are those faculties - just as Indra rules over the faculties (indriya), which are his own.

168. The nine types of Consciousness (vijñāna, Jap. shiki) are : 1-5. The five types of Consciousness relating to the senses, those of sight, hearing, smell, taste and touch. 6. The Thought Consciousness (manovijñāna, Jap. i-shiki), which broadly corresponds to the conscious mind. 7. The Mind Consciousness (kliṣṭamanas, Jap. manashiki). Whereas Thought Consciousness ceases to function in five special conditions (those of deep sleep, the death agony, in forms of meditation that are free of thought, in the Heavens that are free from thought, and in meditations that destroy

The identification of the five Buddhas with the five skandhas, the five types of consciousness and the five types of Knowledge does not exhaust their significance. Their correspondences are manifold and highly complex.[169] They are correlated with the five Elements, the five senses, the five parts of the body, five colours, five shapes, the five cakras, five meditations, and so on, in a long list. For each of these correspondences the same principle applies that we have seen to operate for the skandhas : the constituents of the cosmos (microcosmos as well as macrocosmos) are non-dual with adamantine Enlightenment; they are so many aspects of Suchness (tathatā); each component of the cosmos is a Buddha. The

---

illusion), the Mind Consciousness operates unceasingly at all times and under all conditions. It is the root of all delusion. 8. The Storehouse Consciousness (ālaya-vijñāna, Jap. ariya-shiki), which, in the Tantric schools of Japanese Buddhism, is an aspect of Suchness. Acted upon by ignorance, it produces the phenomenal world. It combines the mutable and the immutable, the fleeting and the eternal, that is to say, Consciousness as it relates to phenomena and to the Suchness of phenomena. It is the Consciousness in which the true and the false are perfectly fused, and while all phenomenal existences arise from it, it is nevertheless inseparable from Suchness. 9. The Undefiled Consciousness (amala-vijñāna, Jap. amarashiki). The Storehouse Consciousness is considered to be imbued with falsity since it is the source of impermanent phenomena. This Consciousness lies beyond the Storehouse Consciousness in the pure and undefiled realm of Suchness. The five types of Knowledge (pañca-jñāna, Jap. gochi) are : 1. The Knowledge of the Essential Nature of the Dharma World (dharmadhātu-svabhāva-jñāna, Jap. hokkai taishō chi), which is the supreme and absolute Knowledge that penetrates every element of the entire cosmos and is totally identified with the Dharma World. It transcends all dichotomies and abides in non-duality. 2. The Great Round Mirror Knowledge (adārśa-jñāna, Jap. dai en kyō chi). Just as a mirror reflects everything impartially and is unchanged by what it reflects, so this Knowledge receives the impressions of all phenomenal entities while itself remaining immutable. In this way everything in the universe is reflected in the Mind of the Buddha, and this constitutes one aspect of his Knowledge. 3. The Knowledge of the Identity of Essences (samata-jñāna, Jap. byōdō shō chi). This is the Knowledge of all things in their fundamental nature. It is the Knowledge that perceives the oneness of all things and the essential identity of self and other-than-self and thus gives rise to an equal and impartial Compassion for all things. 4. The Knowledge of Wondrous Perception (pratyavekṣana-jñāna, Jap. myōkan zatchi). This is the faculty of spiritual discernment whereby the Buddha perceives the elements of the phenomenal world in detail and analyzes the spiritual receptivity of all sentient beings in order to establish levels in the profundity of his preaching that accord with their level of understanding. 5. The Knowledge of the Perfection of Action (kṛtyānu-sthāna-jñāna, Jap. jō shō sa chi), which is the Knowledge that perfects, or produces actions for the spiritual welfare of beings. It is the Knowledge of what is necessary to effect the Liberation of every being. By this Knowledge a Buddha transforms himself into various forms adapted to the comprehension of the many levels of understanding. See MKDJT, p. 620, and BKDJT, p. 1246, s.v., Gochi.

169. See e.g., the table of correspondences in Dasgupta, 1958, p. 57, and cf. ibid., p. 86 for references.

universe in its integral cohesion is Vairocana, the Illuminator, the Great Sun; the universe divided is the five Buddhas. The innumerable divided parts of the world - the directions of space, the divisions of time, the indriyas, the skandhas, the Elements... - are conceptually codified and conventionally reduced to quinary groups, each term of which corresponds to, or is, one of the five Buddhas. In this sense the five Buddhas are nothing other than generic names for the breaths, the senses, the Elements, the regents of the directions... and so on for every aspect of the cosmic structuring.

Fig. 82 : A Nepalese stupa of the five Jina Buddhas. Vairocana has been relocated from the centre of the mandala and appears beside Akṣobhya in a position to the North of East.

Fig. 83 : A Japanese pillar stupa of the Jina Buddhas, whose seed syllables are painted in the directions on the panels that enclose the column.

The five Buddhas give expression to an uncompromizing doctrine of non-duality. Even the passions (kleśa),[170] the dark obscurations of the mind that block the attainment of Awakening, are identified with the five Buddhas [171]: darkness and light are non-dual; the shadows of ignorance are in no way distinct from the Illumination they obscure. All the apparently irreconcilable oppositions that exist within manifested existence are fused within the non-dual body of the Tathāgata.

---

170. Viz., mental darkness (moha), pride (abhimana), jealousy (īrśā), irascibility (krodha) and cupidity (lobha).

171. See Tucci, 1961, p. 53.

f. Borobudur as a Diamond World Mandala.

Many theories have been advanced to explain the symbolic significance of the great stupa of Borobudur in Java.[172] It is a subject that has given rise to a considerable amount of debate, some of it rancorous. Even seemingly straightforward questions of fact such as the number of terraces has been disputed.[173]

One theory that is not known in the West since it has not been translated from the Japanese is that put forward by Toganoo Shoun,[174] a pre-eminent scholar of Shingon Buddhism. He proposes that Borobudur is a three-dimensional representation of the Diamond World Mandala (vajra-dhātu-maṇḍala).[175] Recently the Indian scholar Lokesh Chandra, using a different set of arguments, has independently arrived at the same conclusion.[176] Taken together the evidence put forward by these two researchers seems to establish the identity of the stupa and the mandala beyond any reasonable doubt. The arguments are complicated and of a highly technical nature and are beyond the scope of this study, and all that can be given here is an indication of the way in which the stupa layout corresponds to that of the mandala.

Borobudur consists of a domical stupa supported on three circular terraces that are in turn supported by five square terraces, rising one above the other so as to form a stepped, truncated pyramid, with stairways rising to the upper terraces on each of the four sides. The square terraces are surrounded by ambulatories enclosed by high walls embellished with reliefs and surmounted by niches containing Buddha images. The circular terraces, by contrast, are unenclosed and stand open to the sky. The lowest of the square terraces has a series of reliefs illustrating the operation of the law of cause and effect, the pains of the hells and the pleasures of the heavens that result from different actions (karma), according to descriptions given in the *Mahākarmavibhangga*. The first gallery has two superimposed series of reliefs. The lower row depicts scenes from the Buddha's previous lives taken from the *Jātakas* and the *Avadānas*, and scenes from the Buddha's life taken from the *Lalita Vistara*. The reliefs on the balustrade of the second gallery depict further scenes from the *Jātakas* and the *Avadānas*, while those on the inner wall depict episodes from the *Gaṇḍavyūha* of the *Avataṃsaka-sūtra*, the story of Sudhana's search for the Highest Perfect Enlightenment. This story is continued on the walls and balustrades of the third and fourth galleries. On each of the balustrades

---

172. The literature on the subject is extensive: in 1960 Bosch (1960, p. 167) stated that there were more than 400 works and papers; 20 years later Dumarçay (1978, p. 38) had raised the number to more than 500. For a summary of some of the more influential theories on the meaning of Borobudur, see ibid, pp. 38 ff.

173. E.g., Przyluski, 1936, counts seven terraces, Bernet Kempers, 1959, counts eight, Soekmono, 1976, p. 15, and Seckel, 1964, p. 128, count nine, and Mus, 1935, and Bodrogi, 1973, p. 72, count ten.

174. Toganoo, 1971, pp. 461 ff.

175. The Diamond World Mandala (vajra-dhātu-maṇḍala, Jap. kongō-kai-mandara) is described in the *Kongōchōgyō*. See also MKDJT, pp. 668 ff. and BKDJT, pp. 1369 ff., s.v., Kongōkaimandara, and under the heads of its nine sections; Toganoo, 1932, pp. 189 ff.; Tajima, 1959; and see also the references given above, p. 137, n. 165.

176. Chandra, 1980, pp. 301 ff.

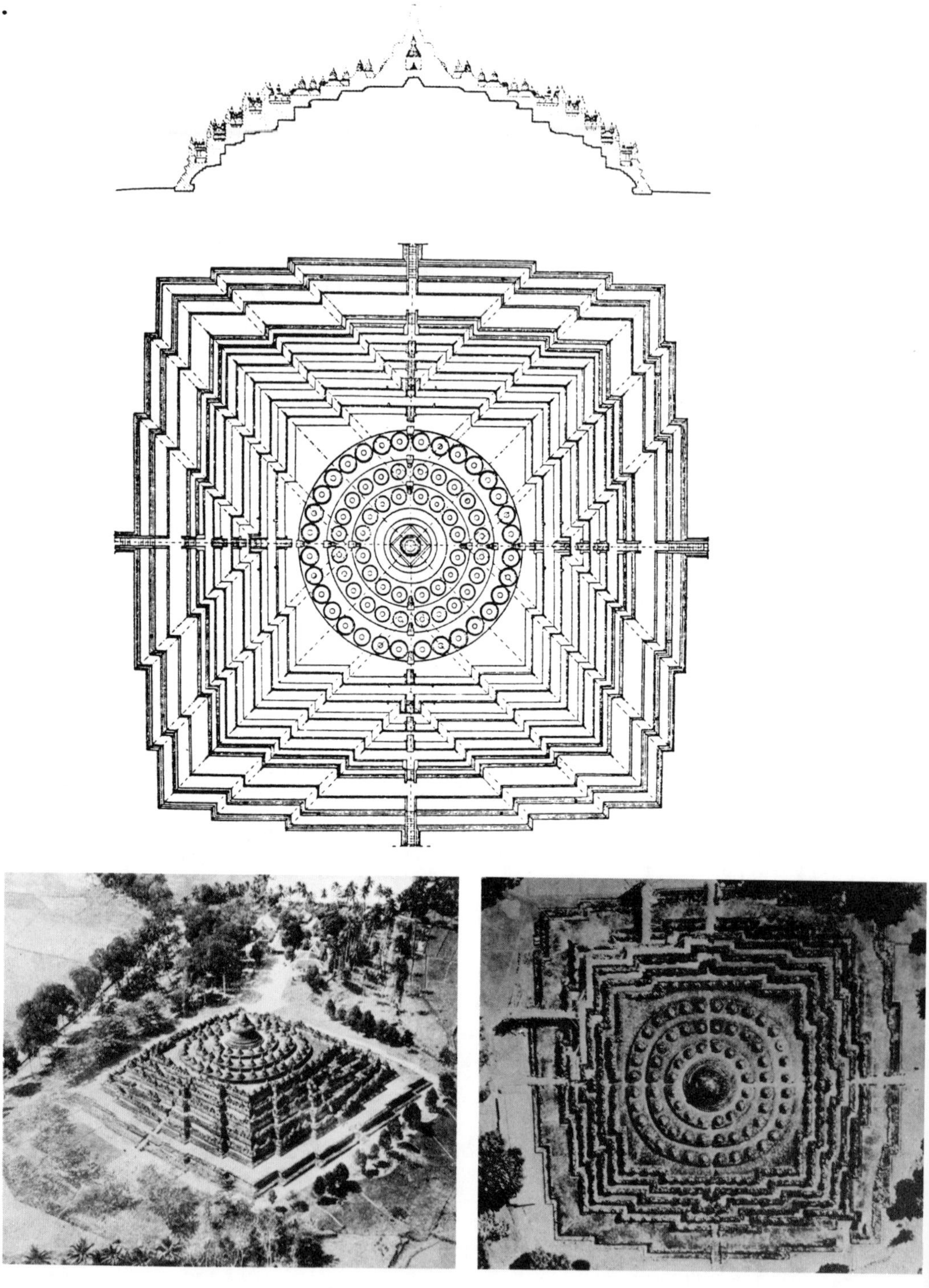

Fig. 84 : Borobudur. a. Section. b. Plan. c. Oblique aerial view. d. Aerial view from directly overhead.

there are rows of Buddha images in niches. The first and second balustrades each have 104 (8 x 13) images, the third has 88 (8 x 11), the fourth has 72 (8 x 9) and the fifth has 64 (8 x 8), to give a total of 432, one of the fundamental cyclic numbers.[177] On the circular terraces there are 72 (32 + 24 + 16) bell-shaped stupas, pierced with a lattice of perforations to reveal a glimpse of Buddhas seated within.[178]

The images of the Buddha on the first four levels are identical on each of the sides in the four directions : those to the East all make the gesture of touching the earth (bhūmisparśa-mudrā), which identifies them as images of the Buddha Akṣobhya; those to the South make the gesture of granting wishes (varada-mudrā), the gesture characteristically made by Ratnasambhava; to the West the images make the gesture of meditation (dhyāna-mudrā), the hand sign of Amitābha; and in the North the hands of the images are held in the gesture of fearlessness (abhaya-mudrā), that of Amoghasiddhi. There are 92 images in each direction. The 64 images in in the niches on the fifth balustrade show the same kind of hand gesture in all four directions, the gesture of teaching (vitarka-mudrā), that held by Vairocana Buddha. The 72 images within the perforated stupas on the three circular terraces all make a gesture that Toganoo has identified[179] as the gesture of the Member of Enlightenment (bodhyaṅgi-mudrā), which symbolizes the Vajra Wheel (vajra-cakra),[180] an alternative to the Wisdom Fist Mudrā held by Vairocana in the Diamond World Mandala.[181] Within the central, crowning stupa there was an image making the earth touching gesture (bhūmisparśa-mudrā), the gesture associated with Akṣobhya.[182]

This allocation of Buddhas is the same as that found in the Diamond World Mandala (see fig. 30), where the four Buddhas surround a central Mahāvairocana in the same directions as at Borobudur. The mandala, however, shows a large number of other divinities. Immediately surrounding Mahāvairocana in the cardinal directions are the four Pāramitā Bodhisattvas; and each of the four Buddhas has a similar entourage of four Bodhisattvas, collectively making up the group of the sixteen Great Bodhisattvas (mahābodhisattva). The mandala contains twelve other Bodhisattvas : the four

---

177. There are 4,320,000 years in a manvantara. See Guénon, 1938.

178. Descriptions of Borobudur are given in Seckel, 1964, pp. 128 ff.; Wagner, 1959, pp. 114 ff.; Bernet-Kempers, 1959, pp. 42 ff.; Bodrogi, 1973, pp. 72 ff.; Holt, 1967, pp. 42 ff.; Mus, 1935, *passim*, Dumarçay, 1978, pp. 21 ff.; Soekmono, 1976, pp. 14 ff.; Coomaraswamy, 1927, pp. 204 ff.; Toganoo, 1971, pp. 463 ff.; Przyluski, 1936, pp. 252 ff.; Zimmer, 1955, 1, pp. 298 ff.; etc.

179. Toganoo, 1971, p. 477. Cf. the *Sādhanamāla* text quoted in Bhattacharyya, 1958, p. 47, saying that Vairocana makes the bodhyaṅgi-mudrā.

180. The bodhyaṅgi-mudrā is held by images of Mahāvairocana Tathāgata in Nepal, Tibet and Japan.

181. The mudrā has without exception been identified as the dharmacakra-mudrā, the gesture of turning the Wheel of the Law, the hand sign made by Śākyamuni. This error has led to most of the confusion concerning the meaning of Borobudur. No one, to my knowledge, has given an adequate explanation of why the Śākyamuni image should appear 72 times on the summit of the monument.

182. Many scholars, however, doubt that this is the original image, but was placed within the stupa to cover up a theft.

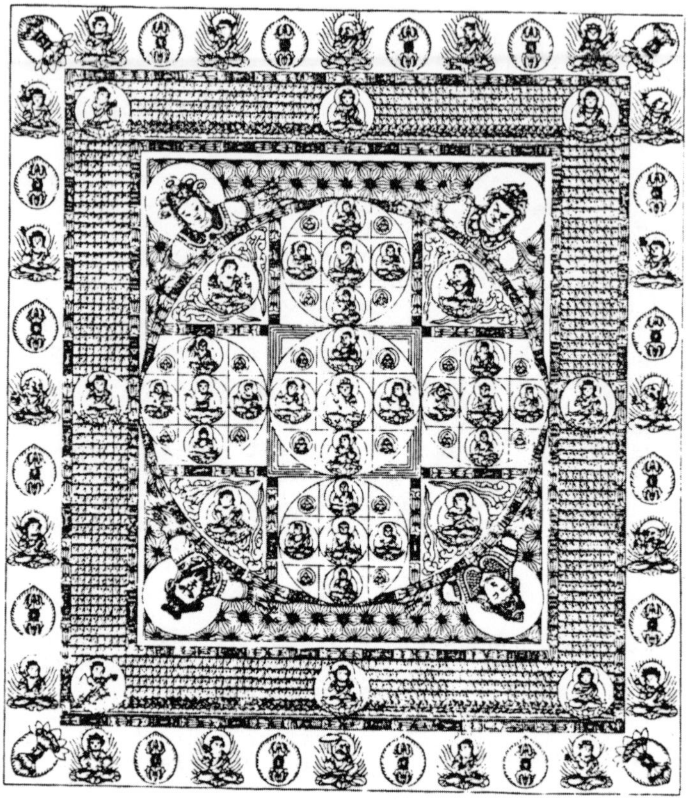

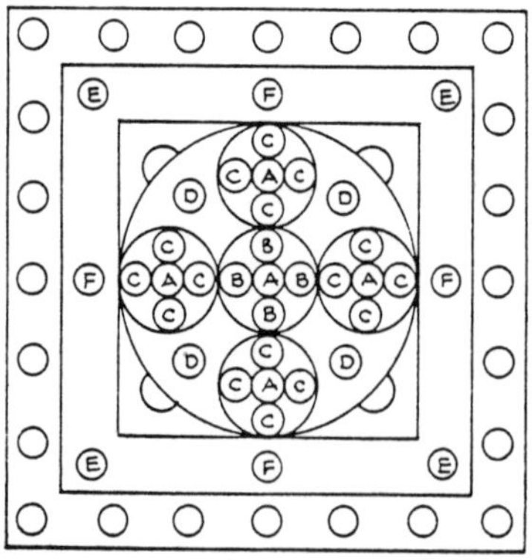

Fig. 85 : Key to the Thirty Seven "Honoured Ones" (Jap. sanjūshichison) of the Diamond World Mandala.

A : The 5 Jina Buddhas.
B : The 4 Pāramitā Bodhisattvas.
C : The 16 Great Bodhisattvas.
D : The 4 Inner Bodhisattvas of Offering.
E : The 4 Outer Bodhisattvas of Offering.
F : The 4 Bodhisattvas of Attraction.

The four large figures who clutch the diagonal edges of the mandala are personifications of the four Elements, Earth, Air, Fire and Water, that support the cosmos. The other figures shown in the mandala are various guardian deities.

inner Bodhisattvas of Offering (pūjā-bodhisattva), located in the diagonal directions within the circle of vajras that encloses the five Buddhas and their retinues; four outer Bodhisattvas of Offering, who are in the diagonal corners of the square band that lies outside the circle of vajras; and four Bodhisattvas of Attraction in the cardinal directions within the same square band. These latter are called Bodhisattvas of Attraction (saṃgraha-bodhisattva, Jap. shō bosatsu) because they represent those qualities of Mahāvairocana which attract men toward Enlightenment. The Buddhas and Bodhisattvas in the Diamond World Mandala number 37, and are collectively called the 37 Honoured Ones (Jap. sanjūshichison). The significance of the mandala resides in these divinities; the other figures in the mandala perform the function of guardians.

Toganoo produces a wealth of evidence to show that the arrangement of images at Borobudur is a variation on a theme commonly encountered in the Ādi-Buddha stupas of Tibet and Nepal, which also have five square stepped terraces with returns and projections like those at Borobudur, pradakṣina galleries at each level, images of the five Jina Buddhas in niches on the top of the balustrades and on the wall surfaces, each in its appropriate direction as at Borobudur, and similar stairways in the cardinal directions. These terraces support a domical stupa containing an image of the primal Buddha (Ādi-Buddha) directly below the axial pillar that rises to form the spire.[183] The Himalayan Ādi-Buddha stupas are specifically identified as sculptured representations of the Dharma World Mandala, that is to say, the Diamond World Mandala.[184] Toganoo claims that Borobudur is an Ādi-Buddha stupa in which the three circular terraces and the crowning stupa replace the domical stupa of the Nepalese and Tibetan type.

---

183. At the centre of the dome there is a small room divided into nine squares so as to give a central space surrounded by eight others in the eight directions. The image of the Ādi-Buddha was placed in the central space and dharma-śarīra verses were placed in the surrounding spaces (Oldfield, 1880, Ch. 8; Hodgson, 1874, p. 30). On the exterior of the dome there are niches, called toran, containing images of the Jina Buddhas, each in his appropriate direction. Vairocana was sometimes placed in a niche to the East of that enshrining Akṣobhya, but was usually not shown. Cf. above, p. 140, fig. 17.

184. In Nepal and Tibet the Ādi-Buddha stupas were called Dharma-World Mandalas (dharma-dhātu-maṇḍala) (Oldfield, 1880, 2, p. 230; Toganoo, 1971, p. 447). In the Vajrayāna the Dharma-World is identified with Samantabhadra; and Samantabhadra, in turn, is identified with Vajrasattva (see MKDJT, p. 1915, s.v., Fugen). The non-duality of their natures is expressed in the dual name Samantabhadra-Vajrasattva (Jap. Fugen-kongōsatta). (See MKDJT, p. 1914, s.v., Fugen-kongosatta). Again, Vajrasattva embodies Diamond Knowledge (vajra-jñāna) and thus includes within himself the whole of the Diamond World Mandala, which is the mandala of Diamond Knowledge. By this series of assimilations Toganoo shows the identity of the Dharma World Mandala and the Diamond World Mandala and also that the Ādi-Buddha stupa is a Diamond World Mandala (Toganoo. 1971, p. 474).

185. "Ādi-Buddha" is a term that is only found in Tibetan and Nepalese Buddhism, but the concept has exact parallels in India in the doctrine of the Dharma-Body Samantabhadra, identified with Vajrasattva as the supreme and original Buddha (paramādya-buddha). Samantabhadra-Vajrasattva, like the Ādi-Buddha, is the root principle of the mind and the supreme root-origin of the physical world. Like the Ādi-Buddha he is the eternal, immutable essence and source of mind on the one hand and phenomena on the other. He is the ultimate non-duality of mind and physical manifestation. The cosmos derives from and is wholly dependent

Fig. 86 : The Kum-Bum, Stupa of the Hundred Thousand Images, Gyantse, Tibet, an example of an Ādi-Buddha Stupa.

The Ādi-Buddha, identified with Mahāvairocana, the central Buddha in the Diamond World Mandala,[185] has two aspects, which are represented by the two Buddhas Akṣobhya and Vairocana. As was shown previously[186] the five Jina Buddhas are correlated with the five constituent aggregates (skandha) of the person[187]: Akṣobhya corresponds to consciousness (vijñāna), Ratnasambhava to sensation (vedanā), Amitābha to discernment (samjñā), Amoghasiddhi to volition (saṃskāra) and Vairocana to form (rūpa).[188] In this schema Akṣobhya Buddha, and not Vairocana, is placed at the centre of the five Buddhas, in accordance with the Vajrayāna teaching that all the things of the three worlds are contained within Consciousness (vijñāna-skandha), that everything is Consciousness Only, and that there is nothing outside of Consciousness. "The five skandhas are the five Tathāgatas. It is taught that four of these are the Knowledge of Consciousness Only".[189] For this reason in the Diamond World Mandala described in the *Guhyasamāja* Akṣobhya appears at the centre and Vairocana is in the East.

In this context the Buddhas Akṣobhya and Vairocana represent complementary aspects of the world. As the aggregate of form (rūpa-skandha) Vairocana represents the sum of phenomenal existences; as the aggregate of consciousness (vijñāna-skandha) Akṣobhya represents the awakened Mind of the Tathāgata. The two Buddhas embody formal manifestation on the one hand and Mind Consciousness on the other, which is to say saṃsāra and nirvāṇa.

Fundamental to the Vajrayāna doctrine is the concept of the non-duality (advaita) of Mind and phenomenal forms.[190] They coexist in an inseparable fusion; they are "distinct yet not distinct". The collocation of Buddhas on the circular terraces at Borobudur conveys this doctrine : the Buddha enshrined within the central stupa is Akṣobhya, representing Mind Only; the 72 Buddhas in the perforated stupas ranged in circles on the round terraces represent 72 aspects of Vairocana as the Buddha who embodies the deployment of Mind into the phenomenal world. Akṣobhya, as Mind Consciousness, is central; the 72 Vairocanas are appropriately peripheral. Taken together Akṣobhya and the 72 Vairocanas represent the non-duality of Mind and phenomena. Together they form the Body of the Ādi-Buddha Samantabhadra-Vajrasattva, which is precisely the Body of the non-

---

upon him as its Principle. He is the unique life-Essence, the innate and animating Principle in every living existence. He is unborn, "without cause", spontaneously existing (svayambhū). He is beyond words, ineffable, and yet "is the most excellent cause of all words; all words are manifested in him". *Monju bosatsu saishō myōgikyō*, Taishō, Vol. 20, pp. 809, 815, 820 & 827, quoted in Toganoo, 1971, p. 486.

186. See above, pp. 136 f.

187. See Bhattacharyya, 1958, pp. 11, 32 & 48, and the quotation from the *Advayavajrasaṃgraha*, ibid, pp. 49 ff. 188. See above, p. 136 f.

189. Snellgrove, 1959, pp. 216 f.; Bhattacharyya, 1958, p. 51 (Akṣobhya) and p. 53 (Vairocana), quoting the *Advayavajrasaṃgraha*; Conze, 1954, pp. 246 ff.

190. The non-duality of forms and Consciousness is conveyed by the Stupa of the Five Elements, described in the following (pp. 372 ff). It combines the shapes of the five Elements making up the world of form with the seed syllable of the sixth Element, Consciousness. On the non-duality of forms and Mind see MKDJT, p. 910, s.v., Shiki shin funi ("The Non-duality of Form and Mind"); BKDJT, p. 2373, s.v., Jū fu ni mon ("The Gate of the Ten Non-Dualities").

duality of form and Mind. The non-duality of Mind and form is the essence of the Ādi-Buddha; he is described as the root-origin which gives birth to all the dharmas of Mind and all the dharmas of form; form and Mind devolve from and depend upon his non-dual Mind and Body.

But why are there 72 Vairocanas ? The Total Knowledge of the Ādi-Buddha has 37 facets, which are personified as the 37 divinities in the Diamond World Mandala. The central and total Knowledge divides itself 36-fold. "The qualities of the Buddha number 36; all are cognate with the Self-Nature Body, together with which they make a total of 37. These 37 comprize the Dharma World Body".[191] Each of these 36 divisions of Knowledge has two aspects : a subjective aspect, which pertains to its visualization in meditation, and an objective aspect, which is its True Form.[192] The 72 images of Vairocana are the qualities of the Knowledge of the Ādi-Buddha Samantabhadra-Vajrasattva, seen from two different viewpoints, that of the Buddhas themselves and that of the meditating subject.

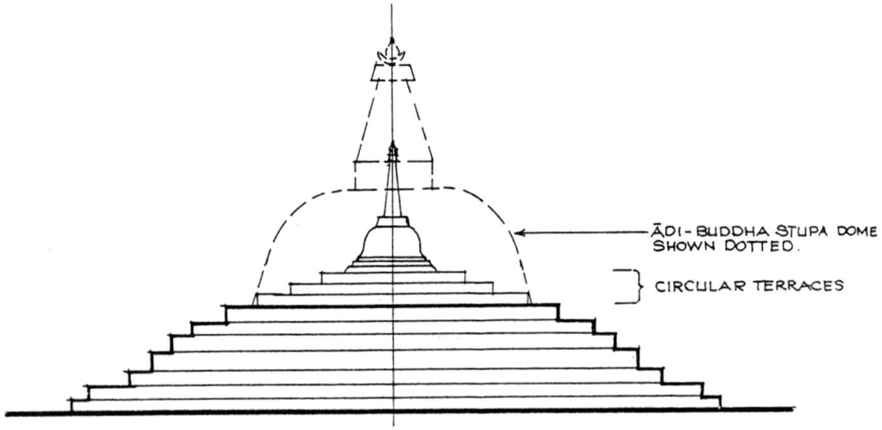

Fig. 87 : The equivalence of the Tibetan Ādi-Buddha stupa and the stupa of Borobudur. The three circular terraces replace the dome.

Akṣobhya and the 72 Vairocanas on the circular terraces of Borobudur form a Diamond World Mandala. The Javanese stupa has the same symbolic significance as the stupa supported on square terraces in Tibet and Nepal. In these the Diamond World Mandala is contained within the stupa dome, whereas at Borobudur the single stupa is divided into 72 smaller stupas. The meaning, however, remains unaltered : the single Dharma World stupa in Nepal and Tibet and the 73 stupas at Borobudur equally represent the Nature-Ocean of Samantabhadra-Vajrasattva.

---

191. *Funbetsushōikyō*, Taishō, Vol. 18, No. 870, p. 291, quoted by Toganoo, 1971, p. 479.

192. These aspects are those "visualized in meditation" (kanshō) and the "True, or Essential Form" (jissō) respectively. See JEBD, p. 140, s.v., Jissō.

The three circular terraces and the central stupa of Borobudur are the exact equivalent of the hemispherical dome of the Ādi-Buddha stupas of Tibet and Nepal. In both the stupa of the supreme Buddha, which is identified with the Diamond World Mandala, is laid out on the summit of the Cosmic Mountain formed by the stepped terraces.

This is more readily comprehensible when it is understood that a distinction can be drawn between Mahāvairocana and Vairocana. Esoteric Buddhist texts[193] describe Mahāvairocana, identified with Samantabhadra-Vajrasattva,[194] as the sum of the five Buddhas including Vairocana; he incorporates the various essences of the five Buddhas within his single Dharma Body of Knowledge. Vairocana, on the other hand, is described as constituting Mahāvairocana's Reward Body and his Body of Form, the body that appears in the world of men. Whereas Mahāvairocana makes the Wisdom Fist Mudrā, Vairocana makes the bodhyaṅgi-mudrā. The Buddha at the centre of the Diamond World Mandala is Mahāvairocana, who is identified with the Ādi-Buddha, Samantabhadra-Vajrasattva; and the Buddhas in the 72 stupas are his various emanations as Vairocana.

Mahāvairocana includes Vairocana within himself and therefore Vairocana does not normally appear among the Buddhas on a stupa. At Borobudur, however, all five Buddhas are shown (Akṣobhya, Ratnasambhava, Amitābha and Amoghasiddhi in their appropriate directions of the fifth terrace) plus Vairocana and Akṣobhya again on the circular terraces and at the centre respectively, together representing Mahāvairocana who is identified with Samantabhadra-Vajrasattva, the Ādi-Buddha.

* * * * *

The 72 Buddhas seated within the stupas on the circular terraces of Borobudur are the two-fold representation of the 37 Honoured Ones of the Diamond World Mandala, the 37 aspects of Total Knowledge. Examining the significance of the 37 divinities in greater detail and more specifically, the Buddhas in the four directions are direct emanations from Mahāvairocana at the centre; the four Buddhas in turn emanate the sixteen Great Bodhisattvas, who represent aspects of the functioning of the active energy of the five types of Knowledge. The four Buddhas also emanate the four Pāramitā Bodhisattvas, each in its corresponding direction, as an offering (pūjā) to Mahāvairocana. Alternately, according to another interpretation, the Pāramitā Bodhisattvas are aspects of Mahāvairocana's Meditation (dhyāna), each of which produces, or "gives birth", to a Knowledge; each is the "Mother" of the Buddha in the same direction.

Further, the sixteen Great Bodhisattvas are the personifications of sixteen stages in the process of perfecting the Buddha Knowledge. The Mahāyāna teaches that Awakening is not the final stage in the progress to total Liberation. The ascent to Awakening is a return to the centre; but beyond the centre is the seventh "ray", outside of space and time, and the Awakened must proceed on this dimensionless and timeless path, deepening and extending his Buddha Knowledge, if he is to win the highest and most perfect Enlightenment (anuttara-saṃyak-saṃbodhi). The two phases of ascent,

---

193. E.g., Śākyamitra's *Kosalā-laṃkāra-tattva-saṃgraha-ṭīkā* and Anandagarbha's *Sarva-tathāgata-tattva-saṃgraha-vyakbyā-tattvāokakarī*, cited in Toganoo, 1971, p. 481.

194. See the *Kongōchōgyō*, Taishō, Vol. 18, No. 865, p. 207, quoted by Toganoo, 1971, p. 481.

individual and supra-individual, up to and beyond Awakening, are codified as fifty two Bodhisattva stages, which are divided into forty prior stages leading up to Awakening, ten stages that follow Awakening, and two final stages within perfect Enlightenment.[195] The sixteen Great Bodhisattvas are hypostases of the stages of attainment which lie beyond Awakening; they personify sixteen aspects of Mahāvairocana's supreme and total Knowledge that are progressively developed by the Awakened in his progress towards the goal of ultimate Buddhahood. Each of the five Buddhas is an aspect of Knowledge and each of his attendant Bodhisattvas is a further differentiation of that aspect : the four Buddhas in the four directions "emanate" their retinue of attendants as so many facets of their own essential nature. Each of the sixteen Great Bodhisattvas represents a step in an hierarchical ascent. Unifying himself in meditation with each of the Bodhisattvas in turn, the sādhaka assimilates the aspect of Buddha Knowledge it personifies and thus realizes his innate Buddha-Nature.[196]

The remaining Bodhisattvas among the thirty seven divinities in the Diamond World Mandala - the eight Bodhisattvas of Offering and the four Bodhisattvas of Attraction - correlate with concepts of sacrifice, and more specifically with concepts of pūjā, the making of offerings to the divinity. In the process of the deployment of the mandala Mahāvairocana first emanates the four Buddhas into the four directions (1). Then, at the same time as they emanate the sixteen Great Bodhisattvas (2), the four Buddhas also emanate the four Pāramitā Bodhisattvas as an offering to Mahāvairocana (3). In response Mahāvairocana emanates the four inner Bodhisattvas of Offering (4); in reply, each of the four Buddhas again emanates a Bodhisattva as a second offering to the central Buddha : these are the four outer Bodhisattvas of Offering (5). Finally, Mahāvairocana answers with the four Bodhisattvas of Attraction. (6)[197]

The formula of reciprocal offering embodied in the mandala is an exemplar of the relationship existing between manifestation and its Principle. Mahāvairocana is the Centre and Source of the manifested universe; the Buddhas and Bodhisattvas who surround him are the deployment of his Buddha-Nature into saṃsāra, the sacrificial act whereby he radiates out into the worlds and into beings. Every grain of sand possesses the Buddha-Nature or, as Esoteric Buddhism expresses it, is the Buddha; each existent thing is resplendent with the glory of perfected Buddhahood : the Buddha and saṃsāra reflect each other in a simultaneous and continuous act of reciprocal sacrifice, each making offerings to the other. Mahāvairocana, who is the Great Sun (Jap. Dainichi) and the source of the Light of Wisdom, shines upon the four Buddhas, irradiating them with splendour. They, in

---

195. See p. 334, and also MS XX-XXI.32 ff.; Soothill and Hodous, 1934, p. 476, s.v.,十地(daśa-bhūmi); Sangarakshita, 1957, pp. 495 ff.; BKDJT, p. 2297, s.v., Jūji; for the Ten Stations. For the 52 stages of the Bodhisattva see BKDJT, p. 1214, s.v., Gojūnii; Soothill and Hodous, 1934, p. 115, s.v.,五十二位; ibid, p. 45, s.v., 十信 ; ibid., p. 53, s.v., 十行 ; ibid, p. 47, s.v., 十地 ; ibid, p. 384, s.v., 等覺 and p. 235, s.v., 妙覺

196. On the sixteen Great Bodhisattvas see Toganoo, 1932, pp. 216 ff.; MKDJT, p. 900, s.v., Jūroku dai bosatsu; ibid, p. 898, s.v., Jūrokusho; BKDJT, p. 1312, s.v., Kongōkaisanjūshichison.

197. Toganoo, 1932, pp. 225 ff. An analysis of the profound import and rich resonances of this symbolism of reciprocal offering would involve a far-ranging excursion into the significance of each of the 37 divinities in the mandala. Their iconography, their names, seed syllables, mudrās, and attributes relate to a complex schema of interlocking and mutually reinforcing meanings. almost endless in their ramifications.

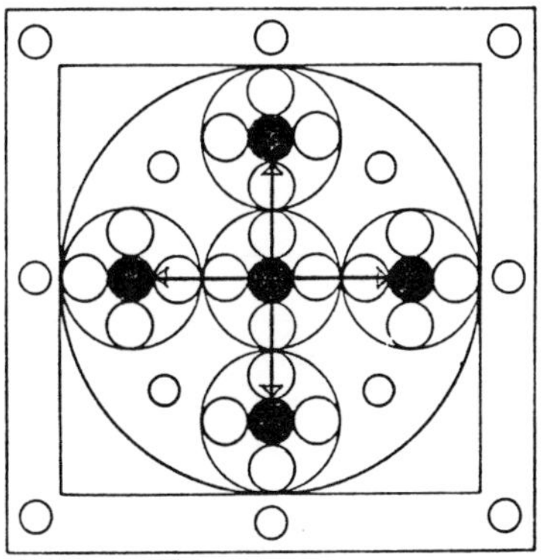

1

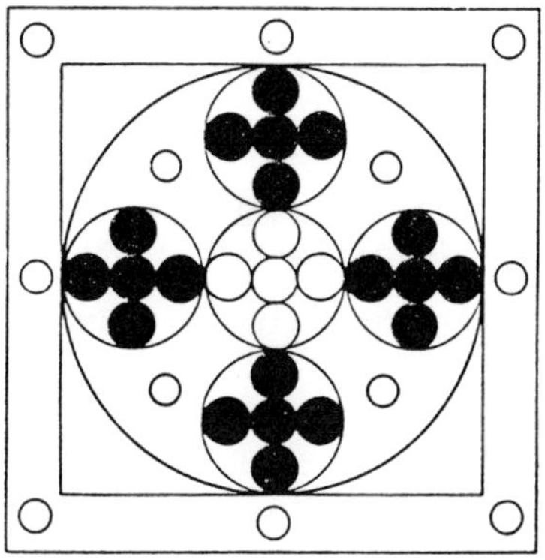

2

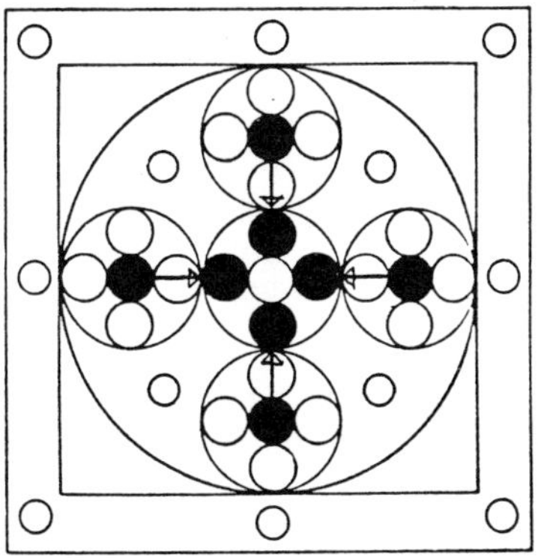

3

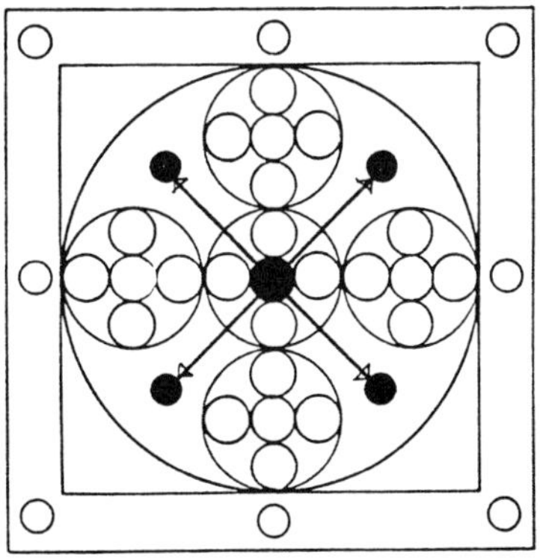

4

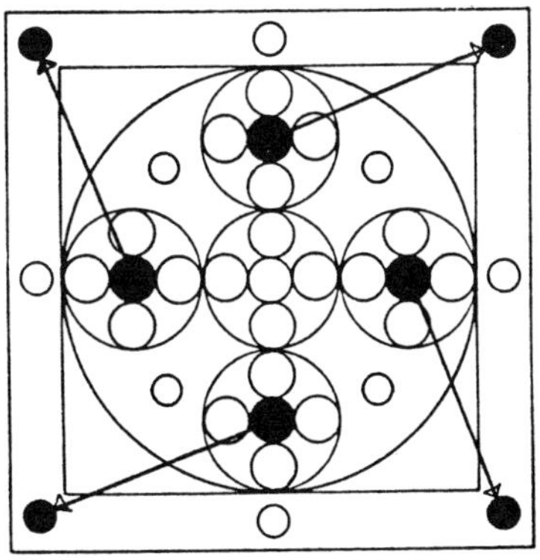

5

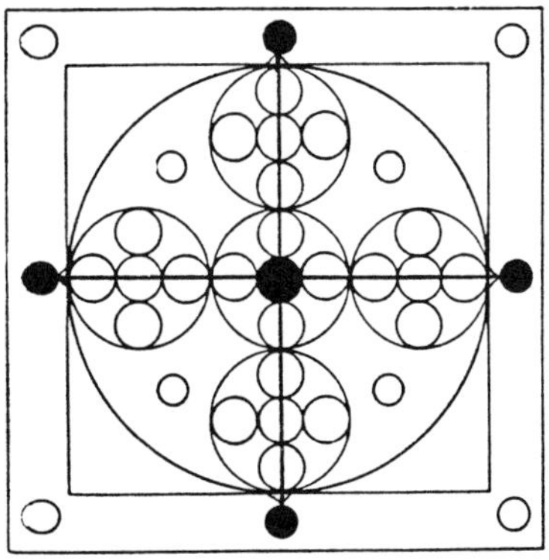

6

turn, reflect this light back to its source, adding light to light. Burning with this increased brilliance the Sun once more shines upon the Buddhas who therefore blaze more strongly and throw yet intenser light upon the Sun, further enhancing its glory... In this way the Essence of Light and its differentiated Qualities shine back and forth upon each other with ever increasing brilliance.[198]

* * * * *

The *Kongōchōgyō* teaches that the layout of the Diamond World Mandala reproduces the Jewel Stupa located in Indra's Heaven at the summit of Mt. Meru. In accordance with this the three circular terraces, which represent the Diamond World Mandala with its 37 divinities, are supported on five square terraces, which represent Mt. Meru. This formula repeats one that is of frequent occurrence in the Himalayan regions in temples, stupas, thaṇka paintings and texts.[199]

The walls enclosing the galleries on the square terraces are sculpted with a profusion of reliefs. These represent the functioning of the essence of Samantabhadra-Vajrasattva throughout all the levels of the cosmos. From the doctrinal standpoint of the Vajrayāna the life of Śākyamuni and his previous births are the activities of Samantabhadra-Vajrasattva. "Śākyamuni Buddha descended to Jambudvīpa as the Transformation Body, (performed) the Eight Events and achieved Enlightenment. All this was the illusory transformation of Samantabhadra-Vajrasattva".[200] Similarly, the friezes depicting the wanderings of Sudhana described in the *Gaṇḍavyūha* of the *Avataṃsaka-sūtra* are, according to the Vajrayāna, depictions of the life of Samantabhadra-Vajrasattva, descended into the world to show the ideal life in the Vajrayāna. Finally, the hell scenes, concealed in the basement of Borobudur, are once again nothing other than depictions of Samantabhadra-Vajrasattva's Body of Form.

The Buddha images and friezes carved on the square terraces of Borobudur represent the functioning of the Ādi-Buddha through every state of existence in the cosmos; likewise, the five Buddhas who appear on the square terraces and on the terraces of the Ādi-Buddha stupas of the Himalayan regions are so many deployments of the Body, Speech and Mind of the supreme Ādi-Buddha Mahāvairocana through the various levels of existence.

---

198. It is to be understood that this reciprocal reflection takes place at a supra-physical and paradigmatic level, since the Diamond World Mandala is the mandala of perfected Knowledge.

199. Chandra, 1980, pp. 310 ff.

200. Amoghavajra's *Jūhachieshiki*, Taishō, Vol. 18, No. 869, p. 286, quoted in Toganoo, 1971, p. 483.

13 THE SACRED ENCLOSURE.

1. THE *CAITYA VṚKṢA*

The peripheral line of the square delineated in the ritual separates a cosmicised space from a surrounding chaos. The area it encloses is a sacred space, a templum in the original meaning of the Latin word, a sacred precinct set apart from the profane, that is to say, from that which is "before (pro) or outside the temple (fanum)".[1]

The primitive exemplar of the Indian sacred space, Buddhist and non-Buddhist, is an area enclosed by a wall or fence and containing a sacred tree and an altar stone.[2] This form of sacred enclosure existed in India's most ancient past : it appears on seals from Mohenjo Daro and also on coins dating from the pre-Buddhist Vedic period.[3] The Pali texts inform us that it was found throughout India at the time when the Buddha was alive and they frequently mention a stone or altar (P. veyaddi, manco) standing beside a sacred tree.[4]

Fig. 88 : The Buddha aniconically represented by a Tree and altar stone-throne. The illustration on the right shows these enclosed within a pavilion, forming a caitya-vṛkṣa.

The ancient symbolism was adopted by Buddhism. In countless panels from Sāñcī, Bhārhut, Amarāvatī and other monuments dating from the aniconic period of Buddhist art, the Buddha is depicted, not anthropomorphically, but by a vacant stone seat at the foot of the Bodhi Tree. In these representations the pre-Buddhist altar stone has become the Buddha's throne.[5]

---

1. OED, s.v., "profane".

2. For two theories concerning the supposed development of this arrangement from a sacred landscape of woods and hills, see Mus, 1937, and Przyluski, 1940, both briefly summarized in Auboyer, 1949, pp. 49-52, and mentioned by Eliade, 1958a, pp. 269 f.

3. Banerjea, 1956, pp. 109 & 174; Coomaraswamy, 1927, p. 45.

4. Eliade, 1958b, p. 270, Coomaraswamy, 1928, p. 23.

5. In these representations the pre-Buddhist altar stone has become the Buddha's throne, but its associations still remain : having burnt away selfhood the Buddha is the sacrifice, occupying the place of the sacrificial Fire, Agni. In some reliefs he is shown by the flames of the triśula burning upon the sacrificial slab.

The closely related symbolic theme of the Tree-Caitya (caitya-vṛkṣa), the Bodhi Tree enclosed within a fence or wall in the manner of an hypaethral sanctuary, is also common in the ancient friezes. The Buddha himself designated the Tree as an appropriate symbol (caitya) to represent him in his absence;[6] and the *Jātakas* tell how, when a seed of the Bodhi Tree miraculously grew to full size as soon as it was planted by Ānanda, the King Aśoka surrounded it with 800 gold and silver jars filled with perfumed water and blue lotuses, placed a throne of seven jewels at its base, enclosed it within a wall and built an adjoining chapel to contain seven precious things.[7] The reference is unequivocally to the setting up of a caitya-vṛkṣa. As a symbol (caitya) the Tree is the equivalent of the Buddha himself and in the caitya-vṛkṣa it is more specifically equated with the Buddha as the axis of the world. The palisade, defining the periphery of cosmic order, establishes the boundaries of the bodhimaṇḍa, the Place of the Buddha's Enlightenment.

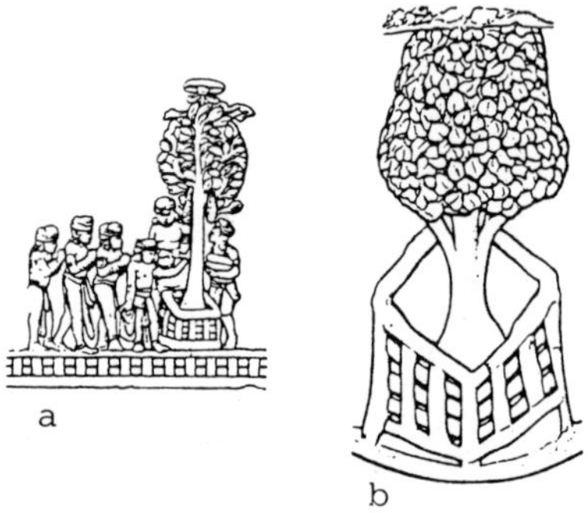

Fig. 89 : The caitya-vṛkṣa depicted in early Buddhist reliefs. a. The sacred tree within a sacred space defined by a vedikā, from a medallion on a railing pillar at Bodhgayā. b. The worship of the sacred tree within a vedikā, Sāñcī.

The meaning of this symbolic schema can be clarified by reference to the cosmogonic model given above. The tree trunk marks the radial axis connecting the felly of our world back to its central hub and source; the stone or altar is the point where it strikes the earth; branches and roots are the superior and inferior states of existence; and the enclosing palisade is the demarked periphery of the cosmos or the boundary of the sacred space measured out upon the ground.

The analogies with the cosmogonic model - tree trunk as radial axis, stone (altar or throne) as earth centre, palisade as the boundary of the cosmos - are enhanced in the Buddhist setting by clear indications of orientation. Hsuan-tsang and the *Jātakas* note that the caitya-vṛkṣas are normally located to the East of towns and temples;[8] the *Mahāvaṃsa* indicates that the seat of the Buddha established in Sri Lanka is turned to the East, while that of the sthavira faces the North;[9] and at the Enlightenment the Buddha takes up his station upon the Diamond Throne (vajrāsana) at the foot of the Bodhi Tree, facing East.[10]

6. *Divyāvadāna* (Cowell and Neil, 1886) cited by Auboyer, 1949, p. 73 Cf. below, pp. 176 f.

7. *Kaliṇga-bodhi-jātaka*, cited in Auboyer, 1949, pp. 52 f.

8. Beal, 1906, p. 172.

9. *Mahāvaṃsa* III.17 ff.; III.22 ff.

10. Coomaraswamy, 1956, p. 25; 1943a, p. 53.

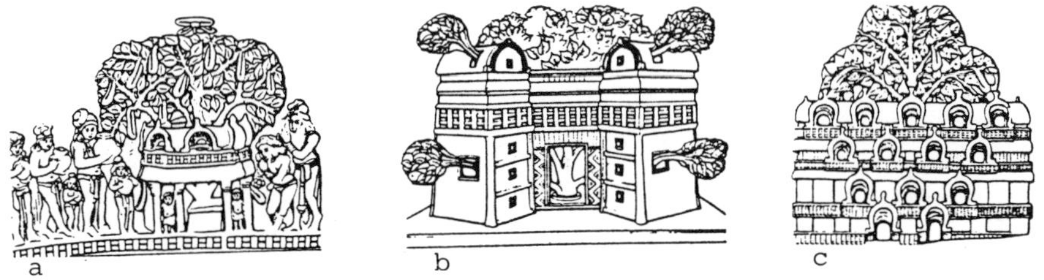

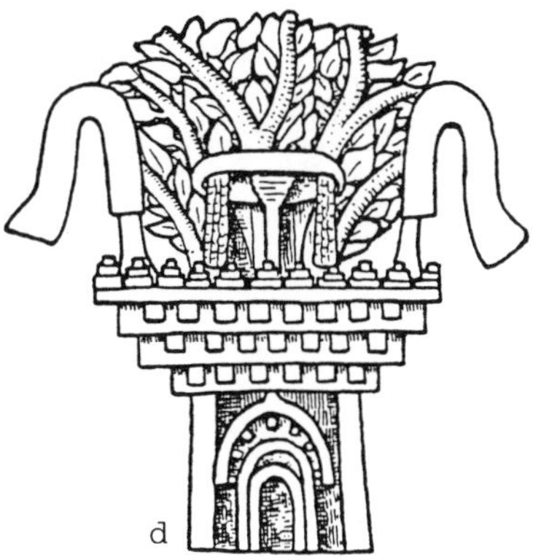

Fig. 90 :
The sacred tree within an hypaethral pavilion (*bodhigara*). a. Aśoka and his retinue watering the tree growing within a *bodhigara*, shown on a lintel at Sāñcī. b. A *bodhigara* depicted on a relief medallion at Mathurā. c. A *bodhigara* shown on a relief panel at Jaggayapeṭa. d. A *bodhigara* depicted on a railing medallion at Mathurā.

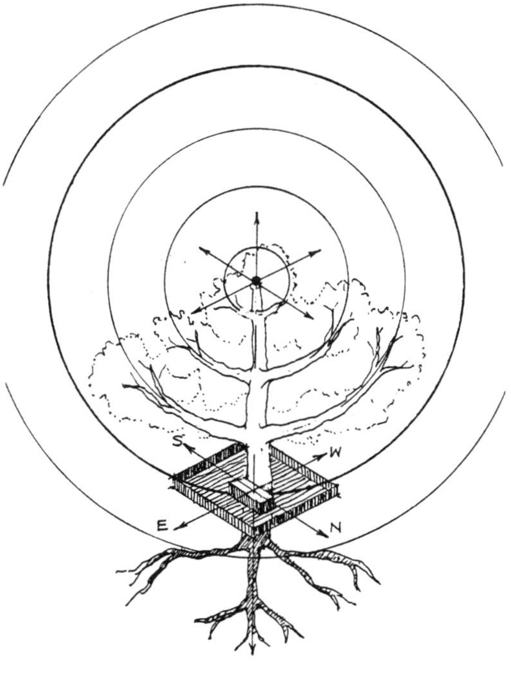

Fig. 91 :
The relationship of the *caitya-vṛkṣa* and the cosmogonic model. The top of the Tree is the cosmogenetic Centre of the cosmos.

Fig. 92 :
A *caitya-vṛkṣa*. The sacred tree, enclosed by a fence, is surrounded by four parasols in the diagonal directions.

The confines of the stupa, marked out by the fence (vedikā) and centred by a post, is a caitya-vṛkṣa. The post and the Tree are explicitly identified in both the Brahmanic and the Buddhist literature.

* * * * *

The words stūpa and caitya are synonymous.[11] Stūpa derives from the root stup, "to accumulate, to gather together";[12] and in a like manner caitya derives from ci, "to pile up, to accumulate",[13] originally used to refer to the piling up, or construction, of a fire altar or funeral pyre,[14] and by this associated with any altar or hallow, with any place where an hierophany of the sacred is deemed to occur, or with any object which is imbued with the numinous, such as a sacred rock, tree, spring or building.[15] In Buddhism, from the earliest times, it had a more specific reference : it signifies an object used to symbolize the Buddha. In the *Kaliṅgabodhi Jātaka* the Buddha is asked what kind of caitya (P. cetiya) can be used to represent him in his absence, and he replies that a Bodhi Tree is an appropriate caitya.[16] In this text caitya means "symbol", in precisely the sense that this term has been defined at the beginning of this study : the caitya - here specified as a Bodhi Tree - is an object that refers to a supra-physical reality. So similarly, any object that serves to recall the Buddha or his Doctrine, any "Reminder", is a caitya.[17]

---

11. Law, 1931, pp. 42 ff., has collected together the various interpretations that orientalists have given the term caitya. These are summarized in Viennot, 1954, p. 89.

12. Bénisti, 1960, p. 47. On the other hand Sivaramamurti (1942, p. 17) and Shah (1951, p. 271) derive it from the root stu, "to worship, to praise".

13. See MacDonell, 1929, s.v. ci. Thus it is that in Shingon Buddhism the word caitya is interpreted as meaning "an accumulation or assembly of felicities"; and Śubhākarasiṃha says that, "All the virtues of all the Buddhas are brought together and abide therein". (Śubhākarasiṃha, p. 628.b). Cf. Toganoo, 1970, p. 479.

14. The early theory advanced by orientalists that interpreted caitya to mean "funeral mound" because of its derivation from the root ci, "to pile up" (see Agrawala, 1965, p. 124; Law, 1931, p. 42) is rejected by Coomaraswamy (1928, p. 24, n. 2), who points out that as used in the epics and the early Buddhist and Jain literature it means "any holystead, altar, shrine, grove, temple..." Cf. Coomaraswamy, 1926a, p. 7, n. 4.

15. Foucher, 1900, p.51; cf. Vallée Poussin, 1937, p. 283; Grunwedel, 1972, p. 21; Pant, 1976, p. 23 ff.

16. Quoted in Coomaraswamy, 1977, 1, pp. 156 f.; and cf. note 6 above. On the tree as caitya, see Coomaraswamy, 1928, pp. 12 ff.; Eliade, 1958b, p. 270; Bosch, 1960, p. 194; Grunwedel, 1972, p. 21; Viennot, 1954, pp. 88 f. In the inscriptions on the stupa at Bhārhut, the term caitya is used in reference to sacred trees (Cunningham, 1868, p. 109; cf. Viennot, 1954, p. 122); and in the inscriptions on the stupas of Amarāvatī and Nāgārjunakoṇḍa, the stupas themselves are called caityas (Sivaramamurti, 1942, pp. 271 & 298, inscr. no. 102; Ramachandran, 1938; Longhurst, 1938, p. 17).

17. See Coomaraswamy, 1977, 1, p. 156, n. 14; 1935a, p. 4 & n. 6; Kramrisch, 1946, pp. 138 & 148, n. 50; Bosch, 1960, p. 193, n. 143; Law, 1931, p. 42.

As a symbol the caitya is an object of contemplation, a focus for the concentration of the mind. In this regard there is another etymological concurrence. There is a hermeneutic connection of ci, "to pile up" (that is, "to edify"), and the closely related root cit, "to regard, to know, to think of, to contemplate".[18] The caitya, as every symbol, is an object of contemplation. With reference to these associations Śubhākarasiṃha writes that, "The Sanskrit word caitya is essentially the same as cita, which according to esoteric interpretations is 'Mind'. The Buddha stupa is 'Mind'".[19]

2. THE PLACE OF ENLIGHTENMENT AND THE DIAMOND THRONE

The foremost sacred enclosure and caitya-vṛkṣa for Buddhists is the Place of Enlightenment (bodhimaṇḍa) at Bodhgayā. This is the sacred space where the Bodhisattva attained Enlightenment, seated upon the Adamantine Throne (vajrāsana) at the foot of the Bodhi Tree. The diamond seat of his Awakening is set at the navel of the world and nave of the World Wheel, and it is here that the stupa is erected. Every stupa rises from the adamantine base of the Buddha's throne; every stupa is built precisely at this same centre of the world, the mid-point of the cosmos where the Buddha attained Awakening. Mythically, and in physical space, this central point of the cosmos is located beneath the Bodhi Tree at Bodhgayā, but metaphysically it is simultaneously stationed at every point of the universe. The Place of Enlightenment (bodhimaṇḍa)[20] is not localized at any one point in space; the Adamantine Seat whereon the Buddha sits when he attains Illumination is not a point fixed in space and time; it is in every place and at every instant, wherever and whenever an ascension is made from this mundane plane of saṃsāra to the "other shore" of nirvāṇa. The bodhimaṇḍa is the visible symbol, positioned in geographical space and in historical time, of an invisible locus of Liberation. It represents a focal point of Consciousness and of being universally,[21] one that transcends all geographical and historical contingencies, all spatial and temporal limitations.

The Throne does not locate a single Awakening but is the site occupied by all the previous Buddhas [22] and by "every Bodhisattva on the day of his Great Awakening".[23] The thousand Buddhas of the present aeon (bhadrakalpa) are seated here in diamond samādhi (vajra-samādhi);[24] it is the same seat that all previous sages (muni) have occupied from the beginning of time.[25]

The place of the Buddha's Enlightenment is the vajra-Seat. We shall see in the following that the vajra, the preeminent symbol of the Buddha's Illumination, is both "diamond" and "lightning".[26] The Knowledge gained by the Buddha at his Enlightenment is diamond-like in its permanence, its

18. Coomaraswamy, 1977, 1, p. 156, n. 14; cf. Sivaramamurti, 1942, p. 19.

19. Śubhākarasiṃha, p. 647.b.

20. Bodhimaṇḍa is translated into Sino-Japanese as dōjō, 道場 , lit., "Place of the Way".

21. Tucci, 1961, p. 40; Coomaraswamy, 1935a, p. 56.

22. *Jātaka* I.71. 23. *Jātaka* I.74; *Buddhacarita* XIII.67.

24. Hsuan-tsang, in Julien, 1857, 1, pp. 458 ff.; Beal, 1911, p. 103; 1906, pp. 115 f.; Auboyer, 1949, p. 89; cf. *Buddhacarita* XIII.68.

25. SPS XIII.67 26. See below, pp. 174 ff.

indestructibility and its radiance; the sudden illumination of this Knowledge is like a flash of lightning. The vajra represents the immutable stability of the Buddha's Total Knowledge, coincident with the centre of the spatial cosmos : the vajra is an axial symbol; its shaft defines the axis of the world.

The Buddha's Throne is adamant, vajra-like, because located at the world's centre. It is "at the navel of the plane of earth; it is possessed of transcendent entirety; no other place on earth but this is the realm of samādhi,[27] the situation of the goal".[28] It is at the umbilicus of the universe; it is the cosmic omphalos.[29] The Throne is also vajra-like because it occupies the place of permanence and indestructibility. The world centre is the point of perfect equilibrium and unshakable stability. He who sits at this central pivot of the universe is established steadfast; he triumphs over motion. "Before he took his seat the Bodhisattva trod down the earth in the four directions; all the regions shook, but when he came to this place, the ground remained calm and stable".[30] The Adamantine Throne is the solid and firm base of the earth; without this foundation the earth would be unstable... "All the Bodhisattvas who wish to subdue the demons and reach the state of Buddha must sit upon this throne (for) if they sit elsewhere the earth would lose its balance... when the earth shakes to its foundations, this place alone is not shaken".[31]

This visible form of the unconquerable (aparājita) seat of Awakening and seat of Victory[32] is a slab of stone (P. pallaṅka) supported on a plain, rectangular base, and is so represented in early Buddhist art.[33] The rock-slab Buddha's Throne (visually and symbolically homologous with the primordial sacrificial altar) is closely associated with the stupa. Hsuan-tsang gives an account of a stupa built at the place where the Buddha combatted demons. The legend records that the demons lifted up a block of stone and invited the Buddha to sit upon it and preach the Dharma to them. Since that time "the infidels have united their efforts to raise this stone, but are unable to budge it from the place where the demons placed it".[34] Elsewhere he tells another story of similar import, about an enormous stone that stood at the summit of a mountain. Descending from the heavens the Buddha sat upon this rock during one whole night, deeply absorbed in meditation. On this stone the gods built a stupa of silver, gold and precious stones.[35]

* * * * *

Hsuan-tsang, describing the Adamantine Throne at Bodhgayā, tells us that it was "constructed at the beginning of the present aeon (bhadrakalpa) and raised up at the same time as the broad earth. Located at the centre

---

27. For samādhi, "at-one-ment" or "consummation", see below, p. 280.

28. *Buddhacarita* XIII.68. The *Nidānakathā* similarly emphasises that the location of the Buddha Seat is at the navel of the World Wheel. Cf. Coomaraswamy, 1935a, p. 42.

29. Senart, 1882, p. 235; *Jātaka* IV.146.

30. Hsuan-tsang, in Julien, 1857, 1, p. 458; cf. *Buddhacarita* XIII.68; *Nidānakathā*; *Mahābodhivaṃsa* 79; Auboyer, 1959, p. 89. For a fuller account, see above, p. 40 f.

31. Hsuan-tsang, in Julien, 1857, 1, p. 139; Beal, 1911, p. 103; Beal, 1906, p. 116. 32. *Jātaka* I.73-77.

33. Coomaraswamy, 1935a, p. 42; Auboyer, 1959, p. 90.

34. Hsuan-tsang, in Julien, 1857, 1, p. 382; Auboyer, 1959, p. 56.

35. Hsuan-tsang, op.cit., p. 440.

of the three thousand great chiliocosms, it descends below the earth to rest upon a Golden Wheel; above, it reaches to the limits of the earth".[36] Chinese inscriptions at Bodhgayā[37] give further details and relate the vajra-Seat to the three Buddha Bodies (trikāya) : 1). Nirmāṇakāya - "In depth the Seat goes down as far as the base of the Golden Wheel; in height it rises above the plane of earth". 2). Saṃbhogakāya - "The Throne rises above the three worlds; its light shines as far as the abode of the gods above; the fire of the kalpa will forever find it hard to reach". 3). Dharmakāya - "Without beginning, without birth or extinction, its traces are universally liberated from the past and the future".

These formulations allude to Buddhist cosmological concepts and more particularly to the Receptacle World (bhājana-loka) described in Vasubandhu's *Abhidharmakośa*[38] : three circles (maṇḍala) are strung one above the other upon a central axis. The lowest of these circles, of immeasurable extent, is the circle of Space (ākāśa-maṇḍala); above this is the circle of the Lower Waters, from which rises the Cosmic Mountain, Meru; and the upper mandala is the Circle of Gold (kañcana-maṇḍala) or Land of Gold (kañcana-bhūmi), that is, Hsuan-tsang's Golden Wheel, which is rimmed by mountains and contains the continents, the seven concentric mountain ranges and seas. It is pierced at its hub by the axial Mountain, whose summit reaches to the celestial regions. The Circle of Gold is the solidified foam of the Waters in the circle that supports it, "stirred by the dawn wind of creation which is impelled by the latent causality of past events"; "it is 'the

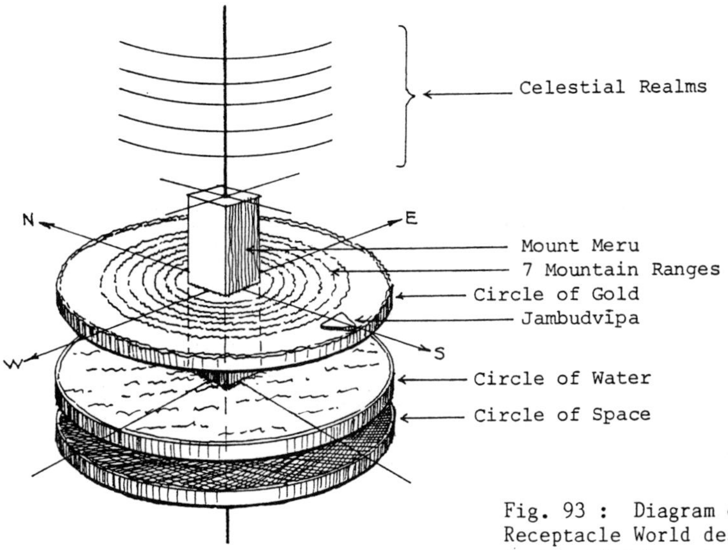

Fig. 93 : Diagram of the Receptacle World described in the *Abhidharmakośa*.

36. Ibid, p. 458 ff.; cf. ibid, pp. 139 ff.; Beal, 1911, p. 103; Auboyer, 1959, p. 74; Coomaraswamy, 1935a, p. 52.

37. Chavannes, 1896, No. 11; cf. Auboyer, 1959, p. 75.

38. *Abhidharmakośa* III.45 ff., in Vallée Poussin, 1926, 2, pp. 138 ff. This cosmology is also outlined in D II.107; Mil 68; and see also Kirfel, 1920, and the other references given below, p. 329, n. 47. See also Coomaraswamy, 1935a, pp. 52 f.; Auboyer, 1959, p. 76.

foundation of the earth', firmly established amidst the possibilities of existence".[39] The symbolism is of pre-Vedic antiquity and is strongly reminiscent of the Brahmanic concept of the Golden Egg : "Agni at one time cast his eyes upon the Waters. 'May I pair with them", he thought. He united with them, and what was emitted as his seed, that became gold. Therefore the latter shines like fire, being Agni's seed, hence it is found in water, for he poured it into the Waters".[40] Agni, cognate with Fire and with Breath, descends into the Waters to awaken the potentialities of form contained therein, and produces the Golden Embryo of the Universe.[41]

In the cosmological schema described in the *Abhidharmakośa* the three circles of Space, Water and Gold, as well as the world they underpin, are upheld and centred by an axis that rises from the Waters in the form of the Cosmic Mountain, Meru. The continental island, Jambudvīpa, the dwelling place of man and the location of Bodhgayā, lies to the South of Meru, so that the cosmological and the geographical centres are not coincident. The inconsistency only appears, however, when the symbolic nature of the axis is forgotten : the metaphysical axis of the universe is present at every point of the cosmos; and the true location of the Adamantine Throne is within each person.

* * * * *

The full implications of the symbolism of the sacred space, here considered in its horizontal significance, will become apparent when the symbolism of the *harmikā* is considered in the following, where it will be shown that the sacred enclosure, centred by the Tree, Post or Throne, is duplicated at the summit of the stupa's dome. The *caitya-vṛkṣa* and *bodhimaṇḍa* marked out at the level of the ground are terrestrial reflections of a supernal exemplar located at the summit of the World Mountain.

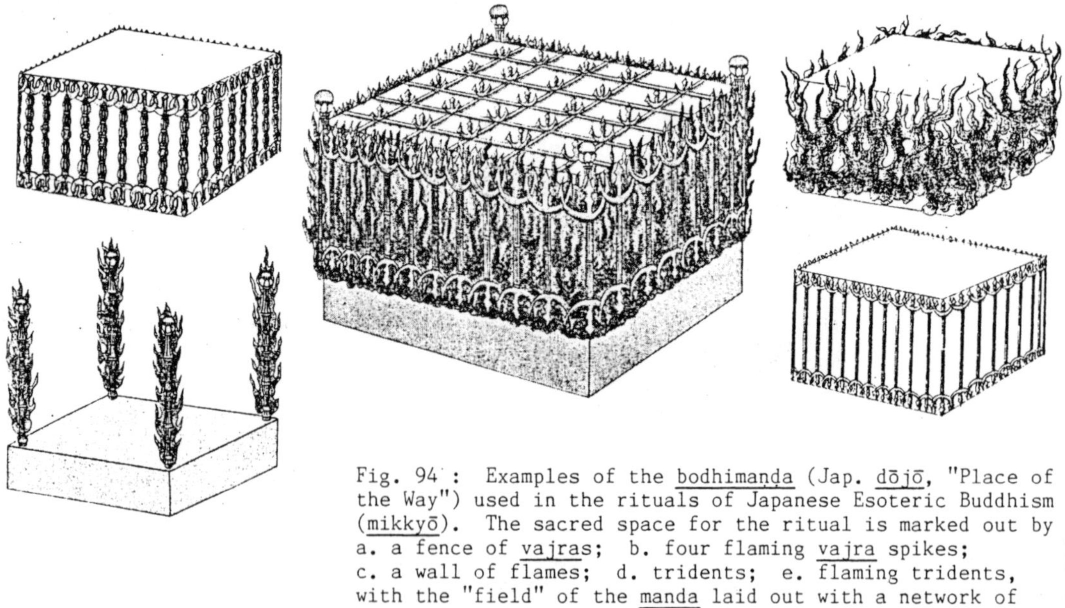

Fig. 94 : Examples of the *bodhimaṇḍa* (Jap. *dōjō*, "Place of the Way") used in the rituals of Japanese Esoteric Buddhism (*mikkyō*). The sacred space for the ritual is marked out by a. a fence of *vajras*; b. four flaming *vajra* spikes; c. a wall of flames; d. tridents; e. flaming tridents, with the "field" of the *manda* laid out with a network of adamantine Breath-threads having *vajras* at the crossings.

---

39. Coomaraswamy, 1935a, p. 53. 40. ŚB II.1.1.5.

41. Cf. Coomaraswamy, 1935a, p. 88, n. 132.

THE PILE

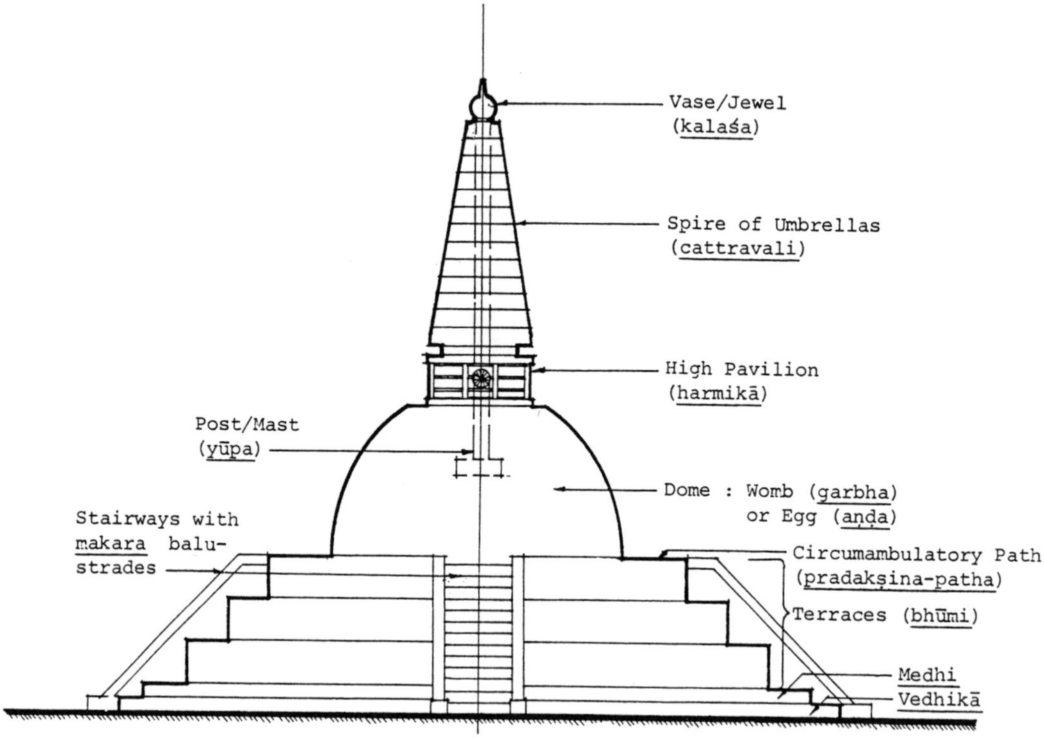
Vase/Jewel
(kalaśa)
Spire of Umbrellas
(cattravali)
High Pavilion
(harmikā)
Post/Mast
(yūpa)
Dome : Womb (garbha)
or Egg (aṇḍa)
Stairways with
makara balu-
strades
Circumambulatory Path
(pradakṣina-patha)
Terraces (bhūmi)
Medhi
Vedhikā

THE PARTS OF THE STUPA

14 THE SYMBOLISM OF THE AXIS.

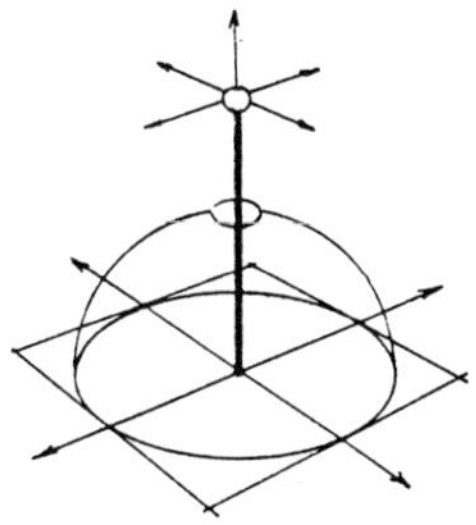

The gnomon-pillar erected in the ritual of demarcation of the stupa plan marks the vertical axis that centres the stupa mass. Symbolically it signifies the axis mundi, and marks the line that connects the mid-point of this world to the mid-points of all the other states of existence and to the unitary and principial point whence they all derive.

The symbolism of the axis mundi is ubiquitous and perennial. It figures in the world outlook of many peoples, disparate in both space and time.[1] It is ritually set up to serve as a line of communication with other planes of existence and as a way of return to their common Source. It is a pathway of ascent, leading upward through the confining carapace of the physical world, passing beyond its limits and bounds to the unlimited and the unbounded. The axial pillar leads to the realm where the shackles of space and time are shaken loose. At the same time it forms a channel for a downflowing of reality into the less-than-real world, an influx that imbues the world with meaning, opening up the finite to the Infinite and time to the Eternal.

This chapter examines the significance of the axis, firstly in its broad Indian context, and then as it more specifically pertains to Buddhism.

1. THE PILLAR AND COSMOGENESIS.

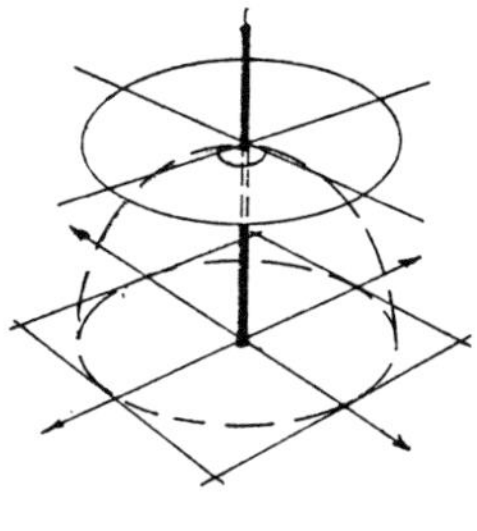

The genesis of the world is described in the Vedas as a "pillaring apart" of Heaven and Earth : "It is by being pillared apart by this Pillar that Heaven and Earth stand fast".[2] Heaven and Earth, originally fused, are split apart and held firm by the World Axis. The symbolic analogue is the rising of the sun : sky and earth which had been confused and indistinct in the darkness of night, become distinct in the light of the dawn. The light separates them and, pillar-like, props them apart[3]:

---

1. The symbolism of the axis mundi is a recurrent theme in the writings of Guénon, Coomaraswamy and Eliade.

2. AV X.8.2.

3. Mus, 1935, p. 346; cf. Bergaigne, 1878, p. 194.

the light of Dawn "divorces the conterminous regions (Sky and Earth) and makes manifest the several worlds".[4] So likewise Heaven and Earth are propped apart by the Column of the Sun at the Dawn of the cosmos.

The pillaring apart of Heaven and Earth by the Column of the Sun coincides with the deployment of Midspace : "The sun is space, for it is only when it rises that the world is seen".[5] The directions of space emanate from the Sun-Pillar, and when the Sun sets space returns into the Void.[6] The Sun-Strut, support of the worlds and origin of the quarters of space, is symbolically raised each morning of the world and removed each evening. In this way the daily drama of the dawn repeats in symbolic miniature the theme of cosmic generation; it images cosmogonic beginnings and the manifestation of the worlds.

With reference to the same symbolic theme Indra enlarges, separates and supports heaven and earth by "making the sun to shine",[7] "engendering the sun and the dawn"[8] and "opening the shadows with the dawn and the sun".[9] He enlarges the two worlds "like the dawn",[10] and causes them "to grow like the sun".[11] "He extends heaven by the sun; and the sun is the prop whereby he struts it".[12] In the Brahmanic sacrificial rituals Agni's column of fire and smoke rising towards Heaven acts as its support.[13] The sacrificial post (yūpa), which is specifically identified with the Dawn, is likewise the support of Heaven.[14] Again, Viṣṇu props up Heaven with a Pillar, first fixing the Eastern "point" of the Earth.[15]

The Solar Pillar is also a Column of Breath. The axial strut of the universe is a pneumatic pillar, a Breath-Post. "Breath is the kingpost (vaṃśa)",[16] at once the principial Pillar of the cosmic house and the pneumatic spine (vertebral column, axis) of the person.[17] The Pillar is identified with the Gale. The diremption of Heaven and Earth is an insufflation. As the dawning Sun differentiates the Worlds so the Dawn Wind inflates and animates them, and the Column of the Gale of the Spirit, of the Breath of Brahman, is raised to support the vault of Heaven.[18]

---

4. RV VII.80; cf. VI.32.2; ŚB IV 6.7.9. The separation of the conjoint principles by light is the theme of the story of the Purūravas and Urvaśi : see ŚB XI.5.1.4.

5. JUB I.25.1-2. 6. JUB III.1.1-2. 7. RV VIII.3.6.

8. RV III.32.8. 9. RV I.62.5. 10. RV X.134.1.

11. RV VIII.12.7. 12. RV X.111.5.

13. Mus, 1935, p. 346, citing Bergaigne, 1878, p. 224.

14. *Idem*. Cf. Bergaigne, 1878, p. 266; Renou, 1928, pp. 52 ff.

15. RV VII.99.1; cf. X.110.4.

16. AĀ III.1.4; cf. Coomaraswamy, 1940, p. 58, and 58, n. 30, where he adduces evidence that vaṃṣa is "kingpost".

17. Cf. ŚB X.2.6.14-15, where the spine, "the one hundred and first part" in relation to the hundred parts of the skeleton, is its Ātman, Spirit or Breath.

18. See above, pp. 58 ff.

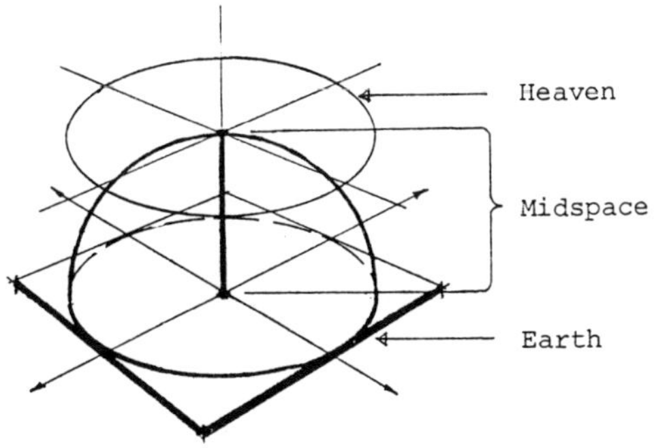

Fig. 95 : The axial Pillar props apart Heaven and Earth to open up Midspace.

2. THE PILLAR AS DEITY.

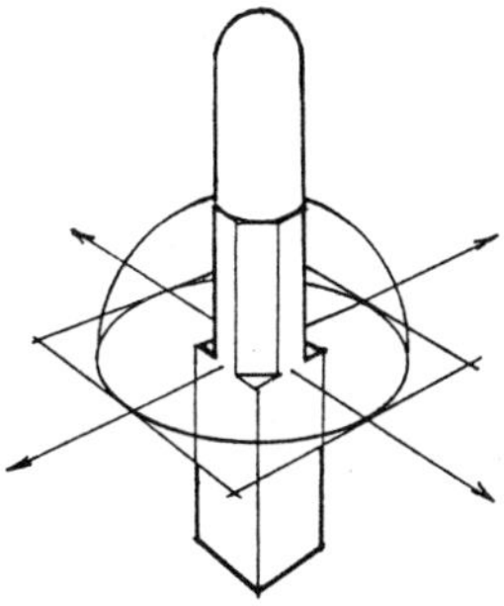

The Pillar of the Dawn or Column of the Sun that figures in the cosmogenetic symbolism of the diremption of Heaven and Earth is the same Pillar (skambha) that is invoked in a hymn of the *Atharva Veda*,[19] which says, "Skambha bears these three worlds, the Earth and the Sky; Skambha bears the wide Midspace, Skambha bears the six vast regions and has pervaded this entire universe". The Skambha is "the Great Being in the midst of the world", "to whom all the gods are joined as the branches around the trunk of the tree".[20] The Pillar includes within itself the totality of manifestation : "The Pillar is all this enspirited (ātmanvat) world,

---

19. AV X.7.1-3, quoted in Kramrisch, 1946, p. 118; cf. Bosch, 1960, p. 93.

20. Kramrisch, 1946, p. 118.

whatever breathes or winks",[21] and "therein inheres all this".[22] This "Pillar of Light extending downwards from the Sun in the zenith to rest on the earth"[23] is a purely pneumatic or spiritual essence,[24] identical with Brahman[25] : "He who knows the Brahman in man knows the Supreme Being and he who knows the Supreme Brahman knows the Skambha".[26] Brahman is the pratiṣṭhar, a term commonly employed in the Vedic texts and expressing the concept of a pillar, support, base of the universe; in the *Mahābhārata* and *Purāṇas* it is described as dhruva,[27] that is, "fixed", "motionless", "firm" and "permanent".[28]

Aspects of this Pillar symbolism are reflected in other mythic and iconographic representations. In the Vedic literature the figure of the Great Mother was associated with a gigantic prop supporting the celestial vault; in some texts she is the personification of that sky-supporting strut, and in others she is the support of the sun.[29] With similar significance Aja-Ekapāda, the "One-Footed He-Goat",[30] is described as the "supporter of the sky".[31] He embodies the lightning[32] and thus "sustains" the two worlds by dispelling the shadows in the instant of his flashing. He is identified with the Sun,[33] is located in the East[34] and is the cosmic support that makes firm the two worlds.[35] He is the solar animal perched on the World Tree[36] and is thereby connected with the ubiquitous tradition that locates in the East a tree whose branches support the rising sun, symbolized by an animal, bird or fruit,[37] and also with an iconography that shows Sūrya, the Sun, as a uniped composed of two parts, one visible and radiating light and the other dark, called "the leg" (pāda), through

---

21. AV X.8.2. 22. AV X.8.6.

23. Kramrisch, 1946, p. 351, quoting AB V.28.1.

24. Coomaraswamy, 1938a, p. 428. 25. Eliade, 1958, p. 115.

26. AV X.7.17.

27. Dhruva is etymologically related to dharma, which is likewise "fixed", "firm", "stable", etc. See also n. 64 in "The Pillar in Buddhism" below, p. 173.

28. Eliade, 1958a, pp. 115-116, where he refers the reader to notes collected by Gonda, 1950, pp. 47f.

29. Przyluski, 1932, p. 95, quoted in Combaz, 1935, p. 114.

30. Mus, 1935, p. 346; Bosch, 1960, p. 207; Macdonell, 1897, p. 73; Keith, 1925, p. 137; Przyluski, 1932, pp. 307-332; Hopkins, 1915, pp.85 & 146; etc. 31. RV X.65.18. 32. Macdonell, 1897, pp. 73f.

33. Henry, 1893, p. 24; Bloomfield, 1894, p. 86.

34. TB III.1.2.8. 35. AV XIII.1.6.

36. Przyluski, 1930, p. 458, quoted in Mus, 1935, p. 346.

37. This evokes the Chinese symbolism of the sacred mulberry tree, called the tree of day, of light and of the sun, the tree which "makes the sun to rise" and is the support of heaven. "It is described as standing in the East, its roots and trunk in the nether-world and its branches and crown reaching up into the sky" (Mai-mai Sze, 1957, 1, p.89; cf. Gieseler, p.174;

which for eight months he sucks up water that redescends during the remaining four months of the year.[38] Sūrya's body is wholly contained within this single leg so that he is one tall pillar (stambha) or solar standard.[39] Aja-Ekapāda is also equated with Varuṇa, who "with his bright foot ascends the vault, with the Pillar holds apart the paired spheres, and upholds the sky".[40]

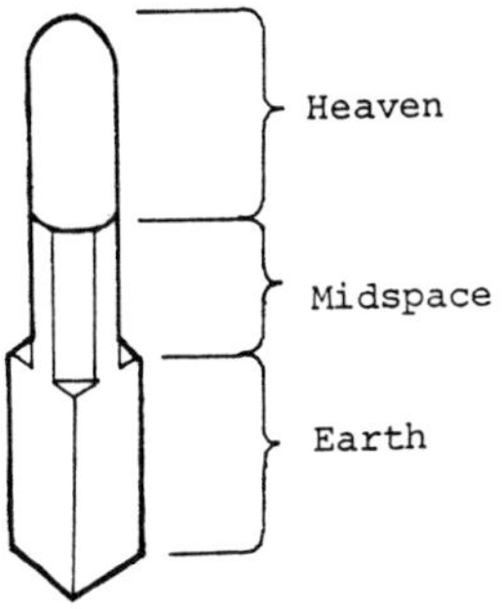

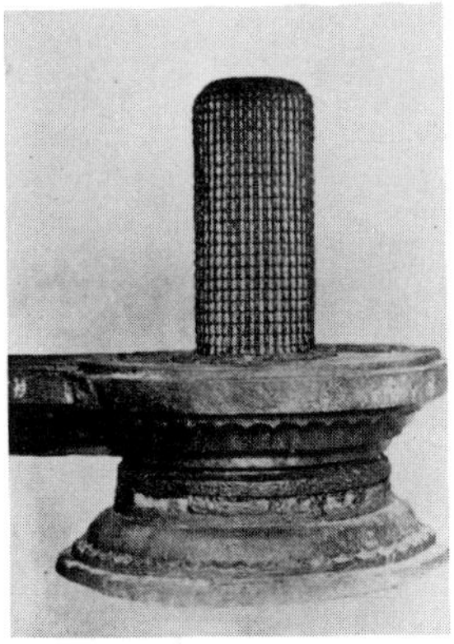

Fig. 96 : The liṅga as cosmos, showing the correspondence of its parts with Heaven, Earth and Midspace.

Fig. 97 : A sahasra-liṅga or "thousand linga", divided into 25 facets each having 40 miniature representations of liṅgas, representing the proliferation of the liṅga into the directions of the universe.

Fig. 98 : A catur-mukha-liṅga, "liṅga with four faces", with heads emerging in the four directions.

Deity as pillar is a recurrent theme in Hinduism. One of the names of Śiva-Rudra is Sthāṇu, "Pillar", and he is described as sthānu-bhūta, "whose essence is a pillar".[41] The identification of Śiva and the pillar as axis mundi is the main significance of the liṅga, pre-eminent symbol of the god. Taken literally it is the phallus, representing the essence of cosmic procreative forces, but its form reveals that it is nothing other than the axial pillar of the universe : square at the base, octagonal at its middle portion and circular at the summit, its parts conform with the shapes associated with Earth (the square), Midspace (the octagon), and Heaven (the circle). Its form subsumes the three worlds, at once separated and joined together within its vertical mass. Identified with the vajra, the lightning, it is the shaft of light, the fiery axis of manifestation that penetrates and fertilizes the yoni, the vulva, the altar, hearth, Mother of the Fire, the Earth.[42]

Bulling, 1952, p.99; Mus, 1935, p.347). This is probably the tree, depicted in the character tung, 東 , "East", that shows the sun, 日 , rising behind a tree, 木 (see Wieger, 1927, p. 282).

38. Mbh VIII.79.78; XII.363.5ff.; cf. Hopkins, 1915, p. 85; Auboyer, 1949, p. 119; Przyluski, 1930, p. 456.

39. Bosch, 1960, p. 208. 40. RV VIII.41.8.

41. Bosch, 1960, p. 187.

42. Zimmer, 1946, p. 128, note by Coomaraswamy; Daniélou, 1964, p.229.

Fig. 99 : Examples from South India of images of Śiva-ekapāda-murti, Śiva in his manifestation as the One-footed God who stands as the central Pillar of the World. Brahmā and Viṣṇu emerge from his sides to form trident (<u>triśula</u>), one of the symbolic forms of Śiva.

Fig. 100 : Two examples of the <u>mukha-liṅga</u>, which show the face of the divinity emerging from the <u>liṅga</u> as the central axis of the universe.

Its axial nature is further indicated by its location within the Hindu temple, where it is positioned on the perpendicular that centres the building and emerges through the finial,[43] a conformation that is mirrored in the cosmo-physiology of man, in whom Tantric *yoga* places a *liṅga* at the centre of each of the *cakras* that are superimposed one above the other along the vertical axis formed by the spinal column.[44]

The strict equivalence of *liṅga* and fiery Pillar is explicitly enunciated in the myth of Śiva's manifestation as a *liṅga* (*liṅgodbhavamurti*), which relates how Brahmā and Viṣṇu quarrelled over who was the mightiest. Suddenly Śiva appeared before them as a fiery *liṅga*, burning with thousands of flames and resembling hundreds of cosmic conflagrations. Whereupon Brahmā, taking his form as a Goose, attempted to fly to the apex of this blazing column, while Viṣṇu, assuming the figure of a Boar, plunged down through the earth to find its foot. After a thousand years they had still

Fig. 101 : Hindu deities manifested from the Pillar.
a. Śiva as Liṅgodbhava-murti.
b. The Nārasiṃha-avatāra of Viṣṇu.

43. Kramrisch, 1946, pp. 168 & 279.

44. Eliade, 1958a, p. 241ff.; Avalon, 1918, *passim*; and below, pp. 317 ff.

not reached its ends and, admitting their failure, bowed down in homage to the supreme god, Pillar of the Universe.[45]

Another expression of this concept is found in the myth of the Nārasiṃha-avatāra of Viṣṇu, in which it is told how Hiraṇyakaśipu, the king of the demons, challenged the god to prove his omnipresence by emerging from one of the pillars of the palace, at the same time drawing his sword and cleaving the pillar. Immediately a terrible roar was heard and Visnu, in a form that was half man and half lion, burst forth from the pillar, seized the blasphemer and tore him to pieces.[46]

In the Vedic texts the symbolism of the "heaven-supporting pillar in the East" finds its classical expression in the person of Agni, the god of the sacrificial fire. He is the Pillar[47] who separates the two worlds by propping them,[48] who "pillars apart Heaven and Earth",[49] who, "established as an angelic pillar, rules-and-wards the firmament".[50] He is "the Pillar of Life at the parting of the ways"[51] who supports the celestial vault above the earth by his flame or smoke,[52] "the Pillar supporting the kindreds (that is, gods and men)".[53] He is the World Tree with a thousand branches[54] who causes the sun to rise into the heavens,[55] who is the standard (ketu) of the sacrifice and as such the equivalent of the dawn, the standard that supports heaven in the East at daybreak.[56]

3. THE PILLAR IN BUDDHISM.

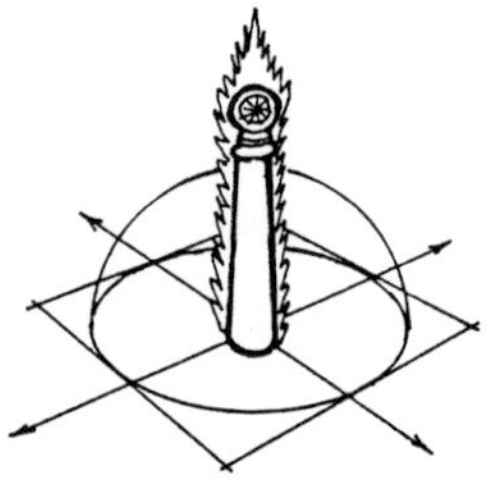

Almost all of the foregoing is valid for Buddhism. As Coomaraswamy has so brilliantly demonstrated in his many writings there is a continuity of symbolic content that runs from Vedic Brahmanism to Buddhism and there is similarly a considerable overlap of the symbolic expressions of later Hinduism and Buddhism. There is a common store of metaphysical symbols whence both traditions draw their spiritual sustenance. All that has been said of Brahman, Agni, Śiva and Viṣṇu as the skambha, the Cosmic Pillar, axis mundi and ontological foundation of the world, is equally true of the Buddha.

---

45. *Liṅga-purāṇa* I.17.5-52 and 19.8ff.; retold in Rao, 1914, p. 105ff.; Sastri, 1916, p. 93 & pl. XVI; Thapar, 1961, p. 78; Larousse, 1959, p. 391; Zimmer, 1946, pp. 128-130.

46. Zimmer, 1955, p. 294 & pl. 203; Rao, 1914, 2, 1, pp. 105ff.; Sastri, 1916, p. 93 & pl. 58; Thapar, 1961, pp. 60f. & pl. 58; Bosch, 1960, p. 188.

47. RV IV.5.1. 48. RV I.67.5; VI.8.3. 49. RV V.29.4.

50. RV IV.13.5. 51. RV X.5.6. 52. RV III.5.10; III.4.6.; IV.5.1; IV.6.2.3; VI.17.7. 53. RV I.59.1-2. 54. RV VI.13.1; VIII.19.33; IX.5.10.

55. RV V.6.4; IV.3.11.

56. RV I.113.19; III.8.8; cf. Mus, 1935, p. 347; Bosch, 1960, p.93; Coomaraswamy, 1935a, pp. 9f. & n. 15.

He likewise is a Pillar of Fire, "glowing with fiery energy",[57] the same igneous power that is displayed in the Twofold Miracle, in the conversion of Kassapa and when he takes his seat above Brahmā on the axis of the world.[58] Among the reliefs from Amarāvatī are to be seen many representations of the Buddha as a fiery pillar, comprizing feet marked with the Wheel of the Dharma and a trident (triśula) head.[59]

Fig. 102 : The adoration of the Buddha as a fiery Pillar.

57. Dh 387. 58. S I,144.

59. Coomaraswamy, 1935a, p.10 and figs. 4-10; cf. Ferguson, 1968, pls. 68 & 70. The trident in itself is an aniconic representation of the Buddha or, more specifically, of his three aspects as Buddha, Dharma and Saṅgha. It is a symbol of fire and can be thought of as representing three aspects of Agni. It is obviously coterminous in meaning with the trident of Śiva, which, among its other significances, is the central vertical axis (suṣumnā) and the two subtle channels (īḍā and piṅgalā) which rise from the fiery mūlādhāra according to the descriptions of the subtle physiology of the human body (see below, pp. 317ff.) When adorsed the trident is the three-prong vajra and when doubled and adorsed it is the five-prong vajra. As will

The representation of the Buddha as a fiery pillar is a survival of the Vedic symbolism and more specifically that embodied in the God of Fire, Agni. The Buddha and Agni are ontologically equivalent persons.[60] The epithet "Awakened at Dawn" is commonly applied to Agni and the Buddha is the "Awakened"; and in the same way that by his pillaring apart of the worlds at the dawn and in the East Agni draws men from the annihilation of confused sleep, so the Buddha similarly awakens them from the sleep of ignorance.

Fig. 103 : The Buddha represented as a Pillar. a. A gatepost from Sāñcī showing the Buddha as a florescent Pillar. It has the Buddha's feet, marked with the Wheel of the Dharma, at its base, and the Wheel (cakra) and trident (triśula) at its head. It stands within a sacred enclosure, indicated by a fence. b. A Buddha Pillar shown in an Amarāvatī relief, with the Dharma Wheel supported by lions in the manner of the Sārnāth pillar. The Buddha throne and footstool, showing the Buddha's feet, stand at its base. c. The Buddha as a fiery Pillar shown in a relief from Amarāvatī.

These analogies, implicit in the early Buddhist literature, are explicitly indicated in the Mahāyāna by the person of the Buddha Ratnaketu ("Jewel Banner" or "Jewel Light"),[61] who embodies the qualities of the Standard of Light. In the *Vedas* the unfurling of the banner denotes the bursting forth of the light of the dawn.[62] Agni is the standard of light

---

be shown, the vajra is the lightning axis of the world, and is specifically identified with the skambha that supports apart Heaven and Earth. For material on the triśula, see Coomaraswamy, 1935a, pp. 13ff.; Saunders, 1960, pp. 157f.; BKDJT, p. 1507, s.v. Sankogeki; Combaz, 1935, pp. 112ff.; Senart, 1882, p. 484.

60. Coomaraswamy, 1935a, pp. 8-10, 14 and notes 11-14.

61. Skt. ketu is both "banner" and "light".

62. RV I.92.1; VII.76.2; cf. Bergaigne, 1878, I, p. 224.

(ketu) raised in the East at dawn, the standard that splits apart and then supports the worlds.[63] The banner of Indra, identified with the Dharma or Order that governs the universe,[64] carried on the eight-wheeled chariot of the Sun,[65] and adorned with the square of ordered space and the circle of ordered time, is raised "in the beginning" and, since Indra is the guardian (lokapāla) of that quarter, in the East, the direction of beginnings.[66] The effulgence of its unfurling scatters the hosts of the Enemy, the children of darkness : the light of ordered cosmos overcomes the obscurity of chaos.[67]

Fig. 104 : The Buddha as a Pillar. The five pillars (vāhalkada) which stand in each of the directions around many early Indian and Sri Lankan stupas represent the Buddha manifested into the four directions of space from the Centre.

Ratnaketu embodies these several symbolisms. As the personification of the Banner of Light he rules over the East, has the ruddy colour of the rising sun and symbolizes the first dawning or unfolding of the Mind of Enlightenment (bodhicitta). Śubhākarasiṃha, writing on the significance of Ratnaketu, explains that in the same way that the unfolding of the general's banner in battle rallies the troops and inspires them to defeat the enemy, so the unfurling of the Mind of Enlightenment routs the forces of darkness; and so likewise the Buddha Śākyamuni, seated beneath the Bodhi Tree in the East at dawn, defeated the hordes of Māra by revealing to them the banner,

---

63. See above, p. 170.

64. As noted above, the word dharma is closely connected etymologically with dhruva, which is "firm", "stable", "fixed", and also "pole", or, more specifically, the Pole Star.

65. The chariot is the day; its eight wheels are the eight divisions (yama) of the day, each of three hours.

66. The square is the foremost of Indra's ornaments. The square on Indra's banner is called the lokapāla, and the guardians of the directions - - Indra, Yāma, Varuṇa and Kuvera - are established at its cardinal points. See Kramrisch, 1947, p. 198.

67. Kramrisch, 1947, *passim*, and 1946, pp. 40f., where references are given.

or the light, of his Wisdom.[68] Ratnaketu reflects the qualities associated with Agni and with Indra's banner : he is the standard erected as the central shaft of the world; he is the rising Sun in the East; he is the revelation of the Dharma that brings order to chaos; he is the light of Wisdom that severs and dispels the darkness of ignorance.

Fig. 105 : The Buddha Ratnaketu, shown making the gesture of touching the earth (bhūmisparśa-mudrā), from the Taizōzuzō version of the Matrix World Mandala. In the standard version of the Mandala the significance of the five Buddhas is rotated (sengen) and in this case Ratnaketu is shown making the sign of bestowing vows (varada-mudrā).

Indra's banner, adorned with the square, is the symbolic equivalent of the "four-square" vajra[69] with which Indra smites the Serpent Vṛtra and pins the Rock at the dawning of the world. Like the banner, the vajra, the Diamond Thunderbolt, was also taken over into Buddhism and there became one of its pre-eminent symbols and the very foundation of the doctrines of the Vajrayāna, the Way of the Vajra. The vajra is a multivalent symbol[70] : clear and transparent like water, it is taken to represent the Void (śūnyatā) it is the pounder or pestle of Knowledge (jñāna) that crushes the defilements of ignorance and passion so as to reveal the eternal and immutable reality of the many dharmas;[71] it is a weapon hurled to destroy the hindrances that block the attainment of Enlightenment, used as Indra did to destroy the Serpent; it is the lightning flash of Awakening; it is the diamond, indestructible, permanent and shining like the Dharma.[72] "Lying beyond words or thought, depending on nothing, showing no dharmas, without beginning, middle or end, inexhaustible, transcending all imperfection, immutable, incorruptible - Knowledge of the Real is like the vajra, which possesses three surpassing qualitites : it is indestructible; it is the most excellent of jewels; and it is the foremost of weapons".[73] "Even when buried in the mud of saṃsāra for innumerable aeons Knowledge is not decayed and never loses its ability to crush the passions; in the same way the diamond, even though buried in the earth for millennia still remains undecayed and unharmed, and is still capable of crushing the encrustations of lust and anger".[74]

---

68. Śubhākarasiṃha, quoted in MKDJT, p. 2026, s.v. Hōdō Butsu. This theme is developed below in connection with the symbolism of the stabilizing of the site. 69. RV IV.22.2.

70. See Saunders, 1960, pp. 184-191; Glasenapp, 1944, pp. 23f.; BKDJT, p. 4234, s.v., Batchira, p. 1309, s.v., Kongō, and 1333, s.v., Kongōsho; MKDJT, p. 655, s.v., Kongō, p. 696, s.v., Kongōsho, and p. 1798, s.v., Bazara; Coomaraswamy, 1935a, pp. 14f. & 42-46.

71. MKDJT, p. 696, s.v., Kongōsho. 72. Saunders, 1960, p. 185.

73. Śubhākarasiṃha, quoted in MKDJT, p. 655, s.v., Kongō.

74. *Idem.*

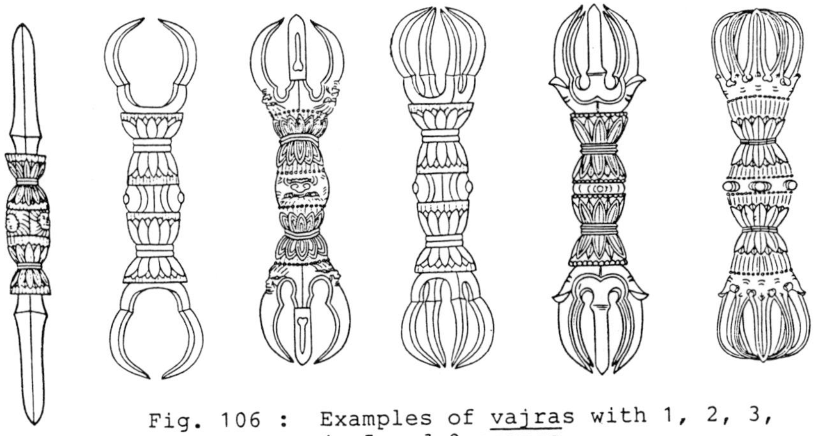

Fig. 106 : Examples of *vajras* with 1, 2, 3, 4, 5 and 9 prongs.

These various qualities of the *vajra* are symbolically embodied in the sceptre-like implement called by the same name and employed in the rituals of the Vajrayāna. It is held in the right hand while the left normally holds its complementary, the bell (*ghanta*). It is not germane to this study to record the many symbolic ascriptions of the different types of the ritual *vajra*, whether in its usual single-, three- or five-pronged varieties, or in its rarer forms having two, four and from six to nine prongs[75] : the lines of the network of their correspondences and associations would, if followed far enough, eventually lead to the most remote corners of the Buddhist doctrine. What is relevant here is that each is an axial symbol, homologous with the Cosmic Pillar.

Fig. 107 : A Dharma Wheel with *vajra* spokes.

Fig. 108 : A Japanese reliquary stupa.

75. MKDJT, 1675, s.v., *Dokukosho* ("single prong pounder"); p. 791, s.v., *Sankosho* ("three prong pounder"); and p. 585, s.v., *Gokosho* ("five prong pounder"). The various types are described in Saunders, 1960, pp. 186ff.

The shaft of the vajra defines the axis of the world or, its equivalent, the axle of the Wheel. The Wheel of the Dharma is frequently shown with vajra spokes, thus identifying the vajra with the radii that connect our plane of existence (the felly) with the Void-point at the hub. In this connection Coomaraswamy has noted that "the point or end of the vajra corresponds to aṇi, the point of the axle tree that penetrates the navel of the Wheel"; further, that akṣa-ja, "axle-, or axis-born", is a kenning for vajra; and also that Kṛṣṇa's cakra, "wheel", is said to be vajra-nabha, in which nabha is "nave" or "navel".[76] The concept is admirably demonstrated by the Japanese reliquary stupa shown in fig.108, in which the lower point of the five-prong vajra penetrates, in the manner of an axle, the hub of a rimbō, or Wheel of the Dharma, while its upper point doubles as the stem of the lotus, which is the symbolic equivalent of the World Tree and an alternate expression of the axis mundi.[77] This example is of particular interest in that it iconographically assimilates the vajra and the stupa. A similar intent is evident in examples of vajras having a stupa form for the head instead of the usual prongs.

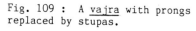

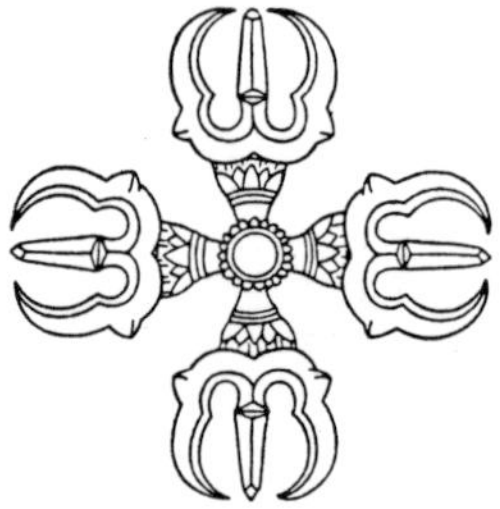

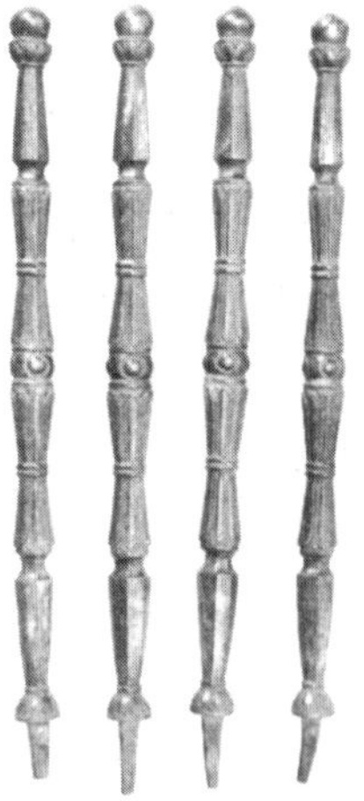

Fig. 109 : A vajra with prongs replaced by stupas.

Fig. 110 : A cross-form vajra (karma-vajra, lit. "action vajra").

Fig. 111 : Vajra spikes.

The cross-form vajra, called the karma-vajra,[78] even more explicitly reinforces these observations. Here the symbols of the Wheel and the vajra coalesce : the twelve prongs of the karma-vajra are the twelve links in the chain of Dependent Origination (pratītya-samutpāda) that constitute the Wheel of Becoming,[79] which, as we have seen, is identified with the Wheel of the Dharma.[80] In the rituals of Shingon Buddhism a karma-vajra is placed at each of the four corners of the mandala where it is symbolically fixed into position by a vertical vajra-spike (Jap. kongō-ketsu) so as to form a combination of three interlocking vajras, two crossing at right angles on the horizontal plane and a third rising as a vertical axis from their point

---

76. Coomaraswamy, 1935a, p.44.

77. For the symbolism of the lotus, see pp. 97ff. & 203ff.

78. Saunders, 1960, pp. 187f.; MKDJT, p. 243, s.v., Kamma-kongō.

79. *Idem*. 80. See above, pp. 85ff.

of intersection : the protective action of the symbol acts in all the directions of space.

It can now be seen that the word vajra carries spatial implications. Its frequent appearance in the names of Bodhisattvas such as Vajrapāṇi ("Vajra Hand"), Vajrasattva ("Vajra Being"), etc., implies that these Bodhisattvas have taken up their station at the still hub of the universe, the locus of the Vajra-Throne of all the Buddhas, the position of diamond-like permanence, immobility and immutability. They have become one with the axle-tree of the world and thereby attained an incorruptible Body of Vajra (vajra-kāya). This state of adamantine durability is iconographically represented by the Buddhas and Bodhisattvas of the Subtle Assembly (sūkṣma-maṇḍala, Jap. misai-e) of the Diamond World Mandala, where each figure is shown seated within a three-prong vajra to indicate the attainment of the Diamond Body, which is the Body of Enlightenment.

Fig. 112 : A Bodhisattva seated within a three-prong vajra to indicate the attainment of the Diamond Body of Enlightenment. The figure comes from the Subtle Assembly of the Diamond World Mandala. In this Assembly all the divinities are shown in their vajra form.

4. COGNATE SYMBOLS OF AXIALITY: THE MOUNTAIN AND THE TREE.

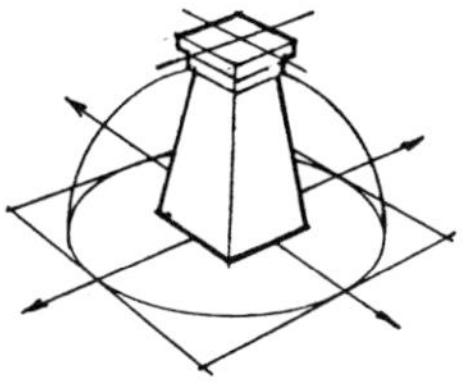

a. The Mountain.

For Hindus and Buddhists alike the sacred Mountain at the centre of the world is Mt. Meru, or Sumeru.[81] The axial nature of this Mountain is cogently expressed in the myth of the Churning of the Milky Ocean. Although ostensibly Hindu, this myth is frequently cited in Buddhist writings and depicted in Buddhist art and is to be taken as also forming part of the Buddhist repertoire of symbols.[82] The story tells how the Gods (deva) and the Titans (asura) interrupted their interminable warfare to cooperate in the churning of the cosmic sea in order to extract the beverage of immortality (amṛta). For the churning rod they used Meru,[83] the mountain pivot

---

81. Cosmological symbolism, which places Mt. Meru at the axial centre of the world, is examined below. See pp. 236ff. & 329ff.

82. It is frequently cited in Shingon Buddhist writings. See above, pp. 105f.

83. "In the original myth Mt. Mandara is used as the churning stick. In South-East Asian variations of the myth Mount Meru usually takes its place". (Heine-Geldern, 1956, p. 4, n.). For our present purposes Mt. Meru and Mt. Mandara are equivalent, being two names for the Mountain that centres the cosmos.

of the world, supported at is lower end by a giant Turtle and steadied at its summit by Viṣṇu. For the churning rope they used the cosmic Serpent Vāsuki,[84] twisting its coils around the mountain. With the Gods at one end and the Titans at the other, they pulled the Snake back and forth, setting the mountain spinning on its axis. Churned by this motion the Milky Ocean began to solidify and from its depths appeared thirteen precious objects. The last of these to emerge was the physician of the Gods, Ghanvantari, holding in his hand the moon, containing amṛta, the drink that confers everlasting life.[85]

Fig. 113 (continued on following page) : The centre and two ends of a relief at Angkor Wat depicting the Churning of the Milky Ocean. Viṣṇu steadies the churning rod, Mt. Mandara, which stands on the back of the Cosmic Turtle lying at the bottom of the Ocean. The Gods and Titans pull at either end of the Cosmic Snake, Vāsuki, who is wrapped around the Mountain in the manner of a churning cord.

In this myth the mountain-churning rod is the axis mundi, an assimilation that is underscored by its iconographical representations : in the numerous Khmer and Cham reliefs depicting this event the churning staff is rarely shown as a mountain, even though it is unambiguously and explicitly described as such in the story, but is usually shown as a pillar, a lotus or a tree.[86] For the Kampuchean sculptor, the mountain, lotus, pillar and tree were equivalent and interchangeable images of the world pivot.

---

84. Vāsuki is another name for Seśa and Ananta, the chthonic Serpent.

85. See Zimmer, 1955. p. 208f., 228f., and pl. 555; Coomaraswamy and Nivedita, 1916, pp. 314-316.

86. See Finot, 1912, p. 190; Bosch, 1960, p. 97, n.53.

This is not the place to go into all the associative ramifications of this story, except to point out that its axial symbolism has reference to both a macro- and a micro-cosmology. Macrocosmically the pillar-mountain is the centrally located *axis mundi*. The Gods and Titans pulling at either end of the Snake hypostatize the tension of cosmic oppositions, the pull and counterpull of universal complementaries; the churning signifies the genesis of the world. Microcosmically the churning-stick is the *suṣumṇā*, the central axis of the body; the Turtle on which it rests is the *mūlādhāra*; the two halves of the Serpent are the *īḍā* and *piṅgalā*; and Viṣṇu seated at the top

Fig. 114 : The subtle physiology of the body, showing the *merudaṇḍa*, the two subtle vectors, *īḍā* and *piṅgalā*, the *mūlādhāra-cakra* at the perineum and the *sahasrāra-cakra* at the crown of the head.

Fig. 115 : The Cosmic Stupa supported on a lotus rising from the Cosmic Turtle.

of the rod-mountain is the *sahasrāra-cakra*, the thousand-petalled lotus at the top of the head. The churning is a thinly-veiled reference to the meditational practices of *kuṇḍalinī yoga*, whereby the ambrosia (*amṛta*) contained within the root *mūlādhāra-cakra* is caused to flow up the *suṣumṇā* to the *sahasrāra-cakra*, whence it flows down to immortalize the body.[87] This physio-cosmological symbolism is not exclusively Hindu but has its Buddhist equivalent in the meditational practices aimed at the activation of the Mind of Awakening (*bodhicitta*) lying dormant within the lowest *cakra*.[88] The symbolism is reflected in the schema of the Buddhist cosmology, where the central Mountain of the world rests upon the Cosmic Turtle, a formula that is expressed in the cosmic stupa shown in fig. 115, which is shown supported on a lotus rising from the back of a turtle.

Relating this symbolism to the cosmic model shown on p. 18 above, the Mountain churning rod is the radius, the cosmic Turtle is the point where it strikes the plane of earth, and Viṣṇu on top of the Mountain is the Centre.

---

87. Dasgupta, 1962, pp. 239ff. 88. Ibid., pp. 93ff.

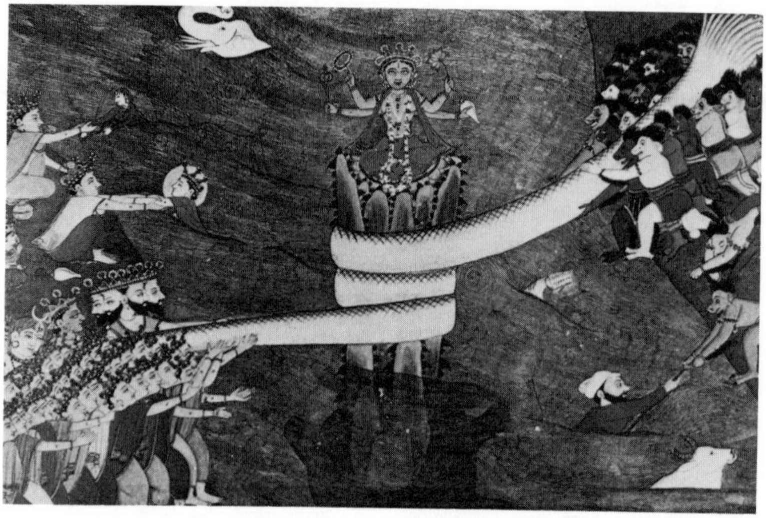

Fig. 116 :
The Churning of the Milky Ocean, shown in an Indian miniature.

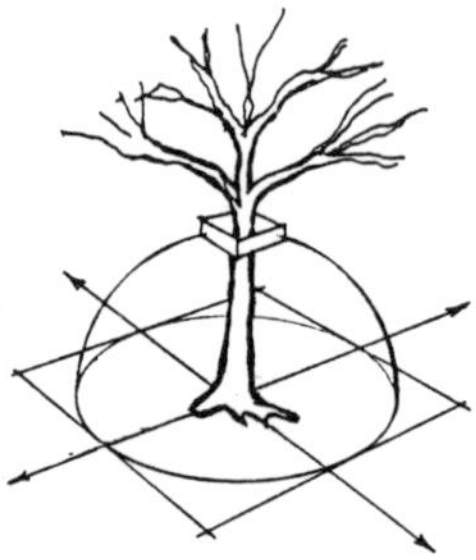

b. The Tree.

The Tree[89] figures the total cosmos : its branches are the heavens; the lower branches or the surface of the ground whence it grows are the plane of earth; the roots, plunging into the subterranean levels, are the hells; and the trunk is the world axis that centres and supports these multiple worlds.[90] Snakes lie coiled among its roots; birds sit among its branches : it connects the chthonic and uranian worlds. Its form embraces all existences, all the worlds, all the multiple states of manifestation, all life. It subsumes the Elements composing the universe : "Its branches are Ether, Air, Fire, Water and Earth".[91] In the *Upaniṣads* it is "this three-fold Brahman, whose name is 'Single Fig Tree', whose radiance is called the Sun";[92] and "the spirant Brahman is, as it were, a great green Tree".[93] A famous passage expresses the "relationship" of Ātman, the Spirit, and jivātman, its manifestation in the individual being, in terms of Tree symbolism : "Two birds, inseparably united companions, dwell in the same tree; the one eats the fruit of the tree, while the other looks on without eating".[94]

---

89. The Tree as axis mundi is an ubiquitous and perennial symbol, one of the richest and most widespread of symbolic themes. A bibliography on the subject would itself fill a volume. See, e.g., Cirlot, 1962, pp. 328ff.; Chevalier and Gheerbrant, 1973, 1, pp.96ff., s.v., Arbre ; Cook, 1974, pp. 9ff.; James, 1966; Butterworth, 1970; Yarden, 1971; Eliade, 1958b, pp. 265-278, and see also his bibliography, pp. 327ff. Viennot, 1954, is of particular interest as relating to Buddhist expressions of Tree symbolism.

90. Guénon, 1958, p. 46. 91. MU VI.4. 92. *Idem*.

93. SA XI.2; cf. Mhv I.69.

94. Muṇḍ. Up. III.1.1; Śveṭ. Up. IV.6; cf. RV I.64.20-21; Coomaraswamy, 1935a, p. 8; Guénon, 1945, p. 41, n. 1.

Fig. 117 : Representations of the Tree from India and Java (Borobudur).

In every symbolic context the Tree is central and axial. It is the perpendicular that centres the cosmos. World Tree and World Axis are coincident. As the Axis, the Tree is prominent among the aniconic representations of the Buddha, who is the humanized type of the Cosmic Pillar. In the *Kaliṅgabodhi Jātaka*, Ānanda requests the Buddha to prescribe a hallow or symbol (caitya, P. cetiya)[95] to which his devotees can make offerings in his absence. The answer is given that a tree is an appropriate and proper substitute for the Buddha's presence, both during his life and after his parinirvāṇa.[96] Similarly, in the *Divyāvadāna*, the Community (saṅgha) proposes to the Buddha that a Bodhi Tree be planted at the gate of the Jetavana Park, both for its protection and as a place for the performance of pūja. The Buddha approves, saying, "This, so to speak, will be my fixed abode".[97]

Fig. 118 : Three examples of the Wish-granting Tree. Borobudur.

---

95. For the meaning of cetiya, see below, p. 221, n. 1.

96. *Kaliṅgabodhi Jātaka* IV.228, in Cowell, 1895. Cf. Coomaraswamy, 1977, 1, pp. 156f.; 1935a, p. 4.

97. *Divyāvadāna*, in Cowell and Neil, 1886, cited by Auboyer, 1949, p. 73.

The Tree appears repeatedly in connection with the major events in the Buddha's life. It is a repetitive reminder that he is the Axis of the World. At his nativity, Māyā, his mother, came to the tree "which supported the mothers of the previous Jinas" : all the Buddhas of the past had been born beneath this same tree.[98] A branch bent down towards her and while she grasped it in her right hand the infant sprang forth from her right side.[99] The Buddha is born at the foot of the World Tree; but the story has further implications that are fully revealed in the iconographic representations of the birth. The pose adopted by Māyā at the nativity, with her right hand raised to grasp the tree branch, is the classic stance of the Yakṣi, or Tree Spirit, and some accounts say that her father was a Yakṣa : Siddhartha is associated with the Tree both by his axial position and by filiation.

a

b

c

Fig. 119 : a. The classic representation of the Yakṣi or Tree Spirit, grasping the branch of the Tree with her upraised right. b. The same stance adopte by Māyā at the birth of the Buddha. The infant Buddha is shown aspersed by two devas. c. The Buddha, represented by a Throne and Tree, assaulted by the hordes of Māra.

The relation of the Buddha and the Tree is again clearly indicated in the account of his first meditation. While his father the king was performing the ploughing ceremony that marks the beginning of the spring, the child prince was left at midday in the shade of a tree. Sitting upright the baby entered the first dhyāna, and when found in the evening the shadow of the tree had not moved.[100] This involves the perennial symbol of the Sun that stands stationary at the summit of the World Tree or the pinnacle of the World Mountain. It is the Sun Door at the entrance to the supra-cosmic realms. When the Bodhisattva enters dhyāna he has withdrawn his senses and his thoughts back to the centre of his being, to the point where the radial axis of the world, here represented by the tree, meets the plane of earthly existence. He is thus directly beneath the solar hub of the universe, the unmoving source of all light.[101]

---

98. Viennot, 1954, p.132, citing the *Lalita Vistara*, XI.

99. *Nidānakathā* II, p. 67. Cf. Viennot, 1954, p. 133.

100. *Nidānakathā* I, p. 74ff.; *Lalita Vistara* XI; Viennot, 1954, p. 133.

101. For the symbolism of the stationary Sun, see above, pp. 24ff.

The Buddha's attainment of Enlightenment is so closely connected with the Bodhi Tree that this is adopted as the specific sign of that event, and to this day the Bodhi Tree is worshipped as the symbol of that literally pivotal occurrence.

The story of the forty-nine days retreat[102] following the Enlightenment makes repeated references to the Tree : the Buddha stands gazing at the Bodhi Tree with unblinking eyes for seven days; he paces out the caṅkrama starting from the Tree; seated beneath the Tree where he received Sujata's offering of food he once more resists the temptations of Māra; and seated beneath the Mucalinda Tree he meditates while sheltered by the Serpent Mucalinda.

* * * * *

The axis is the progenitive origin of the worlds and hence the source of all riches and felicities. This is expressed in the symbolism of the Wish-Granting Tree (kalpa-vṛkṣa), a perennial symbol that finds its specifically Buddhist formulation in the Bodhi Tree that grows in the Land of Supreme Bliss (sukhāvatī), the Pure Land of the Tathāgata Amitābha ("Immeasurable Light") : "... always in leaf, always in flower, always in fruit, of a thousand hues and various foliage, flower and fruit... it is hung with golden strings, adorned with hundreds of golden chains... strings of rose pearls and strings of black pearls... adorned with symbols of the makara, svastika, nandyāvarta and moon... according to the desires of living beings, whatever their desires may be..." Those beings who hear the sound of that Tree moved by the wind, who see it, who smell its scent, who taste its fruits will nevermore suffer diseases of the ear, the eye, the nose or the tongue and "for those beings who are lighted up by the light of that Bodhi Tree, no disease of the body is to be feared". And those beings who meditate upon it will reach Awakening.[103]

Every symbol, however, encompasses two seemingly opposed strata of significance, one life-giving and beneficent, the other life-destroying and maleficent. The withering of leaves on the tree and their regrowth is a similitude of an ever perpetuating regeneration of the worlds; but it is also a metaphor of the fleeting transience of life - all men are as leaves that wither and fall. The tree is not only the Tree of Life, it is also the Tree of the Knowledge of Good and Evil, the Tree as analogy of Time the Devourer. The Tree as cosmos, as the procession of incessant life, yielding all the fruits of existence, in the Buddhist view is at one and the same time the Wisdom Tree (jñāna-druma) "whose roots strike deep into stability... whose flowers are moral acts... which bears the Dharma as its fruit... and... ought not to be felled",[104] and "a vine of coveting" that must be felled at the root.[105] In this latter view the World Tree is an exteriorization of the will-to-life, Eros, Kāma, and the thirst for existence (tṛṣṇa); its felling is the destruction of the Evil One, Māra, Kāmadeva, who is the indwelling Yakṣa of the Tree of Existence. When the Buddha takes up his station at the foot of the Tree he is usurping Māra's throne, trespassing upon the central position of Māra as the personification of the will-to-life, "prime mover of the Tree", support and fulcrum of the Wheel of Existence, and causa causans of its unceasing rotation. We have seen that the Wheel of Existence revolves

---

102. For references see above, p. 41, n. 29.

103. *Mahā-sukhāvatī-vyuhā* 32, in Cowell, Muller and Takakusu, 1984.

104. *Theragāta* 761 & 1094. Cf. Coomaraswamy, 1935a, pp.11f.

105. Coomaraswamy, 1935a, n. 18. There are obvious analogies in this with the relationship of the Biblical Tree of Life and the Tree of the Knowledge of Good and Evil, instrumental in the fall of Adam, located at the centre of the Earthly Paradise. Cf. Guénon, 1958a, Ch. IX ("The Tree in the Midst").

about a hub occupied by the pig of ignorance, the cock of desire-attachment, and the snake of anger, which are the three poisons and basic evils to which all other evils can be reduced, the very constituents of the person of Māra, the Evil One.[106] Seating himself at the foot of the Tree, the Buddha identifies himself with this axle-tree of existence : the poisons are transmogrified; Māra is defeated; the poisonous hub of the Wheel of Existence is transformed into the radiant Centre, abode of the Cakravartin, the "Turner of the Wheel", which thereby becomes the Wheel of the Dharma, the Wheel of the Truth itself. The will to experience is cut away and the true essence of the Tree revealed. So, depending on the point of view, the Tree is regarded as one to be approached with reverence and adoration or as one to be abhorred and cut down at the root - "the conflict is precisely between those principles which are represented by Māra and by Buddha; who, however opposite in nature are one in essence, and therefore at one beyond experience where 'all principles are the same'".[107] "Those who have vision of the Quiddity do not distinguish between the Vortex of Life (saṁsāra) and the Extinction (nirvāṇa)".[108] Ultimately, and in the eyes of the Awakened, the two trees are inseparably joined in non-duality (advaita) : the tree of Māra and the Bodhi Tree are two aspects of one and the same Truth that transcends all dichotomies.

5. STABILIZING THE SITE BY THE PILLAR.

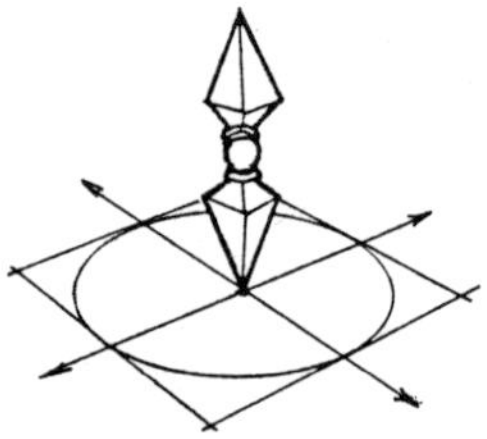

The raising of the gnomon-axis in the rite of laying out the stupa plan equates the cosmo-genetic action of strutting apart Heaven and Earth. It is also a fixing of the Earth, a pacification of the site.

The Vedic cosmogonic myth tells how in the beginning a Mound, Mountain or Rock floated island-like upon the Ocean of universal possibility,[109] wrapped around by the Serpent Vṛtra, "undivided, unawakened, sunk in deepest sleep, outstretched", who had confiscated the Waters of existence and kept them in the hollow of the Rock where he slept, thus "hindering" the making of the world. Indra, hurling his vajra, smote the head of Vṛtra and clove the Rock to allow the Waters to flow free.[110] Indra's demiurgic act is simultaneously threefold : he transfixes the head of the Serpent, he raises the Pillar of the dawning Sun[111] to strut apart the two worlds, and he fixes the primordial Rock to the bottom of the cosmic Ocean. The vajra hurled by Indra is at once the Pillar of the Sun that props Heaven from Earth and the pin or "nail" (kīla) that fastens the Earth upon the Ocean floor. In the beginning, then, the Earth was insecure, "quaking like a lotus leaf, for the gale was tossing it hither and thither..."[112] It was "lacking in foundation or support (pratiṣṭhā)". Indra stabilized this trembling and unfirm ground

---

106. For a description of the Wheel of Existence, see Pallis, 1939, Ch. XI; and above, pp. 84ff.

107. *Cittavisuddhi*, attributed to Āryadeva, in Shastri, JASB, 67, p. 178 quoted in Coomaraswamy, 1935a, n. 18.

108. The theme of the ambivalence of cosmic symbols in the Islamic conte[xt] is demonstrated by Corbin, 1960, pp. 16ff. 109. RV X.89.4.

110. RV II.11.5. See Coomaraswamy, 1935b, pp. 391ff., for other implica[-] tions of this mythic act. 111. See above, pp. 163 ff.

112. ŚB II.1.1.8-9.

he "fixed the shaking mountains and the plains",[113] and thus he is extolled by the hymnist as the one 'Who made the widespread earth when quaking steadfast, Who set at rest the agitated mountains, Who measured out the air's midspace more widely, Who gave the sky support".[114]

There is a mimesis of this myth in the Brahmanic ritual performed to determine the place for the building of the Fire Altar : turning towards the East the performer of the rite throws a yoke pin (śamya) and the point where the pin strikes the ground and remains upright is the central point about which the Altar is constructed.[115]

The myth is also reflected in the Indian rituals performed when a new house is to be built. These rituals are still practised in India to the present day. "Before a single stone can be laid... the astrologer shows what spot in the foundation is exactly above the head of the snake that supports the world. The mason fashions a little wooden peg from the wood of the khadira tree, and with a coconut drives the peg into the ground at this particular spot in such a way to peg the head of the snake securely down... If this snake should ever shake its head really violently, it would shake the world to pieces".[116] The khadira tree supplies the wood of the sacrificial post (yūpa)[117] : peg and post are homologous.

"The transfixing peg is the nether point of Indra's vajra, wherewith the Serpent was transfixed in the beginning".[118] To pin the head of the Serpent in the house building ritual is to repeat Indra's cosmogenetic and stabilizing act. The chaotic and unformed is fixed, cosmicized.[119] Before its transfixing the Serpent moves in cyclic motion, proceeding from the East to the South-West and North, completing the cycle in the course of a year, moving one degree each day. By pinning the Serpent, time is fixed, transformed to the timeless. The world is made stable.[120]

* * * * *

The symbolism is adopted by Buddhism. In the Pali literature "Indra's pin" (indrakīla) is synonymous with "stable order" and "lawfulness"; and its opposite, dassukhīla, is "disorder" or "collapse of justice".[121] Indra's pin is the model of "every instrument or device used to ensure 'security', 'permanence', 'protection'... of every object used to 'fix' or 'secure', or 'to make safe the threshold'".[122] The Indrakīla is also identified with the Rock or Mountain that it pins.[123] In the myth of the Churning of the

---

113. RV X.44.8. 114. RV II.12.2.

115. Eliade, 1957, p. 66, n.15, quoting *Pañcaviṃśa Brāhmaṇa* XXV.10.4 and 13.2. Coomaraswamy, 1938a, p. 431, n. 28, suggests that the mythic paradigm for this mimetic act might be RV X.31.10b.

116. Stevenson, 1920, p. 354; quoted in Coomaraswamy, 1938b, p. 403, n.23; Eliade, 1958b, p. 380; 1957, p. 66; 1959, p. 19; Wales, 1977, p. 26; Bergaigne, 1878, 1, p. 124, n. 1. The ritual is widespread throughout Asia, wherever Indian metaphysical concepts have been entertained. Parallels are to be found as well in many other societies uninfluenced by Indian ideas. A full coverage of this subject would require a separate study. For the ritual in Kampuchean housebuilding, see Porée Maspero, 1954, p. 622, and 1961; and in Sri Lanka, See Liyanaratne, 1976, p. 59 and Coomaraswamy, 1956c, p. 126, both quoting the *Mayamata*; cf. Wales, 1977, p. 142, n.8.

117. AB II.1. 118. Coomaraswamy, 1977, 1, p. 430, n. 28.

119. Eliade, 1957, p. 67; 1959, p. 19.

120. Kramrisch, 1946, p. 62, n. 105; cf. Wales, 1977, p. 42; Boner and Sarma, 1966, pp. xxx-xxxi & I.55-58; Irwin, 1980, pp. 22f. 121. D I.135.

122. Irwin, 1980, p. 23. 123. See Kuiper, 1970. p.110.

Milky Ocean the churning rod is alternately called the Indrakīla or Mt. Mandara, although usually shown iconographically as a pillar (= kīla). The term kīlādri, "pin-hill", occurs in the Buddhist texts; and the hill near Borobudur in Central Java is called the "peg of the world".[124] The pin forming the axis of a Buddha image is called the indrakīla and the stability of the image is said to depend upon it.[125] Indrakīla is also a name of the central mast of the stupa.

* * * * *

By way of a complex interconnection of associations the symbolism of the stabilizing of the earth traces to the Buddhist ritual of "pacifying the site", practised during the seven day ritual for laying out a mandala on the ground, described in the *Dainichikyō*.[126] As was shown, the plan of the stupa is a mandala and the ritual described in the sutra is essentially the same as that for laying out the stupa.[127]

There is a crucial moment on the first day of the seven day ritual when the Earth Gods inhabiting the site upon which the mandala is to be laid out are awakened and asked permission for the use of the ground. This ensures that the site will be stable and immovable. The performer of the ritual kneels upon the ground and strikes the earth with a vajra held in the right hand. Then, transferring the vajra to the left hand and holding it at the breast, he makes the earth-touching sign (bhūmi-sparśa-mudrā) with the right hand, reaching down to rest his fingers upon the ground, while reciting the dhāraṇī of the Earth Goddess and meditating upon her form so as to identify with its essence.[128] He offers incense, flowers, lights and other gifts to the Goddess and to all the Buddhas of the ten directions. Being now assured of a firm ground on which to base it, he proceeds to lay out the mandala.

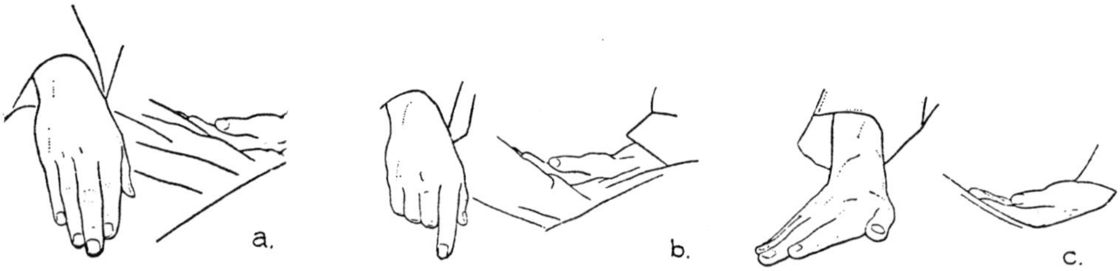

Fig. 120 : The gesture of touching the earth (bhūmisparśa-mudrā) and two of its variant forms. a. The usual form of the earth touching gesture. b. The gesture of designating the earth (Jap. soku chi-in). c. The gesture of the subjugation of the mountain (Jap. anzan-in), that is, of pacifying the earth. The subjugation of Māra equates the pacifying of the ground. (See Saunders, 1960, pp. 81 f.).

Striking the ground with the vajra is symbolically equivalent to Indra's hurling of the vajra to fix the Rock and pin the head of the cosmic Serpent Vṛtra. The vajra is the homologue of the Pillar that struts apart the worlds: it is the Pillar of lightning that flashes forth to illuminate the darkness of chaos, splitting it asunder to form the cosmic strata of Heaven and Earth it is the peg that stabilizes the Earth.

---

124. Kuiper, 1970, p. 110, n. 39.

125. Irwin, 1980, p. 25, citing M XII.125-6. See Acharya, 1946, s.v., Indrakīla(ka). 126. See above p. 104, n. 1, for references.

127. See above, p. 104. 128. MKDJT, p. 974, s.v. Shichi nichi sa dan hō.

Making the earth-touching sign in the ritual relates to an interlocking set of symbols. The earth-touching sign is that made by the previously mentioned Buddha Ratnaketu ("Jewel Banner" or "Jewel Light"), who rules over the East, the direction of the rising sun and the first dawning of the Mind of Enlightenment (bodhicitta).[129] As we saw, the raising of the Jewel Banner (ratnaketu) equates the setting up of the Dawn-Pillar of the world, the Pillar that simultaneously divides the worlds and stabilizes the Earth. The earth-touching sign made by Ratnaketu relates to the same concept. The reference is to the dramatic moment in the myth of Śākyamuni's attainment of Enlightenment beneath the Bodhi Tree when Māra lays claim to the Throne occupied by the Bodhisattva. Śākyamuni touches the earth with his finger tips and calls upon the Earth Goddess to bear witness to the virtues by which he occupies the seat at the centre of the universe. At this the earth trembles in six ways and the Goddess springs forth from the ground and proclaims the Bodhisattva the rightful occupant of the Throne, thereby defeating the demonic hordes and their leader.

Fig. 121 : The Buddha Śākyamuni making the gesture of calling the Earth Goddess to witness, that is, the gesture of touching the earth (bhūmisparśa-mudrā). The gesture is made by reaching down over the right knee, palm inwards, and touching the earth with the finger tips.

By his gesture that calls the Earth Goddess to witness Śākyamuni quells the demonic forces of disruption, instability and disorder so that he can take up his station at the now unshakeable and firm hub of the universe. The action is the symbolic equivalent of Indra's fixing of the Rock and the head of the Serpent by striking them with the vajra. The two mythic actions are cognate, and are explicitly interpreted as such by the Buddhist commentators.[130]

The striking of the earth with the vajra and the making of the earth-touching sign in the seven day ritual are thus seen to be two mutually reinforcing expressions of the symbolism of the stabilizing of the earth. The analogies with the Hindu ritual of pinning the head of the Serpent are apparent. In both rituals the earth is made firm, is cosmicized, by being fixed with a vertical shaft. In both, the amorphous, chaotic flux is immobilized and rendered solid.

The gestures made in the seven day ritual carry further symbolic connotations. Every rite is the outward expression of what is essentially an inward operation.[131] The bodily performance of the ritual is accompanied by its mental counterpart. As the performer of the ritual sets up the mandala on the ground he is simultaneously constructing it in his mind. Every gesture he makes relates to an interior process, and in the context of this inward procedure the gestures used to awaken the gods of the Earth function to awaken the Mind of Enlightenment (bodhicitta), which, because it is immovable and unshakeable, is identified with the Element Earth, similarly characterized by

---

129. See above, pp. 172f.   130. See MKDJT, p. 974.

the qualities of stability, firmness and immovability. The physical act of striking the earth with the vajra is the symbolic equivalent of the meditational process of "activating" the Mind of Enlightenment, bringing it from potentiality to actuality by means of Knowledge, which is symbolically identified with the vajra.

The earth-touching gesture similarly has an interior, microcosmic reference. According to the cosmo-physiological formulations of the Shingon the Element Earth corresponds to the lowermost of the cakras of the body, located below the navel and called the "thigh centre" (Jap. shitsurin).[132] The Mind of Enlightenment (bodhicitta) lies dormant within this centre until awakened by meditational rituals. The thigh centre, the Element Earth and the Mind of Enlightenment are symbolically associated. Placing the hand on the knee in the earth-touching gesture represents the activation of the lowest cakra and the arousal of the Mind of Enlightenment.

There is another and more profound interpretation of this symbolism, involving the concept, basic to the outlook of Shingon Buddhism, of the non-duality (advaita) of Awakening and ignorance. As long as the ritual lasts the body of the performer of the ritual is identified with the Body of Vajrasattva, who personifies Awakening (bodhi) innate within the body and mind of each individual. The earth, on the other hand, is identified with "the great ground of ignorance" (Jap. mumyo daiji) and by striking it with the vajra the ritualist unifies Vajrasattva's Body of Awakening with the ground of ignorance. By this conjunction the innate qualities of the Mind of Awakening are revealed. This explains why the vajra is held at the heart when the yogi makes the earth-touching sign. The vajra symbolizes adamantine Knowledge and the heart is the ground of ignorance in man. Placing the vajra at the heart expresses the non-dual fusion of Awakening and ignorance.[133]

The meaning of these ritual actions has been developed at some length, not only as being pertinent to the study of pillar symbolism, but also to illustrate how symbols form an internally cohesive, consistent and coherent corpus of concepts. The pillar, the standard, the dawn, the East, the earth touching gesture, the vajra, the Element Earth, the thigh cakra in the body, the Mind of Enlightenment and the non-duality of Awakening and ignorance are bound together by an interlocking series of symbolic correspondences and analogies, forming a symbolic whole made up of interrelated and mutually reflecting meanings.

* * * * *

These considerations apply to the stupa. Its central axis is an indrakīla, a spike that fixes the earth and thereby settles the site. The stupa is a stabilizing point that anchors the earth to a solid base. This partially explains the importance of the stupa in Chinese geomancy, which used it as a "pin" to transfix unstable elements in the landscape.

The *Mahāvaṃsa*, telling how a Sri Lankan stupa was located, relates that the king Duṭṭagāmani's spear, having been stuck upright in the ground, could not then be removed but had become firmly fixed into position. Seeing this the king ordered a stupa to be built around this firm axis.[134] The story is the description of an earth-pacifying rite : the spear, coincident with the stupa's axis, is the spike that makes firm the site.

---

131. See above, p. 48. 132. Described in greater detail below, p. 3

133. The above information derives from the MKDJT.

134. *Mahāvaṃsa* XXV.1 & XXVI.9ff. quoted in Mus, 1935, p. 118, n. 2. Cf. *Thūpavaṃsa*, p. 89f.

15 THE SYMBOLISM OF THE DOME.

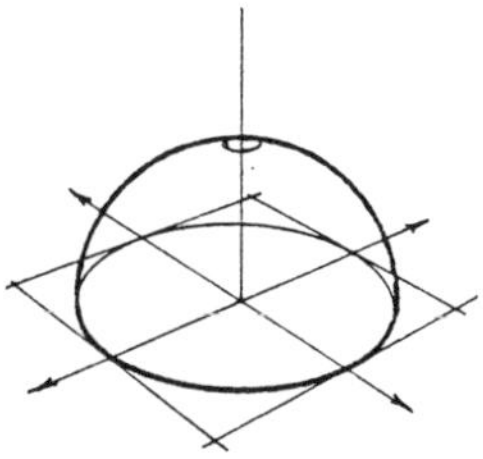

1. THE DOME AS CENTRE AND CONTAINER.

The main mass of the classical form of the Indian stupa consists of a solid, hemispherical dome. From the early times of the *Divyāvadāna* the Buddhist texts have referred to this as the garbha, "womb", "embryo", "container", or, alternately by the equivalent and interchangeable term, aṇḍa, "egg". With this reference the stupa as a whole is called the dhātu-garbha, the "womb of the elements", whence derives dagoba, the most usual designation of the stupa in Sri Lanka.

Fig. 122 : Examples of the stupa dome from India (a and b), Sri Lanka (c and d), China (e and f) and Japan (g). See also fig. 143 of page 222.

With slightly different emphases the symbolism of the womb-egg is also expressed by the cave and the lotus. Each of these symbols, examined in the following, has a twofold significance : on the one hand it refers to the innermost centre of the universe, whether this be conceived macrocosmically or microcosmically, and on the other to its outermost confines. Each symbol is at one and the same time the most interior point and the most exterior container of the worlds. Each is assimilated to the non-dimensional point that is "smaller than a grain of rice, smaller than a grain of barley, smaller than a grain of mustard, smaller than a grain of millet",[1] and yet at the same time is "greater than the earth, greater than the atmosphere, greater than the sky, greater than all the worlds together",[2] which is to say greater than the spheres of gross, subtle and formless manifestation and non-manifestation respectively. It is the most small and simultaneously the most large, in the same way that the dimensionless point is spatially nothing and yet is the principle whence all space derives, or as the number one, the smallest of numbers, principially contains within itself the complete series of numbers.[3] The centre "contains" the circumference : the circumference is a deployment of potentialities, or virtualities, held within the central point which is its principle. The Egg contains the world in potentia, "prior" to its development; but it is also the world itself, its upper half the dome of Heaven and the lower half the supporting Earth. The cosmos is the manifestation of the contents of the Egg; and it is also the Egg itself. The Egg contains the world; it also is the world. Container and content are one.

Viewed from without the stupa-Egg or stupa-Womb is the progenitive source of manifestation, the procreative point whence the worlds are born, the most inward and central spring whence all life flows. But as the pilgrimage of return progresses it is seen that the succeeding circles, increasingly proximate to the centre, contain all that lies outside them. Geometrically expressed, the points on the circumference of the outermost of a series of concentric circles have corresponding points on each of the circles closer to the centre, these being more "packed" as the centre is approached, until finally all are absorbed within the central point, the principle of all the indefinitude of points. Viewed from that centre the circumferences and the centre are coincident; they are all contained within it in their essential unity and non-differentiation. In this view the stupa-Egg constitutes the totality of the Cosmos : the multiplicity of worlds are concentrated and compressed within it.

Viewed from the circumference and from within the confines of the spatio-temporal world, existences, the things of the world, are seen as deployed in space and time; but seen from the centre, which is the locus of the Awakened, they are seen in their non-spatial and atemporal punctuality. They are seen in their non-dimensional momentaneity as they abide in the Infinite which contains all finites and the Eternal which contains all times.

* * * * *

There are several levels of interpretation of the Egg-Matrix symbolism. At one level the symbol represents the container of the manifested universe, its integument marking the confines of manifestation - the Egg-Womb is co-extensive with existences. At another level it is the non-dimensional centre of that manifestation, the principle and point of its existence. Each of these two levels is also bivalent. From one point of view the container demarks the ordered from the chaotic : macrocosmically it is the world defined and measured out in harmonious accordance with the principles governing all things; microcosmically, it is the "field" within the heart-mind that has been cleared of mental obstructions and fenced off from the surrounding confusion and turbulence to provide a serene and stable arena wherein meditational practices can proceed without disturbance. It is a space within the heart-mind where Principle manifests itself. Alternately, the confines it establishes can be viewed as those of limitation and the conditioned, the imprisoning finitudes that the aspirant seeks to escape, forming the house or egg of

---

1. CU III.14.3; cf. Guénon, 1962, p. 225; 1945, p. 41.
2. CU III.14.3; Guénon, 1962, p. 225. 3. *Ibid.*, p. 219.

the cosmos whence the Buddha broke free at his Awakening. These several layers of interpretation are diagrammatically indicated in the accompanying figure.

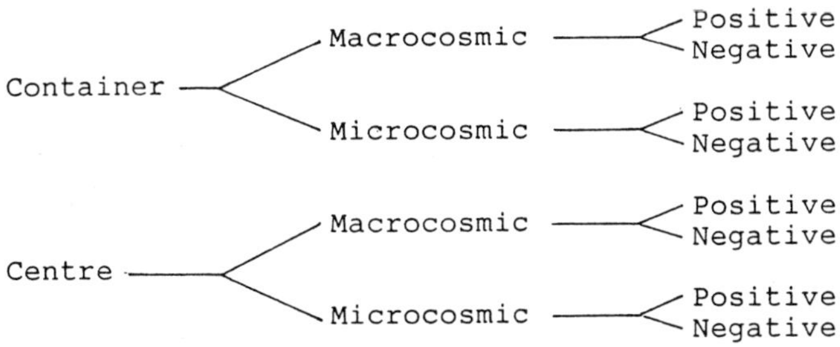

There is, however, yet another level of interpretation where the antinomies of container and centre, macrocosm and microcosm, positive and negative, are reconciled and seen as the non-dual aspects of a single, indivisible Reality. This interpretation is characteristic of those schools of the Mahāyāna which view *saṃsāra* and *nirvāṇa* as inseparably merged. It reverts to the concepts developed in connection with the symbolism of the Wheel : viewed by those who are whirled about on its felly the Wheel of the World is seen to turn on the hub of the three poisons, but in the eyes of the Awakened who have taken up their station at the hub, it is at the same time the Wheel of the Dharma whose axle is Enlightenment and spokes and felly aspects of the Real.

* * * * *

The simultaneity and punctual coincidence of the cosmic circumference and the cosmic centre - of phenomenal existences and their Principle - are indicated by the meanings of the word *ākāśa*, "space". *Ākāśa* fills everything. It is all-pervading and omnipresent. It extends in all six directions and is as much in stone as in air. The world and *ākāśa* are coterminous, and in this sense it can be said that *ākāśa* "contains" the world. But space in its entirety is also to be found at the very centre of the heart. This inner *ākāśa*, abiding within the City of Brahman (*brahmapura*) contains all that is : "In this City of Brahman is a small lotus, a dwelling in which is a small cavity occupied by *ākāśa*";[4] "As large as is this *ākāśa*, so large is that *ākāśa* in the heart. Both heaven and earth are contained within it; both fire and air, both the sun and the moon, the lightning and the stars, and whatever there is in this world and also what is not - all that is contained within it";[5] "All these beings arise out of the space and return into the space. For the space is older than they, prior to them, and is their last resort";[6] and the Self "awakens this rational (cosmos) from out of that space".[7]

The Element *ākāśa* corresponds to *prakṛti*, primordial Substance, from which all existent things are manifested. The manifested world ontologically exists by way of a process of increasing condensation, from Space to Air, to Fire, Water and Earth, the subsequent Element always retaining the qualities of the preceding ones. Sound (*śabda*) is the quality of *ākāśa*, the first and foremost of the Elements in the procession of manifestation : in the beginning was the Word.[8] The innermost heart is the place of *ākāśa*, the place of *prakṛti*, and thus the starting point of the cosmogenetic emanation of the phenomenal world.

---

4. CU VIII.1.1. 5. MU VII.11. 6. CU I.9.1. 7. MU VI.17.
8. Kramrisch, 1946, pp. 163f.

Thus it is that the cella of the Hindu temple, called the garbha-gṛha, the "womb of the house",[9] which is specified as the location of ākāśa and is identified with the City of Brahman, is the navel and nave (nābha) of the building.

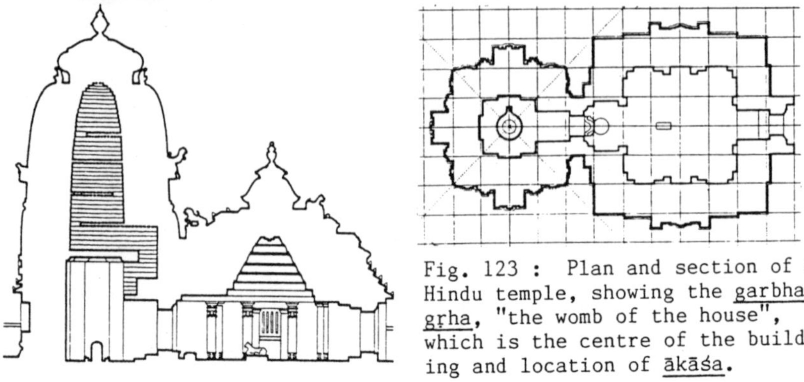

Fig. 123 : Plan and section of a Hindu temple, showing the garbha-gṛha, "the womb of the house", which is the centre of the building and location of ākāśa.

2. THE WOMB *(GARBHA)* AND THE EGG *(AṆḌA)*.

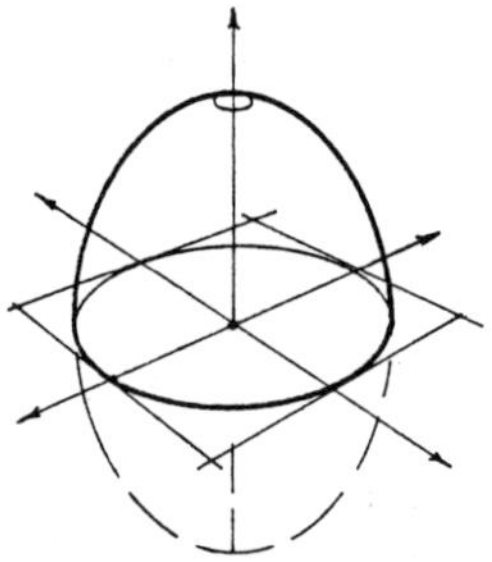

The references to the Womb and the Egg[10] are numerous in the Vedic and the Brahmanic literature. The *Nāsidīya-sūkta* hymn of the *Ṛg Veda*, describing the primordial Waters of Chaos, says, "Darkness there was at first, enveloped in darkness; without distinctive marks, all this was Water. That which was void and enclosed in a shell, that One, by the power of heat (tapas) came into being".[11] "That One", "enclosed in a shell", is the Golden Womb[12] or Golden Egg (hiraṇyagarbha),[13] the same Egg mentioned later in the same hymn : "When the great Waters pervaded the universe, containing an Egg, He (Prajāpati) arose...",[14] and again in the *Atharva Veda* : "In the beginning the Waters, producing a youngling, brought forth an Egg (garbha), which, as it was coming to life, was enveloped in a golden covering";[15] and "Within that impregnable City of the Gods (= the City of Brahman) there exists a golden container, celestial, invested with light".[16] In other texts it says, "Verily, in the beginning this (universe) was Water, nothing but a sea of Water. The Waters desired, 'How can we be reproduced'? They toiled and became heated; a Golden Egg was produced".[17]

9. *Idem.* 10. For the cosmogonic egg in non-Indian societies, see Eliade, 1958b, pp. 413ff.; Chevalier and Gheerbrant, 1973, 3, pp. 299ff., s.v., Oeuf; Cirlot, 1962, p. 90, s.v., "Egg"; Guénon, 1945, p. 101, n. 3; Raglan, 1964, pp. 148f.; Long, 1963, Ch. 3.

11. RV X.129, quoted in Bosch, 1960, p. 51. 12. RV X.82.5.

13. RV X.12.1. 14. RV X.12.7. 15. AV IV.2.8, in Bosch, 1960, p. 54

16. AV X.2.31. 17. ŚB XI.1.6.1.

The frame of reference for this symbolism is the cosmogonic "interaction" of the complementary Principles, Essence (purusa), represented as Breath or Light, and Substance (prakṛti), represented as the Waters.[18] When the Breath enters or the Light shines upon the Waters the possibilities they contain are made manifest, passing from potentiality to act. The Golden Womb or Egg is the progenitive point where the ray of Light or radius of Breath strikes the plane of the Waters; it is the locus of their cosmo-productive union. From this punctual centre, which is the Egg floating on the expanses of the deep, grows the World Tree, whose trunk is the axis of the world and the prop of the firmament and whose branches are the worlds.[19] Alternately, from the Egg rises the Cosmic Pillar, cognate of the Tree : "The great Yakṣa, in the midst of the universe, absorbed in tapas, on the surface of the Waters, in this World Pillar are set whatever gods there be, like the branches of a tree around the trunk".[20] From the Egg is born Prajāpati, whose Body is the manifested universe.[21]

The Egg is identified with the navel of the universe : "The Waters contained the primordial Egg in which all the gods came together. In the navel of the unborn the One was implanted in which all beings stood".[22] In the *Bhagavata Purāṇa* the Golden Egg, lying on the surface of the Waters, contains the Lord Iśvara. He dwells therein for a thousand years, after which time a lotus, as splendid as a thousand suns, springs from his navel. From this lotus, the abode of all living things, Brahmā, the progenitor of the worlds, is born.[23]

The same work gives a variation on this theme : the Lord Viṣṇu, self-absorbed in meditation, sleeps upon the coils of the Serpent Ananta, floating upon the surface of the ocean. From his navel springs a lotus, which opens to reveal Brahmā, the Creator.[24] In these myths the Golden Egg and the navel of the deity, which is the navel of the universe, are to be considered as homologous.

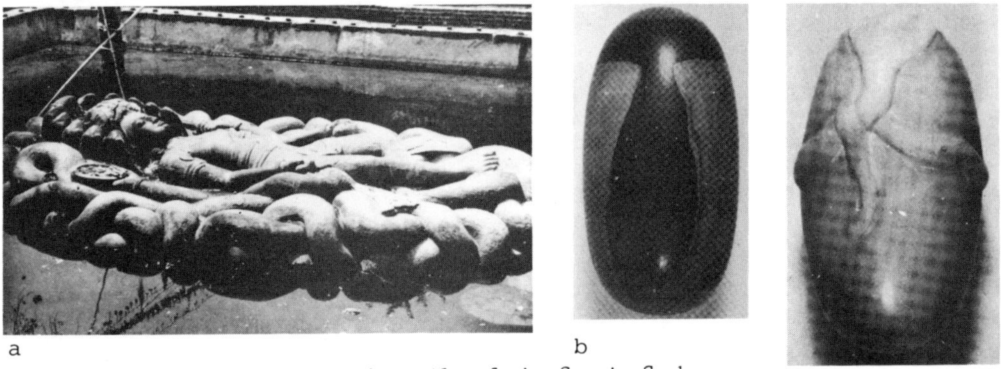

a b c

Fig. 124 : a. Viṣṇu asleep on the coils of the Cosmic Snake, floating on the Waters. b. A liṅga in the form of an egg-shaped stone. d. An egg-shaped liṅga wrapped by a serpent.

---

18. Discussed below, pp. 211ff. 19. Bosch, 1960, p. 55.

20. AV X.82.6. 21. RV X.121.1ff.; ŚB XI.1.6.2. 22. RV X.82.6.

23. *Bhagavata Purāṇa* III.20.14ff.; cf. Bosch, 1960, p. 55.

24. *Bhagavata Purāṇa* I.8.2 and III.8.10; cf. Mbh III.272.44 & XII.207.13; Bosch, 1960, p. 56; Auboyer, 1949, pp. 94f.; Sastri, 1916, pp. 50ff., and fig. 23; Rao, 1914, 1, p. 114; Zimmer, 1955, pp. 12-14 and 165-8, pl. 3, p. 286; 1946, pp. 59 ff.

Located at the centre of the cosmos, the Egg is also identified with the Cosmic Axis. We saw that the Tree and the Pillar rise from the Golden Egg. The same homology is indicated by representations of Śiva's *liṅga* as an egg-shaped stone. In this, egg and axis symbolisms coalesce : the *liṅga*, as *axis mundi*, is figured by the ovoid form developed from the sphere by a bifurcation of its centre so as to form two points joined by an axis.[25] The egg-shaped *liṅga* is sometimes shown with a serpent coiled around it, and this directly associates it with the representations of the stupa entwined by serpents (*nāga*). The chthonic snakes are personifications of the Waters : the egg-stupa and the egg-*liṅga*, each representing the centre and the axis of the worlds, both float upon the Ocean of All-Possibility.

Fig. 125 : Stupas adorned with snakes and snake-knots.

The Golden Egg, or Golden Womb (*hiraṇya-garbha*), is also the container of the world. According to Manu the unmanifested (*avyakta*) and self-existent (*svayambhu*) Lord first created the Waters and then deposited in them a seed, which became a Golden Egg, resplendent as the sun, in which he himself was born as Brahmā, the progenitor of the whole world. He resided within the Egg during one year, and then by his thought divided it into two halves, which were Heaven and Earth. Between them was Midspace, the eight points of the horizon, and the eternal abode of the Waters.[26]

The *Chāndogya Upaniṣad* gives a similar account. In the beginning the Egg was non-existent; then it appeared, grew, and broke open into two halves, one silver, the Earth, and one gold, the Sky. Its amnion is the mountains; its chorion is the mist with clouds; its fluid is the ocean. From it was born the Sun, and "the Sun is Brahman".[27]

In its account of the creation of the universe the *Viṣṇu Purāṇa* tells how in the beginning the primordial Elements, previously chaotic and unconnected, came together and unified to form an Egg, "which gradually expanded like a bubble of water". Within this Egg Mount Meru was the amnion, the cyclic mountains were the chorion, and all the worlds, "the continents and seas and mountains, the planets and divisions of the universe, the gods, the demons and mankind" were contained.[28]

The reference to the bubble of water recalls a passage in the *Mahāvaṃsa* King Duttagāmaṇi asks the architect who is to construct the Great Stupa of Ruwanweli what form it will take. "At that moment Vissakamma[29] entered into

---

25. Cf. Rawson, 1972, pls. 79,376 & 523-30, pp. 113f.; 1973, p. 16 & pl.9.

26. *Manu*, I.5ff.; cf. Bosch, 1960, p. 55; Long, 1963, pp. 124f.

27. CU III.19.1-3; cf. ERE, IV, p. 157; Raglan, 1964, p. 149.

28. *Viṣṇu Purāṇa*, pp. 17f.; cf. Mus, 1935, pp.109f. & p. 110, n. 1; Combaz, 1935, p. 38. 29. Skt. Viśvakarma. Cf. Daniélou, 1964, pp. 314f.

and possessed him. When the master builder had had a golden bowl filled with water, he took water in his hand and let it fall on the surface of the water. A great bubble rose up like unto a half globe of crystal. He said, 'Thus will I make it'".[30] Foucher[31] saw in this a reference to a passage in the *Dhammapada* describing the fleeting nature of the world : "Look upon the world as a bubble : look upon it as a mirage. Him who looks thus upon the world the king of death does not see",[32] but failed to notice that, as pointed out by Mus,[33] the reference is primarily cosmogonic. The globular bubble floating on the waters has the form of the Golden Egg.

The stupa is the Cosmic Egg, the progenitive source of the world, floating on the Waters of All-Possibility. With some stupas the symbolism is explicit : the monolithic rock-cut stupa at Haibak, for example, is surrounded by a moat and its Egg-Dome sat within the waters;[34] reliefs at Sāñcī and early coins show stupas floating on water;[35] and Nieuwenkamp claims, on the basis of the geological and topographical analysis of the site that the stupa at Borobudur originally rose from the midst of an extensive lake.[36]

* * * * *

Early Buddhism emphasises the eschatological and soteriological aspects of Egg symbolism. For the Buddha the Egg is the imprisoning world that cracks open to release the Awakened. In the *Suttavibhaṅga* the Buddha says : "'When a hen has laid eggs, eight, ten or a dozen; when the hen has sat upon them and kept them warm long enough - then, when one of those chicks, the first one to break the shell with the point of its claw or its beak, comes safely out of the egg, what will they call that chick - the eldest or the youngest'? - 'They will call him the eldest, venerable Gautama, for he is the first born among them'. - 'So likewise, O brahman, I alone, among all those who live in ignorance and are as though enclosed and imprisoned in an egg, have burst through this shell of ignorance; I alone have attained to the blessed, the universal dignity of the Buddha. Thus, O brahman, I am the eldest, the noblest among beings'".[37]

This imagery, "of deceptive simplicity",[38] contains a multi-layered symbolism. Enclosed within the egg, the initiate has returned to the centre, has attained a second birth, so as to be classed among the dvīja, the "twice born", those who have undergone a psychic regeneration and resolved within their own being the totality of cosmic possibility. The hatching is a third birth, an escape from the cosmos, a supernatural birth into the supra-cosmic realm.[39] As Mus points out, for the Buddha to speak of the emergence of the "first-born" (jyesta) of the universe from an egg was to remind his listeners of a Brahmanic tradition that would have been familiar to them, that of the Cosmic Egg whence emerge Brahmā, the primordial God of Creation, Prajāpati,

---

30. *Mahāvaṃsa* XXX.11-13; cf. Mus, 1935, p. 109; Dumarçay, 1978, p. 18; Paranavitana, 1946, p. 15.

31. Bénisti, 1960, p. 63; Foucher, 1905, I, p. 63, cited by Mus, 1935, p. 109; cf. Paranavitana, 1946, p. 15.

32. Dh XIII.4 (170), which is parallelled in A IV.137 : "Life is like a dewdrop... a bubble on the water"; cf. D II.246f. : "Like a dewdrop on the tip of a blade of grass when the sun rises, such is the lifetime of men".

33. Mus, 1935, p. 109. 34. Bussagli, 1973, p. 45. For the stupa on the waters see Bénisti, 1960, p. 63. 35. Combaz, 1935, p. 82.

36. Soekmono, 1976, pp. 4f.; Combaz, 1935, p. 83.

37. *Suttavibhaṅga*, *Pārājika* I.1.4; cf. Oldenberg, 1934, pp. 364f.; Mus, 1938, p. 13; 1935, p. 523; Eliade, 1961, p. 77; Oldenberg, 1921, p. 321.

38. Mus, 1938, p. 13.

the Father and Master of Creators, and Agni, the sacrificial Fire and type of the *avatāra*. To break out of the egg is, in the Buddha's parable, to transcend the spatial and temporal bondage of existence, to escape from the thrall of *saṃsāra*.

* * * * *

The symbolism of the *garbha* innate within the being is developed in the Mahāyāna doctrine of the *tathāgata-garbha*, the "Tathāgata Womb".[40] The concept is enunciated in the Vijñānavādin or Yogācāra texts and is a characteristic teaching of the Hua-Yen (Jap. Kegon) sect, but it also occurs in the writings of the Mādhyamika.[41]

The *tathāgata-garbha* is a pure, luminous, spiritual embryo present in all beings, so that it is said that "all beings are the wombs of Buddhahood".[4 The term *tathāgata*, literally "thus come", is here used as a synonym for Suchness (*tathatā*), the eternal Dharma Body (*dharma-kāya*), the Absolute,[43] so that the *tathāgata-garbha* is immanent Suchness, the indwelling Buddha-Nature.[44] It is the potentiality of Enlightenment possessed by every person at the most inward core of his being. It is the *sub-stans*, the support, of the Awakened Mind (*citta-prakṛti*), origin and source of the One Mind (*ekacitta* of all the Buddhas.[45] It is the ground in which the seed (*bīja*) of Enlighten ment takes root and whence it draws its nourishment as it grows to the stage of fruition and is thus the cause (*hetu*) in contrast to the effect, or fruit (*phala*), of Buddhahood.[46] It is the "realm of supreme Wisdom realized in one's innermost self".[47]

The *tathāgata-garbha* is Suchness (*tathatā*) innate within all beings, but a distinction is made between this indwelling Suchness in its defiled state (*samalā-tathatā*), which is the *tathāgata-garbha* of beings in their ordinary condition of ignorance, and Suchness in its purified state (*nirmalā-*

---

39. These concepts, based on elucidations provided by Guénon, are further developed below, pp.201f., where references are given. Mus, 1938, pp. 13f. and Eliade citing him, 1961, p. 78, err in speaking of the hatching as a "second birth".

40. Ruegg, 1969, is the only full length work in a Western language devoted exclusively to the doctrine of the *tathāgata-garbha*. See also Cook, 1977, pp. 44ff.; Suzuki, 1930, pp. 105f., 137f., 177, 182 & 192; Takeda, 1967 pp. 13ff., 36 etc.; Takakusu, 1956, p. 194; Sōgen, 1912, pp. 26f.; Kōshirō, 1961.

41. The concept is of frequent occurrence in the Vijñānavādin texts such as the *Laṅkāvatāra-sūtra*, the *Saṃdhinirmocana-sūtra* and the *Mahāyāna-saṃgraha* (see Cook, 1977, p. 46). The Chinese monk Fa-tsang (613-712), in his "Commentary on the Awakening of Faith in the Mahāyāna" (*Ta-ch'eng chi-hsin lun i-chi*, Taishō, vol. 44, No. 1846, pp. 240-287) established the concept as pivotal in the doctrines of the Hua-Yen sect (see Hakeda, 1967, p. 14). He lists the *Laṅkāvatārasūtra*, the *Ratnagotra-śāstra* and the Awakening of Faith as the sources for the doctrine. For the Mādhyamika version of the doctrine of the *tathāgata-garbha* see Ruegg, 1969, pp. 109, 117, 189, & 405, and Cook, 1977, p. 47. 42. Cook, 1977. p. 44.

43. In the early literature the word *tathāgata* was used as an epithet for the Buddha. In the Mahāyāna it is used in a broader sense to indicate Buddhahood as a Principle. See Hakeda, 1967, p. 13.

44. Cook, 1977, p. 45; Sōgen, 1912, p. 25.

45. Johnston, 1950, p. vii, quoted by Hakeda, 1967, p. 14.

46. Cook, 1977, p. 45. 47. Suzuki, 1930, p. 85; cf. LS 28 (77), 82 (222).

tathatā), which is perfect Buddhahood itself.[48] "... The tathāgata-garbha... is by nature bright and pure, unspotted, endowed with the thirty two marks of excellence, hidden in the body of every being like a gem of great value, which is wrapped in a dirty garment, enveloped in the garment of the skandhas, the dhātus and the āyatanas, and soiled with the dirt of greed, anger, folly and false imagination..."[49] Buddhahood, lying unperceived in the innermost recesses of man's heart, is hidden by coverings of false judgement (parikalpa, vikalpa), not seeing things as they really are, as not subject to individuation, and by irrational attachment (abhiniveśa), which arises from the false judgement that sees things as external to the Mind. The Way of the Buddha is to remove these coverings so as to reveal the pure, immaculate and priceless jewel hidden by these obscuring defilements. When these are removed the Womb is seen to be nothing other than non-discriminative Knowledge (nirvikalpa-jñāna), which Knowledge is a direct perception of Suchness.[50]

The doctrine of the tathāgata-garbha has cosmological as well as soteriological connotations : it is not only the generative source of Buddhahood but also the Womb of the Worlds, the origin and container of all phenomena. "The Mind as saṃsāra is grounded on the tathāgata-garbha".[51] All states of existence are contained within the tathāgata-garbha, but abide there in their pure and undefiled condition, in no way separate from Suchness. These are the only real states; the defiled, which is to say conditioned states, exist solely in illusion; they are, from the beginning, non-existent.[52] When the Wayfarer cuts away the false discrimination that ascribes separateness to the experiential world he perceives that the states of existence eternally abide in the tathāgata-garbha, where they are in no way distinct from Emptiness (śūnyatā) and nirvāṇa.[53]

The tathāgata-garbha is the equivalent of the ālaya-vijñāna, the "Storehouse Consciousness".[54] Ālaya-vijñāna, synonymous with Mind (citta), is a storehouse, or womb,[55] which contains "seeds" (bīja), or potentialities of thoughts, affections, desires and actions (karma),[56] which issue forth from this Mind-repository as "present actions" or experiences (saṃskāra). By this the objective world is "created". These actions and experiences in turn affect and create impressions of new seeds in the ālaya-vijñāna so that the process of bringing forth the phenomena of our experience continues. The seeds whence the world of phenomena (saṃsāra) springs are termed "defiled seeds" (sāśrava-bīja); but the Mind-repository also holds "undefiled seeds" (anāśrava-bīja), from which grow Enlightenment and nirvāṇa : like the tathāgata-garbha, the ālaya-vijñāna is the womb-matrix that gives birth both to the universe and to the Buddhas.

The process whereby the potentialities contained within the seeds of the ālaya-vijñāna evolve into our experience of the sensible and intelligible

---

48. Cook, 1977, p. 46. 49. LS 77 (Suzuki, 1932, pp. 68f.).

50. Suzuki, 1930, p. 106.

51. Aśvaghoṣa, p. 36; cf. *Śrimāla-sūtra*, Taishō, Vol. 12, p. 222b, quoted in Hakeda, 1967, p. 113, n. 12. 52. Aśvaghoṣa, pp. 77f.

53. Cf. Suzuki, 1930, p. 138. 54. Cook, 1977, pp. 46f.; Suzuki, 1930, p.176.

55. In the Chinese texts the terms 藏 (Ch. tsang, Jap. zō), "storehouse", "treasury", and 胎 (Ch. tai, Jap. tai), "womb", are used synonymously, interchangeably, or together to form a compound 胎藏 (Ch. tai-tsang, Jap. taizō) to render garbha. Cf. Suzuki, 1930, p. 176.

56. Suzuki, 1930, p. 177.

world is a rich complexity of doctrinal details[57] and cannot be described here, but expressed in terms of a geometric symbolism the emanation into outward experience of phenomena contained as seed-images within the Mind is a "projection" from a non-dimensional centre. The birth of objective existences from the Womb-Mind is equivalent to the deployment of space and time from a spaceless and atemporal point. The attainment of Buddhahood is a return to that centre, the result of a "turning" or "reversal" (parāvṛtti) to the "base" (āśraya)[58] on which all things depend, namely, the tathāgata-garbha, the Storehouse Consciousness, Mind. It is a turning about in the deepest seat of consciousness, a turning back, going "counter-current" (pratīpa), a re-turning to the Centre, a "revulsion" and conversion from the ego-centric discrimination that separates subject and object. It is the attainment of Mind at the Centre, external to which no thing exists; it is the realization that saṃsāra is Mind Only (citta-mātra).

* * * * *

Shingon Buddhism also teaches that innate within the mind of every being there is a Womb that gives birth to Buddhas. Within this Buddha-Matrix (buddha-garbha) the Mind of Enlightenment (bodhicitta) lies dormant, as a Seed of Consciousness (vijñāna-bīja). The quickening of this Seed is made manifest by an initial arousal of aspiration to attain Buddhahood; having come to life, the Mind of Enlightenment grows within the Womb, nourished by the "ten thousand practices of Great Compassion" (mahā-karuṇā), that is, by the performance of rituals of meditation. The birth of the child is the attainment of Enlightenment; its growth to manhood is the cultivation of Method (upāya), in which the Awakened develops the means to aid, guide and benefit unenlightened beings.[59]

The birth of Enlightenment from the innermost centre of the mind has a macrocosmic counterpart. The Womb is the Principle (理, Ch. li, Jap. ri) of the cosmos.[60] The Buddha born from the Womb is inseparably merged in non-duality with the world . Phenomena are aspects of the Buddha's Three Mysteries : all physical phenomena are aspects of his Body; all mental phenomena are aspects of his Mind; and all manifestations of the Dharma are aspects of his Speech.

These Shingon doctrines are diagrammatically represented in the Matrix Mandala (garbha-maṇḍala), which shows the Womb of Principle, or the Matrix of Great Compassion (mahā-karuṇā-garbha), the womb that gives birth to Buddhas. The layers of the mandala show Buddhas, Bodhisattvas and beings in various stages of maturation within the Womb, the culmination of which process is represented by Mahā-vairocana Buddha at the centre of the mandala, personifying the perfection of Method (upāya). In a complementary interpretation the layers of the mandala are the outward emanation of the Body, Speech and Mind of Mahāvairocana into the multiple states of existence. In this view the figures in the mandala embody aspects of the Buddha's Body, of his Dharma and of his Vow-Mind (purva-praṇidhāna-citta).[61]

* * * * *

---

57. See Sōgen, 1912, pp. 215ff., for a lengthy summary.

58. In Chinese 轉依, chuan-i (Jap. tene, or tenne), lit. "(re)turn-base = Skt. āśraya-parāvṛtti. 59. *Dainichikyō*, p. 610a *et seq*.

60. On the concept of li (Jap. ri), see above, p. 123.

61. See Toganoo, 1932, *passim*; MKDJT, p. 1492, s.v. Taizō mandara.

Fig. 126 : The Matrix World Mandala, which represents the Buddha Mahāvairocana Tathāgata as the all-encompassing Womb and the progenitive Centre of the universe. The layers of Buddhas and Bodhisattvas surrounding Mahāvairocana represent the strata of the cosmos permeated by Mahāvairocana as the Womb-Principle.

These concepts throw light on the meaning of the *garbha* of the stupa. It is the source not only of the phenomenal world (*dharmadātu*) but also of Enlightened Buddhas, who are nourished and protected within its covering until they emerge to succour suffering beings; and it is the source of all the bodily, mental and verbal actions performed by the Buddhas to bring all the beings of the three worlds from darkness into light.

The term *dhātugarbha*[62] also takes on an added significance. In one of its meanings the word *dhātu* is "an element of the body" and hence "bodily remains, relics" so that *dhātugarbha* has generally been taken to mean "relic container", originally applied to the *harmikā* at the top of the stupa's dome where the relics were installed and then by extension to the whole structure. This interpretation, however, only gives a partial explanation of the term. In its primary meaning *dhātu* means "world" or a constituent element of a world.[63] According to its etymological significance, therefore, the term *dhātugarbha* means "the container of the world" or, more precisely, "the container of the elements constituting a world". This was pointed out by Kern as early as the beginning of the century, when he said that "the real meaning of *dhātu* is 'element'... and the *dhātugarbha* is the matrix which contains the elements... the true *dhātugarbha* of the Ādi-Buddha, otherwise called Brahmā the Creator, is *Brahmaṇḍa*, the world egg which contains all the elements and which the horizon divides into two parts. This is the true *dhātugarbha* : the buildings are only its imitation".[64]

---

62. *Dagoba*, which derives from *dhātugarbha*, is the usual name given the stupa in Sri Lanka. See above, p.260. Cf. Brown, 1965, p. 167.

63. Edgerton, 1970, p. 30, s.v. *dhātu*, gives the meaning of *dhātu* as "primordial element", with at least seven different senses :
1. the physical elements, the basic constituents of the physical world, namely, Earth, Water, Fire, Air, Space and Consciousness;
2. elements in the body excusively and specifically;
3. the eighteen constituent elements of the psycho-physical being in its relation to the outside world, namely, the six sense organs, the six sense objects and the six corresponding sensory perceptions;
4. the constituent elements of the mind, "heart" or character and, by extension, the (psychic) character, the nature or natural disposition;
5. sphere, region, world, state of existence, as in *lokadhātu*, "world", *arūpa*-, *rūpa*- and *kāma-dhātu*, the three "worlds" of the formless, form and desire;
6. a mass, abundance, large quantity; and
7. elemental bodily substance, and hence bodily remains, relics.

In summary, what we are dealing with is a world or the constituent parts of a world, whether they be the elements making up a world, a sphere, a state of existence, which is to say a macrocosm, or those that go together to form the microcosm of the individual's physical and mental being. The patriarchs and scholar-sages who translated the Buddhist sutras from Sanskrit to Chinese rendered *dhātu* as 界, *chiai* (Jap. *kai*), "a boundary or limit, a world" (Mathews, 1952), or alternately transliterated it as 馱都 *t'o tu* (Jap. *dato*), defined as "whatever is differentiated, a boundary, limit or region, that which is contained or limited..." (Soothill and Hodous, 1934). Kōbō Daishi says that the term *dhātu* used in the name of the *Vajra-dhātu-maṇḍala* has fou basic meanings : 界, *kai*, "world"; 體, *tai*, "essence", 身, *shin*, "body"; and 差別, *shabetsu*, "what is differentiated". See MKDJT, p. 668, s.v., *Kongōkai mandara*; Burnouf, 1852, p. 511, cited by Combaz, 1935, p. 36.

64. Kern, 1901, p. 154; cf. Mus, 1935, p. 100; Combaz, 1935, p. 36.

3. THE CAVE.

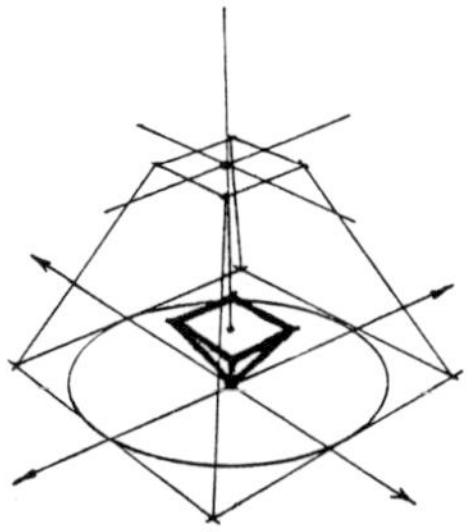

The cave within the mountain is assimilated to the supreme Truth.[65] The Sanskrit word guha, "cave", derives from the root guh, "to cover, to hide", which is synonymous with the root gup, whence gupta, applied to everything having a secret character or to what is not outwardly visible.[66] The cave is the innermost and most hidden centre of the cosmos in the same way that the heart is that of the body. In the Brahmanic tradition the "cave of the heart" is the vital centre of the being, the abode of both the jivātma, the Spirit of Self (ātma) manifested in the human individual, and the paramātma, the supreme and unconditioned Self that is identical with Brahman.[67] Jivātma and paramātma are "the two who have entered into the cave" and "who dwell on the highest summit".[68]

Microcosmically the cave is the central point of the heart, hidden and invisible, containing the seed, or potentiality, of Enlightenment. Macrocosmically it is the central point of the universe, which contains in potentia all the possibilities of manifestation. Enlightenment is an uncovering and growth of the potentialities concealed within its point of origin. This theme is reiterated in Buddhist and pre-Buddhist literature. "Know that this Agni, who is the foundation of the eternal (principial) world and by whom this can be attained, is hidden in the cave (of the heart)".[69] This drawing out of concealed possibility is an initium, a beginning and initiation, a death and a second birth within the concealment and darkness of the cave - and it will be remembered that every change of state takes place in darkness : the Enlightenment of Śākyamuni, for example, takes place in the hours of darkness and is completed at the time of the rising of the sun.[70]

Every Buddhist initiation takes place in the cave of the heart, and the initiatic space - building or mandala - is symbolically identified with the cave. The Buddhist Way, as every other initiatic path, is a series of deaths to selfhood and to the profane world. At his ordination and at each of the stages of Bodhisattvahood the Wayfarer dies to one state of existence and is reborn into a higher state. In this initiatic progress death and birth are two faces of one and the same change of state : what is a death from one point of view is always a birth from another; death in the preceding state is birth into the state that follows.[71]

Entry into the cave is a second birth; emergence from the cave is a third birth. The second birth, which is properly a psychic regeneration, operates in the domain of the subtle possibilities of the human individuality. The

---

65. Eliade, 1958a, p. 235, citing *Kānhupāda*, *Dohākoṣa* 14. On Mountain-Cave symbolism, see Guénon, 1962, Chs. XXIX-XXXIV.

66. Guénon, 1962, p. 218. Guénon also points out that gupta is the equivalent of Gk. kruptos, whence comes "crypt", synonym of "cave". The cave-crypt, i.e., cave-sepulchre, relationship is examined below.

67. Guénon, 1962, p. 220; 1945, pp. 38-41; CU III.14.3 and VIII.1.1.

68. KU III.1; cf. *Brahma-sūtra* I.2.11-12. 69. KU I.17.

70. See, e.g., Warren, 1922.

71. Guénon, 1962, p. 211; 1953, pp. 178ff. For the concept of initiation generally, see Guénon, 1952 and 1953.

third birth, on the other hand, takes place in the spiritual, and no longer the psychic domain : it is an entry into the realm of supra-individual possibilities. The second birth is a birth into the cosmos (corresponding to the birth of the avatāra in the macrocosmic order); it is an entry into the cave, where all the possibilities of the formal realm, both physical and mental, are focussed and contained. The third birth is a birth from the cosmos, a passage from the world of form (rūpa-loka) to the formless world (arūpa-loka). Symbolically, the former is a return to or a concentration within the central point of the circle of the world, an arrival at the peak of the mountain or, according to the symbolism here being discussed, an entry into the cave; whereas the latter is a passage through the apex of the cave, an exit from and leaving behind of the manifested universe in its entirety.

The symbolism of the initiatic cave is reflected in architectural forms. The cella of the Hindu temple, which is a small cubical chamber, unadorned and dark, is called the garbhagṛha, "the womb of the house".[72] "The garbhagṛha is not only the house of the Germ or embryo of the temple; it also refers to man who comes to the Centre and attains his new birth in darkness".[73] It is rahasya, secret and mysterious. The garbhagṛha is the "Cave in the Mountain".[74] The temple is called Guharāja, "King of Caves"; the temple is a mountain; the cella within it is a cave.[75] Deriving from this Indian usage the Burmese term their Buddhist temples "caves" (ku), and the Ānanda temple at Pagan, for example, is so called and has kuharas, "caves" or halls radiating in the four directions from a massive centre.[76] The Buddhist caitya halls at Kārlī, Beḍsā, Ajaṇṭā, Elūrā and elsewhere in India, and the rock cut temples in China, are literally caves, cut into the living rock of hillsides.

Mountain and cave are two archetypes of Buddhist sacred architecture. They are represented by the cave temple and the stupa. The architectural expressions of the two symbols often combine or overlap : the cave temple contains a stupa (the mountain in a cave); and the stupa contains a hollow chamber (a cave in the mountain).[77] The stupa is simultaneously a mountain and a cave.

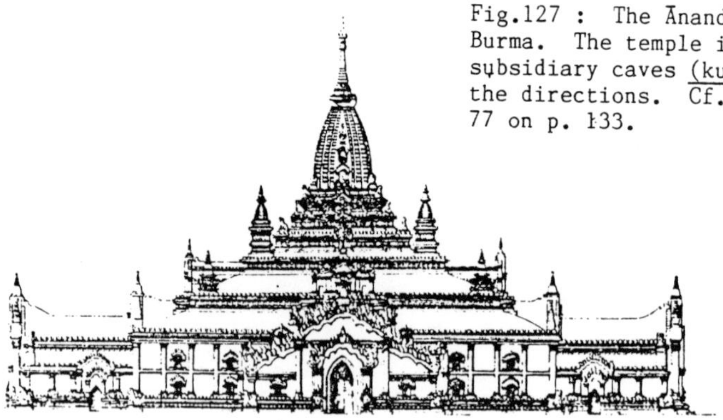

Fig.127 : The Ānanda Temple of Pagan, Burma. The temple is a cave (ku) with subsidiary caves (kuhara) radiating in the directions. Cf. the plan in fig. 77 on p. 133.

72. Cf. above, p. 73. Kramrisch, 1946, p. 162. 74. *Ibid.*, p. 147.

75. *Bṛhat Saṃhitā* LV.17, cited in Kramrisch, 1946, p. 169.

76. Griswold, Kim and Pott, 1964, pp. 26f.; Rawson, 1967, p. 180; Bussagli, 1973, p. 228; Kramrisch, 1946, p. 169, n. 95 and 171.

77. Seckel, 1964, p. 136.

4. THE LOTUS.

The concepts of cosmic containment and centering that are conveyed by the womb, the egg and the cave are most usually expressed in Buddhism by the symbolism of the lotus or the lotus bud, and although the dome of the stupa is not explicitly identified with the lotus in the texts, the ascription can be implied. An analysis of lotus symbolism adds to an understanding of the symbolism of the dome.

As do the womb, the egg and the cave, the lotus lies at the secret centre, in the most occult space (ākāśa) within the inner recesses of the heart.[78] It is the "uncreated depository of Consciousness; in the space that is within the heart lies the Lord of All, the Ruler of the universe".[79] "Now here in this city of Brahman (brahmapura) is an abode, a small lotus flower; within it is a small space. What is within that should be sought, for that,

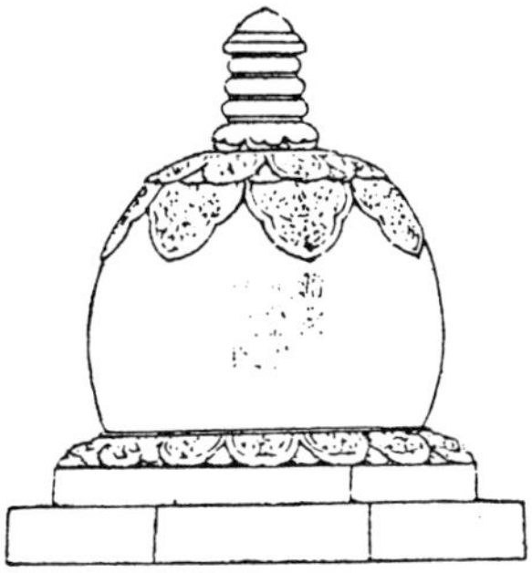

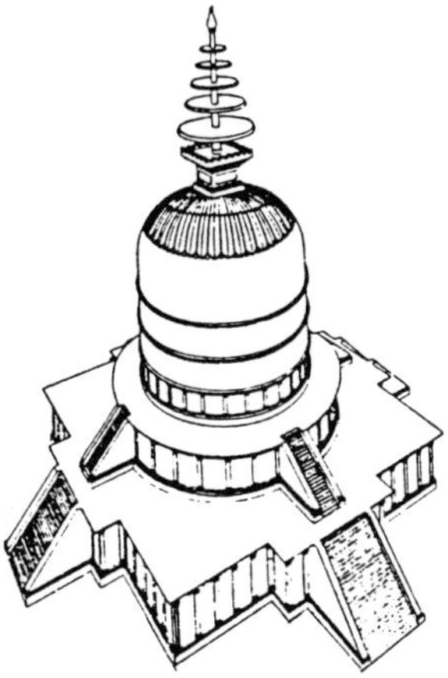

Fig. 128 : Examples of stupas showing the dome emerging from a downward growing lotus, which is the homologue of the inverted Cosmic Tree whose roots are in Heaven and whose branches are the levels of existence.

Fig. 129 : The Bodhisattva Avalokiteśvara (Jap. Kannon Bosatsu), whose cognisance is the lotus, representing the lotus-mind that contains Enlightenment.

Fig. 130 : A lotus opening to reveal the Bodhisattva Tārā, representing the Buddha Nature that abides innate within the heart-lotus, which opens when cultivated by meditational practices.

---

78. CU VII.3.1. On lotus symbolism see Coomaraswamy, 1935a, pp. 17ff. & 39ff.; Bosch, 1960, *passim*; Saunders, 1960, pp. 159ff.; Zimmer, 1955, pp. 158ff.; 1946, pp. 90ff.; BKDJT, pp. 5036ff., s.v., Renge; MKDJT, pp. 2294 ff., s.v., Renge; Chevalier and Gheerbrant, 1973, 3, pp. 141ff., s.v., Lotus; Cirlot, 1962, pp. 184f.; Guénon, 1962, Ch. IX ("Les fleurs symboliques"), pp. 94ff.; Getty, 1962, pp. 192f., s.v., Padma; Ward, 1952, *passim*.

79. BU IV.4.22.

assuredly, is what one should desire to understand... As far, verily as this (world) space (ākāśa) extends, so far extends the space within the heart. Within it, indeed, are contained both Heaven and Earth, both fire and air, both sun and moon, lightning and the stars. Whatever there is of him in this world and whatever is not, all that is contained within it".[80]

In Buddhism the lotus of the heart-mind similarly lies at the innermost centre of the being and when nurtured by meditation and other practices opens to reveal the indwelling Buddha-Nature (buddhatā). In this symbolic formula the flowering of the lotus is the attainment of Enlightenment : the petals open to disclose the Buddha seated on the lotus pericarp. This theme is given explicit plastic expression in the Burmese and Indian bronze lotus buds with hinged petals that open to show a Buddha, a Bodhisattva or a stupa.[81]

The symbolism of the lotus as the birthplace of Buddhas is recurrent in the Mahāyāna literature. The *Mahā-sukhāvatī-vyūha*, for example, describes the lotuses growing in the jewel ponds of the Land of Supreme Bliss (sukhāvatī) : "... from each there proceed thirty six hundred thousand koṭis of rays of light. From each ray of light there proceed thirty six hundred thousand koṭis of Buddhas, with bodies of golden-colour, possessed of the thirty two marks of great men, who go and teach the Law to beings in the immeasurable and innumerable worlds in the eastern quarter. Thus also in the southern, western, and northern quarters, above and below, in the cardinal and intermediate points, they go their way to the immeasurable and innumerable worlds and teach the Law to beings in the whole world".[82] As the ten directions of space are deployed from a centre, so are the omnipresent Buddhas born into the worlds from the lotus.

Another of the Pure Land sutras, the *Amitāyur-dhyāna-sūtra*,[83] describes how those who call upon the name of Amitābha Buddha ("Buddha of Immeasurable Light") are reborn within lotus buds in the Land of Supreme Bliss. When their stock of karma is exhausted the lotus unfolds and the devotee attains the ultimate liberating vision of Amitābha and his Pure Land.[84]

At the centre of being abides the pure and immaculate Mind of Enlightenment (bodhicitta). Its purity is conveyed by the lotus, which is undefiled by the mud from which it grows. This is a concept coeval with Buddhism and it recurs in the earliest Pali literature, in passages such as that which says, "Just as, Brethren, a lotus, born in the water, full grown in the water, rises to the surface and is not wetted by the water, even so, Brethren, the Tathāgata, born in the world, surpasses the world and is unaffected by the world".[85] In the *Milinda Pañho* the purity of nirvāṇa is likened to that of the lotus,[86] and Nāgasena uses the lotus to exemplify the qualities that the Bhikṣu should possess : as the lotus grows in the

---

80. CU VIII.1.1-3.

81. Griswold, Kim and Pott, 1964, p. 34 & fig. 22 on p. 43; Luce, 1969, 3, pls. 425 - 428a; Shorto, 1971, p. 77; Lad, n.d., pl. 48 on p. 212, which shows an Indian example that opens to reveal Vajratāra.

82. MSV 16; cf. Fujimoto, 1955, 1, p. 100.

83. Together with the Larger and Smaller *Sukhāvatī-vyūha-sūtras* the *Amitāyur-dhyāna-sūtra* is one of the three fundamental sutras of the Pure Land schools of Japanese Buddhism, that is, the Jōdo ("Pure Land") and Jōdo Shin ("True Pure Land") schools.

84. DS 22ff.; cf MSV 41.

85. S III. 140; cf. Saunders, 1960, p. 250, n. 8; Coomaraswamy, 1935a, p. 21. 86. Mil IV.66.

water but is undefiled by the water, so the Bhikṣu should be undefiled by the support he receives, by his following of disciples, by fame, honour, veneration or an abundance of requisites; as the lotus remains lifted in the air, so the Bhikṣu should remain far above worldly things; and again, as the lotus trembles in the breeze, so the Bhiksu should exercise self-control in respect of the least evil dispositions.[87]

The lotus is within the heart, at the centre of the being. In a complementary symbolism it grows from the navel of the world. In the Brahmanic mythology it grows from the navel of Prajāpati, whose form is this world, head the Sky, feet the Earth and navel the Atmosphere.[88] In the later Hindu literature the lotus grows from the navel of Viṣṇu, who sleeps upon the Cosmic Ocean supported by the Serpent Ananta ("Endless"); the lotus opens to reveal Brahmā, the progenitor of the worlds.[89] The recumbent Viṣṇu is described as "lotus-navelled" (padma-nābha); and Brahmā is termed the "lotus-born" (abjaja), the "navel-born" (nābhija) and the "lotus-seated" (padmāsana).[90]

The theme of the lotus growing from the navel of the deity is echoed in the Buddhist literature. Immediately prior to his departure from the palace on the night of his Great Renunciation, Siddharta dreams that a lotus rises from his navel up through the worlds to the Akaniṣṭha Heaven, the Heaven of the "Final Limit of Form" and the very summit of the cosmos of formal manifestation (rūpaloka).[91] With equivalent symbolic reference it is told that when the Buddha descended into the womb of his mother Māyā a lotus grew from the waters up to Brahmā's Heaven and all the possibilities immanent within prakṛti lay within this lotus like a drop of nectar.[92] According to a Nepalese tradition, at the beginning of the world the Ādi Buddha manifested himself in the form of a flame rising from a lotus flower.[93]

For Shingon Buddhism also the lotus, which symbolizes Principle, is identified with the heart (hṛdaya), and this in two senses. At one level hṛdaya, from the root hṛi, "vital spirit, the subtle, the recondite", is the pure Mind of the Essential Nature (svabhava-hṛdaya), likened to the lotus which opens to reveal the innate Buddha-Nature (buddhatā). At another level it is the physical heart, whose four arteries and four veins are the eight petals of the lotus. It is an essential concept of Shingon Buddhism that the physical world is intimately and inseparably suffused by its Principle, so that the phenomena of manifestation and their Principle exist in an indistinguishable identity. Conditioned phenomena, in a continual state of flux, and their immutable, unconditioned Principle, are two aspects of a unique Reality that subsumes them both. The Shingon teaches that the lotus is at one and the same time the corporeal, corruptible organ of flesh and blood and the spiritual organ, the abode of Buddhahood, that centres the being.[94]

The Shingon doctrine compares the lotus seed that contains within itself the whole potentiality of the lotus plant and flower to the Mind of Enlighten-

---

87. Mil VII.2-4, quoted by Ward, 1952, pp. 137f.

88. See above, pp. 47ff. 89. See above, p. 194.

90. Coomaraswamy, 1935a, pp. 17f.

91. *Lalita Vistara* , 1, p. 196; Bosch, 1960, p. 56; Foucher, 1917, pp.147ff.

92. Hodgson, 1874, p. 115; Levi, 1905, 3, pp. 163ff.

93. Bosch, 1960, pp. 56f.; Getty, 1962, p. 192.

94. MKDJT, p. 17, s.v. Ajikan; p. 1240, s.v., Shin.

ment (bodhicitta), which is the virtuality of perfected Buddhahood carried innate within every being; the growth of the lotus plant from this seed and the formation of the lotus bud that contains and protects the flower is the growth of the Mind of Enlightenment that takes place when nurtured by the "ten thousand practices of Great Compassion (mahā-karuṇā)"; and the blossoming of the lotus flower is the attainment of Awakening and the deployment of the qualities and skills of Method (upāya).[95]

This concept is represented in the Matrix Mandala, also called the Mandal of Principle and the Lotus Mandala,[96] which shows at its centre an open lotus,[97] with Mahā-vairocana Tathāgata, the hypostasis of Principle,[98] seated on the pericarp, and four Buddhas and four Bodhisattvas, representing the stages in the opening of the Mind-lotus, seated on the eight petals that surround him.[99]

Fig. 131 : The central section of the Matrix World Mandala showing Buddhas and Bodhisattvas seated on the eight petals and pericarp of a lotus.

Fig. 132 : The Pure Land of the Buddha Amitābha (Jap. Amida Butsu).

The panel to the viewer's left of the central lotus in the Mandala shows the Bodhisattva Avalokiteśvara (Jap. Kannon), whose Original Vow (praṇidhāna) was to open the lotus of the Mind within all beings. Accordingly, he is shown holding in his left hand a partially opened lotus, which he is opening with his right hand. The other Bodhisattvas shown in the mansion represent the stages in the process of the Heart-Mind's purification, whereby Avalokiteśvara's Vow is brought to fruition.[100]

* * * * *

95. Śubhākarasiṃha, p. 610.a.20; cf. MKDJT, p. 1563f., s.v. Chudai hachiyo in, and p. 2303, s.v., Renge Mandara; BKDJT, p. 3308, s.v., Taizōkai mandara; Toganoo, 1932, pp. 65ff. 96. Jap. ri mandara and renge mandara respectively.

97. Called the "Central Dais Eight Petal Mansion" (Jap. chudai hachiyo in). See MKDJT, p. 2303, s.v., Chudai hachi yo in.

98. Jap. Ri hosshin. 99. See above, pp.135ff.

100. MKDJT, p. 379, s.v. Kannon in and p. 394, s.v., Kanjizai Bosatsu; BKDJT, pp. 800ff., s.v., Kanzeon Bosatsu and p. 3309, s.v., Taizōkai Mandara; Toganoo, 1932, pp. 161ff.

The lotus is also the container of the universe, as is implied in terms such as padma-garbha, "Lotus-womb", and padma-kośa, "lotus-treasury". The lotus is the cosmos : its filaments are the mountains, distant countries exist on the outer petals, demons and serpents dwell on their underside. On the pericarp there are four oceans centred by Mt. Meru and the great continent of which India is a part.[101]

At the time of the future Buddha's gestation in the womb of Māyā, Brahmā perceived a lotus growing from the lower waters. This lotus contained the quintessence of the world, which Brahmā collected as a drop of elixir. Placing it in a precious vase he offered it to the Buddha-to-be, who drank it and absorbed its essence without difficulty, thus assimilating the quintessence of the universe given to him by the Ancestor of the World (lokapitāmaha).[102]

The Hua Yen (Jap. Kegon) sect[103] teaches the doctrine of the Lotus Womb World (padma-garbha-lokadhātu).[104] This is described in the *Brahmajāla-sūtra*[105] which quotes the supreme Buddha Locana as saying, "I dwell on the lotus throne which contains the worlds and oceans. This throne is surrounded by one thousand petals. Each petal being a world, it makes one thousand worlds. I metamorphose myself producing one thousand Śākyas, conforming to the one thousand worlds. Further, on each petal which is a world there are a hundred million Sumerus, a hundred million suns and moons, a hundred million worlds each in four parts, a hundred million Jambudvīpas, a hundred million Bodhisattva-Śākyas, who are sitting under a hundred million bodhi trees, each of them preaching the qualities and stages of a Bodhisattva... Each Śākya of the remaining nine hundred and ninety nine Śākyas produces thousands and hundreds of millions of Śākyas, who do the same. The Buddhas on the thousand petals are transformations of myself, and the thousands and hundreds of millions of Śākyas are the transformations of these thousand Śākyas. I am their origin and my name is Locana Buddha".[106]

This revelation of Locana Buddha is plastically represented by the huge and famous bronze image housed in the Tōdaiji temple in Nāra, Japan. The image is seated upon a lotus throne, on each petal of which is engraved the figure of Śākyamuni seated on a throne located at the summit of a Great Chiliocosm.[107]

---

101. Zimmer, 1946, p. 52; Ward, 1952, p. 137.

102. Foucher, 1917, pp. 147ff.; cf. Bosch, 1960, p. 56.

103. Ch. Hua Yen, Skt. *Avataṃsaka*, named after the *Avataṃsaka-sūtra* (Taishō, vol. 9, Nos. 278 & 293), which provides its main doctrinal base. Cf. Takakusu, 1956, pp. 108ff.; Steinilber-Oberlin, 1938, pp. 58ff.; Cook, 1977, *passim*; BKDJT, p. 869, s.v., Kegonshu.

104. Jap. renge zō sekai; see BKDJT, pp. 5040, s.v., Renge zō sekai.

105. Jap. *Bommōkyō*, Taishō, Vol. 24, No. 1484. 106. Elisséeff, 1936, p. 91.

107. See the plate in Okazaki, 1977, p. 35 and also Koboyashi, 1975, p. 67, but Koboyashi's description and notations contain errors. For a full and accurate description, see Elisséeff, pp. 92ff. Another illustration is given in BKDJT, Vol. 5, pl. 15221.

Fig. 133 : The Lotus-Womb world described in the *Brahmajāla-sūtra*. A depiction of that World is engraved on each of the petals of the lotus base supporting the image of Locana Buddha enshrined at the Tōdaiji temple, Nāra, Japan. Śākyamuni is shown sitting at the summit of the universe contained within the Lotus-Womb.

It is clear from the above that the lotus and the womb are coterminous in their symbolic significance, and this equivalence is given overt expression in the "intentional language" of Tantric Buddhism, where the lotus is expressly identified with the womb and the female genitals while the *vajra* is the *liṅga*, the *membrum virile*.[108]

Fig. 134 : The Locana Buddha enshrined at the Tōdaiji, Nāra, Japan.

Fig. 135 : The lotus opening to reveal the five-prong *vajra*, representing the deployment of the cosmos from the World Axis, cognate with the Buddha and Enlightenment. The *vajra* and the lotus also represent the essential and substantial principles, the Buddha Method (*upāya*) and Buddha Wisdom (*prajñā*), from whose union the cosmos comes into existence (see below, pp. 212 ff.).

108. Eliade, 1958a, p. 252.

5. THE SPHERE AND THE CUBE.

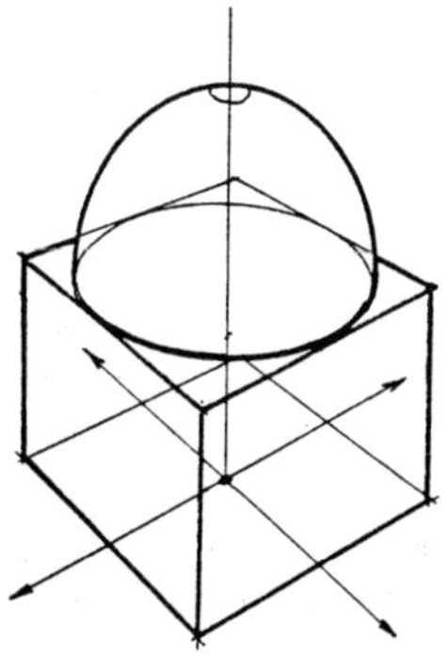

In its most usual form the domical type of stupa shows the hemisphere of the cupola supported on a square base, the medhi. The relation of the hemisphere to the square platform is the three-dimensional equivalent of that which exists between the circle and the square discussed above, where it was seen that in the stupa plan the circle represents the Earth, the Lower Waters, and the square represents Heaven, the Upper Waters. Every symbolism, however, is multivalent, and now in this three-dimensional context the relationship is reversed so that here the activity of the heavens is identified with the circular form, the dome, and the passive qualities of the earth are associated with the square form of the base. Whereas in the plan the dynamic form of the circle was equated with the ever-changing flux of the earth, here it is seen to relate to the cyclic movements of the celestial bodies; and whereas the static form of the square was previously equated with the immutability of Heaven, now it is related to the inert receptivity of Earth. Neither schema precludes the other; they are complementary rather than contradictory.

As in the case of the circle and the square the symbolism of the dome and the base can be interpreted at several levels. The square base is the extended earth, measured out in the directions of space by a procession from Unity to quadrature. The dome, in the likeness of the dome of the sky, relates to the motion of the stars. The base relates to space, the dome to time and, as with the circle and the square, their conjunction is the marriage of these two parameters of the empirical world.

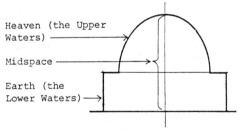

Fig. 136 : The Upper and Lower Waters in the stupa.

Further, and at its highest level of reference, the conjunction of the two forms expresses the union of complementary principles, the essential pole of manifestation on the one hand and its substantial pole on the other. These considerations are developed in the following.

Transposing this, the dome represents the Heaven World, the base the Earth World, and the space enclosed by the dome is the third of the Three Worlds (tribhūmi), Midspace. That is to say, the dome corresponds to the Upper Waters, comprizing the totality of the informal possibilities of manifestation, and the base corresponds to the Lower Waters, comprizing the totality of the possibilities of formal manifestation.

a. The Union of Complementary Principles.

In the cosmogenesis Unity proceeds to multiplicity by way of a diremption. Unity polarizes into two complementary principles,[109] universal Essence and universal Substance.[110] From their "union" or "interaction" the multiple states of existence and all that they contain come into existence. Essence is the active principle of manifestation; and Substance, the sub-stratum, that which "stands below", is the passive principle, the support, of manifestation.

The analogy for this productive conjunction of principles, and one that is to be found in many traditions, is given by the image of light reflecting from water.[111] Essence is compared to the rays of light that shine from the spiritual Sun and reflect from the surface of the Waters of Substance. The sensible and cognizable world is Essence reflecting from the plastic sub-stans of the world.

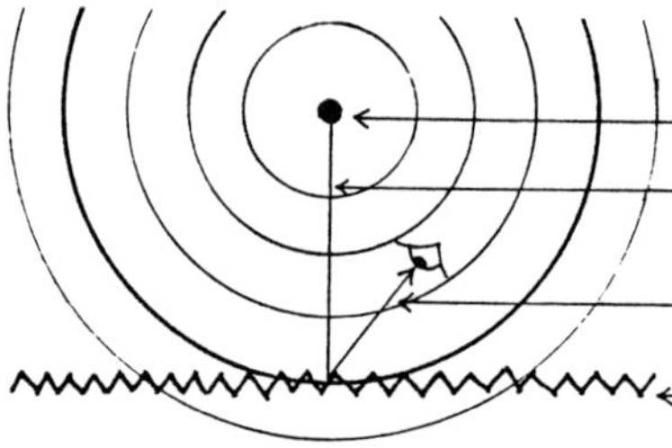

The symbolism can be expressed by way of another analogy taken from the modern world. In the likeness of images thrown upon a screen by a projector, the entities of the world emanate from the Sun and are carried by rays of light, identified with Essence, which reflect from the surface of Substance. In the same way that the viewer of the projected image is not aware of the light source, of the light rays that carry the image, nor yet again of the screen that reflects it, but sees only the one reflected from the other, so also the principles of manifestation and the source whence they originate are apprehended by reflection solely, and themselves remain unmanifested and outside the domain of the sensible or the cognizable.

This analogy is made less imperfect if it is imagined that the forms or images are contained within the light source itself and not, as with a projector, in something external to it. In this manner all entities are principially contained within Unity "prior" (in a logical, not chronological sense) to their emanation. So also it must be imagined that not only the rays of light but also the screen from which they reflect are simultaneously projected from the light source : the light of Essence and the reflecting surface of Substance both proceed instantly by a diremption of primordial Unity.

---

109. The theme of the union of complementary principles is recurrent in the writings of Guénon and Coomaraswamy. See e.g., Guénon, 1958a, Ch. VI ("The Union of Complements"), pp. 27ff. The union of puruṣa and prakṛti has exact parallels in other traditions, e.g., that of Heaven (t'ien) and Earth (ti) in the Chinese tradition.

110. The terms are used as defined by Guénon, 1945, pp. 48f., and 1953a.

111. See Guénon, 1945, pp. 55f.

In a complementary mode of viewing the symbolism[112] the phenomenal forms that arise into existence are thought of not as carried by the light rays, but as being contained within the Waters, which comprize all the possibilities of manifestation in a potential state. These possibilities pass from potentiality to act, are actualized, when the rays of Essence shine upon, or through, the Waters. Or, in another expression, they are realized when the Waters are stirred by the Breath. The forms of the world of our experience are light rays reflected from the waves of the Ocean of Possibility.

Although the production of forms can be spoken of as resulting from the "union" of Essence and Substance, Essence does not enter into its productions. The manner of its production is by way of an "actionless activity".[113] While itself remaining unchanged and unaffected, by its mere "action of presence" it occasions the manifestation of forms, somewhat in the manner in which a catalyst induces a chemical reaction without itself being changed. Essence determines the development of the possibilities lying dormant within Substance, but does not enter into manifestation, so that its immutability is not affected by the differentiation of phenomenal entities. Similarly Substance, while productive of entities, is not itself determined or modified by, but remains outside and below its determinations. The hierogamy of Essence and Substance produces the cosmos; but they themselves do not enter into their productions, remain outside manifestation, and continue free from all limitations.

b. *Puruṣa* and *Prakṛti*.

According to the Brahmanic formulations of this symbolism principial Unity, the source of the manifold entities of the cosmos, is universal Being, personified as Iśvara, the Lord. This is the non-supreme Brahman (apara-brahman), the first affirmation of the supreme Brahman (para-brahman), Non-Being, metaphysically Zero and theologically Godhead, which lies beyond Unity and multiplicity. From Being, Iśvara, proceed the two principles puruṣa and prakṛti.[114]

Puruṣa, "the Male", identified with Prajāpati, is the essential principle of manifestation, and prakṛti is the the substantial principle. Prakṛti is pradhāna, "that which is laid down before all other things"; it is the amorphous, plastic, tenebrous and chaotic support of the worlds. It gives birth to existences and is therefore identified with Māyā, the Mother of Forms, the Great Illusion that generates phenomena, the Earth Mother and Fertility Goddess, all the multifarious and multiform aspects of the cosmic Matrix.

Puruṣa and prakṛti are likened to the primordial Male and Female, personified as the God Śiva and the Goddess Śakti, whose union is productive of the cosmos. Puruṣa is represented by the liṅga, the phallus, and prakṛti by the yoni, the female sex organ; the conjunction of the liṅga and the yoni represents the progenitive syzygy of the conjoint principles. The liṅga marks

---

112. One that more properly belongs to the Aristotelian, as opposed to the Platonic, viewpoint.

113. Guénon, 1958a, pp. 55f. The term "actionless activity" (wei wu wei) is borrowed from the Taoist tradition. It is frequently encountered in Buddhist writings.

114. For the Brahmanic doctrine of puruṣa and prakṛti see Guénon, 1945, Ch. IV, "Purusha and Prakriti"; 1945a, pp. 256ff.

the central axis and the effulgent ray that radiates from the point of Unity; the *yoni* is its symbolic complement, the receptive and substantial support of the cosmos.[115]

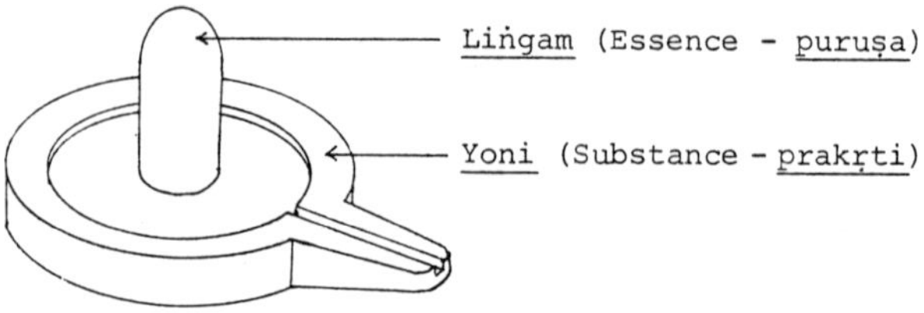

The symbolism is incorporated into the *Vāstu-puruṣa-maṇḍala*, that is, the mandala of *puruṣa*, Essence, immanent within existence (*vāstu*). *Puruṣa*, figured as a man stretched out in the manner of the victim in the Vedic sacrifice, is drawn upon the square of the mandala. He is Prajāpati, sacrificed by the Gods at the beginning of time and thus "incarnated" in the cosmos. *Puruṣa* is imprinted upon the square of *prakṛti*; the two principles are brought together in the mandala, which is thereby identified with the cosmos produced by their union.[116]

c. The Union of Complements in Buddhism.

Although the assimilation is not entirely congruent, it is nevertheless possible to perceive intimations of an analogous formula in the relationship of the Buddha and the Dharma.[117] The Buddha corresponds to the active principle, Essence. Stationed at the hub of the World Wheel, which is also the Wheel of the Dharma, he causes it to turn by his "actionless activity". The word *dharma*, from the root *dhṛ*, "to carry, to bear", means "supporter" and the Dharma, as do the substantial Waters, sustains the universe.[118] It is the *sub-stans* of the worlds and the support of all phenomena, which are therefore also called *dharmas*. From the same root *dhṛ* comes the word *dhāraṇī*, literally "support", referring to the sacred phrases that Tantric Buddhism deems to contain the concentrated essence of the total Dharma. They are considered to be the foundation (*pratiṣṭhā*) of the cosmos. In yet another correlation, the root *dhṛ* is connected in both its etymology and its meaning with another root, *dhru*, whence comes the word *dhruva*, "the pole". By this association Dharma is linked to concepts of axiality.[119]

The assimilation of the Dharma and the supporting Waters is prefigured in the verse of the *Śatapatha Brāhmaṇa* which says that "The Waters are the Dharma",[120] a dictum that is echoed in many passages in the *Vedas* which identify the Waters and *Vāc*, the *Logos*. As do the Waters, *Vāc* "pervades Heaven and Earth".[121] "Separated into many portions", *Vāc* is "assigned to many abodes, widely pervading".[122] It is the Word or Voice "whose cradle is

---

115. On the *liṅga*, see above, pp. 167ff.

116. Kramrisch, 1946, pp. 67ff.; Burckhardt, 1967, p. 25; and above, pp.106ff

117. See Guénon, 1957a, Ch. XXIV ("Le *Triratna*"), pp. 194ff.

118. Guénon, 1957a, 197ff.; Lévi, 1905, p. 160; cf. Hodgson, 1874, p. 72, who equates the Buddha Dharma with *mātra*, "measure" : *mātra* measures space and Dharma "supports form and quality in space". See also Bosch, 1960, p.122 and n. 20.

119. Guénon, 1957a, p. 198, n. 1. This might explain the passage in the *Amitāyur-dhyāna-sūtra* quoted above (p. 122) which describes the ground of

the Waters of the Ocean".[123] "He (Prajāpati) created the Waters from the world of Vāc. Vāc belonged to him. It was created, it pervaded all this. Because it pervaded all this which exists, it (Vāc) was called the Waters".[124] "All this was created by Vāc, and all that existed was Vāc".[125] "This male (puruṣa) Prajāpati desired, may I be multiplied, may I be developed. Having toiled and performed tapas, he first created the *Veda*, the triple science. It became to him a foundation (pratiṣṭhā)... resting on this foundation, he performed tapas. He created the Waters from the world of Vāc".[126] Impregnated by Prajāpati, Vāc gives birth to the first living creatures...[127] and "with this triple science (the *Veda*) he (Prajāpati) entered the Waters (= Vāc). Thence arose an egg".[128] Vāc not only pervades the universe, but also, as do the Waters, sustains it.

With similar reference within Buddhism, the *Saddharma-puṇḍarīka-sūtra* teaches that the Voice (vāc) of the Sutra pervades all space. The entire creation is based upon it. The Voice of the Sutra contains the Body of the Buddha Śākyamuni and the Bodies of all the past and future Buddhas. The Voice of the Sutra gives birth to these Buddha Bodies.[129] The Dharma is not created by the preaching of the Buddha but is the pre-existing and ever-immutable Principle that gives birth to all the Buddhas who preach the Dharma. All the Buddhas are one and consubstantial with the Voice of the Dharma whence they sprang.[130]

* * * * *

In Buddhism generally the Buddha and the Dharma are not truly congruent with the essential and substantial poles of manifestation since they are not seen as conjunct, cosmo-progenitive principles. In Tantric Buddhism, however, the Buddha and the Dharma are specifically identified with puruṣa and prakṛti. The Buddha is assimilated with Method (upāya) as a masculine principle cognate with Essence; the Dharma is assimilated with Wisdom (prajñā) as a feminine principle cognate with Substance; and the Community (saṅgha) is identified with the cosmos produced by their union.[131]

In the doctrines of the Buddhist Tantra the highest and most perfect Enlightenment (anuttara-saṃyak-saṃbodhi) has two aspects : on the one hand Wisdom (prajñā) which is pure Consciousness, the supreme Cognition; and on the other Method (upāya), the "actionless activity" of the Buddha who descends into the world to work there for the Enlightenment of all beings. Wisdom is identified with the Void (śūnyatā), and Method, which acts from compassion for the sufferings of beings, is identified with universal Compassion (karuṇā).[132]

Wisdom is the static and passive principle, the primordial container, support and source of all phenomena (dharma). Method, by contrast, is the active and dynamic principle whose action of presence, the expression of Compassion, brings forth the possibilities of the dharmas that lie in the

---

Amitābha's Pure Land as a banner. 120. ŚB XI.1.6.24.

121. RV X.125.6. 122. RV X.125.3. 123. RV X.125.7.

124. ŚB VI.1.1.9; cf. *Pañchav. Brāhmaṇa* XX.14.2.

125. ŚB VIII.1.2.9; cf. ŚB VII.5.2.21. 126. ŚB VI.1.1.8.

127. *Kāthaka* XII.5. 128. ŚB VI.1.1.10. For other texts relating to Vāc, see Bosch, 1960, p. 53. 129. SPS, cited by Bosch, 1960, p. 123.

130. Cf. Bosch, 1960, p. 162.

131. Dasgupta, 1959, p. 98 & 98 n. 1; Saunders, 1960, p. 154; Hodgson, 1874, p. 127; cf. Getty, 1962, pp. 28 & 197.

132. Dasgupta, 1959, p. 4; 1962, pp. 338ff.; Pallis, 1961.

Fig. 137 : The Bodhisattva Prajñā (Jap. Hannya) who represents Wisdom (prajñā) and the substans of the universe. She carries the Sword of Wisdom that cuts away ignorance to allow the birth of Buddhas.

Fig. 138 : The jewel in the lotus, representing the progenitive union of Wisdom and Method. The symbol is homologous to that of the vajra and the lotus, shown in fig. 135, p. 208.

Fig. 139 : A Tibetan yab-yum image, showing the union of Method (upāya), represented by the Ādi-Buddha, and Wisdom (prajñā), represented by the female Ādi-Prajñā, corresponding respectively to puruṣa and prakṛti, Essence and Substance.

Void of Wisdom.[133]

In their cosmological connotations Method and Wisdom are the equivalents of puruṣa and prakṛti. Wisdom is identified with the primordial Waters; she is also described as the Mother of the Three Worlds, the Mother of the Gods[134] and the Mother of Buddhas. As Ādi-Prajñā, primordial Wisdom, cognate with the Unity of Being, she gives birth to the Ādi-Buddha, the primordial Buddha, and then joins with him in union. She is first his Mother, and then his Consort.[135] The Ādi-Buddha and Ādi-Prajñā are the Father and Mother of the world and in Tibet their union is expressed in an overtly sexual iconography. Yab-yum figures show the Ādi-Buddha, or Method (upāya), as the Father (yab), and Ādi-Prajñā, Wisdom, as the Mother (yum), in sexual union, which represents the non-dual conjunction of the two principles (prajñopāya). In other contexts the two principles are represented by the seed and the ovum, by the male and female sex organs, by the jewel, or vajra, in the lotus, and so on.[136]

* * * * *

Analogous concepts, but lacking the sexual imagery, are expressed in the two mandalas of Shingon Buddhism, the Matrix World Mandala (garbha-kośa-maṇḍala) and the Diamond World Mandala (vajra-dhātu-maṇḍala). The former is also called the Mandala of Principle (Jap. ri mandara) and the latter is the Mandala of Knowledge (Jap. chi mandara).[137] As previously explained, ri, 理, is the Principle or "inner Law" of things. It is the Principle by which

---

133. Dasgupta, 1962, p. 28. 134. *Ibid.*, p. 341. 135. *Ibid.*, p. 340.

136. Eliade, 1958a, pp. 259ff.

137. There is no exact Skt. equivalent for ri. Jap. chi translates jñāna, "Knowledge", and is interchangeably used to designate prajñā, "Wisdom". 138. MKDJT, p. 2271, s.v., Ri mandara.

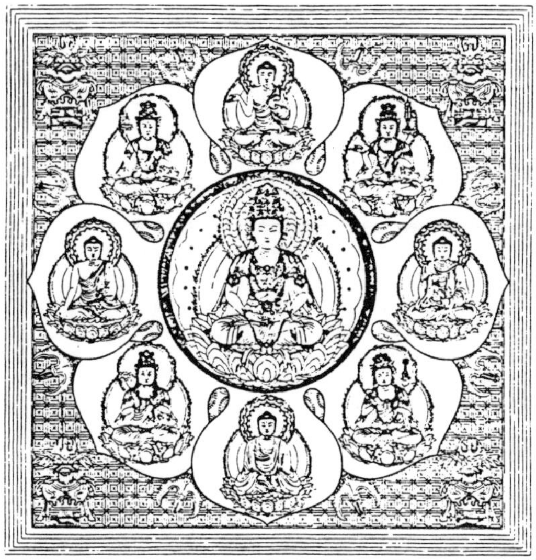

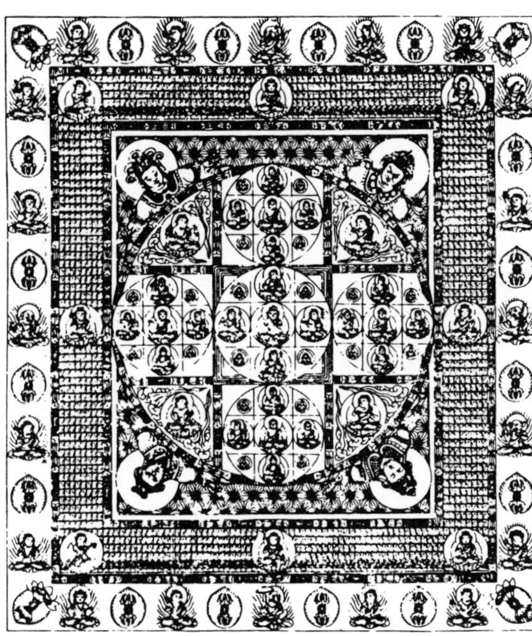

Fig. 140 : The Diamond and Matrix World Mandalas, here represented by their central sections. The mandalas represent two aspects of Enlightenment, those which respectively correspond to the vajra and the lotus, to essential Knowledge (jñāna) and substantial Principle (Jap. ri), to the in-forming and receptive poles of cosmic manifestation. The Shingon school of Buddhism teaches that these aspects are totally merged in an inseparable non-duality (advaita, Jap. funi).

things are what they are and not something else, or the pattern of order that runs through nature. It denotes the plenitude of that which sustains the phenomenal world. Principle thus has obvious analogies with the concept of Dharma as this term has been analysed above. In reference to the mandala it is synonymous with the Matrix that contains, sustains and gives birth to the things of the universe. Principle is all-pervading, unobstructed and omnipresent; it is immanent within all the forms of the cosmos.

The tradition-laden Chinese term li, "Principle", was adopted by the Buddhist translators as a kenning for the Sanskrit śūnyatā, "Void", conceived as the female principle from which forms arise and to which they return. The Matrix Mandala is called the Mandala of Principle because it is the mandala that represents the Void-Principle that pervades the worlds.[138]

The Diamond World Mandala, on the other hand, represents the complementary aspect of Reality, which is Knowledge (jñāna). This is the Buddha Knowledge that discriminates between the existence and the non-existence of the dharmas, the Knowledge that differentiates the ephemeral and mutable aspects of phenomena from the permanence and immutability of their Principle. Phenomenal entities are totally fused within Principle in what is technically termed a "horizontal identity" (Jap. ō-byōdō); the "actionless activity" of Knowledge brings them forth from their indistinction within Principle, and by its discriminating function, perceives them in their "vertical differentiation" (Jap. ju-shabetsu) : by the union of Knowledge and Principle forms issue forth into separate, differentiated existence.[139]

Knowledge, being immutable and indestructible, is represented by the diamond (vajra); Principle is identified with the world-supporting lotus whose opening is the deployment of forms; and therefore the two mandalas that embody them are also termed respectively the Vajra-Mandala (Jap. kongō-mandara) and the Lotus Mandala (Jap. renge-mandara). In Tibetan Buddhism the vajra represents the male phallus[140] and has a significance analogous to that of the liṅga, while the lotus represents the female genitalia. The symbol of a vajra or a flaming jewel supported on a lotus, frequent in both Tibetan and Japanese Tantric Buddhism, represents the union of the conjoint principles, Knowledge and Principle.[141]

* * * * *

Fig. 141 : The vajra and the lotus as the complementary principles of universal manifestation.

Fig. 142 : The sphere and the cube as the complementary principles of manifestation.

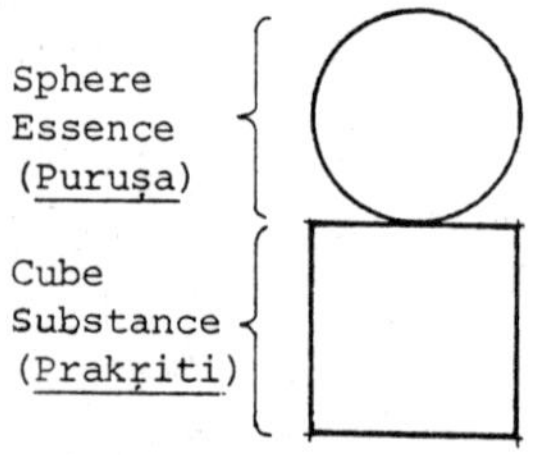

138. MKDJT, p. 2271, s.v. Ri mandara. 139. MKDJT, p. 1599, s.v. Chi mandara. 140. E.g., in the *Hevajra-tantra*, quoted by Dasgupta, 1958, p. 106.

141. It is to be noted that this symbolism differs from that of Wisdom and Method in that here Wisdom (= Knowledge) is conceived as the male principle. Failure to perceive the transposition has led several authors to interpret the symbol of the vajra in the lotus as representing the union of Wisdom and Method, involving the manifestly erroneous assimilation of the vajra and the female principle and the lotus with the active, male principle. This might also relate to the unexplained anomaly that exists in Tibetan iconography, where yab-yum figures invariably show the female (yum) as the active partner (see Bharati, 1965, p. 216), contradicting the texts which describe her as the static principle.

The conjoint principles purusa and prakṛti, Śiva and Śakti, Method and Wisdom, Knowledge and Principle, are symbolized by the sphere and the cube respectively. The sphere, as the least differentiated and most dynamic of geometric forms, is taken to represent the active or male principle, and the cube, as the most differentiated and the most static and stable of geometric forms, is taken to represent the passive, female principle.[142] The juxtaposition of the dome, which relates to the sphere, and the quadrangular base, which relates to the cube, expresses the marriage of the productive principles : the body of the stupa is an image of the world insofar as it is the product of their union.

d. The Symbolism of the Cross.

The complementary principles of universal manifestation, Essence and Substance, arise by a polarization of Unity. The One becomes Two. The Two unite to produce the cosmos. The two phases in the process of generation are shown by upward and downward pointing triangles :

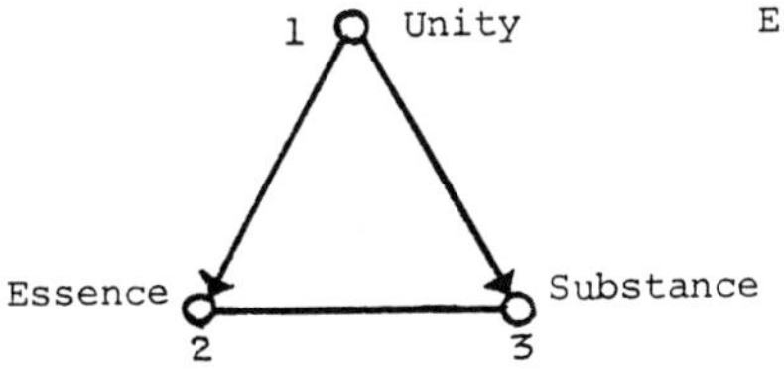

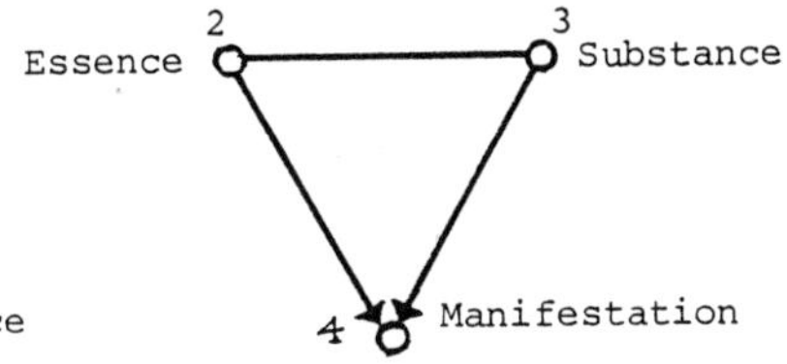

The resultant of the union of Essence and Substance, represented by the lower point of the downward pointing triangle, is the cosmos, comprizing all the phenomenal entities of the physical, the psychic and the formless domains.[143]

As we have seen, the totality of each of the multiple planes of existence making up the universe is subsumed within its centre. Thus, whoever has returned to the centre of his level of existence and has identified himself with that centre has thereby concentrated the manifold entities belonging to that state within the centre of his own being. For this reason he can be taken to represent the whole state of existence that he centres. He is the unified synthesis of its multiplicity. Being reintegrated within the centre of his plane of existence he is also thereby reintegrated within the centre of the human state, and can be considered as the principial or archetypal Man, who typifies the ideal and perfect state within the human condition.[144] It is within this framework of ideas that the lowermost point of the second triangle can alternately be interpreted as signifying a world, or the Man who centres that world.[145]

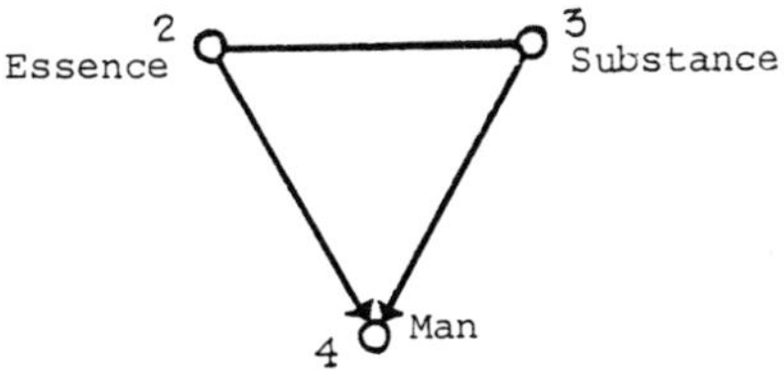

142. Guénon, 1953a, pp. 170ff. 143. Guénon, 1957a, pp. 23ff.

144. *Ibid.*, p. 30ff.; 1958a, pp. 6ff. 145. Guénon, 1957a, p. 37.

If the two triangles are united by their common base to form a quaternary, the fourth term is vertically beneath the first term, which indicates that unified Man is a reflection of principial Unity,[146] expressing a concept that is equally conveyed by the stupa plan. The Man who has returned to the central point of existence combines in himself the two natures of the complementary principles. He is not only their product, but also the medium of their reunification.[147]

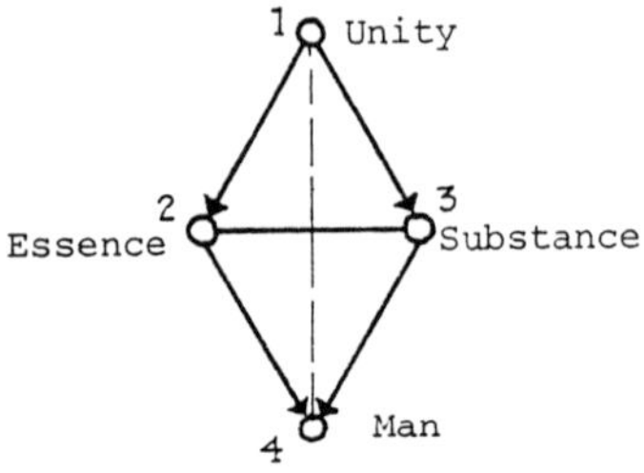

The first and last terms of the quaternary both occupy a central position between the other two, but in an inverse relationship : in both cases they unite and reconcile the complementaries, but in the first case as their principle and in the second as their product. The former case is one of centrifugal polarization, the latter of centripetal unification.[148]

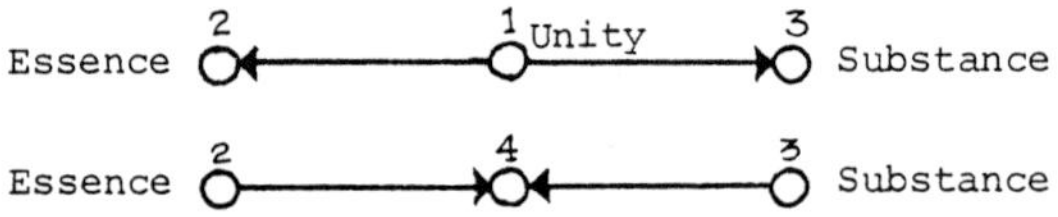

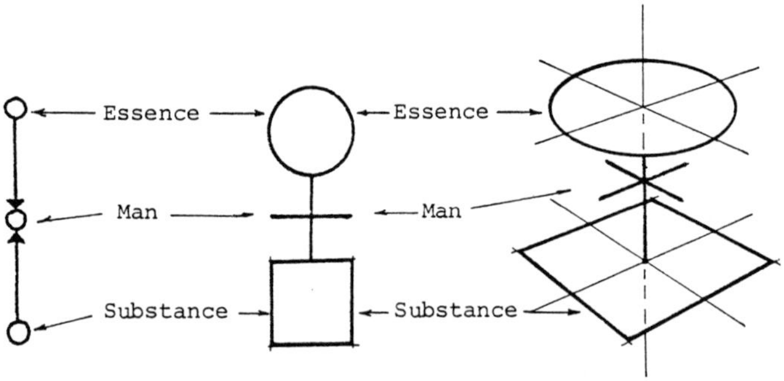

Essence, however, stands above and Substance stands below the things that they produce, so that the relationship of the complementaries and their product is more appropriately shown in a vertical arrangement, with Man standing above Substance, which is his support, and below the down-flowing influence of Essence. In the geometric expression of this disposition, the sphere or circle corresponds to Essence, the cube or square is Substance, and Man is shown by a cross. The cross represents the vertical and one of the two horizontal arms of the three-dimensional cross : the horizontal is a plane of existence and the vertical is the axis that passes through it at its central point. Alternately, in a two-dimensional representation, it is the cross of the four horizontal directions of space. In either case, the

146. Guénon, 1947a, p. 37. 147. Ibid., pp. 29f. 148. Idem.

point where its arms cross is the centre of the plane of existence, the location of perfected Man. It marks the point of mediation, of contact between the worlds, the point where the axis linking the heavenly and the terrestrial realms strikes the plane of earth, and where the supernal influences, passing down the axis, irrupt into the world. When man is identified with the central point, he becomes a mediator between the celestial and terrestrial worlds; he is the visible trace or reflection of the divine, and through him flow the heavenly forces descending from above.[149]

* * * * *

The ternary formed by the complementary principles and their product, Man, embodies a symbolism that occurs in various forms in a large number of traditions. It is the Chinese Taoist Great Triad of Heaven, Earth and Man, in which Heaven (<u>t'ien</u>) equates Essence, Earth (<u>ti</u>) equates Substance,[150] and Man, representing the "ten thousand things", that is, the totality of manifestation, is the offspring of their marriage or, to use the Taoist formula, the "Son of Heaven and Earth".[151]

The Three Jewels (<u>triratna</u>) of Buddhism, namely the Buddha, the Dharma and the Community (<u>saṅgha</u>), embody an analogous symbolism. As seen above, the Buddha corresponds to the active component of the triad, the Dharma is the supporting substratum, and the Saṅgha is the third term of the ternary, representing the centrally located section of humanity and, by extension, the cosmos. The ideal type of the members of the Buddhist Community is the <u>arhat</u>, the Worthy, who has perfected his humanity by returning to the centre of his state of existence. He corresponds to Man in the Great Triad.

The Buddhist concepts of kingship provide another example of the schema. The king is symbolically located at the centre of his realm, which is structured in the image of Indra's Heaven of the 33 Gods (<u>trāyastriṃśa</u>) on the summit of Mt. Meru, where Indra, the prototypic King, is enthroned at the axial pivot surrounded by his retinue of gods in the 32 directions of space : the 4 cardinals, the 4 ordinals, and then their intermediate divisions and subdivisions. The geometric structuring of Indra's Heaven is in turn reflected in the layout of the terrestrial kingdom, divided into directionally oriented provinces and centred by the sovereign's palace.

The king is located at the centre of the kingdom, which is a similitude of the cosmos. Throughout Buddhist Asia the monarch is accordingly addressed by epithets that affirm his central position in the world. The Burmese king, for example, was called "Centre of the Earth" and "Centre of the Universe".[152] Situated at midpoint of his realm and the midpoint of the cosmos he occupies the point where the principles unite. He is the visible product and living embodiment of their conjunction. Symbolically, and in his performance of rituals, the king combines the natures of the Buddha and the Dharma. In some ritual contexts he is equated with the Buddha himself; in others he is seen as a Bodhisattva who will attain Buddhahood in the next birth.[153] In the likeness of the Buddha he is a <u>cakravartin</u>, a turner of

---

149. *Ibid.*, p. 31.

150. Confusion can arise from a failure to distinguish Heaven and Earth (<u>t'ien</u> and <u>ti</u>) of the Chinese tradition and Heaven (<u>svarloka</u>) and Earth (<u>bhūloka</u>) in the Brahmanic schema of the Three Worlds. The former correspond to <u>puruṣa</u> and <u>prakṛti</u>, the universal principles that stand outside of manifestation, while <u>svarloka</u> and <u>bhūloka</u> correspond to the Upper and Lower Waters, those of formless and formal possibility respectively, and both within manifestation. 151. Guénon, 1957a, pp. 82ff.

152. Tambiah, 1976, p. 103. 153. *Idem.*

the Wheel, and thereby identified with the Buddha as the "motionless Mover" whose "action of presence" initiates the movement of the World Wheel. On the other hand, and expressing his possession of the Dharma-Nature, he is called the "Dharma-King" (dharma-rāja). The Buddha's Law is made manifest in his person; he is the perceptible similitude of Principle. He acts as the mandatory of the Law and as the executive (kartṛ) of the cosmic Norm. He translates the Dharma into regulatory action. As the earthly embodiment of the Dharma, the cosmic principle that orders chaos, he is the source whence radiates the temporal Law that regulates the kingdom and lacking which it would disintegrate into disorder.

* * * * *

The geometry of the stupa embodies the triad comprizing the complementary poles and Man as the product of their union. The spherical form of the dome represents the Essential principle, identified with the Buddha, with Method (upāya), with the Diamond World of Knowledge. The cube-related form of the base is the Substantial principle, identified with the Dharma, with Wisdom (prajñā), and with the Matrix World of Principle. The six-armed cross formed by the vertical axis and the four directions of space on the horizontal plane is the cosmos as it abides in wholeness within its centre, or it is perfected Man, identified with the Sangha, with the arhat, or with the Buddhist king. The same symbolism is also reflected in the stupa plan, where the circle, the square and the cross of the directions correspond respectively to Essence, to Substance and to the resultant of their marriage.

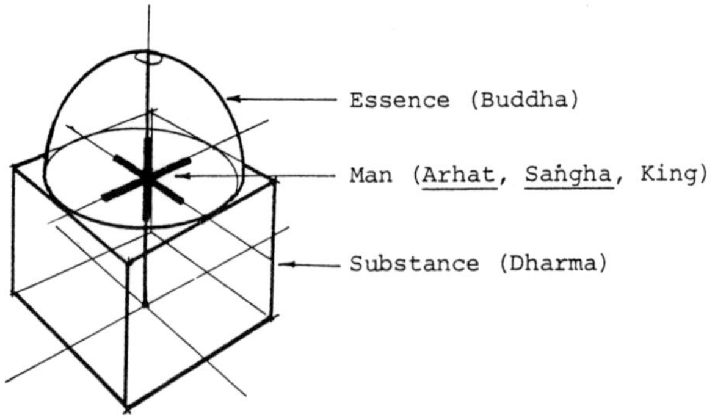

16 THE SYMBOLISM OF THE SUPERSTRUCTURE.

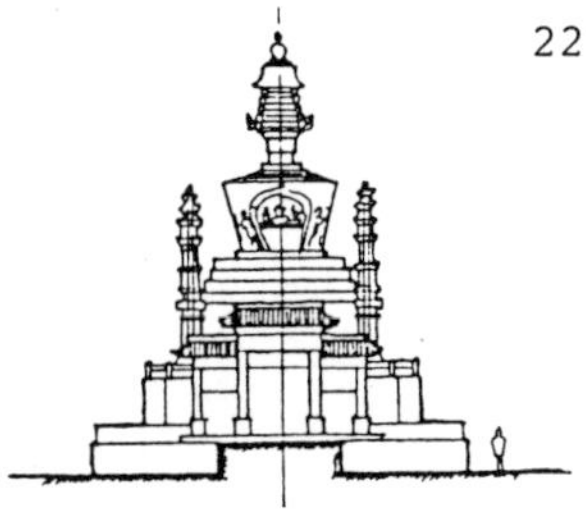

1. THE STUPA TYPES.

The stupa has many variant forms. For the purposes of this study they are classified under three heads :

1) The dome-stupa. The predominant visual element is the dome. The prototypic form is seen at Sāñcī; it is the type that predominates among the early stupas of India and in Sri Lanka, Burma and Thailand. Variant forms are seen in Tibet and in the type of stupa called the Prabhutaratna Stupa (Jap. tahō tō, lit. "Many Jewels Stupa") in Japan (see fig. 144, i).

2) The terrace-stupa. The dome is diminished and raised upon a podium formed by a truncated, stepped pyramid. The terrace-stupa is common in Tibet and Nepal, in Burma, in Central and South East Asia. The preeminent example of the type is Borobudur in Java.

3) The tower-stupa. A multi-layered, tower-like structure, usually referred to as a "pagoda".[1] There are two main forms. One, of brick or masonry, indicates the layers by a series of relatively inconspicuous cornices or by windows; the other, of timber, expresses its storeys by a series of strongly articulated roofs. In both types an almost vestigial stupa stands as a finial upon its summit. The former type is exemplified by Bodhgayā and by the masonry towers of China; the latter, once common in China, is now mainly to be seen in Japan, where it exists in large numbers.

---

1. It is usual to distinguish stupas and pagodas, with the latter term being applied to the multi-storeyed towers found most characteristically in the Far East. This usage is not adopted in this thesis, since the word "pagoda" bears no relation in derivation or meaning to anything in the Buddhist vocabulary. It is a Portuguese neologism, possibly a corruption of the Sanskrit bhagavat, "blessed", or the Persian but Kadah, "idol house" (Willetts, 1965, p. 392; Encyclopaedia Britannica, s.v., "Pagoda"). The terms commonly used in the Indian Buddhist literature are stūpa and caitya (or thūpa and cetiya in Pali). These are used with local variations of pronunciation throughout Buddhist Asia. In the Chinese literature they are transliterated as 窣都婆 (Ch. su t'u po; Jap. sotoba), which is abbreviated to 塔 (Ch. t'a, Jap. tō), literally "tower", and as 支提 (Ch. chih t'i, Jap. shidai) respectively. Early Chinese texts designated monuments containing relics (śarīra) as su t'u po (stūpa), and those without them as chih t'i (caitya), regardless of their form. Later, however, the terms are used indiscriminately and as synonyms, thus returning to the practice followed in the ancient Indian texts, such as the *Divyāvadāna*, p. 242, where there is a passge in which the terms stūpa and caitya are both applied to the monument that is erected over the relic-ashes of the Buddha Kṣemankara (Bénisti, 1960, pp. 48 &74), and the *Bodhisattvabhūmi* (BKDJT, p. 3832, s.v., Tō; Toganoo, 1970, p. 472; Bénisti, 1960, p. 240; all quoting the *Makasogiritsu (Mahāsaṃghika-vinaya)*, Taishō, Vol. 22, No. 1425, 33, p. 1452; also Vallée Poussin, 1937, pp. 283f.; Foucher, 1905, 1, p. 60; Combaz, 1935, p. 30; BKDJT, p. 1876, s.v., Shidai). Considerable confusion can arise from the erroneous use of the term caitya to designate "caitya halls", that is, hollow structures containing a stupa, such as the famous rock cut cave "temples" at Kārlī, Elūrā, Ajaṇṭā, etc. Cf. Griswold Kim and Pott, 1964, p. 59, n. 9.

Fig. 143 : Examples of dome-stupas from Thailand (a), Sri Lanka (b), Japan (c), Tibet (d), India (e and h), China (f), Burma (g and j), and Afghanistan (i).

Fig. 144 : Dome-stupas from Thailand (a, b and e), China (c) and Japan (d, f and g).

Fig. 145 : Terrace-stupas from Java (Borobudur) (a), Burma (b and d) and Thailand (c).

Fig. 146 : Examples of tower-stupas. a. The Bodhgayā stupa, India. b. A tower-stupa shown on the so-called "Bodhgayā plaque", dating from the 1st or 2nd Century B.C., the oldest known example of the tower type of stupa. c. A small votive tower-stupa from India. d. A Burmese copy of the Bodhgayā stupa. e - j. Examples of tower-stupas from China.

Fig. 147 : Further examples of tower-stupas from China (a - k) and Japan (l - m). The Japanese tower-stupas are typical of those built in China during the T'ang Dynasty, none of which has survived.

2. THE STUPA AS MOUNTAIN.

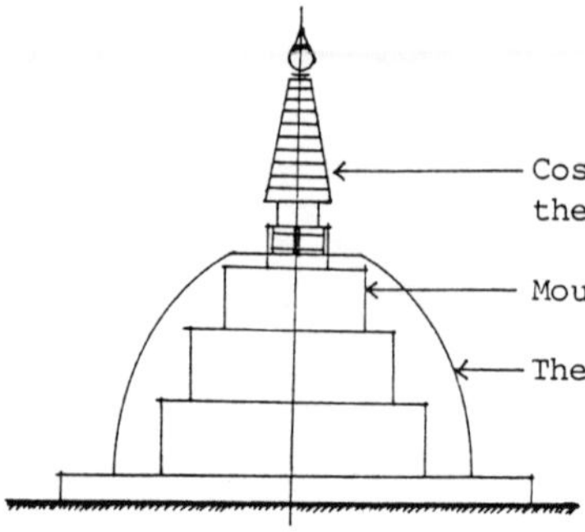

In his monumental work on Borobudur Paul Mus has established beyond reasonable doubt that every domical stupa implicitly contains the Cosmic Mountain. Within the curve of the cupola stands a hidden Meru.[2] The presence of this interior Mountain is evidenced by the harmikā located at the apex of the dome. As shall be shown in the following[3] the harmikā is "the citadel of the gods" (deva-kotuva) and represents Indra's Heaven, the Trāyastriṃśa, that stands upon the summit of Mt. Meru. The harmikā is the tip of the Mountain peak emerging from the Egg.[4] In accordance with this significance the sun and the moon are represented on the sides of the harmikās of many Tibetan and Sri Lankan stupas, since in Buddhist cosmology the Sun and the Moon are said to circle the Cosmic Mountain. Tibetans assimilate the stupa spire to the Cosmic Tree, which grows from the summit of Meru,[5] presupposing the existence of the Mountain in the cupola.[6] Also, in some Sri Lankan stupas the Mountain is present within the dome in physical as well as symbolic fact, figured by square blocks of stone placed within chambers on the central axis deep within the construction.[7] Mediaeval Sinhalese inscriptions and chronicles refer to stupas as "mountains", even when there is nothing in their location to suggest this nomenclature.[8] To this day stupas in Sri Lanka carry names such as Abhayagiri, Dakhinagiri, Vessagiri, etc., in which giri is "mountain".

The stepped pyramid is likewise a Mountain. The form of the terrace-stupa is that of the prāsāda, which is specifically a Mountain.[9] The Burmese terrace-stupas are described as "mountains";[10] and the Angkorian temples, which are closely related to the terrace-stupa in both their form and significance, are specifically built to represent the Mountain of the World. Heine-Geldern says that "Practically every temple in South East Asia, whether Hindu or Buddhist... (was) considered as the image of a mountain, usually, though not invariably, of Mt. Meru. In ancient Cambodia a temple was quite ordinarily referred to as 'giri', 'mountain'".[11] The same is also true of South East Asian terrace-stupas.

---

2. Mus, 1935, pp. 107ff. 3. See p. 247 f.

4. See below, pp. 257ff; Mus, 1935, p.113. 5. See below, pp. 256ff.

6. Mus, 1935, p. 116.

7. Paranavitana, 1946, p. 23 and pl. V; Hocart, 1927, p. 179; Mus, 1935, p. 108. It is relevant to the considerations concerning the symbolism of the summit of the Mountain developed in the following, that in some cases these Merus show a small reliquary (karaṇḍuva) in the form of a stupa on their summits. 8. Paranavitana, 1954, p. 205. 9. Mus, 1935, p. 115.

10. Griswold, Kim and Pott, 1964, p. 34. 11. Heine-Geldern, 1965, p. 3.

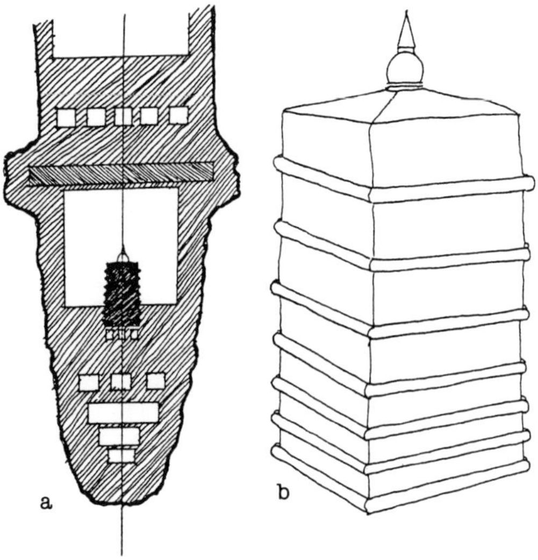

Fig. 148 : The Meru stone in the relic chamber of the Tōpāväva dāgaba, Sri Lanka.
a. Section through the relic chamber.
b. The stone, with a stupa on its summit.
See Paranavitana, 1946, pp. 22 ff., for a full description.

a

b

c

d

d

e

Fig. 149 :
Tower-stupas and temples as Mountains. a. A Burmese "Mountain-temple". b. The <u>śikhara</u> of the Hindu temple is the Cosmic Mountain. c. Bodhgayā. d. The Balinese "Meru". e. The Japanese stupa, called a <u>shumisan</u>, a "Mount Sumeru".

The tower-stupa of the Bodhgayā type is the visual and symbolic equivalent of the Hindu temple, which also is identified with the Cosmic Mountain.[12] "The temple... is always the One Mountain, an image of manifestation in its hierarchy along the central axis of being".[13] The Hindu temple is named Meru, the Mountain pivot of the World, Mandara, the Mountain Churning Rod, and Kailaśa, the Mountain abode of Śiva. The same assimilation applies in the case of tower-stupas of the type in which the storeys are articulated with roofs : the many-tiered temple-stupa of Bali is termed a "Meru",[14] just as the Japanese tower-stupa, of similar form, is called shumisan, "Mount Sumeru".[15]

3. THE MOUNTAIN IN THE EGG - THE EQUIVALENCE OF THE STUPA TYPES.

The Egg of the dome-stupa conceals a Mountain. The paradigmatic model for this symbolic construct is found in texts such as the previously cited passage from the *Viṣṇu Purāṇa* in which the World Egg, floating like a bubble on the primeval Waters, is said to contain Mt. Meru, "like its amnion".[16]

In the terms of cosmological symbolism and insofar as it is the container of the world, the Cosmic Egg cannot exist unless its halves are held apart by the Mountain Axis. In turn, the presence of the Mountain Axis necessarily presupposes the existence of the World Egg. The cosmogenesis is a separation of the two halves of the World Egg by the Mountain Axis - remove the Mountain and the Egg returns into non-existence; its bifurcated foci are reunified.

The two halves of the Cosmic Egg are Heaven and Earth, the complementary and principial poles of the universe, by whose "interaction" the phenomenal universe comes into existence. These halves, Heaven and Earth, are propped apart by the World Axis. Expressing this symbolism geometrically, the ovoid has two foci, which lie on its axis. These foci represent the bifurcation of a point-centre; the axis that joins them is also that which separates them, and if they were not separated by this axis they would return to the undivided unity of the point-centre whence they derived and the volume of the ovoid would simultaneously return to the undifferentiated unity of the sphere. The existence of the ovoid depends on the axis.

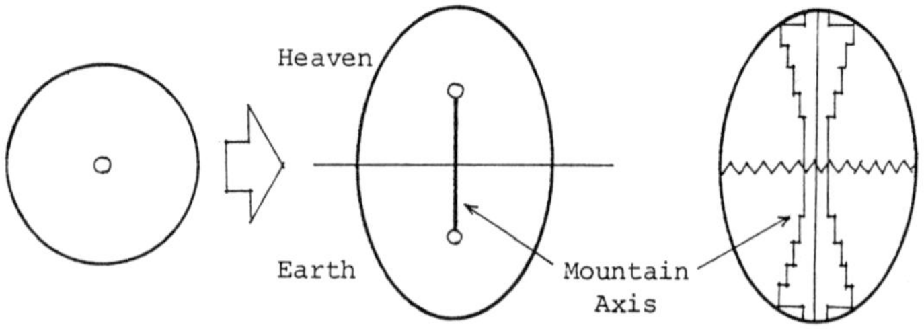

Fig. 150 : The Mountain in the World Egg.

---

12. Kramrisch, 1946, pp. 161ff. 13. *Ibid.*, p. 168.

14. Heine-Geldern, 1956, p. 3. 15. MKDJT, p. 3834, s.v., Tō.

16. See above, p. 194.

Similarly, the existence of the World Egg depends on its axis, which is the Mountain.[17] Without the Mountain to prop them apart Heaven and Earth would merge back into non-differentiation. This is to say that the World Egg and the World Mountain that separates its halves are concomitant. They are mutually dependent and necessarily co-exist. The Cosmic Egg cannot exist without Mt. Meru, and the Mountain cannot exist without the Egg that surrounds it.

Transposed to the context of the symbolism of the stupa this concept entails a most important consequence : the stupa dome, identified with the World Egg, necessarily presupposes the existence of a supporting Mountain-Axis; and in return the stupa Mountain necessarily presupposes the existence of the Cosmic Egg. Therefore the stepped pyramid of the terrace-stupa and the storeys of the tower-stupa, which have been shown to represent the Mountain, must both be considered as supporting an invisible, but nevertheless symbolically existent dome. The superstructure of every stupa is enclosed within an unseen bubble. Symbolically, the Egg and the Mountain co-exist in every stupa, but in the domed stupa only the Egg and in the terrace-stupa and the tower stupa only the Mountain is visible. The dome on the one hand and the the terraced pyramid and the tower on the other are two aspects of one and the same cosmological schema : the dome is the Egg in which the Mountain-Axis is invisibly contained; and the other two types are Mountains, contained within the invisible hemisphere of the Egg. The emphasis is different but the symbolism is the same.

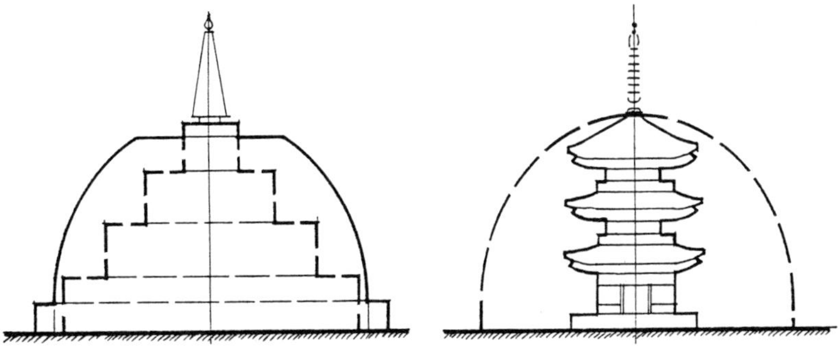

Fig. 150 : a. The invisible Mountain in the Egg of the domical stupa.
b. The invisible Egg enclosing a tower-stupa.

The concept is cogently conveyed by the diagram of circles that determine the elevation of the Japanese tower-stupa : the geometry reflects the symbolic content. So also Mus, following Foucher, who pointed out the curved, dome-like profile of Borobudur, put forward the thesis that this monument was enclosed within an invisible, bubble-like dome.[18] He could have gone further and posited the existence of a similar symbolic dome for every stupa that has the form of the Mountain.

* * * * *

---

17. Mus has shown that the four preeminent symbols of the axis in Brahmanism - the Pillar, the Tree, the Mountain and the primordial Person (puruṣa-prajāpati) - are equivalent and interchangeable, so that the presence of an axis always presupposes the symbolic presence of them all.

18. Mus, 1935, pp. 99ff.

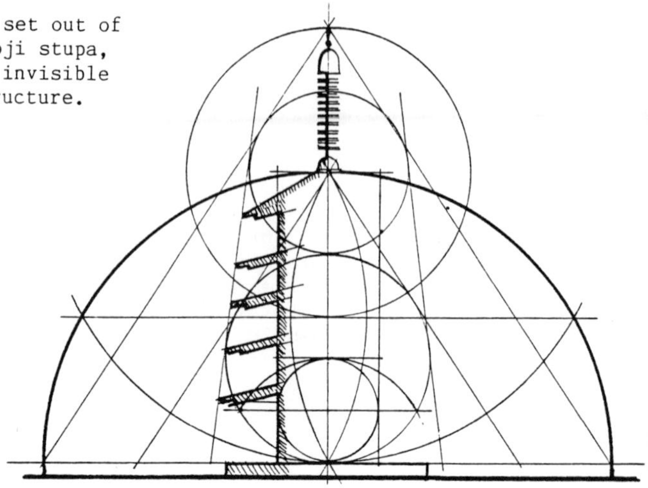

Fig. 151 : The geometric set out of the elevation of the Daigoji stupa, Kyōto, Japan, showing the invisible dome that encloses the structure.

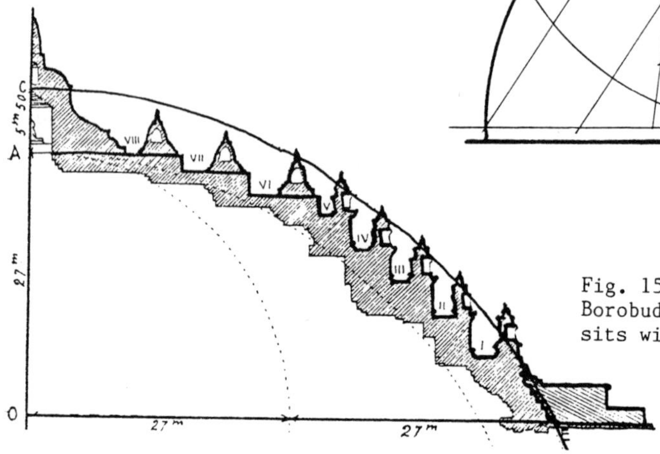

Fig. 152 : A cross section through Borobudur, showing how the monument sits within an invisible sphere.

If the stepped terraces and the towers of stupas are enclosed within an invisible Egg-shell then the generally accepted theory of the development of the stupa requires revision. Historians trace the development of the stupa from the Sāñcī type, taking this as the original form from which all others derived. Seckel voices the generally held view when he says that "all forms of the stupa and pagoda, in all the countries of Asia, are directly

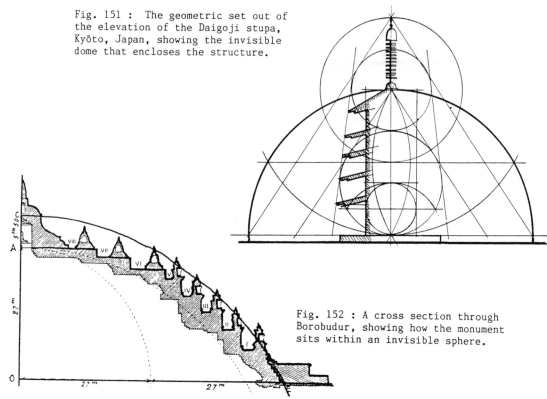

Fig. 153 : The evolution of the Indian stupa into the Far-Eastern tower-stupa according to Seckel (1964, p. 114). From left to right : the basic Indian type; the later Indian type (Gandhāra); Chinese multi-storeyed stupa; multi-storeyed Chinese tower-stupa.

or indirectly derived from the Sāñcī type of stupa".[19] The historians claim to discern a series of morphological changes whereby the supporting base of the stupa becomes increasingly prominent at the same time as the dome diminishes. They say that at an early date the circular base of the prototypic Sāñcī type of stupa was replaced by a square socle; this was divided into layers, which were progressively enlarged until the terrace-stupas of the Tibetan and Burmese type evolved, in which the original stupa dome had been raised to the summit of a large stepped pyramid.

The development of the tower-stupa is similarly explained in terms of an elevation of the base. The socle was enlarged and hollowed out to form a cella containing a Buddha image. The stupa, now consisting of a stupa raised above a shrine room, stood at the centre of a square vihāra, made up of a series of monks' cells. These were brought inwards, closer and closer to the stupa base, until they were attached to its sides. Contracting still further the cells were then incorporated within the mass of the stupa base so as to stand beneath the dome. At the same time the terraces were converted to sanctuaries by the addition of roofs. In the next step these monks' cells, converted into chapels or niches, were superimposed to form a multi-storeyed tower, with the stupa rising higher and higher as the supporting sanctuaries proliferated. The tower-stupa at Bodhgayā is the end product of this process in India.

Fig. 154 : The evolution of the Chinese tower-stupa from the Indian prototype according to Willetts (1965, p. 393). From left to right : ceramic model of a Chinese watch tower, Han period; the Sāñcī dome-stupa; reliquary in the shape of a stupa, Gandhāra; two representations of stupas in wall paintings at Tun Huang (5th-6th Centuries); relief of a multi-storeyed tower-stupa at Yunkang (early 6th Century).

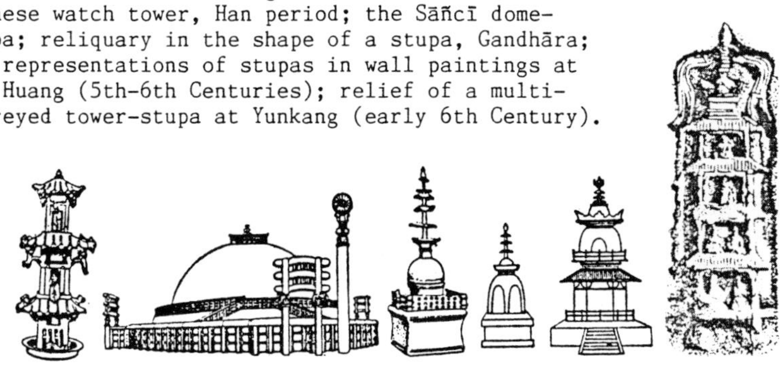

From India, say the historians, the form migrated to China, where it combined with the indigenous pavilion towers to produce the multi-storeyed "pagodas" that are so numerous in the Far East. "This combination of stupas and vihāras", says Combaz, "is basically the origin of all the transformations undergone by the stupa in the course of its travels through Asia".[20]

---

19. Seckel, 1964, p. 106. The classic works on the development of the stupa are Combaz, 1932, 1933 and 1935. See also Goetz, 1959, pp. 74ff.; Seckel, 1964, pp. 103ff.; Longhurst, 1928 and 1936. Pant, 1976, discusses the development of the Indian forms; Willetts, 1965, pp. 392ff., the Chinese; Rawson, 1967, the S.E. Asian; Marchal, 1947, the Kampuchean; Rajanubhab, n.d., those of Thailand.

20. Combaz, 1932, pp. 188f.

The theory of its development supposes that the stupa, at first firmly established on the ground, was progressively elevated to the top of a terraced pyramid or to the summit of a stack of sanctuaries. As it rose higher it simultaneously diminished in size, until in the Far Eastern towers it became a mere vestige, reduced to the status of a diminutive and visually insignificant finial. What was least significant in the beginning - the base - became the dominating element; and the components that contained the very essence and significance of the stupa - the dome, the harmikā and the spire - were relegated to comparative unimportance. If this account is true then the history of the stupa is a record of an erosion of meaning.

The vestigial dome on top of the tower of the Chinese stupa.

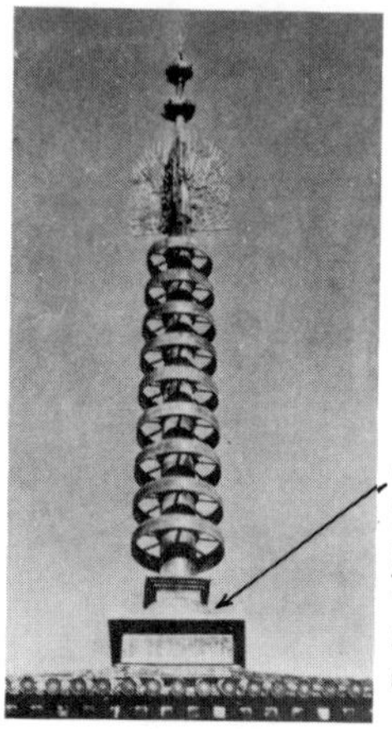
The "upturned bowl" (fuku-bachi), the vestigial dome in the Japanese stupa.

Fig. 155 : Vestigial dome-stupas at the summit of tower-stupas from China and Japan.

It would require a separate study to demonstrate the inconsistencies in both the chronological and morphological data on which the theory is based. It must suffice here to point out that the supposed evolution of the stupa types is inconsistent with their symbolism. The domical and tower stupas express the same symbolism, but in precisely opposite ways : in one the perceptible Egg envelops an imperceptible Mountain; in the other the expression is reversed and an imperceptible Egg encloses a perceptible Mountain. The types are to be regarded as related but distinct and as independent and separate variations on a single symbolic theme.

* * * * *

This interpretation involves a seeming paradox. The Mountain formed by the stepped pyramid of the terrace-stupa is enclosed within an invisible dome; but at its summit stands a domical stupa : there is a dome built upon a dome, a stupa standing upon a stupa. The apparent inconsistency will be resolved when the significance of the harmikā is examined in the following, where it will be shown that the stupa is the Dharma and the locus of the preaching of the Dharma is precisely at the summit of the Mountain. The stupa in which the Diamond World Mandala is revealed, for example, stands on the Mountain peak; the stupa is the Body of the Buddha, whose normal abode and place of preaching is the Mountain top, a symbolism that is expressed in the Far Eastern practice of placing the Buddha image, and in some cases its equivalent, the stupa, upon an altar platform built in the likeness of Mt. Meru. These are considerations that will be developed in what follows.

Fig. 156 : A Burmese example of a stupa standing on the summit of the Cosmic Mountain.

4. THE SYMBOLISM OF THE LEVELS.

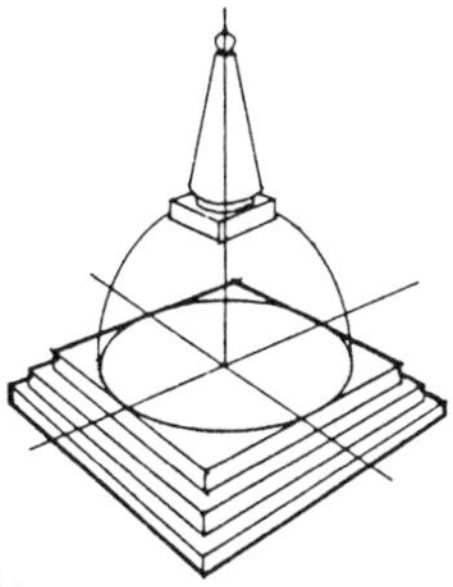

a. The Spatial Significance of the Levels.

The bases of terrace-stupas are divided into 3, 4 or 5 levels; tower-stupas are divided into storeys, almost invariably of an odd number, and counting from 3 to as many as 13 or more. In their general significance these layers relate to the concepts of spatial deployment analyzed in the first volume of this study.

Fig. 157 : Examples of terrace-stupas with multi-levelled bases from Angkor, Tibet and Thailand.

The stepped base of the terrace-stupa and the storeyed pile of the tower-stupa both represent Mt. Meru, the Cosmic Mountain, which is identified with the World Pillar (*stambha*), "in whom Earth, Midspace and Sky are set",[21] and "of whom Earth is the basement and Midspace the belly... and the Sky the head".[22] As does the Pillar it supports the three layers of the world. It props apart Heaven and Earth, and their diremption creates extended space, the intermediate world, Midspace (*antarikṣa*) : "At first these two worlds (Heaven and Earth) were together; and when they parted asunder the space which is between (*antar*) them became that Midspace".[23]

---

21. RV X.7.12; cf. X.7.3, 8, 22 & 35. 22. RV X.7.32.

23. ŚB VI.1.2.23.

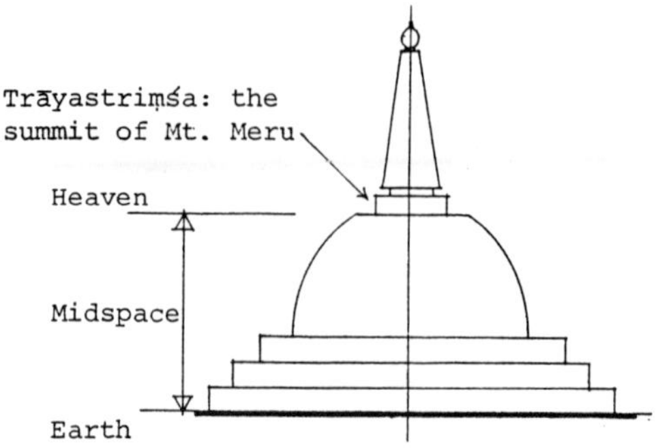

Fig. 157 : The dome-stupa as Mt. Meru, the Cosmic Mountain.

Midspace extends from the surface of the Earth to the first of the heavens,[24] the Trāyastriṃśa Heaven of Indra at the summit of Meru. That is to say, Midspace is vertically coextensive with the Cosmic Mountain : its height is exactly that of the Mountain. The Mountain summit marks the plane of transition from the intermediate world of space to the celestial world and, since they are identified with the Mountain, the stepped pyramid of the terrace-stupa and the pile of the tower-stupa define the vertical extent of Midspace. The body of the stupa is homologous with spatial extension. The levels of the pyramid and the storeys of the tower are divisions of space.

The directions of space number from four upwards : the four directions of space plus the centre is five; the four directions plus the Zenith and the Nadir is six; the six directions plus the centre is seven; the four cardinal directions and the four ordinals together make up the eight directions; these plus the centre give nine; and so on. Herein lies the meaning of the stupa terraces and storeys.

The levels of the stupa body reiterate the symbolism of spatial deployment that was embodied in the plan, but now that symbolism is expressed in a linear and vertical mode. The plan of the stupa, laid out from a centre and according to the directions of space, incorporated a symbolism wherein time was rendered static. Temporal succession was transmuted into space.

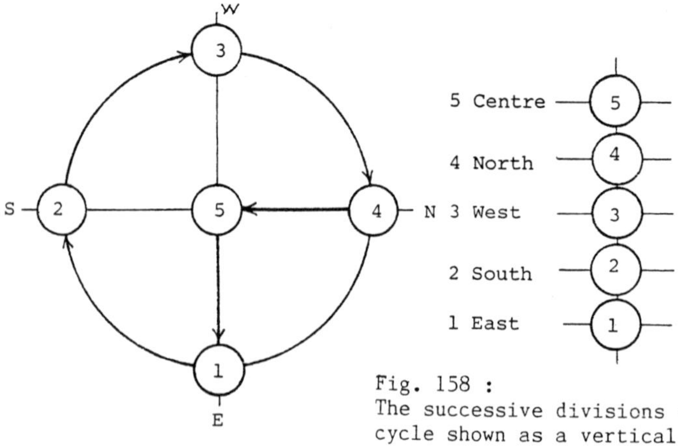

Fig. 158 :
The successive divisions of the cycle shown as a vertical hierarchy.

24. It is emphasized that svarloka, the Heaven-World, the Sky, is not synonymous with Heaven (t'ien) in the Chinese Great Triad of Heaven, Earth and Man. Svarloka is the realm of the heavens, and is located within manife ation; Heaven (t'ien) is one of the complementary principles of manifestatic and as such lies outside it. See also p. 219, n. 150.

The cycles were expressed in their simultaneity, geometrically compressed into a timeless instant. Now, in the vertical superimposition of levels, the symbolism of the plan is repeated, but in a manner that reveals its temporal and successive aspect. The levels show the orients as they devolve in time, one following the other. They are shown in their hierarchy : in the plan the quarters were equal, but here they are placed one above the other as the steps in an ascending progress to Heaven.

We have already met with prototypic examples of this mode of symbolic thought : the seven steps of the Buddha at his Nativity and his nine double paces in the caṅkrama were seen to be simultaneously a traversal of the directions and an ascent to the summit of the worlds; the five layers of the Vedic altar, placed one upon the other in a vertical stack, are the five directions and the five seasons; the cycle of the sun through the quarters is an ascent to the cosmic apex. The principle is clearly apparent at Borobudur, where the four lower terraces show the Buddhas of the four directions in their corresponding positions on the four faces. The fifth terrace, by contrast, shows Vairocana, the Buddha of the Centre, on all four faces. The five directions are stacked one upon the other.[25]

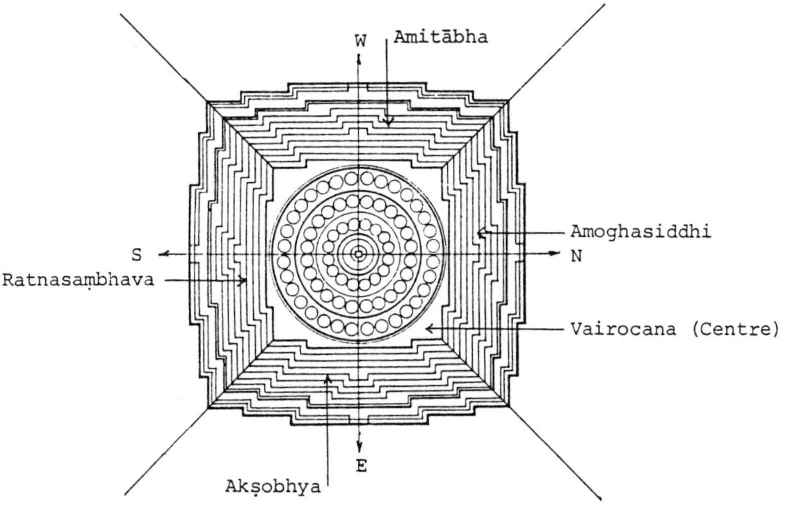

Fig. 159 : The allocation of the Buddhas of the five directions on the terraces of Borobudur.

The path to the summit of the Mountain is a spiral. Each layer of the stupa is one turn of a helix described upon a cylinder whose axis coincides with that of the stupa. The ritual of pradakṣina, the circumambulation of the stupa, performed upon the ambulatories of the terrace-stupa, follows this circular and upward course. Walking clockwise, to follow the cycle of the sun, and mounting from one level to the next, the pilgrim traces a spiral ascent to the mountain top. In the tower-stupa the same path can be climbed by way of flights of steps concealed within the building and running in a spiral up and around the central axis.

---

25. See above, pp. 141ff.

b. The Cosmological Significance of the Levels.

In a more specific significance the levels of the stupa represent the levels on the slopes of Mt. Meru. According to Buddhist cosmology,[26] the slopes of Meru have four or five levels, depending on how they are counted : the realms of Serpents (nāga), Fairwings (suparṇa) or Garudas, Demons (dānava, rakṣasa), Spectres (yakṣa), and of the four Regents of the Directions.[27] This latter can be taken as a fifth level, or alternately as located on the summit of Meru, in the four directions around the city of Indra and his 32 attendant gods at the centre.[28]

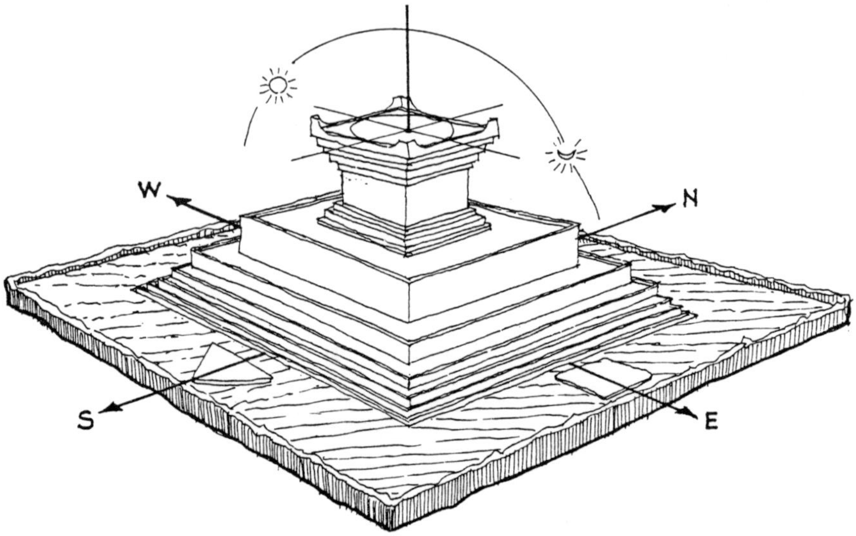

Fig. 160 : The Buddhist cosmos, with Mt. Meru at the centre surrounded by seven mountain ranges and the Iron Enclosing Mountains. Jambudvīpa, the continent of men, lies in the Salt Ocean to the south of Mt. Meru.

This configuration obviously only relates to stupas with four or five levels. For stupas with another number of levels a different schema is relevant. Mt. Meru, the central mountain of the universe, is surrounded by seven concentric circles of mountain ranges, separated from each other by seas. Enclosing the whole system is an eighth mountain chain, the Iron Mountains, which mark the boundary of the cosmos with the Void. Jambudvīpa, the "continent" or "island" (dvīpa) inhabited by men, is located to the South of Meru in the Salt Ocean that separates the seventh and eighth mountain ranges. The seven mountain ranges that stand between Jambudvīpa and Mt. Meru rise towards the centre. The height of each chain is double that of the preceding and the intervening seas increase in width proportionally. Viewed from Jambudvīpa the tops of each mountain range would just be visible. Kirfel writes that "the whole system, viewed in profile, produces the effect of an enormous pyramid with seven levels...",[29] or, in the metaphor employed by Mus, "like sheaths, one within the other, expanded telescopically... with

26. References for the Buddhist cosmology are given on p.329, n. 47.

27. Their names and their subjects are listed on p.329, n. 49.

28. Kirfel, 1920, pp. 188f.; Mus, 1935, p. 355.

29. Kirfel, 1920, p. 27.

the Mountain (Meru) itself appearing from the summit".[30] That this is no mere figure of speech is shown by fig.161, taken from the Powun-gaung caves in Upper Burma, which depicts the world in cross section : the seven mountain ranges, "like a decreasing series of organ pipes", are arranged on either side of Mt. Meru, represented by a central tower.[31]

This cosmological symbolism is translated into architectural forms. The city of Dipavati is described in the *Mahāvastu* as having seven enclosing walls of gold, each topped with a balustrade of a different colour. The

Fig. 161 : Depiction of Mt. Meru in a relief from the Powun-gaung caves, Upper Burma.

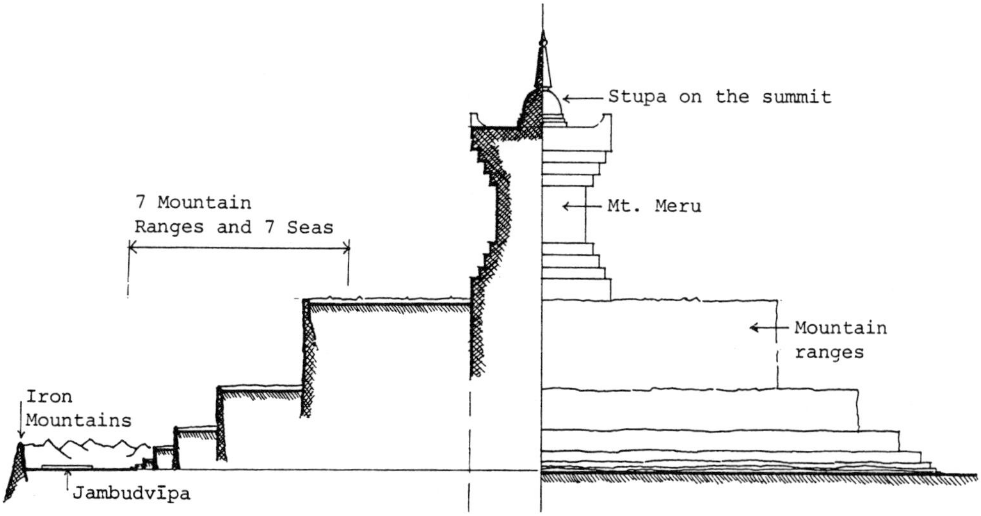

Fig. 162 : Section and elevation of the Buddhist cosmos.

30. Mus, 1935, p. 356. 31. *Ibid*, p. 358f.

city of Kusāvatī, mentioned in the *Vinaya* of the *Mūla-sarvastivādins*, also had seven enclosing walls.[32] The ancient Indian prāsādas, or palaces, repeat the formula. Pali writings make frequent use of the term satta-bhūmaka-pāsāda, "a seven-storeyed pavilion".[33] None has survived in India, but the Sat Mahal Pāsāda, a solid seven storeyed pyramid, still stands in Sri Lanka.[34] The Lohaprāsāda, built by Duṭṭhagāmaṇi, is described in the *Mahāvaṃsa* as originally having had nine storeys (nava-bhūmaka) but was reconstructed with seven storeys after it burned down.[35]

Fig. 163 : The Sat-mahal-pāsāda, a seven storeyed tower at Polonnāruwa, Sri Lanka.

Mus, following Przyluski, has pointed out Mesopotamian parallels which undoubtedly embody a cognate symbolism and throw light on its meaning. The layout of Mesopotamian cities such as Ecbatana and Uruk[36] duplicates the Buddhist cosmology. The cities are enclosed within seven walls of seven colours, rising towards the centre, where there stood a tower, representing the Cosmic Mountain. These seven walls signified the pathways traced by the movements of the seven planets upon the ecliptic. Each of the walls was capped by crenellations, which marked the successive positions of the planet's rising on the celestial horizon. The profile of the crenellations delineates the sinuous curve of the planet's progress, the peaks and troughs of which were taken to represent the complementary aspects - light and dark, beneficent and malefic - of the planet's passage.[37] That this symbolism is not remote from the subject of our study is indicated by the fact that the harmikās of early Buddhist stupas show exactly the same pattern of crenellations.

---

32. *Ibid*, p. 329; Przyluski, 1932a, p. 180.

33. E.g., in the *Jātakas*, the *Aṭṭhakathā* of the *Dhammapada*, the *Mahāvaṃsa*, etc. 34. Rhys Davids, 1903, p. 70; Mus, 1935, p. 320; Przyluski, 1936, p. 251.

35. *Mahāvaṃsa* XXVII; cf. XXXIII.6; XXXVI.25 (where it is reduced to five storeys); VI.102; XXVI.124; etc. See Mus, 1935, p. 320.

36. Relevant to the discussion of the symbolism of the rainbow (pp. 286 ff. below) is the fact that the ideogram used to designate the city of Uruk is that which signifies "rainbow".

37. The peaks and troughs correspond to the upward and downward pointing triangles which combine to form the Seal of Solomon. See Mus, 1935, pp. 334ff.; and for the symbolism of the Seal of Solomon, see Guénon, 1962, 225f.

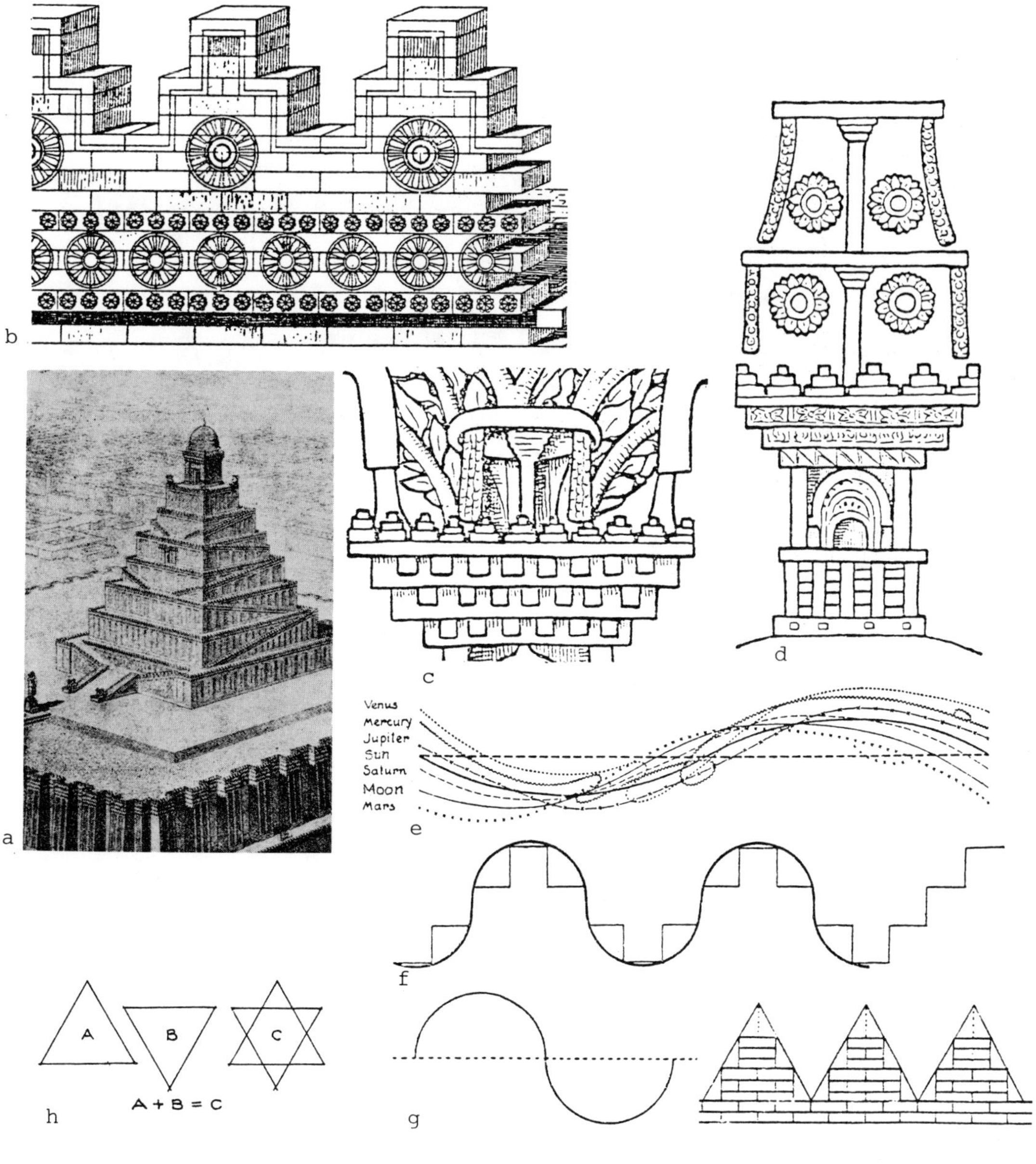

Fig. 164 : a. Mesopotamian ziggurat. b. Detail of Mespotamian crenellations. c and d. Examples from reliefs at Mathurā and Bhārhut of harmikās surmounted by crenellations of the Mesopotamian type. e. The curves described by the planets in relation to the ecliptic. f. The planetary curves translated into crenellations. g. The peaks and troughs of the planetary curve. h. The peaks and troughs represented as upward- and downward-pointing triangles, combined in the Seal of Solomon. See also the following page.

i

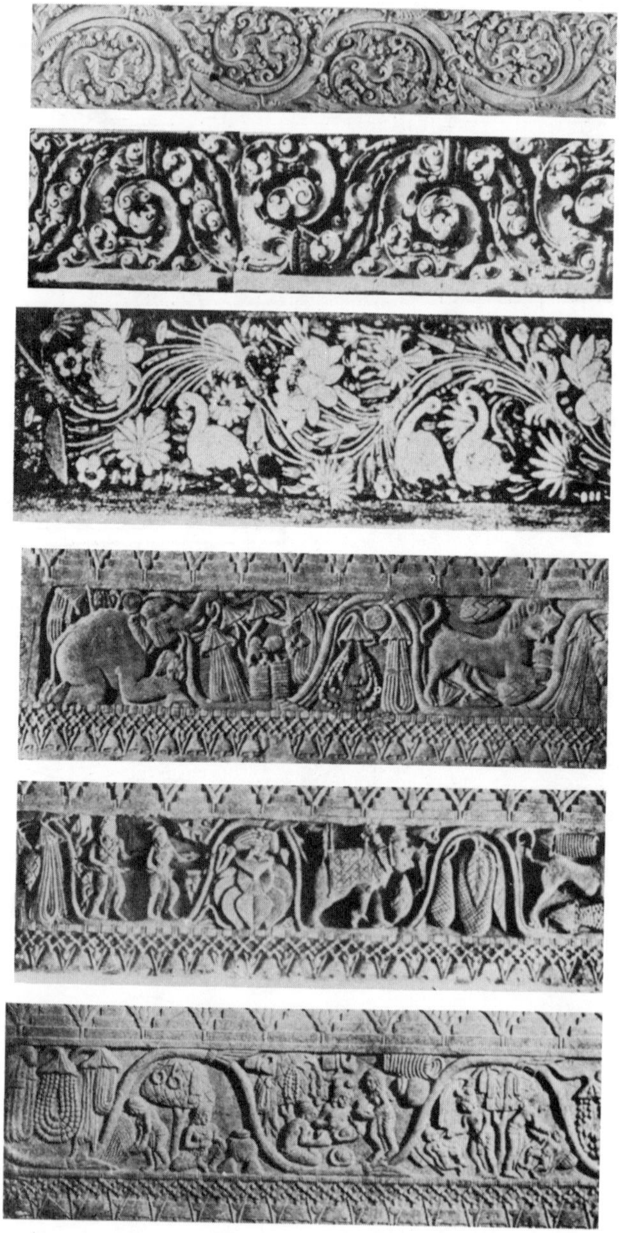

j

Fig. 164 (cont.) : The curve of the planets' progress expressed as a scroll ornament, a recurrent motif in Indian and Indian-influenced architecture. i. Four examples of the scroll shown in vertical panels. j. Horizontal panels showing variations on the scroll motif. In the three lower panels the association of the scroll theme with the planet's movements is emphasised by the presence of the same crenellation pattern that appears on the harmikās of early stupas and on the walls of Mesopotamian cities.

The cosmo-chronographic symbolism of the Mesopotamian seven-walled city was duplicated in the seven-layered ziggurat. The seven layers of the ziggurat and the seven walls of the city are symbolically equivalent : the seven levels are the city walls retracted and compressed onto the central tower-Mountain; or, alternately, the city walls are an expansion, a deployment, of the levels of the ziggurat.

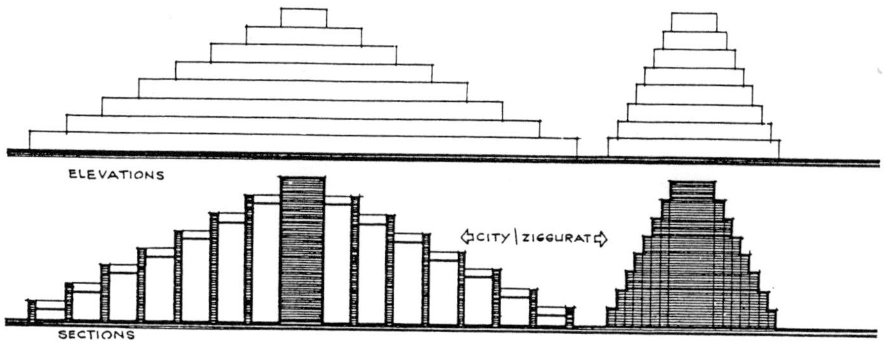

Fig. 165 : Diagrammatic representation of the relationship of the seven-walled Mesopotamian city and the ziggurat.

In the Mesopotamian astronomical symbolism each of the four planets Jupiter, Mercury, Mars and Saturn ruled a direction of space. This was not to suggest that they simultaneously divided the celestial space : at no time do they appear together on the horizon at the four points of the compass. The square of the directions over which they preside is not defined upon the terrestrial horizon but upon the celestial equator and successively, in the course of the annual cycle. Their governance of the four quarters is linked to the displacement of the sun; they appear at the critical points where the sun changes direction, that is, at the solstitial and equinoctial points, which cosmologically correspond to the cardinal directions. The Mesopotamian planetary schema was completed by three other planets, Venus, the Sun and the Moon. Venus was the Queen of Heaven, the Mother Goddess, located at the apex of heaven; the Sun was at the Centre; and the Moon was in the Nadir.[38]

The assimilation of the planets and the directions in this manner is evident in early Buddhist iconography. The four wheels on the four sides of the Aśokan pillar at Sārnāth are centred by cabochons, which Przyluski has identified with the four planets of the directions. As we have seen the pillar originally supported a Sun Wheel at its summit.[39]

The coincidence of the Mesopotamian and Buddhist formulae is undeniable. Is it therefore valid to ascribe planetary associations to the seven storeyed Buddhist stupa? The seven layers undoubtedly have reference to the seven mountain ranges of the Buddhist cosmology, but nowhere do the Buddhist texts correlate the mountain ranges with the planets. Kirfel tried to establish correspondences,[40] but his efforts merely point up the difficulties

---

38. Przyluski, 1932; Mus, 1935, pp. 147ff. 39. *Idem*.

40. Kirfel, 1920, p. 188.

involved.[41] Although the Mesopotamian and Buddhist schemata are obviously affiliated, it is possibly wiser not to view the levels of a seven-storeyed stupa as the direct and conscious employment of a planetary symbolism, but rather as the expression of mythological formulae which reflect the astronomical schema, such as that of the Buddha's seven steps at his Nativity.

That myth[42] now reveals a wider significance. The seven steps retrace the progress of the sun on the ecliptic; they traverse the six positions of the sun in its pathway of return to the summit of the heavens.[43] They also retrace the analogous paths of the Moon and the five planets, Mars, Mercury, Saturn, Jupiter and Venus, each having its separate cycle and together representing so many divisions of Time, the Year. The movements of the planets encapsulate the totality of time; other than by way of their motion time is not measurable, which is to say, not existent. The Buddha's steps to the summit of the universe at once encompass all the directions measured out by the extension of space, and all the cycles of time measured out by the orbits of the planets. He steps from rung to rung on the ladder of the orients; he simultaneously ascends the ladder of the planetary spheres.[44]

* * * * *

Fig. 166 : Examples of Japanese tower-stupas with three, five and thirteen storeys. Others exist having seven, nine and eleven storeys.

The same significances attach to nine-storeyed stupas. Indian astronomy counts seven or nine planets : the seven-fold schema is increased to nine by the addition of Rāhu and Ketu, the ascending and descending nodes of the moon's orbit.[45] Eleven storeyed stupas involve a further development of the cosmological correspondences. The surrounding mountain chains, cognate with the planetary orbits, rise in steps one behind the other to the

---

41. There are some traces of a relationship. The *Jātakas*, for example, place the sun at the summit of the mountains called Yugandhara, but the correspondences are obscured by the simple fact that the lists of names of the seven mountain ranges do not agree from one text to another. See Mus, 1935, p. 354.

42. Mentioned above, p. 40, and described in greater detail below, pp. 275ff. 43. Cf. below, pp. 277ff.

44. The assimilation is not merely metaphorical. See below, 286ff., on the symbolism of the rainbow-bridge. 45. For the symbolism of Rāhu and Ketu, see below, pp. 311 ff.

central Mountain; the slopes of the Mountain have four levels, the realms of the Serpents, the Fairwings, the Demons and the Spectres. The eleven storeys are the seven encircling mountains plus these four kingdoms. By the same reasoning the stupa with thirteen storeys is the same with the circles of the two additional planets, Rāhu and Ketu, counted into the total.

In these cosmological schemata of 7, 9, 11 or 13 storeys the Trāyastriṃśa Heaven and the kingdoms of the four Regents of the Quarters are not numbered among the storeys. They are taken to be on the summit, not the slopes, of Meru. They are not considered to be in the Midspace, but already within the celestial world.

* * * * *

The symbolism of the multiple storeys reiterates the spatio-temporal symbolism that has been seen to operate throughout the stupa. Once again space and time are married within the fabric of the architecture. The cycle of the planets, whose rhythms are the very pulse of the manifested universe, are merged into the spatial configuration of the mountain levels. Space and time, the coordinates of the cosmos, are once more fused within the building form.

* * * * *

Further significance adheres to the number of levels forming the "Mountain" of the stupa. Quite apart from their term by term correspondence with cosmological entities the pyramids and towers also have meaning in that numbers themselves embody a profound symbolism. In the traditional Indian view the quantitative aspect of number - number used for counting - is negligible in relation to its qualitative, which is to say symbolic, aspect. The true significance of numbers resides in their ability to express universal and principial relationships (Gk. logoi).

For Buddhists, a stupa with three levels or three roofs would, by its association with the number 3, evoke the relationships inhering within the Three Jewels (triratna) of the Buddha, the Dharma and the Saṅgha. For Chinese Buddhists it would additionally evoke all the symbolic relationships that are associated with the analogous Chinese symbolism of the Great Triad of Heaven, Earth and Man.[46]

So likewise a stupa with five levels conveys the concept of the hierogamous union of the celestial principle (3) and its terrestrial complement (2), which the number 5 comprizes.[47] Five, as the middle number of the first nine numbers, is the number of the centre, a significance that is expressed by its ideogram, 五 , which derives from the depiction of a simple cross, †

---

46. For the relation of the Triple Jewel and the Great Triad, see above, pp. 212ff. It must be emphasised that it is the number of roofs, and not a correlation of the roofs taken separately that is in question here. Heaven and Earth are the principles of manifestation and lie outside its confines; by contrast, the layers of the stupa refer to entities that are within manifestation. It is not possible, therefore, to identify the three levels of a three storeyed stupa with Heaven, Earth and Man except inasmuch as the Triad is reflected in every triple-portioned entity. Cf. above, p. 219, n. 150 and 234, n.24.

47. For a brilliant analysis of the symbolism of numbers in China, see Granet, 1950, pp. 148ff. See also Chevalier and Gheerbrant, 1973, under the separate heads of the numbers : Trois, Cinq, etc.

referring to the four directions plus the centre, with the addition of strokes above and below to represent Heaven and Earth.[48] The directions are five in number and the Chinese classified all the "ten thousand things" that make up the totality of manifestation - elements, colours, flavours, musical tones, viscera, metals, planets, flora, fauna, the senses - into quinaries. Every thing in the universe was allocated to one of the five directions.[49] The five storeyed Chinese stupa incorporates the cosmos not only in an abstract manner but also in the specific and concrete sense that every one of the ten thousand things, which is to say all the phenomena comprized within corporeal and subtle manifestation, are correlated with its levels.

For Indians the number seven, by way of its association with the seven directions (the six directions plus the centre) symbolizes the totality of space and the totality of time. It brings together the numbers 3 and 4, the numbers of Heaven and Earth (with its 4 cardinal points) : it is the number of the universe in movement.

Similar associations adhere to stupas with nine storeys. For the Chinese nine is the number of yang and the preeminent number of the deployment of space, with reference to the eight directions and the centre : the "magic square" (Ch. lo shu), which, in a manner analogous to that of the Vāstu-puruṣa-maṇḍala in India, was the metaphysical foundation for the planning of the Emperor's Palace (the Hall of Light, Ch. ming t'ang),[50] the Chinese city, and the "well-field" system of laying out farms.[51] It was also the number of the celestial spheres and, symmetrically, the number of the infernal circles and the Nine Springs, the abode of the dead. The Chinese imperial throne had nine steps, the Taoist baton had nine nodes, the imperial towers had nine storeys.[52]

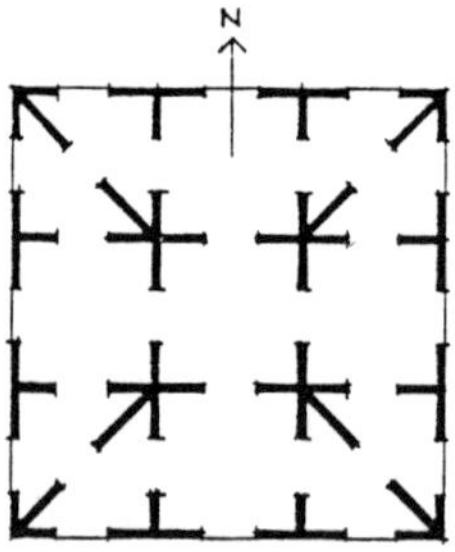

4	9	2
3	5	7
8	1	6

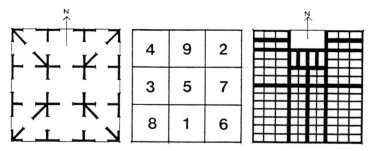

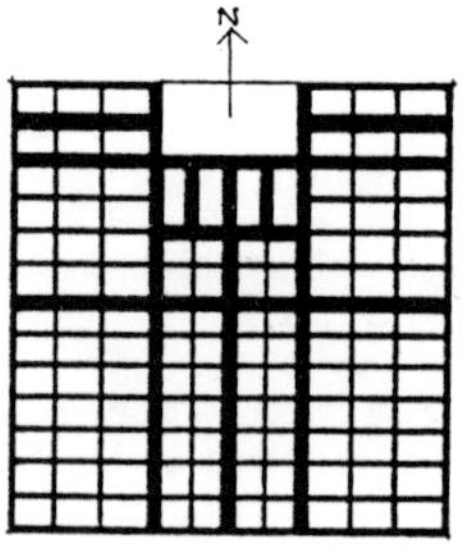

Fig. 167 : a. Diagrammatic plan of the Hall of Light (ming t'ang), the residence of the Emperor that stood at the centre of the Chinese kingdom.
b. The Chinese "magic square", one of the principal bases of Chinese architectural planning.
c. The plan of the Chinese city of Ch'ang An, based on the square divided into nine.

---

48. Wieger, 1965. p. 107.

49. See Granet, 1950, pp. 375ff.; and on the correlation of the five directions, the five "elements" (or more correctly, "processes"), etc., see Needham, 1956, pp. 261ff.; Forke, 1925, pp. 227ff.; etc.

50. See Soothill, 1951, and Granet, 1950, *passim*; Maspero, 1946; Guénon, 1957a, Ch. XVI ("Le Ming Tang").

51. Wheatley, 1971, p. 132f. 52. Chevalier and Gheerbrant, 1973, 3, pp. 261ff., s.v. Neuf.

These various associations are symbolic in the true sense. There are, as well, a multitude of secondary associations. The Buddhist texts delight in lists of ternaries, quinaries, septenaries and other numerical groups. The Buddhist dictionaries list literally hundreds of items under the head of each number. There are three Wisdoms, three mysteries, three sections, three jewels, three vehicles... five Buddhas, five kinds of Knowledge, five kinds of *dharma-kāya*, five Bhodisattva practices... and so on. The number of components built into the stupa would inevitably act as a mnemonic device : each time a Buddhist who has embarked upon a path of practice sees a stupa he is reminded of the doctrines and the meditations that pertain to his stage of the Way.

17 THE SYMBOLISM OF THE HARMIKĀ.

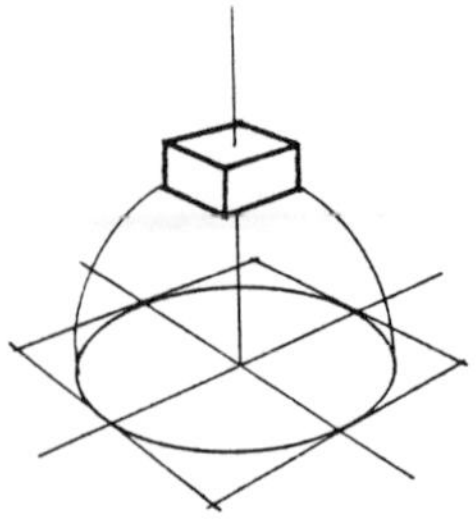

The harmikā[1] is the structure built at the summit of the dome or tower, marking the place where the central axis emerges from within the edifice. Bas-reliefs and votive stupas dating from the early centuries of the Buddhist era show that the ancient, prototypic form of the harmikā was a square laid out around a Bodhi Tree or a Parasol and bounded by a fence or an hypaethral pavilion.[2] Etymology indicates the nature of this bounded area : the word harmikā is closely related to harmya (P. hammiya), "pavilion"

Fig. 168 : The harmikā as a fence enclosing a tree, parasol or sacrificial post, at Sāñcī and in reliefs from Amarāvatī.

---

1. Archaeologists refer to the harmikā as the "tee", which is an anglicised form of hti, the name by which the harmikā is known in Burma. See Longhurst, 1928, p. 126.

2. See Combaz, 1932, pp. 195ff.; 1933, pp. 113ff.; and below, pp. 256ff. One form of the harmikā, typified by those on the reconstructed stupas at Sāñcī and one shown in an Amarāvatī bas-relief, consists of a post-and-railing balustrade enclosing a Bodhi Tree or its symbolic equivalent, a Parasol. Another, as shown in a bas-relief from Mathurā, takes the form of an hypaethral pavilion, with windows and doors and having a distinctive roof composed of an inverted stepped pyramid surmounted by a flat, crenellated terrace. Like the fence-type harmikā the pavilion harmikā is also built to surround a Bodhi Tree or a Parasol. In some cases, exemplified by those on the reliefs shown in fig. 169 (b), the pavilion and the fence are associated (Combaz, 1932, pp. 195ff.; 1933, pp. 113ff.).
In its later development in India the structural details and the doors and windows of the pavilion disappear and the fence is no longer free-standing. Little by little the harmikā becomes a cubic block topped by a cornice of stepped overhangs, and then, as at Elūrā and Ajaṇṭā, the cube and its cornices are elaborated by a series of returns. This is a formula

and correctly signifies a kiosk or belvedere erected upon the upper terrace of a multi-storeyed building.[3] This is also the meaning of the word given in the traditional Buddhist exegeses : Buddhaghoṣa, for example, says that

a

b(1)

b(2)

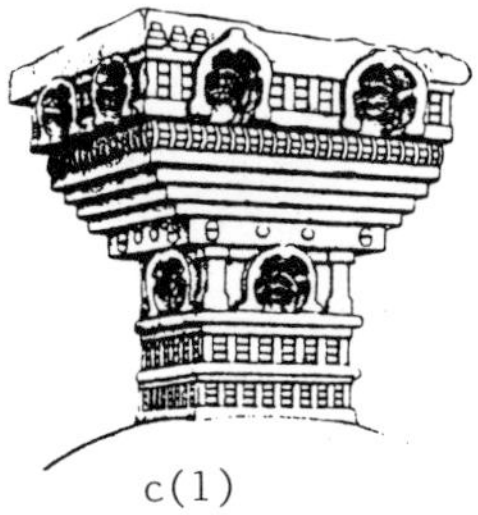

c(1)

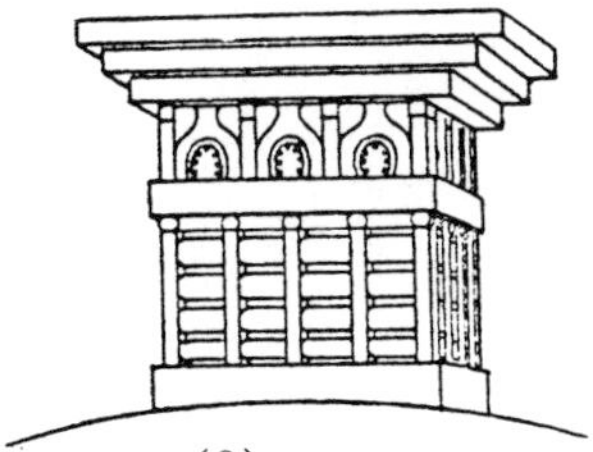

c(2)

Fig. 169 :
a. The harmikā as an hypaethral pavilion enclosing a tree, shown in a relief from Mathurā.
b. The harmikā as hypaethral pavilion and fence combined, shown in reliefs from Bhārhut.
c. The same shown in reliefs from Bhāja and Ajaṇṭā.

---

that is retained in the stupas of Burma and Tibet.

Indian stupas of the middle ages usually show the cubic type of harmikā with a cornice and plinth and sometimes decorated with a representation of the posts and rails of the prototypic balustrade. This type of harmikā also appears in the ancient Sinhalese stupas, where the faces of the harmikā are ornamented with a railing pattern of pilasters and cross bars, with the centre of each face showing a circular disc, referred to in the *Mahāvastu* as a "sun" (*Mahāvastu* XXVI.66; Paranavitana, 1946, p. 34). The tradition of showing railings and suns on the harmikā is maintained in Sri Lanka to the present day.

The cube with plinth and cornice also became the standard form of the harmikā in the stupas of Nepal, Tibet, Burma, Thailand and in the Lamaist stupas of China. In Java the harmikā is a simple block in the shape of a truncated pyramid with a square, or, exceptionally, an octagonal base. As an alternative some Javanese stupas, such as those at Caṇḍi Sewu, have a harmikā in the form of an elaborately profiled pedestal.

Although greatly reduced in size and visual importance the harmikā still exists in the storeyed stupas of the Far East as a small cube surrounding the "upturned bowl" (Jap. fukubachi). Despite its diminutive size it here retains the same important symbolic significance as its more visually prominent counterparts.

In Burma, successive enlargements by encasing the original stupa produced a form in which the harmikā disappeared as the base, dome and pinnacle merged into a single, flowing profile without a perceptible differentiation of parts (Combaz, 1933, pp. 114 & 118f.; 1932, pp. 196ff.).

Many theories have been put forward to explain the significance of the

Fig. 170 : a, b and c. The harmikā as a stepped roof rising above a cube ornamented with a fence pattern, shown on stupas at Ajaṇṭā and Kārli. d and e. The cube of the harmikā elaborated by returns in stupas at Elūra and Ajaṇṭā. f. The harmikā of the Thai stupa, showing eight columns representing the Noble Eightfold Path. g, h and i. The cubic harmikā of the Nepalese stupa, ornamented with eyes on each face.

"the term harmikā designates the pavilion installed upon the top level of a terraced prāsāda".[4] The harmikā is alternatively referred to as a deva-kotuva (or in Sinhalese hataräs-kotuva), in which kotuva usually denotes "an area enclosed by a fence or wall" : the deva-kotuva is "an enclosure of the gods",[5] that is to say, a sacred enclosure. Again, in the Sinhalese chronicles it is termed "the four-cornered (that is, square) enclosure (caturaśra-koṣtha)".[6]

The iconographic and archaeological indications concur : the harmikā is a space defined by the walls of a pavilion or by a fence and centred by a tree or parasol or some other axial symbol. This is precisely the form of the sacred enclosure now familiar to us from the foregoing analysis of the stupa plan.[7] The schema of the prototypic harmikā duplicates the elementary form of the Buddhist templum, the cosmicised space laid out around an axis mundi. Here at the apex of the stupa dome a second and similar sacred space is defined; the same spatial symbolism of cosmic structuring is repeated at a higher level. But why should a sacred precinct be located in such an unlikely and inaccessible place as the summit of a cupola? For the answer we must turn to the Vedic altar and its derivative, the Hindu temple.

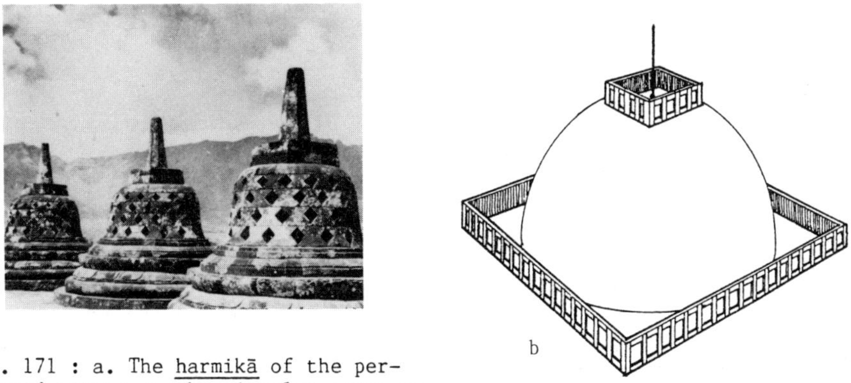

Fig. 171 : a. The harmikā of the perforated stupas on the circular terraces at Borobudur.
b. The superimposition of sacred enclosures.

---

harmikā : for Fergusson it was a reliquary casket (Fergusson and Burgess, 1910, p. 70; Fergusson, 1935); Senart (1882, pp. 414ff.) saw it as a fire altar; Jouveau-Dubreuil. (1922, *passim*), following Havell (1915, pp. 47 & 49), claimed that it was the "chimney" of a sacred fire hut; in the view of Przyluski (1935, pp. 199ff.) it was the equivalent of the coping stone of a Brahmanic tomb; Combaz (1932, pp. 114ff.) saw it as a fenced pavilion built to enclose a Bodhi Tree; Mus (1935, pp. 113ff.) identified it as Indra's palace at the summit of Mt. Meru; and Fabri (1930 & 1932, *passim*) traced it to Mesopotamian forms of ornament.

3. Combaz, 1932, p. 194 (quoting Foucher) and p. 194, n. 3; 1933, p. 100; Acharya, 1946, p. 608, s.v., harmya, gives "an edifice, an upper room, a turret... etc... a palace".

4. Quoted by Combaz, 1932, p. 98.

5. Paranavitana, 1946, pp. 31 & 33; Coomaraswamy, 1977, 1, p. 437.

6. Paranavitana, 1946, p. 31; Parker, 1909, p. 337; Govinda, 1976, pp. 19 & 31. 7. See above, pp. 153ff.

1. THE *HARMIKĀ* AS HIGH ALTAR - THE *ĀMALAKA*.

The Sinhalese chronicles call the harmikā a "high altar" (P. muddha-vedi).[8] This ultimately refers to the Vedic High Altar (uttara-vedi), one of the altars set up for the performance of the Vedic sacrifice.[9] It is a square altar built at the Eastern side of the Altar Ground (vedi) : "The altar ground (vedi) is the Earth; the High Altar (uttara-vedi) is the Heaven World".[10] Symbolically the High Altar stands at the summit of the vertical axis represented by the East-West spine of the altar layout.

The symbolism of this arrangement of altar hearths recurs in the Hindu temple where the High Altar, the Altar of Heaven, is placed at the summit of the temple, above the flattened area on top of the superstructure (śikhara).[11]

In the Hindu temple of the Northern (nagara) type the position of the High Altar is marked by a ribbed coping stone, called the āmalaka, which sits upon the flat shoulder course at the top of the śikhara. By contrast, the High Altar in the Southern (draviḍa) type of Hindu temple is represented by a High Temple (kṣudra-alpa-vimāna or harmya, which latter term, as seen above, relates to harmikā). The High Temple is placed at the summit of the truncated pyramid that forms the body of this style of Indian architecture.[12]

The significance of the āmalaka, the ring-stone with a cogged rim that crowns the Northern type of temple, is unambiguous.[13] Kramrisch has shown that the āmalaka corresponds to the uppermost of the three self-perforated bricks (svayamātṛṇṇā) which are placed at different levels of the Vedic altar to represent the three worlds of Earth, Midspace and Heaven.[14] Located at the top of the temple, the āmalaka represents the celestial world. Its association with the supernal realms is indicated by the word āmalaka, which is the name of a tree that bears fruit having a similar shape to the cogged ring-stone of the temple.[15] In the Hindu myths the Āmalaka is the primordial Tree, the first to grow in the world, and sacred to the great gods of the Hindu Trinity : Viṣṇu sits at its foot, Brahmā above, and Śiva at a still higher level; the devas are its leaves, flowers and fruits; the Sun rests in its branches.[16]

---

8. Paranavitana, 1946, p. 31.

9. For a description of the Vedic High Altar, see above, pp. 45ff., and below, p. 366.

10. ŚB VII.3.1.27. 11. Kramrisch, 1946, p. 146.

12. *Ibid.*, pp. 180, 184 & 242. The form of the High Altar is reminiscent of the shrines shown in the early Buddhist reliefs of Bhārhut and Sāñcī. See Kramrisch, 1946, p. 195.

13. For a discussion of the meaning of the āmalaka, see Kramrisch, 1946, pp. 348ff.

14. The significance of the self-perforated bricks is discussed in Coomaraswamy, "*Svayamātṛṇṇā* : Janua Coeli", 1977, 1, pp. 465ff.

15. The word āmalaka is from the root mal, "to hold, to gather", with reference to its function : it is the loadstone that holds together the pi[llars] of the śikhara and the ringstone that clasps the temple's neck. It is also written with a short a (amalaka) and amala is "stainless, without impurity"; the Buddhists call it the amala-śila, "the stone of purity", and also amala-sāra, "pure Essence". See Kramrisch, 1946, p. 354; Beal, 1906, pp. 136f.; Foucher, 1905, p. 356.

16. *Skanda Purāṇa*, XII.9-23, cited by Kramrisch, 1946, p. 356.

a

b

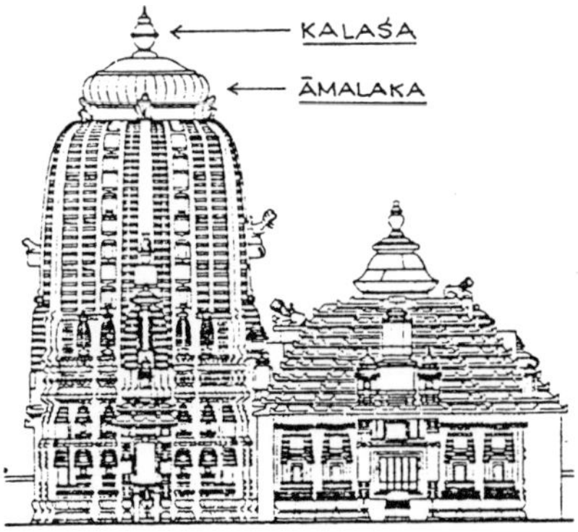

c

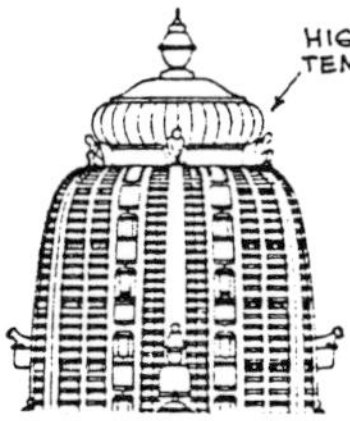

d

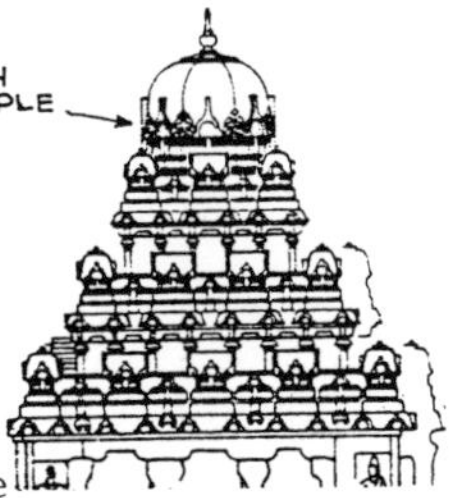

e

Fig. 172 : a and b. Hindu temples of the Northern (nagara) and Southern (dravida) types.
c and d. The High Altar at the summit of Hindu temples of the Northern and Southern types.
e. The āmalaka, or cogged load-stone, of the Hindu temple, supporting the golden vase (kalaśa).

Just as the Āmalaka Tree supports the Sun, so the load-stone of the temple supports the golden vase (kalaśa), the symbol of the Sun: "The golden kalaśa, a high seat on the summit of the god's dwelling, looks as if it were the sun's orb that had risen on the lordly mountain of sunrise".[17] The āmalaka is "the disc of the Sun... like the pericarp of the sky lotus, of which the petals are the directions of the compass and the filaments the solar rays";[18] its emanating sectors are "the rays of the Sun spread like the filaments of the lotus of the zenith".[19] The golden vase is cognate with the "one Sun that never leaves the Meru",[20] the Sun that stands stationary at the top of the Mountain at midday.[21] The golden Sun-vase stands at the centre of the āmalaka, whose radiating sectors are the Sun's rays or the petals of a Sun-lotus, opening to disclose a pericarp bearing the golden vase that contains the beverage of immortality (amṛta).

The āmalaka is a common iconographic element in Buddhist art and is used extensively in Buddhist architecture,[22] where it frequently occurs as a column capital.[23] Used in this location it has the same significance as the āmalaka that appears at the summit of the Hindu temple : it is the stationary Sun at the top of the Cosmic Pillar. This significance is frequently emphasised by enclosing the āmalaka within a fence, the presence of which can be indicated in several different ways : in some places the surrounding fence is solid and the āmalaka is not visible; in others the balustrade is reduced to a mere framework so as to display the Sun-lotus

---

17. Ep. Ind. XIII, 45, 56, cited by Kramrisch, 1946, p. 355. Many other inscriptions liken the kalaśa to the sun. See *ibid.*, n. 192.

18. *Ibid.*, p. 351 and n. 174, where the reference is given.

19. BU VI.3.6.; Kramrisch, 1946, pp. 351 & 355. 20. AB XIV.6.44, Comm.

21. Cf. above, pp. 24f. 22. Kramrisch, 1946, p. 354, n. 188.

23. The pillars of such famous Buddhist monuments as Bedṣā, Nāsik, Kārlī, etc., are capped by āmalakas. The so-called "cushion" capitals of pillars in the Hindu cave temples of Bādāmī, Elūrā and Elephanta are in fact representations of the āmalaka.

within;[24] in some the four thin corner posts are replaced by caryatids of ganas[25] or yakṣīnis;[26] and in yet others the āmalaka is exposed to full view by raising it above the fence.[27]

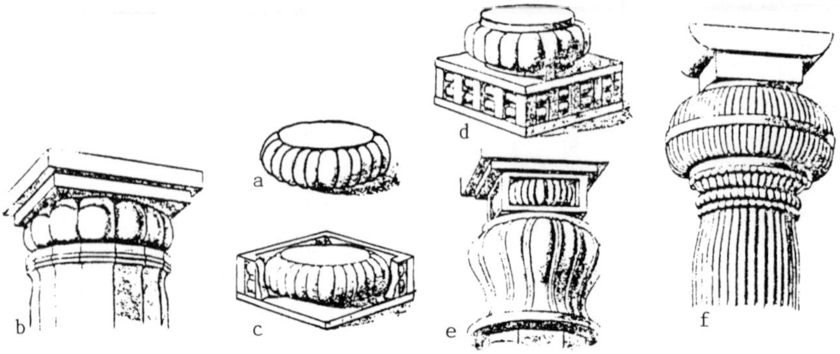

Fig. 173 : Varieties of the āmalaka column capital. In a. and b. the āmalaka is exposed to view; in c. it is enclosed within a fence and is not visible; in d. the āmalaka is made visible by raising it above the fence; in e. the fence is a mere framework, open at the sides to show the āmalaka within; and in f. the āmalaka forms a "cushion" capital. See also the illustrations on the facing page.

The fence that surrounds the āmalaka has the same significance as that which encloses the stupa's harmikā. The identity is demonstrated by the presence on many āmalaka-capital pillars of the same inverted pyramid of overhanging slabs that rises above the harmikā of the ancient Indian stupas.

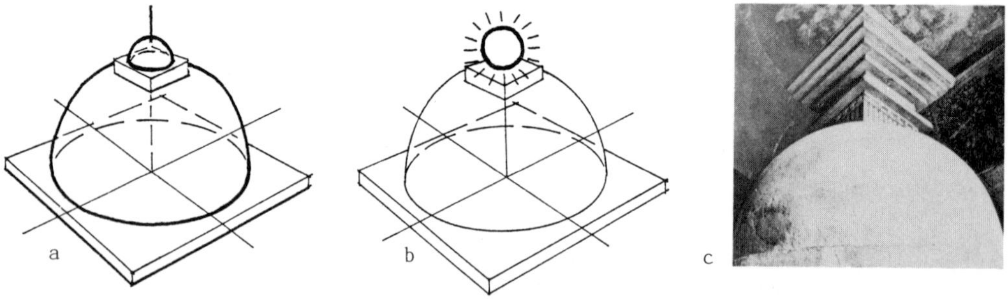

Fig. 174 : a. The stupa as two superimposed Eggs. b. The harmikā as the Sun. c. The inverted pyramid of overhanging slabs rising above the harmikā, Ajaṇṭā. The same motif appears on the column capitals shown in fig. 175.

The evidence suggests that the harmikā of the stupa and the āmalaka at the summit of the Hindu temple or the top of the column are symbolically equivalent. The assimilation is further justified by indications given in the early architectural manuals, which use the term aṇḍa, "egg", as a synony for āmalaka. The harmikā is similarly identified with the egg : one of the

24. As shown at Nāsik, Bedṣā, Kārlī, etc. 25. Shown, e.g., in vihāra 3 at Nāsik and caves 1 and 2 at Ajaṇṭā.

26. Shown in cave 26 at Ajaṇṭā. See Kramrisch, 1946, p. 353 and n. 185
27. Brown, 1965, p. 11.

Fig. 175 : Columns with āmalaka capitals. a. Āmalakas forming "cushion" capitals. b - g. The āmalaka shown within a fence, opened at the sides.

common names of the stupa, dhātugarbha - in which garbha can be translated either as "womb" or "egg" - was originally applied to the harmikā alone and was only later used for the structure as a whole.[28] The āmalaka and the harmikā are both "eggs".

* * * * *

The reference to the egg or womb leads back once more to associations with the Sun, for the *Chāndogya Upaniṣad* teaches that the Sun, which is Brahman, is born from the Cosmic Egg.[29] In the same manner the Sun-vase (kalaśa) emerges from the āmalaka-egg.[30]

* * * * *

The āmalaka of the Hindu Temple is the stationary Sun at the summit of the World Mountain. The temple is identified with Mt. Meru, the support of the Sun, the Sun that neither rises nor sets, symbol of the ultimate state of illumination of the seeker : "For one who thus knows the secret doctrine of Brahman, it does not set nor does it rise; for him, it is day, once for all".[31] The Hindu temple, built in the likeness of the cosmic Meru, is "the Mountain where the sun rests at midday";[32] the mountain is the support of "the One Sun that never leaves the Meru", the Sun that is the "illuminator of the regions",[33] the step-way (sopārna-marga) to release (mukti).[34] The kalaśa, the water jar that tops the finial of the temple is "the sun's orb, arisen on the lordly mountain of sunrise".[35]

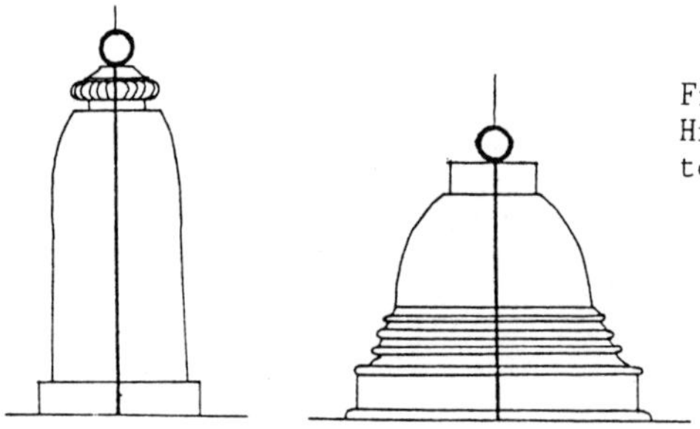

Fig. 176 : The symbolic equivalence of the Hindu temple and the stupa : the Sun at the top of the Pillar.

The same symbolic considerations apply to the stupa. The body of the stupa is Mt. Meru and the harmikā at its apex locates the supernal Sun that stands stationary at its summit. The full import of this symbolism will become apparent when the significance of the Sun Door is examined in the following.[36]

---

28. Govinda, 1976, p. 30; Kramrisch, 1946, p. 354; Fergusson and Burgess, 1910, 2, p. 344, and cf. above, pp. 200ff.

29. CU III. 19.1-3. 30. See below, pp. 343f.

31. CU III.2.3; cf. Kramrisch, 1946, p. 355.

32. From the Deopara inscription quoted above.

33. AB XIV.6.44, Comm.

34. Buddhist stone inscription, Ind. Ant. XVII, p. 308, quoted in Kramrisch, 1946, p. 355 and n. 196.

35. Inscriptions on the Mahādeva temple at Ittagi, Ep. Ind. XIII, pp. 46 & 56, quoted Kramrisch, 1946, p. 355. See *idem*, n. 192 for other inscriptions similarly likening the kalaśa to the sun.

36. See below, pp. 268 ff.

Fig. 177 : The High Altar at the summit of the Mountain-tower of the Southern type of Indian Hindu temple. Kailasanatha temple, Elūrā.

a

b

c

Fig. 178 : a. The Tree growing from the top of Mt. Meru, shown in a relief from Borobudur. b. A living tree growing from the caitya-vṛkṣa formed by the harmikā of a Nepalese stupa. c. An Amarāvatī relief showing a Tree growing from a stupa harmikā.

2. THE *HARMIKĀ* AS *CAITYA-VṚKṢA*.

In the following it will be shown that the spire that emerges from the dome of the stupa at the centre of the harmikā has a multivalent meaning. It is at one and the same time identified with a sacrificial post (yūpa), with a parasol, and with the World Tree. The three forms are assimilable : post, parasol and Tree are homologous and interchangeable symbols.[37] The sacrificial post is specifically identified with the Tree, the Lord of the Forest (vanaspati) from which it is cut;[38] and the form and significance of the parasol exactly parallel those of the Tree.[39] The symbolism of the Tree inheres within the other forms.

a

Fig. 179 : a. The Tree growing from the summit of the World Mountain, shown in a gunungan, used in the Javanese wayang. b. The Tree growing from the harmikā in an Amarāvatī relief.

The spire is the Tree of Enlightenment.[40] In Tibet the term for the axial pillar of a stupa is srog-shing, literally "life wood", which corresponds to "Tree of Life".[41] In many early depictions of stupas the spire is shown in the form of a tree.

Since the spire is identified with the Cosmic Tree the harmikā, which in early stupas has the form of a fence or an hypaethral pavilion, has all the characteristics of a caitya-vṛkṣa, a walled or fenced area forming a sanctuary for a sacred tree.[42] The harmikā is a caitya-vṛkṣa at the top of the World Mountain.[43]

The symbolism interconnects with that of the harmikā as High Altar. It will be remembered that the prototypic form of the caitya-vṛkṣa is a sacred enclosure centred by a tree having an altar or throne at its foot. The harmikā marks the location of the Buddha throne or the Buddha altar, at the foot of the Tree of Enlightenment. That is to say, it marks the location of the bodhimaṇḍa.

---

37. See below, pp. 320ff. 38. See below, pp. 322f. 39. See pp. 327f.

40. Govinda, 1976, pp. 14, 31, 38 and 48.

41. Tucci, 1932, pp. 40f.; Irwin, 1980, p. 16. 42. See pp. 153ff.

43. One form of the caitya-vṛkṣa is the bodhighara, an overhanging platform or gallery built around a Bodhi Tree. From this platform devotees poured water onto the Tree as an act of worship (Coomaraswamy, 1930). Irwin (1980, p. 19) has suggested that the harmikā derives from this.

3. THE *HARMIKĀ* AS *BODHIMAṆḌA*.

The harmikā demarks a sacred space at the summit of the Mountain. This is the centre of the world, the hub of the Cosmic Wheel, the location of the bodhimaṇḍa where the Buddha attained Enlightenment, where he eternally reveals the Dharma, and where, Sun-like, he shines to irradiate the worlds.

As we have seen[44] the place of the Buddha's Enlightenment, the bodhimaṇḍa, physically and geographically is at Bodhgayā, which is identified with the navel of the world; but metaphysically the place of Enlightenment is at the apex of the cosmos, at the summit of the Cosmic Mountain. This is clearly shown in the ritual procedures of Shingon Buddhism, which include a meditation on the bodhimaṇḍa.[45] The ritual commences with a meditation on the Receptacle World[46] : the circles (maṇḍala) of the five Elements are visualized as standing one above the other in the reverse of their

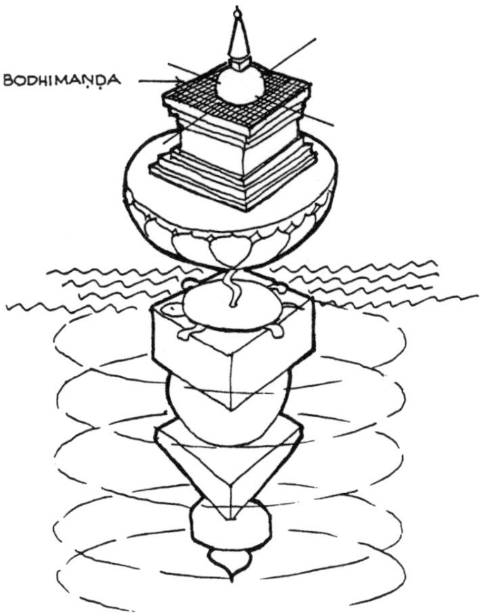

Fig. 180 : The meditation on the bodhimaṇḍa in Shingon Buddhism.

---

44. See above, p. 157.

45. Jap. dōjōkan, lit., "Visualization of the Place of the Way". The meditation is described in MKDJT, p. 1660, s.v., Dōjōkan, and under the headings of its component meditations, viz. p. 263, s.v., Kikaikan, "Visualization of the Receptacle World"; p. 2307, s.v., Rokakukan, "Visualization of the Jewel Stupa"; p. 2096, s.v., Mandarakan, "Visualization of the Mandala"; etc.

46. Jap. kikaikan. Cf. the description of the Receptacle World according to Vasubandhu's *Abhidharmakośa* given above, p. 159.

usual order, so that the lowest circle is Space (ākāśa), above which rest the circles of Air, Fire, Water, and Earth. Above the Earth circle lies the Milky Ocean containing a Golden Turtle from whose back grows a great lotus supporting Mt. Meru, which is surrounded by the seven mountain ranges and their seven intervening seas, the Iron Enclosing Mountains and the Salt Ocean, and the continents in the four directions.[47] On the summit of Meru is the place of Enlightenment,[48] identified with the Jewel Stupa (Jap. hōrōkaku), which contains the Diamond World Mandala,[49] having the Great Sun Buddha (Mahāvairocana, Jap. Dainichi) at its centre, surrounded by his attendant retinue of Buddhas, Bodhisattvas and gods.

The Diamond World Mandala is revealed by the Great Sun Buddha within the Jewel Stupa that stands at the centre of Indra's Heaven on the summit of Mt. Meru. In the pre-Buddhist mythology the centre of the Mountain summit was occupied by Indra, who is cognate with the Sun. In the context of Shingon Buddhism Indra is replaced by the Great Sun Tathāgata. In both the Brahmanic and Buddhist formulations the personification of the Sun sits upon the Mountain peak, illuminating the universe with his progenitive rays. Mahāvairocana, as was Indra previously, is the Sun standing still at the apex of the Cosmic Axis.

* * * * *

Parallel considerations are indicated by other meditational practices in Shingon Buddhism. Several texts describe rituals in which the initiate visualizes a Buddha or Bodhisattva seated upon a lotus at the summit of Mt. Meru. One such is a meditation on the Bodhisattva Avalokiteśvara : a seed syllable is visualized on the back of the Cosmic Turtle; it changes to the golden Mountain, Meru, made of the four jewels and surrounded by seven mountain ranges. Vairocana sits within the Mountain and from the pores of his skin flows a rain of fragrant milk, which runs down into the eight seas between the mountain chains. On the summit of the Mountain is an eight-petalled lotus supporting a Jewel Stupa, within which a seed syllable shines with a great light, illuminating all the Buddha Worlds throughout the cosmos. From within this great light appears the Bodhisattva Avalokiteśvara, with one thousand hands and one thousand eyes...[50]

---

47. Cf. the description of the Buddhist cosmology given below.

48. I.e., the bodhimaṇḍa, Jap. dōjō. 49. See pp. 341f.

50. Jap. Senjūsengen Kanjizai Bosatsu, Skt. Sahasrabhuja-Avalokiteśvara Bodhisattva. The description comes from the *Kongōchōyuga Senjūsengen Kanjizai Bosatsu shugyōgikikyō*, I, quoted in BKDJT, p. 2151, s.v., Shumidan; cf. *Kongōchōrengebushinnenjugiki*, Taishō, Vol. 18, No. 873, p. 299.

A. The Diamond World Mandala.

B. The Jewel Stupa in the Diamond World Mandala.

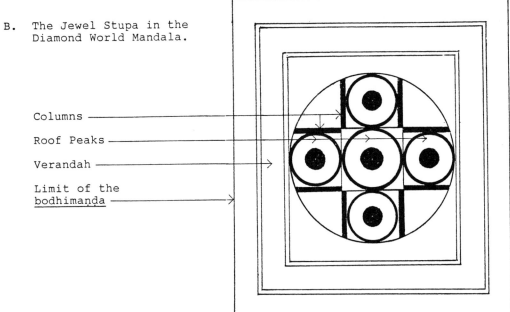

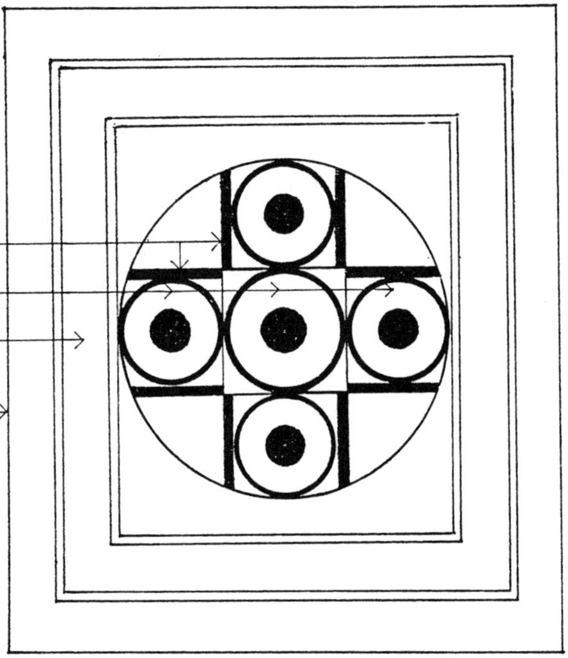

Fig. 181 : The Diamond World Mandala is laid out within the Jewel Stupa (hōrōkaku) within the bodhimaṇḍa on the summit of Mt. Meru. The Jewel Stupa is described in the *Ryakushutsukyō*, 1, as having eight columns and five roof peaks. The five roof peaks correspond to the circles encompassing the five Buddhas and their retinues, and the eight columns are the eight vajras that are tangential to these circles. Surrounding the Stupa is a verandah, where the 1,000 Buddhas of the bhadrakalpa sit.

4. THE MOUNTAIN SUMMIT.

The Mountain links the worlds. It is the channel of communication between the realms of existence. The focal point of this interchange is the Mountain tip. In numberless myths of many peoples the gods or ancestors descend to the tops of mountains to communicate with men or to enter the terrestrial domain. In Hindu mythology the chariots of the gods, the sky travellers, alight upon the summit of the World Mountain, the point of contact between men and gods. The shapes of the Hindu temple are named for the chariots that rest upon their summits : Triviṣṭapa, the chariot of Indra; Vairāja, the chariot of Brahmā as the personification of the Cosmic Intellect, Virāj, the non-supreme aspect of Brahman in whom the totality of manifestation inheres; the Kailaśa of Śiva; Puṣpaka of Kuvera; and Maṇika of Varuṇa.[51]

Similarly, in the Vedic fire sacrifice, performed upon the summit of an altar piled up in the likeness of the Cosmic Mountain, the gods are invited by means of incantations to descend onto this sacred mountain top. The performer of the ritual "is able to watch the coming of the gods with his spiritual eye. They appear in swiftly moving cars drawn by celestial horses... and having come, the deities take their places on the seats prepared for them on a litter made of blades of holy grass (kuśa). As honoured guests they partake of the holy oblations, and when dismissed, depart".[52]

In the rituals connected with the Diamond World Mandala the Great Sun Buddha, together with the four Buddhas and a retinue of attendant Bodhisattvas, is invited to come down from above and take his station within the Jewel Stupa on the top of the Meru peak.[53] This is a ritual repetition of the Great Sun Buddha's revelation of the Dharma. He descends the axis of the world, retracing the path of his attainment of Final Liberation, until he comes to the Heaven of Indra at the top of the Cosmic Mountain, the point of contact with the worlds below, and there reveals the Truth for the sake of beings dwelling in the Worlds of Desire (kāma-loka). The revelation is twofold, verbal and geometric : he preaches the Sutra of the Diamond Summit (*Vajra-śekhara-sūtra*, Jap. *Kongōchōgyō*) and simultaneously emanates the Diamond World Mandala in the directions of space.[54]

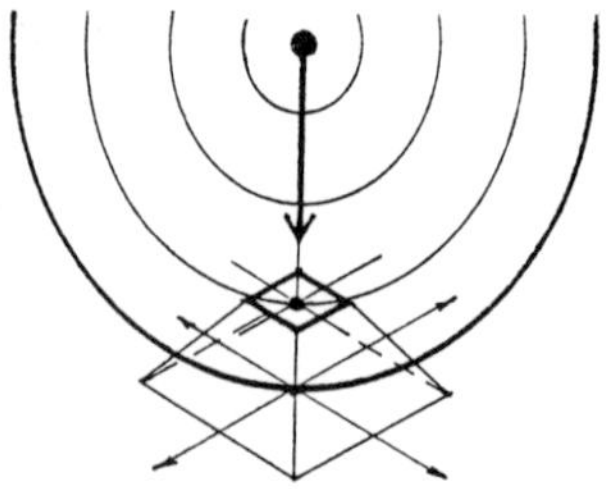

Fig. 182 : Descent to the Mountain summit.

51. Kramrisch, 1946, pp. 277-280. 52. Zimmer, 1955, pp. 37f.

53. Tucci, 1961, pp. 87ff.; Toganoo, 1932, p. 196.

54. MKDJT, p. 706, s.v. *Kongōchōgyō*.

a

c

b

Fig. 183 : a. The stupa at Borobudur represents a stupa-pavilion standing at the summit of the Cosmic Mountain. b. A stupa on top of the Mountain in a Burmese example. c. An Indian drawing of a pavilion on the summit of Meru.

This descent to the Mountain summit is an instance of the universally recurrent theme of the descent of the divine Principle to the central navel of the world, to the point whence the corporeal world of spatial extension originates. The World of Form (rūpa-loka) is the subtle world of mental phenomena, existing in time but not in space. The top of the Mountain is the point on the axis of the world where it emerges into its spatial mode of existence, which is to say, into corporeality. The dissemination, or spatial projection, of the Truth from the Jewel Stupa is thus symbolically equivalent to the emanation of space from the omphalos on the Mountain peak - and the ritual of bringing the Buddhas down into the mandala is thereby seen to have a twofold significance : it re-enacts the process of the epiphany of the Dharma; and also the genesis of the spatio-corporeal cosmos.

The progenitive source of the world is located at the summit of the axial Mountain. "The summit of the cosmic mountain is not only the highest point of the earth; it is also the earth's navel, the point at which the creation began".[55] Eliade cites numerous examples of this symbolic construct from non-Indian traditions;[56] and, providing an explicit architectural expression of this concept, many temples in Java and elsewhere in Further India are conceived as mountains topped by a liṅga.[57] With analogous import

---

55. Eliade, 1954, p. 16. 56. *Idem*; Wheatley, 1971, p. 492.

57. Stern, 1934, *passim*, Bosch, 1960, pp. 165f.; Wales, 1977, p. 114; Heine-Geldern, 1956, p. 3; Coedes, 1963, p. 43. Cf. above, p. 256f.

the Chinese Buddhist cosmology places a large, multi-storeyed stupa at the centre of the summit of Meru;[58] and in Burma terraced pyramids representing Mt. Meru are surmounted by stupas.[59]

* * * * *

The Mountain top is the point of communication between the worlds and it is from here that the transcendent Truth enters the world of men. Thus, in the Mahāyāna, the Buddha preaches the sutras on the summit of Gṛhadrakuṭa, the Vulture Peak. This is parallelled in Pali texts where the Buddha is said to occupy the summit of Meru. One such reference occurs in the legend of the Buddha : it is recounted that immediately after his Great Awakening the Buddha perceived the profundity of the Truth he had realized and hesitated to put in motion the Wheel of the Dharma, thinking that it would not be understood. At this the gods cry out, "the world is lost", and Brahmā prays to him to preach the Doctrine. In his prayer Brahmā says, "As from a mountain's rocky pinnacle the folk around are clear to view, so Sage, from the Palace of Truth, from its topmost heights, survey with eye all-seeing the folk beneath, poor thralls of birth and swift decay, whose doom is that same sorrow thou no more will know".[60] At his Awakening the Buddha ascended to the Palace of Truth (P. dhamma-mayam-pāsādam) at the summit of the Mountain. In a similar vein a text in the *Saddharma-ratnavali* says that the Buddha ascends the Meru of Wisdom and there enters the Palace of Wisdom.[61] At least six passages in the Pali Canon repeat the metaphor.[62]

a

Fig. 184 : a. The altar stand supporting the image and the supporting base of the stupa both represent the Cosmic Mountain.
b. A Japanese Sumeru platform (Jap. shumidan), the stand that supports an image. It is named for and built in the likeness of Mt. Meru, or Sumeru. c. A Japanese "yoga-stupa" (Jap. yuga-tō). The five pinnacles on the roof represent the five roof peaks of the Jewel Stupa (Jap. hō-rōkaku) that stands at the summit of Mt. Meru.

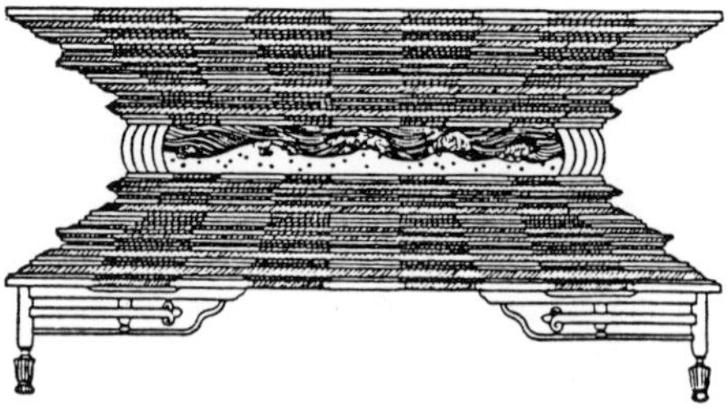

b

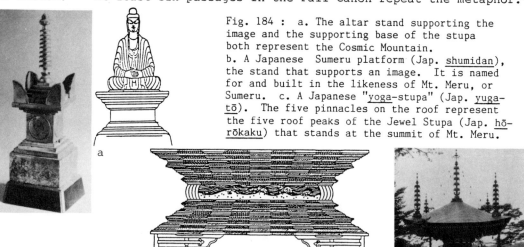

c

58. Combaz, 1935, p. 65; cf. below, p. 328, and also the "jewel stupa" of Indra's Heaven where the *Kongōchōgyō* (*Vajra-śekhara-sūtra*) is revealed and the Culamani stupa which contains the hairtuft (śikha) of the Buddha. See below.

59. The Sinbyume stupa, for example, is topped by a stupa that represents the Culamani ("Hairtuft Jewel"), the stupa that enshrined the Buddha's hair relic in the Trāyastriṃśa Heaven of Indra. Wales, 1977, p. 140, gives related examples.

60. Paranavitana, 1954, pp. 204f., quoting Chalmers.

61. *Saddharma-ratnavali*, Colombo Edn., 1925, p. 276, cited by Paranavitana, 1954, p. 205.

62. For references, see Paranavitana, 1954, p. 206, n. 25.

The symbolism is explicitly demonstrated in the Buddhist temple altar (Jap. dōjō, "Place of the Way", i.e., the bodhimaṇḍa), which supports the image of a Buddha or Bodhisattva. It is called the Meru Platform (Jap. shumidan) and is shaped in the likeness of the Mountain, being narrowest at mid-height, where a panel is decorated with wave patterns to represent the waters of the Great Ocean that encircles Mt. Meru.[63]

* * * * *

The harmikā stands at the summit of the World Mountain. Several etymologies and symbolic themes coalesce in this concept. The Sanscrit word for "mountain summit" is śikhara, which also designates the crowning cupola of the Hindu temple (which is identified with the Mountain) and, by extension, its tower.[64] The word śikhara derives from śikha, "hairtuft", and more specifically refers to the hairtuft worn by Hindus at the scapula foramen to mark the location of the "aperture of Brahman" (brahmarandhra), the point where the axis of the body (merudaṇḍa, brahmadaṇḍa) emerges from the top of the head.[65] The same associations are connected with the word stūpa, which in its literal sense also means "topknot" or "crest";[66] whence its derivative, stūpikā, which is the topmost finial of a building, the portion of its axis that emerges above the capstone.[67] As does śikha, the term stūpa signifies the hairtuft at the topmost point of the human body; by way of

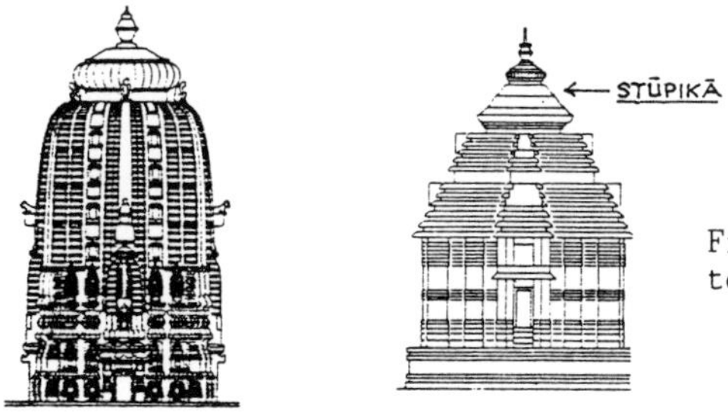

Fig. 185 : The śikhara of the Hindu temple and a stūpikā or finial.

analogy it comes to indicate the topmost point of the building; and finally it is applied to the edifice as a whole : the building is named for its crowning and focal element.[68]

---

63. Jap. shumi transliterates Sumeru, an alternative name of Meru. For a description of the Meru Altar, see BKDJT, p. 2515, s.v., Shumidan; MKDJT, p. 1097; Saunders, 1960, pp. 132ff.; *Hōbōgirin*, 1, 1-3, s.v., Sendaiza.

64. Mallaya, 1949, pp. 267ff.; Kramrisch, 1946, p. 154, n. 66.

65. See below, p. 317. This is the point that locates the microcosmic equivalent of the Sun Door, discussed in the following.

66. Macdonell, 1929, s.v., stūpa; Coomaraswamy, 1977, 1, pp. 386f.; Mallaya, 1949, pp. 9 & 268f. This last work gives a full list of references to the Brahmanic texts using the word stūpa in this sense.

67. Mallaya, 1949, p. 270.

68. On this identification see Coomaraswamy, 1977, 1, p. 450, n. 53; 2, p. 283f., s.v., cetiya, & p. 288, s.v., thūpa. The use of the word stūpa to designate a building form is exclusively Buddhist. In the Brahmanic literature the term is used in its literal sense only, and never with reference to architecture (Burnouf, 1876, p. 314; Bénisti, 1960, p. 47). The architectural use of the term and the building form it designates are coeval : it first appears on an Aśokan inscription of the 3rd century B.C., the time of the first proliferation of stupas (Bloch, 1951, pp. 28 & 34; Bénisti, 1960, p. 47).

a

b

c

Fig. 186 : a. A Bhārhut relief showing the Buddha's topknot enshrined in the Assembly Hall of the Gods in Indra's Trāyastriṃśa Heaven on the summit of Mt. Meru.
b. A Tibetan thaṇka depicting Śākyamuni cutting his hair tuft. Indra floats in the sky above him, holding the dish in which he receives the hair and carries it to the Trāyastriṃśa Heaven.
c. The adoration of the Buddha's topknot by the Gods of the Trāyastriṃśa Heaven. A god holds a parasol, a sign of royalty, above the hair. Sāñcī.

Śikhara is synonymous with śekhara (Jap. chō), the word used in the name of the *Vajra-śekhara-sūtra* (Jap. *Kongōchōgyō*), "The Sutra of the Diamond Summit", which refers to the summit of Mt. Meru, the location of Indra's Heaven, where Mahāvairocana Tathāgata preaches the sutra and reveals the Diamond World Mandala within the central Jewel Stupa.

The symbolic construct relates to other mythic formulations. At the time of his Great Renunciation the future Buddha cut off his hairtuft (śikha) as a sign of his severance from the worldly life. Grasping his sword in his right hand he seized his hair with the other and cut it off together with a jewel, the emblem of his princely rank. Throwing the topknot and diadem into the air, he said, "If I am to become a Buddha, let them stay in the sky; but if not, let them fall to the ground". The god Indra, perceiving them with his divine eye, caught these sacred objects in a jewelled casket and enshrined them within a stupa in his Trāyastriṃśa Heaven on the summit of Mt. Meru.[69] The myth contains a complexity of interconnecting connotations : the stupa on the top of the Mountain; the topknot hairtuft, which equals the stupa and the śikhara; the revelation of the *Kongōchōgyō* in the stupa in Indra's heaven; the symbolism of the uṣṇīṣa and the thousand petalled lotus (uṣṇīṣa-kamala) that it contains[70] - these, and a whole range of other meanings come together in this legend, not only clarifying the significance of the harmikā, but also typifying the manner in which symbolic constructs involve an extended and intricate network of mutually reflecting and mutually reinforcing references.

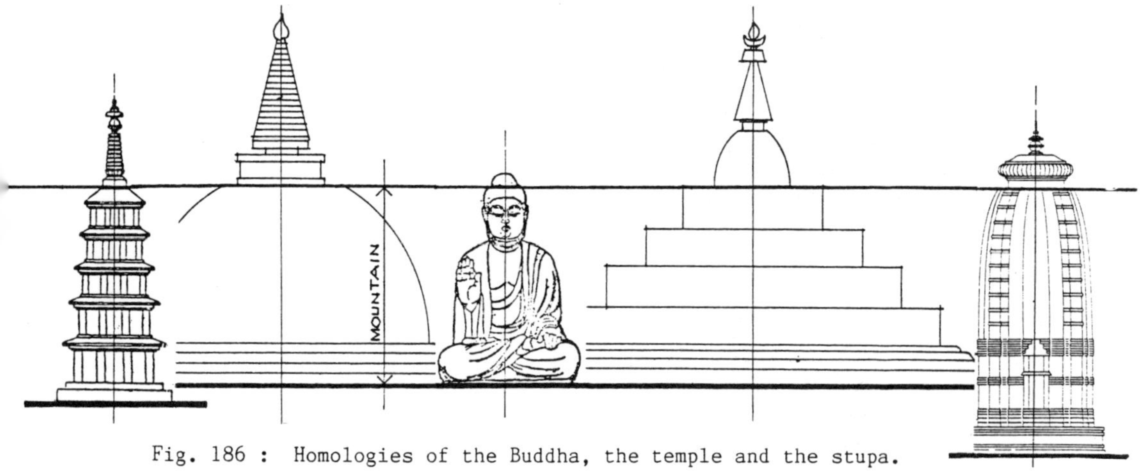

Fig. 186 : Homologies of the Buddha, the temple and the stupa.

69. *Jātaka* I.64; Zimmer, 1955, pp. 191f. On the symbolism of the hairtuft jewel (culamaṇi), see BKDJT, p. 840, s.v., Keishu, and cf. SPS, pp. 275ff.

70. See below, p. 318 and above, pp. 92ff.

5. THE SUPERIMPOSED ALTARS.

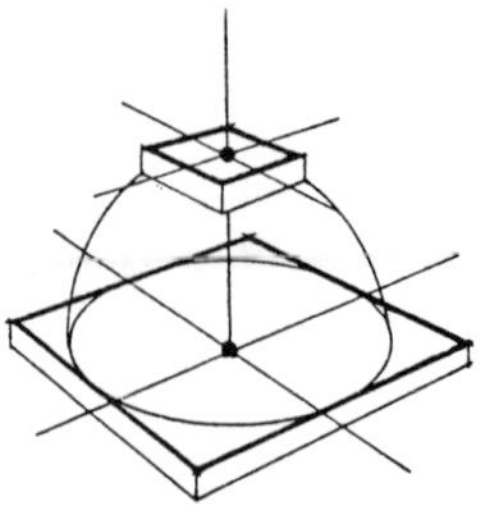

The harmikā is a High Altar raised upon the summit of the Cosmic Mountain. It is an image at a higher level of the sacred enclosure that forms the stupa plan. The lower of these two sacred spaces was brought to life by a seed (dhātu) buried at its centre; the upper enclosure is similarly fecundated. Seeds are placed within deposit boxes at the level of the earth so as to fecundate the stupa womb; other seeds are similarly placed within the harmikā.

a

b

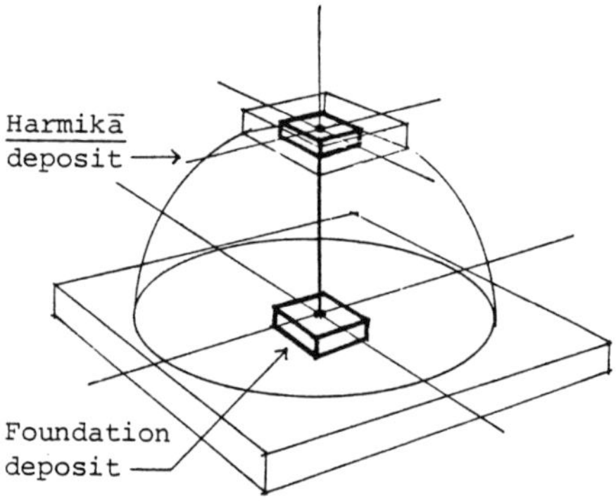

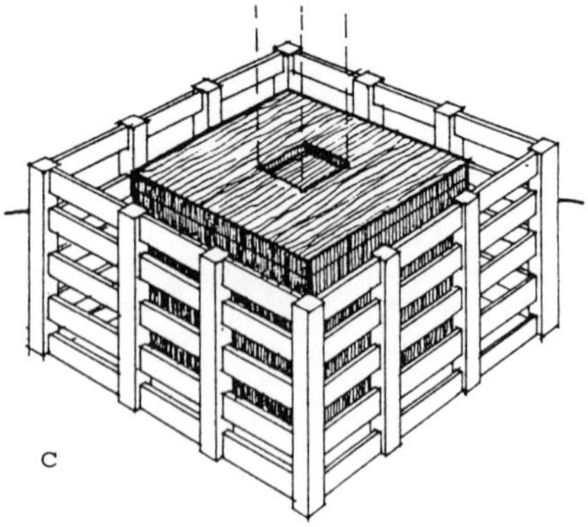

c

Fig. 187 : a. The harmikā of the Sri Lankan stupa, which encloses a deposit box containing a yantragala in the form of a mandala. The harmikā is ornamented to represent a fence and is marked with a sun disc.
b. Superimposed deposits.
c. The harmikā deposit box enclosed within a fence in the ancient form of Indian and Sri Lankan stupa.

At the centre of the harmikā lies a deposit box.[71] The main stupa at Sāñcī provides the prototypic example : the fence of the upper altar surrounds a heavy stone box with a lid.[72] The same arrangement applies in the

71. Fergusson and Burgess, 1910, 2, p. 344; Volwahsen, 1969, p. 90.

72. Marshall, 1918, pp. 33f.; Paranavitana, 1946, pp. 19 & 31.

case of Sri Lankan stupas, but in these the fence is represented on the walls of the deposit box itself. Into this box was lowered a yantragala of sacred stone, its surface hollowed into a mandala-like arrangement of recesses to contain the relics and votive offerings.[73]

The practice has its counterpart in the building of the Hindu temple, where three ritual deposits are made during the course of the construction. The first is placed within the ground at the centre of the site upon the foundation stone (ādhāraśilā); another is placed within the wall near the entrance doorway; and a third is placed at the summit of the building, vertically above the foundation deposit.[74] The crowning deposit and the foundation deposit are analogous,[75] and in South-East Asia take the form of a stone slab divided into compartments in the manner of a mandala and as

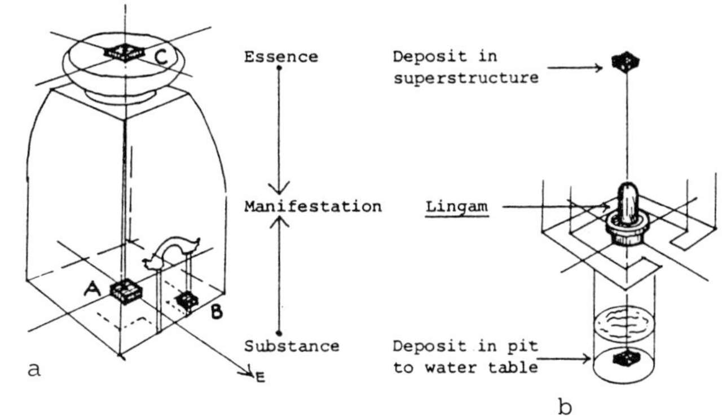

Fig. 188 : Location of the ritual deposits : a. in the Indian Hindu temple ; b. in the Javanese Caṇḍi.

previously described for the foundation stone.[76] The same arrangement is found in the caṇḍis of Java, where boxes containing the pripih (precious stones, seeds, pieces of metal, etc.) were placed in a pit beneath the main image and again in the superstructure above it.[77] In Bali the central pillar of a Meru, or temple, is hollowed out immediately below its tip to receive nine gems, the central one of which denotes the presence of Śiva, and metal sheets inscribed with characters representing the various gods. A similar deposit is made at the base of the pillar.[78]

The symbolic intent of the superimposed ritual deposits in the Hindu temple is not difficult to discern. The foundation deposit, buried in a pit that often descends to the water table and is filled with water,[79] pertains to the Waters of Substance (prakṛti); the deposit at the summit pertains to the vivifying presence of Essence (puruṣa); and the liṅga or image that is located between them on the vertical axis is the result of their union. The complementary poles of Heaven and Earth marry to generate the divinity, who is primordial Man. The temple embodies not one, but three altars, those of the chthonic, mundane and celestial planes, of the bhūr-, bhūvar- and svar-lokas. There is an altar for the plane of earth, an altar for the dome of the sky, and another for the column that pillars them apart.

---

73. Brown, 1965, p. 168. 74. See above, pp. 129ff.

75. Dagens, 1970, p. 394, gives Sanscrit references, and see also *ibid.*, pp. 20, 192ff., and 394ff. 76. See above p. 129. 77. Soekmono, 1976, p. 17.

78. Heine-Geldern, 1930, 4, p. 61; Covarrubias, 1937, p. 268; Combaz, 1935, p. 146; Kramrisch, 1946, p. 279; Dumarçay, 1978, pp. 60f.

79. See Coedes, 1935, p. 45.

The rites that established the foundation of the stupa are repeated at the top of the dome. A foundation stone was laid down within the earth as a solid structural and symbolic base for the pillar, physically present or metaphysically implied, that rises from it to support the sky. At the apex of the sky a new foundation is established to support the celestial column that lies beyond the Sun. The crown of the edifice, says the *Divyāvadāna* , should be raised on new masonry.[80] Arriving at the summit of the dome of heaven, the builder is on the roof of the cosmos : transcending the universe he lays the foundation for a supra-mundane mansion.

6. THE SUN DOOR.

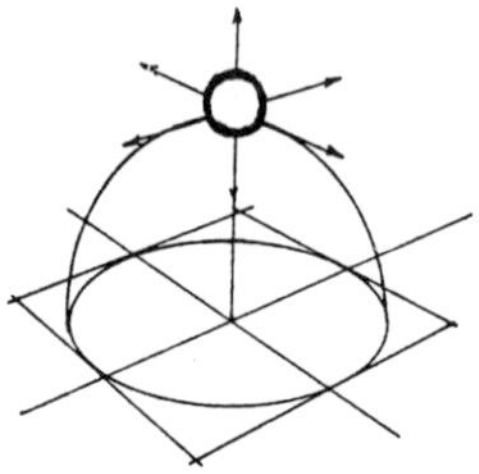

The harmikā locates the supernal Sun, standing immobile at the apex of the Cosmic Egg and the summit of the Mountain. It is by way of this Sun that nirvāṇa is attained. Liberation, in both the Brahmanic and Buddhist traditions, is symbolically expressed as a passage through a Sun Door.[81] It is "through the hub of the wheel, the midst of the Sun, the cleft in heaven, that all is covered over by rays that one is altogether liberated".[82] "The Sun is the World Gate which admits the Knower into paradise, but it is a barrier to the ignorant".[83] Passing through the Sun Gate the Knower leaves the defined and measured world of order (cosmos) and enters the undefined Empyrean, the Brahma-World. The *Bṛhadāranyaka Upaniṣad* describes the ascent of the Knower through the hubs of the three-wheeled cosmic Chariot, through the wheels of the Gale, the Moon and the Sun, which "open up" for his upward going : "Verily, when a person departs from this world, he goes to the Gale (vāyu). It opens out for him there like the hole of a chariot wheel. Through that he goes upwards. He goes to the Sun. It opens out there for him like the hole of a lambara (a musical instrument). Through that he goes upwards. He reaches the moon. It opens up there like the hole of a drum. Through that he goes upwards. He goes to the world free from grief, free from snow. There he dwells immortal years".[84]

Microcosmically, the symbolism is expressed in terms of the nāḍis, the subtle vectors or "arteries" of the heart which channel the solar rays and the life breaths[85] : "Even as a great extending highway runs between two villages, this one and that yonder, even so the rays of the Sun go to both these worlds, this one and that yonder. They start from yonder Sun and enter into these arteries (nāḍi). They start from these arteries and enter into yonder Sun..."[86] The *Upaniṣad* goes on to describe the spiritual ascension up the axis within the lesser world of the individual being : "But when he

---

80. *Divyāvadāna*, 244.12. 81. This is another theme that has been extensively and profoundly analyzed by Coomaraswamy. See e.g., his essays *Svayamātṛṇṇā* : Janua Coeli" and "The Symbolism of the Dome" in 1977, 1, and "Eckstein" (1939). The following considerations once again rely heavily on his writings. Cf. Guénon, 1962, Ch. LVIII, "Janua Coeli". 82. JUB I.3.5-6.

83. CU VIII.6.5; cf. JUB I.5 and III.14; Iśa Up. 15-16; etc.

84. BU V.10.1. 85. On the nāḍis, see below, pp. 317 ff.

86. CU VIII.6.2.

thus departs from this body, then he goes upwards by these very rays... he goes to the Sun. That, verily, is the Gateway of the world, an entering in for the wise but a barrier for the foolish. On this there is one verse. A hundred and one are the arteries of the heart, one of them leads to the crown of the head. Going upward through that one becomes immortal : the others serve for going in various directions".[87] The vertical vector, coincident with the suṣumṇā, and rising from the heart to pass through the Sun at the brahmarandhra or foramen, "extends to immortality", which is to say, extends to the Brahma World beyond the Sun. "The rays of Him (the Sun) are endless, who as its lamp indwells the heart... of which one standeth upward, breaking through the solar orb and overpassing into the Brahma World; thereby men attain their final goal"[88] and "win beyond the Sun".[89]

The Sun Door is a barrier (nirodha) standing between the unconditioned and the conditioned : in the Vedic texts it marks the junction of the supreme (para) and the non-supreme (apara) Brahman; it is the line of demarcation between the cosmos subject to the limitations of space and time, and the supra-cosmic Empyrean which lies in the dimensionless and timeless Brahmaloka. "I will tell thee that, which knowing, ye perceive the door of the world of heaven and having successfully come unhurt to the end of the Year, shall speedily attain the world of heaven";[90] "It is thus the immortal that lies beyond this (Year, Prajāpati, temporal existence)".[91] In Buddhism it is "the end of the world" in both the existential and temporal senses.[92] "There is no release from sorrow unless World's End is reached. So should a man become... a 'world-ender'".[93] With reference to this concept the Buddha is termed the "World-Ender" (lokantagū).[94]

The Sun Door is a barrier for the foolish.[95] For Knowers it is the Gate of Life but for the nescient it is the portal of Death : whoever "thinking, 'He is one, and I another', is not a Knower, but as it were a beast to be sacrificed to the gods".[96] The question is asked, "Who is qualified to pass (arhati) through the midst of the Sun?"[97] In the Brahmanic formulations it is the Qualified or Worthy (arhat), Agni,[98] who in other contexts is himself the Sun Door or Gate of Fire,[99] who "ascended, reaching the sky; opened the doors of heavenly light; and is the ruler of the heavenly realm".[100] Similarly, the Buddha opened the doors of immortality[101] and thus, like Agni, has become a "Door God",[102] a Guardian of the same Door at which the Buddhas are said "to stand and knock".[103] Having passed on forever, the Way remains open behind him,[104] and the Buddhist Worthies (arhat) are those who have passed beyond the further reaches of saṃsāra.

* * * * *

At first sight the symbolism of the Solar Gate at the apex of the World Egg seems incompatible with the physical world that we know by way of the senses. The Sun Door, the metaphysical centre of the heavenly sphere in this solar symbolism, is not coincident with the physical and visible centre of the turning of the stars. The celestial sphere appears to revolve about an axis that is not vertical but set obliquely to the plane of the earth; its apex, approximately located by the Pole Star, lies in the Northern sky.

---

87. CU VIII.6.5-6.
88. MU VI.30. 89. CU II.10.5. 90. JUB IV.15.1. 91. ŚB X.2.6.4.
92. A II.48.50. 93. Idem. 94. Sn 1128-1134
95. CU VIII.6.15; and cf. n. 81 above. 96. BU I.4.10.
97. JUB I.6.1; cf. KU II.21. 98. RV I.127.6; II.3.1; X.10.2.
99. JUB IV.11.5. 100. AB III.42. 101. Mv I.7; D II.33; M I.167.
102. AB III.4.2. 103. S II.58. 104. Mus, 1935, p. *277.

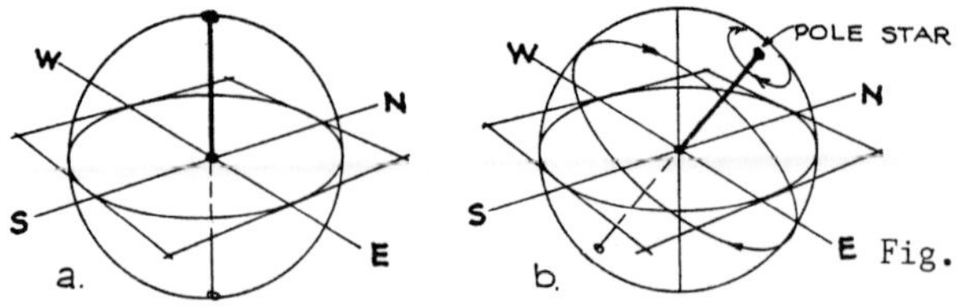

Fig. 189 : Solar (a) and polar (b) symbolism.

Therefore, according to one mode of symbolic expression, the exit from the universe is located there, at the hub of the turning wheel of the constellations : the symbolism is no longer solar, but polar.[105] Alternately, the two symbolisms are combined and reconciled. The oblique pole of the celestial sphere, joining its fixed polar extremities, runs in a North-South direction; projected down onto the plane of earth it coincides with the North-South axis. The Northern extremity of the pole, point of the celestial centre in the polar symbolism, is thus identified with the North as the point that locates the winter solstice in the solar symbolism; and by

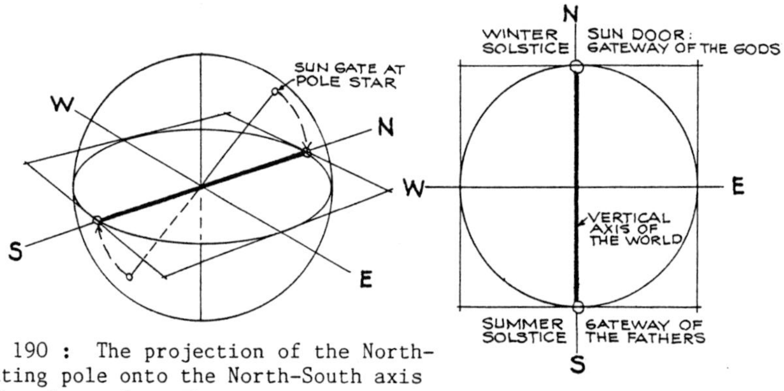

Fig. 190 : The projection of the North-pointing pole onto the North-South axis of the plane of earth.

a corresponding upward projection, its Southern extremity is identified with the South point, that which coincides with the summer solstice. The solstitial and polar axes are equated; the solstitial axis is now also the pole of the year; the poles of the spatial and temporal worlds are homologized. In this schema the North-South axis has become the equivalent of the vertical axis of the world; the cosmic section has been projected onto plan.

This marriage of the solar and the polar modalities of celestial symbolism involves a relocation of the Gate of Cosmic Exit. It no longer stands at the pivotal hub of the celestial sphere nor at the zenith, vertically above the point of crossing of the directional axes, but is equated with the North point upon the plan, that is, with the point where the North-South axis cuts the periphery of the cosmos. This is the location of the Gateway of the Gods, the Gate that gives access to the Pathway of the Gods (devayāna) leading to the supernal realms lying beyond the cupola of the cosmos. The South, its directional and symbolic complementary, locates the Gateway of the Forefathers, the Gate that gives access to the Pathway of the Forefathers (pitryāna), leading back into the cosmos. The Gateway of the Forefathers is the Gateway passed through by unregenerate men : it is simultaneously an exit and an entry. The Comprehensor, entering the world through the Gate

105. Guénon, 1968, p. 134.

way of the Forefathers, ascends to the Northern Gate and passes through, never to return unless to aid and guide those who follow; but the ignorant fall back to the Southern Gate, pass out through the same Gate whereby they entered and are reborn into yet another level of existence. The Northern Gate is an exit solely; the Southern Gate is both an entry and an exit, for to pass through this portal is at once to pass from one level of cosmic rebirth to another : it is a death to one world and simultaneously a rebirth into another state within the ever-turning Wheel of Suffering. "At what time those who tend towards Union (without having effectively realized it) quit manifested existence, either never to return or destined to return to it, I will teach thee, O Bharata. Fire, light, daytime, waxing moon, the half year when the sun ascends towards the North, it is under these luminous signs that those go to Brahman who know Brahman. Smoke, night, waning moon, the half year when the sun descends towards the South, it is under these shadowy signs that there pass to the sphere of the moon those who later will return (to new states of manifestation). These are the two permanent Paths of the manifested world, the one bright, the other dim; by the one they go to return no more (from the unmanifested to the manifested); by the other they go to return again (into manifestation)".[106]

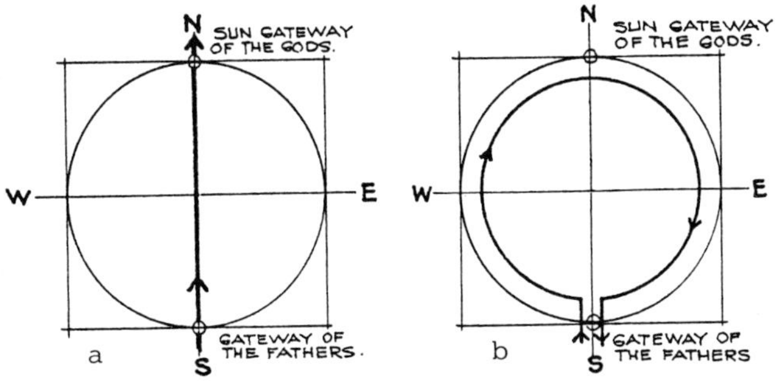

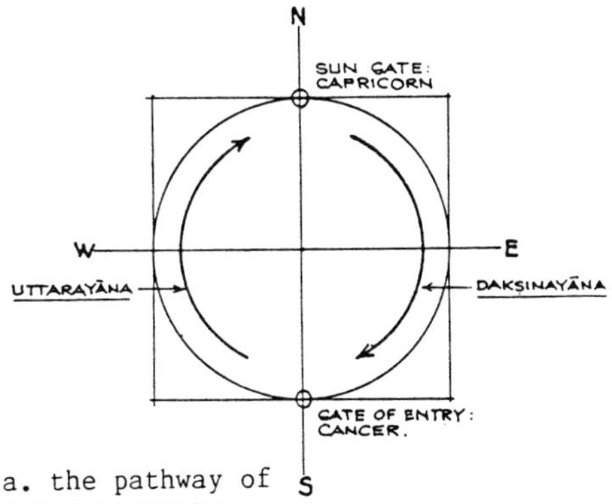

Fig. 191 : The two pathways through the cosmos : a. the pathway of the Comprehensor; b. the pathway of the unregenerate.

Fig. 192 : The ascending and descending courses of the sun.

The Comprehensor's ascent from the Southern Gate of Entry to the Northern Gate of Exit is symbolically prefigured in the ascending course (_uttarayāna_) of the sun in its annual cycle, in which it climbs from the sign of Cancer in the South to the sign of Capricorn in the North; the descent of those who fail to achieve Enlightenment, on the other hand, is the symbolic equivalent of the descending course of the sun (_dakṣinayāna_) in the reverse direction, towards the South.

The Sanscrit word for "North" is _uttara_, which is literally "the highest point" and the ascending march of the sun (_uttarayāna_) is a movement towards that point. But the North is the direction of the winter solstice and the South is that of summer. In terms of the seasons the ascent to the North would therefore seem to be an approach to the side of winter and lesser light, and in this sense the lowest point of the cycle. The _avatāra_ is born at the winter solstice, which corresponds to the North, and ascends towards the light of summer in the South. However, the contradiction is only apparent. The symbolism is applied at two levels : the march of the sun belongs to the celestial order, while the succession

106. BG VIII.23-26. The same teaching is given more extensively in CU V.10.1-6. Cf. CU IV.15.5; BU 6.2.15-16; RV I.72.7; II.2.4; ŚB I.9.3.2; and see Guénon, 1945, Ch. XXI, pp. 148ff.; Radhakrishnan, 1953, p. 432.

of the seasons belongs to the terrestrial order, and following the general law of symbolic analogy the correlation of two different levels entails an inversion of relationship, so that what is highest in the celestial realm becomes the lowest in the terrestrial, and vice versa.

Initiation rites reflect this symbolism. To accord with the spatial symbolism of axial ascent, the initiate would need to enter the initiatic space - cave, hut or building - from below, at a point on the floor directly beneath the ridge pole, then ascend the axis and leave through the mid-point of the roof.[107] The practical difficulties posed by this ascent

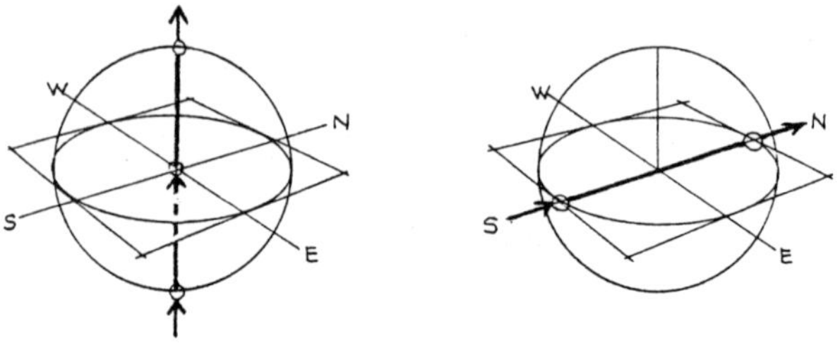

Fig. 193 : Vertical ascent represented on the horizontal plane.

are overcome by transposing the symbolism, as above, to the horizontal plane. The initiate enters the ritual space by an entry in the South, which is symbolically at the foot of the vertical axis, and proceeds to the exit in the North, which is symbolically at its summit. Here he quits the universe. His entry by the Southern door is a second birth, a birth into the cosmos; and his exit by the Northern door is a third birth, out of the cosmos.[108]

* * * * *

Some Vedic and Buddhist formulations introduce a variation on the theme of the Gateway of the Gods in the North : the Gateway is not in the North, but in the North-East; and accordingly the Gateway of the Forefathers is not in the South but in the South-West. This expresses the same symbolism but with an added and more explicit reference. In the annual cycle through the seasons the sun ascends from the North of winter to the South of summer by passing through the East of spring; and in its descent it passes from the South of summer through the West of autumn to the North of winter. In this the East is the side of light and life and the West is the side of darkness and death. Consequently the Gate of the Gods is located in the North to accord with the polar symbolism, but is inclined towards the side of light and life, the East, while the Gateway of the Forefathers, located in the South, is inclined towards the West, the direction of darkness and death. Thus it is that on some stupa foundation stones, marked with the cross of the four directions, the NE-SW axis is also added to indicate the positions of entry and exit. The symbolism likewise explains the importance attached to the North-East in Buddhist monastery, temple and town planning. To cite but one example, from Japan, an enormous temple and monastic complex of the Tendai school is built upon Mt. Hiei to the North-East of Kyōto, a city that is laid out on strict North-South axes of orientation. In the popular imagination the Hiei group of temples protects the city from malevolent influences coming from that direction, but esoterically it marks and guards the city's Sun Door leading to the realms of Enlightenment.

* * * * *

107. For the symbolism of the cave, see above, pp. 201 ff.

108. The second and third births correspond to the lesser and greater mysteries of the Greeks.

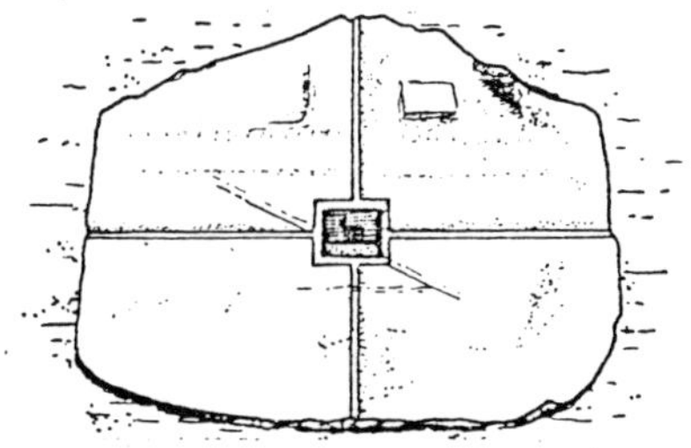

Fig. 194 : Foundation stone of a Japanese tower-stupa. The stone, on which the "heart-pillar" (Jap. shin-bashira) rests, has a recess for a deposit, grooves indicating the cardinal directions, and a secondary groove indicating the directions of the Gates of the Forefathers and the Gods.

The Gateway of Exit is located at the winter solstice in the North. The North point is the polar equivalent of the Solar Gate that leads out of the cosmos. Again, the North is the point that marks the end of the year; it is the extreme position of the sun prior to its descent into the South and summer. The end of the year is equated with the Door of Heaven, as is indicated in the previously cited text : "I will tell thee that, which knowing, ye perceive the door of the world of heaven and having successfully come unhurt to the end of the Year, shall speedily attain the world of heaven";[109] and "it is thus the immortal that lies beyond this Year".[110] Again, "He alone gains the Year who knows its doors; for what were he to do with a house who cannot find his way inside?... Spring is a door and likewise winter is a door thereof. This same Year the sacrificer enters as a world of Heaven".[111] "The two ends of the Year are winter and spring"[112] and he who is filled with the magical power of asceticism (tapas) "swiftly goes from East to Northern ocean".[113]

The North, location of the sign of Capricorn, is the "end of the world" in the spatial, temporal and soteriological senses, and this as much for Buddhism as Brahmanism : "There is no surcease from sorrow until world's end (loka-nirodha) is reached";[114] and thus it is that at his parinirvāṇa the Buddha is "headed North" (uttara-sīso).[115]

109. JUB IV.15.1. 110. ŚB X.2.6.4. 111. ŚB I.1.6.19.

112. JUB I.35. 113. AV XI.5.6. 114. A II.48-50.

115. D II.137.

18 ASCENT.

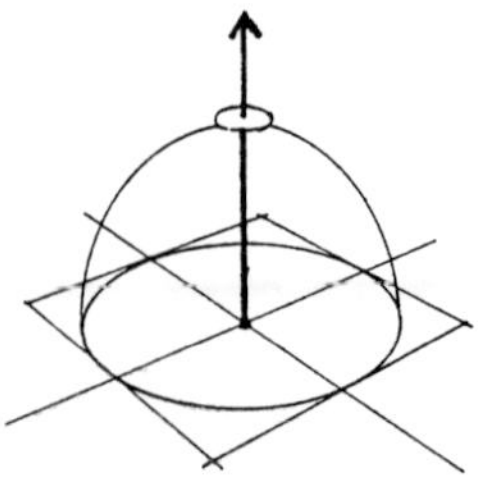

1. THE SYMBOLISM OF ASCENSION.

The central axis of the world is the pathway to Liberation. The central pole leads upwards to the Gateway of Escape, the Sun Door that opens out of the cosmos. For Hindus and Buddhists alike the spiritual way is an ascension of the axis of the world.[1] This "difficult ascent" (dūrohana)[2] is symbolically enacted in the Brahmanic ritual of vājapeya, in which the sacrificer climbs a sacrificial post (yūpa). The post is cut from a tree that is specifically felled for the purpose. During its felling the priest cries to it, "'Graze not the sky! hurt not the air! unite with the earth!' For verily that tree which they cut for the stake is a thunderbolt (vajra)".[3] The post is assimilated to the Cosmic Pillar : "With thy crest thou hast touched the sky; with thy middle thou hast filled the air; with thy foot thou hast steadied the earth".[4] It is assimilated to the thunderbolt (vajra)[5] and to the Cosmic Tree : "Lord of the Forest, raise thyself up on the loftiest spot on earth".[6] At the summit it carries a wheel rim of wheaten flour, symbol of the Sun Gate.[7] The sacrificer ascends to heaven by climbing the sacrificial post. Placing a ladder against it, he addresses his wife : "'Come, wife, ascend we to the sky!' She answers : 'Ascend we'".[8] These ritual words are exchanged three times and the sacrificer climbs the ladder. Reaching the top he touches the wheaten wheel and spreading out his arms like wings cries, "We have come to heaven, to the gods; we have become immortal".[9] "Verily the celebrant of the rite makes it a ladder and a bridge to attain the world of heaven".[10]

Ascending the post the sacrificer follows the pathway opened up by Agni in the beginning : "Agni rose aloft touching the sky; he opened the door of the world of heaven... him he lets pass who is the Comprehensor thereof",[11] and "Were the sacrificer not to ascend after him, he would be shut out from the world of heaven".[12] For those, however, who are not Comprehensors thereof, the door is shut. For them the post bars the way. "By means of the sacrifice the Gods gained that supreme authority they now yield. They spake, 'How can this (world) of ours be made unattainable to men?'... They barred the way (yopaya) by means of the sacrificial post (yūpa), they disappeared : and because they barred the sacrifice therewith, therefore it is called yūpa".[13] The Gods barred the way by setting the post point downwards, but men and Ṛṣis dug it out and set it upright, saying, "Rise erect, O Lord of the Forest", "Aloft to our aid do thou stand like Savitṛ the God (the Sun)", and thus gained a vision of heaven. "In that the

---

1. On the symbolism of ascension, see Eliade, 1960, Ch. V; 1958b, pp. 102ff.; 1964a, pp. 487ff.; 1961, pp. 47ff.; 1958a, pp. 318ff.

2. See Eliade, 1947; 1960, pp. 115ff. 3. ŚB III.6.4.13.

4. ŚB III.7.1.14. 5. ŚB III.6.4.18-27 & III.6.4.13, cited above.

6. RV III.8.3.

7. Auboyer, 1949, p. 79, n.4. The wheel is wheaten because "among plants wheat comes nearest to man, (for) it has no skin" (ŚB V.2.1.8). To pass through the Sun is to be "sun-skinned", i.e., the skin of the ego is flayed. 8. ŚB V.2.1.10. 9. TS I.7.9; etc. 10. TS VI.6.4.2.

11. AB III.42. 12. TS V.6.8.1. 13. ŚB III.2.2.2. On the meaning of yopaya as "to block or bar the way", see Coomaraswamy, 1977, 1, p. 402, n. 62; and also Eggeling, 1882, XXVI, p. 36, n. 1.

post is fixed upright (it avails) to the foreknowledge of the sacrifice and for the vision of the world of heaven". "The post is the thunderbolt (vajra); it stands erect as a weapon against him whom we hate", that is, the Enemy, Death.[14]

The difficult ascension (dūrohana) after Agni[15] is imitated in countless other climbing rites,[16] each of which is a ritual expression of the concept that "As one would keep climbing up a tree by steps... he keeps ascending these worlds"[17] and "ascending these worlds, he reaches that goal, that support".[18]

A similar symbolism is preserved in Buddhism.[19] The stupa's central axis equates the sacrificial post whereby the sacrificer climbs to the supra-empirical states; but in Buddhism it is not Heaven, but Awakening, that lies at the summit.

The *Majjhima-Nikāya*, describing the Buddha's nativity, relates that "as soon as he was born, the Bodhisattva placed his feet flat on the ground and, turning towards the North, took seven steps, sheltered by a white parasol. He contemplated the regions all around and said, with the voice of a bull[20] : "I am at the summit of the world, I am the best in the world, I am the eldest in the world; this is my last birth; for me there will never again be another existence".[21] The *Nidānakatha* adds further details. Emerging from Māyā's right side the Bodhisattva was received by the four regents of the directions. Standing upright, he faced the East. The thousands of worlds around him were "like an open and level place"... He contemplated the four directions, the nadir and the zenith and in these ten directions he saw no one equal to him. "This is the North (uttara disā, lit. "the upper region")", he said and took seven steps in that direction, accompanied by an entourage of gods, who held his parasol, his fan, and the other insignia of his royal rank. Stopping at his seventh step he cried out, with a voice like a lion's roar, "I am at the summit of the world...etc."[22] The myth is repeated with variations in other texts : the Buddha takes seven steps to the North, or in four, six or ten directions.[23]

The pole star in the Northern sky locates the point that is pierced by the pivotal axis that centres the rotation of the celestial sphere. In terms of polar, as opposed to solar symbolism, this is where the summit of the dome of heaven lies; here, in the North, is located the Gateway of Exit, the doorway of escape from the cosmos. With his seven steps towards the

---

14. AB II.1-2; cf. Coomaraswamy, 1977, 1, pp. 402 f.

15. AB IV.20-22; TS V.6.8.

16. E.g., JUB III.1.3.9; PB XVIII.10.10; ŚB V.2.1.5ff.; etc. The question is discussed by Coomaraswamy, 1977, 1, pp. 470ff., and see also the references given from Eliade in n. 1 above.

17. JUB I.3.2. 18. ŚB I.9.3.10.

19. For folklore equivalents, sometimes disguised, see Penzer and Tawney, 1924, 1, p. 153; 2, p. 387; 8, pp. 68ff.

20. The myth has been examined on pp. 40 and 242 ff., above. The "Bull of the World" signifies the leader of the herd of creatures and the "voice of the bull" is the voice of the leader of men. 21. M III.123.

22. Fausböll, *Jātaka* I.53; Rhys Davids, 1880, p. 67; Mus, 1935, p. 483.

23. Lamotte, 1944, 1, pp. 16ff., lists the texts.

North the Buddha mounts to the summit of the universe, pacing out as he ascends the directions of space, here superimposed as rungs upon a ladder. His steps are an upward progress to the apical eminence of the universe. With his seventh step he reaches the top of the Mountain, the point whence spatial extension deploys. The reiterated references to orientation, the primacy of the North, the inspection of the directions, the role of the regents of space - emphasise that the referent of this symbolism is spatial deployment and that the Buddha's seventh step is a transcendence of the spatial condition and a return to the centre of the universe.

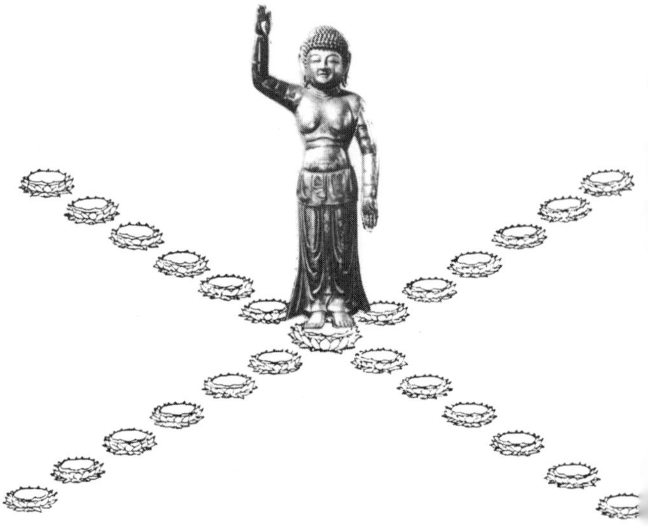

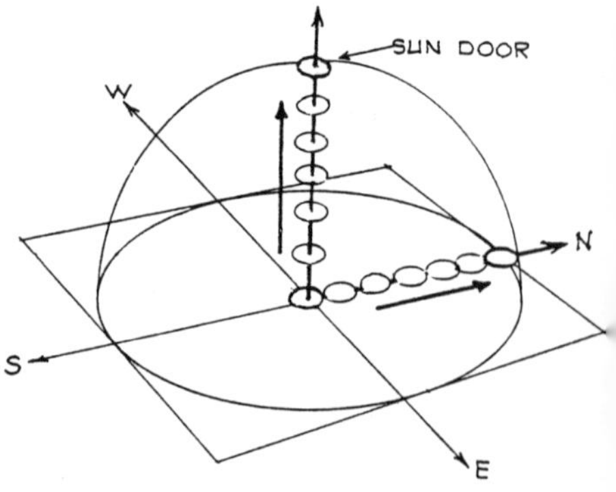

Fig. 195 : The Buddha's nativity. The infant Buddha stands upon superimposed lotuses, representing the steps he takes to encompass the whole universe and ascend to the Sun Door.

Fig. 196 : The seven steps in the four directions taken by the infant Buddha at his birth. He points upwards and downwards to indicate his preeminence in all the levels of existence, both above and below.

Fig. 197 : The Buddha's seven steps to the North are equivalent to seven steps to the Sun Door at the zenith of the cosmos.

To reach "the summit of the universe" (lokagge) is also to reach its point of origin, the"eldest" place, so that the Buddha can declare, "I am the eldest in the world". He has become contemporary with the world's beginning; the Buddha and the cosmos are coeval. "He has abolished Time and the Creation, and finds himself in the a-temporal instant that precedes the cosmogony".[25]

---

25. Eliade, 1960, p. 114; 1961, p. 76.

At each step taken by the Buddha a lotus springs up to support his foot. "(The Bodhisattva), who was like the constellation of the seven Ṛṣis (the Great Bear), calmly took seven firm steps, and beneath his feet lotuses appeared, uncrushed and tall..."[26] In Indian symbology the flowering of the lotus represents the deployment of the directions of space; its petals open out from a centre that locates the midpoint of the world.[27] The seven lotuses that mark the footsteps of the Buddha are to be thought of as strung like beads upon the line that marks the axis of the cosmos so as to form a series of superimposed worlds. The placing of the lotuses side by side in a line towards the North is a conventional representation of a vertical ordering : the lotuses stand one above the other on a vertical line leading to the cosmic apex. Just as the ascent of the sun in its annual course is from the Southern gate of cosmic access to the Northern gate of cosmic exit, so the Buddha ascends through the levels of the universe.

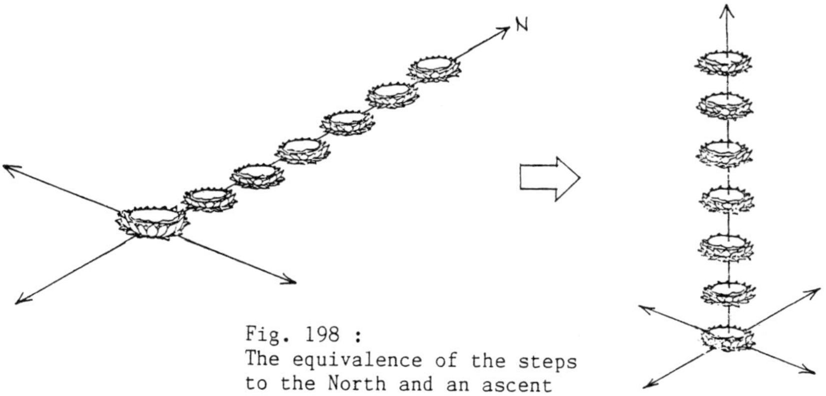

Fig. 198 :
The equivalence of the steps to the North and an ascent of the vertical axis of the universe.

The opening of lotuses at each of his seven steps shows that the Buddha assimilates and establishes sovereignty over each of the seven levels of the universe. Before he commences his ascent the Buddha contemplates the four directions and sees that his equal does not exist at that plane of existence. Moving up through the levels of the cosmos he repeats this process at each of them in turn - he assures himself of his sovereignty over the extended universe at every level of existence. This paradigmatic action establishes his overlordship of space and also of time, since the directions are homologous with the seasons, the year and the Great Year.[28] The symbolic references are reinforced when the text compares the Buddha to the seven Rsis, which are the stars that revolve about the Pole.[29]

The symbolism of the seven steps is parallelled in another Buddha legend. In the account of the forty nine days that follow the Buddha's attainment of Enlightenment it is told how for seven days he stood gazing at the Bodhi Tree with unblinking eyes. At the end of this time the gods began

---

26. Aśvaghoṣa I.33; Cowell, 1893, p. 5; 1894, p. 5; Nandargikar, 1911, p. 7. See also Mus, 1935, p. 483, n. 3. Cf. *Lalita Vistara* VIII; Viennot, 1954, p. 134. 27. See above, pp. 97ff.

28. See above, pp. 46 ff., and cf. Mus, 1935, pp. 489f.

29. See above, p. 65.

to wonder and to have doubts, asking, "Is this all that happens on the attainment of Buddhahood....?" Knowing their thoughts the Buddha performed a great miracle by causing a crystal portico with ten thousand columns to appear.[30] "Then... he spent seven days walking up and down in that jewelled cloister which stretched from East to West".[31] "In the second week[32] the Tathāgata took a long walk taking in the regions of the three thousand great thousands of worlds... and in the fourth week the Tathāgata took a short walk from the sea in the East to the sea in the West".[33]

A famous railing at Bodhgayā encloses the place of the Buddha's promenade (caṅkrama).[34] The railing was described by the Chinese pilgrim Hsuan Tsang : "To the North of the Bodhi Tree is the place where the Buddha walked. When the Buddha had attained full Awakening he did not rise from his seat but remained there for seven days in meditation. When he rose he went to the North of the Bodhi Tree and walked for seven days, coming and going from East to West, on a space of about ten paces. Extraordinary flowers, eighteen in number, appeared at the places of his footsteps. Later a brick platform, about three feet high, was erected on this spot".[35]

The legend of the caṅkrama repeats the symbolism of the seven steps. The contingent details are different - the walk is along the East-West axis, not on the axis leading to the North, and a diurnal and solar symbolism replaces an annual and polar one - but the essential significance of the two legends is the same. In the drama of the nativity the Bodhisattva takes seven steps; in the caṅkrama the number increases to eighteen. With meticulous detail Mus has shown that the eighteen-fold division of the caṅkrama is in fact nine double paces (18 = 9 x 2), and that there are two ways of numbering the planetary spheres, either as seven or as nine, when Rāhu and Ketu, the "planet" of the eclipse and its "tail", are added.[36] We have seen that each of the planetary spheres corresponds to a direction and in the same way that the seven steps of the Buddha at his nativity simultaneously traverse the seven planetary spheres and the seven directions of space, so similarly the nine double steps of the caṅkrama pace out the eight directions and the centre that correspond to the nine planetary spheres.

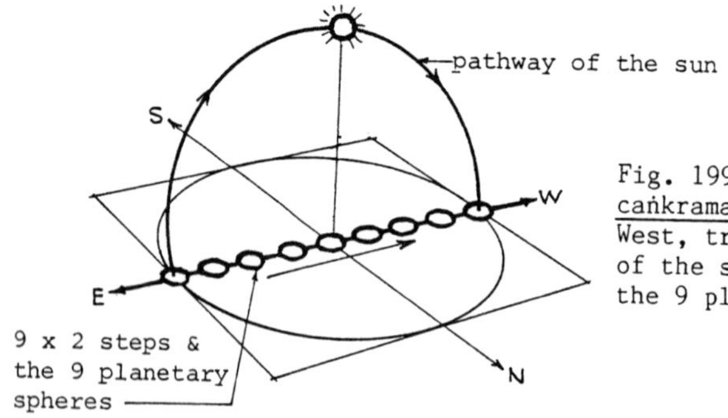

Fig. 199 : The 9 x 2 steps of the caṅkrama, proceeding from East to West, trace the diurnal movement of the sun and its passage through the 9 planetary spheres.

---

30. Alabaster, 1871, pp. 161ff.; cf. Mus, 1935, p. 477.

31. Rhys Davids, 1880, p. 106. 32. The chronology of the seven weeks' retreat varies from text to text. 33. *Lalita Vistara*, Foucaux, 1884, 1, p.314

34. For descriptions of the railings enclosing the caṅkrama at Bodhgayā, see Coomaraswamy, 1927, p. 32 and p. 32, n. 8 for references. See also Goetz, 1959, p. 57. 35. Julien, 1857, pp. 470f.; cf. Beal, 1906, pp. 122f.

36. See Mus, 1935, p. 487; Senart, 1882, p. 141, n. 4.

The walk "from the sea in the East to the sea in the West" follows the daily course of the sun, passing by way of the Zenith from the place of its rising to the place of its setting.[37] As previously explained,[38] this daily course of the sun is a measuring out of the four directions. The walk from the Eastern to the Western oceans encompasses the whole expanse of earth, environed by waters in the four directions. The same idea is conveyed by the legend of the Buddha's dream, in which he sees himself as a giant holding the two oceans in his arms.[39] The same symbolism inheres in the ritual of the cakravartin's consecration (abhiṣeka), in which he is aspersed with waters taken from the four seas to indicate his dominion over the total extent of earth;[40] it is also apparent in the legend that tells us that prior to his unblinking contemplation of the Bodhi Tree the Buddha bathed in the four oceans.[41]

* * * * *

In a complementary expression of the concept of ascension to the Sun Door, the Buddhist literature makes many references to arhats who "move at will", who have the power of flight and rise up to break through the roof plate of the house. The Brahmanic prototype of the ascending arhat is Marut who "having done what had to be done (that is, 'having stood free from determination, free from conception, free from the love of self'), departed by the Northern course of the sun, for there is no way thither by a side path. This is the path to Brahman here in the world. Bursting open the Sun Door, he rose on high and departed".[42] With the same symbolic import the Buddhist texts speak of arhats who "fly through the air, breaking through the roof of the palace"[43] or, "flying at their own will, break and pass through the roof of the house and rise up into the air";[44] and the arhat Moggallāna, "breaking through the round of the roof plate, sprang into the air".[45]

The locus classicus of this symbolic construct is the story of the Buddha's breaking through the ridge plate of the world at the time of his Enlightenment.[46] Seated beneath the Bodhi Tree, Śākyamuni concentrates and integrates his mind (samādhi) and in contemplation ascends the Cosmic Axis until, as the sun rises, he breaks free from the world of space and time, emerging through the roof plate (kaṇṇikā) of the cosmos, symbolically conceived as a house, and sings his triumphant song of victory :

> "Seeking the builder of the house
> I have run my course in the vortex
> Of countless births, never escaping the hobble (of death);
> Ill is repeated birth after birth!
> Householder, art seen!
> Never again shalt thou build me a house.
> All of the rigging is broken,
> The peak of the roof (kaṇṇikā) is shattered :
> Its aggregations passed away,
> Mind has reached the destruction of cravings".[47]

---

37. Cf. the myth of the Sun Pillar in Lake Anavatapta, p. 26, above.

38. See above, pp. 30 ff. 39. A III.240.

40. See above, pp. 92 f., and below, pp. 345ff.

41. *Buddhacarita*, XV.III; Cowell, 1894, p. 159. 42. MU VI.30; Coomaraswamy, 1977, 1, p. 473. 43. *Jātaka* III.472. 44. DhA I.63.

45. DhA III.66; *Jātaka* IV.228-229; Eliade, 1960, p. 190; Coomaraswamy, 1977, 1, p. 457. 46. See above, p. 41.

47. See Coomaraswamy, 1943a, p. 54; 1956a, p. 28; Warren, 1922, p. 83

In a brilliant series of scholarly masterpieces[48] Coomaraswamy analyzed this theme of breaking through the roof plate and showed that the roof plate is symbolically identified with the Sun Door that leads out of the cosmos. The circular roof plate (kaṇṇikā) is the structural member that holds together the rafters at the apex of a domed or conical roof. To the roof plate, or "king post", the rafters (or "beams" in both senses) converge in the manner of spokes to the hub of a wheel or ribs to the pole of a parasol or the rays, or beams, of light to the sun : wheel, parasol, sun and circular roof plate are coincident in symbolic meaning, variations on a theme of radiation from a centre. Whatever has been said on the significance of the wheel, the parasol and the sun is equally applicable to the circular roof. The roof form is charged with a potency of metaphysical meaning; the architectural element resonates with a rich reverberation of significance. The kaṇṇikā is the Sun Gate, the doorway or exit through which the Worthy (arhat) the "movers-at-will", leave the world. It is the "Door of the Summit" (agga-dvāra), "the Doorway to Buddhahood", since the Buddha is himself the Summit (agga).[49]

The symbolism of the Cosmic House whose roof beams come together at the roof has, when interpreted at the microcosmic level, a significance that pertains directly to the core concern of Buddhist doctrine, namely, the attainment of Awakening by the concentration of mind achieved by meditation (dhyāna). The equivalent and precursive Brahmanic teaching is expressed in terms of an explicit architectural symbolism : "The Breath of Life (prāṇa = the Spirit, Brahman, the Gale) is a Pillar. And just as (in a house) all the beams are met together (samāhita) in the king post, so it is that in the Breath (the functions of) the eye, the ear, the intellect, the tongue, the senses and the whole self are unified (samāhita)".[50] Coomaraswamy points out that samāhita is literally the same as to be "in samādhi", since both words derive from sam-ā-dhā, "to put together, to make to meet, to con-centrate, to resolve", and hence to resolve to a common principle. Samādhi is "composition, consent", and in Yoga the "consummation" of dhyāna, an at-one-ment, integration or unification.[51] In modern colloquial parlance the Awakened is one who has "put it all together", in a total and cosmic sense. He has returned to the centre of his being, which is coincident with the centre of the universe, where the senses are withdrawn into the Source whence they flowed outward to their objects, and where space and time are likewise withdrawn into the principial point whence they devolved into existence. The reintegration of being and the universe in contemplation is a reversal of the procedure from unity to quadrature, from the one to the many, whereby the worlds and the beings who dwell in them come forth into existence. They return to the principial point and are once more subsumed within their own true nucleus of origin.

There are Buddhist equivalents to the above-cited Brahmanic text : "Just as every one of the rafters of a building with a domed roof go up to its roof plate, incline towards its roof plate, and are assembled at its roof plate, and the roof plate is called the apex of all, even so, your Majesty, every one of these skilful habits (P. kusalā-dhammā)[52] inclines towards samādhi, leans towards samādhi, and bears upon samādhi".[53] The same idea is

---

48. See the references given in n. 1, p. 274 above, and esp. Coomaraswamy, 1977, 1, pp. 459ff.; see also "Pali kaṇṇikā : Circular Roof Plate", *ibid.* 49. A II.7; D III.147; cf. Coomaraswamy, 1977, 1, p. 7, n. 16. For the agga-dvāna, "Door of the Summit", see 1945b, p. 473, n. 12.

50. AĀ III.2.1; SA VIII. 51. Coomaraswamy, 1977, 1, p. 456, n.61.

52. Defined in Mil II.1.9 (33); see Coomaraswamy, 1977, p. 457, n. 63.

53. Mil II.1.13 (38). Cf. pp. 62 ff. above, where this symbolism is related to the indriyāni.

repeated in the *Majjhima-Nikāya* : "Just as the roof plate of a dome mansion is the peak that ties together and holds together, just so the sheltering roof of the skilful habits (is the peak that ties together and holds together) the six states of consciousness".[54]

The identification of the act of breaking through the roof plate with the attainment of samādhi through meditation explains why, in the above-quoted story of the arhat Moggallāna's flight through the roof plate his ascension is said to have been dependent on his first having "clothed the body with the raiment of contemplation".[55]

The breaking through the roof plate of the world is the culmination of an ascension up the cosmic axis. This ascent is expressed as a "flight" or a "climbing".[56] The power of flight is a recurrent theme in the early Buddhist writings. "Just so, O king, can the Bhikkhu, who has the power of flight and has mastery over his mind, when he has made his mind rise up to the occasion, travel through the sky by means of his mind".[57] This power of flight is listed as one of the siddhis, or transcendental powers, in both the Hindu and Buddhist traditions : in Buddhism it is the first of the "four magical powers of translation" (gamana),[58] and Patañjali gives it as one of the powers attained through the practice of Yoga.[59] "The Sacrificer, having become a bird, soars to the world of heaven".[60] Numerous texts speak of the wings that one must possess to attain to the top of the sacrificial tree,[61] of the "Gander whose seat is in the light",[62] of the sacrificial horse that, in the shape of a bird, carries the sacrifice to heaven,[63] and so on.[64] The Muni of the *Ṛg Veda* declares : "Exhilarated by the sanctity of the Muni we have mounted upon the wind; behold, mortals, (in them) our forms!... The steed of the wind, the friend of Vāyu, the Muni is instigated by the deity..."[65] The Buddhist legends say that Lake Anavatapta can only be reached by those possessing the power of flight. The Buddha and the arhats are able to fly there "in the twinkling of an eye". The Hindu myths give similar accounts of the Ṛṣis.[66]

Coomaraswamy has indicated the true nature of this power of flying. It implies wings, which are characteristic of angels "as being an intellectual substance independent of local motion; an intellectual substance, as such, being immediately present at the point to which its attention is directed"[67] : "Intellect is the support of birds".[68] The images of flight and "wings" signify intelligence, "the understanding of secret things and metaphysical truths"[69] : "Intelligence (manas) is the swiftest of birds";[70] and "he who understands has wings".[71]

---

54. M I.322-3. 55. Dh III.66; *Jātaka* IV.228-9; Eliade, 1960, p. 108; Coomaraswamy, 1977, 1, p. 452.

56. Eliade has devoted considerable attention to the phenomenon of spiritual "flight" and "climbing" in various traditions. See e.g., Eliade, 1964a, pp. 407ff.; 1960, pp. 90ff.; 1958a, pp. 327ff.; and see also Guénon, 1945, pp. 148ff.; 1962, pp. 235ff.

57. Mil III.7.9 (85). 58. Vis 396. 59. *Yoga-sūtra* III.45.

60. PB V.3.5. 61. JUB III.13.9. 62. KU V.2. 63. ŚB XIII.2.6.

64. Eliade, 1964a, pp. 407ff. 65. RV X.136.3-5.

66. Eliade, 1958a, p. 327. 67. Coomaraswamy, 1977, 1, p. 452.

68. RV VI.9.5; etc. 69. Eliade, 1960, p. 105; 1958a, p. 329.

70. RV VI.9.5. 71. PB IV.1.13.

Power of flight is the prerogative of arhats, the Worthy; it is also possessed by kings, magicians, sages and mystics of every kind.[72] The kings of South-East Asia were carried shoulder high and their feet never touched the ground; like gods and arhats they "flew through the air".[73] Eliade has pointed out that this symbolism is susceptible of a dual interpretation : it refers both to transcendence and to the gaining of freedom,[74] these being the two aspects of an ontological mutation of the human being, and a "rupture of the plane of experience".[75] Flight and ascension are symbolic formulae. They are not to be thought of as bodily, but as a purely spiritual locomotion.

So closely is the power of flight associated with the arhats, the Worthies, in the Theravāda outlook of the Sinhalese that from the word arhat they have derived the verb rahatva, "to disappear, to pass instantly from place to place".[76] The arhats are kamacarin, "movers-at-will", those who "no longer need to move at all in order to be anywhere".[77] In Tantric Buddhism the same idea is embodied in the Dākīnīs, "who walk through the air" and "go to heaven".[78]

It is to be understood that whatever form its expression might take in the myths and legends, the flight of Buddhas and arhats, metaphysically considered, is always vertical and up the axis of the cosmos, through the Sun Door to the realm of immortality. The Awakened One who flies through the roof plate of the Cosmic House can claim that he has "obtained blessedness, the universal dignity of the Buddha".[79]

2. THE SYMBOLISM OF THE STAIRWAYS.

Terrace stupas typically have stairways in each of the four directions. In South-East Asia, and occasionally elsewhere, these flights of steps have snake-balustrades, whose ophidian nature is indicated by the makara heads or serpent heads (normally five- or seven-fold) with which they terminate. The motif is common in both Hindu and Buddhist architecture and expresses a complex symbolism that is shared by the two traditions. It pertains to the theme of ascension.

The most impressive and famous examples of the serpent-balustrades are those on the causeways leading over the moats to the great gateways of the Bayon at Angkor Thom,[80] where rows of devas on the one side and asuras on the other clutch the bodies of seven-headed serpents (nāga). It was assumed by earlier scholars that this was a vast depiction of the Churning of the

---

72. Eliade, 1960, p. 100. 73. Hocart, 1923, p. 80. Roman, Islamic and Chinese parallels are given in Eliade, 1960, pp. 99f.

74. Eliade, 1960, p. 106; 1958a, p. 329; 1957, p. 79.

75. Eliade, 1960, pp. 108f.

76. Hocart, 1923, p. 80; cf. Eliade, 1958a, p. 329; 1960, p. 108.

77. Coomaraswamy, 1946, p. 184; cf. Eliade, 1960, p. 108.

78. Van Durme, 1932, p. 374, n. 2.

79. *Sutta-vibhanga* I.1.4, cited in Mus, 1938; cf. Eliade, 1957, p. 79; 1952, p. 238.

80. Examples on a smaller scale are to be found at Prah Khan and Bantaei Chmar.

a

b

c

Fig. 200 (above) : The stairways of a Burmese stupā (a), of stupas from Afghanistan (b) and at Borobudur, Java (c).

(below) : Examples of serpent-balustrades terminating in a makara- or serpent-head. a. Caṇḍi Mendut, Java. b. Angkor Wat, Kampuchea.

a

b

Milky Ocean : the body of the snake is to be thought of as wrapped around the central temple, which represents the Cosmic Mountain, and is pulled by the Gods on the one side and the Titans on the other so as to twirl the Mountain in the manner of a churning rod and thus extract the beverage of immortality (amṛta).[81]

Fig. 201 : The serpent balustrades at Angkor Thom. The body of the serpent on one side of the causeway is held by asuras and that on the other side is held by devas.

Later scholars, led by Mus, have tendered an alternative interpretation the serpent is the rainbow, representing a passageway, a bridge of communication, between Earth and Heaven.[82] The mythic paradigm is found in the story of the Buddha's descent from Indra's Heaven, where he had gone to instruct his mother, Māyā. Having stayed there for three months, preaching the Dharma to her and to the gods, he returned to earth by a rainbow ladder, created by the gods. The ladder of his descent was threefold : the central flight, used by the Buddha himself, was of seven colours and seven precious stones; the flanking steps, used by the gods Indra and Brahmā who accompanie the Buddha as he descended, were of silver and gold; and the whole was supported on the backs of two serpents... and the ladders were as three rainbows to the eyes of men on earth".[83]

---

81. For the Churning of the Milky Ocean, see also above, pp. 177f. Cf. Groslier, 1956, pp. 155f.; Chevalier and Gheerbrant, III, p. 252, s.v., Nāga; Wheatley, 1971, p. 483; Coedes, 1963, p. 47, who sees the gateway at the end of the causeway as the churning rod, rather than the temple proper. This in no way alters the symbolism.

82. See Mus, 1937, p. 69 : "...at Angkor Thom there is not one serpent but two. Gods and titans each carry their own. Further, instead of pulling against each other, they are in two parallel rows facing those who arrive. It is quite clear that they are not churning anything..."; and see also Wales, 1977, pp. 123f. Mus' theory is now accepted by many scholars : see e.g., Giteau, 1951, pp. 156ff.; Boisselier, 1966, p. 103, n. 3.

83. DhA III.125; cf. Zimmer, 1955, pp. 240 & 336; Luce, 1969, p. 240.

The two interpretations are not necessarily incompatible but can be shown to have a common reference; and they can also be shown to apply not only to the balustrades on either side of the causeways at Angkor Thom but to every example of serpent-balustrade, including those which flank the stairways of terrace-stupas.

a

b

c

d

Fig. 202 : a. The Buddha's descent from the Trāyastriṃśa Heaven. The Buddha is represented aniconically, by footsteps at the top and bottom of the triple ladder.
b. A dragon- or serpent-balustrade from Vietnam.
c. Stairways in the four directions of a Burmese stupa.
d. Tibetan stupa with stairways in the four directions. Such stupas are called "stupas of the descent from heaven" and represent the Buddha's descent from the Trāyastriṃśa Heaven. (See Combaz, 1932, pp. 238f., and Tucci, 1932, pp. 21ff.).

The two myths relating to the serpent-balustrade - the churning of the ocean and the descent of the rainbow bridge - are two expressions of an archetypal theme that recurs in various forms in the mythologies of many peoples.[84] The meaning of this theme, which in its Hindu-Buddhist context involves a rich profusion of fusions and interconnections, directly relates to the symbolism of the ascent of the stupa levels.

---

84. Guénon, 1962, Ch. LXIV ("Le pont et l'arc-en-ciel"). The theme of the rainbow-bridge or rainbow-ladder appears in the myths of peoples as widely separated as Iran and North America, China and Africa. For the Scandinavians the rainbow is the Pifrost bridge, for the Japanese the floating bridge of Heaven; for the Pygmies, Hawaiians, Maoris and many peoples of Polynesia, Melanesia and Indonesia it is the bridge of the gods that joins Heaven and Earth. See Chevalier and Gheerbrant, 1973, 1, pp. 117ff., s.v., Arc-en-ciel; Eliade, 1964a, pp. 131ff. ("Ascent of the Rainbow"), where further references are given. The rainbow-snake assimilation is similarly widespread.

a. <u>The Symbolism of the Rainbow Bridge</u>.

The symbolism of the rainbow relates to that of the bridge. Connecting the "banks" of Heaven and Earth, the bridge spans the river or sea of Mid-space; it links this shore of saṃsāra, the domain of birth and death, to the further shore of nirvāṇa, the domain of deathlessness.[85] To cross the bridge is to ascend the vertical axis of the world, passing upward to the Sun Gate.[86]

The rainbow is likewise a bridge, but corresponds to the arched bridge rather than the straight.[87] The difference between the two symbolic expressions - the straight bridge and the arched - is that between the way of the vertical axis that leads directly to the Sun Door, and the "peripheral" way that leads through a series of hierarchical states, following a spiral that unwinds around the central axis. This corresponds to the spiral progress marked out in the ritual circumambulation (pradakṣina) of the terrace-stupa : ascending by the stairway in the East, the direction of sunrise and beginnings, the devotee turns to the left at each terrace and walks in a clockwise direction with his right side to the stupa, thus passing successively through the directions of space at ever higher levels.[88]

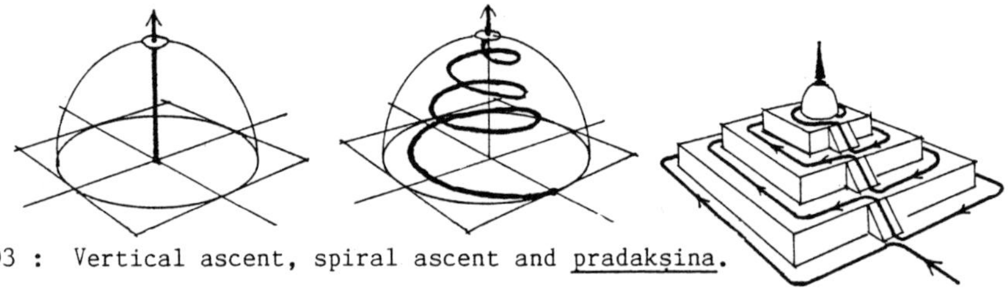

Fig. 203 : Vertical ascent, spiral ascent and pradakṣina.

The rainbow relates to this spatial symbolism by way of its seven colours, or, more precisely, its six colours and white. The six colours of the rainbow are the three primaries - red, yellow and blue - and the three complementaries - orange, purple and green. Placed on the circumference of a circle the three primaries will be found at the three points of an equilateral triangle; the three complementaries will be at the points of a second triangle which is the reverse of the first, in such a way that

---

85. In Vedic formulations the bridge is homologous to the Breath-thread (sūtrātman) that traces to the Sun. The word for "bridge" in the *Ṛg Veda* is setu, "line", from root si, "to attach", with reference to early bridges made of ropes, which literally tied one bank to the other. See Guénon, 1962 p. 379; D.L. Coomaraswamy, 1944. The bridge is the ray of the Sun's light, the beam (in both senses), the trunk of the Tree, that connects the worlds. In this it is to be understood that the bridge, as with all symbols of the axis mundi such as the axle of the cosmic chariot, is to be thought of as vertical.

86. For the symbolism of the bridge, see Guénon, 1962, Ch. LXIII ("Le symbolisme du pont"); also D.L. Coomaraswamy, 1944, *passim* ; Chevalier and Gheerbrant, 1973, 3, p. 47, s.v., Pont.

87. The curved bridges of Shintō shrines in Japan are of this type, referring to the Floating Bridge of Heaven, described in the myths as a rainbow.

88. Cf. above, p. 235.

each primary colour is placed at a diametrically opposed position to its complementary;[89] each complementary occupies a position of the arc joining the points of the two primaries by whose combination it is produced; the other nuances of colour in the spectrum correspond to all the other points on the circumference; and, finally, the seventh "colour", white, occupies the centre.

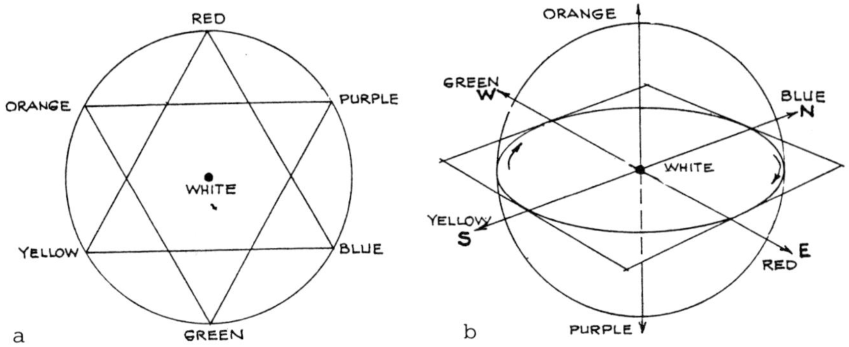

Fig. 204 : a. The wheel of the colours; b. the colours and the seven directions of space (one schema).

Laid out in this way the seven colours form a wheel with six spokes, which is the two dimensional equivalent of a three-dimensional cross having six branches emanating from a centre. In this way the colours correspond to the seven directions of space. In this schema the "colour" white plays the same role in relation to the six colours as the centre plays in relation to the six directions. It is located at the point where all oppositions are resolved in unity. In the same way that the dimensionless centre is the principial point whence the six directions proceed, so also white, which is "colourless", synthetically contains all colours and is the principle whence they derive : the six colours and the nuances that are formed by their mixture are merely a differentiation of white light, just as the directions of space are only the development of the possibilities contained in the primordial point.[90]

By way of these associations the seven colours of the rainbow-staircase are assimilated to the seven directions of space. The ascent of the rainbow stairway is symbolically equivalent to the seven steps taken by the Buddha at his nativity. It is a progress through the six directions back to the seventh "direction", the dimensionless and spaceless point of Unity; it is a return to the hub of the six-spoked Wheel of the World; it is a transcendence of the spatial condition. The Buddha's descent of the rainbow-staircase, coming down from the celestial spheres to the world of men, is yet another expression of the genesis of the spatio-temporal world from its Principle; it is a descent from the point-summit of the universe into the world of spatial and temporal differentiation.[91]

89. The figure thus formed is the previously mentioned Seal of Solomon, a basic symbol in every tradition.

90. These considerations are taken almost verbatim from Guénon, 1962, Ch. LVII ("Les sept rayons et l'arc-en-ciel"), which contains further elucidations.

91. Cf. above, pp. 275ff.

A variation on the theme of the colours and the directions is found in the Vajrayāna, where the five Jina Buddhas, each representing an aspect of Total Knowledge and each ruling over one of the directions of space, are correlated with five colours, namely, the three primaries (yellow, red and blue) and black and white. These are the colours of the five Elements and in the same way that all physical phenomena are compounded from the five Elements so also all colours (= forms, rūpa)[92] are produced by the mixture of black and white and the three primaries.[93] To indicate that he comprizes within himself the five types of Knowledge, the five Elements and the five directions of space, the Buddha Mahāvairocana sits on a white lotus[94] and his body radiates a light of five colours.[95] With the same import the Bodhisattva Vajrasattva (Jap. Kongōsatta Bosatsu) is similarly shown with a nimbus and aureole of five colours.[96]

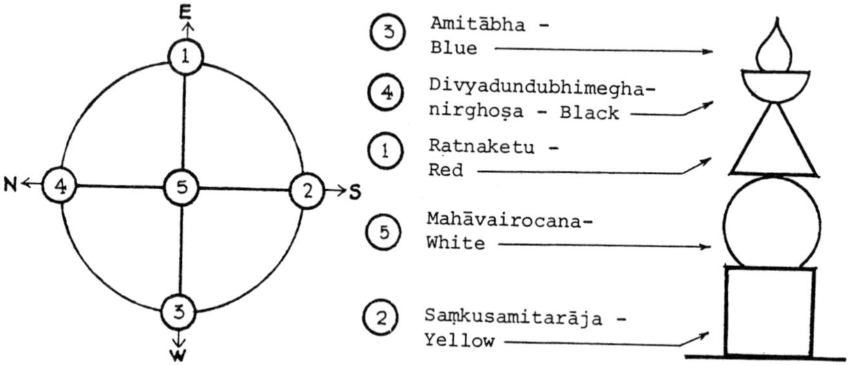

Fig. 205 : The correlation of the five Buddhas of the Matrix World and the directions, the shapes of the Stupa of the Five Cakras (Jap. gorintō) and the five colours.

Fig. 206 : The Buddhist divinities Vajrasattva (Jap. Kongōsatta), on the left, and Mahāvairocana (Jap. Dainichi) of the Diamond World, each shown emitting a nimbus of light made up of five colours.

92. See below, p. 289, n. 97. 93. BKDJT, p. 1189, and MKDJT, p. 590, s.v., Goshiki.

94. According to the descriptions given in the *Tenjinrinhon* of the *Dainichikyō*, quoted in MKDJT, p. 1523, s.v., Dainichi Nyorai.

95. Śubhākarasiṃha 4, quoted MKDJT, p. 1523.

96. Getty, 1928, p. 29; Rowland, 1947, p. 48, n. 6.

The rainbow-stairway of seven colours passes from this world of differentiated colours and forms,[97] the world of contrasts, to the domain of the pure and colourless light of Perfect Knowledge, the Knowledge that sees all differentiations in their integral cohesion and all oppositions in their coincidence. The Buddhas emanate a five- or seven-coloured light to indicate their possession of Perfect Knowledge. They "shine both by night and day, and shine with a five-fold brightness".[98] At the time of his Enlightenment the body of Śākyamuni issues "a halo, resplendent with many colours, proceeding to a fathom's length all around his person",[99] with "rays of six different colours which issue forth from his body and race hither and thither over places and pagodas, and deck them, as it were, with the yellow sheen of gold, or with the colours of a painting".[100] The *Amitāyur-dhyāna-sūtra* speaks of "rays of five colours" that issue from the Buddha's mouth,[101] and the passage could be matched by many others describing the emanation of a five- or seven-coloured ray of light from the Buddha's ūrṇā, from his mouth or tongue, from the pores of his skin, or from his entire body. Tibetan texts speak of the "Rainbow Body" (Tib. jai-lüs), the highest spiritual state attainable by the yogin while still in the physical body.[102] The divine gurus of Tibet are described as "seated within the halo of a five-hued rainbow",[103] and the *Bardo Thödol*, describing after-death experiences, says that if the dead man is able to concentrate his mind on Vairocana Buddha he will finally merge with him "in a halo of rainbow light".[104] The stupa, homologous with the Buddha's body,[105] is also described as emanating a seven-coloured light. The stupa that miraculously rises from out of the earth in the *Saddharma-puṇḍarīka-sūtra*[106] consists of seven precious substances, which Kern identifies with the seven colours of the rainbow and with the seven planets.[107] The Pure Land sutras describe the splendours of Amitābha's Pure Land, Sukhāvati, by means of the same formula : the trees, ponds, pavilions, etc., are all fashioned from seven jewels.[108]

The rainbow connects the world of saṃsāra to the "Other Shore" of nirvāṇa. It is the pathway that separates the supernal and the sacred realms from the mundane and the profane. Hence the rainbow is specifically identified with the Pathway of the Gods (devayāna) leading to the Brahmaloka.[109] Similar connotations inhere within the symbolism of the so-called "boundary path" (Jap. kaidō) of five colours that encloses the central eight-petalled lotus in the Japanese Matrix World Mandala. The band of five colours is described as a boundary (Jap. kyōkai, lit., "world boundary or limit") and a path (Jap. dō) : it marks the border of the Dharma World (dharma-dhātu)

---

97. The Chinese character se, 色 (Jap. shiki), "colour", is used to translate Skt. rūpa, "form". Colour and form are seen as coincident; the world of differentiated colour is that of differentiated forms.

98. Dh 387, XXVI.5. Cf. the "Miracle of the Six Rays" in Coedes and Archaimbault, 1973, pp. 184ff. 99. Rhys Davids, 1880, p. 124.

100. Warren, 1906, p. 92. See also Hardy, 1860, pp. 179f.; Mus, 1935, p. 587; Rowland, 1947, p. 46, n. 3. For pre-Buddhist parallels see Rowland, 1947, p. 48, n. 4. 101. ADS I.6.

102. Evans-Wentz, 1958, p. 318, n.3; Eliade, 1965, p. 43.

103. Evans-Wentz, 1958, pp. 262 & 276f.

104. Evans-Wentz, 1957, pp. 105ff.; Eliade, 1965, pp. 37ff.

105. See below, pp. 360ff. 106. SPS XI (Kern, 1884, p. 227).

107. Kern, 1884, p. 227, n. 3. 108. See, e.g., ADS *passim*.

109. Senart, 1875, p. 225.

where the five Buddhas reside; and it is the path used by the Buddhas and Bodhisattvas and by the performer of the rite when they enter and leave the mandala.

Fig. 207 : The rainbow arch that demarks the sacred area of the Tibetan altar.

Fig. 208 (above) : The "boundary path" (Jap. kaidō) of five colours that encloses the central eight petal lotus of the Matrix World Mandala.

Fig. 209 (below) : a. A detail from a Tibetan thaṅka, showing the "rainbow border" of five colours that frames the central section of a mandala.
b. A detail of the Wheel of Existence showing the five-colour rainbow border that separates the realms of existence.

a

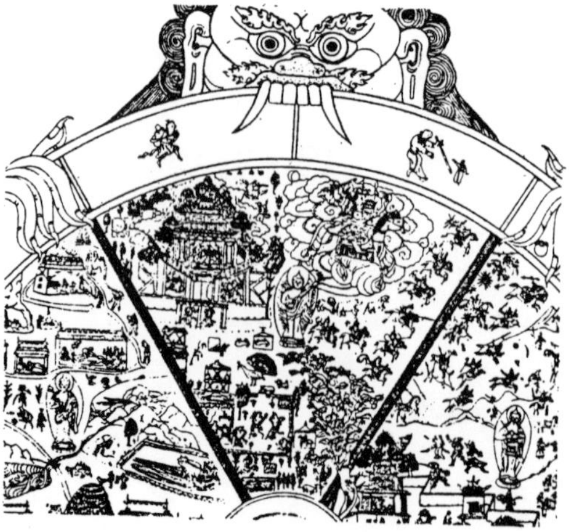

b

The five colours mark the confines of a sacred space : a five-coloured cord is stretched between vajra-spikes to demarcate the boundaries of the mandala when it is being laid out upon the ground;[111] a "rainbow border" of five colours frames Tibetan mandalas; the six realms shown in paintings of the Wheel of Existence[112] are separated by "rainbow-coloured cordons";[113] and the sacred area of the Tibetan altar is sometimes placed behind a rainbow arch.[114]

The symbolism has a temporal as well as a spatial reference. According to one version of the Hindu-Buddhist cosmology, Jambudvīpa, the continent where men dwell, is one of seven continents that occupy the seven directions around Mt. Meru.[115] Four of these continents lie in the cardinal directions, one is in the Nadir, another in the Zenith, and the seventh is coincident with Meru itself. Mt. Meru has seven "faces", each having one of the colours of the rainbow and each turned to one of the continents. Meru itself, designated as "the White Mountain", is the seventh and central "face".[116] The seven continents do not exist simultaneously but emerge successively in the course of cyclic periods, sometimes represented symbolically as six millennia : in the seventh millennium manifestation returns to its Principle. As in every formulation concerning cycles, the schema equally applies to cycles of greater or lesser duration : it applies, for example, to the cycle of the week, with its six days followed by a day of rest. So also a kalpa contains two complete cycles of seven manvantaras each.[117]

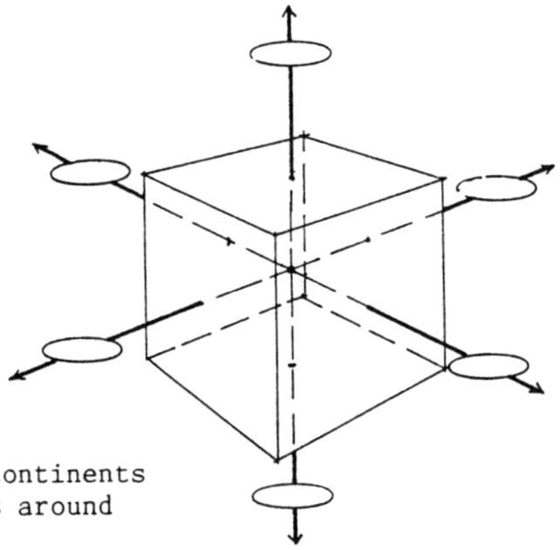

Fig. 210 : The continents in the directions around Mount Meru.

---

110. MKDJT, p. 207, s.v., Kaidō; p. 591, s.v., Goshiki kaidō; BKDJT, p. 1190, s.v., Goshiki kaidō.

111. MKDJT, p. 674, s.v., Kongōketsu. Cf. Tucci, 1961, p. 87.

112. See above, pp. 84ff.

113. Waddell, 1895, p. 103; Rowland, 1947, p. 49.

114. Evans-Wentz, 1958, pl. II, shows a photo of an altar at the Pemiondu Mon temple in Sikkhim, described as "a rainbow and haloed shrine symbolical of the celestial hierarchies".

115. *Viṣṇu-purāṇa* II.2 (Wilson, 1840, pp. 135ff.).

116. The colour of the face of Meru turned to our world of Jambudvīpa is made of sapphire and is blue. In India it is said that the blue colour of the sky is produced by the reflection of light from Meru.

117. Guénon, 1950, pp. 57-59.

There is another way in which the rainbow-stair is linked with the turning of the wheel of time. The seven and five colours of the rainbow are homologous with the seven and five planets. The rainbow is the ecliptic on which the planets trace their paths.[118] Not only does this tie in with the previously analyzed symbolism of the ecliptic, with its Gates of Entry and Exit corresponding to the signs of Cancer and Capricorn, but also provides a connection to the myth of the Churning of the Milky Ocean, since, in one of its meanings, the movement of the Serpent around the Mountain churning rod is the movement of the planets upon the ecliptic. In another of its meanings it refers to the movements of the heavenly bodies as they turn about the Pole Star.[119]

As well as being a transcendence of space the ascent of the staircase of the stupa is thus also a trancendence of time. Rising up the rungs of the ladder of cyclical succession, the initiate returns to the timeless, and colourless, centre of the rainbow.

b. The Rainbow Serpent and the Rainbow *Makara*.

The identification of the rainbow and the serpent (nāga) is a frequent theme in Indian literature. The assimilation is indicated iconographically by the snake's seven or five heads, which correspond to the seven or five colours of the rainbow. The myths sometimes speak of two serpents, with reference to a double rainbow defining the pathway to the Empyrean. These are expressed architecturally by the two serpent-balustrades that flank the stairway.

Fig. 211 : Examples of nāgas and nāgīs, shown with five- and seven-headed serpent halos.

The rainbow-serpent indicates the way of spiral ascent to the Sun Door. This is one significance of the frequently encountered symbolic theme of a snake coiled around an axis, seen, for example in the caduceus-like Brahmanic rod (brahmadaṇḍa), the sword of the Buddhist divinity Fudō Myō-ō (Acalanatha Vidyarāja), the serpent twisted around the Mountain in the myth

118. Mus, 1935, p. 334, n. 1 and p. 330. Cf. above, pp. 238ff.

119. See, e.g., Wales, 1977, p. 124.

of the Churning of the Milky Ocean, the seven-headed serpent Mucalinda wrapped protectively seven times about the body of the meditating Buddha (who personifies the World Axis), and stupas embellished with knotted snakes.

Most examples of ophidian balustrades, however, terminate not with the heads of serpents but with those of the aquatic monster, the makara. The iconography changes but the symbolic reference remains the same. The makara, like the serpent, is identified with the rainbow.[120]

The makara and the serpent both represent the Waters. The association of the nāgas with water is a commonplace of Asian mythology and needs no detailed demonstration. The Cosmic Serpent, Ananta, the Endless, is identified with the substantial Waters; nāgas inhabit sub-aquatic paradises in rivers, lakes and seas; they control the rain, granting or withholding it; they change into rain clouds and produce rivers. They are the guardians of the life-giving energy (rasa) contained in the waters and from this they produce the Elixir of Immortality (amṛta), for whose possession they engage in deadly combat with the Sunbird, Garuḍa. In Buddhism the Gods of the Waters, Varuṇa and Sāgara, are serpent-kings (nāga-rāja); and the nāgas were the custodians of the *Prajñā-pāramitā-sūtras* until Nāgārjuna recovered them by journeying to the nāga palace beneath the ocean.[121]

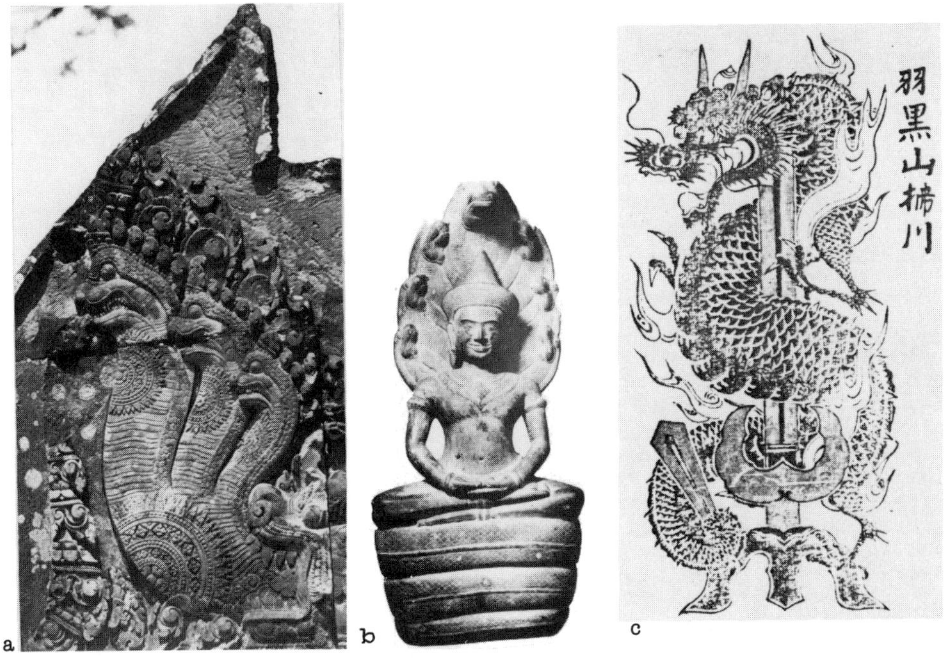

Fig. 212 : a. A five-headed nāga ornamenting a lintel at Banteay Srei, Angkor.
b. A Mucalinda Buddha. The Buddha sits upon the coils of the serpent Mucalinda, who spreads his hoods to protect him from a violent storm. Mucalinda represents the subterranean realms of existence.
c. The Wisdom Sword of Acalanatha Vidyarāja (Jap. Fudō Myō-ō), entwined by a flaming serpent.

---

120. Vogel, 1924 and 1926, *passim*.

121. This information is taken from Vogel, 1924.

The makara similarly stands for the Waters. It combines in its horrific features elements taken from the crocodile, the elephant and the serpent, which are all, in the Indian view, connected with water. It comprizes the same aquatic associations as does the nāga. Throughout the Sanskrit literature the ocean is termed makarālaya, "the abode of makaras". The makara is the mount of the God of the Waters, Varuna, and also of the Goddes Gaṅgā. It is the vehicle and cognizance of the Yakṣas,[122] and in Tantric Hinduism it dwells within the abdominal cakra (svadhiṣṭhāna-cakra), which is associated with the Element Water; in this location the makara is the vehicle of the seed syllable of the Element Water, vaṃ.[123]

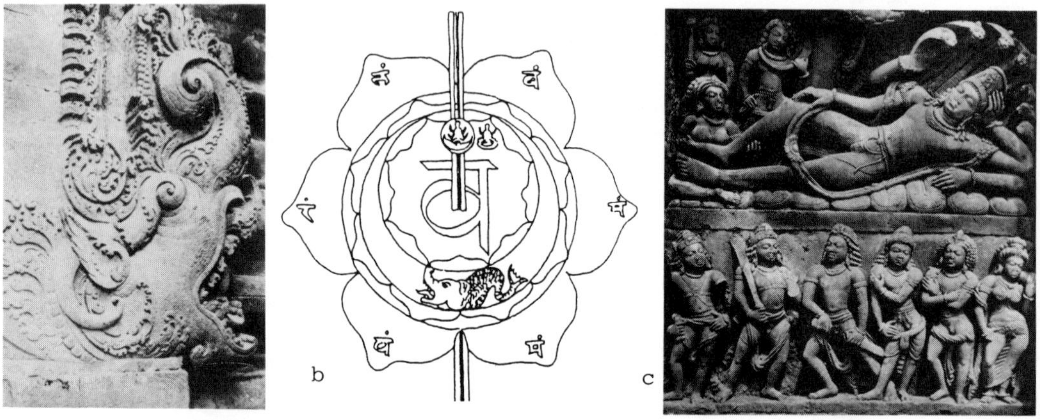

a b c

Fig. 213 : a. A makara head, comprizing elements of the crocodile, the elephant and the serpent, all associated with the Waters. The head is adorned with an intricate scrollwork, indicative of both fiery breath and foliage. b. The abdominal centre (svadhiṣṭhāna-cakra), with a makara bearing the seed syllable of the Element Water, vaṃ. c. Viṣṇu asleep upon the Cosmic Serpent Ananta. Below him stand the five Paṇḍava brothers and their common wife, Draupadī, the protagonists in the *Mahābhārata*.

In these formulations the makara and the serpent are associated with the waters of the earth, lying in lakes and seas; but in the context of rainbow symbolism they are also connected with the waters of the heavens, carried in clouds and falling from above as rain or dew. The arch of the rainbow is compared to a channel that siphons the lower waters upwards to the apex of its curve and then releases them as rain, which falls down to fructify the earth. Similarly, the body of the makara or serpent is a conduit to carry the waters upward to the heavens. In a typical expression of this symbolic concept, the people of Java say that a vast rainbow-snake arches over their island. This serpent has the heads of antelopes (equivale to the makara)[124] at its two ends, one of which swallows the Indian Ocean in the South and the other the waters of the Java Sea in the North. Sucking up these waters into its body it then releases them to flow down onto the land as rain.[125]

122. Coomaraswamy, 1931, p. 13.

123. Avalon, 1958, p. 119; Govinda, 1959, p. 142.

124. On the equivalence of deer and makara heads, established by reference to the Chinese Dragon, which is also identified with the rainbow, see Bosch, 1941, pp. 585ff.; 1960, pp. 130ff.; and cf. Combaz, 1939, pp. 136ff.; de Visser, 1913, pp. 1-25.

125. Auboyer, 1949, pp. 118f.

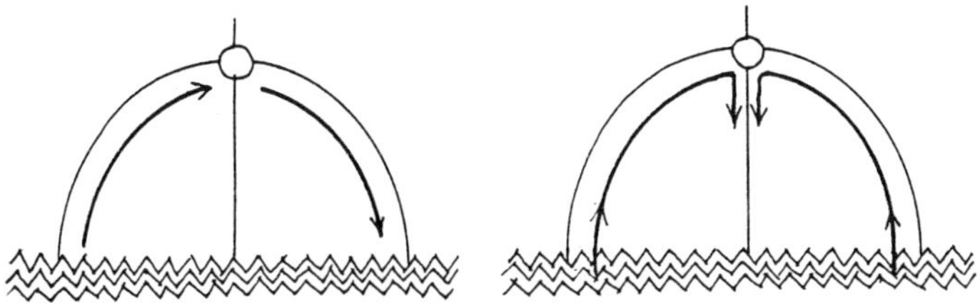

a

b

c

Fig. 214 : a. Two diagrammatic representations of the ascending and descending Waters.
b. Examples of makara heads.
c. A Javanese kālamakara, with deer heads substituting for makaras.

c. The Upward and Downward Flowing Waters.

Acting as a conduit the rainbow-body of the serpent or makara conveys the underlying, chthonic waters to the sky, whence they fall to the earth as rain. The physical analogy is with the process of evaporation whereby the heat of the sun "draws up" water to the sky, from where it pours down once again to earth. The cycle of the waters involves phases of upflowing and downflowing : the waters rise from the earth to the heavens and, in a complementary movement, fall from the heavens back to earth. The down-pouring of the life-giving rain, symbolically equivalent to the down-shining of the life-giving light of the sun, is universally taken to represent the flowing of celestial influences from above. In the complementary movement of ascent the vapourized water represents the rising of terrestrial influences towards the heavens.[126]

a

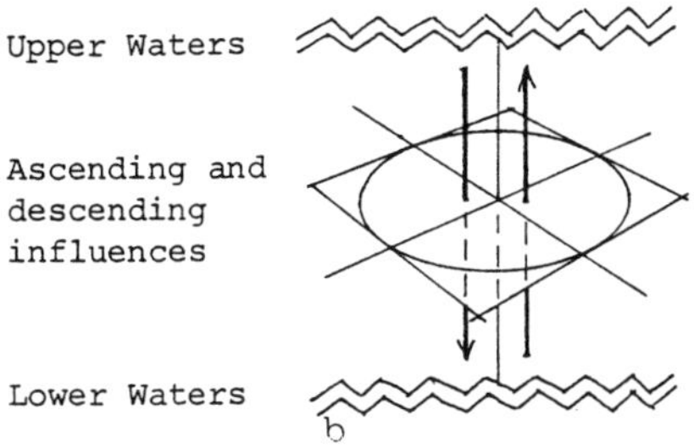

b

Fig. 215 : a. A makara-rainbow from Java. b. The ascending and descending currents of the cosmos.

The symbolic significance of this upward and downward counterflowing can be interpreted at several levels. Firstly, the passive, low-lying waters and the waters carried by the clouds respectively represent the Lower Waters and the Upper Waters. Taken inclusively and in their widest significance the Waters represent All-Possibility or Substance (prakṛti), the passive principle of manifestation and the potential aspect of Being, containing within itself the sum total of the possibilities of manifestation

126. Guénon, 1962, pp. 362f. and 363, n. 3.

in both its formal and informal modes.[127] The cosmo-genetic process involves a diremption of the Waters : the Lower Waters are those which contain the sum of the possibilities of form, that is to say, all the individual states of existence; and the Upper Waters are those which contain the sum of the informal possibilities, that is, all the supra-individaul states. Viewed in this framework of reference the rising of the waters from below represents the "transformation" of the Lower to the Upper Waters, a passage from the formal to the informal states; and, by contrast, the downflowing of the waters represents the reverse passage from the informal states to the worlds of form.

Secondly, at the most universal level of meaning the upward and downward flowing waters represent the interaction of forces or currents emanating from the complementary poles of manifestation, namely, puruṣa and prakṛti, Heaven and Earth, Essence and Substance. This is the significance of the double spiral,[128] found, for example, at the ends of the rainbow shaped torana-lintels at Sāñcī. The two spirals represent the forces emanating from the two poles of the World Egg, one unrolling upwards and the other downwards, produced by the Egg's rotation around the axis that joins the two poles. The actions and reactions produced by the upward and downward flowing currents of force actualize the innumerable modifications of the virtualities contained within the Egg.[129] The same significance inheres within the double svastika, whose counter-posed arms represent the contrary movements of the upward flowing influences of Earth and the downward flowing influences of Heaven.

Fig. 216 : Spirals adorning the ends of the gate lintels at Sāñcī.

The spirals uncoiling around the axis from the two poles equate the coils of the rainbow-snake, an assimilation expressed in symbols such as certain forms of the Brahmanic rod (brahmadaṇḍa) and the caduceus, in which the two snakes turning about the rod are the two contrary forces emanating from the two poles and proceeding around the axis mundi.

---

127. All-Possibility contains the sum total of the possibilities of manifestation, both formal and informal, but does not include the possibilities of non-manifestation, which lie beyond Being. For the distinction of non-manifestation and manifestation and of formal and informal possibilities see p. 5, n. 21, above.

128. Guénon, 1957a, Ch. V ("La double spirale").

129. *Ibid.*, pp. 47f.

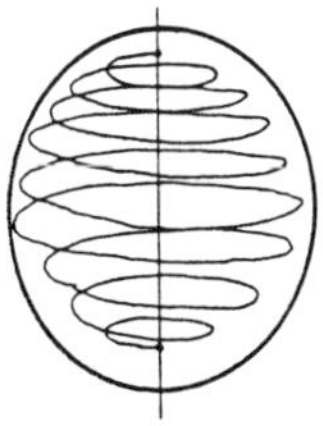

a

b

c

d

Fig. 217 :
a. The ascending and descending spirals emanating from the poles of the Cosmic Egg. b. The double spiral, representing the spirals of cosmic influence shown in the previous figure. c. A *makara* with spiral body. d. A *nāga* spiral in the ceiling of an Indian temple, Bādāmī.

This brings the meaning of the Churning of the Milky Ocean into clearer focus. The *asuras* and the *devas* who pull the snake in opposite directions represent the states of darkness and light respectively, or those states that are lower and higher than the human state or, alternately, the "powers" of Substance, which is below, and of Essence, which is above : their interaction produces the manifested worlds.[130] The opposition of the *devas* and the *asuras* relates to the twofold significance of the serpent, the *devas* corresponding to the descending movement, going from the essential towards the substantial pole, while the *asuras* correspond to the ascending movement around the axis, going from the substantial pole towards the essential.[131]

Fig. 218 :
In the Hindu-Buddhist pneuma-physiology the two subtle "arteries" or vectors (*nāḍi*), the *iḍā* and the *piṅgalā*, which carry the upward and the downward flowing Breath, spiral round the axis of the body, the *merudaṇḍa*. See below, pp. 299 f.

At another level of interpretation the ascending and descending motions are the complementary phases of the manifestation of the worlds from their Principle, the descending motion, or catabasis, corresponding to their "evolution" into existence, and the ascending motion, or anabasis, corresponding to their "involution" back into the point of Unity whence they

---

130. For other aspects of this symbolism, both maleficent and beneficent, see Guénon, 1958a, pp. 11ff.; 1953a, Ch. XXX.

131. Guénon, 1958a, p. 51; cf. Coomaraswamy, 1935b, pp. 402ff., and esp. p. 404.

derived. The former is the coming out of phenomena into manifestation and the latter is their return into non-manifestation. This is the univeral spiration,[132] the expiration and inspiration of the Spirit or Breath, the outbreathing being manifestation, the inbreathing the return into the One, the alternate phases which are the days and nights of Brahmā, the kalpa and pralaya, the "births" and "deaths" of the worlds.[133]

d. The Marriage of the Currents.

The concept of the "interaction" of the cosmic forces of currents emanating from the two principial poles of the universe is expressed in terms of a productive union. The fall of rain is a consequence of a marriage of Heaven and Earth[134] : "Yonder world thence gave rain to this world as a marriage gift".[135] This is the union of conjoint principles "at the end of the Sky, at the top of the Tree, where Heaven and Earth embrace".[136]

The symbolism is mythically conveyed in the Vedic accounts of the rain-producing conjunction of Mitra and Varuṇa, who "are the leaders of the waters"[137] and who "must favour thee with rain".[138] In several places in the *Ṛg Veda* the two gods are together invoked to send rain,[139] and whereas in later Hinduism and Buddhism it is Varuṇa alone who is the God of the waters and the rain and who rules over the aquatic nāgas, in these early texts the rains are the joint production of the two gods.[140]

The two gods form a progenitive pair (mithunam), Mitrāvaruṇau, which Coomaraswamy terms "a syzygy of conjoint principles, in which Mitra is the male and Varuṇa the female partner, an 'opposition' or 'polarity' which is that of Day to Night, of Light to Darkness".[141] Mitra is the Sun and Varuṇa the (dark) Sky, and the Sun[142] is the husband of the Sky.[143] The Sun inseminates the Sky[144] and "forms his likeness in the womb of the Sky",[145] in the same way that "Mitra inseminates Varuṇa".[146] In the *Mahābhārata*[147] it is asked, "What is the universe and the non-universe... what is Mitra, what is Varuna?" and the reply is given, "... the female and the male, the former being prakṛti (Substance) and the latter puruṣa (Essence); similarly Mitra is puruṣa and Varuṇa is prakṛti". Verses chanted in honour of the two gods are addressed to Heaven and Earth. "Heaven and Earth, one should know, are the favourite resort of Varuṇa and Mitra, by means of

---

132. The word is connected with "spiral" and spiritus, "breath".

133. Guénon, 1957a, p. 52. 134. PB VII.10.1-4; VIII.2.10.

135. JB I.145.

136. JUB I.3.2. This relates to the "intercourse of creatures" (bhūtānāṃ ca maithunam), ritually expressed in S.E. Asia and elsewhere by the sexual intercourse of the king and a nāgi at the summit of the temple-mountain. See Bosch, 1960, pp. 92f.; Vogel, 1926, p. 37.

137. TS VI.4.3.3. 138. ŚB I.8.3.13.

139. E.g., RV III.62.16; V.63.1; V.63.3. Cf. Gonda, 1972, p. 34.

140. E.g., Mbh II.9, etc. Cf. Daniélou, 1964, p. 119.

141. Coomaraswamy, 1942, p. 38.

142. For Mitra as the Sun, see Gonda, 1972, Ch. V ("Mitra and the Sun"), pp. 54ff., and also p. 130. 143. Coomaraswamy, 1942, p. 40.

144. JB II.241. 145. RV I.115.5. 146. PB XXV.10.10; SB II.4.4.19.

147. MBH XII.306.38.

their favourite resort he thus appropriates them cryptically".[148] The rain-producing conjunction of Mitra and Varuṇa is an instance of all the progenitive and productive unions of the complementary principles of manifestation, puruṣa and prakṛti, Heaven and Earth, Essence and Substance. The diremption of Sky and Earth brings drought; but when they marry "they enliven one another; with the smoke (of the sacrifice) this world enlivens that (world), with rain that (world) enlivens this".[149]

Mitra, who is the Sun, gives light and heat, while Varuṇa, assimilated to the Waters, produces vapour. From their union comes the rain. The upward and downward movement is specified in the texts : "In that he (fire) leaps up and down, that is his form as Mitra and Varuṇa";[150] which the commentary explains by saying that "Flaming fire flares upward, it sinks down through the extinction of the flame. In the former case it exhibits its form as Mitra (the Sun) because of its being elevated through the erection of him who has seen Mitra; in the other, Varuṇa, because of the downward movement of the water, which is associated with Varuṇa.[151]

Macrocosmically the non-dual biunity of principles represented by the mixta persona Mitrāvaruṇau produces life-bestowing rain. The symbolism also has a microcosmic application, as is indicated by a most evocative passage in the *Śatapatha Brāhmaṇa* : "When Sky and Earth are in harmony, then indeed it rains[152]... may he (Mitrāvaruṇau) who rules over the rain favour thee with rain. Now he that rules over the rain is undoubtedly that blowing one (the Gale, Vāyu); and he it is true blows as one only; but on entering into man he becomes... two, the prāṇa and the apāna.[153] And Mitra and Varuṇa are assuredly the prāṇa and the apāna; and hence he says by that (prayer), 'May he who rules over the rain favour thee with rain'".[154]

The progenitive marriage of Mitra and Varuṇa is that of the two Breaths in the yogin. Mitra is identified with prāṇa, the vital air that rises, ascending respiration, and Varuṇa is identified with apāna, the vital air that descends, descending respiration.[155] "Mitra, indeed, is the up-breathing

---

148. PB XIV.2.4, quoted in Gonda, 1972, p. 31.

149. AB IV.27. For elaborations of this theme see Coomaraswamy, 1942, pp. 65ff. As this passage indicates the concept of the ascending and descending currents also has reference to the sacrifice. Cf. "The food offered in the sacrificial fire goes up to the Sun... the sap which flows therefrom rains down... the Sun rains down with his rays... (and) the offering properly cast in the fire goes toward the Sun; from out of the Sun comes rain". (MU VI.37). The sacrifice mimetically replicates the mythic paradigm.

150. AB III.4.5.

151. Quoted by Gonda, 1972, p. 31. The rays of the sun descend from the heavens; the vapours rise from the earth; but Mitra's flame rises and Varuṇa's waters descend (cf. also Mitra as prāṇa, the rising Breath, and Varuṇa as apāna, the descending Breath, discussed in the following). The contradiction is apparent only, and exemplifies the reversal of relations entailed by a transposition of the symbolism from a metaphysical to a physical level of reference. The same consideration applies to the seeming paradox of Mitra's association in other texts with the apāna, "the way downwards, the breath that leaves the body through the anus" (Mbh XIV.42.34) and thus with the organ of excretion (apāna) and the excretory functions. See Gonda, 1972, pp. 124-6 for sources. 152. Cf. AĀ III.1.2.2-4; ŚB I.7.2.16.

153. Cf. ŚB I.1.3.2. 154. ŚB I.8.3.12.

155. ŚB III.2.2.13; IX.5.1.56; XII.4.1.9. Alternately, and with similar import, Mitra is prāṇa and Varuṇa is udāna, expiration, the vital air that is projected outwards.

(*prāṇa*), Varuṇa is the down-breathing (*apāna*)".[156] The marriage of *prāṇa* and *apāna* is the microcosmic equivalent of the marriage of Sky and Earth;[157] and the assimilation of the progenitive conjunctions, Mitrāvaruṇau and *prāṇāpānau*, is a commonplace in the Vedas.[158] The unified pair Mitrāvaruṇau, identified with *prāṇāpānau*, is the unified Breath in man, which produces "rain" in the *yogin*.

The nature of this interior "rain" produced by the Breath-Gale, which is the syzygy of the up- and down-flowing Breaths, is clarified by reference to the psycho-physiological structure of the human organism, in which *prāṇa* and *apāna* are said to be carried in the two subtle channels or "arteries" (*nāḍi*), *iḍā* and *piṅgalā*.[159] These two channels, passing from the root centre (*mūlādhāra*) in the vicinity of the perineum, twine up the axis of the body, the *merudaṇḍa*, in the manner of the serpents of the caduceus.

According to the schema of correspondences adduced by the Buddhist Tantra, the *bodhicitta* is carried by the two breaths flowing through the *iḍā* and *piṅgalā* to the lotus in the crown of the head (*uṣṇīṣa-kamala*), where it is identified with the Moon; by contrast, the Fire-force in the *nirmāṇa-cakra* in the navel region is identified with Sun. The *bodhicitta*-Moon holds *amṛta*, the Nectar of Immortality, which flows from there by way of a duct, the *śaṃkhinī*,[160] opening into the palatal region. The lower mouth of this duct, located in the upper palate, is called the Door of Vairocana, or the tenth gate (*daśana-dvāra*), the other nine gates being the orifices of the body. The *amṛta* trickles down from the Moon through this Door of Vairocana and in the normal course of events is consumed by the Solar Fire of the *nirmāṇa-kāya* in the navel *cakra*. The Solar Fire is Rāhu, the Eclipse, who devours the sixteenth digit of the Moon, which is *amṛta*, so that the man falls a victim to mortality. If, however, the downflow of *amṛta* can be checked by shutting the Door of Vairocana so as to save it from the destructive Fire of Time (*kālāgni*), and if instead the *yogin* drinks the Elixir, then he will cheat death and become immortal. The texts describe techniques for closing the tenth gate, such as the *khecari-mudrā*, in which the *yogin*'s tongue is turned back into the hollow of the palate to close the duct running down from the *uṣṇīṣa*-lotus.[161]

The symbolism of the rainbow reappears in this context. The Tantric texts speak of the drop (*bindu*) which, when union (*samapatti*) is effected, descends from the top of the head and fills the sexual organs with a jet of five-coloured light. The instruction is given : "During union he (the *yogin*) must meditate on the *vajra* and the lotus (*padma*), considering them as filled with five-fold light".[162]

---

156. ŚB XII.9.2.12.

157. Cf. Coomaraswamy, 1942, pp. 65ff. Like Mitra and Varuṇa, the Aśvins are also identified with Sky and Earth (ŚB IV.1.5.16) and with *prāṇa* and *apāna* (See Rao, 1914, p. 543).

158. "References to Mitrāvaruṇau as *prāṇāpānau* (or *prāṇodānau*) are too many for separate citation" (Coomaraswamy, 1942, p. 38).

159. See below pp. 317ff.

160. This duct is described as a serpent with heads at both ends and corresponds to the pair of *makara* heads that are shown emerging from the upper jaw of the Face of Glory in some depictions.

161. Dasgupta, 1962, pp. 239ff. For the *khecari-mudrā*, see also Eliade, 1958a, p. 247.

162. Candrakirti, Commentary on the *Guhya-samāja-tantra*, quoted by Tucci, 1934, p. 349 Cf. Eliade, 1965, p. 40.

e. The Symbolism of the Gander.

The formula is otherwise expressed in the symbolism of the Gander (haṃsa). The rhythm of inhalation and exhalation is the manifestation of the "inner Gander", the Sunbird, who plunges down into the Waters and again flies upwards to the Sky, the "Golden Bird indwelling the heart and Sun",[163] "the Gander whose seat is in the light",[164] who is "a blazing fire"[165] that "has entered into the ocean",[166] who goes "to and from the outer (world)... the Gander unique in the midst of the world".[167] He is "the Gander in the Sky, the pervader of Midspace... who leads the outbreath (prāṇa) upward, and casts inwards the in-breath (apāna)",[168] and of whom it is said that "Not by any outbreath or inbreath does any mortal live, but on another do they live on which these (breaths) do both depend".[169]

Fig. 219 : The inner Gander, whose body is fiery Breath.

The ingoing breath (apāna) makes the sound haṃ, the outgoing breath (prāṇa) makes the sound sa, and the yogin who listens to the Gander murmuring its own name in the inflow and the outflow of his breathing realizes the Bird's indwelling presence, since haṃ-sa-haṃ-sa... is also sa-'haṃ-sa-'haṃ..., "This is I". Having become one with the Sunbird of his Breath, the yogin is called a parama-haṃsa, "a great Gander".[170]

The haṃsa within the yogin is none other than Viṣṇu, the Cosmic Gander whose inbreathing and outbreathing is the manifestation and dissolution of the worlds, the Gander that sings, "Many forms do I assume. And when the Sun and Moon have disappeared, I float and swim with slow movements on the boundless expanse of the Waters. I am the Gander. I am the Lord. I bring forth the universe from my essence and I abide in the cycle of time that dissolves it".[171]

---

163. MU VI.34. 164. KU V.2. 165. MU VI.35. 166. Śveṭ. Up. VI.15.
167. Śveṭ. Up. III.18 & VI.15. 168. KU II.2.2-3. 169. KU II.2.5.
170. Zimmer, 1946, p. 47.
171. *Matsya-Purāṇa* CLX VII.13-25, quoted in Zimmer, 1946, pp. 47f.

a

b

c

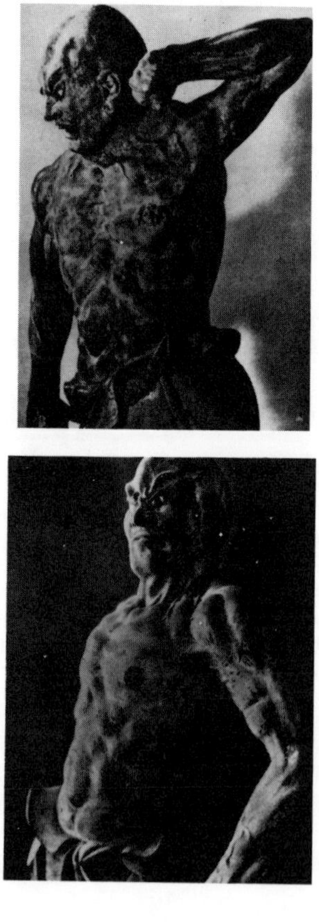

d

Fig. 220 :
a. The Bodhisattva Samantabhadrāyu (Jap. Fugen Emmei, "Fugen of Long Life"). He rides upon the elephants of the four directions (dig-gaja, see below, p. 315), who carry vajras in their trunks, assimilating them with the adamantine Breaths. The elephants stand upon the Wheel of the World, its spokes indicating the deployment of the directions, supported on 100 small elephants who represent the Lower Waters that uphold the cosmos. In the drawing on the left the Regents of the Directions stand on the heads of the dig-gajas. The image identifies the Breaths and the directions of spatial emanation.

b. A Japanese drawing showing the union of the Breaths, represented by two forms of the elephant-headed god, Ganeśa (Jap. Kangiten). One represents the outward and the other the inward flowing Breath.

c. The Ni-ō, "Kings of Virtue", are guardians placed to the left and right of Buddhist temple gateways. As two aspects of Vajradhara, who personifies the qualities of the vajra, they embody a complex symbolism involving the concept of the inflowing and outflowing Breaths correlated with the syllables a and um̱, whose union forms the syllable aum̱, signifying non-dual Enlightenment. One has his mouth open and the other has it closed to indicate the counterflowing of the Breaths. Their bodies are carved to convey the impression that they are inflated with Breath.

The Gander is the Breath. It sits upon the Cosmic Egg (brahmaṇḍa) that floats upon the Waters and is thus equated with the Dawn-Wind of creation.[172] As the progenitive Breath it is the vehicle of the God-Creator, Brahmā, who in Shingon Buddhist iconography is shown seated on a gander having heads in the four directions, two stretched upwards and two downwards, two with open mouths and two with mouths closed, to represent the alternations of the outflowing and the inflowing breaths.[173]

Fig. 221 : A Japanese image of the four-headed Brahmā riding on four ganders, two with their heads raised and two with heads lowered and one of each type with its mouth closed and one of each type with its mouth open, representing the upward and downward flowing of the macro- and micro-cosmic Breaths, correlated with the cosmo-genetic deployment of the directions of space.

The open and closed mouths representing prāṇa and apāna are found again in the embracing pair of elephant-headed gods, the Kangiten, used in secret rituals involving breath control (prāṇayāma), the object of which is the attainment of Diamond Breath (vajra-prāṇa), identified with the Gale of Immortality.[174] The elephants' trunks represent the subtle arteries, iḍā and piṅgalā, that carry the breaths in the body of the yogin, and the attainment of their fusion in the Diamond Breath is indicated by a single prong vajra held at the end of the trunk. This is seen, for example, in depictions of Fugen Emmei (Samantabhadrāyu), the Fugen of Long Life, who embodies the immortality achieved by control of the breath.[175]

The theme is repeated in the iconography of the "Virtuous Kings", (Jap. Niō), who stand as wrathful, semi-naked and extremely muscular guardians at either side of temple gateways in the Far East. They represent two aspects of the Bodhisattva "Vajra Holder" (Vajradhara, Jap. Kongōshu), embodiment of the qualities of the vajra. One of the Kings, shown with his mouth open, is identified with the syllable a and the upward flowing breath, and the other, with mouth closed, represents the syllable uṃ and the downward flowing breath. Together they are the non-dual syzygy of the syllable auṃ and the vajra-Breath.[176] Cognate concepts are conveyed by the karashiki, "Chinese Lions", which similarly act as gatekeepers and are shown, one with mouth open and one with teeth clenched, on either side of the temple entrance or flanking the altar.

* * * * *

172. Guénon, 1945, p. 56, n. 2. 173. MKDJT, p. 2070, s.v., Bonten.

174. MKDJT, p. 384, s.v., Kangiten.

175. MKDJT, p. 1911, s.v., Fugen Emmei.

176. BKDJT, p. 4019, s.v., Niōson; Sawa, 1971, pp. 129f.

These various concepts come together in the symbolism of the stairway of the stupa and its two rainbow-serpent balustrades. The stairway is the rainbow bridge that connects this terrestrial world with the celestial realms. An ascent of the stairway is a climbing of the Mountain-Axis, rising to the Sun Door on its peak, represented by the finial stupa that stands upon the summit of the truncated pyramid formed by the terraces. Reversing the movement, a descent of the stairway is a downflowing of spiritual influences from the celestial realms to the plane of earth. The stairways of the stupa are axial passageways to the solar Empyrean at the summit of the Cosmic Axis; they are also pathways for the descent of the sacred. They are the steps whereby the Buddha comes down from the heavens into the world of men.

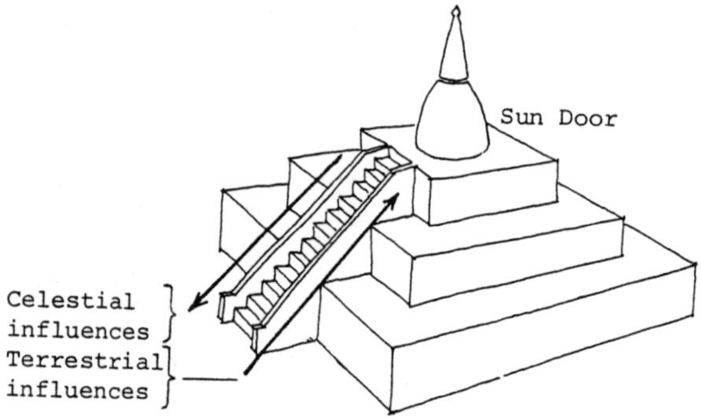

Fig. 222 : The ascending and descending influences in the stupa.

Fig. 223 : A snake coiled round a <u>linga</u>, which is the cognate of the World Egg and the <u>axis mundi</u>.

The rainbow-serpent balustrades of the stupa stairway form part of the same symbolic construct. Their lateral positions, to right and left of the steps, correspond to those of the right and left hand spirals that coil around the central axis, which latter is identified with the stairway itself.[177] The balustrades are to be regarded as a variation on the theme of the serpent coiled around the axis, otherwise expressed by myths such as the Churning of the Ocean, Mucalinda wrapping the Buddha in his coils and by such symbols as the Brahman's rod (<u>brahmadaṇḍa</u>), the two arteries of the subtle body coiling around the spinal axis, the snake that coils around the <u>liṅga</u> in the <u>mūlādhāracakra</u>, the <u>nāga</u> stones of South India, the snakes knotted in festoons upon the stupa, and so on. In their macrocosmic reference they are the channels that carry the counterflowing currents from the essential and substantial poles of the universe; they convey the interacting energies of the Upper and Lower Waters; and they symbolize the interplay of all the contrary movements and contrary forces of the universe. Microcosmically, they signify <u>prāṇa</u> and <u>apāna</u>, the upward and downward moving phases of the Breath, which are the homologues in the body of the <u>yogin</u> of the ascending and descending currents in the body of the cosmos.

---

177. The same symbolism is embodied in the ladder, whose two strings have the same significance as the balustrades. See Guénon, 1962, p. 339.

a
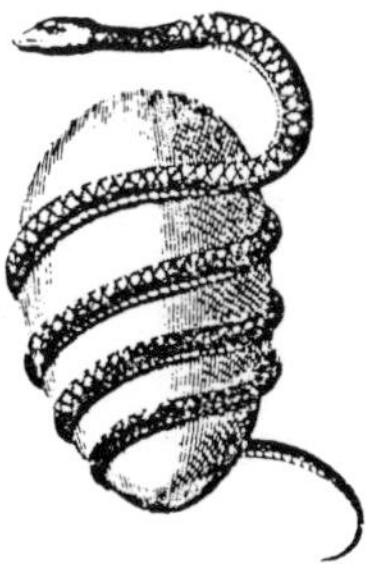
b

Fig. 224 : a. A serpent coiled around the World Egg. The symbol equates that of the serpent coiled around the liṅga in the previous illustration. b. Serpent stones in South India, showing snakes twined about an invisible axis in the manner of the caduceus.

f. The *Kālamakara*.

These contrary currents are reconciled and integrated within a superior principle, represented macrocosmically by the Sun at the summit of the Mountain, microcosmically by the uṣṇīṣa-lotus at the summit of the merudaṇḍa and within the upper part of the skull, and in the stupa by the crowning harmikā or its equivalent at the summit of the stupa's axis. This conjunction of opposing currents in a principle that contains them both in a non-dual syzygy is represented by another motif that closely relates to that of the serpent-balustrade, namely, the kālamakara.

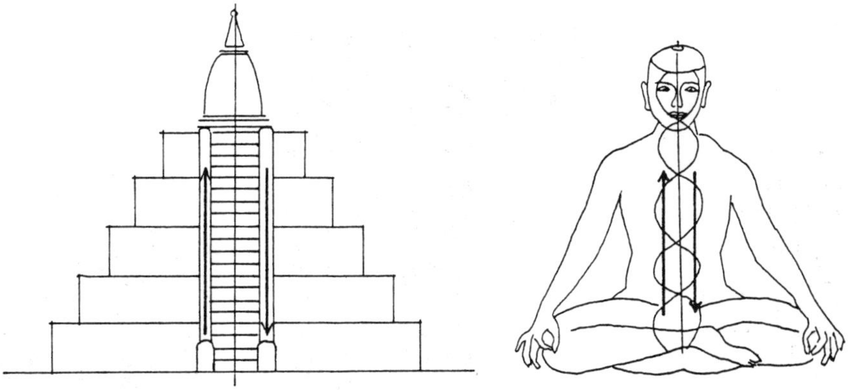

Fig. 225 : The ascending and descending forces in man and in the stupa.

* * * * *

Every change of state is a death to the preceding and a rebirth into the succeeding state.[178] Each, therefore, is a prefiguration of the final death and rebirth which is the attainment of Enlightenment. The ascent from

178. See above, p. 201.

one terrace of the stupa to the next represents just such a change of state, and hence the steps leading from each level to the next in South East Asian stupas are sometimes embellished with the kālamakara, the decorative motif that typically adorns the doors and windows of Indian temples.

The kālamakara consists of a combination of makaras and a Face of Time, Kāla-mukha, more usually called a Face of Glory (kīrttimukha). The Face is a fearsome, mask-like visage located at the apex of the lintel arch. From its mouth to either side it spews forth a serpent body that runs outwards and downwards to frame the opening. These two serpent bodies, wreathed in flames or foliage, terminate in makara heads, located at the feet of the jambs.[179]

The significance of the makara-jambs equates that of the makara-balustrades that flank the stupa stairways. Here again the two makara bodies, to the right and left of the doorway, are the channels that carry the contrary movements of the cosmic currents. They convey the rhythmic alternation of cosmic antinomies, the contrasting phases of inhalation and exhalation, expansion and reintegration, kalpa and pralaya.

b

d

a

c

Fig. 226 :
a - d. Examples of kālamakaras from Javanese caṇḍis.
e. A Buddha image framed by a kālamakara.

e

179. Or, alternately, they are located at the springing of the arch.

These two opposing forces channelled by the bodies of the counterposed makaras coalesce within the Face of Glory that is set at the centre of the transome. The Face represents the coincidentia oppositorum, in its malefic aspect. To pass beneath the jaws of the Face is to be swallowed by Time.[180] His mouth gulps down living things, but at the same time pours forth a profusion of foliage. The jaws destroy but are also the source of rain, of the water that brings life and fertility.[181] The Face of Glory is the Mask of destruction and creation, death and life, darkness and solar light.

a b

Fig. 227 : a A kālamakara in the Japanese Matrix World Mandala, where it marks the point of entry into the sacred precincts. b. The rain producing union of opposites.

* * * * *

The dual nature of the Face of Glory is conveyed in the myth that describes its origin. It tells how Jalandhara, a mighty asura who had conquered all the worlds, in the pride of his power sent Rāhu, the Demon of Eclipsing Darkness, to demand from Śiva his bride, Pārvati. In reply Śiva opened his third eye and flashed forth a tremendous burst of power, which assumed the form of an horrendous demon, possessed of an insatiable and raging hunger. Seeing Rāhu, the monstrous apparition rushed toward him with jaws agape ready to devour him. Rāhu, terrified, flew for refuge to Śiva, who commanded the monster to let him be. Deprived of its prey, the fiendish vision was still tortured by his immense hunger, so the Lord bade it feed upon the flesh of its own feet and hands. So great was the demon's voracity that having consumed its own extremities it did not cease its meal but continued to eat until only its face remained. Śiva watched this bloodcurdling banquet with ecstatic bliss, delighted with this projected image of his own world-annihilating power, and declared, "You will be known henceforth as 'Face of Glory', and I ordain that you shall abide forever at my door. Whoever neglects to worship you shall never win my grace".[182]

Elsewhere the Demon Rāhu is identified with the Face of Glory,[183] and in this myth the Face is shown to be a reflex of this Demon of Darkness and at the same time a part of Śiva's own nature, a projection of his illuminated Consciousness.

* * * * *

The Face of Glory combines in its angry countenance the features of the aquatic and chthonic animal, the makara, and those of the solar and celestial animal, the lion. It is called the Siṃha-mukha, "Face of the Lion", and the lion is cognate with the Sun; it is the cognizance of Sūrya, the Sun God, and is emblazoned on his banner. The Mask is also the Rāhur-mukha, "Face of Rāhu", and Rāhu is the son of a lioness, Siṃhika. Rāhu is called Svarbhānu, "Splendour of Radiance", the asura who "struck the Sun with darkness, and stricken with darkness he did not shine".[184] The

---

180. For the theme of swallowing by a monster, see Eliade, 1960, pp. 219ff. 181. Combaz, 1939, pp. 50f., & 101; Auboyer, 1949, p. 119.

182. *Skanda-purāṇa* II.XVII.X.10ff.; XI.36-44; retold by Zimmer, 1946, p. 330. 183. See below, pp. 309, 311 ff.

184. ŚB V.3.2.2; cf. RV V.40.5-6.

a

b

Fig. 228 : a. A stupa framed by a <u>kālamakara</u>. b. An image of the Buddha standing beneath a <u>kālamakara</u>. c and d. Two examples from Bali of Faces of Glory with a single eye.

c,d

"darkness" is the "Upper Darkness", the principial indistinction of non-manifestation.[185] Behind the Mask of Death is the Sun, the Eye of All.[186]

The Sun, cognate with the Breath of Life, is also Death : "Now that man in yonder orb (the Sun)... is no other than Death; - his feet have stuck fast in the heart, and having pulled them out he comes forth; and when he comes forth then that man dies",[187] and, "inasmuch as the Sun is Death, his offspring here below are mortal".[188] The Sun, generator of his children, is also their devourer.[189] The Sun, who measures out the cycles of Time, is identified with Prajāpati, the Year, who both "killeth and maketh alive",[190] who unifies some things and separates others".[191] He is "the One-to-be-Known, the all-devourer, the all-producer".[192]

---

185. See Guénon, 1952, Ch. XXXI ("Les deux nuits"). The Upper and Lower Darknesses, which are Non-manifestation and the Substantial Principle of manifestation respectively, should not be confused with the Upper and Lower Waters, which represent the possibilities of informal and formal manifestation. These latter are both contained within the Lower Darkness. Cf. the diagram in n. 21, p. 5, above.

186. RV VII.63.1. Accordingly the Face is sometimes shown with but a single eye. 187. ŚB X.5.2.13. 188. ŚB II.3.3.7. 189. PB XXI.2.1; cf. parallel texts in Coomaraswamy, 1940, p. 47.

190. AV XIII.3.3; cf. I Sam. II.6 and I Kings V.7. 191. AĀ III.2.3.

192. BG XIII.6.

Generation and destruction are the inseparable aspects of the divine. The God has two faces : he gives birth and he kills. The teaching that all produced things are subject to decay and death is the very basis of the Buddhist Dharma : where there is birth, there inevitably follows old age, disease and death. The Enemy is Time (kāla) : he is the insatiable and voracious glutton, engulfing all existences; and Time is Śiva in his manifestation as the "Black One" (kāla) and Rudra, "The Howler", the personification of dark, tamasic aspects of the divine. For Buddhists, kāla is Yama, the King of the Dead, who in his Tibetan form as Shindje is the Kīrttimukha who devours the living contents of the Wheel of Existence.[193]

* * * * *

The Face of Glory is the devouring Sun. It is the visible appearance of the Sun Door, which is a portal of death for the ignorant but a Gate of Life for Comprehensors.[194] In the Indian zodiac the makara is the sign that corresponds to Capricorn, which lies to the North, in the position of the winter solstice. The makara is thereby identified with the Gate of Cosmic Exit, the Gateway of the Gods, cognate with the Sun Gate.[195] The zodiacal makara is the Face of Glory, and its location at the Northern apex of the celestial circle is symbolically conveyed by the location of the Face at the apex of the doorway's arch.

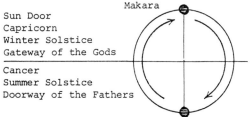

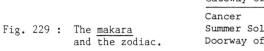

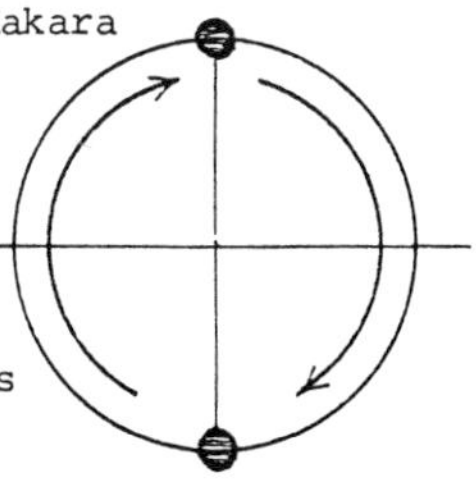

Fig. 229 : The makara and the zodiac.

This clarifies the meaning of doorways adorned with the kālamakara motif. On the one hand the Face of Glory, the sign of the Sun Door, is apotropaic, repulsing the unworthy with its terrible visage; but the Worthies (arhat) know that the way to the deathless is through the Doorway of Death : the Door of Death is the Door of Deliverance. Death is not destruction but transformation. The Face marks the transition point and the locus of the sacrifice : he who would pass beyond the Sun Door must be devoured, his selfhood swallowed, offered in a willing act of sacrifice. Then the other, glorious side of the Mask is revealed and life, emanated from Principle, returns to Principle. The other side of the monster's Mask is the Face of Glory.

The motif of the monster-Face of the makara set in the zodiacal sign of Capricorn traces to Vedic formulations. The symbolism of the God Varuṇa encompasses the same concepts. Varuṇa is "the Seizer" (graha)[196] who "seizes the sick man",[197] "seeks after these creatures... seizing on them"[198]

---

193. See above, p. 85f. 194. Above, pp. 209 f.

195. Guénon, 1962, p. 171. Cf. above, p. 271. 196. JUB IV.1.7.

197. TS II.3.11.1; V.2.1.3; AB VII.15. 198. ŚB II.3.2.10.

and on the sacrificer's children,[199] and "seizes him who is seized by the Evil One".[200] "Seizer" (graha) is a synonym of makara and also of śiśumāra, "the crocodile". The sacrificer wears an amulet "in order that the celestial Varuṇa may not strike fear into him... and Varuṇa does not slay him in his pride, neither does the makara, the graha or śiśumāra hurt him".[201] The word śiśumāra is both "child killer" and "crocodile", and Varuṇa, the Cosmic Crocodile, "into whose maw the seven rivers flow",[202] lies in the river, his head facing into the current, waiting to seize the children of the sacrificer.[203] He is the Crocodile (śiśumāra) who "ascended to Heaven", where he lies in wait with jaws agape and turned counter-current against the river of the sacrificer's path leading to the celestial regions.[204] The assimilation of Varuṇa as the devouring Crocodile lying at the Doorway to the heavens with the Face of Glory at the apex of the arch is further evidenced by the fact that Śiśumāra, the Crocodile, is also called śarkara, a term used to designate the uppermost self-perforated brick (svayamātṛṇṇā) of the Vedic fire altar, locus of the Sun Door, of the constellation Capricorn, the celestial makara,[205] and of the Face of Glory.

The makara-crocodile is Varuṇa's sinister and terrific aspect, identified with devouring Time and Death. It is the fearsome Varuṇa to whom the hymnist prays, "Stay thou here and be not angry; steal not our life from us, O thou wide-ruler";[206] and "Give us not as a prey to death, to be destroyed by thee in wrath..."[207] This is Varuṇa the Binder, who ties the wicked in his noose (pāśa), the "Lord who punishes".[208] Varuṇa carries the noose[209] and is closely associated with bonds and knots. To be bound by Varuṇa's cord is to be caught in the snare of Death. Birth, which is a receiving of name-and-form (nāma-rūpa), is a loosening of the Death-cord; Liberation, which is a transcendence of name-and-form, is the total untying of Varuṇa's knots.[210]

Fig. 230 : A Japanese Buddhist drawing of Varuṇa (Jap. Suiten, "Water God") holding his attribute, the noose, in the left hand. He rides on a turtle in the primeval Waters and wears a serpent (nāga) crown.

---

199. TS VI.6.54. 200. ŚB XII.7.2.18. 201. SA XII.21 & 28.

202. RV VIII.69.2. 203. TS VI.6.5.4.

204. PB VIII.6.8-9; XIV.5.14-15; JB I.174-5; III.193; AB II.19.3. Cf. Coomaraswamy, 1942, p. 28, n. 22 & p. 30, n. 22.

205. For the homology of the Sun Door and the sign of Capricorn, see above, p. 271 ; and for the term śarkara, see Coomaraswamy, 1977, 1, p. 485, n. 3. 206. RV I.24.11. 207. RV I.25.1-2.

208. *Manusmṛti* IX.245, quoted by Daniélou, 1964, p. 119.

209. See above, pp. 120ff.

210. The symbolism of knots, cords and bonds is discussed above, pp. 111ff. See Muṇḍ. Up. III.2.8.

g. The Astronomical Symbolism of the *Kāla-makara*.

The equivalence of the Face and the zodiacal sign of the makara, that is, Capricorn, introduces an astronomical significance into the symbolism of the kāla-makara motif. The Face occupies the location of the winter solstice in the North, the point of the sun's maximum withdrawal in the ascending phase of the annual cycle. It also marks the place of the beginning of the descending phase of the sun's movement towards the summer solstice of Cancer. We have seen that these two phases of the sun on the circle of the ecliptic, one ascending and the other descending, symbolize the cosmic inbreathing and outbreathing, which is the alternation of the "births" and "deaths" of the universe and also the counterplay of cosmic influences deriving from the principial poles of the cosmos. The makara bodies depicted on the door jambs signify these countervailing currents; and the Face at their place of junction locates their reabsorption into the One.[211]

Fig. 231 : The nodes of the moon's orbit.

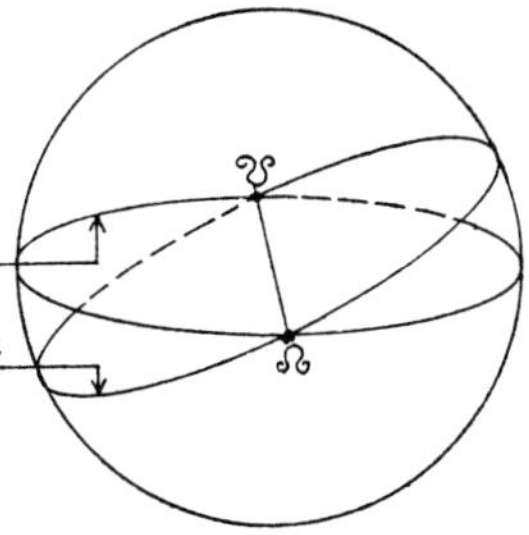

There is another way in which the kāla-makara motif refers to the astronomical symbolism of ascending and descending cycles. As mentioned above,[212] the Face of Glory is also the Face of Rāhu (rāhur-mukha). Rahu is the Demon of the Eclipses. The circle of the moon's orbit intersects with the ecliptic at two diametrically opposed points called the "nodes". The point where the moon passes from the Southern to Northern latitudes is the ascending node and the other is the descending node. Rāhu personifies the ascending node of the moon's orbit and his body, Ketu, severed from his head, is the moon's descending node.[213] Whenever a conjunction of the sun and the moon takes place at or near the nodes, there is a solar or lunar eclipse. The nodes are not stationary, but move along the ecliptic in a direction contrary to that of the sun, the moon and the planets, taking about eighteen and a half years to make a complete revolution. Because of this the eclipses also gradually move through the signs of the zodiac.[214]

---

211. These indications explain the apparent paradox that has worried some orientalists (e.g., Auboyer, 1949, p. 117) in connection with the "palace on a single pillar" spoken of in the Sinhalese chronicles. The column is said to "terminate with a makara" (*Culavaṃsa* II.11; see also Auboyer, 1949, p. 117 & p. 80, n. 3), which seems to contradict the aquatic associations of the makara. There is no anomaly. Located at the top of the axial pillar of the world, the makara occupies the position of the Sun Door; in this position the makara reveals its solar aspect. The monster at the pillar summit is the Face of Glory (kīrttimukha), the solar transformation of the aquatic monster. 212. See p. 307.

213. The expressions "dragon's head" (caput draconis) and "dragon's tail", represented by the signs ☊ and ☋ respectively, are still used in astronomy to designate the ascending and descending nodes of the moon's orbit. Also, the time taken for the moon to return to one and the same node is still called a "draconic month" (Hartner, 1938, p. 121).

214. Hartner, 1938, p. 122.

As the ascending and descending nodes of the moon's orbit Rāhu and Ketu embody a further example at yet another level of reference of the symbolism of the ascent and descent of the cosmic currents, but here expressed in its malefic aspect.

Rāhu consists of tamas, Darkness; his shape, visible only at the time of an eclipse, is like the circle of the sun and the moon; alternately, he has the shape of a serpent.[215] As the Demon of the Eclipses, he is the Devourer; he personifies a temporal cycle whose culmination is the death or annihilation of the sources of light, the sun and the moon. The Face of Glory - the Face of Rāhu - is the gluttonous face of Time, who devours life. The Face of Glory is also the Grasa-mukha, in which gras is "to devour" and "to eclipse"; and likewise, the Kāla-mukha is both the "Face of Time" and the "Face of Death", for Time (kāla) is Death. Mahākāla, "Great Time", is the great God Śiva in his terrifying (ugra) and wrathful form, the form he assumes to destroy the worlds.

h. The Symbolism of Passage through the Doorway.

The identification of the Face of Glory with Rāhu, the Eclipse, connects the kāla-makara to the theme of the falling of rain, examined above in connection with the rainbow. Typically the lower jaw is missing from the monster's face. The iconographic reference is to the myth of Rāhu. As we have seen, Rāhurmukha, "Face of Rāhu", is a cognomen of the Face of Glory.[216] The head is that of Rāhu, the Eclipse. The myth tells how the gods made an agreement with the asuras that if they helped to churn the Milky Ocean they would receive an equal share of the Nectar of Immortality (amṛta) that would be produced; but when the amṛta appeared from the Ocean Viṣṇu took it from the asuras and gave it to the gods. At this Rāhu, assuming the form of a god, seized the amṛta and began to drink it. The Sun and the Moon perceived his deception and denounced him to Viṣṇu, who promptly cut off Rāhu's head at the level of the jaw. But the amṛta had already worked its effect and the immortal head lived on, and forever since has pursued his intransigent enemies, the Sun and the Moon, in order to devour them. When the two great luminaries are partly swallowed they are eclipsed, but always slip from Rāhu's jawless mouth to shine once more.[217]

Fig. 232 : A Javanese kīrttimukha.

---

215. Varāhamihira's *Bṛhatsaṃhitā* V.1-3, quoted by Kramrisch, 1946, p. 325.

216. *Ibid.*, p. 324. 217. *Ibid.*, p. 325; Hartner, 1938, p. 131.

In this myth the head of Rāhu is severed at the level of the mouth. Since he lacks a lower jaw the amṛta that Rāhu drinks does not pass into his body but drips from his head like rain. In one of its meanings this symbolic construct refers to the falling of the "inner rain" which is the flow of amṛta from the upper palate of the yogin. As we saw, when correctly controlled by the yogin this Elixir flows down to render his body immortal, and so likewise, in the symbolism of the kāla-makara, the amṛta, channelled through the serpent door-jambs, which are the two nāḍis of the right and the left, fall from the palate of the jawless monster's head. This life-giving rain is iconographically represented by the cascades of jewels that are shown flowing from the monster's mouth.

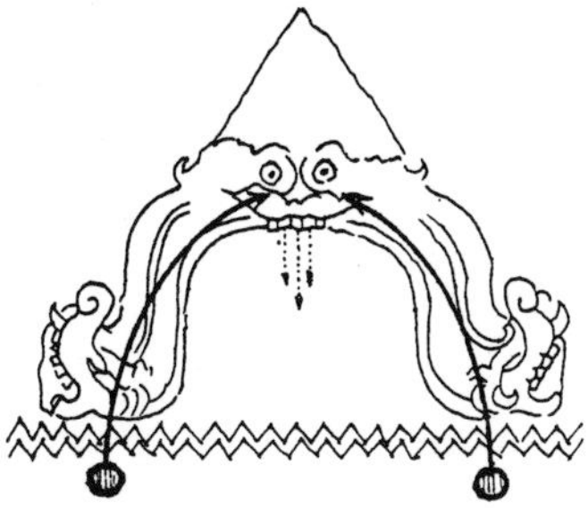
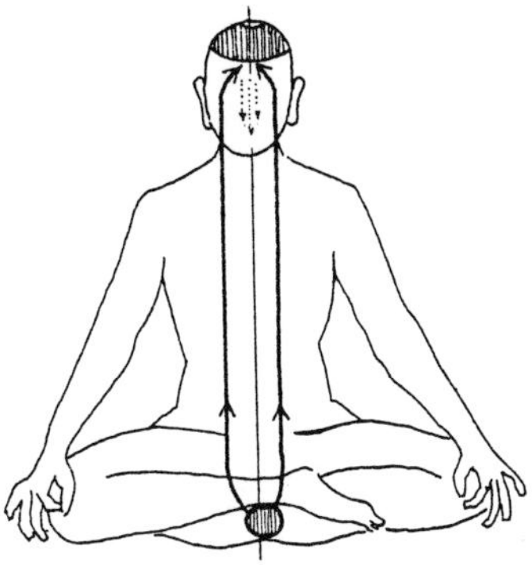

Fig. 233 : The downflow of amṛta in the kālamakara and in the yogin.

At the macrocosmic level of interpretation the theme of the monster who releases the downflowing rain of amṛta from his jawless mouth is parallelled in the Vedic Serpent Vṛtra, whose jaws were smitten by Indra's bolt when he released the waters of life.[218] With jaws shut tight the Dragon-Serpent enveloped the world[219] and covered all;[220] jawless, he breathes out his splendour, wealth and sovereignty into existence.[221] Vṛtra's outbreathing is the exhalation of the Spirit; it is the universe made manifest. So also the Face, its cheeks distended in a furious outblowing, inflates the worlds; from its jaws stream fiery scrolls of animating Breath.

Varuṇa, as Death and the Seizer, like Vṛtra also restrains the Waters; to him belong the stagnant Waters, for "whatsoever parts of flowing waters do not flow, these are withheld by Varuṇa"[222] and "it is to Varuṇa that those waters belong which, whilst being part of flowing water, do not flow"[223] : "The Great Varuṇa has hidden the sea".[224] When appeased, Varuṇa is the giver of the living, flowing Waters; he causes the rivers to flow, and they stream unceasingly according to his ordinance;[225] by his occult power the rivers swiftly pouring into the ocean do not fill it;[226] and he ascends to heaven as a hidden ocean.[227] And, with clear reference to the symbolism of the rainbow and its seven colours, just as the seven rivers flow from the mouth of Vṛtra when made to gape by Indra's vajra, so also "from thy (Varuṇa's) mouth flow the seven rivers, as through a deep channel".[228] Here again it is Indra who rescues and "unlooses" the victims "bound" by Varuṇa.[229]

---

218. See above, pp. 64f. 219. TS II.4.12.2. 220. RV I.32.7.
221. Cf. RV I.80.6. 222. ŚB V.3.4.12. 223. ŚB V.3.4.12.
224. RV IX.73.3. 225. RV II.28.4. 226. RV V.85.6. 227. RV VIII.41.8.
228. RV VIII.58.12. 229. Dumézil, 1934, pp. 79ff.

Therefore to pass through the doorway beneath the gaping jaw of the kīrttimukha is to pass through the celestial rain that pours down from the jawless mouth of the monster; it is to pass through a shower of death-defeating Elixir. Passage through the doorway is the symbolic equivalent of a lustration in amṛta; whoever enters the sacred precinct is made immortal; he passes from the realm ruled by Time and Death to the domain of the timeless and the deathless.

* * * * *

The same meanings inhere within other symbols adorning doorways. Indra, the God of the life-bestowing and life-sustaining rain, is frequentl shown at the centre of the lintel, holding his bow, which is identified with the rainbow. To pass beneath Indra's bow, the rainbow, is a transition from the terrestrial to the celestial worlds by way of the bridge of the rainbow-snake. It is also to pass through the lustrating rain of amṛt that Indra showers upon the earth.

The symbolic themes of Indra and his rainbow, the rainbow-snake, and the Churning of the Milky Ocean, come together in the architecture of the gateways of Angkor Thom, which stand at the end of the causeways balustere with serpents held by the devas and the asuras. The angles of the facades show Indra mounted on a giant three-headed elephant.[230] In a variation of the same symbolism, the Khmers also chiselled rainbow designs on the lintels of doorways leading into their temples. Frequently the figure of Indra was added in the centre of the bow, sometimes seated on a three-headed elephant or alternately on a Face of Glory (kīrttimukha).[231]

Fig. 234 :
A lintel at Banteay Srei, Angkor, showing Indra riding his elephant Airāvata. With his vajra he smites the serpent Vṛtra to release the Waters, which pour down upon the plants, animals and men below. The scene is framed by a rainbow-serpent arch.

Indra is carried by his elephant, Airāvata, whose name is also that of the rainbow and the lightning-thunderbolt (vajra). By etymology and and myth Airāvata is related to the Waters and the life-fluid of the universe.[232] As do the Waters, Airāvata and his elephant kin support the cosmos. It is recounted that when Garuḍa, the Golden Sunbird, emerged from

230. Coedes, 1963, pp. 47f. 231. *Ibid.*, p. 48; de Coral Rémusat, 1936.

232. Zimmer, 1946, p. 104, traces the connections.

his egg at the beginning of time, Brahmā took the two halves of the egg shell, one in each hand, and chanted over them seven sacred incantations. From the shell in his right hand emerged Airāvata, followed by seven other bull elephants; and from the shell in the left hand came eight elephant cows. The sixteen elephants, the ancestors of all pachyderms, support the universe in the eight directions of space and are called dig-gajas, the "Elephants (gaja) of the Directions (dik)".[233] As supporters of the universe elephants are often shown as caryatids supporting temples and stupas. Airāvata's connection with the supporting Waters is indicated in other ways. Airāvata was one of the precious things that rose from the depths as the gods and the titans churned the Milky Ocean.[234] He is the King of the Serpents (nāga-rāja) : "They (the nāgas) that have Airāvata for their king - the snakes, shining forth in battle - are like unto thunder-clouds impelled by lightning-attended wind... they glow in the upper sky like the Sun... these scions of Airāvata... Who would wish to move in the army of the sunbeams without Airāvata ?"[235]

a

b

Fig, 235 : a. A Japanese Buddhist drawing of Indra (Jap. Taishakuten) riding on Airāvata. Indra holds the vajra with which he smites Vṛtra to release the Waters; and Airāvata carries a single prong vajra in his trunk, referring to the adamantine nature of his inflowing and outflowing breaths. b. The elephant frieze at the base of the Kailaśanatha temple, Elūrā. The elephants represent the Waters on which the temple, as the embodiment of the cosmos, floats.

The ancestral elephant Airāvata emerged from the Waters at their churning, and in the Indian myths the elephants are closely associated with the clouds and rain. "The elephant", says Zimmer, "is a rain cloud walking on the earth",[236] and because of this assimilation the elephant is frequently used in rain-making rituals.[237] The elephants were at one time winged and moved through the sky like clouds until condemned to walk upon the ground as a punishment for their misdemeanours.[238]

The identification of elephants and clouds explains their presence on the lintels of Hindu and Buddhist structures, where they are shown one on either side of the Goddess Lakṣmi, aspersing her with water pouring from

233. Zimmer, 1955, p. 160; 1946, pp. 104f.

234. Mbh I.17ff.; *Viṣṇu-purāṇa* I.9; *Matsya-purāṇa* CCXLIX.13-38; etc. See also the references from Zimmer in the previous note.

235. Mbh *Pausya-parvan* III, quoted by Vogel, 1926, p. 62.

236. Zimmer, 1946, p. 109. 237. E.g., *ibid*., pp. 105ff.

238. *Ibid*., p. 106.

their trunks or from vases held in their trunks.[239] Appearing in this aspect the Goddess is called Gaja-Lakṣmi, "Lakṣmi of the Elephants". Alternately, the elephants flank a stupa, or some other representation of the Buddha in either iconic or aniconic form.[240] The aspersion of Lakṣmi has its equivalent in the Buddhist myth : at his nativity the future Buddha and his mother are washed by two streams of water flowing from the trunks of sky-elephants,[241] or alternately from seven or nine dragons or serpents.[242] The Hindu and Buddhist parallels are so close that the Gaja-Lakṣmi is employed on the ancient Indian stupas to represent the aspersion of Māyā;[243] but whether it appears in a Hindu or a Buddhist context the theme of water pouring from the elephants' trunks is an abhiṣeka, a lustration with the ambrosial rain that confers immortality, with the Waters of Life, falling from celestial elephant-clouds.

Fig. 236 ;
a. Gaja-Lakṣmi, Lakṣmi aspersed by elephants.
b. Indra riding on Airāvata.

The identification goes further : the Sanskrit word nāga means both "snake" and "elephant"; in myth and symbol their meanings coalesce. They both are linked with the Waters; transposed to the level of celestial reference, the snake is the rainbow and the elephant is the cloud, both equally the source of the life-giving rain and dew. The elephant's trunk is associated with the rainbow-serpent both by its ophidian shape and by its ability to suck up water. The primordial elephant Airāvata has seven trunks, reminiscent of the nimbus of seven serpent heads that adorns the heads of nāgas, of those which similarly appear behind the heads of Rāhu

---

239. Lintels showing the Goddess aspersed by flanking elephants are a feature of the earliest Buddhist architecture, and span the gateways of monuments of the 1st and 2nd centuries B.C. From then on it has regularly appeared in Hindu and Buddhist art and architecture up to the present day.

240. E.g., at Kaṇherī, where it is shown with the Buddha Tree and Throne, the aniconic representations of Enlightenment.

241. Warren, 1922, p. 46.

242. See e.g., Seckel, 1964, pp. 266-7, caption to pl. 55.

243. Foucher, 1934, *passim*.

and Ketu, the seven heads of the serpents that form the balustrades at the Bayon, and the seven heads of Mucalinda who protects the meditating Buddha.

Thus the trunks of the elephants flanking the Goddess Lakṣmi are visually, functionally and iconographically synonymous with serpent-makaras and thereby with the two halves of the cosmic rainbow; they are the channels that carry the spiritual currents through the body of the universe and through the body of man. The connection of the elephant with the rainbow, the serpent, the makara and the nāḍis is also indicated by the presence of Airāvata within the mūlādhāra, the root plexus within the perineum, the cakra or node that lies within the Lower Waters of microcosmic man.[244]

The symbolism of the Gaja-Lakṣmi and its variations parallels that of the Face of Glory. The lustrations of the Buddha, the stupa or the Goddess by the two elephants shows that they have achieved the realms of immortality; they are wholly immersed in the ambrosial Elixir. They figure the state of deathlessness atttained by the worshipper when he passes through the portal. Stepping beneath the elephants he is aspersed with the Water of Immortality that flows from their trunks. In entering the sacred enclosure he is showered with the Waters of Life and is washed free of his mortality.

3. THE INTERIOR ASCENT.

The correspondence of the macrocosm and the microcosm is a fundamental proposition of the Hindu and the Buddhist doctrines. "In this fathom-length body, furnished with perception and consciousness", says a Pali text, "there is contained the world",[245] and this is a theme that is repeated on many occasions throughout the Mahāyāna and Vajrayāna literature. The human body is the total universe in miniature. A strict analogy exists between their physical components, their divisions, their structuring, their proportions. The spinal column is Meru, the cosmic Mountain that pivots the world, and is therefore called the merudaṇḍa, the "Meru rod" or "Meru staff". Rising from the perineum it passes through a series of "wheels" (cakra), which are the counterparts in the human body of the celestial planes ranged on the slopes of the Mountain. It emerges at the brahmarandhra, the "cavity of Brahman", at the apex of the head, a luminous point of light, cognate with the Sun, the uncreated, unborn and eternal origin of all things. Here is located the Centre of being, the Principle whence his existence devolves.[246] The aim of yogic practice is to climb the Mountain of one's body, ascending stage by stage through planes of increasing luminosity, to the total Effulgence of the Sun.

According to the psycho-physiology (or pneuma-physiology) of the Indian traditions, the body is traversed by an indefinitely large number[247] of subtle vectors, luminous "arteries" or "canals" (nāḍi),[248] by which prāṇa, the vital Breath, circulates through the body. Three among them

---

244. Avalon, 1958, pp. 334 & 355, and see pl. II; Govinda, 1959, p. 142.

245. *Ayuttara* IV.45-6. 246. Tucci, 1961, pp. 108f.

247. They are said to number 300,000, 200,000, 80,000 and, most commonly, 72,000, but these numbers must be taken as symbolical.

248. Cf. above, p. 60. The nāḍis belong to the subtle form and should not be confused with the corporeal arteries or nerves, although they have correspondences with the latter. See Guénon, 1945, pp. 97f.; Eliade, 1958a, p. 234.

are of special importance : the suṣumnā,[249] the median vector, coincident with the central axis of the body; and, on either side, the iḍā and piṅgalā, which run respectively from the right and left nostrils to meet in the perineum. Through these, as we have seen, flow the two "breaths", prāṇa and apāna, the vehicles of citta, "mind", the principle of the psyche's volitional, affective and thinking activities.[250] The suṣumnā joins the root cakra, the mūlādhāra, with the thousand-petalled lotus (sahasrāra) at the crown of the head, passing through the cakras, numbered five according to the Hindu *Tantras*[251] and three according to the Buddhists.

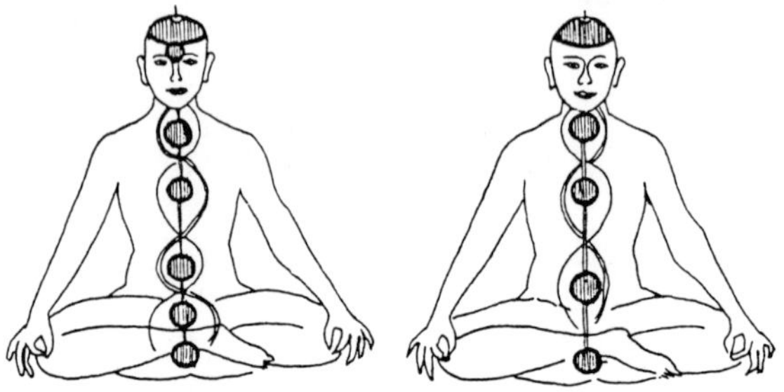

Fig. 237 : The subtle pneuma-physiological centres (cakra) in the body according to the Hindu and Buddhist schemata. The Hindus number five cakras between the root cakra (mūlādhāra-cakra) in the perineum and the thousand petal lotus (sahasrāra) at the summit of the head; the Buddhists number three centres.

A cakra is defined as the place "where the nāḍis meet like spokes in the nave of a chariot wheel",[252] and the Buddhist aspirant is told "to meditate on the four cakras,[253] each of which is formed like an umbrella or the wheel of a chariot".[254] The psycho-physical complex is a chariot of fire, with wheels set upon the suṣumnā as on an axle. The three cakras of the Buddhist schema are located in the umbilical, cardiac and laryngeal regions, and are the sites of the three Buddha Bodies : the "apparitional Body" or the "measured Body" (nirmāṇa-kāya) in the stomach cakras; the Dharma Body (dharma-kāya) in the heart cakra; and the "Body of Majesty" (saṃbhoga-kāya) in the cakra of the throat.[255]

In the yoga techniques of Buddhist Tantra the outflowing of the mind (citta) to its objects is forcibly reversed by arresting[256] the flow of the two breaths, prāṇa and apāna, which carry it out from its source through the iḍā and piṅgalā. By a simultaneous control of thought and respiration the mind is concentrated and the breaths redirected into the base of the median channel, the suṣumnā. From here the citta, now

---

249. The term suṣumnā does not appear in the Buddhist texts, where the term avadhūtī is used instead. See Eliade, 1958a, p. 240.

250. Tucci, 1961, p. 113.

251. For an exhaustive description of the cakras in Hindu *Tantra*, see Avalon, 1958. 252. Mund. Up. II.2.6.

253. There are four cakras if the mūlādhāra is included.

254. Evans-Wentz, 1958, p. 191; cf. Govinda, 1959, p. 193.

255. For the Buddha Bodies, see Suzuki, 1930, pp. 142ff. & 308ff.

256. The word hatha in hatha-yoga means "violence", referring to the force with which the breath's flow is redirected.

257. According to some texts the heat is obtained by a "transmutation" of sexual energy. See Evans-Wentz, 1958, pp. 316ff.

visualized as a flame fanned by the two breaths into a state of brilliant and fiery incandescence,[257] passes up through the cakras, being progressively purified by an ever intenser burning, until it finally reaches the lotus at the crown of the head (uṣṇīṣa-kamala), where it is absorbed within the supreme beatitude of the One.[258]

The two subtle vectors of the right and the left, the iḍā and the piṅgalā, and the breaths which they carry, are identified with a series of complementary principles representative of all the contraries and oppositions within the cosmos : Wisdom (prajñā) and Method (upāya), female and male, the ovum and the seed,[259] the moon and the sun, and so on.[260] In the lotus of the head at the apex of the being these principles unite; the Male and the Female are fused as in sexual union; Wisdom and Method are inseparably merged (prajñopāya) in the non-duality (advaita) of the Great Bliss (mahā-sukha) of the Void.

This merging in Unity is not, however, the ultimate goal of the yogin's practice. The ascending realization is followed by a descent. The breaths, now transformed into the Elixir of Enlightenment (amṛta), flow down through the cakras and thence to the lower parts of the body. By this inner "aspersion" with the Water of Life the body and mind of the yogin are identified with the vajra; the total being has been filled with the fiery effulgence of Enlightened Consciousness. The final end of the Adamantine Path (vajrayāna) has been achieved.[261]

Iḍā and piṅgalā are equated with the Moon and the Sun,[262] and Eliade draws attention to the significance of their merging in the axial suṣumnā. The rhythm of the sādhaka's inbreathing is the course of the sun, that is, the day; and that of this outbreathing is the course of the moon, that is, the night. His breathing relates him to the cosmic cycles; and when the two breaths are united in the "middle path",[263] the median vector that "devours time",[264] the sun and moon are joined, the opposites are reintegrated and time is transcended. The sādhaka enters the atemporal state which the *Tantras* term "that in which there is neither day nor night". He has reached the locus of the coincidentia oppositorum, the nunc stans.[265]

---

258. Tucci, 1961, p. 113; David Neel, 1965, p. 221; Govinda, 1959, pp. 171ff. Analogous methods and symbolism are found in the kuṇḍalinī-yoga of Hindu tantrism but in this there are numbered five cakras plus the mūlādhāra and the sahasrāra. See Avalon, 1958; Rawson, 1973, pp. 25ff.; Eliade, 1965, pp. 117ff.; 1958a, pp. 245ff.; Tucci, 1961, pp. 114ff.

259. Eliade, 1958a, p. 239; Dasgupta, 1958, p. 119, who cites the *Sadhanamala*, the *Hevajra-tantra* and the *Heruka-tantra*.

260. Eliade, 1958a, p. 237. The import of these homologies was indicated above, pp. 210 ff.

261. See n. 258 above. There are numerous variations on this basic meditational schema, which employ a rich divergence of symbolic expression, often deliberately obscured in the texts by an ambiguous terminology that can only be interpreted by initiates (see Eliade, 1958a, pp. 249ff.). For other aspects of the technique, such as the arousal of the śakti in the nirmāṇa-kāya, see Dasgupta, 1962, pp. 92 ff.

262. See Bagchi, 1934, pp. 82ff.; Dasgupta, 1958, pp. 107f.; 1962, p. 239.

263. Buddhism is termed "the Middle Path" (Jap. chūdō), or lit., "the Way of the Centre".

264. *Hathayoga-pradīpikā*, IV.16-17, cited by Eliade, 1961, p. 88.

265. Eliade, 1961, pp. 87ff.

19 THE SYMBOLISM OF THE SPIRE.

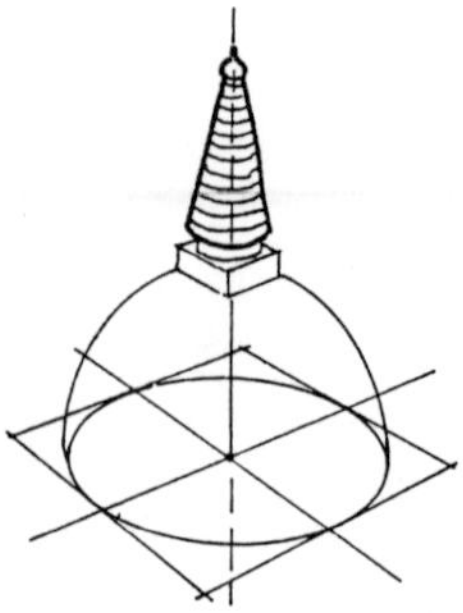

1. THE POST OR MAST.

The pole or mast (yūpa, yaṣṭi), support of the stupa finial, takes two forms. In some cases it penetrates deeply into the body of the dome or traverses it entirely; in others it rises from a supporting stone (yantragala)[1] set into a shallow cavity upon the summit. Both methods are attested by examples in various regions of Central and South East Asia, India, China and Japan.[2] The yūpa of the great Svayambhūnātha stupa in Nepal is a wooden post rising from the base of the dome;[3] the yūpa of the Kaniṣka stupa is described as an iron pillar that was hoisted by winches to be set into the apex of the tower.[4] The yūpas of Japanese tower-stupas (termed "heart pillars", shin-bashira) are of three types : they are set into pits dug deep into the ground; they rise from the surface of the ground; or they are suspended by chains from the external columns. In each case they emerge from the uppermost roof to form the spire (Jap. sōrin); in no case are they structural : excavations of the 8th Cent. Hōryuji stupa revealed that the central column had rotted away beneath ground level without affecting the stability of the building.[5]

It has been shown in the preceding that the prototypic harmikā is a sacred space enclosed by a fence or by the walls of an hypaethral pavilion and centred by a Parasol or Tree, in which latter case the harmikā is a caitya-vṛkṣa. The spire that crowns the stupa, in whatever outward form it might take in its later developments, retains the meanings that inhere within these symbols of axiality.[6]

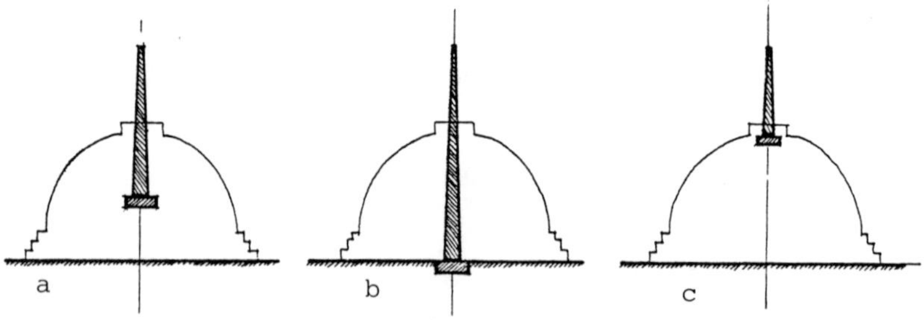

Fig. 238 : The mast or post in the dome-stupa, where it either penetrates the dome (a), traverses it (b), or rises from the harmikā (c).

---

1. Cf. above, p. 129. 2. Combaz, p. 52. 3. *Ibid.*, p. 53; 1932, p. 245.

4. *Ibid.*; 1933, p. 201; 1935, p. 53. 5. Kidder, 1972, pp. 99f.

6. For the development of spire types, see Combaz, 1933, pp. 119ff.

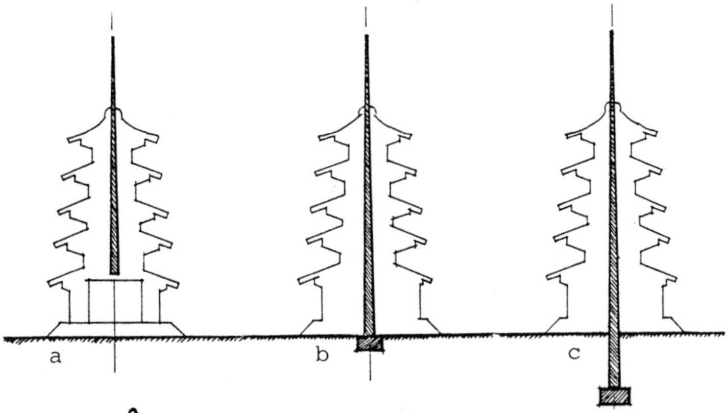

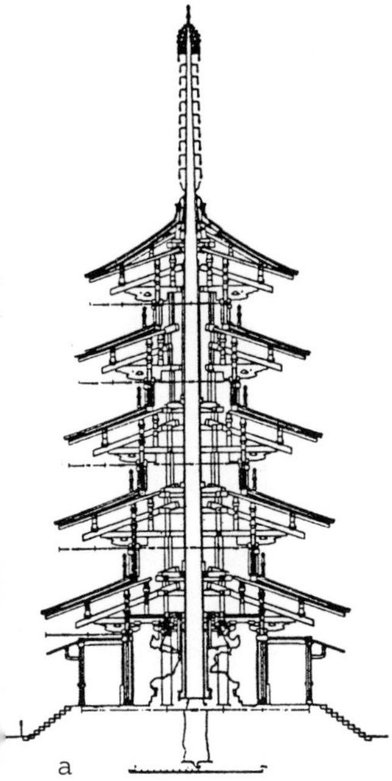

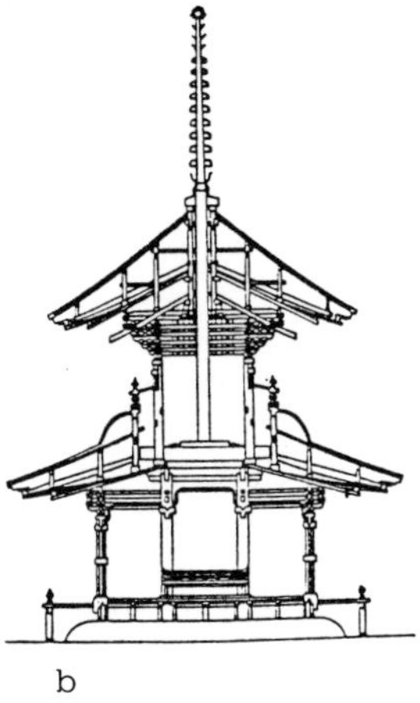

Fig. 239 : The mast or post in the tower-stupa, where it either stands suspended above the ground (a), rises from a foundation stone level with the ground (b), or sits into the ground (c).

Fig. 240 : a. A section through the stupa at the Hōryuji, Nara, showing the "heart pillar" (shin-bashira), which was originally set deeply into the ground, but now stand above ground level, supported from above. b. A section through a Japanese "Prabhutaratna stupa" (Jap. Tahō-tō), showing the "heart pillar" suspended above the ceiling of the shrine room at ground floor level.

2. THE SPIRE AS SACRIFICIAL POST (*YŪPA*).

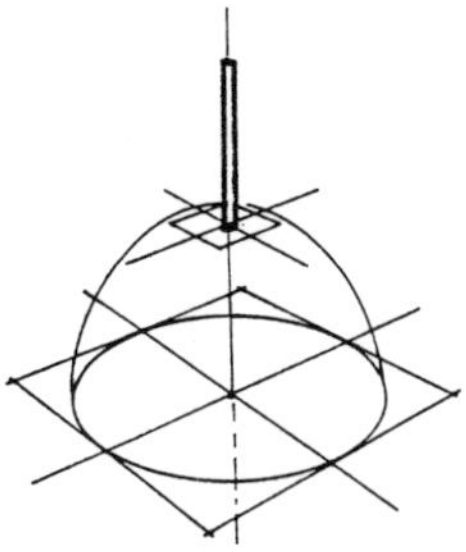

The post that supports the umbrellas of the spire is called the yūpa,[7] which literally means "post" but more specifically refers to the Vedic sacrificial post. The sacrificial post was square at the bottom, octagonal at the middle section and curved at the top, representing Earth, Midspace and Heaven respectively.[8] This is precisely the form of the liṅga[9] and also

7. The term occurs in connection with the stupa in the early text, the *Divyāvadāna* 244, quoted by Combaz, 1935, p. 51; cf. Foucher, 1905, 1, p. 96. Most scholars have thought it to be scribe's error, but Irwin (1980, p. 13) has shown that it also occurs in another early text, the *Mahāvaṃsa*. On the Vedic sacrificial post, see Banerjea, 1940.

8. Irwin, 1980, p. 14 and p. 32, n. 14, gives references. On the cosmological symbolism of the square and the circle, see above, pp. 101ff.; for the cube and the sphere, see pp. 209ff.; and for the symbolism of the octagon, see p. 167. Cf. Agrawala, 1965, pp. 121ff. 9. See above, pp. 167ff.

that of the finial posts of early Sri Lankan stupas.[10] Such a stupa post is locally called a "peg of Indra" (indrakīla, P. indha-khīla), that is, Indra's vajra, with which he smote the Serpent Vṛtra's head and fixed the Mountain Rock at the beginning of the world.[11] There is a further assimilation : the sacrificial post is sometimes simply described as octagonal ("The sacrificial post is eight-cornered; for the Gayātri metre has eight syllables, and the Gayātri is Agni's metre"),[12] and the yūpas of early stupas often take this same form.[13]

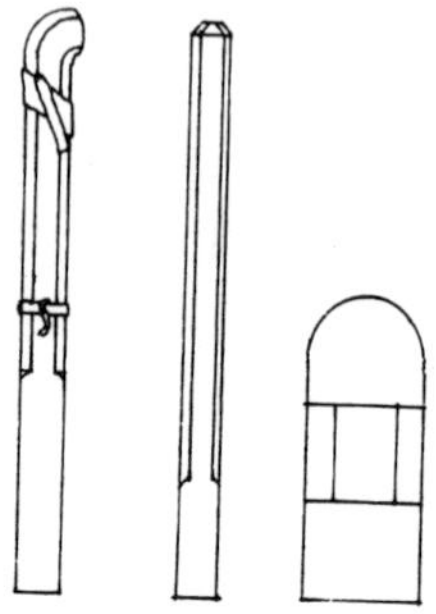

Fig. 241 : The Vedic sacrificial post (yūpa) (a), the axial yūpa of the stupa (b), and a liṅga. Each is circular above, octagonal at its mid-section and square below, representing the Three Worlds of Heaven, Midspace and Earth respectively.

These correlations indicate a complex pattern of interlocking symbolic concepts. Firstly, by its association with the Vedic yūpa the finial post of the stupa is assimilated with the World Tree. Addressing the sacrificial post, the ritualist says, "Rise erect, O Lord of the Forest",[14] and elsewhere he further specifies that it is the Tree growing on the summit of the world, which in the symbolism of the stupa, is the location of the harmikā : "Lord of the Forest, raise thyself up on the loftiest spot on earth".[15] The same identifications are made in the *Śatapatha Brāhmaṇa*.[16]

The yūpa is also identified with the vajra. Like the yūpa the vajra is described as "eight-angled" (aṣṭaśri),[17] and the natural crystalline structure of the diamond (vajra) is octagonal.[18] In keeping with this symbolism the Pali word attansa, literally "eight-angled", also signifies "diamond" and "pillar".[19] "The post is the thunderbolt (vajra)", is a repeated refrain in the *Śatapatha Brāhmaṇa*,[20] alluding not only to the axial symbolism of the vajra but also and more specifically to its function as "Indra's pin" (indra-kīla) : "For he who has set up the sacrificial post has hurled the vajra... Indra, forsooth, is the deity of the sacrifice... and he (the sacrificer) thereby connects it (the sacrificial post) with Indra".[21] The stupa post is the vajra spike that pins the Mountain of the Cosmos.

---

10. Paranavitana, 1946, pp. 36f.; cf. Gail, 1980, p. 260.

11. See above, p. 184. 12. ŚB V.2.1.5; cf. III.7.1.28.

13. E.g., at Amarāvati, the Sri Lankan stupas, Borobudur, etc. See Paranavitana, 1946, p. 35; Combaz, 1933, p. 54; Gail, 1980, p. 260.

14. RV I.36.13. 15. RV III.8.3; cf. Auboyer, 1949, p. 94 and above, pp. 256 ff., where the symbolism of the yūpa and its assimilation with the World Pillar (skambha) is further elaborated. 16. ŚB III.6ff.; cf. Irwin, 1980, p. 14. 17. AB II.1; KB X.1. In RV IV.22.2, on the other hand, the vajra is "four-edged" (catur-aśri).

18. Guénon, 1962, p. 290; Coomaraswamy, 1939, p. 71. 19. *Idem.*

20. E.g., ŚB III.6.4.13; III.7.1.14. 21. ŚB III.7.1.17.

The connection of the stupa post with the liṅga, suggested by their morphological similarity, is given credence by other evidence. The Nepalese still refer to the axial pillars of their stupas as liṅgas.[22] In Hindu architecture the liṅga is not infrequently used as a finial in a manner similar to that of the yūpa standing at the stupa summit. Rising from the āmalaka in the position more usually occupied by the kalaśa, it is called the ākāśa-liṅga,[23] in which ākāśa is the dimensionless space of the void point.[24] Again, the Brahmanic aiḍūka is described as consisting of a liṅga standing upon three platforms.[25]

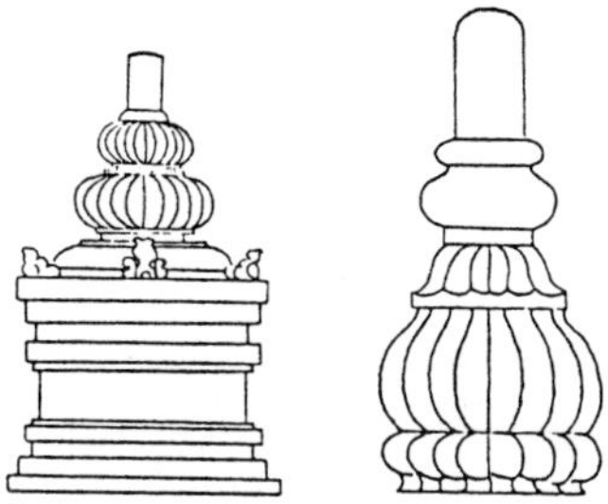

Fig. 242 : Examples of liṅga finials on Indian and Javanese stupas.

Finally, the assimilation of stupa post and liṅga is explicit in Java, where there exist many examples of stupas having liṅgas for finials, and where there is also a type of stupa, called a liṅga-stūpa, which shows the same sequence of sectional shapes - square, octagonal and circular - as does the liṅga.[26] The liṅga-topped stupa relates to the considerations developed previously in connection with the harmikā as the High Altar.[27]

---

22. Irwin, 1980, pp. 25f. 23. Dhaky, 1974.

24. Cf. the discussion of the kalaśa as the Void Point below, pp. 346 f. On the meaning of ākāśa, see Coomaraswamy, "Kha and Other Words Denoting 'Zero' in the Indian Metaphysics of Space", in 1977, 2, pp. 220ff.

25. Irwin, 1980, p. 27, and Roth, 1980, pp. 199f., both citing the *Viṣṇudharmottara Purāṇa* III.84.1-7. On the relation of the stupa and the aiḍūka, see Goswamy, 1980, pp. 2-3; Coomaraswamy, 1927, p. 30; Shah, 1951; Allchin, 1957; Roth, 1980, pp. 1999f.; Pant, 1976, pp. 18-22 & 60; Agrawala, 1964, p. 224; Pal, 1971.

26. Van Lohuizen-de Leeuw, 1980, p. 281. 27. See above, pp. 250ff.

Fig. 243 : Javanese Mountain-<u>caṇḍis</u> surmounted by stupas with <u>liṅga</u> finials.

3. <u>THE SPIRE AS PARASOL.</u>

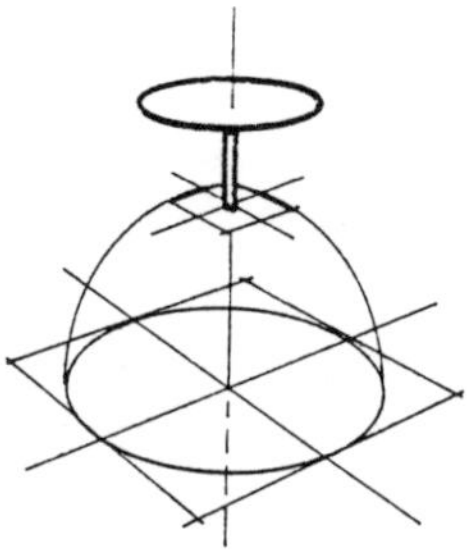

The ancient stupas at Sāñcī show a simple parasol emerging from the centre of the space enclosed by the <u>harmikā</u>'s fence. This is a theme that is repreated with variations in countless stupas throughout the ages. However far removed they might seem from those early prototypes, the later forms of the spire, such as the ribbed cone of the Sri Lankan stupas and the superimposed discs of the Tibetan and Japanese stupas, developed as a proliferation of umbrellas, placed one above the other. The spire is inseparably connected with the parasol, and its symbolism must be interpreted accordingly.

The parasol is an <u>imago mundi</u> : its canopy is Heaven, its pole is the cosmic axis, and the surface from which it rises is Earth.[28] As a cosmic image it is prominent among the aniconic images of the Buddha. Reliefs from the early stupas figure the Buddha by a throne sheltered by a parasol and fronted by footprints. The reference is cosmic : the parasol is Heaven, the throne is Midspace and the footprints are Earth.[29]

---

28. For the symbolism of the parasol see Chevalier and Gheerbrant, 1973, 3, p. 362, s.v., <u>Parasol</u>; Coomaraswamy, 1938b. 29. Auboyer, 1949, p. 67.

The form and the significance of the parasol duplicate those of the dome : the ribs come together at the pole as do rafters at the roof plate. The canopy of the umbrella is the symbolic equivalent of the stupa cupola; the point where the pole of the parasol pierces the canopy corresponds precisely to the point, defined by the harmikā, where the pole emerges from the summit of the stupa garbha.[30]

a b c

Fig. 244 : a. The single and triple parasols on the stupas at Sāñcī.
b. The Tree and the Parasol associated in images of Bodhistattvas at Borobudur, Java.

* * * * *

The *Saddharma-puṇḍarīka-sūtra* and the *Lalita Vistara* both say that the gift of a parasol to a stupa is an act that brings much merit to the donor.[31] The *Mahākarmavibhanga* says that those who give parasols will be born as cakravartin-kings.[32] A passage in the *Mahāvastu* tells how in a previous birth the Buddha erected a parasol above a stupa and as a result of that act escaped rebirth in the evil realms during twenty four cosmic expansions and reabsorptions, was then born as a cakravartin-king, then among the gods as the chief of the Maruts, and finally as the Fully Awakened One. "This (the gift of a parasol... is efficacious, fruitful, and leads to immortality (amrta)".[33]

To donate a parasol is to acknowledge that the Buddha is the supreme and universal monarch whose Law rules the cosmos. Throughout Asia from earliest times the parasol has been the emblem of kingship, and thus comes to represent the Buddha as Cakravartin. The form of the parasol with its radiating ribs recalls the wheel, which is the symbol of the Buddha located at the centre of the revolving wheel of the world.[34] The *Lalita Vistara*

---

30. The significance of this superimposition of cosmic symbols has been indicated above, pp. 266ff. 31. Combaz, 1932, p. 199; 1935, p. 57.

32. *Mahākarmavibhanga* LXIV.144, cited by Combaz, 1932, pp. 199f.; 1935, p. 57.

33. *Mahāvastu* I.13, p. 267, from the chapter entitled *Chattravastu*, "The Section of the Parasol", translated by Bénisti, 1960, 61ff.

34. See above, p. 96.

recounts how in a dream the future Buddha saw a parasol rise out of the ground and spread its light over the three worlds, presaging the manner in which his Dharma would penetrate and regulate all things. The Buddha is "the master of the world, the Teacher who bears the threefold parasol, the heavenly parasol, the earthly parasol and the parasol of Deliverance".[35]

The *Mahāvaṃsa* , describing the building of the Great Stupa in Sri Lanka, tells how King Duṭṭhagāmaṇi conferred his kingly power upon the stupa by placing a parasol, his sign of sovereignty, upon its summit.[36] The presence of the parasol is a recognition of the regal status of the stupa. Placed above the stupa the parasol indicates the royal nature of the form it shelters : the stupa embodies the Dharma that governs the cosmos; it is the visible form of the Buddha as king, as the Cakravartin who centres the universe and who sets the Wheel turning by his preaching. It is the sign of the Buddha's spiritual authority and temporal power.[37]

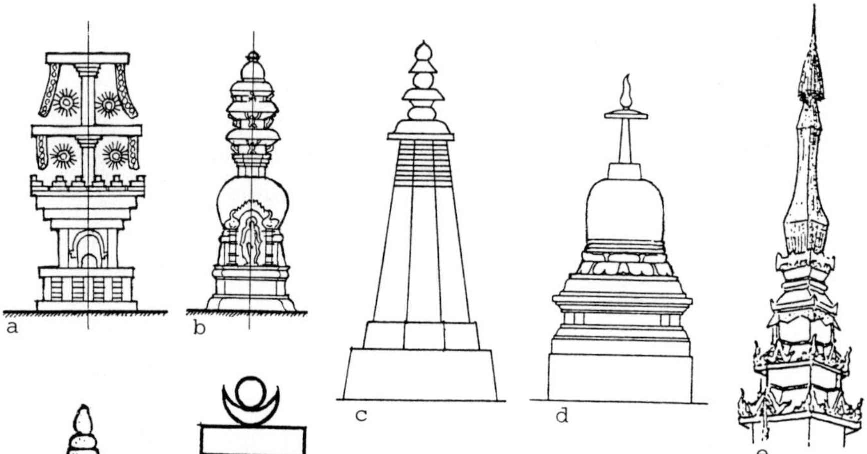

Fig. 244 : Examples of parasols from India (a and b), Java (c, d and f), Burma (e) and Tibet (g). The illustration on the right (h) shows the Buddha with a parasol emerging from his head as an extension of the meru-daṇḍa.

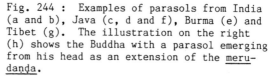

35. *Mahāvaṃsa* XXXI.91f.

36. *Ibid.*; cf. Combaz, 1932, p. 199, 1935, p. 57; Bénisti, 1960, p. 60. See also *Mahāvaṃsa* XXXI.111, where Duṭṭhagāmaṇi offers a white parasol to the Buddha relics.

37. See above, pp. 88 ff. Cf. Combaz, 1932, p. 199; Bénisti, 1960, p. 60.

4. THE SPIRE AS COSMIC TREE.

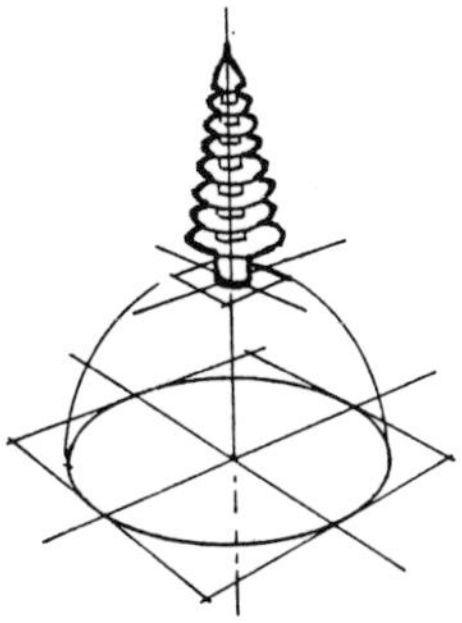

As a symbol of the cosmos the parasol is assimilable to the World Tree.[38] The pole corresponds to the trunk; the canopy, or canopies, which are so many superimposed supernal worlds, correspond to the branches.[39] The assimilation is evidenced by iconography. Reliefs from Amarāvatī show a proliferation of umbrellas which are indistinguishable from trees. Bosch has brought together comparable examples.[40] In later stupas, where the finial has become a series of superimposed discs or a grooved cone the two symbols are shown separately, with the honorific umbrella fixed above the Tree.[41]

a

b

c

Fig. 245 : a and b. Amarāvatī reliefs in which the proliferation of parasols from the harmikā has the form of a tree. c. In the Tibetan stupa the parasol and the spire discs are distinguished and shown separately.

The finial emerging from the harmikā is specifically designated as the Tree of Enlightenment. It is the Supernal Tree whose branches are the layered heavens, corresponding to states of consciousness attained in meditation, spreading one over the other in innumerable planes above the summit of Mt. Meru. It is the equivalent of the Āmalaka Tree of Hinduism, in whose branches Brahmā, Viṣṇu and Śiva dwell, described in the *Skanda Purāṇa* : "The Sun is in its branches, the gods are in their ramifications and in its leaves, flowers and fruits. Thus the Āmalaka is the support of

---

38. See above, p. 256. 39. Govinda, 1976, pp. 14f.; cf. 31,32 & 38.

40. Bosch, 1960, p. 161. 41. Govinda, 1976, p. 14.

all the gods".[42] The āmalaka, as we have seen, is the crown of the Hindu temple and equivalent to the harmikā of the stupa. It is the Sun-Tree growing from the peak of Meru.

Fig. 246 : A Tree growing from the stupa harmikā. See also the illustrations on pp. 255 and 256.

The Tibetan legends associated with the Chinese mountain Wu-t'ai Shan, sacred to Wen-chu (Mañjuśrī) and identified in its symbolic significance with the axial Mountain of the universe, tell us that on the top of the Mountain there was a five-fold caitya, from which grew a Jambu tree. When the Buddha illuminated the tree with a golden beam of light that shone from his ūrṇā, the tree gave forth a lotus flower, which opened to reveal Mañjuśrī.[43] The story parallels that of Brahmā's birth from a lotus sprung from Viṣṇu's navel; and the five-fold caitya is reminiscent of the five-roofed Jewel Stupa on the summit of Meru, wherein the Diamond World Mandala is revealed by Mahāvairocana.[44]

5. THE SYMBOLISM OF THE SPIRE DISCS.

The spire of the stupa is the Cosmic Parasol, the Tree of Enlightenment, the sacrificial Post, rising from the sacred enclosure, the High Altar, at the summit of the Mountain. The spire is typically divided into a series of horizontal layers indicated by some convention such as grooves or discs. These layers are the multiple canopies of the Parasol, the branches of the Tree, or the levels of ascent on the Pillar.

We have seen that the harmikā, the "citadel of the gods" (devakotuva) at whose centre the spire is erected, is the location of Indra's Heaven of the 33 Gods, the Trāyastriṃśa, which stands at the summit of Mt. Meru.[45] Mus has demonstrated that the uppermost of the layers of the spire corresponds to the Heaven of the Final Limit of Form, the Akaniṣṭha.[46] These two heavens, the Trāyastriṃśa and the Akaniṣṭha, are positioned at the lower and upper extremities of the series of celestial regions that are strung one above the other upon the World Axis that extends upward from the top of the Cosmic Mount. The spire rises into these supernal realms that lie above the Mountain summit; its layers represent their superimposed strata. The number and nature of these heavens is specified in the numerous texts that describe the Buddhist cosmology.

---

42. *Vaiṣṇava Khanda* XII.9-23, in Kramrisch, 1946, p. 356.

43. Bosch, 1960, p. 186, where sources are given.

44. See above, p. 259, fig. 181. 45. See p. 226.

46. Mus, 1935, pp. 523 & 716, citing Hodgson, 1874. Cf. Senart, 1882, p. 416; Waddell, 1895, p. 263.

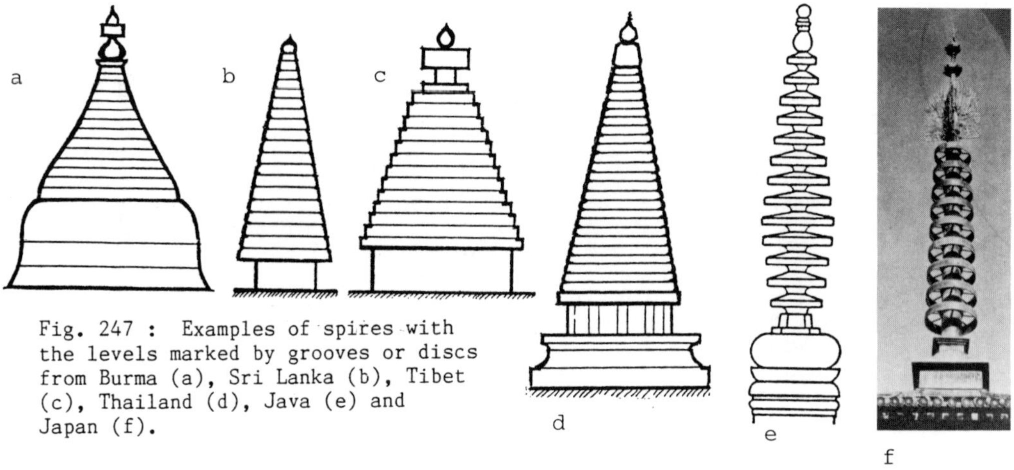

Fig. 247 : Examples of spires with the levels marked by grooves or discs from Burma (a), Sri Lanka (b), Tibet (c), Thailand (d), Java (e) and Japan (f).

6. THE BUDDHIST COSMOLOGY.

The Buddhist cosmos is divided into three worlds (trai-dhātuka, trai-lokya)[47] : the World of Desire (kāma-loka), the World of Form (rūpa-loka), and the Formless World (arūpa-loka). Together they make up the totality of the states of existence wherein deluded beings transmigrate in a succession of births and deaths, determined by the inexorable laws of causality. The World of Desire includes all those planes of existence where the inhabitants are subject to sensual cravings, those in which food, sexuality and sleep exist, ranging from the lowest hells through the six migratory realms[48] to the six Heavens of Desire.

The lowest of the six Heavens of Desire is the Heaven of the Four Celestial Kings (catur-mahā-rāja-kāyika), that is, the heaveṇ of the Regents of the Four Directions,[49] located on the sides of Mt. Meru. On the summit of Meru is the Heaven of the 33 Gods (trāyastriṃśa), ruled by Indra. These two heavens are called the Heavens of the Earth-Dwelling Gods (Jap. jigoten).

---

47. The Buddhist cosmology is described in Buddhaghoṣa's *Visuddhimagga* (see Ñānamoli, 1964). A similar, but more elaborate description is found in Vasubandhu's *Abhidharmakośa*, Ch. III (see Vallée Poussin, 1926). The classic analysis is Kirfel, 1920. See also BKDJT, p. 2513, s.v. Shumisen; Evans-Wentz, 1957, pp. 61-66; MacGovern, 1923, pp. 48ff.; Ishizuka and Coates, 1949, pp. 89ff.; Gombrich, 1975, pp. 132ff.; Beal, 1971, pp. 36ff.; Elisséeff, 1936, pp. 82ff.; Coedes and Archaimbault, 1973; ERE, IV, s.v. Cosmogony and Cosmology - Indian; Heine-Geldern, 1956, p. 2; Wales, 1977, pp. 29ff.; Viennot, 1954, pp. 101ff.; Sarkisyanz, 1965, p. 83 (which is inaccurate); Coomaraswany, 1931, p. 14 (on water cosmology); James, 1969, pp. 46ff.; Tambiah, 1976, pp. 9ff. and 1970; Gokhale, 1966.

48. See above, pp. 85f., and the caption to fig. 36, p. 83.

49. The Regents of the Four Directions are Dhṛtarāṣtra, commander of the gandharvas and piṣācas in the East; Virūḍhaka, commander of the kim-bhāndas and pretas in the South; Virūpākṣa, commander of the nāgas and the pūtanas in the West; and Vaiśravaṇa, commander of the yakṣas and rākṣasas in the North. Each is served by eight generals, who together make up the group of 32 generals.

Above them are the four Heavens of the Sky-Dwelling Gods : the Heaven of Time (yama); the Heaven of Contentment (tuṣita), where the future Buddha, the Bodhisattva Maitreya, resides; the Heaven of Joyful Transformations (nirmāṇa-rati); and the Heaven of Free Transformations by Others (para-nirmitavaśa-vartin).[50]

Above the six heavens of the World of Desire are the heavens of the World of Form. The beings dwelling in these heavens are no longer subject to desires or passions, but nevertheless still possess forms of an etherial nature. The World of Form is divided into the Heavens of the Four Meditations (catur-dhyāni-bhūmi),[51] which correspond to states of consciousness attained in meditation. An ascent through these heavens is a passage to ever more refined and rarefied levels of consciousness and a withdrawal of consciousness towards its Centre. The World of Form comprizes eighteen levels,[52] three in each of the first three Meditations, and nine in the fourth. The five highest of these levels are called the Pure Abodes (suddhāvāsakāyika),[53] and the uppermost of these is the Heaven of the Final Limit of Form (akaniṣṭha),[54] which is the heaven of the Non-Returners (anāgāmin).[55]

Beyond the Heaven of the Final Limit of Form is the third of the Buddhist Worlds, the Formless World (arūpa-loka), which includes those states of manifestation that do not possess any vestige of form but are nevertheless relative in that they are still subject to the workings of causation. The Formless World includes four heavens, which once again correspond to stages in meditation :

1) The Heaven of Limitless Space (ākāśānantyāyatana), attained in meditation by the negation of all physical phenomena.

2) The Heaven of Pure Consciousness (vijñānānantyāyatana), in which empty space is negated.

3) The Heaven of Nothingness (ākiñcayāyatana), in which Pure Consciousness is negated.

4) The Heaven of Neither Consciousness nor Non-Consciousness (naivasaṃjñānasaṃjñā-āyatana), in which both Consciousness and the absence of Consciousness are negated. In this heaven the mind is severed from both Consciousness and the non-Consciousness of nothingness. This heaven is the uttermost limit of the domain of manifestation; "beyond" this realm lies the unmanifested, the world of the Buddhas, immutable, eternal, totally unconditioned and free from the workings of causality.

* * * * *

---

50. The names of the four Heavens of the Sky-Dwelling Gods refer to pleasures enjoyed by the inhabitants. For details, see MacGovern, 1923, p. 66.

51. The four meditations are counted as five in the *Abhidhamma* , where the second meditation is divided into two parts, viz., the meditation that suppresses ratiocination (P. vitakka) and that which suppresses reflection (P. vicāra). See Paranavitana, 1954, p. 223; Coedes and Archaimbault, 1973, p. 17, n. 1, and p. 171, n. 2.

52. Or sixteen according to the Siamese text, the *Traibhūmi Braḥ R'vaṅ*. See Coedes and Archaimbault, 1973, pp. 6f.

53. BKDJT, p. 1229, s.v., Goshōgoten.

54. MKDJT, p. 11, s.v., Akanida; BKDJT, p. 1742, s.v., Shikikukyōten.

55. Described below, pp. 330ff.

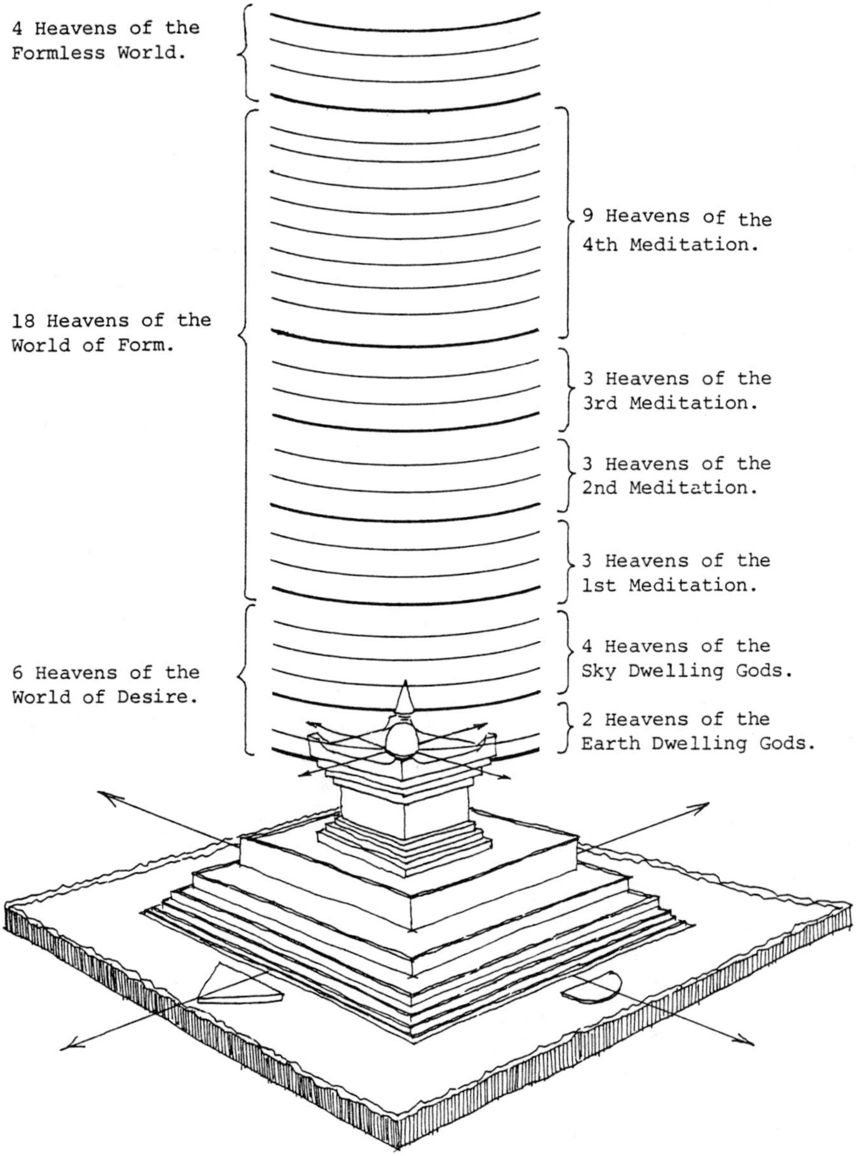

Fig. 248 : The Buddhist cosmology, showing the hierarchy of heavens.

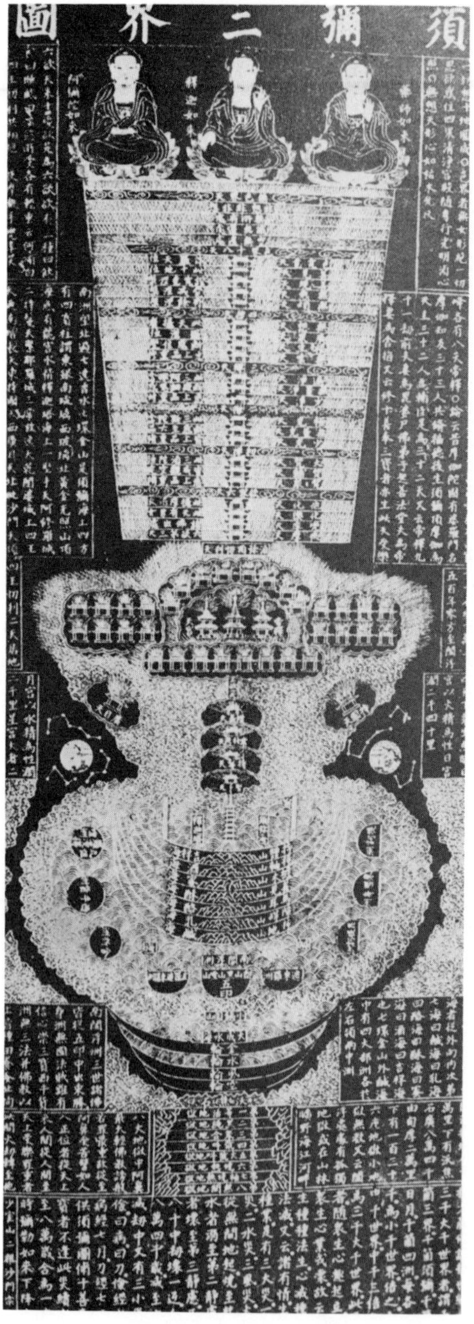

Fig. 249 : The Buddhist cosmology, shown in Chinese and Tibetan paintings.

Nowhere do the Buddhist texts specifically correlate the layers of the spire with the heavens. We have seen, however, that the *harmikā* and the topmost level of the spire mark the lower and upper limits of the celestial realms up to the summit of the World of Form, and it is therefore reasonable to assume that the layers between are the intervening celestial realms, even though the number of spire layers (almost without exception an odd number, 5, 7, 9, 11 or 13) is not that of the heavens above the Trāyastriṃśa, which can be counted either as 8 (the four Heavens of the Sky-Dwelling Gods plus the four Heavens of the World of Form) or as 22 (if the 18 levels of the Meditation Heavens are counted separately). As shown in the accompanying figure it is possible to selectively juggle the layers and the heavens to establish a correspondence, but this is to enter the domain of arbitrary assimilations. If, as seems beyond reasonable doubt, the layers of the spire indicate the hierarchy of states of existence and states of consciousness that constitute the celestial realms of the Buddhist cosmos, they must be considered to do so in a manner that is conventional, rather than numerical.

Formless Heavens	1	4	1	4
Heavens of Form	4	4	4	4
Sky Dwellers	1	1	4	4
Earth Dwellers	1		2	1
	7	9	11	13

Fig. 250: Various ways of counting the Buddhist Heavens to accord with the number of discs of the stupa spire.

7. THE *AKANIṢṬHA* HEAVEN AND THE STAGES TO *NIRVĀṆA*.

The top layer or disc of the spire represents the Akaniṣṭha, the Heaven of the Final Limit of Form. This is the level attained by Non-Returners (*anāgāmin*). Theravāda Buddhism specifies four levels of attainment in the progress of the *sādhaka* : firstly, the stage of the Stream-Enterer (*śrotāpanna*), the stage of those who have abandoned false views and entered the stream of sanctification; secondly, the stage of Once-Returners (*sakṛdāgāmin*), those who will attain Enlightenment in one more rebirth in the World of Desire; thirdly, the Non-Returners (*anāgāmin*), who will never again return to the World of Desire and who dwell in the Heaven of the Final Limit of Form; and fourthly, the stage of the *Arhats*, who are forever freed from the cycle of rebirth, who have overcome all cravings and defilements and have attained perfect Knowledge.[56]

The *Sarvāstavādin Vināya* specifies that the number of discs is to be from one, two, three, four... up to thirteen, and says that if the stupa is erected for an *Arhat* the discs should number four; three for a Non-Returner; two for a Stream-Enterer; one for a Once-Returner; and for "a simple, good man" no parasol is to be put up.[57] The same text elsewhere stipulates that a stupa erected for a *pratyeka-buddha* should not have more

---

56. Each of the four stages has a level of progressing towards its attainment and the level of attainment itself, to give a total of eight stages in four pairs. See JEBD, p. 290, s.v., *Shisōhachihai*; p. 96, s.v., *Hachikenjō*; BKDJT, p. 1770, s.v., *Shiyōshika*.

57. *Mūlasarvastivāda Vināya*, Taishō, Vol. XXIV, No. 1451, p. 291, quoted in BKDJT, p. 2834, s.v., *Tō*; translated into French in Bareau, 1960, p. 236. Cf. Roth, 1980, pp. 184f.

than thirty discs, while one for a Buddha should have an indeterminate number, "more than a thousand if it is very high, so as to obtain infinite merit".[58] The text indicates a clear correlation of the levels of the stupa spire and the transcendent levels in the attainment of nirvāṇa.

There are similar indications in the doctrines of the Mahāyāna and the Vajrayāna, where the ascent to nirvāṇa is expressed in terms of fifty two stages of the Bodhisattva (bodhisattva-bhūmi).[59] The first forty of these, termed the Prior Stages (Jap. jizen), lead up to the attainment of Awakening; the next ten stages, called the Ten Stations (daśa-bhūmi),[60] are those in which the Wisdom of Enlightenment is increased and perfected; and the last two stages, called the stage of Similar Enlightenment and the stage of Wondrous Enlightenment, are two levels of the supreme and perfect Awakening (anuttara-saṃyak-saṃbodhi).[61]

The levels of the spire are correlated with the Stations. As in the above, these are most usually counted as ten,[62] but there exist alternate lists. One of these enumerates nine true Bodhisattva Stations followed by a tenth stage, which is that of Buddhahood.[63] Theravāda texts list seven Bodhisattva Stations leading to the stage of the arhat, which correspond to a list of seven bhūmika given in the *Akṣyupaniṣad*,[64] and the Tibetan and Chinese versions of the Mahāyāna text, the *Karandavyūha*, list seven Stations instead of the ten given in the Sanskrit version of the same work.[65] A Tibetan text, the *Kriyāsaṃgraha*, correlates the thirteen discs of the Tibetan stupa with thirteen powers of the Buddha,[66] and Bénisti has identified these as thirteen bhūmi or Stations in the ascent of the Bodhisattva.[67]

There seems to be a clear indication in this that the seven, nine or thirteen discs of the stupa spire can be taken to represent the Bodhisattva Stations, the stages in the Bodhisattva's ascent to perfect Awakening.

* * * * *

Two interpretations of the meaning of the layers of the spire have been given : according to one they are a conventional representation of the heavens that lie superimposed above the summit of Mt. Meru; and according to the second they are the Stations of the Bodhisattva, the levels he passes through in his progress towards perfect Enlightenment. From one viewpoint the two schemata are concordant, since they both express stages of ascent towards the complete attainment of Buddhahood; but from another viewpoint they seem irreconcilable, since in the former they are levels leading up to Awakening and in the latter they are stages that follow Awakening, those in which the qualities of Awakening are developed and perfected. The contradiction is apparent rather than real, and involves doctrines concerning the place of Enlightenment now to be examined.

---

58. *Mūlasarvastavāda Vināya*, Taishō, Vol. XXIV, No. 1495, p. 652; Bareau, 1960, p. 236. 59. For the 52 stages of the Bodhisattva, see BKDJT, p. 1214, s.v., Gojūnii. 60. For the Ten Stations, see BKDJT, p. 2297, and MKDJT, p. 864, s.v., Jūji, and *ibid*., p. 871, s.v., Jūji Bosatsu.

61. The penultimate stage is called "similar" because it differs from the ultimate stage "to a very small degree". Ishizuka and Coates, 1949, p. 180.

62. See above, p. 150. 63. Soothill and Hodous, p. 47, s.v., 十地; Edgerton, 1970, p. 411, s.v., bhūmi. 64. For references see Edgerton, 1970, p. 411, s.v., bhūmi. See also Przyluski and Lamotte, 1932, *passim*; Przyluski, 1936, p. 254; Paranavitana, 1954, p. 223.

65. Dayal, 1931, Ch. VI; Przyluski, 1936, pp. 254f.

66. See below, pp. 367ff. 67. Bénisti, 1960, p. 101.

8. THE *AKANIṢṬHA* AS THE PLACE OF ENLIGHTENMENT.

The uppermost layer of the spire's horizontal courses represents the Heaven of the Final Limit of Form. In the Theravāda formulations this heaven, as we have seen, is the dwelling place of the Non-Returners (anāgāmin), those who are in the penultimate stage before the attainment of the final stage of the arhat, the Worthy, he who has entered nirvāṇa. This is to say that the Akaniṣṭha Heaven is the place where Non-Returners achieve Enlightenment. This heaven is the locus of Liberation.

The Mahāyāna texts similarly teach that the Akaniṣṭha is the place where nirvāṇa is attained. It is in this heaven that all Buddhas have attained Awakening. "The idea that the Bodhisattva attains his supreme Enlightenment when he is reborn in the Akaniṣṭha Heaven... recurs throughout the *Laṅkāvatāra (-sūtra)*".[68] This same sutra also speaks of the "downflowing" (niṣyanda) Buddha,[69] who dwells within the Akaniṣṭha and exerts his influence within the world of men indirectly and by reflection. This Buddha causes a "maturing" in those he seeks to save, thereby gaining them access to the Akaniṣṭha, where they are perfected and gain Liberation.[70]

The Vajrayāna teaches the same doctrine. According to Śubhākarasiṃha, the Palace of the Vajra Dharma World (vajra-dharma-dhātu) in the Akaniṣṭha Heaven is "the place where Buddhas have attained Awakening since ancient times".[71] In the Shingon doctrine the Heaven of the Final Limit of Form is the abode of the Bodhisattvas of the Ten Stations : "The Heaven of the Fourth Meditation is the abode of the five types of Non-Returner,[72] (whose heavens are) called the five Pure Abodes. Beyond these is the abode of the Bodhisattvas of the Ten Stations, similarly called a Pure Abode. This is said to be the heaven of Maheśvara" and "Beyond and above these (the five Pure Abodes of the Non-Returners) is the Station of the Bodhisattvas who are working to receive Buddhahood. This is also called a Pure Abode Heaven. Most of the Bodhisattvas (who dwell there) will become Buddhas in one more birth".[73]

The Tendai School of Japanese Buddhism identifies Maheśvara's Palace in the Akaniṣṭha Heaven with the Palace of the Mind of Radiant Light (Jap. kōmyōshinden), which is at one and the same time the bodhicitta innate within the yogin and the Mind of Vairocana (Jap. birushana shin). In this context the word akaniṣṭha, "final limit of form", is not taken to refer to the heavens but to the Buddha's Mind, which is "the ultimate end of form" because all forms, all dharmas, flow from, and ultimately return to it : the Akaniṣṭha is the One Mind without Form (Jap. musō ichishin), the Principle of all phenomenal forms. To ascend to the Akaniṣṭha is to attain the One Mind : the Akaniṣṭha is the place of Enlightenment.[74]

* * * * *

---

68. Suzuki, 1930, p. 375.

69. The niṣyanda-Buddha corresponds to the saṃbhoga-kāya. The Chinese translators rendered niṣyanda-buddha and saṃbhoga-kāya by the same characters, 報佛 , Ch. pa fo, Jap. hō butsu, "Reward Buddha". See Suzuki, 1930, pp. 322 & 325ff.

70. Suzuki, 1930, p. 324; cf. Mus, 1935, p. 526.

71. MKDJT, p. 2078, s.v. Kongō hō kai gu.

72. For the five types of Non-Returner, see JEBD, p. 88, s.v., Goshu fugen.

73. Śubhākarasiṃha, 5, quoted in BKDJT, p. 1229, s.v., Gōshōgoten.

74. BKDJT, p. 1093, s.v., Kōmyōshinden.

Other texts locate the place of Enlightenment at a higher level among the heavens. The *Abhidharmakośa*, for example, distinguishes two places where nirvāṇa is attained, the Akaniṣṭha Heaven and the Heaven of Neither Consciousness nor Non-Consciousness.[75] Nirvāṇa in the Akaniṣṭha Heaven corresponds to the attainment of the seventh Station among the Ten Stations of the Bodhisattva.[76] It is the station of the arhat, the place of nirvāṇa as this is conceived in the Hīnayāna. On the other hand, nirvāṇa in the Heaven of Neither Consciousness nor Non-Consciousness is the full acquisition of perfect Enlightenment as conceived in the Mahāyāna, the nirvāṇa that results from the attainment of all the Ten Stations of the Bodhisattva. According to this doctrine Enlightenment is achieved at the bhavāgra, literally, "the highest point of existence", the summit of the universe.[77] Although the terms akaniṣṭha and bhavāgra are practically synonymous they do not refer to the same heaven : the term bhavāgra does not refer to the highest heaven in the World of Form, but to the highest heaven of the Formless World, the Heaven of Neither Consciousness nor Non-Consciousness.[78] Further, the word bhavāgra closely relates to the almost equivalent term bhūtakoṭi, "the limit of the real",[79] identified with the tathāgata-garbha, with the Void (śūnyatā) and with nirvāṇa.[80]

9. THE *LOCI* OF ENLIGHTENMENT.

It can be seen from this that there are different teachings concerning the place where Enlightenment is attained. It shifts along the axis mundi according to the context in which it is viewed. In some formulations nirvāṇa is attained at the foot of the Bodhi Tree and at the level of the earth; elsewhere it is described as being attained at the summit of the World Mountain, in Indra's Heaven and at the peak of the World of Desire; or it occurs in the Akaniṣṭha Heaven, at the summit of the World of Form; or again, in the Heaven of Neither Consciousness nor Non-Consciousness, at the summit of the Formless World.

These four loci of liberation, ranged one above the other on the axis of the world, correspond to four points within the stupa. The central point at ground level (A), the point of origin for the setting out and orientation of the plan, locates the bodhimaṇḍa visible to the eyes of men on the plane of earth; the place where the axis emerges from the stupa dome (B), marked by the harmikā, is the bodhimaṇḍa on the Mountain top; the uppermost disc of the spire (C) locates the Akaniṣṭha Heaven; and the jewel or vase at the pinnacle of the spire (D) locates the bhūtakoṭi, the point where the Buddhas make their exit from the cosmos and enter the Void.

---

75. Vallée Poussin, 1926, p. 213.

76. Przyluski, 1936, p. 254, citing the *Abhisamāyalaṃkāra*. See also Dayal, 1932, p. 271.

77. Edgerton, 1970, s.v., bhavāgra. Cf. Burnouf, 1852, 1, p. 309.

78. *Idem*; Mus, 1935, p. 528.

79. Edgerton, 1970, s.v., bhūtakoṭi : bhūta is "real, true, not false"; koṭi is "end" or "goal". The Chinese translation, 實際 , (Ch. shih chi, Jap. jissai), is also literally "the limit of the real". See Suzuki, 1930, p. 429.

80. *Laṅkāvatāra-sūtra*, II, XXVIII, 138 (77), (Suzuki, 1932, p. 69); cf. Suzuki, 1930, p. 259.

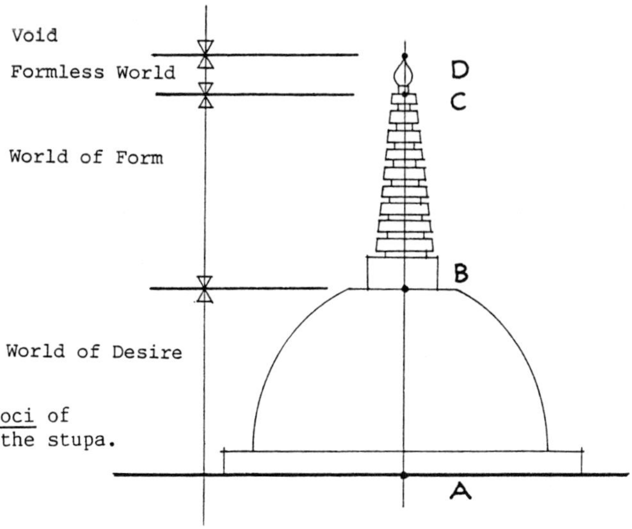

Fig. 250 : The loci of Enlightenment in the stupa.

Each of these positions locates a point of transition from one world to another. The central point at ground level marks the place where the mundane world is left and the vertical ascent begins. The harmikā marks the point of transition from the World of Desire to the World of Form.[81] The uppermost disc of the spire is the point of transition from the World of Form to the World of the Formless. The tip of the spire is the point where the Formless World - and the cosmos in its entirety - is left behind, and the realm of the Void is entered.

The Buddha attains nirvāṇa by a meditational ascent of the cosmic axis, rising to the pinnacle of existence, where he breaks out of the universe into the realm of totally unfettered Freedom. The nature of this ascension to Enlightenment, being ineffable, can only be conveyed to the unenlightened by analogy, that is, by way of a reflected image. The point where the stupa's axis meets the ground is just such a reflection. It is the "trace" in the mundane world of the ultimate place of Enlightenment. This midpoint of the plan is a vertical projection onto the "field" or "ground" of human existence of the perpendicular Way that leads to the pinnacle of the world, where the Buddhas escape the cosmos and are liberated. Coincident with the bodhimaṇḍa at Bodhgayā and the centre of the plane of man's universe, the locus of the Adamantine Throne is the terrestrial cognizance of the upward path to Awakening. The unenlightened recognize nirvāṇa by its reflection at the centre of their world.

The point at the centre of the stupa's plan reflects the higher point of Illumination located at the summit of the Mountain. This in turn is a reflection of a yet higher locus of attainment at the centre of the Akaniṣṭha Heaven; which yet again is an image of the final and true place of Awakening, the highest of the heavens of the Formless World.

---

81. This does not accord with the cosmology, which specifies four heavens above that of Indra in the World of Desire. Nevertheless, in all traditions, including Buddhism, the top of the Mountain is the place of transition to the extra-terrestrial realms.

Each of these points of transition is located at the summit of a world, or sphere, which can be likened to a dome. The stupa thus comprizes not one but several cupolas. The visible dome of the garbha is enclosed within a series of invisible counterparts, lying one within the other in concentric layers, each typifying an indefinite number of domes representing the heavens and the states of meditational consciousness that make up the supernal realms. The Path to Buddhahood leads upwards through their successive summits. To ascend from one plane of consciousness to the next is to pass through the apex of a cupola, at the point where it is pierced by its axis. The Buddha's escape from the World of Desire at its ridgepole is a breaking free that is repeated at ever higher levels, upward through the Heavens of the World of Form to its final limit at the Akaniṣṭha, and thence through the Formless Heavens to the ultimate summit of the total cosmos, the Heaven

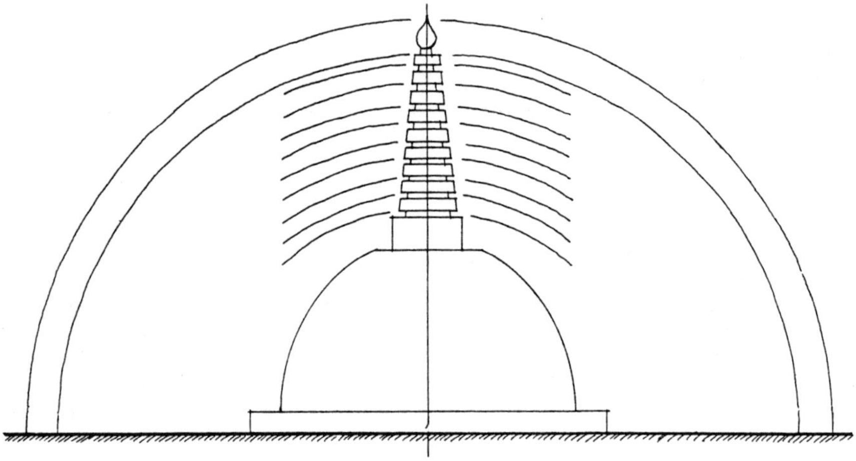

Fig. 251 : The layers of invisible domes enclosing the stupa.

of Neither Consciousness nor Non-Consciousness. There, at the utmost zenith of manifestation, the Buddha attains the Highest Perfect Awakening (anuttara-saṃyak-saṃbodhi) and passes to the Void (śūnyatā).

The image of superimposed domes is given tangible architectural expression in the Indian caitya-caves, where the axis of the stupa stands directly beneath the point of convergence - the roof plate or kaṇṇikā - of the rafters of the domical cave roof.[82] The cupola of the stupa is enclosed within the cupola of the cave; the roof repeats the form of the stupa Egg (aṇḍa) as though it were a second shell. Of similar significance are the single or double-roofed cetiyas, also dome shaped, that are conjectured to have enclosed the Thūparāma and other early stupas in Sri Lanka.[83] It is not unreasonable to assume that the vault of the sky served as the upper dome in the case of unenclosed stupas.

---

82. For descriptions of the caitya-temples, see Zimmer, 1955, pp. 247ff and 289ff.; Volwahsen, 1969, pp. 89ff.

83. Paranavitana, 1946, pp. 83ff.

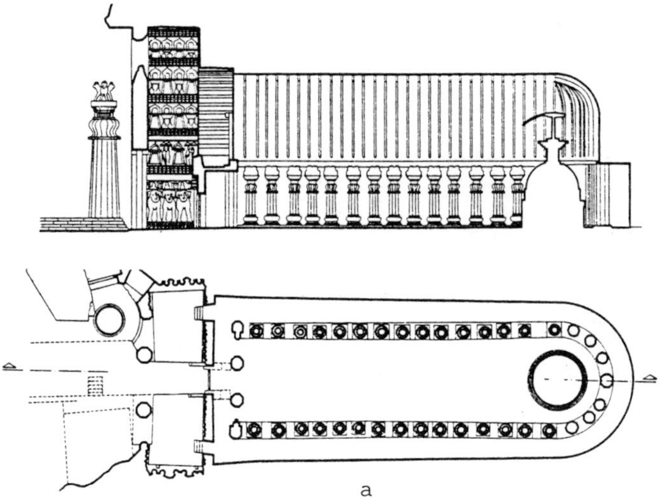

a

b

c

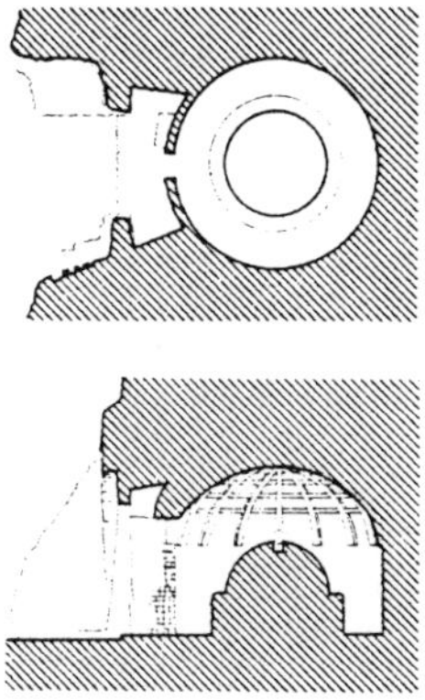

d

e

f

Fig. 252 : Rock cut caitya-halls with false rafters coming together at the roof plate directly above the vertical axis of the stupa. a and b. Plan, section and interior view of the rock cut caitya-hall at Kārli. c. The cave-temple at Bhāja. d. Plan and section of the small cave-temple at Guntupalle. d and e. Caitya-halls at Ajaṇṭā.

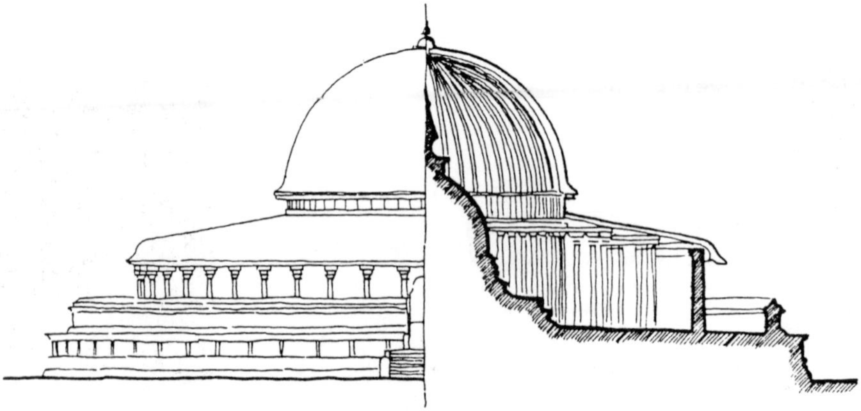

Fig. 253 : Paranavitana's conjectural reconstruction of the domed cetiya that originally enclosed the Thūparama in Sri Lanka.

In summary, the topmost pinnacle of the stupa spire marks the position of the doorway leading out from the Formless Heavens to the Void; the highest of the spire discs locates the doorway from the World of Form to the Formless World; the harmikā marks the doorway from the World of Desire to the World of Form; and the central point of the stupa's plan is the reflection of these transcendent points upon the plane of earth.

10. THE TWOFOLD REVELATION OF THE DHARMA.

The superimposition of the places of Awakening has its counterpart in the Vajrayāna doctrine of the descending revelation of the Dharma. According to this teaching Mahāvairocana, the "Great Sun" Buddha, first revealed the *Vajra-śekhara-sūtra*, the "Sutra of the Diamond Summit" (Jap. Kongōchōgyō),[84] in the Akaniṣṭha Heaven, which in the Shingon is alternately called the "Heaven of the Summit" (Jap. yuchōten). The Akaniṣṭha is ruled over by Maheśvara (Śiva) and the Sutra is preached within his palace, the "Palace of the Diamond Dharma-World" (vajra-dharma-dhātu).[85] The Sutra is revealed here for the sake of the Bodhisattvas of the Ten Stations, the Non-Returners who have reached the final stages in the ascension towards full Awakening. This is the revelation of the Sutra in its most subtle and ethereal form, manifested in rarified modes appropriate to the understanding of Bodhisattvas who are at the threshold of the Formless. According to the Buddhist doctrine of Expedient Means (upāya) the Buddha reveals the Truth in ways that are suitable for the levels of comprehension of his hearers. Whereas the revelation of the Sutra in its least formally limited expression is suitable for aspirants who have reached the highest among the heavens of the World of Form, it is necessary to reveal it once more for the sake of those who are still enmeshed in the World of Desire. For this purpose the Great Sun Buddha descends the axis of the world to the summit of the Cosmic Mountain, where he once again reveals the Truth for the sake of men.

---

84. The term śekhara (Jap. chō), "summit", in the name of the sutra, is synonymous with śikhara, a name of the Hindu temple and, as was shown in the preceding, closely related to the word stūpa. See above, pp. 262ff.

85. Jap. hōrō kaku. See MKDJT, pp. 2038f., s.v., Hōrō kaku; pp. 668ff., s.v., Kongōkai mandara; BKDJT, p. 1434, s.v., Kongōkai mandara; Toganoo, 1932 pp. 207ff.

This second revelation is a reflection of the first : in the same way that the first preaching of the Sutra takes place in Śiva's Palace of the Diamond Dharma-World at the summit of the World of Form, the second revelation is made within the Jewel Stupa (kūṭāgāra) in Indra's Heaven at the summit of the World of Desire.[86]

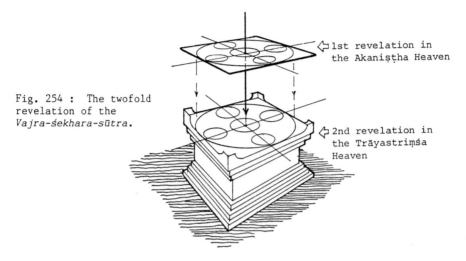

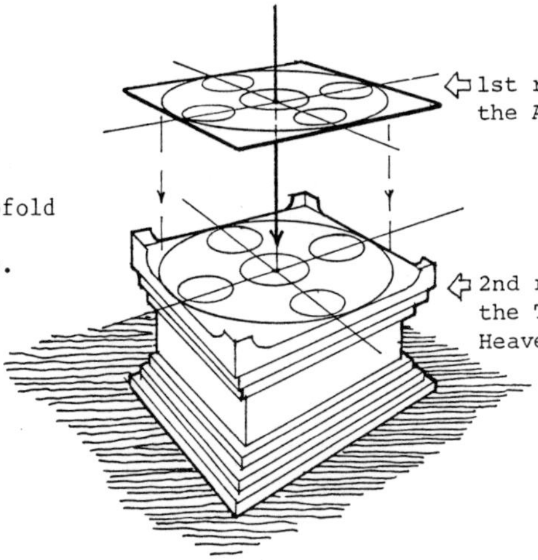

Fig. 254 : The twofold revelation of the *Vajra-śekhara-sūtra*.

The preaching of the Sutra is accompanied by the revelation of the Diamond World Mandala, and paintings of this mandala show the Buddha Mahāvairocana seated within the Jewel Stupa, with its roofs, columns and verandah, on the summit of Meru and surrounded by his retinue of Jina Buddhas, Bodhisattvas and Gods.

In the same way that the mandala at the top of Meru is the reflected trace at a more corporeal level of an ethereal mandala revealed in Śiva's Palace at the summit of the World of Form, so also the loci of Enlightenment superimposed on the axis of the stupa can be viewed as representations at varying levels of subtlety of the ultimate place of Awakening.

86. See above, p. 337, n.81, where it was explained that although Indra's Heaven is not the highest heaven in the World of Desire, its location upon the summit of the World Mountain entitles it to be so considered in the present context.

20 THE SYMBOLISM OF THE PINNACLE.

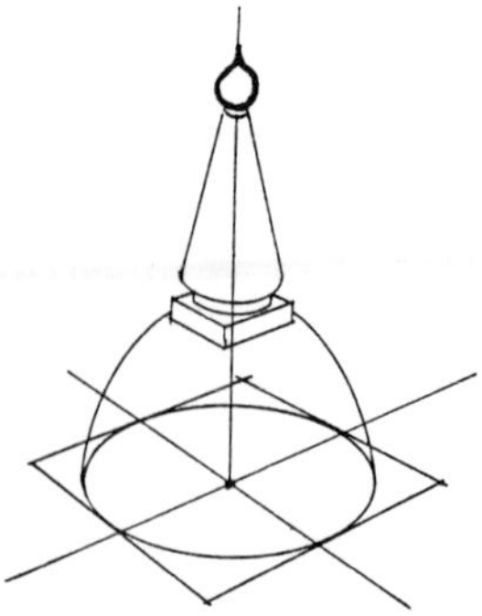

The stupa pinnacle is commonly terminated by a vase (kalaśa) or by a jewel (maṇi). In both cases the reference is to the station of perfected Enlightenment, the fulfilment of the ultimate goal of every Buddhist doctrine and practice.

a

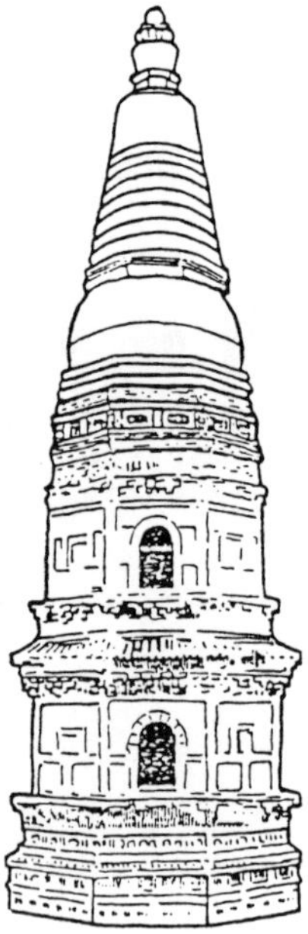

b

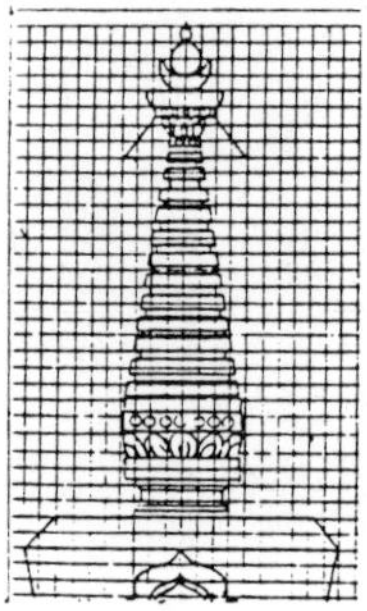

c

d

e f g

Fig. 255 : Examples of jewel and vase pinnacles from Japan (a and d), China (b), Tibet (c), Java (e), and India (f and g).

Fig. 256 (below) : Examples of vases from a. A relief at Amarāvatī. b. The Matrix World Mandala. c. and f. Reliefs at Borobudur. d. Sāñcī. e. The abhiṣeka rites of Japanese Shingon Buddhism.

a

b

c

d

e

f

1. THE VASE.

In Buddhist iconography the full vase[1] symbolizes the plenitude of the Enlightened Mind. The mind of the ignorant and foolish is likened to a half-filled pot.[2] A complementary imagery emphasises the pot's emptiness, signifying the Void (śūnyatā) : beings should strive to empty their hearts, so as to become containers of the Truth of the Void.[3] The receptacle of Buddha Wisdom, the Wisdom Jar (Jap. kembyō), is a wish-bestowing vase, a vase of plenty (pūrṇa-kalaśa), that contains treasure and fulfils desires.[4] "The Enlightened Mind is a divine vase, which grants the desires of all beings".[5]

* * * * *

a

b

c

Fig. 257 : a. A Japanese reliquary vase. Its function is the same as that of the reliquary stupa.
b. A vase-stupa depicted on a panel at Borobudur.
c. The vase (kalaśa) at the pinnacle of a Hindu temple.

The kalaśa appears at the summit of the Hindu temple. Its significance there sheds light on its meaning at the top of the stupa spire. The golden kalaśa at the summit of the temple is the Sun resting on the peak of the Mountain at midday.[6] "The golden kalaśa, a 'high seat', on the summit of the god's dwelling, looks as if it were the sun's orb that had arisen on the lordly mountain of sunrise".[7] It is the vase filled with the Nectar of Immortality (amṛta-kalaśa), the vase that confers immortality because "Viśvakarman made the kalaśa from the different parts (kalā) of the various gods".[8]

The kalaśa rising from the āmalaka of the Hindu temple lies on the vertical axis that centres the structure. It is directly above the nidhi-kalaśa, the vase of treasures (nidhi) built into the foundation. The figure of a Golden Man was immured within the temple base. Here again at the temple's highest point another Golden Man, the prāsāda-puruṣa, is placed

---

1. On the symbolism of the vase, see Chevalier and Gheerbrant, 1973, 2, p. 113, s.v., Coupe, and 4, p. 56, s.v., Pot; Saunders, 1960, pp. 192ff.

2. *Suttinipāta*, 721. 3. Glasenapp, 1944, p.99.

4. See Bosch, 1960, p. 112. 5. *Rokujūkegonkyō*, 59, Taishō, Vol. IX, no. 278, p. 776. 6. See the Deopara inscr. of Vijayasena, Ep. Ind. p. 314, in Kramrisch, 1946, p. 355. 7. Ep. Ind. XIII, pp. 46 & 56 in *idem*. Cf. above, p. 253. 8. *Mahā-nirvāṇa-sūtra* V.181, cited *ibid.*, p. 349.

within the vase, the symbol of the man who has been transformed, spiritualized, made immortal. The treasures of the lower deposit, symbolically located within the Lower Waters, recur at the summit, where the aspects of divinity they represent infuse the water within the jar and transform it into the Elixir of Immortality (amṛta).[9]

* * * * *

The vase at the pinnacle of the stupa finial has analogous meanings. The Sun that stands stationary at the Mountain summit is located at the leve of the harmikā; but in the same way that the place of Enlightenment is reflected at a number of levels, so also the Sun at the centre of Indra's Heaven is the reflection of a higher Sun that lies at the Doorway to the Voi The kalaśa is the visible sign of this invisible Solar Gate.

As in the Hindu temple the stupa vase is the amṛta-kalaśa, the vase that contains the Nectar of Immortality. The significance of the vase chang according to its position, at the top or bottom of the Pillar. At the base of the Pillar it is the vase of plenty (pūrṇa-kalaśa), overflowing with vegetation, jewels, pearls and other treasures.[10] In this position it is associated with the lower Waters and with Earth;[11] it is the equivalent of the Golden Womb (hiraṇya-garbha), the source of all health, life, opulence and fertility. It contains the rasa, the life-giving and regenerating sap of the world Waters, cognate with the soma liquid. By contrast, when locate at the topmost point of the stupa it is the amṛta jar containing the purifie and concentrated essence of the rasa that has risen through two stems from the Waters below. The finial kalaśa is the symbolic equivalent of the pillar's inverted pot capital, homologue of the downward growing lotus from which the waters of life stream down.[12] The symbolism reflects that analyze in a previous place[13] : from the utmost summit of the total cosmos flows dow the life- and benefit-bestowing moisture. The stupa is bathed in the Elixir of Life.

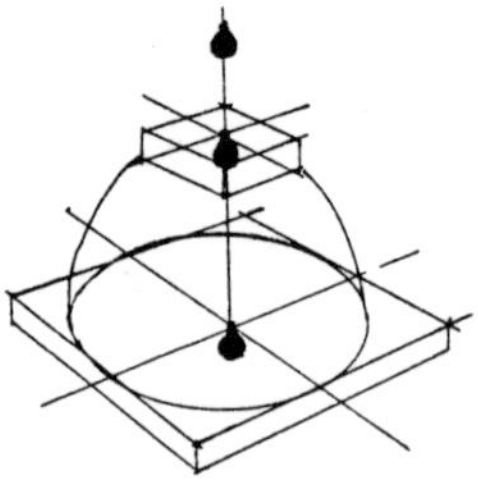

Fig. 258 : Vases within the stupa.

The two vases, the pūrna-kalaśa and the amṛta-kalaśa, the vase of the Waters and the vase of the summit, are often both physically present within the stupa, in the same way as they are in the Hindu temple. Vases are placed at three places within the stupa, one at the ground, another at the level of the harmikā, and a third at the pinnacle of the finial. Their locations mark the transition points in the spiritual ascent. The vases placed at each of these levels contain precious substances that represent t qualities of Buddhahood. The vase buried in the ground at the base of the stupa axis contains these qualities as potentialities, the potentialities o

---

9. *Ibid.*, p. 350.

10. Coomaraswamy, 1931, pp. 37ff.; Lamotte, 1944, 2, p. 177.

11. "The Earth Goddess is the kalaśa", says the *Dainichikyō*, 5, *Himitsumandarahon*, quoted in BKDJT, p. 4356, s.v., Byō.

12. Cf. above, p. 203, fig. 128. 13. See above, pp. 295ff.

Enlightenment that lie innate within the body of the cosmos and the body of the aspirant. The finial vase, located at the summit of the stupa, represents these same potentialities of Enlightenment in their full development, now shining out in splendour like the sun.

This significance of the vase correlates with that of the vases used in the initiatic rites (abhiṣeka) in Shingon Buddhism. Five vases, called "jewel vases" (Jap. hōbyō) or "Wisdom Vases" (Jap. kembyō), are placed at the centre and the four corners of the mandala in which the rite is performed.[14]

Fig. 259 : The One Sign Assembly of the Diamond World Mandala, with initiatic vases in the four corners. The Buddha Mahāvairocana occupies the position of the fifth and central vase, but its presence is nevertheless implied.

14. The four corner vases are shown in the Central Eight Petal Section of the Matrix World Mandala (see fig. 52, p. 100) and in the One Sign Assembly of the Diamond World Mandala. In each case the central, fifth vase is not shown since its position is occupied by Mahāvairocana Tathāgata, but its presence is implied and is specified in the sutras.

The five vases contain twenty precious things : five jewels, five medicines, five types of grain and five perfumes, representing all the precious things of the world, which in turn are the similitudes of the precious qualities of Enlightenment. They also contain perfumed water, which represents the Water of Total Knowledge, here divided among the five vases to indicate its five aspects, which correspond to the five Jina Buddhas.[15] When in the initiation ceremony water is poured from the vases onto the head of the initiate he thereby symbolically receives, in a virtual mode, the five kinds of Buddha-Knowledge. In this way the esoteric tradition is transmitted from one age to the next in a line of unbroken succession.[16]

The ritual of anointment with the Water of Knowledge reenacts an archetypal initiation. Descriptions of the highest of the Ten Stations of the Bodhisattva connect it with the symbolism of life-giving rain. Termed the Station of the Dharma Cloud (dharma-megha-bhūmi), or of Dharma Rain, it is the Station where the pāramitā of Knowledge (jñāna-pāramitā) is perfected, the Station in which the immeasurable virtues of the Bodhisattva permeate, like a cloud, the whole of the Dharma World. Like a great and all-pervading cloud of Knowledge the Bodhisattva rains down the amṛta of the Dharma to nourish all the beings of the Dharma World.[17] The Tenth Station is also called the Station of Initiation (abhiṣeka-bhūmi),[18] because at this level, which corresponds to the Heaven of Neither Consciousness nor Non-Consciousness, the Buddha confers the highest Awakening upon the Bodhisattva by sprinkling his head with the Water of Knowledge.[19] Beyond the highest of the Formless Heavens where this rite takes place lies the Void, the abode of perfected Buddhas; by this ritual of aspersion the Bodhisattva gains entry to that realm.

The vase at the top of the finial mast incorporates these formulae. It is the vase of initiation that holds the Water of the Buddha's Wisdom. It signifies the attainment of the Highest Perfect Awakening. The vase of the stupa spire, like the initiation vases used in the abhiṣeka rite, are filled with precious things. It is the single vase that subsumes within its form the sum of all the aspects of Buddha Knowledge.

* * * * *

The vase is the Sun that divides the manifested world, in both its formless and formal modes, from the unmanifested Void. This is indicated in Shingon Buddhism by the assimilation of the finial vase with the Void Point (Jap. kūden). The concept has both spatial and sonorous connotations : the Void Point is the dimensionless centre, the state without limiting conditions, the principial Void whence all manifestation devolves into spatiall extended existence; and it is also the anusvāra, literally "the following sound", in Sanskrit, indicated by a point, or point and semicircle, ँ, (called nāda and bindu, the anunāsika, and in Japanese "the upturned moon and point", gyōgatten), placed above the syllable to show that its sound loses itself in a final ṃ sound, never being suppressed altogether but prolonging itself indefinitely even when it has become indistinct and impercept

---

15. The seed syllable of the Element Water is vaṃ, which is also the seed syllable of Knowledge.

16. See MKDJT, p. 284, s.v., Genbyō; p. 2029, s.v., Hōbyō; BKDJT, p. 4356 s.v., Byō; p. 480, s.v., Karasha; p. 1278, s.v., Gōbyō; p. 998, s.v., Genbyō. For the rite of abhiṣeka, see above, pp. 92f.; MKDJT, pp. 409ff., s.v., Kuanjō; BKDJT, p. 811, s.v., Kanjō; Ishizuka and Coates, 1949, pp. 172ff.

17. BKDJT, pp. 2297ff., and MKDJT, p. 847, s.v., Jūji.

18. See Edgerton, 1970, s.v., bhūmi (4).

19. Cf. *Kōbō Daishi Zenshu*, II, Ch. 59.

ible. When added above a seed syllable (which is a sonorous symbol signifying some ultimately ineffable concept), the Void Point represents the absorption of the syllable's referent back into the unmanifested state, that is to say, into the Void.[20] To give an example, the syllable a represents the Mind of Enlightenment (bodhicitta), lying innate but unrealized within the yogin. By the addition of the Void Point the syllable becomes aṃ, which represents Enlightenment transposed into the Great Void, that is, Enlightenment in its fully realized state.[21]

* * * * *

Fig. 260 : The Void Point.
a. The seed syllable aṃ as drawn in the Shingon rituals in Japan. The Void Point is added to the Sanskrit syllable a. b. The spire of the Tibetan stupa, terminating in a Sun and Moon Finial, representing the nāda and bindu, or Void Point.

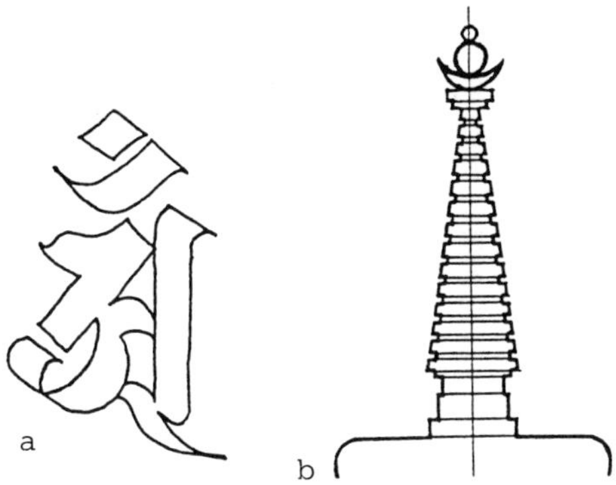

In many stupas, and particularly those in China, the terminal vase takes the shape of a gourd. For the Chinese this would give the architectural element an added resonance of meaning since the Taoists see the gourd as a symbol of immortality. The sacred gourd grows on the isle of the immortals, where its vine connects Earth and Heaven. Its seeds are the food of immortality and are ritually eaten at the time of the spring equinox, the time of renewal and regeneration. Apart from these Chinese associations, the shape of the gourd has cosmic reference : its two spheres are the dirempted portions of the World Egg and its shape is that of Mt. Meru; it is also reminiscent of the Taoist alchemist's crucible, the container of the Elixir of Life. Microcosmically, it is assimilated to the cave of the heart. Placed as a roof finial on the entrance pavilions to Chinese secret societies, the gourd signifies that this is the entrance to an abode of immortality. Precisely the same meaning adheres to it when it is located at the topmost point of the stupa.[22]

The two halves of the gourd are analogous to the two superimposed spheres that very often take the place of a vase on the spire of the Japanese stupa. These represent the last two of the fifty two stages of the Bodhisattva, namely, the stage of Similar Enlightenment and the stage of Wondrous Enlightenment.[23] This significance relates to another Shingon teaching regarding seed syllables. Two superimposed dots added to a syllable indicate

---

20. See MKDJT, p. 3266, and BKDJT, p. 646, s.v., Kūden; Guénon, 1945, p. 118, n. 1; Govinda, 1959, p. 133.

21. Śubhākarasiṃha, 10, quoted in MKDJT, p. 326, s.v., Kūden, says, "Aṃ is the seed syllable of the perfection of Enlightenment. The syllable a is bodhicitta, and the Void Point added above it is the Great Void, and this is the perfection of Enlightenment".

22. See Chevalier and Gheerbrant, 1973, 1, p. 116, s.v., Courge.

23. See above, p. 334, n. 61.

a

b

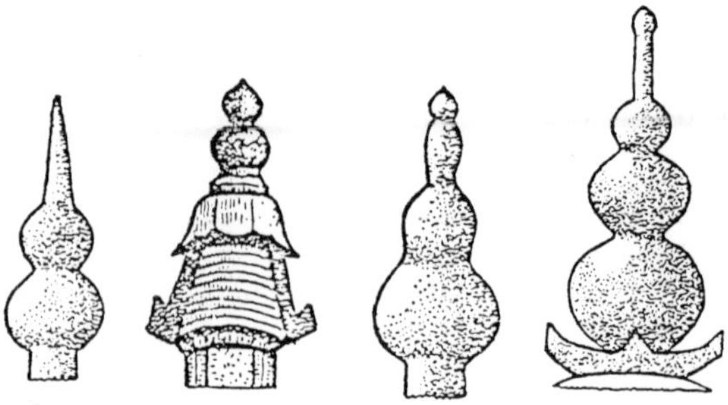

Fig. 261 :
a. The seed syllable *aḥ*, with the *nirvāṇa* points added to the syllable *a*.
b. The *nirvāṇa* points on the pinnacle of the Japanese stupa.

Fig. 262 :
Examples of gourd finials on Chinese stupas.

that it ends with the unvoiced aspirate *ḥ*, called the *visarga*. In the Vajrayāna these dots are called "*nirvāṇa* points" (Jap. *nehanden*). The exegetes of the Vajrayāna take the *visarga* to mean "Liberation" or "Extinction", since the verbal preposition *vi-* expresses separation, dispersal, privation, as in "asunder, apart, off, away, without"; and *sarga*, from the root *sṛg*, means "to discharge, to utter, let go, release".[24] Thus *visarga* is practically synonymous with *nirvāṇa*, which is likewise "liberation, extinction, a blowing out, an expiration".[25] In this way the expiration of the breath in the forming of the *ḥ* sound is associated with the ultimate expiration that is *nirvāṇa* and, being unvoiced, is identified with the serene and eternal silence of that state. The addition of the "*nirvāṇa* point to a seed syllable indicates that the concept it symbolizes has been transposed to the level of *nirvāṇa*. The syllable *a*, for example, is the Mind of Enlightenment. The addition of the points indicates that this Mind, which lies dormant within the ignorant, has been actualized and that Enlightenment has been attained.[26]

These concepts relate directly to the "*nirvāṇa* points" found at the top of the stupa. It will be seen in the concluding sections of this study that the stupa embodies the Buddha's Dharma; it represents the totality of the Buddha's sonorous utterance. The *nirvāṇa* points at the summit of the stupa transpose this body of Dharma sound from the physical to the metaphysical plane.

2. THE JEWEL.

A jewel (*maṇi*) at the apex of the stupa spire carries meanings analogou to those of the vase.[27] The two symbolisms converge: like the vase, the jewel grants all wishes; and the *kalaśa* is called a "jewel vase" (Jap. *hōbyō*).

---

24. Macdonell, 1929.

25. See above, p. 59.

26. MKDJT, p. 1781, s.v., *Nehanden*.

27. On the symbolism of the jewel, see Saunders, 1960, pp. 154ff.; BKDJT, p. 4132, s.v., *Nyoihōshu*; Govinda, 1959, p. 57ff.

b c

Fig. 263 : a. The Bodhisattva Cintāmaṇi-Avalokiteśvara (Jap. Nyoirin Kannon, "Jewel Wheel Avalokiteśvara"), who personifies the qualities of the wish-granting Jewel.
b. A jewel stupa. b. A flaming jewel at the summit of the Stupa of the Five Elements (Jap. gorintō).

In the Stupa of the Five Elements (Jap. gorintō)[28] the flaming jewel at its summit represents the Element Ether (ākāśa, "Space"). Ether is the quintessential and central Element and in some contexts is taken to represent perfected Consciousness, the state of Freedom attained by transcending the qualities of aggregation represented by the other four Elements. In answer to the question, "Where do Earth, Water, Fire and Air come to an end?" the Buddha replies, "Not thus, O monk, is the question to be put, but : Where is it that these Elements find no footing? - And the answer is : in the invisible, infinite, all-radiant Consciousness (P. viññānam). There neither Earth not Water, neither Fire nor Air can find a footing".[29] This is the Consciousness identified with nirvāṇa by Buddhaghoṣa in the *Visuddhimarga*;[30] it is synonymous with Enlightenment. The flaming jewel is the Enlightened Mind, the bodhicitta, whose radiance illumines the worlds, penetrating all things with light. Identified with Illumination, it is the Wish-Granting Jewel (cintāmaṇi, Jap. nyoihōshu) that signifies the ability of the bodhicitta to give birth to the qualities of Buddhahood. Its effulgence is the light of the Dharma that enlightens beings, the light which, like the Water of Knowledge poured from the Jewel Vase, confers immortality on those on whom it falls. It is the attribute and cognizance of several Bodhisattvas. It is held by Samantabhadra, (who also carries the Jewel Vase that contains the Dharma Water of bodhicitta), by Mañjuśrī, Ratnasambhava and several forms of Avalokiteśvara, who assumes aspects that specifically embody the qualities of the Wish-Granting Jewel.[31] Carried by Kṣitigarbha (Jap. Jizō) to the infernal realms, the radiance of the Jewel illuminates the darkness and eases the sufferings of those who dwell there.

---

28. See below, pp. 372ff.

29. D, *Kevaddha-Sutta*, quoted in Govinda, 1959, p. 58.

30. Govinda, 1959, p. 58.

31. E.g., the Bodhisattva Cintāmaṇi Avalokiteśvara (Jap. Nyoirin Kannon Bosatsu).

The etherial jewel, the philosopher's stone sought by the alchemists as the ultimate end of the Great Work,[32] is identified with the diamond (vajra). The diamond symbolizes the irresistible and invincible power of the Buddha's Knowledge (prajñā), which cuts away and crushes the passions and ignorance.[33] Capable of cutting all other substances, it cannot be cut by them.

The triple jewel (triratna) symbolizes the Buddha, the Dharma and the Saṅgha (the Buddhist community). With this reference the jewel at the summit of stupas and other Buddhist buildings in the Far East are often shown emitting a three-pointed flame.[34]

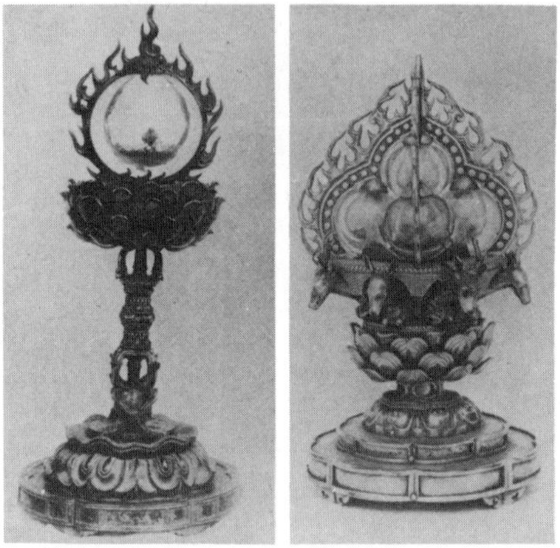

Fig. 264 : Two examples of Japanese jewel-reliquaries, which are forms of the stupa.

Fig. 265 : A jewel finial on a Buddhist building in Japan.

The similarity of the rounded shapes of the dome-stupa, the vase and the jewel reflects an overlapping of their symbolic meanings. In some cases this isomorphism is intentionally utilized to produce an iconographic ambiguity, so that it is difficult to tell which of the three forms is being represented. In some contexts the vase and the jewel are used as stupas : in Japan, for example, the "Jewel Relic Stupa" (Jap. hōju shari tō) has the shape of a jewel; and the "Jewel-Vase Stupa" (Jap. hōbyōtō) and the "Stupa Bowl" (Jap. tōmari) are stupas in the form of vases. In the *Mānasāra*, the *Mayamata* and other *Śilpas* finial vases and jewels are designated stūpi.[35] The "pot-shaped" stupa is one of the six shapes of stupa recognized in Sri Lanka in early times.[36]

The significance of the three forms overlap and mutually reflect. The rotundity of the vase, like that of the dome-stupa, refers to an all-containing and cosmic plenitude. The vase or jewel placed at the peak of the stupa repeats the form it surmounts. The stupa is crowned by its symbolic homologue; the stupa's culminating element replicates it meaning in miniature.

32. Guénon, 1962, p. 290; Govinda, 1959, p. 59.

33. For the symbolism of the vajra, see above, pp. 174ff.

34. Saunders, 1960, p. 154.

35. Pisharati, 1936, *passim*; Acharya, 1946, s.v., stūpi; Combaz, 1935, pp. 99f.

36. Parker, 1909, p. 337; Paranavitana, 1946, p. 27. The other shapes are bell-, bubble-, heap of paddy-, lotus-, and (possibly) āmalaka-shape.

Fig. 266 : Stupas in the form of vases.

* * * * *

In the same way that the vase has a twofold significance depending on whether it is located at the top or the bottom of the World Axis, so also the jewel changes its meaning according to its position. At the base of the World Axis the jewel is connected with the Waters and is identified with the pearl. Eliade has brought together references from many cultures connecting the pearl with the Waters, with the moon, with the feminine or substantial principle, with fecundity and birth.[37] To this list can be added Indian mythic formulae linking the jewel and the serpent, and thus pertaining to the themes developed in the chapter on the rainbow-serpent : a Buddhist test locates the origin of the Wish-Granting Jewel (cintāmaṇi), here called the Jewel of Diamond Wisdom (vajra-jñāna), within the brain of a giant makara;[38] elsewhere it is described as having been fashioned from the heart of a Garuḍa by a Serpent King (nāga-rāja);[39] and again it is said to have come from the brain of a nāga.[40] Similar associations are evident in Indian myth and folklore, where nāgas are said to wear jewels or pearls on their heads.[41]

These values are transformed when the jewel is located at the top of the World Axis. In this position it is the diamond, or vajra, as is evidenced by the terminology used of Sri Lankan stupas, where the vase-shaped crystal at the top of the spire is called the "vajra-circle" (P. vajira-cumbata).[42] The vajra is not only the diamond but also the World Axis, so that the apical vajra-jewel is both the summit and the summation of the axial pillar on which it stands. It is the point-source whence the pillar-axis emanates; and the qualities ascribed to the vajra-pillar are subsumed within its crowning jewel. Positioned at the highest

---

37. Eliade, 1961, pp. 128ff.; 1958b, pp. 439f.

38. *Zappōzōkyō*, quoted in BKDJT, p. 4132, Nyoihōshu; cf. Saunders, 1960, p. 155.

39. *Kambutsusammaikaikyō*, quoted in BKDJT, p. 4133, s.v., Nyoihōshu; cf. Saunders, 1960, p. 155.

40. *Daichidoron*, *idem*.

41. Vogel, 1926, pp. 25f.

42. Paranavitana, 1946, p. 40.

point of the stupa, the vajra-jewel is the unique Principle of the whole edifice and thus the unique Principle of the whole cosmos. It is akṣara (both "indestructible" and "indivisible"), symbol of the indestructible and indivisible unity of the Principle of manifestation.

The jewel at the top of the mast is at the apex of an invisible dome that encloses the stupa. Cognate with the Sun,[43] it is the eckstein, which is at once "keystone" and "diamond", of this imperceptible carapace. It is the "capstone", "coping stone" and "corner stone"[44] of the unseen cupola, coincident with the Sun Door. The corner stone is also a "cornered stone", which is to say a faceted stone, which once again links it to the vajra, likewise "four-cornered" or "eight-cornered".[45]

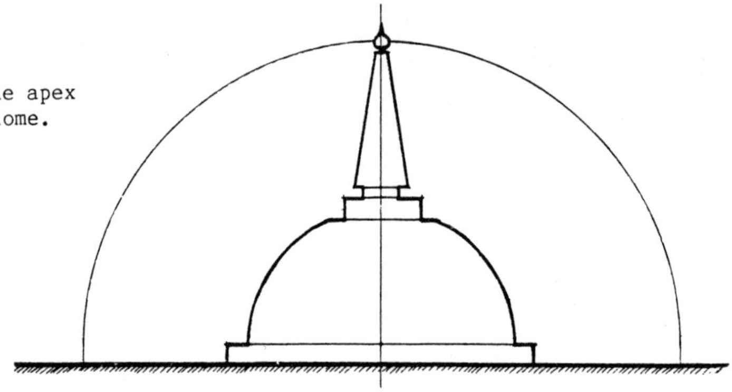

Fig. 267 : The jewel at the apex of the stupa's invisible dome.

* * * * *

Having ascended the levels of the stupa in meditation, the yogin has reached the ultimate pinnacle of its structure. From here he steps into the Void. He has achieved total Enlightenment and realized the Buddhahood that lay concealed within him. He steps beyond the symbol into Silence.

---

43. The flaming jewel is called a "sun gem" (suramaṇi) in Tibet, Burma and China. See Beal, 1871, p. 11 and p. 11, n. 1.

44. Coomaraswamy, 1939, pp. 66ff.; Guénon, 1962, Ch. XLIII ("La Pierre angulaire"), pp. 278ff. Coomaraswamy distinguishes between the cornerstones as foundation stones, placed at the four angles of the building, and *the* cornerstone, placed at its crown. It is this latter, apical cornerstone that is here identified with the jewel of the stupa.

45. The vajra is "four-cornered" in RV IV.22.2; and the yūpa, identified with the vajra, is "eight-cornered". See above, p. 320.

21 THE FUNCTION OF THE STUPA.

The stupa has three main functions : as a reliquary containing the Buddha's ashes or some other symbol of his Dharma; as a memorial marking the location of an event in the Buddha's life; and as a votive offering. In each of these functions the stupa acts as a symbol intimating concepts belonging to the metaphysical order of reality.

1. THE STUPA AS RELIQUARY.

When the Buddha entered parinirvāṇa his body was cremated and the ashes collected. Eight kings quarelled over their possession until the Brahmin priest, Droṇa, restored peace by dividing the relics into eight portions. Each king carried his share to his own country and there enclosed it within a stupa. Droṇa also erected a stupa to enshrine the vessel that had held the ashes, and the villagers who lived close to the site of the cremation built a tenth stupa to contain the embers of the cremation fire.[1]

According to sacred tradition the relics enshrined in one of these stupas later passed into the hands of Serpent Kings (nāga-rāja) while the other seven parts were miraculously brought together in the city of Rājagṛha, where the elders of the Saṅgha had them deposited in a subterranean chamber to await their dissemination throughout the Buddhist world by the pious king, Aśoka.[2] Recovering the ashes from the underground repository and from the Serpents,[3] Aśoka divided them into 84,000 parts and enshrined them in stupas in every part of India.[4]

For the most part stupas follow the pattern indicated in these early legends and contain either a portion of the ashes or some other object associated with the Buddha or his Dharma : his nail or hair clippings,[5] objects used by the Buddha, such as his alms bowl, staff or robe,[6] copies of the sutras, sacred formulae (dhāraṇī), seed syllables (bīja), the ashes of saints, Buddha images or mandalas.

---

1. D II.165-167. See BKDJT, p. 3832, s.v., Tō, and p. 1063, s.v., Kōshō Baramon, where further references are given. Cf. *Thūpavaṃsa* 38-39; *Nihon no Bijutsu*, 10, No. 77, p. 17; Przyluski, 1935, Combaz, 1935 p. 10; Paranavitana, 1946, p. 3.

2. *Thūpavaṃsa* 24; *Mahāvaṃsa* 31.17ff.; Vogel, 1926, pp. 125ff.; Paranavitana, 1946, pp. 3-4; etc.

3. For Aśoka's visit to the Nāga Kings to obtain the ashes, see Przyluski, 1935, pp. 356ff.

4. BKDJT, p. 3832, s.v. Tō; *Thūpavaṃsa* V; Przyluski, 1935, pp.352 and 366; Dutt, 1962, p. 109; *Nihon no Bijutsu*, 10, No. 77, p. 17; Bénisti, 1960, p. 49; Mus, 1935, p. 192; and cf. below, pp. 366ff.

5. See the stories recorded in the *Vinaya*s of hair and nail clippings enshrined in stupas during the lifetime of the Buddha in Bareau, 1960, pp. 231 & 262. Cf. BKDJT, p. 3832, s.v., Tō.

6. The texts distinguish stupas containing ashes (stūpa-śarīraka) and those enshrining objects once used by the Buddha (stūpa-paribhogika). Memorial stupas which do not contain a relic are called uddesika-stūpas. See *Kālingabodhi-Jātaka* IV.228; Bénisti, 1960, p. 50; Seckel, 1964, p. 103; Sivaramamurti, 1942, p. 20; Vallée Poussin, 1937, p. 284; Coomaraswamy, 1935a, p. 4; Zimmer, 1955, p. 233; Combaz, 1932, p. 172.

The ashes or alternate deposits are added to the stupa as a "seed" that brings the architectural body to life. Inseminating the womb (garbha) they quicken the dead mass of the masonry. The *Culavaṃsa* , describing the Tamil invasions of Sri Lanka, depicts the invaders as disembowelling the stupas and depriving them of life by tearing out the relics. Jīvita, "life", is the term used in the history : the sacred deposit constitutes the life of the construction.[7]

The relics are able to enliven the stupa because they are imbued with the qualities - the numinous - of the Dharma. "When deposited within the stupa a relic of the Tathāgata, whether a hair of his head or beard, a tooth, a finger nail, or even a single particle of his ashes, works as if the treasure of the Tathāgata's Dharma were deposited there".[8] Every school of Buddhism, mutatis mutandis, teaches the doctrine of the identity of the Buddha's Body and his Dharma.[9] The relics, as representing either parts of his Body or aspects of his Word, are so many traces of the Truth, portions of the eternal Dharma gifted to men as aids to their Enlightenment. As a reliquary the stupa exists to proclaim the immanent presence of these particles of the Buddha's Law.

* * * * *

The stupa frequently functions to enshrine portions of the ashes remaining from the Buddha's cremation. Excavations of the early stupas in Afghanistan, Sri Lanka and various parts of India have shown that the greater number contained this form of relic.[10] The presence of the ashes in the stupa relates to a complex schema of interlocking and mutually reflecting symbolisms involving several of the themes developed in this study. One aspect of this schema pertains to the symbolism of cremation.[11]

The burning of the Buddha's body is an image of a metaphysically consumated combustion. It is the corporeal mimesis of a prior spiritual process. The cremation symbolizes a sublimation : the fire burns away the bonds of selfhood and Liberation is achieved.[12]

The cremation is the external projection of an inward conflagration. The Buddhist *Tantras* describe the fiery nature of the Śakti who lies dormant within the nirmāṇa-cakra, the subtle centre located in the umbilical region. When awakened she reveals her presence by the sensation of a great fire, which burns upwards in a fiery ascent through the dharma-cakra and the saṃbhoga-cakra to the uṣṇīṣa-kamala at the top of the head. From there, having burnt everything in her path, she returns to her starting place.[13] Numerous Hindu and Buddhist texts[14] describe breathing

7. *Culavaṃsa* LXXX.68ff.

8. *Tsa t'a kun to kin*, Taishō No. 699, p. 801, quoted in Tucci, 1932, p. 28. 9. See pp. 366ff., below.

10. Not all stupas contain relics, the notable examples being the monolithic stupas in the caitya-caves of India.

11. Cf. Chevalier and Gheerbrant, 1973, p. 130, s.v., Cremation.

12. The concept of the passage through fire as a purification and regeneration is widespread. Its Buddhist expression could be matched by parallels from many other sources. See Chevalier and Gheerbrant, 1973, 2, pp. 309ff., s.v., Feu. It is a common theme in alchemical symbolism. See Eliade, 1956, *passim*.

13. Dasgupta, 1962, p. 101; Eliade, 1958a, p. 246. Hindu yoga employs a similar symbolism : see Avalon, 1958, pp. 241f.; Eliade, 1958a, p. 246.

14. E.g., *Jaiminīya-Brāhmaṇa* III.3.1; *Kauṣītaki-Brāhmaṇa* XXIII.5; *Majjhima-Nikāya* I.244; etc., cited by Eliade, 1958a, pp. 232ff.

and other exercises for the production of "inner heat" (tapas),[15] engendered to burn away impediments to Enlightenment. The presence of this heat was a prerequisite for the successful performance of the Vedic Soma sacrifice,[16] and in Tibetan Buddhism a candidate's degree of advancement in the technique was judged by his ability to dry out wet sheets applied to his naked body or his ability to melt snow.[17]

The symbolism is ritually expressed in the fire sacrifice[18] of Shingon Buddhism. Adapted from Vedic prototypes, the Buddhist ritual involves setting fire to 108 sticks and the burning of offerings in the flames. The sticks represent ignorance, the passions, suffering and karma; the offerings are the obstacles that stand in the way of Deliverance; and the fire is the Fire of Knowledge that consumes these defilements and impediments. The offerings are sacrificed to the Mind King (Jap. shinnō), the Mind of Enlightenment (bodhicitta) that resides at the innermost centre of the sacrificer's being.[19] To be efficacious the ritual must be performed outwardly and mentally at the same time : the Fire of Knowledge is visualized as burning in the heart; the sacrificer identifies his body with the sacred enclosure wherein the ritual is performed, his speech with the hearth, and his mind with the fire.

The Buddha is the paradigm and type of those who have passed through the transforming fire. He says, "I kindle a flame within me...my heart is the hearth, the flame the dompted self".[20] He is the embodiment of the Fire of Knowledge.[21] "I have become a flame", he declares.[22] He is the "master of the element fire",[23] and is repeatedly described as "burning".[24] He is represented with flames issuing from his body,[25] surrounded by a fiery halo,[26] with a flame emerging from the top of his head,[27] and as a Pillar of Fire.[28] The accounts of his life tell how he subdued a fierce dragon inhabiting the fire temple of the Brahmanic fire-worshippers by assuming his own fiery form and fighting fire with fire;[29] and also how in Sri Lanka he caused the hide on which he sat meditating to flame forth

---

15. For a full discussion of inner heat (tapas) see Eliade, 1960, pp. 106ff.; 1979, pp. 232ff.; cf. Govinda, 1959, pp. 159ff.

16. Eliade, 1958a, pp. 107ff.

17. David-Neel, 1965, pp. 216ff.; Samdup and Evans-Wentz, 1958, pp. 156 and 196ff.; Eliade, 1958a, p. 331; Blofeld, 1970, p.223.

18. Jap. goma, transliteration of Skt. homa, from the root hu, "to pour into the fire". Alternately, Jap. funshō, "burning". For the Shingon Buddhist fire sacrifice, see MKDJT, pp. 638ff., and BKDJT, pp. 1294f.

19. Śubhākarasimha, 20; *Sonshōki*; the *Naigomahon* of the *Yugakyō*; quoted in MKDJT, p. 638.

20. S I.169. 21. MKDJT, p. 1588, s.v., Chikua. 22. Vin II.28.

23. Vin I.25. On the "mastery of fire", see Eliade, 1958a, pp. 320 ff.; 1960, pp. 92ff. 24. E.g., D XXVI.5 (387).

25. Cf. Rowland, 1949; Eliade, 1965, p. 34.

26. See e.g., pl. 28, etc., in Thapar, 1961. The flaming halo is a commonplace in Japanese Buddhist art. Fudo Myō-ō and other divinities are shown in the midst of flames.

27. Examples are numerous. See e.g., Bowie, Diskul and Griswold, 1072, pp. 59ff., and pl. 49; Snellgrove, 1978, pls. 155, 163, 177, etc.

28. See Coomaraswamy, 1942, p. 161, and above, pp. 171ff.

29. Vin I.25.

on all sides, expanding over the whole island and driving out the Yakṣas who dwelt there.[30] At Śrāvastī flames burst forth from the upper part of his body.[31]

The Buddha is the humanized type of Agni, the Sacrificial Fire.[32] At his cremation he is simultaneously the devouring fire and the holocaust. His apparitional, factitious body (nirmāṇa-kāya) is burnt away so as to reveal his true Dharma-Body (dharma-kāya). The ashes are the visible and remaining traces of this transformation. Their presence in the stupa testifies that the Buddha has passed through the self-consuming conflagration of Perfect Knowledge.

Fig. 268 : The Buddha Amitābha (Jap. Amida Butsu) seated within a halo of swirling flames.

Fig. 269 : The flame (jyotiṣ) issuing from the Buddha's uṣṇīṣa.

Fig. 270 : The Buddha surrounded by a halo of flames.

30. *Thūpavaṃsa*, 79-80; cf. *Mahāvaṃsa* I. 31. See p. 54 above.

32. Coomaraswamy, 1942, p. 160; 1944, p. 55.

2. THE STUPA AS MEMORIAL.

Not all stupas contain relics.[33] So-called uddesika-stūpas, commemorative stupas erected at places associated with some important event in the life of the Buddha, are of this type.[34]

In the *Mahāparinibānna Sutta* the Buddha designates four places that should be visited by believers after his parinirvāṇa, namely, the place of his nativity, of his attainment of Enlightenment, of the preaching of his first sermon, and the place of his parinirvāṇa. He adds that a stupa should be erected at each of these sites, so that "the hearts of many shall be made calm and glad".[35]

In accordance with this prescription stupas were erected in India at Kapilavastu (the place of the nativity), at Bodhgayā (the Enlightenment), at the Deer Park at Vārāṇāsī (where the first sermon was preached), and at Kusinagara (the place of the parinirvāṇa).[36] The number of places of Buddhist pilgrimage was then increased to eight by adding the locations of the four great miracles, namely, Śrāvastī (the place of the "twin miracles"), Sāṃkāśya (where the Buddha descended from the Trāyastriṃśa Heaven), Vaiśali (place of the parileyyaka retreat) and Rājagṛha (where the Buddha subdued the mad elephant).[37] In Tibet stupas are classified into eight distinctive types, each associated with one of these eight events.[38]

The stupa erected to mark the location of an event in the life of the Buddha is not a memorial in the usual sense of the word. The memorial stupa functions as a true symbol. The event is important insofar as it offers insights into the nature of Reality and thereby assists the Wayfarer to pass from this to the farther shore. A spatial symbolism inheres within the accounts of each of the eight events.[39] We have seen that at his birth the future Buddha is received into a net held by the guardian deities of the four directions of space. He takes seven steps, which are symbolically equivalent to a return by way of the six directions of space to the progenitive source point of the universe. The story of the Enlightenment is also replete with spatial references : the Bodhisattva takes up his station at the central point of the cosmos beneath the Bodhi Tree, the axis mundi, and in meditation ascends that axis until he breaks through the ridge pole of the cosmic house. At the third Event, the preaching of the first sermon in the Deer Park at Vāraṇāsī, he sets in motion the Wheel of the Dharma which, in one of its meanings, is a

---

33. See above, p. 354, n. 10. Cf. Tucci, 1932, p. 24.

34. Combaz, 1932, pp. 172f. Cf. above, p. 353, n. 6.

35. D V.8 & 12; II.140-3; cf. Coomaraswamy, 1935a, p. 6.

36. BKDJT, p. 3835, s.v., Tō.

37. Luce, 1969, p. 148; Tucci, 1932, pp. 23f. Tucci gives two lists drawn from Tibetan texts. Other lists of eight stupas associated with famous places are given, e.g., the "stupas of the eight great miracles" (aṣṭa-mahāsthāna-caitya) listed in the JEBD, s.v., Hachidai reitō. (The JEBD errs, however, in equating these stupas with those built to house the Buddha relics divided among the eight kings after his parinirvāṇa. Cf. Tucci, 1932, p. 23). See also the list given in the *Pa ta lin t'a min hao kin*, Taishō, Vol. 32, No. 1685, p. 773, cited in Tucci, 1932, p. 23.

38. Tucci, 1932, pp. 23f; cf. Combaz, 1932, pp. 248ff.

39. The spatial symbolism of each of these events is developed in greater detail above, pp. 39ff.

model of the spatial deployment of the worlds. Finally, his entry into parinirvāṇa is an ascension of the central axis of the universe, the final reenactment of the drama of release prefigured at the Enlightenment.

The commemorative stupa embodies the spatial component of the myth in a tangible, geometric form. It marks the Event, not as an episode that takes place in historical time, but rather as one that occurs at the position of the central axis of the cosmos. In this way the occurrence and the place of the occurrence are identified : the stupa positions the Event, locates it, fixes it to a point in space, and thereby pins the myth to a punctual, timeless Present. It expresses a temporal occurrence in a spatial mode, transforming a successive and sequential phenomenon into one of timeless instantaneity. By "geometrizing" the temporal event its eternal quality is intimated, in the same way that by abstracting all spatial elements from the temporal or "successive" arts, such as music or the chant, that is, by converting space into time, an intimation of the spaceless quality of the Infinite is conveyed. This is to say that the memorial stupa functions as a symbol, communicating some sense of the Eternal that inheres within every episode in the Buddha's myth. In a quite literal sense the stupa establishes the point of the Buddha legend.

Looking at them from a complementary point of view, and using an Eliadean terminology, the eight Events are an irruption of the sacred into the profane. The nativity, the Illumination, the first sermon and the parinirvāṇa are mythic crises, scenes in an archetypal and timeless drama enacted to reveal aspects of the Truth. In these four Events the Buddha breaks through the obstructions barring the passage to the Real. Similarly, the four miracles, as disruptions of the "normal" and dislocations of the "natural", are manifestations of the supra-normal and the supra-natural. Thus each of the places where one of the Events occurred locates a hierophany, a point of fracture in the barriers separating the worlds. The *locus* of the Event is a sacred space, whose confines demark the source of an epiphany. The stupa, as a place-marker that defines this sacred space, positions a point of hierophany, it locates a place of communication between the worlds, a place where the Buddha revealed a glimpse of the realm of the Real.

3. THE STUPA AS VOTIVE OFFERING.

The building of a stupa is a meritorious act.[40] Numerous texts in the Mahāyāna Canon describe the merits to be acquired by the building of stupas,[41] ranging from rebirth in a Pure Land to the acquisition of long life. The *Saddharma-puṇḍarīka-sūtra* teaches that those who construct stupas, "even little boys who in playing erect here and there heaps of sand with the intention of dedicating them as stupas to the *Jinas*", will attain Enlightenment.[42]

In Tibet there are three types of work undertaken to acquire merit : the making of statues and paintings, the copying and transcribing of the doctrine in the form of sutras or dhāraṇīs, and the construction of temples and stupas (Tib. mCod rten, pronounced chorten).[43]

---

40. Zimmer, 1955, p. 234; Griswold, Kim and Pott, 1964, pp. 24ff.; Combaz, 1932, p. 173f.

41. A list of relevant texts and quotations from them are given in BKDJT, p. 3839, s.v., Tō.

42. SPS II.50

43. Tucci, 1932, p. 25.

The merit that accrues from building a stupa derives from the fact that the stupa is symbolically identified with the Dharma. The building of a stupa is a means of propogating and reaffirming the Dharma : "Shining with the beneficent influence of the True Dharma, like a beacon the stupa blazes the enlightening magic of the Buddhist faith to the four quarters". As we saw, the term "dharma" does not simply mean the Buddha's sermons;[44] it is the Law or Principle that governs the universe.[45] The Buddha's teachings, recorded in the sutras, are but one mode of expressing this wholly transcendent and essentially ineffable Law; the stupa expresses the same truth in a complementary mode. To build a stupa is therefore to disseminate the Truth.[46]

Whoever donates a stupa is munificent (dānapati); he is a sacrificer (yajamāna). He observes the precept of liberality (dāna) and attains the perfection of giving (dāna-pāramitā), the first of the six or ten perfections on the path to Enlightenment. He has chosen the good of others rather than his own and has thereby performed an act of renunciation that partially reflects the total Renunciation of the Buddha.

Tibetan and Indian stupas frequently carry inscriptions saying that they have been constructed "so that all beings may attain Buddhahood".[47] The reference is to the vow (praṇidhāna) taken by a Buddhist when he enters the Way. He vows to seek Liberation not for himself alone but for "all beings". It is a vow of sacrifice : he resolves not to enter nirvāṇa until accompanied by every last creature; it is a vow that will be fulfilled on the day of the Supreme Enlightenment, appointed as the ultimate goal of the total universe. The stupa is therefore built with a twofold aim : so that merit may be acquired; and so that this merit may be turned over to others (pariṇāmanā).

Fig 271 :
The adoration of the Buddha, aniconically represented by a stupa, shown in a relief panel from Amarāvatī.

44. Zimmer, 1955, p. 234. 45. See above, p. 212.

46. See Tucci, 1932, p. 27f., for references to Tibetan sources.

47. *Ibid.*, p. 30.

22 SYNTHESIS.

1. THE IDENTITY OF THE STUPA AND THE BUDDHA.

Hindu and Buddhist thinking assumes the existence of a strict analogy between the macrocosm and the microcosm, that is, between the "world" constituted by the individual being on the one hand and the total cosmos on the other. The *Tantras* describe a highly complex cosmo-physiology in which the bodily organs and functions are equated with cosmic counterparts - the directions, the planets, the constellations, the gods, and so on.[1] The gods who dwell in the heavens also abide in the *cakras* of the human body and rule over the senses;[2] Mt. Meru is contained within the body as the *merudaṇḍa*, the spinal axis;[3] the centre of the world lies within the heart, like a cave within the Mountain;[4] the breaths are the cosmic Winds[5] and the directions of space, and in the same way that the world is woven by the Air (*vāyu*)[6] man is woven by his breaths.[7] The identity of the body and the cosmos is realized by the practice of meditational techniques : "Imagine the spinal column of thy body to be Mt. Meru, the four chief limbs to be the four continents, the minor limbs to be the sub-continents, the head to be the world of the *devas*, the two eyes to be the sun and the moon...etc."[8]

The cosmic body realized by these meditational means is the Body of the Buddha, which is identified with the total cosmos.[9] It is also the body of the stupa, since the stupa is likewise identified with the universe.[10] The stupa is at one and the same time the body of the whole world and the Body of the Buddha, which is the body of perfected Man, of the Buddha as the universal type or norm of the human.

The homology of the stupa and the Body of the Buddha is expressed by an identification of their respective parts. In Tibetan the axis of the stupa is termed "the line of Brahma (*ts'ans t'ig*), which is the equivalent of *brahma-sūtra* or *brahmadaṇḍa*, both of which are used to refer to the spinal column,[11] which in turn is identified with Mt. Meru in the tantric texts, where it is taught that the Buddha's spine was a single column of bone, fixed and motionless, so that he could not turn his head but must turn his whole body, "like an elephant".[12] The supporting base of the stupa is identified with his legs and thighs, and the *Kriyāsaṃgraha* calls it "the platform of the legs (*jaṅgha-vedi*)".[13] In South East Asia the plinth is alternately called the Adamantine Throne (*vajrāsana*), thus

---

1. Eliade, 1958a, p. 236.
2. Wales, 1977, pp. 43f.
3. *Kāṇhupāda, Dohākoṣa*, 14, cited by Eliade, 1958a, p. 235.
4. See above, p. 201.
5. CU III.13.1-5; AV XI.4.15.
6. BU III.7.2; Eliade, 1958a, pp. 117 and 235; 1957, pp. 76f.; 1937, *passim*.
7. AV X.3.13.
8. Evans-Wentz, 1958, pp. 324ff.; Eliade, 1958a, p. 236.
9. See above, pp. 52ff.
10. See above, pp. 17ff.
11. Tucci, 1932, p. 17.
12. Eliade, 1958a, p. 235.
13. Bénisti, 1960, p. 97.

identifying it with the Buddha Throne.[14] In Tibet the base is the Buddha's legs, the dome is his torso, and the harmikā is his head,[15] and accordingly the Nepalese paint eyes on the four sides of the harmikā to represent the the eyes of the Ādi Buddha.[16] The eyes are also the sun and the moon, which the Indian tradition identifies with the eyes of the Great Person (mahā-puruṣa), who is at once Prajāpati and the Buddha.[17] The stupa spire rising from the harmikā is the Buddha's crown and has the significant name cūdāmaṇi, a word that designates the shining jewel worn at the top of the Buddha's head.[18] The pinnacle of the Nepalese stupa is said to be the jyotiṣ, the flame that burns on the Buddha's uṣṇīṣa;[19] in Tibet a jyotiṣ-shaped pinnacle crowns the summit of the spire;[20] and the finials of Thai stupas closely resemble the flame shown above the uṣṇīṣas of Sukhotai images, which is an adaptation of the Sinhalese ketumala.[21] In Kampuchea the stupa is called "the sacred body" and its parts are given names such as "the shoulder of the sacred body", "the nāga's coil", and so on, which are the names of the corresponding parts of the Buddha image.[22]

Fig. 272 : The assimilation of the Body of the Buddha and the stupa (see Mus, 1935, p. 105).

Fig. 273 : The Nepalese stupa, with eyes painted on the harmika.

Fig. 274 : The assimilation of the Body of the Buddha and the Tibetan stupa.

---

14. See above, pp. 157ff.; Shorto, 1971, p. 77. Shorto's article is concerned to establish the identity of the stupa and the Buddha image in South East Asia.

15. Cf. Volwahsen, 1969, p. 90; Govinda, 1976, p. 6. Volwahsen gives medhi = abdomen, aṇḍa = upper torso and harmikā = head. Burckhardt, 1967, p. 130, also errs in correlating the cubic part of the stupa with the torso and the dome with the head.

16. Levi, 1905, 2, p. 4; Mus, 1935, p. 124. 17. See above p. 52.

18. Waddell, 1895, p. 263; Levi, 1905, 2, p. 2; Mus, 1935, p. 124.

19. See above, p. 355. 20. Waddell, 1895, p. 263.

21. Mus, 1935, p. *83; Shorto, 1971, p. 76.

22. Carbonel, 1973, p. 229.

The stupa is the Body of the Buddha. "The stupa is the Buddha, and the Buddha is the stupa", says a Pali text[23] and in several places elsewhere it is said that the stupa is the external appearance, the form, of the Buddha (buddha-bimba)[24]: "The Body of the Buddha seen from without is a stupa; seen from within it is a prāsāda".[25] The *Lalita Vistara* tells us that the Buddha is "the caitya of the world",[26] and when the Buddha attains Awakening, the gods declare : "The profit gained here below by the gods of the earth has been beautiful and great. There where the greatest of beings has walked, there where all the dust grains of the earth have been illuminated, the three thousand worlds have come together to form a caitya, which is his body".[27]

In many regions of South East Asia the terms for "stupa" and "Buddha" are the same,[28] and in Bangkok the assimilation of the Buddha image and the stupa is so complete that the cloisters of temples are lined with Buddha images whose socles contain funerary urns, in the same way as do the stupas of Thailand.[29]

The stupa that miraculously appears in the sky when Śākyamuni preaches the *Saddharma-puṇḍarīka-sūtra*[30] is the Dharma-Body (dharma-kāya) of the Buddha. This teaching is implied in the sutra itself[31] and is explicitly

Fig. 275 : The assimilation of the stupa pinnacle and the flame (jyotiṣ) that issues from the Buddha's uṣṇīṣa.

---

23. Bénisti, 1960, p. 51; Auboyer, 1961, pp. 182ff.; Carbonel, 1973, p. 229.

24. *Hemacandra* II.358, cited by Vallée Poussin, 1898, p. 220; Combaz, 1935, p. 75; Mus, 1935, p. 234; Bénisti, 1971, p. 144.

25. *Song hyang Kamāhāyanikan*, a late Javanese text, quoted in Mus, 1935, pp. *82 and 105; Combaz, 1935, p. 76; Bénisti, 1960, p. 51.

26. *Lalita Vistara*, in Foucaux, 1884, 1, p. 353; Lefman, 1902, 2, *Varienten*, etc.

27. *Lalita Vistara*, Foucaux, 1884, 1, p. 307; cf. Bénisti, 1960, p. 51; Mus, 1935, p. 234.

28. Carbonel, 1973, p. 231.

29. *Idem*, quoting an oral communication from Bareau.

30. See above, p. 55.

31 See Mus, 1935, p. 234; cf. Vallée Poussin, 1925, p. 263.

enunciated in the teachings of Shingon Buddhism, where the Jewel Stupa represents the Dharma-World Vairocana and the two Buddhas Śākyamuni and Prabhutaratna, who sit side by side within the stupa, are two aspects of Vairocana, namely that in the Matrix World (garbha-dhātu) and that in the Diamond World (vajra-dhātu) respectively.[32]

Fig. 276 : The stupa that appears in the sky at the time of Śākyamuni's preaching of the *Saddharma-puṇḍarīka-sūtra*. The Buddhas Śākyamuni and Prabhutaratna, representing the Matrix and the Diamond Worlds, sit within the stupa, which is the non-dual fusion of the two Worlds. The mandala on the left shows the emanation of the layers of existence from the stupa, which represents the cosmogenetic Principle of the cosmos.

The identification of the stupa and the Buddha Body is conveyed in iconography. In Buddhist art the stupa and the Buddha image are interchangeable. The two symbols are sometimes juxtaposed to show their equivalence, as in a frieze at Amarāvatī showing a row of alternating Buddha images and stupas; the stupa is depicted receiving worship and offerings in the manner of an image; and the stupa substitutes for the image in the early aniconic art. Many relic chambers contain a Buddha image as the stupa's "life" or innermost essence,[33] a concept also conveyed by the Buddhas visible within the pierced domes of the seventy two stupas on the upper terraces of Borobudur. Images shown on the outside of a stupa dome are a revelation or emergence of this indwelling presence. Of equal significance are the metal stupas from South India that open to reveal a Buddha contained within,[34] a variation on the metal lotuses whose petals unfold to show a Buddha or a stupa.[35]

32. BKDJT, p. 3489, s.v., Tahō Nyorai.

33. E.g., at Amarāvatī, Gummadidduru, Nāgārjunakoṇḍa (see Bénisti, 1960, p. 81), and in the crowning stupa at Borobudur.

34. Ramachandran, 1954, p. 56, pl. XII, 1 & 2, and pl. XIII, 3.

35. See above, p. 204, and for references, p. 204, n. 81.

When the Sinhalese chronicles speak of the relics as the "life" of the stupa[36] it is implied that they animate the stupa in the way a body is animated.[37] This being so, it is not difficult to understand why the stupa is worshipped as the Buddha and why clothes and food are offered to it as if to a living person.[38]

Fig. 277 : Buddhas and stupas juxtaposed in a frieze at Amarāvatī.

a b

c d

Fig. 278 : The adoration of the stupa. In b. the stupa is worshipped by elephants, and early Buddhist art shows many examples of animals paying homage to the Buddha in the form of a stupa.

---

36. See above, p. 354.

37. *Idem*; Mus, 1935, p. *82; Bénisti, 1860, p. 51.

38. Bénisti, 1960, p. 51.

a

b c

d

e

f

g, h

Fig. 279 : a - c. A bronze stupa that opens to reveal a Buddha seated within. d. A Japanese stupa opening to reveal a Jewel within, representing the Buddha-Nature innate within the being. e. A stupa from Borobudur with a Buddha image on its front surface shown as if emerging from within the the stupa. f. A similar stupa within the rock cut caitya-hall at Elūrā. g and h. The perforations of the 72 stupas on the circular terraces at Borobudur allow a partial view of the Buddhas contained within.

2. THE IDENTITY OF THE STUPA AND THE DHARMA.

The Buddha has said, "Who sees the Dharma sees me, who sees me sees the Dharma".[39] He describes himself in terms that elsewhere he uses in reference to the Dharma : he is "unknowable" (ananuvedya); invisible to both gods and men; and those who see him in any form or think of him in words do not see him at all.[40] The Buddha and the Dharma he preaches are two aspects of one and the same reality. A Pali text from Kampuchea, the *Dhammakāya*,[41] assimilates the Buddha and the Dharma by means of a table that equates elements of the Dharma and various parts of the body of the Buddha. The "divine ear" of the Dharma corresponds to the ear of the Buddha; the bases of supernormal power (iddhipāda) correspond to his feet; the Ten Recollections are his ten fingers, and so on.[42] A Laotian work, the *Saddavimāla*, similarly equates the parts of the Buddha's body with sections of the canonical texts and with letters of the alphabet, which correlate with those sections.[43]

The sacred texts are the verbal embodiment of the Dharma; the stupa is its architectural embodiment. The stupa is the architectural equivalent of the scriptures. Aśoka built 84,000 stupas throughout his kingdom, one for each of the 84,000 sections or chapters of the Pali Canon. It is related that Aśoka asked the monk Moggaliputta Tissa what was the extent of the Law preached by the Buddha. The bhikkhu replied that there are 84,000 sections of the Dharma, and the king said, "I will pay homage to each of them with a vihāra (containing a stupa)", and gave 84,000 pieces of gold to the kings of 84,000 cities for their construction.[44] The Dharma is the Buddha made manifest in his Word, and each section of the Dharma is a portion of the Body of the Buddha, that is, of his Dharma Body (dharma-kāya); together, these sections make up a verbal replica of his person. "The 84,000 sections of the Law are the image of the perfectly accomplished Buddha".[45] The 84,000 stupas constructed by Aśoka together make up the total Dharma-Body of the Buddha.

The correlation of the divisions of the Law with an equal number of stupas is a continuation of Brahmanic precedents. It will be remembered that the 10,800 bricks of the Vedic altar are the 10,800 paṅkti of the *Ṛg Veda*, and 1,200 syllables are chanted into each of the 360 enclosing stones to give a total of 432,000, the number of syllables in the *Ṛg Veda*.[46] The Vedic altar is the sum of the syllabic sounds making up the sacred doctrine, the revealed word of Brahman. So similarly, by constructing stupas throughout his kingdom, Aśoka was building in masonry the great body of the total Dharma. To construct the Vedic altar is to build up the Body of Prajāpati, that is, the Body of Brahman (brahma-kāya); to construct the 84,000 stupas is to assemble the Body of the Dharma (dharma-kāya); and it is significant in this respect that the Pali texts use the two words, brahma-kāya and dharma-kāya, as synonyms.[47]

---

39. S III.120 40. M I.140-141.

41. The *Dhammakāya* forms the second part of Fasc. 13 of the *Sutta-Jātaka-nidānānisaṃsa*. It is summarized in a fragment recovered from a Burmese stupa and translated by Coedes (n.d.). For additional information, see Coedes, 1940, p. 329.

42 *Idem*. 43. Finot, 1919, pp. 77ff.

44. *Mahāvaṃsa* V.77-80; cf. Mus, 1935, p. 279.

45. *Culavaṃsa* LXIV.31. 46. See above, p. 46.

47. CF. Mus, 1935, pp. 280f.

Each of the 84,000 stupas is a portion of the Law; but again, each is the totality of the Law, since the total Dharma is reflected in each of its parts. Every stupa is an embodiment of the Dharma in its entirety. The conceptual framework for the equation of the part and the whole is provided by the doctrine of the Dharma as sound. According to the teachings of the Vajrayāna the Dharma is the Law or Norm that produces in the minds of those who hear it an understanding of the principles governing all things. The doctrines enunciated in the sutras are Dharma in this sense, since they operate to produce an understanding of the underlying Truth of phenomena.

* * * * *

Not only does the stupa represent the Dharma as a whole but its component elements are correlated with specific teachings contained within the Dharma. A typical example of the manner in which the parts of the stupa are associated with doctrinal concepts is given in the Tibetan text, the *Vaidūrya gy s'el*,[48] and shown in the accompanying illustration. The

Fig. 280 :
The correlation of the parts of the stupa and the doctrine according to the *Vaidūrya-gy s'el*. The four sides of the first level of the base represent the four types of Mindfulness (smṛtyupasthāna), those of the body, sensation, mind and things; the four sides of the second level are the four types of Renunciation (prahāna); the third level represents the four factors of miraculous power (ṛddhi-pāda); and the four sides and centre of the fourth tier represent the five faculties (pañcendriya). The base of the dome represents the five facülries raised to the level of powers (pañca-bāla), while the dome itself incorporates the seven members of Enlightenment (bodhyaṅga); the harmikā indicates the Eightfold Noble Path (aṣṭāṅgamarga); the mast represents the ten kinds of Knowledge (jñāna); the thirteen umbrellas are the thirteen powers of the Buddha (dasa-bala plus the three applications of memory, āvenika smṛtyupasthāna); and the large parasol at the top of the mast is the Great Compassion (mahā-karuṇa) of the Buddha towards all sentient beings. The moon and the solar disc at the very summit of the structure represent the pure thought of Enlightenment (bodhicitta) and the four types of transcendent Knowledge (mahāvyutpati) respectively; and lastly, the finial point represents the the supernormal faculties (abhijñā). The text ascribes similar associations to the accessory and decorative elements of the stupa. The stone pillars (stambha) represent the Buddha's fourfold intrepidity (vaiśāradya); the stairs are the Buddha's four defenses (catvāryārakṣyāni); the makara flag (makaradhvaja) that flies from the top of the mast indicates victory over the four types of demonic force (māra); and so on for the flower garlands, the strings of bells and flags, the decorative parasols, and every other adjunct of the stupa.

---

48. A Commentary on the *Vaidūrya dkarpo*, translated by Tucci, 1932, pp. 41ff., and summarized in Combaz, 1935, p. 76 and in Govinda, 1976, pp. 54ff. Cf. Saunders, 1960, p. 253, n. 12.

equations shown there are not arbitrary. Up to the level of the harmikā the associations given in the Tibetan text follow in closest detail the doctrinal enumerations given in several places in the Pali *Abhidhamma*.[49] Another text, the *Kriyāsaṃgraha*,[50] relates the measurements and proportions of the stupa to doctrinal concepts, as shown in fig. 281.

In his analysis of a Sri Lankan stupa Govinda claims that the total number of stupa elements and their corresponding doctrinal categories,

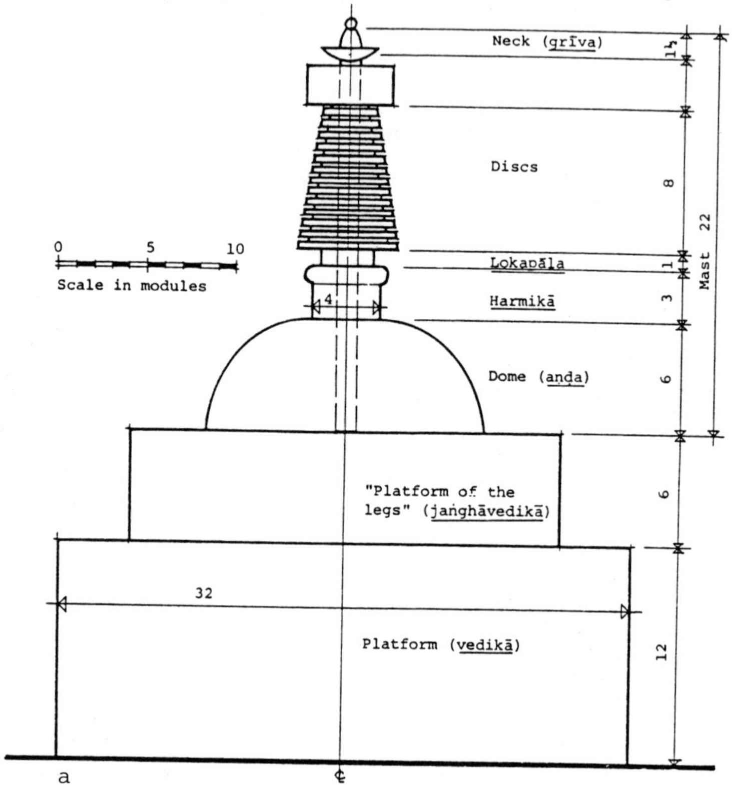

Fig. 281 : The correlation of the dimensions of the stupa with doctrinal concepts according to the *Kriyāsaṃgraha*. a. The "Heap of Grain" form of dome. The platform (vedikā) on which the stupa sits is 32 modules (mātrikā) wide and 12 modules high, with reference to the 32 marks of the Great Person (mahāpuruṣa) and the 12 links in the Chain of Dependent Origination. The so-called "platform of the legs" (jaṅghāvedikā) has a height of 6 modules, which represent the 6 types of Consciousness (anusmṛti). The dome is also 6 modules high, referring to the 6 types of transcendent Knowledge (abhijñā), and the harmikā is 3 modules high signifying the 3 Vehicles (yāna) of the Buddhist doctrine, and 4 modules wide, relating to the Four Noble Truths. The total length of the mast is 22 modules, indicating the 22 steps of thought (cittopāda); the part of the mast that supports the discs measures 8 modules, which are the Eight Noble Members (āryāṣṭāṅghika); the 13 discs are the 13 bhūmi, the

49. E.g., Anuruddha's *Abhidhammatha-saṅgaha* VII.3; Govinda, 1976, p. 58. The categories of the parts of the Tibetan stupa diverge in certain respects from the Pali texts. Govinda, 1976, pp. 59ff., gives details of correspondences and divergencies.

50. Kuladatta's *Kriyāsaṃgraha*, translated in Bénisti, 1960, pp. 94ff. See also Roth, 1980, pp. 195f.

counting from the base to the thirteenth umbrella, is 60 [= 5x(3+3+3+3)] and these are the 60 elements of spiritual development. Govinda relates these to the 15 (= 5x3) heavens (6 in the kāma-loka, 5 in the rūpa-loka and 4 in the arūpa-loka) and to the 30 [= 5x(3+3)] classes of beings (10 in the kāma-loka, 16 in the rūpa-loka and 4 in the arūpa-loka).[51] He also claims that Borobudur is laid out according to the schema of these same progressive steps in the Theravāda spiritual ascent.[52]

* * * * *

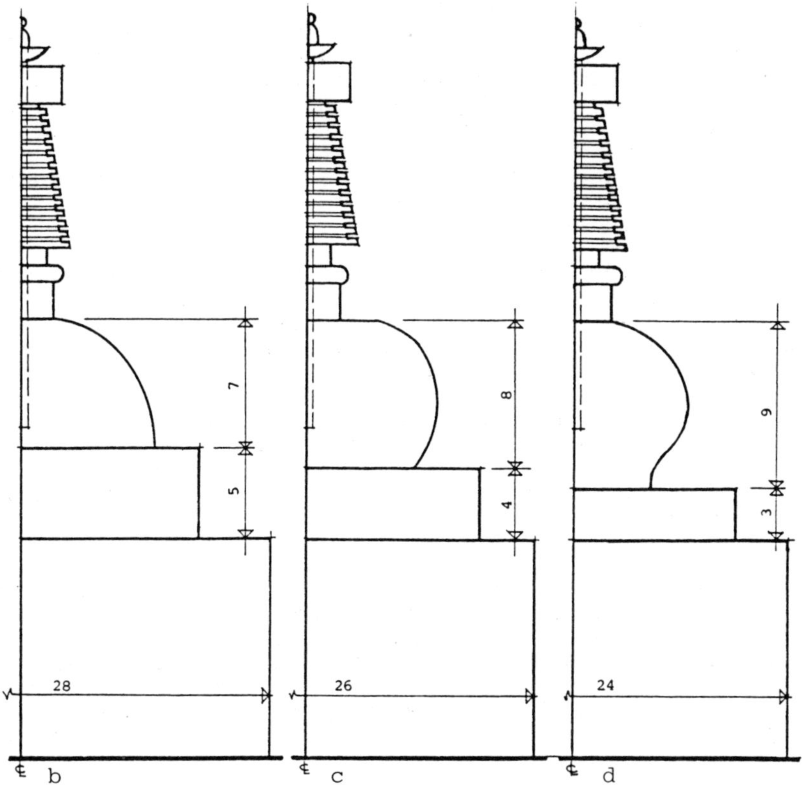

neck (grīva) of 1½ modules is relative truth (samvṛtisatya) and absolute Truth (paramartha-satya). The finial is Great Compassion. b. In later parts of the same text alternate and additional correspondences are detailed. In the case of the stupa with a "Bowl-form" dome hte ground platform (vedikā) of 28 modules equals the 10 powers (bala) plus the 18 things that are exclusive to a Buddha (āveṇika). The "platform of the legs" is 5 modules, which correspond with the 5 powers (bala), and the dome is 7 modules high, relating to the 7 members of Awakening (bodhyaṅga). c. The stupa with a "Bulb-form" dome. The platform is 26 modules wide, which refers to the 10 types of Knowledge (jñāna), the 12 powers (vasītā) and the 4 abilities (vaiśāradya), the 4 modules of the "platform of the legs are the 4 Noble Truths, and the 8 modules of the dome are the 8 Liberations (vimokṣa). d. The stupa with a "Vase-form" dome. The 24 modules of the platform correlate with the 12 Perfections (pāramitā) plus the 12 sacred formulae (dhāraṇī), the 3 modules of the "platform of the legs" are the 3 Liberations (vimokṣa), and the 9 modules of the dome are the 9 articles of discourse (pravacana).

---

51. Govinda, 1976, pp. 64ff.

52. *Idem*. Govinda also develops a series of relationships that inhere within the numerical schema described in the Tibetan text.

In considering these correspondences a distinction is to be drawn between anagogic symbols on the one hand and signs, functioning by way of an association of ideas, on the other, the former having a metaphysical and the latter a physical referent.[53] When the parts of the stupa are correlated with the Four Noble Truths, the Twelve-Linked Chain of Dependent Origination, the Four Powers, etc., the stupa is made to function as a didactic or mnemonic sign serving to remind the viewer of these doctrinal formulations. In this capacity the stupa is a sign. But insofar as these formulations refer to the Dharma, which is essentially ineffable, they are themselves metaphysical symbols and, by way of their association with these formulations, the parts of the stupa acquire metaphysical layers of significance. The Dharma is identified with the Body of the Buddha; the Dharma-Body (dharma-kāya) is both the body of the doctrine and the ultimate Body of the Buddha. Hence the identification of the parts, proportions and measures of the stupa with aspects of the doctrine structures it in accordance with metaphysical paradigms. The correlation of the constituent elements of the stupa with numerical codifications of the Dharma is a true symbolism.

The ascription of doctrinal concepts and stages of meditation to the elements of the stupa is a spatialization of the doctrine. By their incorporation within the stupa, concepts and practices are given a spatial dimension; they are related to the directions of space, to a centre, and to a vertical axis, the pathway of ascension.

The stupa is seen to embody the Dharma in several ways : it is identified with the Wheel of the Law, which is the symbolic expression of the manner of the Dharma's functioning as the Law of the cosmos; it embodies the sound of the Dharma; and it incorporates doctrinal codifications in its layout and measurements.

* * * * *

In innumerable texts the Dharma is equated with light : the Buddha's Awakening is an Illumination, and his preaching of the Dharma is an irradiation of the worlds. The stupa as Dharma is thus a source of light; it is a Beacon of the Law,[54] and in many places it has been a common custom to light up the stupa with a profusion of lamps.[55] The Bhārhut stupa, for example, has niches covering the dome with a network of radiance.[56] The stupa propogates the doctrine; it shines with the radiance of the Dharma, illuminating the four quarters.[57]

The building of a stupa is a renewal of the preaching of the Dharma. According to a Tibetan text, the stupa is built to allow all creatures to see the Buddha, to hear the Law spoken once again, and to reverence the Community (saṅgha), which has received the Law and faithfully trans-

---

53. See above, Introduction, for the use of the word "symbol".

54. "Ein Leuchtterm des Weltgezetzes", as de Groot terms it (de Groot, 1919, quoted in Combaz, 1935, p. 77).

55. Combaz, 1935, p. 77; Govinda, 1976, p. 5.

56. Zimmer, 1955, p. 329. The pattern of the illumination is significant : in one circle there are 120 niches, each intended to hold five lamps, so as to give a total of 600 in the band.

57. For the equivalence of Light and the Word (= Dharma) in various traditions, see Guénon, 1953, Ch. XLVII ("Verbum, Lux et Vita"), pp. 294ff.; cf. Coomaraswamy, 1977, 2, pp. 185 and 192f.

mitted its teachings. The building of a stupa is a "gift of the Law" (dharmadāna).[58] It is precisely because the stupa equals the Dharma that Buddhist literature, both Hīnayāna and Mahāyāna, abounds in texts that enjoin and prescribe homage (vandanā) to the stupa.[59]

Fig. 282 : The stupa identified with the Dharma. The stupa is delineated by lines made up of the Chinese characters that are readings from a Buddhist sutra, the *Saishō-ō-kyō*.

58. Tucci, 1932, p. 28, citing Cordier, Catal. 1, p. 358, n. 129, fol. 155.

59. *Idem.* As example texts Tucci cites *Mahāvastu* II.37ff.; *Svayambhū-purāṇa* 126-127; *Aśokavadānamāla* X; *You jao fo t'a kun to kin*, Taishō, Vol. XVI, No. 700.

3. THE IDENTITY OF THE STUPA AND THE BUDDHA IN SHINGON BUDDHISM.

The most explicit expression of the identity of the stupa and the Buddha is contained in the teachings of Shingon Buddhism, which unambiguously postulate the homology of the being, the Buddha, the Dharma, the cosmos and the stupa. The theoretical basis for these assimilations is the doctrine of the six Elements,[60] namely, Earth, Water, Fire, Air, Ether (or Space) and Consciousness, the irreducible components of all manifested existences, both formal and informal, physical and mental.

Theravāda Buddhism teaches that the six Elements, like the phenomena they compose, are subject to change, impermanent, and thus lacking in self-nature or an abiding reality.[61] The exoteric schools of the Mahāyāna teach that they have two aspects : one, perceptible to the senses, which is mutable, transient and only relatively real; and another, sensibly imperceptible, which is immutable, permanent and unconditioned. The former pertains to the realm of saṃsāra, and merely possesses a quasi-reality in relation to the latter, which abides in the realm of Suchness and the absolutely real.

Shingon Buddhism rejects the Theravādin view because it denies the reality of phenomena, and it rejects the Mahāyāna view because it draws a distinction between the phenomenal and the real : the Comprehensor knows that the phenomenal and the real, saṃsāra and nirvāṇa, are non-dual; the ignorant alone see them as distinct. The Shingon teaches that ultimate reality presents two aspects, one that changes momently and one that remains forever permanent. The unenlightened see them as separate and irreconcilable, but in the clear vision of the Enlightened they are the inseparable faces of a single, undifferentiated Truth. Ultimate reality embraces both the relative and the absolute; both are facets of the Real.[62]

Esoteric Buddhism, the Shingon, posits the extreme paradox : the phenomena of the world, just as they are in their mutability and fleeting transience, are indistinguishable from Suchness, in its adamantine and unchangeable permanency. And since phenomena are composed entirely of the six Elements, these also dwell simultaneously and inseparably in the two realms of the relative and the absolute. Thus, even though the Elements combine and recombine in a ceaseless flux of changing pattern, they neverthless constitute the very essence of Suchness : they are, in themselves, permanent and immutable, universally omnipresent, eternal and indestructible.[63]

All things come into existence by dependent origination from the six Elements.[64] Kōbō Daishi writes, "All things are produced from the six Elements. The four Dharma Bodies (dharma-kāya)[65] and everything in

---

60. Ṣaḍ dhāvata, Jap. roku dai, lit. "the six greats", so called because all things that exist are compounded from them.

61. See Karunadasa, 1967, *passim*. 62. See below, pp. 376ff.

63. MKDJT, p. 2320, s.v., Rokudai; p. 2322, s.v., Rokudai taidai; BKDJT, p. 296, s.v., Engi; p. 2033, s.v., Shingonshu; p. 5070, s.v., Rokudai.

64. *Idem*. 65. To establish the non-duality of Suchness and phenomena Shingon Buddhism teaches that each of the Buddha Bodies is an aspect of the supreme dharma-kāya and therefore calls them the nirmāṇa-dharma-kāya, the saṃbhoga-dharma-kāya, and so on.

the Three Worlds are produced from them. All the *dharmas*, from the uppermost limit of the Dharma Body to the lowest of the six realms are produced from them. Even though the *dharmas* are differentiated as subtle and gross and distinguished as large and small, they all come out from the six Elements. Therefore the Buddha teaches that the six Elements are the essential nature of the Dharma World". And again he says, "From the six Elements are produced all the Buddhas, all beings, the physical world, the four types of Dharma Body and the Three Worlds".[66]

In the whole of the manifested world there are no phenomena apart from the six Elements; all *dharmas*, whether gross, subtle, formless or unmanifest, are produced from them. They completely pervade the *dharmas* at every level of existence; they are omnipresent throughout the Dharma World. This is expressed in the doctrine of the "unobstructedness of the six Elements"[67]: the six Elements are eternally and unchangeably without hindrance; they are unified, merged, mutually interpenetrating and all-pervading.

From this basis it follows that there is a total interfusion of all things. Physical phenomena, which arise by dependent origination from the first five of the six Elements (Earth, Water, Fire, Air and Ether), interpenetrate with the phenomena of mind, which arise from the sixth Element, Consciousness : the body is inseparably fused in non-duality with the mind; the Body and Mind of the Buddha are merged; the body and mind of the being are merged with the Body and Mind of the Buddha; and the being and the Buddha are merged with the total universe.

In the view of the Enlightened Buddhas there is no differentiation of self and other-than-self : the Element Earth of his Body is merged with the Element Earth throughout the whole universe; the Element Water of his Body pervades the Element Water universally; and so on for each of the six Elements. The Elements of his Body and Mind are fused with the world; the Body of the Buddha is the body of the cosmos; both are composed of, and arise from, the six Elements; and hence the Buddha Body is called the "Dharma Body of the Six Elements".[68]

The first five of the six Elements correlate with five forms : Earth with the cube, Water with the sphere, Fire with the pyramid, Air with the hemisphere and Ether with the jewel-form. Placed one above the other these make up the "Stupa of the Five *Cakras*" (Jap. *gorintō*), a stupa found in countless thousands in Japan. The Element Consciousness, which does not lie within the bounds of form, is not represented, but since, according to Shingon doctrine, form (*rūpa*) and mind (*citta*) are non-dual, the five Elements with form are inseparable from the sixth, which is immanent within them all, and is present by implication in the stupa form. It is common to inscribe the seed syllables of the five Elements, namely, *a*, *va*, *ra*, *ha* and *kha*, on the front faces of the corresponding forms of the stupa, while its reverse side shows the single syllable *vaṃ*,[69] which is the seed syllable of Consciousness, elongated to pass

---

66. Kōbō Daishi, commenting on the *Dainichikyō* and quoted in MKDJT, p. 2322, s.v., *Rokudai taidai*.

67. Jap. *rokudai muge*. See MKDJT, pp. 2322f., s.v., *Rokudai taidai*.

68. Jap. *rokudai hosshin*. See BKDJT, p. 1388, s.v., *Gorin*.

69. Normally the seed syllable for Consciousness is *huṃ*, but this refers more specifically to Consciousness as it lies innate and unrealized within the mind of the unenlightened being, whereas *vaṃ* is Consciousness that has been fully realized in Awakening.

through each of the five parts of the stupa so as to indicate its interpenetration with each of them.[70]

In Shingon the supreme Buddha is Dainichi Nyorai, the "Great Sun" Tathāgata (Mahāvairocana).[71] In accordance with the doctrine of the unobstructedness of the six Elements the Dharma Body of Dainichi is assimilated to the cosmos; the Dharma Body of Dainichi and the Dharma World (<u>dharma-dhātu</u>)[72] are both nothing other than the six Elements. Hence the stupa of the Five <u>Cakras</u>, which is to say the Stupa of the Five Elements, represents the <u>Body</u> of Dainichi Nyorai and the body of the universe, for which reason it is also called the Stupa of the Dharma World Body (Jap. <u>hokkai shari tō</u>).[73]

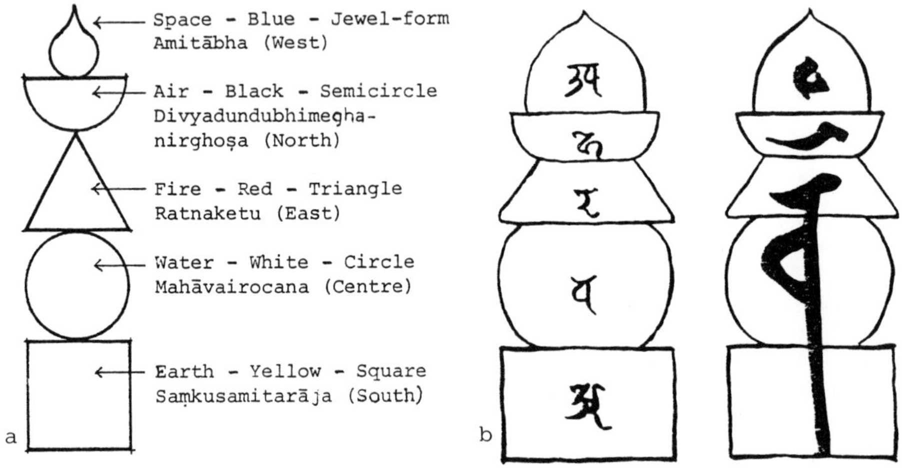

Fig. 283 : a. The Stupa of the Five Elements (Jap. <u>gorintō</u>) showing the correlations of the five Elements with the five shapes, the five colours and the five Buddhas of the Matrix World.
b. The Stupa of the Five Elements inscribed with seed syllables. On the front of the stupa are written <u>a</u>, <u>va</u>, <u>ra</u>, <u>ha</u> and <u>kha</u>, which are the seed syllables of the five Elements Earth, Water, Fire, Air and Space, and also those of the five Buddhas of the Matrix World. On the back of the stupa is written the single syllable <u>vaṃ</u>, which is the seed syllable of the sixth Element, Consciousness, and also of Mahāvairocana in the Diamond World. The stupa thus indicates the non-duality of physical phenomena and Mind and of the Matrix and Diamond Realms.

---

70. MKDJT, p. 652; BKDJT, p. 1389, s.v., <u>Gorintō</u>; Saunders, 1960, pp. 168ff.; Glasenapp, 1944, p. 107. 71. Cf. above, pp. 25.

72. Jap. <u>hokkai</u>. As previously indicated the word <u>dharma</u> (Jap. <u>hō</u>) is susceptible to interpretation at different levels : at one level it is the wholly transcendent Law, at another it is synonymous with "things" or "phenomenal entities". In Buddhism generally the Dharma-World (<u>dharma-dhātu</u>) is transcendent; it is the World of Suchness. In Shingon Buddhism, by contrast, the term refers to this world of sensible <u>dharmas</u> which, in the esoteric view, is non-dual with the transcendent World of the Dharma. Similar considerations apply to the term <u>dharma-kāya</u>, "Dharma Body". See BKDJT, p. 4557 and MKDJT, p. 1991, s.v., <u>Hokkai</u>; and p. 2019, s.v., <u>Hosshin</u>.

73. Jap. <u>shari</u> is <u>śarīra</u>, "body", but also means "relic", so that <u>hokkai shari tō</u> can also be taken to mean "the Stupa of the Dharma World Relic" : in the same way that other stupas contain relics, this one contains the Dharma World.

The being and the Buddha are non-dual (advaita, Jap. funi); the stupa of the Elements is also homologous with the human body. The five Elements of the stupa are the five cakras located on the spinal axis. The Earth cakra is located in the lower part of the body, including the legs; the Water cakra is in the stomach region; the Fire cakra is in the chest; the Air cakra is in the region of the face; and the cakra of the Element Ether is located at the crown of the head. In the meditational practices associated with this schema[74] the sādhaka first meditates upon the Element Earth, visualizing it as the syllable a and in the form of a yellow square located at the perineum; next he visualizes Water as the syllable va and in the form of a white circle at his navel; Fire as the syllable ra and a red triangle at his heart; Air as the syllable ha and as a dark blue (or black) half-moon shape between the eyebrows; and finally he visualizes Ether as the syllable kha and as a sky-coloured jewel at the top of his head. In this way the yogin identifies his body with the stupa, and thereby with the Body of Dainichi and with the cosmos.[75]

Fig. 284 (above) :
A Japanese drawing showing the correlation of the parts of the Stupa of the Five Elements and the cakras in the body. The upper pair of hands make the mudrā of Mahāvairocana in the Diamond World; the lower pair make his mudrā in the Matrix World. The two small circles drawn in the jewel of the fifth Element, Space (ākāśa), correspond to nirvāṇa points and represent the attainment of Enlightenment

Fig. 285 (left) :
Examples of the Stupa of the Five Elements (Jap. gorintō).

---

74. The so-called "Meditation on the Five Cakras" (Jap. gorinkan).

75. MKDJT, p. 651, and BKDJT, p. 1388, s.v., Gorinkan; MKDJT, p. 650, and BKDJT, p. 1388, s.v., Gorin.

According to Shingon tradition[76] the esoteric sutras were preached not by Śākyamuni in the world of men, but by the Dharma Body of Mahāvairocana (Dainichi) to the Bodhisattva Vajrasattva (Jap. Kongōsatta), who sealed them within an iron stupa in South India, where they lay until hundreds of years after the parinirvāṇa of Śākyamuni, when they were recovered by the Indian master, Nāgārjuna. In a vision the sage was directed by Vairocana Buddha to the stupa containing the doctrine. By performing rituals revealed to him in his vision, Nāgārjuna caused the stupa to open, revealing a radiant interior, wondrously adorned with flowers, jewels and canopies, fragrant with incense and filled with the sound of chanting. Having pacified the wrathful deities who guarded the doorway, Nāgārjuna entered the stupa and the door closed behind him. For many days he stayed within the stupa memorizing the sutras it contained. Having committed them to memory he came out from the stupa, which closed after him, and proceeded to write down the sutras he had memorized. This was the first transmission of the esoteric doctrine in the world of men.[77]

The Shingon school gives several interpretations of the symbolism of this legend. According to one of these Vairocana personifies perfected Buddhahood as it lies beyond all limiting conditions, and Vajrasattva represents Buddhahood insofar as it is the principle of the conditioned and the mutable and, as pertaining to the unenlightened being, is Enlightenment lying innate but unrealized within the mind, the so-called Mind of Enlightenment (bodhicitta). When Mahāvairocana preaches the doctrine to Vajrasattva he transmits it from its state of eternal immutability to the innermost core of the mind of each being, where it lies concealed until uncovered by meditation. The stupa is the very Body of Vairocana and the embodiment of Enlightenment; and since Enlightenment is innate within the mind of the being, so also is the stupa. Hence Śubhākarasiṃha calls the iron stupa "the Buddha-stupa in the Mind"[78] and explains that the Sanskrit word caitya, synonymous with stupa, is etymologically equivalent to citta, "mind" : the caitya, or stupa, is the Mind of the Buddha and, by association, the Mind of Enlightenment (bodhicitta) innate within the minds of all beings.[79] Nāgārjuna's entry into the iron stupa is the realization of his innate Mind of Enlightenment; it is the revelation of his fundamental and inherent Buddha-Nature. The door of the stupa represents the obstacles of ignorance, delusion and passion that obstruct the realization of one's innate Buddhahood.[80]

According to a complementary interpretation Nāgārjuna's entry into the stupa is an exemplar of esoteric practices in which the sādhaka concentrates his mind upon a symbol (in this case a stupa) and unifies himself with it so that there is an immediate realization of the essential meaning of the symbol : the metaphysical referent of the symbol is directly grasped and incorporated within oneself. The iron stupa is the stupa of the Dharma World, created as an illusion by the divine power of Vairocana and used by Nāgārjuna as an object of meditation in order to gain the Knowledge of the Universal Dharma World. Having attained this Knowledge in samādhi, Nāgārjuna transmitted it in the esoteric sutras.

---

76. Recorded by Amoghavajra in the *Kongōchōgiketsu* as a tradition orally transmitted to him by his master Vajrabodhi and quoted in MKDJT, p. 1706, s.v., Nantentō. 77. *Idem*.

78. *Idem*, quoting Śubhākarasiṃha.

79. Śubhākarasiṃha, quoted by MKDJT, p. 1647, s.v., Sotoba.

80. MKDJT, pp. 1705ff., s.v. Nantentettō.

This interpretation involves a concept that is one of the most profound insights of Esoteric Buddhism, namely that the attainment of union (yoga) by contemplative concentration on a symbol such as a stupa is not a process of transcending the illusory to attain the real, that is, it is not an eradication of the impermanent and mutable form of the symbol so as to perceive the immutable and permanent reality that lies beyond these illusory externals. Esoteric Buddhism teaches that the mutable forms are also real at their own level, and union achieved in meditation is a perception of the non-dual inseparability of the mutable and the immutable. The iron stupa is both an existing entity, even if illusory, and is at the same time the Palace of the Universal Dharma World wherein Vairocana eternally dwells as the Self-Nature Dharma World Buddha. This is the same stupa that the sādhaka contemplates in the rituals of the visualization of the Dharma World Stupa, which is identified with Vairocana Buddha. This meditation is a reenactment of the opening of the iron stupa by Nāgārjuna and of his receiving the transmission of the doctrine.

* * * * *

With the Shingon doctrine of the non-duality of the body of the stupa and the Body of the Supreme Buddha Mahāvairocana we reach the furthest reaches of the meanings of symbolism. In this doctrine the symbol is no longer a sensible image or reflection of a supra-sensible Reality. It is, on the contrary, that Reality itself. The symbol and its referent coincide. The stupa, just as it is, in its ephemeral, physical form, is in no way distinct or separate from the immutable, supra-physical Dharma-Body of the Buddha. The Buddha is wholly present in the architectural form.

Fig. 286 : Examples of the Stupa of the Five Elements.

ABBREVIATIONS.

A	*Aṅguttara-Nikāya*. Woodward and Hare, 1932.
AA	Artibus Asiae.
AĀ	*Aitareya Āranyaka*. Keith, 1909.
AB	*Aitareya Brāhmaṇa*. Keith, 1920.
AD	Architectural Design, London.
ADS	*Amitāyur-dhyāna-sūtra*. Cowell, Muller and Takakusu, 1894.
Ait. Up.	*Aitareya Upaniṣad*. Hume, 1931; Radhakrishnan, 1953.
Arthaśāstra	Kautilya's *Arthaśāstra*. Shamasastry, 1923.
Asvaghoṣa	"Awakening of Faith in the Mahāyāna". Hakeda, 1967. Cf. Suzuki, 1900, and Richard, 1907.
AV	*Atharva Veda*. Whitney and Lanman, 1905; Griffith, 1916.
BEFEO	Bulletin de l'École Française d'Extrême-Orient. Hanoi-Paris.
BG	*Bhagavad Gīta*. Nikhilananda, 1944; Radhakrishnan, 1948.
BKDJT	*Bukkyō Daijiten*. Mochizuki, 1954.
BKJT	*Bukkyō Jiten*. Tokyo, 1966.
Brahma Sutra	Vireswarananda, 1962; Radhakrishnan, 1960.
BSOS	Bulletin of the School of Oriental and African Studies. London.
BSSB	*Brahma-Sūtra Śankara-Bhaṣya*. Apte, 1960.
BU	*Bṛhadāraṇyaka Upaniṣad*. Hume, 1931; Radhakrishnan, 1953.
Buddhacarita	Asvaghoṣa's *Buddhacarita*. Cowell, Muller and Takakusu, 1894.
CU	*Chāndogya Upaniṣad*. Hume, 1931; Radhakrishnan, 1953.
Cūlavaṃsa	Geiger and Bode, 1912.
D	*Dīgha-Nikāya*. Rhys Davids, 1899.
Dh	*Dhammapada*. Radhakrishnan, 1950.
Dha	*Dhamma Atthakathā*. Norman, 1906.
Divyāvadāna	Cowell and Neil, 1886.
ERE	Hasting's Encyclopaedia of Religion and Ethics. London.

ET	Études Traditionelles. Paris.
HJAS	Harvard Journal of Asiatic Studies. Cambridge, Mass.
Hōbōgirin	Lévi, Takakusu and Demiéville, 1929.
HOS	Harvard Oriental Series.
Īśā Up.	*Īśā*, or *Īśāvāsya Upaniṣad*. Hume, 1931. Radhakrishnan, 1953.
JA	Journal Asiatique. Paris.
JAAC	Journal of Aesthetics and Art Criticism.
JAOS	Journal of the American Oriental Society.
Jātaka	Cowell, 1895.
JEBD	Japanese-English Buddhist Dictionary.
JRAS	Journal of the Royal Asiatic Society.
JUB	*Jaiminīya Upaniṣad Brāhmaṇa*. Oertel, 1896.
Jūjushinron	Kōbō Daishi's *Himitsu Mandara Jūjushinron*.
Kauṣ. Up.	*Kauṣītaki Upaniṣad*. Hume, 1931; Radhakrishnan, 1953.
KB	*Kausītaki Brāhmaṇa*. Keith, 1920.
KU	*Katha Upaniṣad*. Hume, 1931; Radhakrishnan, 1953.
Lalita Vistara	Lefman, 1902.
LS	*Lankāvatāra-sūtra*. Suzuki, 1932.
M	*Majjhima-Nikāya*. Horner, 1954.
Mahāvaṃsa	Geiger and Bode, 1964.
Mahāvastu	Jones, 1949.
Mānasāra	*Mānasāra Śilpaśāstra*. Acharya, 1927.
Manu	*Manava Dharmaśāstra*. Buhler, 1886.
Mayamata	Dagens, 1970.
Mbh	*Mahābhārata*. Roy, 1893; Sukthankar, 1933.
MCB	Mélanges Chinoises et Bouddhiques.
Mil	*Milinda Pañho*. Rhys Davids, 1890.
MS	Asaṅga's *Mahāyāna-sūtrālaṃkāra*. Lévi, 1907.
MSV	*Mahā-sukhāvatī-vyūha*. Cowell, Muller and Takakusu, 1894.
MU	*Maitri Upaniṣad*. Hume, 1931; Radhakrishnan, 1953.
Muṇḍ. Up.	*Muṇḍaka Upaniṣad*. Hume, 1931; Radhakrishnan, 1953.
Nidānakathā	Rhys Davids, 1880.
Nirukta	Sarup, 1921.
PB	*Pañcaviṃsa Brāhmaṇa*.

Praśna Up.	*Praśna Upaniṣad.* Hume, 1931; Radhakrishnan, 1953.
PTS	Pali Text Society Translation Series.
QJMS	Quarterly Journal of the Mythic Society.
RV	*Ṛg Veda.* Griffith, 1963.
S	*Saṃyutta-Nikāya.* Rhys Davids and Woodward, 1917.
SA	*Śāṇkhāyana Āraṇyaka.* Keith, 1908.
Sāyaṇa	*Ṛg Veda Saṃhitā,* with Sāyaṇa's Commentary. Pradhan, 1933.
ŚB	*Śatapatha Brāhmaṇa.* Eggeling, 1882.
SBB	The Sacred Books of the Buddhists.
SBE	The Sacred Books of the East.
SBH	The Sacred Books of the Hindus.
Sn	*Sutta-Nipāta.* Fausböll, 1881.
SPS	*Saddharma-puṇḍarīka-sūtra.* Kern, 1884.
Śubhākarasiṃha	*Dainichikyōshō.*
SV	*Sukhāvatī-vyūha.* Cowell, Muller and Takakusu, 1894.
Śveṭ. Up.	*Śveṭāsvatara Upaniṣad.* Hume, 1931; Radhakrishnan, 1953.
Taishō	Takakusu and Watanabe, 1927.
TB	*Taittirīya Brāhmaṇa.* Mitra, 1959.
Thūpavaṃsa	Jayawickrama, 1971.
TS	*Taittirīya Saṃhitā.* Keith, 1914.
TU	*Taittirīya Upaniṣad.* Hume, 1931; Radhakrishnan, 1953.
Vin	*Vinaya-Piṭaka.* Horner, 1938.
Vis	*Visuddhi-Magga.* Rhys Davids, 1920.
Viṣṇu Purāṇa	Wilson, 1840.
VS	*Vājasaneyi Saṃhitā.* Griffith, 1927.
Yoga-sūtra	Patañjali's *Yoga-sūtra.* Mitra, 1881; Prasada, 1924; Woods, 1914a; 1914b.

LIST OF WORKS CITED.

Acharya, P.K.
1927a Indian Architecture According to the *Mānasāra Śilpaśāstra*. London.

1927b *Mānasāra* on Architecture and Sculpture. Sanskrit Text with Critical Notes. 5 Vols. Oxford University Press, London.

1934 Architecture of *Mānasāra*. London.

1946 An Encyclopaedia of Hindu Architecture. London.

Agrawala, V.S.
1965 Indian Art. Varanasi.

Alabaster, H.
1871 The Wheel of the Law. Buddhism Illustrated from Siamese Sources. London.

Allchin, F.R.
1957 Sanskrit *Eḍūka*, Pali *Eḷuka*. BSOAS, 20, 1 ff.

Allen, Douglas
1978 Structure and Creativity in Religion. Mouton, New York.

Altizer, T.J.J.
1963 Mircea Eliade and the Dialectic of the Sacred. Philadelphia.

Amitāyur-dhyāna-sūtra.
("The Sutra of the Meditation on the Buddha of Immeasurable Light", Jap. *Kammuryōjubukkyō*). Taishō, Vol. 12, No. 365. English translation Cowell, Muller and Takakusu, 1894.

Apte, V.M.
1960 *Brahma-Sūtra Shānkara-Bhāshya*. Bādarāyana's *Brahma-Sūtra* with Shankaracharaya's Commentary. Bombay.

Auboyer, Jeannine
1949 Le trône et son symbolisme dans l'Inde ancienne. Paris.

1959 Le caractère Royal et Divin du trône dans l'Inde ancienne. In Sacral Kingship, Studies in the History of Religions, (Supplement to Numen), IV. Leiden.

1961 La vie quotidienne dans l'Inde ancienne. Paris.

Avalon, Arthur (see also Sir John Woodroffe).
1958 The Serpent Power. 6th edn. Madras.

Bagchi, P.C.
1934 Some Technical Terms of the *Tantra*s. Calcutta Oriental Journal, I, 2 (Nov.), 75-88.

Banerjea, J.N.
1940 Indian Votive and Memorial Columns. Journal of the Indian Society of Oriental Art, 18.

1956 The Development of Hindu Iconcography. Calcutta.

Bareau, André
1960 La construction et le culte des *stūpa* d'après les *Vinaya-piṭaka*. BEFEO, 50, 239-274.

Beal, S.
1869 Travels of Fa Hian and Sung Yun from China to India (A.D. 400 and A.D. 518). London.
1871 A Catena of Buddhist Scriptures from the Chinese. London.
1906 Buddhist Records of the Western World. London.
1911 Life of Hiuen Tsiang. London.

Belvalkar, S.K., and Ranade, R.D.
1927 History of Indian Philosophy. 2 Vols. Poona.

Bénisti, Mireille
1960 Étude sur le *stūpa* dans l'Inde ancienne. BEFEO, 50, 37-116.
1971 Les *stūpa* aux cinq piliers. BEFEO, 58, 131-162.

Bergaigne, A.
1878 La religion vedique d'après les hymnes du *Ṛg Veda*. 4 Vols. Paris, 1878-1897.
1978 Vedic Religion. Trans. V. Paranjpe. 4 Vols. in 1. Delhi.

Bernet Kempers, A.J.
1959 Ancient Indonesian Art. Harvard Uni. Press, Cambridge, Mass.

Bharati, A.
1965 The Tantric Tradition. London.

Bhattacharya, T.
1963 Study of *Vāstuvidyā* or Canons of Indian Architecture. Delhi.

Bhattacharyya, B.
1931 *Guhyasamāja Tantra* or *Tathāgataguhyaka*. Gaekwad Oriental Series, 53. Baroda. (Skt. with Eng. Introduction).
1958 The Indian Buddhist Iconography. Calcutta.
1964 An Introduction to Buddhist Esoterism. Varanasi.

Blacker, C., and Loewe, M.
1975 Ancient Cosmologies. London.

Bloch, J.
1951 Les inscriptions d'Aśoka. Paris.

Blofeld, John
1970 The Way of Power. London.

Bloomfield, M.
1894 The Hymns of the *Atharva Veda*. SBE, 42. London.

Bodrogi, Tibor
1973 The Art of Indonesia. London

Boerschmann, Ernst
1925 Chinesische Architektur. 2 Vols. Berlin.

Boiselier, Jean
1963 Le statuaire du Champa. Paris.

1966 Le Cambodge. Manuel d'archéologie d'Extrême Orient, Pt. 1 : l'Asie du Sud-Est, Vol. 1. Paris.

Boner, Alice, and Sarma, S.R.
1966 *Śilpa Prakāśa*. Medieval Orissan Text on Temple Architecture by Rāmacandra Kaulācāra. Leiden.

Bosch, F.D.K.
1941 L'arc-à-biche à Java et à Champa. BEFEO, 31, 2-3.

1960 The Golden Germ. An Introduction to Indian Symbolism. Indo-Iranian Monographs, 2. 's-Gravenhage.

Bose, N.K.
1932 The Canons of Orissan Architecture. Calcutta.

Bowie, T., Diskul, M.C.S. and Griswold, A.B.
1972 The Sculptures of Thailand. The Asia Society. New York.

Boyd, Andrew
1962 Chinese Architecture and Town Planning. London.

Brown, Percy
1965 Indian Architecture. Vol. 1 : Buddhist and Hindu. Bombay.

Buhler, A
1886 The Laws of Manu *(Manava Dharmaśāstra)*. SBE, 25. Oxford.

Bulling, A
1952 The Meaning of China's Most Ancient Art : An Interpretation of Pottery Patterns from Kansu (Ma Ch'ang and Pan Shan) and their Development in the Shang, Chou and Han Periods. Leiden.

Burckhardt, Titus
1958 Principes et methodes de l'art sacré. Lyon.

1967 Sacred Art in East and West. Its Principles and Methods. Translated by Lord Northbourne. London.

Burnouf, E.
1852 *Saddharma Puṇḍarīka* (Le Lotus de la Bonne Loi).

1876 Introduction a l'histoire du bouddhisme indien. Paris.

Bussagli, Mario
1973 Oriental Architecture. New York.

Butterworth, E.A.S.
1970 The Tree at the Navel of the World. Berlin.

Carbonnel, J.P.
1973 Le *stūpa* Cambodgien actuel. Arts Asiatiques, 26, 225-240.

Chandra, Lokesh
1980 Borobudur : A New Approach. In Dallapiccola, 1980, 301-319.

Chapin, H.B.
1949 A Hitherto Unpublished Great Silla Pagoda. Artibus Asiae, 12, 2, 84-88.

Chavannes, Edouard
1896 Les inscriptions chinoises de Bodhgayā. Revue de l'Histoire des Religions, 34, 1. Paris.

Chevalier J and Gheerbrant, A. (eds.)
1973 Dictionnaire des symboles. 2nd edn. 4 Vols. Paris.

Chhanda, R.
1921 Four Ancient *Yakṣa* Statues. Journal of the Department of Letters, University of Calcutta, 4.

Chou Yi-liang
1945 Tantrism in China. HJAS, 8, 241-332.

Cirlot, J.E.
1962 A Dictionary of Symbols. London.

Clark, Walter E.
1937 Two Lamaistic Pantheons. Harvard-Yenching Institute Monograph Series, 3 & 4. Harvard University Press, New York. Reprinted in one vol., 1965.

Coedes, G.
n.d. *Dhammakāya*. Adyar Library Bulletin, 20, 3-4.

1935 Discovery of the Sacred Deposit of Angkor Wat. Annual Bibliography of Indian Art and Archaeology, 10, 43-47.

1940 Études Cambodgiennes, XXXIII. La destination funéraire des grands monuments Khmer. BEFEO, 40. (Hanoi, 1941).

1952 Un *yantra* récemment découvert à Angkor. JA, 465-477.

1963 Angkor. An Introduction. London.

Coedes, G. and Archaimbault, C.
1973 Les Trois Mondes *(Traibhūṃi Braḥ R'van)*. BEFEO, 89. Paris.

Combaz, Gisbert
1932 L'Évolution du *stūpa* en Asie. MCB, 2, 1932-1933.

1933 L'Évolution du *stūpa* en Asie. MCB, 3, 1933-1934.

1935 L'Évolution du *stūpa* en Asie. MCB, 4, 1935-1936.

1937 Masques et Dragons en Asie. MCB, 7, 1937-1945, 1-328.

1939 L'Inde et l'Orient classique. 2 vols. Paris.

Conze, Edward
1967 Thirty Year of Buddhist Studies. London.

1973 The Shorter *Prajñāpāramitā* Texts. London.

1975 Further Buddhist Studies. Oxford.

Conze, Edward (ed.)
1954 Buddhist Texts Through the Ages. Oxford.

Cook, Francis H.
1977 Hua Yen Buddhism. The Jewel Net of Indra. University Park, Penn., and London.

Cook, Roger
1974 The Tree of Life. Symbol of the Centre. London.

Coomaraswamy, A.K.

1926a The Origin of the Buddha Image. Art Bulletin, 9.

1926b The Indian Origin of the Buddha Image. JAOS, 46.

1927 History of Indian and Indonesian Art. New York.

1928 *Yakṣas* (1). Smithsonian Miscellaneous Collections, 80, 6.

1930 Early Indian Architecture : 1. Cities and City Gates; 2. *Bodhi-gharas*. Eastern Art, 2, 208-235.

1931 *Yaksas* (2). Smithsonian Miscellaneous Publication, 3059.

1935a Elements of Buddhist Iconography. Cambridge, Mass.

1935b Angel and Titan : An Essay in Vedic Ontology. JAOS, 55, 373-419.

1935c The Darker Side of Dawn. Smithsonian Misc. Collections, 94.

1937 The *Yakṣa* of the *Veda* and *Upaniṣads*. QJMS, 28 (1937-1938).

1938a *Nirmāṇakāya*. JRAS, 81-84.

1938b *Uṣṇīṣa* and *Chatra*. Poona Orientalist, 3.

1938c Notes on the *Katha Upaniṣad*. New Indian Antiquary, 1, 43-56, 83-108, 199-213.

1939 Eckstein. Speculum, 14, 66-72.

1940 The Sun-kiss. JAOS, 60, 46-67.

1942 Spiritual Authority and Temporal Power in the Indian Theory of Government. American Oriental Society, New Haven, Connecticut.

1943a Hinduism and Buddhism. New York.

1943b The Symbolism of Archery. Ars Islamica, 10, 104-119.

1944a The Iconography of Durer's "Knots" and Leonardo's "Concatenation". The Art Quarterly, 7, 109-128.

1944b Sir Gawain and the Green Knight : Indra and Namuci. Speculum. 19, 104-125.

1945a Spiritual Paternity and the "Puppet Complex". Psychiatry, 8, 287-297.

1945b Some Sources of Buddhist Iconography. B.C.Law Volume, Poona, 469-476.

1946 Figures of Speech or Figures of Thought. London.

1947 Time and Eternity. Artibus Asiae Supplement, 8. Ascona.

1956a La Sculpture de Bhārhut. Paris.

1956b Buddha and the Gospel of Buddhism. Bombay.

1956c Mediaeval Sinhalese Art. 2nd edn. New York.

1976 The Vedas. Essays in Translation and Exegesis. Prologos, Beckenham (being a reprint of A New Approach to the Vedas: An Essay in Translation and Exegesis, London, 1933, and The *Ṛg Veda* as *Land-Nama-Bok*, London, 1935).

1977 Selected Papers : 1. Traditional Art and Symbolism; 2. Metaphysics. Bollingen Series, 89, Princeton, New Jersey.

Coral-Rémusat, Gilberte de
1936 Animaux fantastiques de l'Indochine, de l'Insulinde et de la Chine. BEFEO, 36, 427 ff.

Corbin, Henry
1960 Avicenna and the Visionary Recital. London.

Covarrubias, Miguel
1937 Island of Bali. London.

Cowell, E.B.
1893 The *Buddhacarita* of Asvaghoṣa. Anecdota Oxoniensia, Aryan Series, 1-7. Oxford.

1894 The *Buddhacarita* of Asvaghoṣa. In Cowell, Muller and Takakusu, 1894.

1895 The *Jātaka*, or Stories of the Buddha's Former Births. 6 Vols. Cambridge, 1895-1907.

Cowell, E.B., Muller, M. and Takakusu, J.
1894 Buddhist Mahāyāna Texts. SBE, 49. London.

Cowell, E.B. and Neil, R.A.
1886 *Divyāvadāna*. Cambridge.

Cunningham, A.
1868 The *Stūpa* of Bhārhut. London.

Dagens, Bruno
1970 *Mayamata*. Traité Sanskrit d'architecture. Pondicherry.

Dainichikyō.
Dai birushana jōbutsu shimpen kaji kyō (Mahā-vairocana-bhisaṃbodhi-sūtra). Taishō, Vol. 18, No. 848. Trans. Śubhākarasiṃha.

Dainichikyōshō.
(Śubhākarasiṃha's "Commentary on the *Dainichikyō*"). Taishō, Vol. 39, No. 1796.

Dallapiccola, Anna L. (ed.)
1980 The Stupa. Its Religious, Historical and Architectural Significance. Franz Steiner Verlag. Wiesbaden.

Danielou, Alain
1964 Hindu Polytheism. London.

Darian, Steven
1976 The Other Face of the *Makara*. Artibus Asiae, 38, 29-34.

Dasgupta, S.
1958 An Introduction to Tantric Buddhism. Calcutta.

1962 Obscure Religious Cults. 2nd edn. Calcutta.

David-Neel, Alexandra
1965 Magic and Mystery in Tibet. 2nd edn. New York.

Dayal, H.
1931 The Bodhisattva Doctrine in the Buddhist Sanskrit Literature. London.

de Champeaux, G.
1966 Introduction au monde des symboles. Paris.

de Groot, J.J.M.
1952 Der Thupa das heiligste Heiligtum des Buddhismus in China. Abhandlungen Preuss, Ak. Wiss. Phil. Hist. Klasse, 11.

de Jong, P.E. de J.
1952 Minangkabau and Negri Sembilan, Socio-Political Structure in Indonesia. The Hague.

Devendra, D.T.
1958 The Symbolism of the Sinhalese Guardstone. Artibus Asiae, 21, 259-268.

de Visser, M.W.
1913 The Dragon in China and Japan. Amsterdam.
1935 Ancient Buddhism in Japan. 2 Vols. London.

Dhaky, M.
1974 The *Ākāśaliṅga* Finial. Artibus Asiae, 36, 307-315.

Dumarçay, Jacques
1978 Borobudur. Oxford University Press, Kuala Lumpur.

Dumézil, G.
1934 Ouranos-Varuṇa. Paris.
1940 Mitra-Varuṇa. Paris.

Dutt, Sukumar
1962 Buddhist Monks and Monasteries of India. London.

Edgerton, Franklin
1924 The Meaning of *Sankhya* and *Yoga*. American Journal of Philology, 45, 1, 1-46.
1970 Buddhist Hybrid Sanskrit Grammar and Dictionary. Yale University Press, New Haven. Repr. New Delhi.

Eggeling, Julius
1882 The *Śatapatha-Brāhmaṇa*. SBE, 12, 26, 41, 43 & 44. London, 1882-1900.

Eliade, Mircea
1937 Cosmical Homology and Yoga. Journal of the Indian Society of Oriental Art. (June-Dec.), 188-203.
1947 *Dūrohaṇa* and the "Waking Dream". In Iyer, 1947, 209-213.
1952 Le temps et l'Éternité dans la pensée indienne. Eranos-Jahrbuch, 20, 219-252.
1956 The Forge and the Crucible. New York.
1957 Centre du monde, temple, maison. In Le symbolisme cosmique des monuments religieux, Serie Orientale Roma, 14, Rome.
1957a The Sacred and the Profane. The Nature of Religion. New York.
1958a Yoga. Immortality and Freedom. New York.
1958b Patterns in Comparative Religion. New York.

Eliade, Mircea (cont.)
1958c Rites and Symbols of Initiation. New York.

1959a Cosmos and History. The Myth of the Eternal Return. New York.

1959b Methodological Remarks on the Study of Religious Symbolism. In Eliade and Kitagawa, 1959, 86-107.

1960 Myths, Dreams and Mysteries. London.

1961 Images and Symbols. London.

1963 Myth and Reality. New York.

1964 Myth and Reality. In Sykes, 1964, 2, 748-753.

1964a Shamanism. Archaic Techniques of Ecstasy. London.

1965 The Two and the One. London.

1970 Two Tales of the Occult. New York.

1973 The Dragon and the Shaman. Notes on a South American Mythology. In Sharpe and Hinnells, 1973, 99-105.

1979 A History of Religious Ideas. 1. From the Stone Age to the Eleusinian Mysteries. London.

Eliade, Mircea and Kitagawa, J.M.
1959 The History of Religions. Chicago.

Eliot, Sir Charles
1932 Hinduism and Buddhism. London.

1935 Japanese Buddhism. London.

Elisséeff, Serge
1936 The *Bommokyō* and the Great Buddha of Tōdaiji. HJAS, 1, 1, 84-95.

Evans-Wentz, W.Y.
1957 The Tibetan Book of the Dead. 3rd edn. London.

1958 Tibetan Yoga and Secret Doctrines. Oxford.

Evola, J.
1951 The Doctrine of Awakening. London.

Fabri, C.L.
1930 Un élément Mesopotamien dans l'art de l'Inde. Journal Asiatique, 207.

1932 Mesopotamian and Early Indian Art : Comparisons. Mélanges Linossier, 1. Paris.

Fausböll, V.
1881 The *Sutta-Nipata*. SBE, 10. Oxford.

Féer, Léon
1883 Contes Indiens. Les Trentes-deux Récits du Trône *(Batriś-Siṃhāsan)*. Paris.

Fergusson, J.
1868 Tree and Serpent Worship. London.

1935 The *Harmikā* and the Original Buddhist *Stūpa*. Indian Historical Quarterly, 11, 2.

Fergusson, J. and Burgess, J.
1910 History of Indian and Eastern Architecture. 2 Vols. London.

Fernando, W.B.M.
1974 Evolution of the *Chattravalla* in Ceylon. Artibus Asiae, 36, 75-80.

Filliozat, J.
1933 La force organique et la force cosmique dans la philosophie médical de l'Inde et dans le Veda. Revue Philosophique, 58.

1947 Le symbolisme du monument du Phnom Bakhen. BEFEO, 44, 1947-1950. Paris.

Finot, L.
1912 Bulletin de la Commission Archéologique de l'Indochine. Paris-Hanoi.

1919 Récherches sur la littérature Laotienne. BEFEO, 17, 77-81.

Finot, M.L.
1903 Phnom Baset. BEFEO, 3, 1.

Forke, Alfred
1925 The World Conception of the Chinese. Probsthain's Oriental Series. London.

Foucaux, Ph. (ed.)
1884 Le *Lalitavistara* ou Développement des Jeux, contenant l'histoire du Bouddha Cakyamouni depuis sa naissance jusqu'à sa predication. AMG, 6 & 9. Lyons, 1884-1892.

Foucher, A.
1900 Étude sur l'iconographie bouddhique de l'Inde. 2 pts. Paris. 1900-1905.

1905 L'Art gréco-bouddhique du Gandhāra. 2 Vols. Paris. 1905-1918.

1909 La Grande Miracle du Bouddha a Śrāvastī. Journal Asiatique, 1.

1917 The Beginnings of Buddhist Art. London.

1934 On the Iconography of the Buddha's Nativity. Memoirs of the Asia Society of India, 46. Delhi.

1949 La vie du Bouddha, d'après les textes et les monuments de l'Inde. Paris.

Franz, H.G.
1980 Stupa and Stupa-Temple in the Gandhara Regions and in Central Asia. In Dallapiccola, 1980, 39-58.

Frédéric, L.
1959 Indian Temples and Sculpture. London.

Fujimoto, Ryukyo
1955 An Outline of the Triple Sutra of Shin Buddhism. 2 Vols. Kyoto.

Furuta, Shokin
1964 The Philosophy of the *Chashitsu* : the Garden. The Japan Architect, (May), 78-82.

Fuyokyō.
Taishō, Vol 3, no. 186.

Gail, Adalbert
1980 Cosmical Symbolism in the Spire of the Ceylon *Dagoba*. In Dallapiccola, 1980, 260-266.

Gangoly, O.C.
1946 Indian Architecture. Bombay.

Gaster, T.H.
1954 Myth and Story. Numen, 1, 184-212.

Geiger, W. and Bode, M.H.
1912 The *Cūlavaṃsa*. PTS. London.

1912a The *Mahāvaṃsa* or the Great Chronicle of Ceylon. PTS. London.

Getty, Alice
1962 The Gods of Northern Buddhism. Oxford,1928; repr. Tokyo.

Ghoshal, U.N.
1959 A History of Indian Political Ideas. Bombay.

Giteau, Madeleine
1951 Le Barattage de l'Ocean au Cambodge. Bulletin de la Société des Études Indochinoises, Saigon, n.s., 26, 2.

1969 Bornage rituel des temples bouddhiques du Cambodge. Publications de l'École Française d'Extrême-Orient, Paris.

Glasenapp, Helmut von
1944 Mystères bouddhiques. Paris.

Goetz, Hermann
1959 India. Art of the World Series. London.

Gokhale, B.G.
1966 Early Buddhist Kingship. The Journal of Asia Studies, 26, 1, 15-22.

Gombrich, R.F.
1975 Ancient Indian Cosmology. In Blacker and Loewe, 1975, 110-142.

Gonda, Jan
1950 Notes on *Brahman*. Utrecht.

1962 Les religions de l'Inde. 2 Vols. Paris.

1972 The Vedic God Mitra. Leiden.

Gordon, Antoinette K.
1959 The Iconography of Tibetan Lamaism. 2nd edn. Rutland, Vermont, and Tokyo.

Goswamy, B.N.
1980 The Stupa. Some Uninformed Questions about Terminological Equivalents. In Dallapiccola, 1980, 1-11.

Govinda, Anagarika
1959 Foundations of Tibetan Mysticism. London.

Govinda, Anagarika (cont.)

1961 The Psychological Attitude of Early Buddhist Philosophy. London.

1976 Psycho-cosmic Symbolism of the Buddhist Stupa. Emeryville, California.

Granet, Marcel

1950 La Pensée Chinoise. Paris.

Griffith, R.T.H.

1916 The Hymns of the *Atharva-Veda*. Benares, 1916-1917.

1927 *Vājasaneyi Saṃhitā* : The White *Yajur Veda*. Benares.

1963 The Hymns of the *Ṛg Veda*. 2 Vols. 2nd edn. Benares.

Griswold, A.B.

1967 Towards a History of Sukhodaya Art. Bangkok.

Griswold, A.B., Kim, Ch. and Pott, P.H.

1964 Burma, Korea, Tibet. Art of the World Series. London.

Groslier, B.Ph.

1956 Angkor. Paris.

1962 The Art of Indo-China. London.

1970 Indochina. Asian Civilizations Series. London.

Groslier, G.

1921 Récherches sur les Cambodgiens. Paris.

Grunwedel, Albert

1972 Buddhist Art in India. Delhi, 1901; repr. 1972.

Guénon, René

1938 Quelques remarques sur la doctrine des cycles cosmiques. ET, 226, 345-354.

1945 Man and His Becoming According to the Vedanta. London.

1945a Introduction to the Study of the Hindu Doctrine. London.

1946 Les principes du calcul infinitésimal. Paris.

1947 Autorité spirituelle et pouvoir temporel. Paris.

1950 Le Roi du Monde. Paris.

1952 Initiation et réalization spirituelle. Paris.

1953 Aperçus sur l'initiation. Paris.

1953a The Reign of Quantity. London.

1957 Les états multiples de l'être. Paris.

1957a La Grande Triade. Paris.

1958 The Symbolism of the Cross. London.

1962 Symboles fondamentaux de la science sacrée. Paris.

1970 Formes traditionelles et cycles cosmiques. Paris.

1977 Études sur la Franc-maçonnerie et le Compagnonnage. 2 Vols. Paris.

Guérinot, A.
1926 La religion Djaina. Paris.

Hakeda, S. Yoshito
1972 Kukai. His Major Works. Columbia Uni. Press. New York.
1967 The Awakening of Faith. Attributed to Asvaghoṣa. Columbia University Press. New York.

Hardy, R.S.
1860 Manual of Buddhism. London.

Hartner, Willy
1938 The Pseudoplanetary Nodes of the Moon's Orbit in Hindu and Islamic Iconographies. Ars Islamica, 5, 1, 113-154.

Harvey, G.
1925 History of Burma. London.

Hastings, James (ed.)
1911 Encyclopaedia of Religion and Ethics. London.

Havell, E.B.
1920 A Handbook of Indian Art. London.

Hayley, F.A.
1923 Sinhalese Laws and Customs. Colombo.

Heesterman, J.C.
1957 The Ancient Indian Royal Consecration. The Hague.

Heine-Geldern, Robert
1930 Weltbilt und Bauform in Sudostasien. Wiener Beitrage zur Kunst und Kultur Asiens.
1956 Conceptions of State and Kingship in South-East Asia. Data Paper No. 18, South East Asia Program, Cornell University, New York.

Henry, Victor
Les Hymnes *Rohita*. Paris.

Hocart, A.M.
1923 Flying Through the Air. Indian Antiquary, 80-82, repr. in The Life Giving Myth, London, 1952, 28-32.
1927 Kingship. Oxford.
1927a The Four Quarters. Ceylon Journal of Science, 1, 3.

Hodgson, B.H.
1874 Essays on the Languages, Literature and Religion of Nepal and Tibet. London. Repr. Varanasi, 1971.

Hoens, D.J.
1951 *Śānti*: A Contribution to Ancient Religious Terminology. The Hague.

Hokodaishōgonkyō.
(Lalitavistara). Taishō, Vol. 3, No. 187.

Holt, Claire
1967 Art in Indonesia. Cornell Uni. Press, New York.

Hopkins, B.
1915 Epic Mythology. Strasbourg.

Horner, I.B.
1938 The Book of the Discipline *(Vināya Pitaka)*. PTS. 5 Vols. London. 1938-1952.

1954 The Middle Length Sayings *(Majjhima Nikāya)*. PTS. 3 Vols. London. 1954-1956.

Hume, R.E.
1931 The Thirteen Principal *Upaniṣads*. 2nd edn. London.

Irwin, John
1980 The Axial Symbolism of the Early Stupa : An Exegesis. In Dallapiccola, 1980, 12-38.

Ishizuka, R. and Coates, H.H.
1949 Hōnen. The Buddhist Saint. 5 Vols. Kyoto.

Iwano, S. (ed.)
1934 *Kokuyaku Issaikyō Indo Senjubutsu* ("The Complete *Tripiṭaka* in Japanese Translation - Indian Texts"); *Mikkyōbu* ("Esoteric Buddhist Section"). 5 Vols. Tokyo.

Iyer, K. Bharata
1947 Art and Thought. A Volume in Honour of the Late Dr. Ananda Coomaraswamy on the Occasion of his 70th Birthday. London.

James, E.O.
1966 The Tree of Life : An Archaeological Study. Leiden.

1969 Creation and Cosmology. A Historical and Comparative Enquiry. Leiden.

Japanese-English Buddhist Dictionary.
1965 Daitō Shuppansha, Tōkyō.

Jayawickrama, N.A.
1971 The Chronicle of the *Thūpa* and the *Thūpavaṃsa*. SBB, 28. London.

Johes, Clifford R.
1973 Source Material for the Construction of *Natya Maṇḍap* in the *Śilpaśāstra* and the *Tantrasamuccaya Śilpaśāstra*. JAOS, 93, 2.

Johnston, E.H.
1950 *Ratnagotara-vibhāga-mahāyānottara-tantra-śāstra*. Patna.

Jones, J.J.
1949 The *Mahāvastu*, Translated from the Buddhist Sanskrit. 2 Vols. SBB, 16 & 17. London.

Jouveau-Dubreuil, G.
1922 Vedic Antiquities. London.

Julien, Stanislas
1853 Houei-Li et Yen-Thsong. Histoire de la vie de Hiouen-Tsang et de ses voyages dans l'Inde; suivie de documents et d'éclaircissements geographique tirés de la relation originale de Hiouen-Tsang. Paris.

Julien, Stanislaus (cont.)

1857 Mémoires sur les contrées Occidentales, traduit du sanskrit en chinois, en l'an 648... 2 Vols. Paris.

Karunadasa, Y.

1967 Buddhist Analysis of Matter. Colombo.

Keith, A.B.

1908 *Sāṅkhyāyana Āraṇyaka*. London.

1909 *Aitareya Āraṇyaka*. Anecdota Oxoniensia Aryan Series, 9. Oxford.

1914 *Taittirīya Saṃhitā* : The Veda of the Black Yajur School. HOS, 18 & 19. Cambridge, Mass.

1920 *Ṛg Veda Brāhmaṇas* : The *Aitareya* and *Kauṣītaki Brāhmaṇas* of the *Ṛg Veda*. HOS, 25. Cambridge, Mass.

1925 The Religion and Philosophy of the *Veda* and *Upaniṣads*. HOS, 32. Cambridge, Mass. Repr. Delhi, 1970.

Kern, H.

1884 The *Saddharma-puṇḍarīka* or the Lotus of the Good Law. SBE, 21. Oxford.

1896 Manual of Indian Buddhism. Grundriss der Indo-Arischen Philologie, Band 3, Heft 8, Strassburg.

1901 Histoire du Bouddhisme dans l'Inde. AMG, Bibl. d'Études, 10 & 11, Paris. 1901-1903.

Kidder, J. Edward

1972 Early Buddhist Japan. London.

Kirfel, W.

1920 Die Kosmographie der Inder. Leipzig.

Kielhorn, F.

n.d. Deopara Inscriptions of Vijayasena. Epigraphica Indica, 1.

Kōbō Daishi (Kūkai)

Himitsu Mandara Jūjushinron ("Commentary on the Ten Stages of Mind in the Esoteric Mandala"). Taishō, Vol. 77, Nos. 24-5.

Hizōki ("A Record of the Secret Treasure"). In *Kōbō Daishi Zenshū* ("The Collected Works of Kōbō Daishi"), 2, 1-70.

Kōbō Daishi Zenshū.

("The Collected Works of Kōbō Daishi"). Tokyo.

Kongōchōgyō.

Bussetsu issai nyorai shinjisshō daijō genshō sammai dai kyō ō kyō (Skt. *Vajra-śekhara-sūtra*). Taishō, Vol. 18, No. 882. Trans. Dānapala.

Koboyashi, Takeshi

1975 Nara Buddhist Art : Tōdaiji. Tokyo.

Kramrisch, Stella

1946 The Hindu Temple. 2 Vols. Calcutta.

1947 The Banner of Indra. In Iyer, 1947, 197-201.

1954 The Art of India. London.

Kuiper, F.B.J.
1970 Cosmogony and Conception : A Query. University of Chicago, History of Religions, 10.

Lad, P.M. (ed.)
1956 The Way of the Buddha. Ministry of Information and Broadcasting, New Delhi.

Lamb, Alistair
1961 *Chandi Bukut Batu Pahat*. Monographs on South East Asian Subjects, 1. Singapore.

Lamotte, Étienne
1944 Le Traité de la Grande Vertu de Sagesse de Nāgārjuna (*Mahāprajñāpāramitāśāstra*). Louvain.

Larousse Encyclopaedia of Mythology.
1959 London.

Law, B.C.
1931 *Cetiya* in the Buddhist Literature. Studio Indo-Iranica.

Leclère, A.
1906 Les livres sacrés du Cambodge. AMG, 20. Paris.

Lefmann, S.
1902 *Lalita Vistara*. 2 Vols. Hallé. 1902-1908.

Legge, J.
1886 A Record of the Buddhist Kingdoms, Being an Account by the Chinese Mônk Fa-Hien of his Travels in India (A.D. 399-414). Oxford.

Le May, Reginald
1938 A Concise History of Buddhist Art in Siam. Cambridge.
1954 The Culture of South East Asia. London.

Lévi, Sylvain
1905 Le Nepal. 3 Vols. Paris.
1907 Asaṅga's *Mahāyāna-sūtrālaṃkāra*. Bibliothèque de l'École des Hautes Études, 150 & 190, 1907 & 1911.
1915 Le catalogue géographique des *yakṣa* dans le *Mahāmāyurī*. Journal Asiatique, 11, 5.
1898 La doctrine du sacrifice dans les *Brāhmaṇas*. Paris.

Lévi, Sylvain and Takakusu, J. (eds.)
1929 *Hōbōgirin*, dictionnaire encyclopédique d'après les sources chinoises et japonaises. Tokyo. Since 1929.

Lin, Li-kouang
1935 Puṇyodaya (Na T'i), un propagateur du tantrisme en Chine et au Cambodge à l'époque de Hiuan-tsang. Journal Asiatique, 227, 83-100.

Ling, Trevor
1973 The Buddha. Buddhist Civilization in India and Ceylon. London.

Lipsey, Roger (ed.)
1977 Coomaraswamy. Selected Papers. See Coomaraswamy, 1977.

Livingstone, Ray
1962 The Traditional Theory of Literature. University of Minnesota, Minneapolis.

Liyanaratne, J.
1976 Le *Purāṇa Mayamata*, manuel astrologique singhalese de construction. École Française d'Extrême-Orient, 109. Paris.

Long, Charles H.
1963 Alpha. The Myths of Creation. New York.

Longhurst, A.H.
1928 The Development of the Stupa. Journal of the Royal Institute of British Architects, 36, 4, 135-149.

1936 The Story of the Stupa. Colombo.

1938 The Buddhist Antiquities of Nāgārjunakoṇḍa. Memoirs of the Archaeological Survey of India, Delhi.

Luce, G.H.
1969 Old Burma - Early Pagan. 3 Vols. Published for Artibus Asiae and the Institute of Fine Arts, New York Uni., New York.

Luce, G.H. and Pe Maung Ting
1923 Glass Palace Chronicle of the Kings of Burma (*Hmannan Yazawin*). Oxford.

Ludowyck, E.F.C.
1958 The Footprint of the Buddha. London.

Luk, Charles (Lu K'uan Yu)
1966 The *Śūraṅgama Sūtra (Leng Yen Ching)*. London.

Lunet de Lajonquière
1902 Inventaire descriptif du Cambodge. Paris. 1902-1911.

McCune, E.
1962 The Arts of Korea. Tokyo.

MacDonald, A.W.
1957 Notes sur la claustration villageoise dans l'Asie du Sud-Est. Journal Asiatique, 254, 2.

Macdonell, A.A.
1897 Vedic Mythology. Grundriss, 3, 1A, Strasbourg. Repr. Varanasi, 1971.

1929 A Practical Sanskrit Dictionary. London.

McGovern, W.M.
1923 Manual of Buddhist Philosophy. 1. Cosmology. London.

1968 An Introduction to Mahāyāna Buddhism. Varanasi.

Mahā-prajñā-pāramitā-śāstra.
See Lamotte, 1944.

Mahā-sukhāvatī-vyūha.
Jap. *Daimuryōjukyō*. Taishō, Vol. 9, No. 276. English translation : Cowell, Muller and Takakusu, 1894 ("The Greater *Sukhāvatī-vyūha*").

Mahathera, P.V.
1962 Buddhist Meditation in Theory and Practice. Colombo.

Makasogiritsu.
Skt. *Mahāsaṃghika-vinaya*. Taishō, Vol. 22, No. 1415.

Mallaya, N.V.
1949 Studies in Sanskrit Texts on Temple Architecture With Special Reference to *Tantrasamuccaya*. Annamalai.

Marchal, H.
1938 Les déformations de la tète de Kāla dans le décor Balinais. Revue des Arts Asiatiques, 22, 4.

1948 The Head of the Monster in Khmer and Far Eastern Decoration. Journal of the Indian Society of Oriental Art, 6, 97 ff.

1947 Note sur la forme du *stūpa* au Cambodge. BEFEO, 44, (1947-1950), 581-590.

Marshall, Sir John
1918 A Guide to Sanchi. Calcutta.

1918a A Guide to Taxila. Calcutta.

Maspero, H.
1946 Le Ming T'ang et la crise religieuse chinoise avant les Han. MCB, 8-9, (1946-1951).

Mathews, R.H.
1952 Chinese-English Dictionary. Revised edn. Cambridge, Mass.

Mikkyō Daijiten.
1971 ("Encyclopaedia of Esoteric Buddhism"). 6 Vols. Kyoto.

Mitra, R.
1859 The *Taittirīya Brāhmaṇa* of the Black *Yajur Veda*, with the Commentary of Śāyana Archarrya. 3 Vols. Calcutta. 1859-1890. (Sanskrit).

1881 The *Yoga* Aphorisms of Patañjali, with the Commentary of Bhoja Rāja. Bibliotheca Indica, 93, Calcutta. 1881-1883.

Mochizuki, Shinkyo (ed.)
Bukkyō Daijiten ("Encyclopaedia of Buddhism"). Tokyo.

Moertono, S.
1968 State and Statecraft in Old Java : A Study of the Later Mataram Period, 16th to 19th Century. New York.

Muir, J.
1868 Original Sanskrit Texts on the Origin and History of the People of India, their Religion and Institutions. London.

Mus, Paul
1928 Le Buddha paré. Son origine indienne. Śākyamuni dans le Mahāyānisme moyen. Études indiennes et indo-chinoises, 2, BEFEO, 28, 1-2, 147 ff.

1935 Barabudur. Esquisse d'une histoire du bouddhisme fondée sur la critique archéologique des textes. 2 Vols. Hanoi-Paris. Repr. in 1 Vol., New York, 1978.

Mus, Paul (cont.)

1937 Angkor in the Time of Jayavarman VII. Indian Art and Letters, 1.

1938 La Notion de temps réversible dans la mythologie bouddhique. L'Annuaire de l'École Pratique des Hautes Études, Section des Sciences Religieuses, 1938-1939. Melun.

Nāgārjuna

Mahā-prajñā-pāramitā-śāstra. See Lamotte, 1944.

Ñānamoli, Bhikkhu

1964 Buddhaghoṣa, 'The Path of Purification' (*Visuddhimagga*). 2nd edn. Colombo.

Nandargikar, G.R.

1911 The *Buddhacarita* of Asvaghoṣa. Poona.

Needham, Joseph

1956 Science and Civilization in China. Vol. 2 : History of Scientific Thought. Cambridge.

1959 Science and Civilization in China. Vol. 3 : Mathematics and the Sciences of the Heavens and Earth. Cambridge.

Nihon no Bijutsu. ("The Art of Japan")

1967 *Nihon no Bijutsu*, 8, 16. An issue devoted to *Butsugu*, ("Buddhist altar equipment")

1969 *Nihon no Bijutsu*, 10, 77. An issue devoted to *Tō*, ("The Stupa").

Nikhilananda, Swami

1944 *Bhagavad Gīta*. New York.

Nitschke, Gunter

1966 *Ma*. The Japanese Sense of Place. AD, March, 117-156.

1974. *Shime*. Binding and Unbinding. AD, Dec. 747-791.

Norman, H.C.

1906 *Dhammapada* Commentary *(Dahmmapada Atthakathā)*. PTS. 4 Vols. London. 1906-1914.

O'Connor, S.J.

1966 Ritual Deposit Boxes in South East Asian Sanctuaries. Artibus Asiae, 28, 1, 53-60.

Oertal, H.

1896 The *Jaiminīya* or *Talavakāra Upaniṣad Brāhmaṇa*. JAOS, 16, 79-260.

Okazaki, Joji

1977 Pure Land Buddhist Painting. Tokyo and New York.

Oldenberg, H.

1921 Le Bouddha, sa vie, sa doctrine, sa communité. Trans. into French from the German by A. Foucher. Paris.

Oldenberg, H. and Muller, Max

1892 The *Grihya-sūtras*. SBE, 29 & 30. London.

Oldfield, H.A.
1880 Sketches from Nipal. 2 Vols. London.

Pal, P.
1971 The *Aiḍūka* of the *Viṣṇudharmapurāṇa* and Certain Aspects of Stupa Symbolism. Journal of the Indian Society of Oriental Art, 4, 1, 49-62.

Pallis, Marco
1939 Peaks and Lamas. London.

Pant, Sushila
1976 The Origin and Development of Stupa Architecture in India. Varanasi.

Paranavitana, S.
1946 The Stupa in Ceylon. Memoir of the Archaeological Survey of Ceylon, 5. Colombo.

1954 The Significance of the Sinhalese "Moonstone". Artibus Asiae, 17, 3, 196-231.

Parker, H.
1909 Ancient Ceylon. London.

Parmentier, Henri
1906 Nouvelles notes sur le sanctuaire de Po-Nagar à Nhatrang. BEFEO, 6, 3-4.

1909 Découverte d'un nouveau depôt dans le temple de Pô-Nagar de Nha-Trang. BEFEO, 9, 2.

1918 Inventaire des monuments chams de l'Annam. Paris.

1935 La construction dans l'architecture Khmère classique. BEFEO, 35, 2.

Penzner, N.M. (ed.) and Tawney, C.H.
1924 The Ocean of Story, Being C.H.Tawney's Translation of Somadeva's *Kathā Sarit Sāgana* (or Oceans of Streams of Stories). 10 Vols. London. 1924-1928.

Perry, Whitall N.
1971 A Treasury of Traditional Wisdom. London.

Pisharati, K.R.
1936 *Stupi*. Indian Culture, Oct., 353.

1937 Hindu Architecture According to *Tantra Samuccaya*. Journal of the Indian Society of Oriental Art, 5, 204-207.

Porée-Maspero, L.
1961 *Krŏn Pāli* et les rites de la maison. Anthropos, 56, 1-6, 179-251, 548-628, 883-929.

Pott, P.H.
1952 The Influence of Tantric Buddhism on Ancient Indonesian Civilization. Marg, 57, 3, 53 ff.

Pradhan, S.
1933 *Ṛg Veda Saṃhitā* with Śāyana's Commentary. Calcutta.

Prasāda, Rāma
1924 Patañjali's *Yoga-Sūtras* with the Commentary of Vyāsa and the Gloss of Vāchaspatimiśra. SBH, 4. Allahabad.

Prematilleke, L.
1966 Identity and Significance of the Objects Held by the Dwarves in the Guardstones of Ancient Ceylon. Artibus Asiae, 28, 155-161.

Przyluski, J.
1923 La légende de l'empereur Açoka (*Açoka Avadāna*). AMG, Bibliothèque d'Études, 32. Paris.

1929 Les *Salvas*. Journal Asiatique, 214.

1930 Deux noms indiens du dieu Soleil. Rapson Studies, BSOS, 6, 2, 1930-1932.

1932 Unipèdes. Études Indiens et Chinois, 2. Paris. 1932-1933.

1932a Le symbolisme du pilier de Sārnāth. Mélange d'orientalisme publié par la Musée Guimet à la Mémoire de Raymond Linossier, 2, 481 ff.

1935 The *Harmikā* and the Origin of the Buddhist *Stūpa*. The Indian Historical Quarterly, 11.

1935a Le partage des reliques du Buddha. MCB, 4, 413-467.

1935b La ville du *Cakravartin*. Influences babylonniennes sur la civilization de l'Inde. Rocznik Orjentalistyczny, 5, 165-185.

1936 Les sept terraces du Barabudur. HJAS, 1, 251 ff.

1940 La participation. In Nouvelle Encyclopédie Philosophique. Paris.

Przyluski, J. and Lamotte, E.
1932 Bouddhisme et *Upaniṣad*. BEFEO, 32, 141-169.

Radhakrishnan, S.
1929 Indian Philosophy. 2 Vols. 2nd edn. London.

1944 The *Bhagavadgīta*. London.

1950 The *Dhammapada*. London.

1953 The Principal *Upaniṣads*. London.

Raglan, Lord
1964 The Temple and the House. London.

Rahula, W.
1956 History of Buddhism in Ceylon. Colombo.

Rajanubhab, Prince Damrong
n.d. A History of Buddhist Monuments in Siam. Bangkok.

Ramachandran, T.N.
1954 The Nāgapaṭṭiṇam and other Buddhist Bronzes in the Madras Museum. Bulletin of the Madras Government Museum, Madras.

Ramachandran, R.
1938 Nāgārjunakoṇḍa. Memoirs of the Archaeological Survey of India. Delhi.

Rambach, P. and de Golish, V
1955 The Golden Age of Indian Art. London.

Randhawa, M.S.
1964 The Cult of Trees and Tree Worship. New Delhi.

Rao, T.A.Gopinath
1914 Elements of Hindu Iconography. 2 Vols. Madras.

Rawson, Philip
1972 Tantra. 2nd edn. London.

1973 Tantra. The Indian Cult of Ecstasy. London.

1967 The Art of South East Asia. London.

Rénou, L.
1928 Les maitres de la philologie vedique. Annales de la Musée Guimet, Bibl. Études, 38.

Reynolds, Frank
1972 The Two Wheels of the *Dhamma* : A Study of Early Buddhism. In Smith, 1972.

Rhys Davids, C.A.F.
1920 *Visuddhimagga*. 1-2, Pali Text, PTS. London.

1920a The *Visuddhimagga* of Buddhaghoṣa. PTS. London.

1924 Buddhist Psychology. Oxford.

Rhys Davids, C.A.F. and Woodward, F.L.
1917 The Book of the Kindred Sayings (*Samyutta-Nikāya*). PTS. 5 Vols. London. 1917-1930.

Rhys Davids, T.W.
1880 Buddhist Birth Stories. London

1881 Buddhist *Suttas*. SBE, 11. London.

1890 The Questions of King Milinda (*Milinda Pañho*). SBE, 25 & 36. London.

1889 Dialogues of the Buddha (*Digha-Nikāya*). 3 Vols. London. 1889-1921.

1903 Buddhist India. London.

Rhys Davids, T.W. and Stede, W.
The Pali Text Society's Pali-English Dictionary. PTS. London.

Rice, Tamara Talbot
1965 Ancient Arts of Central Asia. London.

Richard, Timothy
1907 The Awakening of Faith in the Mahāyāna Doctrine - The New Buddhism. Shanghai. Repr. London, 1961.

Roth, Gustav
1980 The Symbolism of the Buddhist Stupa. In Dallapiccola, 1980, 183-209.

Rowland, Benjamin Jr.
1938 Buddha and the Sun God. Zalmoxis, 1, 68-84.

Rowland, Benjamin Jr. (cont.)

1938a The Wall Paintings of India, Central Asia and Ceylon. Boston.

1947 Studies in the Buddhist Art of Bamiyan : the Bodhisattva of Group E. In Iyer, 1947, 46 ff.

1953 The Art and Architecture of India. Penguin Books, London.

1953a The Four Beasts : Directional Symbolism in Ceylon. The Art Quarterly, (Spring).

1962 The Iconography of the Flame Halo. Bulletin of the Fogg Museum of Art, 11, 10-16.

Roy, P.C.

1893 The *Mahabharata* of Krishna-Dvaipayana Vyasa. 12 Vols. Calcutta. 1893-1894.

Ruegg, D.S.

1969 La théorie du *tathāgatagarbha* et du *gotra*. Publication de l'École Française d'Extrême Orient. Paris.

Saliba, A.

1976 *Homo Religiosus* in Mircea Eliade. An Anthropological Evaluation. Leiden.

Samdup, Lama K.D. and Evans-Wentz, W.Y.

1958 Tibetan Yoga and Secret Doctrines. Oxford.

Sangharakshita, Bhikshu

1957 A Survey of Buddhism. Bangalore.

Sarcar, H.

1960 Studies in Early Buddhist Architecture in India. Delhi.

Sarkisyanz, E.

1965 Buddhist Backgrounds of the Burmese Revolution. The Hague.

Sarup, L.

1921 The *Nighantu* and *Nirukta* of Yaska. Oxford.

Sastri, H. Krishna

1916 South Indian Images of Gods and Goddesses. Madras.

Saunders, E. Dale

1960 *Mudrā*. A Study of Symbolic Gestures in Japanese Buddhist Sculpture. London.

Sawa, Takaaki

1965 *Mikkyō no Bijutsu*. ("The Art of Esoteric Buddhism"). Tokyo.

1972 Art in Japanese Esoteric Buddhism. New York and Tokyo.

1971 *Butsuzō Zuten*. ("The Iconography of Buddhist Images"). Tokyo.

Schrieke, B.

1955 Indonesian Sociological Studies : Selected Writings of B. Schrieke. The Hague.

Seckel, Dietrich

1964 The Art of Buddhism. Art of the World Series. London.

Sekai Bijutsu Zenshū.
("A Collection of the Art of the World").
1962 Sekai Bijutsu Zenshū, 2 : Nihon ("Japan"); 2 : Asuka-Hakuhō. Tōkyō.

Senart, E.
1882 Essai sur la légende du Bouddha, son caractère et ses origines. Paris.

Shah, Priyabal
1951 *Aiḍūka*. Journal of the Oriental Institute, 1, 3, 1951-2.

Shamasastry, R.
1923 Kautilya's *Arthaśāstra*. 2nd edn. Mysore.

Sharpe, Eric J. and Hinnells, John R.
1973 Man and His Salvation. Manchester.

Shorto, H.L.
1963 The 32 Myos in the Medieval Mon Kingdom. BSOS, 26, 3, 572-591.
1971 The Stupa as Buddha Icon. In Watson, 1971, 75-81.

Sickman, L. and Soper, A.
1956 The Art and Architecture of China. London.

Sivaramamurti, M.
1942 Amarāvatī Sculptures in the Madras Government Museum. Bulletin of the Madras Government Museum, Madras.

Smart, W.M.
1931 Textbook on Spherical Astronomy. London.

Smith, Bardwell L. (ed.)
1972 The Two Wheels of the *Dhamma*. AAR Studies in Religion, 3, American Academy of Religion, Penn.

Smith, John E.
1965 The Structure of Religion. Religious Studies, 1, 1.

Smith, Vincent A.
1911 A History of Fine Art in India and Ceylon. Oxford.

Snellgrove, D.L.
1957 Buddhist Himalaya. Oxford.
1959 The Notion of Divine Kingship in Tantric Buddhism. In Sacral Kingship, Studies in the History of Religions (Supplement to Numen), 4.
1961 *Hevajra-Tantra* : A Critical Study. 2 Vols. London.
1971 Indo-Tibetan Liturgy and its Relationship to Iconography. In Watson, 1971, 34-46.

Snellgrove, D.L. (ed.)
1978 The Image of the Buddha. Serindia Publications, UNESCO. Paris and Tokyo.

Soekmono, Dr.
1976 *Chandi Borobudur*. A Monument of Mankind. The Unesco Press. Amsterdam and Paris.

Sogen, Yamakami
1912 Systems of Buddhist Thought. Calcutta.

Somadeva. See Penzner and Tawney, 1924.

Soothill, W.E.
1951 The Hall of Light. London.

Soothill, W.E. and Hodous, L.
1934 A Dictionary of Chinese Buddhist Terms. London.

Soper, C.
1947 The "Dome of Heaven" in Asia. The Art Bulletin, 29, 225-248.

1949 Aspects of Light Symbolism in Gandhāran Sculpture. Artibus Asiae, 1949, 12, 252-283, & 314-330; 1950, 13, 63-85.

Speiser, C.
1965 Oriental Architecture in Colour. London.

Srinavasan, S.
1979 Mensuration in Ancient India. Varanasi.

Steinilber-Oberlin, E.
1938 The Buddhist Sects of Japan. Their History, Philosophical Doctrines and Sanctuaries. London.

Stern, Ph.
1934 Le temple-montagne Khmer, le culte de *liṅga* et le *devarāja*. BEFEO, 34, 161 ff.

Stevenson, M.
1920 Rites of the Twice-born. London.

Stutterheim, W.F.
1956 Studies in Indonesian Archaeology. Koninklijt Instituut voor Taal-, Land-, en Volkenkunde, Translation Series. The Hague, Hijhoff.

1931 The Meaning of the Hindu-Javanese *Candi*. JAOS, 51, 1-15.

Śubhākarasiṃha. See *Dainichikyōshō*.

Sukhāvatī-vyūha.
Jap. *Amidakyō*. Taishō, Vol. 12, No. 366. English trans. in Cowell, Muller and Takakusu ("The Smaller *Sukhāvatī-vyūha*").

Sukthankar, V.S.
1933 *Mahābhārata*. 24 Vols. Poona.

Suzuki, Beatrice Lane
1936 The Shingon School of Mahāyāna Buddhism, Part 2 : The *Mandara* : The *Taizōkai*. The Eastern Buddhist, 7, 1 (May, 1936), 1-38; 7, 2 (June, 1937), 177-212.

Suzuki, D.T.
1900 Asvaghoṣa's Discourse on the Awakening of Faith in the Mahāyāna. Chicago.

1930 Studies in the *Laṅkāvatāra Sūtra*. London.

1932 The *Laṅkāvatāra Sūtra*. London.

Sykes, G. (ed.)
1964 Alienation. The Cultural Climate of Modern Man. New York.

Sze, Mai-mai
1957 The Tao of Painting. A Study of the Ritual Disposition of Chinese Painting. 2 Vols. London.

Tajima, R.
1959 Les deux grands Mandalas et le doctrine de l'ésoterisme Shingon. Tokyo and Paris.

Takakusu, J.
1956 The Essentials of Buddhist Philosophy. 3rd edn. Honolulu.

Takakusu, J. and Watanabe, K. (eds.)
1927 *Taishō Shinshu Daizōkyō*. ("Taishō Edition of the Buddhist *Tripiṭika* in Chinese"). 100 Vols. Tokyo.

Tamaki, Koshiro
1961 The Development of the Thought of *Tathāgata-garbha* from India to China. Journal of Indian and Buddhist Studies, 9, 1, 378-386.

Tambiah, S.J.
1970 Buddhism and the Spirit Cults in North-East Thailand. Cambridge University Press, London.

1976 World Conqueror and World Renouncer. A Study of Buddhism and Polity in Thailand Against a Historical Background. Cambridge University Press, London.

Tawney, C.H. : See Penzner and Tawney, 1924.

Taw Sein Ko
1913 The Evolution of the Burmese Pagoda. In Burmese Sketches, Rangoon.

Thapar, D.R.
1961 Icons in Bronze. London.

Thiounn, S.E. Okhna Veang
1906 Programme des fêtes du couronnement de S.M. Prea Bat Samdach Prea Sisowath. Paris.

Toganoo, Shoun
1932 *Mandara no Kenkyū*. ("A Study of Mandalas"). Kōyasan.

1971 *Rishukyō no Kenkyū*. ("A Study of the *Prajñā-pāramitā-naya-sūtra*"). Koyasan.

Tsao t'a kun to kin.
Taishō, No. 699.

Tucci, G.
1932 *Mc'od rten* e *ts'a ts'a* nel Tibet Indiano ed Occidentale. Indo-Tibetica, 1. Rome.

1934 Some Glosses upon the *Guhyasamāja*. MCB, 3, 339-353.

1938 Il Simbolismo archittectonico dei tempi di Tibet occidentale. Indo-Tibetica, 3-4. Rome.

1961 The Theory and Practice of the Mandala. London.

Vallée-Poussin, L. de la
1925 Bouddhisme. Opinions sur l'histoire de la dogmatique. Paris.

1898 Bouddhisme. Études et materiaux. London.

1926 L'*Abhidharmakośa* de Vasubandhu. Paris.

1937 *Staupikam*. HJAS, 2, 276-289.

van Durme, P.J.
1932 Notes sur le Lamaisme. MCB, 1, 263-319.

van Lohuizen de Leeuw
1956 South East Asian Architecture and the Stupa of Nandangarh. Artibus Asiae, 19.

1980 The Stupa in Indonesia. In Dallapiccola, 1980, 277-300.

Vasubandhu : See Vallée-Poussin, 1926.

Viennot, Odette
1954 Le culte de l'arbre dans l'Inde ancienne. Paris.

Vireswarananda, Swami
1962 *Brahma-Sūtras*. Calcutta.

Vogel, J.P.
1924 Serpent Worship in Ancient and Modern India. Acta Orientalia, 2, 279-312.

1926 Indian Serpent Lore or the *Nāgas* in Hindu Legend and Art. London. Repr. Delhi, 1972.

1929 Le *makara* dans le sculpture de l'Inde. Revue des Arts Asiatiques, 6, 3 (Sept.).

1936 Buddhist Art in India, Ceylon and Java. Oxford.

Volwahsen, Andreas
1969 Living Architecture - India. London.

Waddell, L.A.
1895 The Buddhism of Tibet or Lamaism. London.

Wagner, F.A.
1959 Indonesia. The Art of an Island Group. London.

Ward, William E.
1952 The Lotus Symbol : Its Meaning in Buddhist Art and Philosophy. JAAC, 40, 2, 135-146.

Watson, W. (ed.)
1971 Mahayanist Art After A.D.900. Colloquies on Art and Architecture in Asia, 2. University of London, London.

Wales, H.G. Quaritch
1931 Siamese State Ceremonies. London.

1953 The Mountain of God. London.

1977 The Universe Around Them. Cosmology and Cosmic Renewal in Indianized South-east Asia. London.

Warren, Henry Clark
1922 Buddhism in Translation. Harvard Oriental Series, 3. Abridged verion containing only the life of the Buddha. Cambridge, Mass.

1953 Buddhism in Translation. Cambridge, Mass.

Waley, Arthur
1937 The Book of Songs. London.

Wheatley, Paul
1971 The Pivot of the Four Quarters. Edinburgh.

Whitney, W.D. and Lanman, C.R. (eds.)
1905 *Atharva Veda*. Cambridge, Mass.

Wieger, L.
1965 Chinese Characters. 2nd edn. London.

Willetts, W.
1965 Foundations of Chinese Art. London.

Williams, C.S.
1960 Chinese Symbolism and Art Motives. New York.

Wilson, H.H.
1840 The *Viṣṇu Purāṇa*. London. Repr. Calcutta, 1961.

Winstedt, R.O.
1947 Kingship and Enthronement in Malaya. JRAS, Malayan Branch, 20, 1.

Woodroffe, Sir John (see also Avalon, Arthur)
1954 *Tantrarāja Tantra*. A Short Analysis. Madras.

Woods, James H.
1914a The *Yoga Sūtras* of Patañjali as Illustrated by the Comment Entitled "The Jewel Lustre" or *Maṇiprabha*. JAOS, 34, 1-114.

1914b The *Yoga* System of Patañjali. Harvard Oriental Series, 17. Cambridge, Mass.

Woodward, F.L and Hare, E.M.
1932 The Book of the Gradual Sayings (*Aṅguttara Nikāya*). PTS. 5 Vols. London. 1932-1939.

Wu, Nelson
1963 Chinese and Indian Architecture. New York and London.

Yarden, L.
1971 The Tree of Light. A Study of the Menorah. London.

Zimmer, Heinrich
1946 Myths and Symbols in Indian Art and Civilization. Bollingen Series, 6. New York.

1955 The Art of Indian Asia. Bollingen Series, 39. 2 Vols. New York.

1956 Philosophies of India. New York.